This is the third volume in the major six-volume Commentary on Homer's *Iliad* prepared under the General Editorship of Professor G. S. Kirk. It opens with two introductory chapters: the first on Homeric diction (on which emphasis is maintained throughout the Commentary); the second on the contribution that comparative studies have made to seeing the Homeric epics in sharper perspective. Like its companion volumes, the Commentary deals with the cultural background of the poem and with linguistic and thematic points. Dr Hainsworth confronts in an intentionally even-handed manner the serious problems posed by the ninth, tenth, and twelfth books of the *Iliad*, seeking by means of a succinct discussion and a brief bibliography of recent contributions to furnish the user with a point of entry into the often voluminous scholarship devoted to these questions. The Greek text is not included.

This Commentary is an essential reference work for all students of Greek literature, and archaeologists and historians will also find that it contains material of value to them.

The Iliad: a commentary

Volume III: books 9–12

THE ILIAD:
A COMMENTARY

GENERAL EDITOR G. S. KIRK

Volume III: books 9–12

BRYAN HAINSWORTH

UNIVERSITY LECTURER IN CLASSICAL LANGUAGES,
UNIVERSITY OF OXFORD,
AND FELLOW OF NEW COLLEGE

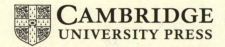

CAMBRIDGE
UNIVERSITY PRESS

Published by the Press Syndicate of the University of Cambridge
The Pitt Building, Trumpington Street, Cambridge CB2 1RP
40 West 20th Street, New York, NY 10011-4211, USA
10 Stamford Road, Oakleigh, Victoria 3166, Australia

First published 1993
Reprinted 1996

Printed in Great Britain at the University Press, Cambridge

A catalogue record for this book is available from the British Library

Library of Congress cataloguing in publication data
Kirk, G. S. (Geoffrey Stephen)
The Iliad, a commentary.
Includes bibliographical references and indexes.
Contents: v. 1. Books 1–4   v. 3. Books 9–12
Bryan Hainsworth.
1. Homer. Iliad.   2. Achilles (Greek mythology) in
literature.   3. Trojan War in literature.   I. Homer.
Iliad.   II. Hainsworth, Bryan.   III. Title.
PA4037.K458 1985   883'.01   84-11330

ISBN 0 521 23711 4 hardback
ISBN 0 521 28173 3 paperback

This volume
is dedicated to the memory of
Eric Yorke
Friend and Tutor

CONTENTS

Contents

COMMENTARY

FIGURES

xi

PREFACE

Students of *Altertumswissenschaft* everywhere owe much to the continuing commitment of publishers, to the Fondazione Lorenzo Valla and the Clarendon Press for a commentary on the *Odyssey* and to the Cambridge University Press for undertaking at Geoffrey Kirk's instigation an even grander commentary on the *Iliad*. A commentary on either poem of Homer, unless it has a very narrow focus, must nowadays be the work of several hands; such is the pressure of other duties in English-speaking lands on those who would willingly devote all their time to the old poet. Though each of the General Editor's collaborators has had a free hand and with it an inescapable responsibility the commentary is in a sense a co-operative venture. In detail Richard Janko, Nicholas Richardson and Mark Edwards and of course the General Editor suggested many improvements and generously made their own work available to me, but in a deeper sense the concept of an Iliadic commentary that shaped vols. I and II (see the outline in vol. I xv–xxv) has shaped my own work. The same assumptions are made about unity of conception, though I follow Danek in relieving Homer of responsibility for book 10; about the broad integrity of the text, though the easy accessibility of the scholia in Erbse's edition is a constant reminder how much we take on trust; and about the profound influence of oral techniques of composition on the linguistic and narrative style of the epic. These are assumptions universally understood and therefore discountable if not *in toto* universally accepted.

Nothing in format or conventions will surprise. One particular convention, however, is worth mention. Akhilleus and Hektor live in the mind of every reader for whom the *Iliad* is a poem as well as a text, and expressions of the kind 'Akhilleus says' or 'Hektor does' flow easily from the commentator's pen. Such expressions are shorthand for the cumbrous 'the poet represents his character Akhilleus saying, etc.', which it would be tedious to repeat more frequently than is necessary to remind the reader that when history becomes heroic poetry it becomes fiction. The *Iliad* relates events as they were conceived and structured in the poet's mind; how that was done it is the primary function of commentary to elucidate, while recognizing that the completeness of the picture and sequence of events is subject to fallibility, indifference, and the poet's own evaluation. The latter is the province of narratology, an art too novel for its application to Homer yet to have produced consensus; my debt on this front to de Jong will be evident. Indebtedness to the thoughts and insights of others inevitably weighs heavily on this commentary. It is lightened only by the thought that bibliography is an inescapable problem for any late twentieth-century commentator on a major classical text. It would be easy to compile a list of two or three hundred items, in the manner of a doctoral thesis, or indeed twice that number, but such a list is of little real help to the majority of users. The bibliography that precedes the commentary is exactly what it is entitled, a list of works cited frequently enough to justify the abbreviation of their titles; it has no pretence to be exhaustive even as a list of indispensable Homerica. In the commentary itself no attempt is made to cumulate secondary literature, but the work of Burkert, Chantraine, M. W. Edwards, Fenik, Latacz, Meister, Redfield, Schein, and the contributors to *Archaeologia Homerica*, to name the most obvious, has left its mark on every page. References are made, not to cite a source, but to indicate where further information beyond what is appropriate to a commentary may be found or to provide a point of entry into always voluminous scholarship.

Finally thanks are due, for their patience as well as their labours, to the officers of the Cambridge University Press and especially to their copy-editor, the ever-vigilant Susan Moore.

J. B. H.

Bladon, Oxon., January 1991

ABBREVIATIONS

Books

Adkins, *Merit and Responsibility*   A. W. H. Adkins, *Merit and Responsibility: A Study in Greek Values* (Oxford 1960)

Ameis–Hentze   K. F. Ameis and C. Hentze, *Homers Ilias* (Leipzig 1868–1932; repr. Amsterdam 1965)

Amory Parry, *Blameless Aegisthus*   A. Amory Parry, *Blameless Aegisthus: a Study of* ἀμύμων *and Other Homeric Epithets* (Leiden 1973)

Ap. Soph., *Lex.*   *Apollonii Sophistae Lexicon Homericum*, ed. I. Bekker (Berlin 1833)

Apthorp, *MS Evidence*   M. J. Apthorp, *The Manuscript Evidence for Interpolation in Homer* (Heidelberg 1980)

Arch. Hom.   *Archaeologia Homerica: Die Denkmäler und das frühgriechische Epos*, edd. F. Matz and H.-G. Buchholz (Göttingen 1967–   )

Arend, *Scenen*   W. Arend, *Die typischen Scenen bei Homer* (Berlin 1933)

Austin, *Archery*   N. Austin, *Archery at the Dark of the Moon: Poetic Problems in Homer's Odyssey* (Berkeley and Los Angeles 1975)

Boedeker, *Aphrodite*   D. D. Boedeker, *Aphrodite's Entry into Greek Epic* (Leiden) 1974

Bolling, *External Evidence*   G. M. Bolling, *The External Evidence for Interpolation in Homer* (Oxford 1925, repr. 1968)

Bowra, *Tradition and Design*   C. M. Bowra, *Tradition and Design in the Iliad* (Oxford 1930, repr. Westport 1977)

Bowra, *HP*   C. M. Bowra, *Heroic Poetry* (Oxford 1952)

Bremer, *HBOP*   *Homer: Beyond Oral Poetry*, edd. J. M. Bremer, I. J. F. de Jong, and J. Kalff (Amsterdam 1987)

Burkert, *Religion*   W. Burkert, *Greek Religion: Archaic and Classical* (Oxford 1985); Engl. trans. by J. Raffan of *Griechische Religion der archaischen und klassischen Epoche* (Stuttgart 1977)

Chantraine, *Dict.*   P. Chantraine, *Dictionnaire étymologique de la langue grecque* (Paris 1968-80)

Chantraine, *GH*   P. Chantraine, *Grammaire homérique* i–ii (Paris 1958–63)

Commentary   *A Commentary on Homer's Odyssey*, vol. i, by A. Heubeck, S. West, and J. B. Hainsworth (Oxford 1988); vol. ii, by A. Heubeck and A. Hoekstra (Oxford 1989); vol. iii by J. Russo, M. Fernández-Galiano, and A. Heubeck (Oxford 1991)

Cook, *Troad*   J. M. Cook, *The Troad: an Archaeological and Typographical Study* (Oxford 1973)

Crespo, *Prosodia*   E. Crespo, *Elementos antiguos y modernos en la prosodia homerica* (Salamanca 1977)

Cuillandre, *La Droite et la gauche*   J. Cuillandre, *La Droite et la gauche dans les poèmes homériques* (Paris 1944)

Danek, *Dolonie*   G. Danek, *Studien zur Dolonie*, Wiener Studien, Beiheft 12 (Vienna 1988)

Davies   M. Davies, *Epicorum Graecorum Fragmenta* (Göttingen 1988)

de Jong, *Narrators*   I. J. F. de Jong, *Narrators and Focalizers: the Presentation of the Story in the Iliad* (Amsterdam 1987)

Delebecque, *Cheval*   E. Delebecque, *Le Cheval dans l'Iliade* (Paris 1951)

Denniston, *Particles*   J. D. Denniston, *The Greek Particles* (2nd edn, Oxford 1951)

Dodds, *Greeks and the Irrational*   E. R. Dodds, *The Greeks and the Irrational* (Berkeley and Los Angeles 1951)

Edwards, *HPI*   M. W. Edwards, *Homer, Poet of the Iliad* (Baltimore and London 1987)

Erbse,   H. Erbse, *Scholia Graeca in Homeri Iliadem*, vols. i–v (+ index vols.) (Berlin 1969–87)

Erbse, *Funktion der Götter*   H. Erbse, *Untersuchungen zur Funktion der Götter im homerischen Epos* (Berlin 1986)

Espermann, *Antenor, Theano, Antenoriden*   I. Espermann, *Antenor, Theano, Antenoriden: ihre Person und Bedeutung in der Ilias* (Meisenheim am Glan 1980)

Fagles   *Homer: the Iliad*, trans. R. Fagles (New York 1990)

Fenik, *Iliad X and the Rhesos*   B. C. Fenik, *Iliad X and the Rhesos: the Myth*, Collection Latomus 73 (Brussels–Berchem 1964)

Fenik, *TBS*   B. C. Fenik, *Typical Battle Scenes in the Iliad* (Hermes Einzelschriften 21, Wiesbaden 1968)

Fenik, *Tradition*   B. C. Fenik, ed., *Homer: Tradition and Invention* (Leiden 1978)

Fenik, *Homer and the Nibelungenlied*   B. C. Fenik, *Homer and the Nibelungenlied: Comparative Studies in Epic Style* (Cambridge, Mass. 1986)

Finley, *World*   M. I. Finley, *The World of Odysseus* (2nd edn, Harmondsworth 1979)

Foley, *Traditional Oral Epic*   J. M. Foley, *Traditional Oral Epic: the Odyssey, Beowulf, and the Serbo-Croatian Return Song* (Berkeley and Los Angeles 1990)

Foxhall and Davies, *Trojan War*   L. Foxhall and J. K. Davies, edd., *The Trojan War: its Historicity and Context* (Bristol 1984)

Fränkel, *Gleichnisse*   H. Fränkel, *Die homerischen Gleichnisse* (Göttingen 1921, repr. 1977)

Friedrich, *Verwundung* W. H. Friedrich, *Verwundung und Tod in der Ilias* (Göttingen 1956)

Friis Johansen, *Iliad in Early Greek Art* K. Friis Johansen, *The Iliad in Early Greek Art* (Copenhagen 1967)

Frisk, *GEW* H. Frisk, *Griechisches etymologisches Wörterbuch* (Heidelberg 1954–72)

Goodwin, *Syntax* W. W. Goodwin, *Syntax of the Moods and Tenses of the Greek Verb* (2nd edn, London 1929)

Greenhalgh, *Early Greek Warfare* P. A. L. Greenhalgh, *Early Greek Warfare: Horsemen and Chariots in the Homeric and Archaic Ages* (Cambridge 1973)

Griffin, *HLD* J. Griffin, *Homer on Life and Death* (Oxford 1980)

Hainsworth, *Flexibility* J. B. Hainsworth, *The Flexibility of the Homeric Formula* (Oxford 1968)

Hainsworth, *Od.* A. Heubeck, S. R. West and J. B. Hainsworth, *A Commentary on Homer's Odyssey* vol. I (Oxford 1988)

Hatto, *Traditions* A. T. Hatto, ed., *Traditions of Heroic and Epic Poetry* (London 1980–9)

Higbie, *Measure and Music* C. Higbie, *Measure and Music: Enjambement and Sentence Structure in the Iliad* (Oxford 1990)

Hoekstra, *Modifications* A. Hoekstra, *Modifications of Formulaic Prototypes* (Amsterdam 1965)

Hoekstra, *SES* A. Hoekstra, *The Sub-Epic Stage of the Formulaic Tradition* (Amsterdam 1969)

Hoekstra, *Epic Verse before Homer* A. Hoekstra, *Epic Verse before Homer* (Amsterdam 1979)

Hoekstra, *Od.* A. Heubeck and A. Hoekstra, *A Commentary on Homer's Odyssey* vol. II (Oxford 1989)

HSL *Catalogue* R. Hope Simpson and J. F. Lazenby, *The Catalogue of Ships in Homer's Iliad* (Oxford 1970)

HyDem, HyAp, HyHerm, HyAphr, HyDion *Homeric Hymns* to Demeter, Apollo, Hermes, Aphrodite, Dionysus

Janko, *HHH* R. Janko, *Homer, Hesiod and the Hymns* (Cambridge 1982)

Kakridis, *Researches* J. T. Kakridis, *Homeric Researches* (Lund 1949)

Kiparsky, *Oral Poetry* P. Kiparsky, *Oral Poetry: Some Linguistic and Typological Considerations*, in B. A. Stolz and R. S. Shannon, edd., *Oral Literature and the Formula* (Ann Arbor 1976)

Kirk, *Songs* G. S. Kirk, *The Songs of Homer* (Cambridge 1962)

Kirk, *Myth* G. S. Kirk, *Myth: its Meaning and Functions* (Cambridge, Berkeley, and Los Angeles 1970)

Kirk, *HOT* G. S. Kirk, *Homer and the Oral Tradition* (Cambridge 1976)

Krischer, *Konventionen* T. Krischer, *Formale Konventionen der homerischen Epik* (Munich 1971)

Kullmann, *Quellen*   W. Kullmann, *Die Quellen der Ilias* (Wiesbaden 1960)

Kurt, *Fachausdrücke*   C. Kurt, *Seemännische Fachausdrücke bei Homer* (Göttingen 1979)

Language and Background   *The Language and Background of Homer*, ed. G. S. Kirk (Cambridge 1964)

Latacz, *Kampfdarstellung*   J. Latacz, *Kampfparänese, Kampfdarstellung und Kampfwirklichkeit in der Ilias, bei Kallinos und Tyrtaios* (Munich 1977)

Lawrence, *Fortification*   A. W. Lawrence, *Greek Aims ln Fortification* (Oxford 1979)

Leaf   W. Leaf, *The Iliad* I–II (2nd edn, London 1900–2)

Leumann, *HW*   M. Leumann, *Homerische Wörter* (Basel 1950)

LfgrE   *Lexicon des frühgriechischen Epos*, edd. B. Snell and H. Erbse (Göttingen 1955–)

Lexicon Iconographicum   *Lexicon Iconographicum Mythologiae Classicae*, edd. H. C. Ackermann and J. R. Gisler (Zurich 1981–)

Lohmann, *Reden*   D. Lohmann, *Die Komposition der Reden in der Ilias* (Berlin 1970)

Lorimer, *HM*   H. L. Lorimer, *Homer and the Monuments* (London 1950)

L–P   E. Lobel and D. L. Page, *Poetarum Lesbiorum Fragmenta* (Oxford 1955)

LSJ   H. Liddell, R. Scott, and H. S. Jones, *A Greek–English Lexicon* (9th edn, Oxford 1940)

Meister, *Kunstsprache*   K. Meister, *Die homerische Kunstsprache* (Leipzig 1921, repr. Stuttgart 1966)

Monro, *HG*   D. B. Monro, *A Grammar of the Homeric Dialect* (2nd edn. Oxford 1891)

Moulton, *Similes*   C. Moulton, *Similes in the Homeric Poems*, Hypomnemata 49 (Göttingen 1977)

M–W   R. Merkelbach and M. L. West, edd., *Fragmenta Hesiodea* (Oxford 1967)

Mueller, *Iliad*   M. Mueller, *The Iliad* (London 1984)

Murray, *Rise*   G. Murray, *The Rise of the Greek Epic* (4th edn, Oxford 1934)

Nagler, *Spontaneity*   M. N. Nagler, *Spontaneity and Tradition: a Study in the Oral Art of Homer* (Berkeley and Los Angeles 1974)

Nagy, *Best of the Achaeans*   G. Nagy, *The Best of the Achaeans: Concepts of the Hero in Archaic Greek Poetry* (Baltimore 1979)

Nickau, *Zenodotos*   K. Nickau, *Untersuchungen zur textkritischen Methode des Zenodotos von Ephesos* (Berlin 1977)

Nilsson, *GgrR*   M. P. Nilsson, *Geschichte der griechischen Religion* I (3rd edn, Munich 1967)

Nilsson, *HM*   M. P. Nilsson, *Homer and Mycenae* (London 1933)

OCT   Oxford Classical Texts: *Homeri Opera I-V*: i–ii (*Iliad*) edd. D. B. Monro and T. W. Allen (3rd edn, Oxford 1920); iii–iv (*Odyssey*) ed. T. W. Allen (2nd edn, Oxford 1917–19; v (*Hymns*, etc.) ed. T. W. Allen (Oxford 1912)

Page, *HHI*   D. L. Page, *History and the Homeric Iliad* (Berkeley and Los Angeles 1959)

Page, *Odyssey*   D. L. Page, *The Homeric Odyssey* (Oxford 1955)

Page   D. L. Page, *Poetae Melici Graeci* (Oxford 1962)

Parry, *MHV*   A. Parry, ed. *The Making of Homeric Verse*. The Collected Papers of Milman Parry (Oxford 1971)

Peristiany, *Honour and Shame*   *Honour and Shame: the Values of Mediterranean Society*, ed. J. G. Peristiany (London 1955)

RE   *Paulys Real-Encyclopädie der classischen Altertumswissenschaft*, edd. G. Wissowa et al. (Stuttgart 1893–   )

Redfield, *Nature and Culture*   J. M. Redfield, *Nature and Culture in the Iliad: the Tragedy of Hector* (Chicago 1975)

Reinhardt, *IuD*   K. Reinhardt, *Die Ilias und ihr Dichter*, ed. U. Hölscher (Göttingen 1961)

Richter, *Furniture*   G. Richter, *The Furniture of the Greeks, Etruscans and Romans* (London 1966)

Risch, *Wortbildung*   E. Risch, *Wortbildung der homerischen Sprache* (2nd edn, Berlin 1973)

Ruijgh, *L'Élément achéen*   C. J. Ruijgh, *L'Élément achéen dans la langue épique* (Assen 1957)

Sacks, *Traditional Phrase*   R. Sacks, *The Traditional Phrase in Homer* (Leiden 1987)

Schadewaldt, *Iliasstudien*   W. Schadewaldt, *Iliasstudien* (3rd edn, Darmstadt 1966)

Schein, *Mortal Hero*   S. L. Schein, *The Mortal Hero: an Introduction to Homer's Iliad* (Berkeley and Los Angeles 1984)

SCHS   *Serbo-Croatian Heroic Songs*, ed. and trans. A. B. Lord and others (Cambridge, Mass., 1954–   )

Schulze, *QE*   W. Schulze, *Quaestiones Epicae* (Gütersloh 1892)

Schwyzer, *Gr. Gr.*   E. Schwyzer, *Griechische Grammatik*, i–iii (Munich 1939–53)

Scott, *Simile*   W. C. Scott, *The Oral Nature of the Homeric Simile* (Leiden 1974)

Shewan, *Lay of Dolon*   A. Shewan, *The Lay of Dolon* (London 1911)

Shipp, *Studies*   G. P. Shipp, *Studies in the Language of Homer* (2nd edn, Cambridge 1972)

Strasburger, *Kämpfer*   G. Strasburger, *Die kleinen Kämpfer der Ilias* (Frankfurt 1954)

Studies Palmer   *Studies in Greek, Italic and Indo-European Linguistics offered to*

Leonard R. Palmer, edd. A Morpurgo Davies and W. Meid (Innsbruck 1976)

Studies Webster   Studies in Honour of T. B. L. Webster I edd. J. H. Betts, J. T. Hooker, and J. R. Green (Bristol 1986)

Thalmann, *Conventions*   W. G. Thalmann, *Conventions of Form and Thought in Early Greek Epic Poetry* (Baltimore and London 1984)

Thompson, *Motif Index*   S. Thompson, *Motif Index of Folk Literature* (Copenhagen 1955-8)

Thornton, *Supplication*   A. Thornton, *Homer's Iliad: its Composition and the Motif of Supplication* (Göttingen 1984)

Trümpy, *Fachausdrücke*   H. Trümpy, *Kriegerische Fachausdrücke im griechischen Epos* (Basel 1950)

van der Valk, *Researches*   M. H. A. L. H. van der Valk, *Researches on the Text and Scholia of the Iliad* I–II (Leiden 1963–4)

van Thiel, *Ilias und Iliaden*   H. van Thiel, *Ilias und Iliaden* (Basel and Stuttgart 1982)

Ventris and Chadwick, *Documents*   M. Ventris and J. Chadwick, *Documents in Mycenaean Greek* (2nd edn, Cambridge 1973)

Vermeule, *Aspects of Death*   E. Vermeule, *Aspects of Death in Early Greek Poetry and Life* (Berkeley and Los Angeles 1979)

von Kamptz, *Personennamen*   H. von Kamptz, *Homerische Personennamen* (Göttingen 1982)

Von der Mühll, *Hypomnema*   P. Von der Mühll, *Kritisches Hypomnema zur Ilias* (Basel 1952)

Wace and Stubbings, *Companion*   A. J. B. Wace and F. H. Stubbings, *A Companion to Homer* (London 1962)

Wackernagel, *Untersuchungen*   J. Wackernagel, *Sprachliche Untersuchungen zu Homer* (Göttingen 1916, repr. 1970)

Wathelet, *Traits éoliens*   P. Wathelet, *Les traits éoliens dans la langue de l'épopée grecque* (Rome 1970)

Wathelet, *Dictionnaire*   P. Wathelet, *Dictionnaire des Troyens de l'Iliade* I–II (Liège 1988)

Webster, *Mycenae to Homer*   T. B. L. Webster, *From Mycenae to Homer* (2nd edn, London 1964)

West, *GM*   M. L. West, *Greek Metre* (Oxford 1982)

West, *Theogony*   M. L. West, *Hesiod, Theogony* (Oxford 1966)

West, *Works and Days*   M. L. West, *Hesiod, Works and Days* (Oxford 1978)

West, *Catalogue*   M. L. West, *The Hesiodic Catalogue of Women* (Oxford 1985)

West, *Od.*   A. Heubeck, S. R. West, and J. B. Hainsworth, *A Commentary on Homer's Odyssey* I (Oxford 1988)

West, *Ptolemaic Papyri*   S. R. West, *The Ptolemaic Papyri of Homer* (Cologne and Opladen 1967)

Whallon, *Formula, Character, and Context*   W. Whallon, *Formula, Character, and Context: Studies in Homeric, Old English, and Old Testament Poetry* (Washington, D.C., 1969)

Whitman, *HHT*   C. H. Whitman, *Homer and the Heroic Tradition* (Cambridge, Mass., 1958)

Willcock   M. M. Willcock, *The Iliad of Homer* I–II (London 1978–84)

Willcock, *Companion*   M. M. Willcock, *A Companion to the Iliad* (Chicago 1976)

Wyatt, *ML*   W. Wyatt, *Metrical Lengthening in Homer* (Rome 1969)

Journals

AJP	*American Journal of Philology*
BSA	*Annual of the British School of Archaeology at Athens*
Class. et Med.	*Classica et Mediaevalia*
CPh	*Classical Philology*
CQ	*Classical Quarterly*
GGN	*Nachrichten von der Gesellschaft zu Göttingen* (phil.-hist. Klasse)
IF	*Indogermanische Forschungen*
JHS	*Journal of Hellenic Studies*
LCM	*Liverpool Classical Monthly*
Mnem.	*Mnemosyne*
Mus. Helv.	*Museum Helveticum*
REG	*Revue des études grecques*
RhM	*Rheinisches Museum*
SMEA	*Studi micenei ed egeo-anatolici*
TAPA	*Transactions and Proceedings of the American Philological Association*
WS	*Wiener Studien*
YCS	*Yale Classical Studies*

NOTE

| indicates the beginning or end of verses; occasionally it marks the caesura. The abbreviation '(etc.)' when the frequency of a word or formula is cited means that other grammatical terminations are included in the total. For 'Arn/A', 'Did/A', etc., see vol. I 41–3.

INTRODUCTION

1. Formulas

The creation of the *Iliad* on the assumptions that underlie this commentary is not easily described, for our knowledge of ἀοιδή is limited and, it must be said, speculative. The *Iliad*, said Aristotle (*Poetics* ch. 23), was μία πρᾶξις πολυμερής; it had a unity but a great many parts. Aristotle admired the unity, and he was quite right to do so. For an ἀοιδός 'The Trojan War' was, in crude terms, a bundle of stories: the rape of Helen, the gathering at Aulis, the wrath of Akhilleus, the Amazons, the Aethiopians, the death of Akhilleus, the suicide of Aias, the wooden horse, etc., each story a bundle of incidents, duels between heroes, *aristeiai*, heroic deaths, raids, rescues, quarrels, etc., and a vast apparatus of names and genealogies, and each incident itself a bundle of themes or motifs. (See vol. II 15–27.) In this form much of the material would have been as familiar to his audience as it was to the singer. What the singer could do, for which he commanded respect and attention (cf. *Od.* 8.479–81, 17.518–20), was to turn impalpable themes and motifs of arming, fighting, arriving, eating, or the like into dactylic hexameter verse. He had a special language for the purpose (see Vol. IV 8–19) and a special way of combining it into sentences.

Accounts of Homeric diction have usually attempted to describe, from a synchronic standpoint, certain phenomena in the text. Methodologically, no doubt, that was correct. It was the method of M. Parry's *L'Epithète traditionnelle dans Homère* (Paris 1928 = *MHV* 1–190), the seminal work of this part of Homeric criticism. By extracting a sample of conspicuous diction from the text, defined as expressions 'which are regularly used under the same metrical conditions to express a given essential idea', Parry was able to claim that it was virtually certain that almost all such expressions were traditional pieces of diction. He called them 'formulas.' The term had been used non-technically in Homeric studies for many years, but its choice, though quite inevitable, seriously oversimplified conceptions of Homeric composition when it was subsequently elevated into the key element of a theory.[1]

---

[1] (*MHV* 270). D. L. Page put it more bluntly: 'there is a stock-in-trade, the vast number of traditional formulas, to be learnt only by a long apprenticeship; and there is a technique,

Parry's typical formulas were expressions like κῦμα κελαινόν (9.6) or βοὴν ἀγαθὸς Διομήδης (9.31), nouns or personal names with a perpetual ('ornamental') epithet. These served well for his primary argument. Such expressions typically fall into sets: there will be an expression filling each of the principal cola of the verse, especially those in its second half, and only exceptionally will there be more than one expression for each colon. It must be accepted that such a pervasive yet economical provision of metrical diction is an aspect of the evolution of ἀοιδή. However, that sort of diction is not the whole nor even a major part of what Homer sang, and when Parry proposed (in *HSCP* 1930 = *MHV* 266ff.) as a model of Homeric composition (which he took to be oral composition in performance) one of formulas falling into sentence-patterns, it was necessary to understand 'formula' in a wider sense, as any sort of repeated word-group, and to presume the formular status of expressions where it was not demonstrable. The model implied that any verses composed in this way would contain very little non-formular diction. Methodologically the distinctive feature of the Parry model is that it assigns to the formula an absolute priority.

In its stark form such a model does not commend itself for aesthetic reasons, being inimical to the freedom of thought and expression which the poetry of Homer seems to exemplify; but it tackled an aspect of Homeric diction that does not yield to normal critical methods and invited refinement. Even for scholars who accepted its implications the model posed two important problems: (1) how to integrate into the model of composition the many expressions which were not formulas in the sense Parry had defined, and (2) how to describe exactly what a formula *is* (as opposed to defining a class of expressions in the text which the scholar wished to study). No solution to either of these problems has yet been propounded to general satisfaction.[2]

For a tradition of heroic narrative poetry that is long extinct how much diction could be non-formular without invalidating the model cannot be known, but the very nature of the Parry model stimulated attempts to describe the formula in such a way as to embrace, it was hoped, material that on a strict definition was not formular at all by showing that the non-formular diction was similar to indisputable formulas. Hence the invention of the 'formular phrase' and the 'formula by analogy'.[3]

---

the craft of using and adapting formulas and systems of formulas, to be acquired only by long experience' (Page, *Odyssey* 139). This model is strongly criticized by Foley, *Traditional Oral Epic* 52–120.

[2] See the discussion in Austin, *Archery* 14–26.

[3] A. B. Lord, *The Singer of Tales* (Cambridge, Mass., 1960) 4 ('formular phrase'), J. A. Notopoulos, *AJP* 83 (1962) 337–68 ('formula by analogy'). M. N. Nagler's 'pre-verbal Gestalt', *TAPA* 98 (1967) 269–311, is the ultimate extension of this line of argument.

So long as attention lingered on the noun-epithet expressions denoting gods and heroes it did not matter much whether the formula was thought of as a repetition in the text or as something in the composer's mind for which repetition in the text was evidence. A 'formula by analogy', however, unless it is adduced, implausibly, as an argument that the expression is an under-represented formula, is implicitly an attempt to enter the poet's way of thinking; he is thought to be creating new diction while retaining the syntax and phrase-structure of the old. In the end these modifications, which were designed to save Parry's model, so modified it as to turn it on its head, making the structures, patterns, and other generative processes of the poetical grammar primary and the formulas an incidental result of their use.[4]

Understanding, as Aristarchus taught, begins from the text. Consider then a few verses from the beginning of Phoinix' discourse at 9.434ff., verses that express thoughts which are neither alien to the heroic world of the *Iliad* nor, like scenes of battle, central to it. In such a passage, it is suggested, the poet composed easily in the traditional style but *composed*, rather than recreating some well-rehearsed episode.

εἰ μὲν δή | νόστον γε | μετὰ φρεσί, | φαίδιμ' Ἀχιλλεῦ,
βάλλεαι, | οὐδέ τι πάμπαν | ἀμύνειν | νηυσὶ θοῇσι
πῦρ ἐθέλεις ἀΐδηλον, | ἐπεὶ χόλος | ἔμπεσε θυμῷ,
πῶς ἂν ἔπειτ' | ἀπὸ σεῖο, | φίλον τέκος, | αὖθι λιποίμην   437
οἶος; | σοὶ δέ μ' ἔπεμπε | γέρων ἱππηλάτα Πηλεὺς   438
ἤματι τῷ | ὅτε σ' ἐκ Φθίης | Ἀγαμέμνονι πέμπε   439
νήπιον, | οὔ πω εἰδόθ' | ὁμοιΐου πολέμοιο,
οὐδ' ἀγορέων, | ἵνα τ' ἄνδρες | ἀριπρεπέες | τελέθουσι.

Phoinix, as it happens, uses no *hapax legomena*. However, he uses a number of phrases that do not recur and several words or tight word-groups both of which singly fill a colon: νόστον γε, βάλλεαι, ἀμύνειν, σοὶ δέ μ' ἔπεμπε, οὐδ' ἀγορέων. There is a strong enjambment between 437 and 438, which throws the pathetic word οἶος into relief, and the main caesura of 439 is overridden; elsewhere the phrases into which the sentences fall closely follow the colonic structure of the hexameter. However it arrives upon the singer's lips, what arrives is a minimal unit of composition shaped according to the structure of the verse.

εἰ μὲν δή (8× *Il.*, 7× *Od.*): a formula, but not specifically a verse-formula.

---

[4] This is in essence the position taken by M. N. Nagler *TAPA* 98 (1967) 269–311, *Spontaneity* 1–19. The generative processes described by Nagler are, so to speak, the low-level rules of the poetical grammar.

μετὰ φρεσί(ν) (11× *Il.*, 8× *Od.*), cf. ἐνὶ φ. (28× *Il.*, 42× *Od.*): a pair of functionally synonymous expressions differing only in the metrical effect of the initial sound.

φαίδιμ' Ἀχιλλεῦ (4× *Il.*, 1 *Od.*): a formula with generic epithet, cf. φ. Ὀδυσσεῦ (5× *Od.*)).

νηυσὶ θοῇσι (7× *Il.*, 3× *Od.*): a short common-noun formula showing typical characteristics, mobile between positions 1, 3, and 9, augmented by preposition παρά, noun and epithet separated, expanded to νήεσσι θ., word-association persisting in other differently shaped cases; a metrical duplicate is attested – νηυσὶν ἐΐσῃς (1× only).

πῦρ ... ἀΐδηλον: noun and epithet separated, cf. π. ἀ juxtaposed (2× *Il.*).

ἐπεὶ χόλος ἔμπεσε θυμῷ (3× *Il.*): a half-verse formula.

ἔμπεσε θυμῷ (5× *Il.*, 1× *Od.*): a member of a long series of expressions made up of verb (–∪∪) + θυμῷ, and of a shorter series based on ἔμπεσε (ἔ. πέτρῃ, ἔ. πόντῳ).

φίλον τέκος (11× *Il.*, 4× *Od.*): a formular mode of address with variants φίλε τέκνον, τέκνον φίλε (-ον).

γέρων ἱππηλάτα Πηλεύς (4× *Il.*): an archetypal formular expression, ἱππηλάτα (an original vocative case) Πηλεύς expanded by γέρων, cf. γ. ἱ. Οἰνεύς, γ. ἱ. Φοίνιξ.

ἤματι τῷ ὅτε ... (19× *Il.*, 3× *Od.*): the formular element of a sentence pattern.

νήπιον ... (19× *Il.*, 5× *Od.*): a runover word, followed by explanatory clause, a sentence-pattern.

ὁμοιΐου πολέμοιο (6× *Il.*, 2× *Od.*): an ossified formula incorporating a gloss.

οὐδ' ἀγορέων: 'recent' form of gen. pl. when out of its traditional pattern, cf. οὔτ' ἀγοράων |, *Od.* 4.818.

ἀριπρεπέες: the localization is typical for a word of this shape.

From passages such as this it is evident that any theory seeking to explain the relation of Homeric diction to Homeric composition must attempt to integrate at least the following phenomena:

(i) A significant part of the vocabulary of the poem consists of *hapax legomena* or uniquely occurring grammatical forms, and a large part of its diction is not formular in a strict sense;

4

(ii) many words and word-types, especially longer words, have a preferred location in the verse.

(iii) a majority of phrases, e.g. verb + object or noun + epithet, conform to the basic cola of the verse (see Introduction to vol. 1, 26–30);

(iv) many sentences conform, at least partially, to certain patterns: they begin and end at certain points in the verse, they locate subject and predicate at certain points, they overrun the verse-end and are extended by participial, relative or other clauses;

(v) much diction represents the use of minimal statements, i.e. oft repeated but very simple thoughts of the type 'strike with the spear', 'his limbs collapsed', or 'he seized the armour', which do not have a fixed verbal expression;

(vi) the expression of such minimal statements makes frequent use of synonymous or quasi-synonymous words;

(vii) many phrases relate to each other in that they share besides a common structure common elements of vocabulary;

(viii) within the verse and sentence many phrases recur many times and appear to exist as units (formulas);

(ix) many formulas, as it were as lexical units, may enter into phrase and sentence patterns;

(x) many lines (constructed according to (ii), (iii), and (iv)), couplets, and groups of lines appear to exist as autonomous units of expression;

(xi) many formulas, especially noun + epithet formulas, incorporate a contextually redundant element, e.g. a so-called *epitheton ornans*;

(xii) 'ornamental' epithets may be confined to certain heroes, objects, or ideas, or may be applied to a range of nouns ('generic' epithets);

(xiii) some effort is expended to ensure that such sets of formulas are extensive enough to fill the cola most frequently required;

(xiv) formulas for a given idea, where their attestation in the poem is sufficient to reveal it, usually occur in such a way that enough *and only enough* exist to fill certain popular cola and combinations of cola in the verse;

(xv) some expressions appear to be derivative from formulas;

(xvi) formulas agglomerate over limited areas of text;

(xvii) formulas become obsolete and are reinterpreted or replaced.

These aspects of Homeric diction are briefly discussed in the numbered sections below.

How the apprentice ἀοιδός learned his diction, what he learned, and in which order can only be guessed at. No doubt it was unsystematic. Logically priority goes to the bringing together of verse-cola, sentence patterns, and basic ideas of heroic poetry (iii, iv, and v above). We may call these the high-level rules of the poetical grammar. The basic ideas then give rise to repeated forms of expression – and a problem. It is convenient for many purposes to define a formula, in the first instance, as an expression repeated in a text. Nothing more is required, for example, for examining the extension and economy of groups of name–epithet formulas. Yet the objectivity of this definition is illusory. Most discussions of formular usage sooner or later use the repetition of the phrase as evidence for 'formula' in the sense of a word-group that exists before it is employed in the same way as a word exists. A formula in this sense must always represent a leap in the dark, into the poet's mind. The leap is justified by the illumination shed on the way in which Homeric language is organized and functions. The formular link, which may be strong or weak, between words may arise by mere force of repetition or by the convenience or serendipity of the expression, or it may be acquired by the apprentice poet as an already existing unit of speech.

This conclusion introduces a diachronic dimension into the nature of Homeric diction, If formulas existed as such for, it may be, many generations before Homer, then a formula has a history. The phrase is repeated and becomes a formula because it is useful and also because it is at the time an effective expression. But the ability of successive ἀοιδοί to adapt such formulas to the insensible evolution of language and *a fortiori* to changes in the basic dialect of their art was limited: formulas could become unmetrical, unintelligible, or merely mechanical associations of words – clichés in the strict sense. Inertia is the principal reason for keeping such expressions, though in moderation 'glosses' (unintelligible words) may add a 'heroic' colour to the diction: her epithet δασπλῆτις adds a special kind of terror to the Ἐρινύς. At a given time, therefore, e.g. when the *Iliad* was composed, 'formulas' – if that is the right word – at every stage of their history from the first tentative repetition of a pleasing word-group to the mechanical reproduction of an unintelligible gloss will be found. We are fortunate if we can suggest the stages reached and the processes involved.

(i) *Hapax legomena*

A true *hapax legomenon* seems to present a special problem for those who believe that the techniques of composition used in the Homeric poems are mainly those of oral poetry. The techniques of oral poetry are generic and formular, the *hapax legomenon* by definition is not. It may not even bear any relation of sound, sense, or form to the formular part of the diction, and it would be gratuitous and implausible to claim that more than a handful make their sole appearances by chance. On the contrary, *hapax legomena*, being an aspect of the vitality of the *Kunstsprache*, and of the willingness of ἀοιδοί to experiment with their lexicon, must be accommodated in any satisfactory account of Homeric diction.[5] Here then the question is how *hapax legomena* can be deployed in a sentence otherwise made up of formular elements by a composer who relies heavily on such elements. When it is put in that way the problem posed by a *hapax legomenon* for the singer is not radically different from that posed by an otherwise unused grammatical form of a regular part of his lexicon. The unique grammatical form will indeed bring with it the verbal associations of the regular forms, but since the associated words and phrases would be built around the particular metrical shape of the regular forms they are likely to be as much a hindrance as a help in handling the unusual form.

The scale of the problem presented by true *hapax legomena* and by many uniquely occurring grammatical forms is quite serious. The printed text of the *Iliad* is made up of some 111,500 words, i.e. segments of text marked off by verse-ends or spaces, or about 63,000 if particles, pronouns, and prepositions are ignored. Many of these 'words' are repeated, but about 11,000, or more than one in six, are found once only. About 2,000 of them according to M. Pope are true *hapaxes*, lexical items occurring just once in the poem.[6]

(ii) Localization

The Homeric verse is traditionally described by its outer metric as a sequence of six dactylic feet with catalexis and optional substitution of − for ∪∪. The colometric studies initiated by H. Fränkel in 1926 describe the verse by its inner metric as a sequence of cola. The interrelations of cola (see vol. 1 18–23) are as supple as the alternations of spondees and dactyls in the traditional description and have this advantage, that it is shown how verbal units of composition 'come naturally to make the sentence and the verse'. The ἀοιδός does not fit words into a schema; his units of thought present themselves to him as, or as part of, a colon located in a specific part of the

---

[5] See M. M. Kumpf, *Four Indices of the Homeric Hapax Legomena* (Hildesheim 1984) for statistics, N. J. Richardson in Bremer, *HBOP* 165–84, for argument, Edwards, vol. v 53–5. Edwards concludes his discussion of *hapax legomena* with these words: '[Homer] was also completely at ease in employing in his verse words which are not only non-formular but which must be considered (on our limited evidence) foreign to the usual epic vocabulary.' M. Pope, *CQ* 35 (1985) 1–8, draws attention to new coinages in Homer.

[6] 'Word' is used here as a publisher might speak of a 'book of 80,000 words'. The composer's vocabulary or lexicon of course is very much shorter: ἔγχος is one entry in the lexicon but supplies 205 'words' to the text of the *Iliad*. Statistics are mine. I am indebted to the Revd A. Q. Morton, formerly of the University of Edinburgh, for making available to me computerized word-lists and indices.

verse.[7] The units need not be formulas. *Il.* 1.4, for example, contains no formulas (= repeated phrases), yet falls easily into the characteristic cola of the hexameter:

$$\text{ἡρώων} \mid \text{αὐτοὺς δὲ} \mid \text{ἑλώρια} \mid \text{τεῦχε κύνεσσιν}^8$$

For a minority of verses in the *Iliad* the poet has used no resources more arcane than these, for example Diomedes' opening words in reply to Agamemnon in book 9 (verse 32):

$$\text{Ἀτρεΐδη, σοὶ πρῶτα μαχήσομαι ἀφραδέοντι}$$

The verse practically composes itself. Ἀτρεΐδη is put in the initial position in 32 of its 35 occurrences in the *Iliad*, and μαχήσομαι immediately after the caesura in all of its 5 occurrences. That conforms to the normal practice for words of their respective shapes. ἀφραδέοντι is a unique *form* in the *Iliad*, but forms shaped $-\cup\cup-\cup$ normally fall at the verse-end. πρῶτα may be thought *a priori* to be a free form, but no less than 29 of its 35 occurrences are in the third foot.[9]

Localization often applies to the word group rather than the single word. Formulas indeed show an enhanced tendency towards localization resulting from their use in patterns of sentence construction (see §iv).[10] The unexpected locations of the words in the clumsy formula ἐς ῥ' ἀσαμίνθους βάντες (10.576) in the first half of the verse are comprehensible only if the expression is understood as a block – without the verb and preposition ἀσαμίνθους goes to the verse-end, where it belongs. Formulas are prominent in the second half of the verse where the metrical pattern is stricter and draw words out of the positions which in isolation they would naturally occupy. Strings of particles gravitate towards the beginning of the verse; prepositions and shorter adjectives must always be taken with their nouns: the measure $-\cup\cup-$, if augmented, moves to the second half of the verse: ἀχνύμενος in first–second, ἀχνύμενός περ in fifth–sixth, and καὶ ἀχνύμενός περ in third–fifth foot.

Localization is thus a primary resource for the singer. It is not pure gain, however, for it may happen occasionally that the singer's thought seeks

---

[7] H. Fränkel, 'Der kallimachische und der homerische Hexameter', *GGN* (Phil.-hist. Kl.) 1926, 197–229 (= *Wege und Formen frühgriechischen Denkens* (Munich 1960, with revisions) 100–56). For a historical sketch of subsequent scholarship see Foley, *Traditional Oral Epic* 74–84, or M. W. Edwards, *Oral Tradition* 1 (1986) 174–80.

[8] Cf. Edwards on 17.605 Ἕκτορα δ' Ἰδομενεὺς μετὰ Λήϊτον ὁρμηθέντα: 'A verse including three proper names in different syntactical relationships to the same sentence must be rare; but the metrical shapes of all three make the cola very easy to handle.'

[9] E. G. O'Neill Jr, *YCS* 8 (1942) 105–78, provides the essential statistics of localization (after correction from his Table 29 for natural quantity at the verse-end), updated by J. R. S. Beekes, *Glotta* 50 (1972) 1–10.

[10] Here as elsewhere the general statement may conceal idiosyncratic behaviour on the part of some formulas, see Hainsworth, *Flexibility* 50, 54.

expression in words and phrases that would naturally fall in the same place. If the diction is kept one expression must be displaced by the other into an unexpected position: ἀπὸ κρατερῆς ὑσμίνης by ὄσσε φαεινώ, 16.645; τόδε μακρὸν ἐέλδωρ by ἐκτετέλεσται, *Od.* 23.54; παρὰ τάφρον ὀρυκτήν by τείχεος ἐκτός, 9.67, 20.49. The results are not the most elegant of verses (see also §xv). A complicated example is ὄσσε κελαινὴ νὺξ ἐκάλυψε (5.310 = 11.356): both ὄσσε κάλυψε and νὺξ ἐκάλυψε are formular; κελαινή, only here with νύξ, appears to be inspired by another rearranged pair of formulas, νὺξ ἐρεβεννή and νὺξ ἐκάλυψε > ἐρεβεννή νὺξ ἐκάλυψε (3×).

The relation between metrical units and sense units is complex and, except in the case of enjambment,[11] has not been exhaustively explored. The cola of the verse may not define the syntactical units of the sentence, but syntactical units often coincide with cola. For present purposes it should be noted that the cola in the second half of the verse are frequently merged or their separation reduced to mere word-division: ἐρίγδουπος πόσις Ἥρης, ἔπεα πτερόεντα προσηύδα. However, should the division of the cola coincide with the bucolic diaeresis, the handling of diction may be strongly affected. A phrase may terminate, or be continued to verse-end: ὤχθησαν δ' ἀνὰ δῶμα Διὸς θεοί (οὐρανίωνες), Ἀτρείδης δ' ἀν' ὅμιλον ἐφοίτα (θηρὶ ἐοικώς). Epithets that fall between the caesura and the diaeresis are commonly generic and may not be juxtaposed with their noun: δουρικλυτός, λευκώλενος, Διῒ φίλος; but noun–epithet formulas that fall between the middle of the fourth foot and the verse-end regularly have special epithets: πολύμητις Ὀδυσσεύς, etc.

(iii) Phrase patterns

Localization of single words, it is evident *a posteriori*, is a resource whose potential is soon overtaken by more immediately useful linguistic habits. Words are not used alone but in phrases and sentences. Provided that phrases – any phrases, whether wholly new or wholly ossified – fall into an appropriate rhythm, they slip into place in the hexameter in the same way as a single word of the same shape.

Phrases have their internal patterns. In *Iliad* 1.1 the patronymic Πηληϊάδεω + Ἀχιλῆος with single -λ- has a congener in Λαερτιάδεω Ὀδυσῆος with -σ-; in 1.2 the phrase ἄλγε' ἔθηκε (which actually recurs at 22.422) is one out of many 'object – ∪ + verb ∪ – ×' phrases, e.g. in Agamemnon's *aristeia* (11.91–263) ἦτορ ἀπηύρα, φηγὸν ἵκοντο, μῦθον ἐνίσπες, λαὸν ἄνωχθι, πολλὰ δ' ἔδωκε, χίλι' ὑπέστη.

Such patterns in the shaping of phrases are formular in the sense of being

---

[11] For enjambment see the monograph of Higbie, *Measure and Music*. She discusses competition for localization on pp. 173–80.

fixed and repetitious, but that label must not be affixed to the words themselves that are patterned; *any* metrically suitable words – common, rare, or *ad hoc* inventions – may enter the pattern. For the same reason the singer is not dependent on formulas in the strict sense even in areas where such formulas are conspicuous. He uses the name Ἀχιλλεύς with an epithet 92 times in the *Iliad* and 68 times without one, but since more of the qualified occurrences of Ἀχιλλεύς enter into long complex formulas than the unqualified occurrences enter into formulas of any sort, it is right to conclude that the poet is just as happy using the name *tout court* as in a name–epithet formula.

Examples of phrase patterns: neuter adjective + αἰεί giving −∪∪−−: ἀσκελές/ἀσφαλές/ἐμμενές/νωλεμές/συνεχὲς αἰεί, etc.; a form in -θι + postposition πρό: οὐρανόθι πρό, Ἰλιόθι πρό, ἠῶθι πρό; monosyllabic noun preceded by an epithet −∪∪−: εἰλίποδας βοῦς, χαλκοβατὲς δῶ, κυδάλιμον κῆρ, ἀκάματον πῦρ, etc.; nouns or adjectives linked by repeated τε and placed at the verse-end: μέγα τε δεινόν τε, χερσίν τε ποσίν τε, κλισίας τε νέας τε, etc.; noun + preposition + epithet filling the first half: νῆας ἐπὶ γλαφυράς, χειρὸς ἀπὸ στιβαρῆς, ἀσπίδ᾽ ἐνὶ κρατερῇ, etc. (note the importance of the two initial consonants of the epithet).[12]

Phrase patterns are naturally thought of as short, but intriguing longer examples are found: e.g. Ἕκτορά τ᾽ ἀμφὶ μέγαν καὶ ἀμύμονα Πουλυδάμαντα (11.57), Νέστορα τ᾽ ἀμφὶ μέγαν καὶ ἀρήϊον Ἰδομενῆα (11.501). It should be noted that the two occurrences are in close proximity (see §xvi).

How far patterns beyond those of syntax help to form phrases is a more impalpable subject. Quasi-homonyms, such as δῆμος and δημός, interact: πίονα δῆμον – πίονα δημῷ; but that is obviously a very limited resource. Examples of assonance that are certain are also rare: ἧφι βίηφι, ὅνδε δόμονδε. Parry noted the repeated vowel sequence in θῆλυς ἀϋτή – ἡδὺς ἀϋτμή, to which add ἠπύτα κῆρυξ; D. G. Miller has drawn attention to several similar assonances.[13] But exceptions are numerous. A pleasing sound is perhaps a reason for keeping an expression rather than a template for its creation.

(iv) Sentence patterns

Parry's examination of name–epithet formulas included a succinct discussion how the formulas were worked into sentences, predominantly by the localization of a verb or verb–object group before the verse-end formula

---

[12] J. A. Russo, *YCS* 20 (1966) 219–40, lists thirty examples of phrase patterns (called by him 'structural formulas'). Other examples are cited in vol. i 26–30, in Edwards, *TAPA* 97 (1966) 115–79, and for the last colon S. E. Bassett, *TAPA* 36 (1905) 111–24.

[13] D. G. Miller, *Homer and the Ionic Epic Tradition* (Innsbruck 1982) 57–69.

(*MHV* 42–55). Localization steers a word to a particular part of the verse; the sentence pattern simultaneously builds it into the expression of a complete thought.

The opening verses of book 1 illustrate points ii–iv:

Μῆνιν ἄειδε, θεά, | Πηληϊάδεω Ἀχιλῆος |
οὐλομένην, | ἣ μυρί᾽ | Ἀχαιοῖς | ἄλγε᾽ ἔθηκε

There is an unusual break in the second foot of the first verse of *Il.* 1; otherwise the phrases into which the sentence falls fill the cola (marked by |) into which the normal verse falls. Light enjambment, with completion of the clause in the first or second foot of the second verse, is characteristic of the Homeric sentence (seven instances, for example, in the first twenty verses of book 11).

Πηληϊάδεω Ἀχιλῆος occurs 6×, by virtual necessity always between caesura and verse-end, in each case preceded by the noun on which the genitive depends. Similar name–epithet formulas in the genitive case are used in the same way (*MHV* 61). It is a trite summary of these data to describe the pattern of the clause as noun ... + noun–epithet formula in the genitive case at the verse-end. Does the summary describe a reality or a mere accident? The reality of a pattern in the use of the relatively infrequent genitive case is borne out by the data cited by Parry for the use of name–epithet formulas in the nominative case, where, of course, it is the verb that precedes the formula. In these clause-patterns *any* noun-phrase and *any* verb of suitable shape may be combined. The clause will come more naturally together if the noun or verb is a common one, but all that is required is the appropriate metrics. In the syntagma (verb ∪ − ∪∪) + (name–epithet subject expression − ∪∪ − ×) in the second half most verbs and expressions are quite usual and doubtless came together without much effort on the composer's part, but ἐφίλατο Παλλὰς Ἀθήνη, 5.61, happens to be unique. Only in that verse, in the *Iliad*, does Παλλὰς Ἀθήνη enter this clause-pattern and the augmented first aorist form ἐφίλατο is unique in Homer. But ἐφίλατο occupies not only the position of the verb in this clause-pattern but also the slot reserved in the verse for words of shape ∪ − ∪∪.

The sentence of 1.1–2 is formally completed within the first verse but is extended with progressive enjambment by the addition of an epithet, οὐλομένην, which in its turn is explicated by a relative clause. This type of sentence structure has many parallels, e.g. Ζεύς ... | σχέτλιος, ὅς ..., 9.19; γυναῖκας ... | Λεσβίδας, ἃς ..., 9.129; βουλῆς ... | κερδαλέης, ἥ τίς κεν ἐρύσσεται ἠδὲ σαώσει, 10.43–4.

The most important clause and sentence boundary is the verse-end, for about two out of five Homeric verses are unenjambed; subsidiary boundaries coincide with those of the metrical cola. In the middle or second half of the verse, sentence boundary may have a serious effect on what follows. The last two feet can accommodate only the shortest clauses or sentences if necessary enjambment is not to ensue. Short sentences in that position, however, are not infrequent: ἦ τι μάλα χρεώ, οὐδέ με πείσει, ἦρχε δ' Ὀδυσσεύς, εἴ ποτ' ἔην γε. Strings of particles and pronouns effectively postponing the beginning of the following sentence to the beginning of the next verse are also common, e.g. the notorious αὐτὰρ ἔπειτα, but also (in book 9) ἀλλ' ἔτι καὶ νῦν, εἰ δέ κεν αὖτε, ὄφρα σε μᾶλλον, ὡς καὶ ἐγὼ τήν, οὐδ' ἄν ἔτ' αὖτις, ἀλλὰ πολὺ πρίν, πὰρ δ' ἄρα καὶ τῷ, ἀλλ' ἔτι μᾶλλον, ὁππότε κέν μιν. In spite of the necessary enjambment that is entailed the singer finds it easy to bring back an important word from the following sentence into the last colon: αὐτὰρ Ἀχαιούς, ἂν δ' Ἀγαμέμνων, ἀντί νυ πολλῶν, οὐδέ τι μῆχος. A longer sentence filling the whole second half is sometimes used to complement the thought of what precedes: τοῦ γὰρ κράτος ἐστὶ μέγιστον, σὺν γὰρ θεῷ εἰλήλουθμεν, σὺ γὰρ βασιλεύτατός ἐσσι, τὸ γὰρ γέρας ἐστὶ γερόντων.

(v) Minimal statements

In principle the apparatus outlined in §§ii–iv would enable an ἀοιδός to sing what no ἀοιδός had sung before, but it is obvious that he was not put under such pressure continuously. What he sang was to a large extent thematically determined, and because his thoughts were similar so was his language. In such circumstances it was inevitable that much of his diction through its convenience or through sheer repetition hardened into formulas. 'Formula', it must here be stressed, is not an absolute term. In Homeric diction there is a gradient of linguistic similarity among the expressions we read in the text, and even when similarity has become identity there are degrees in the coherence of the formular group. One begins therefore with what may be called 'minimal statements', events or actions given expression by a single verb with its subject, object, or other complement.

The realization even of a simple idea may cut across grammatical categories: 'share' + 'honour' appears as (ὁμοίης) ἔμμορε τιμῆς, τιμῆς ἔμμοροί εἰσι, and ἥμισυ μείρεο τιμῆς; but the reader's attention is more likely to be caught where the syntax of the expressions is constant. The effect of a wound in the *Iliad* is usually instantaneous. The victim collapses; his limbs, knees, might, heart, or soul are undone (λύεσθαι). The idea may be put very simply: λύτο γούνατ(α), λύντο δὲ γυῖα, λέλυντο δὲ γυῖα, λύθη μένος, βίη λέλυται, and in the active voice λύε γυῖα, λῦσε δὲ γυῖα, λῦσε μένος, λῦσεν δὲ μένος, γούνατ' ἔλυσε. The nouns may be combined: λύτο γούνατα καὶ φίλον ἦτορ, λύθη ψυχή τε μένος τε. Epithets or prepositions may expand the simple phrase: φίλα γυῖα λέλυνται, λύθεν δ' ὑπὸ γυῖα, λύθεν δ' ὑπὸ φαίδιμα γυῖα, ὑπὸ γυῖα λέλυνται, ὑπέλυντο δὲ γυῖα, ὑπὸ γούνατ᾽ ἔλυσε, ὑπέλυσε δὲ γυῖα, ὑπέλυσε μένος καὶ φαίδιμα γυῖα.

The spirit departs and the victim dies: λίπε δ᾽ ὀστέα θυμός, λίπ᾽ ὀστέα θυμὸς ἀγήνωρ, λίπη λεύκ᾽ ὀστέα θυμός, λίπη ψυχή τε καὶ αἰών.

A corpse must not be abandoned to the enemy; it must be seized by the most convenient limb and pulled out of their reach: ποδὸς ἕλκε, ἕλκε ποδός (ἐκ ποδὸς ἕλκ᾽ 11.398 is different), (ὑφ᾽) ἕλκε ποδοῖιν, λαβὼν ποδὸς (ἐξερύσασκε/ἧκε), ποδῶν λάβε, ποδῶν ἔλαβε, ἔχεν ποδός.[14]

Dexterous handling of language such as this relies on the singer's *copia verborum* combined with the resources of the *Kunstsprache* in declension, conjugation, and word-formation, together with a few transformational rules. So the poet will say (λύτο etc.) γούνατ(α) in place of γυῖα where metre requires it (but by the rule of economy (§xiv) not γοῦνα, which has no metrical utility beside γυῖα). γούνατα, 'knees', and γυῖα, 'limbs', are not synonymous but may replace each other in the expression of this thought. 'He trembled', however, is always expressed by γυῖα: ὑπό τ᾽ ἔτρεμε γυῖα, τρόμος ἔλλαβε γυῖα. Now from the λύτο γούνατα and λίπε ὀστέα series a transformational rule may be extracted: ∪∪ – ∪∪ – ∪ > ∪∪ – ∪∪ – ∪∪ – ∪ by the addition of an epithet in the fourth or fifth foot: hence we may predict (and find, 8.452) τρόμος ἔλλαβε φαίδιμα γυῖα.

The epithets add emotional colour to such expressions but as descriptions they tell us nothing that we did not know already; they exemplify the amplitude of the epic style (§xi).

(vi) Synonyms

The epic diction is fertile in synonyms. When Dionysius Thrax defined synonymy as συνώνυμόν ἐστι τὸ ἐν διαφόροις ὀνόμασι τὸ αὐτὸ δηλοῦν, οἷον ἄορ ξίφος μάχαιρα σπάθη φάσγανον (*Gram. Gr.* p. 36.5(7)) he took his examples, or most of them, from Homer. Perhaps he did not take τὸ αὐτὸ δηλοῦν too literally; Seleucus Homericus (*F.H.G.* III 500) wrote a book paradoxically entitled Περὶ τῆς ἐν συνωνύμοις διαφορᾶς, and that represents the attitude of the Homeric scholia too. As a heuristic principle it is doubtless the better course to assume that even where words designate the same object they differ in their overtones; their focus – and therefore the contexts in which they are most appropriate – may differ, or they may say something of the speaker's state of mind or of his intention, or they may separate levels of style.

Agamemnon took a 'sword' (ξίφος, 11.29) but it was with his 'hanger'

---

[14] For other examples see 10.154–4n. (χαλκός + λάμπειν/λάμπεσθαι), 13.471–5n. (χώρῳ ἐν οἰοπόλῳ), 19.61–2n. (ὀδὰξ ἕλον οὖδας).

(ἄορ < ἀείρω; for 'hanger' = sword see *NED* s.v.) that he slew Iphidamas at 11.240. The technical point of these two synonyms is precise; the one has initial consonant, the other initial vowel, cf. κῆδος – ἄλγος, κῦδος – εὖχος, μοῖρα – αἶσα, γαῖα – αἶα, πλοῦτος – ὄλβος, φωνή – αὐδή, φῶτα – ἄνδρα, κύπελλον – ἄλεισον, ὄμματα – φάεα, τεύχεα – ἔντεα, Πηλεΐδης – Αἰακίδης, Κυλλοποδίων – Ἀμφιγυήεις, ἔγχεος αἰχμή – δουρὸς ἀκωκή, ἀκαχήμενος ἦτορ – τετιημένος ἦ., ἐνὶ φρεσί – μετὰ φ., etc. See also §13 below. The same alternation appears in adjectives, though the decorative nature of many epithets means that the need for synonyms is not so exigent: ἐρεμνός – κελαινός, ἠΰκομος – καλλίκομος, ἀγακλυτός – περικλυτός. Several of these pairs combine words that are common at all stages in the evolution of the Greek language with words that are restricted to the archaic epic (and its derivative genres). It cannot be shown, but it is surely likely, that many of these words were obsolete in the vernaculars of Homeric times. If so, their use in the epic would be recognized as characteristic of epic style, but it is doubtful if the singer sought them out for that reason. Simply as part of the poetical grammar the archaic synonyms would occur often enough by random effects to give the diction its other-worldly feeling.

When the words cited in the preceding paragraph enter into formulas their synonymy serves the purpose of extending the formular system and filling cola that would be impossible with the primary term alone (cf. §xiii).[15] Thus δόρυ μακρόν ∪∪ – ∪, δόρυ μείλινον ∪∪ – ∪∪, but χάλκεον ἔγχος – ∪∪ – ∪, and αἰχμή χαλκείη – – – – –. There is a difference between the weapon as a whole or any part of it (ἔγχος), the shaft (δόρυ), and the head (αἰχμή), but the difference is hardly visible in use. Moreover, this rather loose and extensive system has permitted the emergence of δόρυ χάλκεον and μείλινον ἔγχος, expressions in which the narrow sense of the primary formulas has been inverted. The oft-quoted series πατρὶς ἄρουρα, πατρίδα γαῖαν, πατρίδος αἴης, πατρίδι γαίη shows the effect of the final colon on phrase formation, for the different grammatical cases enter into quite different sentence patterns.

Other examples: ταχὺν ἰόν but πικρὸν ὀϊστόν; μέθυ ἡδύ but οἶνον ἐρυθρόν; ἅλα δῖαν, but εὐρέα πόντον; θοὸν ἅρμα but περικαλλέα δίφρον; μέγα (ϝ)ἄστυ but πόλιν εὐρυάγυιαν – the device is conspicuous where short noun–verb expressions are required; χέεν ἀχλύν but ἠέρα χεῦε and κατέχευεν ὀμίχλην.

Synonyms are essential for formular doublets of the 'make war and do battle' type, a numerous class (see §ix).

Overlapping the poet's use of synonyms is his use of indirect reference.

---

[15] The most extensive study is H. A. Paraskevaides, *The Use of Synonyms in Homeric Formulaic Diction* (Amsterdam 1984).

This may be stylistic *variatio*, e.g. to avoid the repetition of a noun in the same or adjacent sentences: thus νηλέϊ χαλκῷ beside δουρὶ φαεινῷ, and ὀξέϊ χαλκῷ beside ὀξέϊ δουρί. The general word, however, may serve for the specific term where the latter is metrically impossible; thus νώροπι and αἴθοπι χαλκῷ (but not νηλέϊ χαλκῷ) refer to a helmet and supply an important dative formula which would be impossible with the specific nouns (κόρυς, κυνέη, πήληξ, τρυφάλεια).

(vii) Substitution

It is sometimes obvious that the singer will take a phrase and change a single word in it: τὸ (ὃ) γὰρ γέρας ἐστὶ γερόντων/θανόντων, γέγηθε δέ τε φρένα ποιμήν/Λητώ, μέγα πῆμα/χάρμα πόληΐ τε παντί τε δήμῳ; σχέτλιοί ἐστε, θεοί, δηλήμονες/ζηλήμονες (see 24.33n.) is almost at the level of a pun. At 12.404 the poet, describing the course of a spear, sang Αἴας δ' ἀσπίδα νύξεν ἐπάλμενος· οὐδὲ διάπρο ...; a similar verse occurs at 7.260, but with ἡ δὲ διάπρο; even more remarkable is the substitution at. *Od.* 8.322 ἦλθε ... ἦλθ' ... for ἠδὲ ... ἠδ' at *Il.* 20.34 in a series of divine names. Or one verse may seem to act as a template for another: ἀπὸ δ' ἕλκεος ἀργαλέοιο | αἷμα μέλαν κελάρυζε· νόος γε μὲν ἔμπεδος ἦεν 11.812–13 = 16.528–9 to μέλαν, then ... τέρσηνε· μένος δέ οἱ ἔμβαλε θυμῷ; ἕζετ' ἔπειτ' ἀπάνευθε νεῶν 1.48 = *Od.* 6.236 with κίων for νεῶν and consequently a quite different syntax.

Though striking evidence for the basic orality of the Homeric style these are atypical examples and hardly justify a place among the resources of ἀοιδή. Better instances of substitution as a technical device in a wider but still restricted area are provided by the whole-verse formulas that introduce speeches and resume the narrative after them: τὸν/τὴν δ' ἠμείβετ' ἔπειτα with twenty-seven different (and interchangeable) subjects, τὸν/τὴν δ' αὖτε προσέειπε with twenty-two subjects, τὸν/τὴν/τοὺς δ' ἀπαμειβόμενος προσέφη with nine subjects (see *MHV* 10–16).

Substitution, exemplified by a series of expressions with one term in common, creates 'formulas by analogy': θυμός, localized in the fifth foot, is the subject of eight different verbs scanned ∪ − ×, and of seven verbs scanned − ∪∪ when placed at the verse-end. In both cases there is a strongly formular member of the set which may be regarded as the starting-point of the series: θυμὸς ἄνωγε etc. (13×) and ἤθελε θυμός (9×). The singer, familiar, let us say, with θυμὸς ἄνωγε creates, say, θυμὸς ἰάνθη by substituting the word he requires. The nearer the phrases in sense the more obvious it is that a closer relationship exists than that implied by the common phrase pattern: ἆλτο χαμᾶζε generates ἆλτο θύραζε with a similarly formed adverb. ἔκβαλε and ἔκπεσε are the active and passive expressions of the same thought: ἔκβαλε/ἔκπεσε δίφρου, ἔκβαλε/ἔκπεσε χειρός, cf.

ἔμβαλε/ἔμπεσε πόντῳ, ἔμβαλε/ἔμπεσε θυμῷ; the middle voice ἐμβάλετο cannot be substituted, hence ἔνθετο/ἔνθεο θυμῷ.

Some uses of the generic epithet (§xii) may be classed as substitutions.

(viii) Formulas proper

Sections ii–vii sought to exemplify some aspects of the traditional poetic grammar that informs the language of the *Iliad*. At that level, the basic level, the tradition of ἀοιδή was a tradition of habits, techniques, minuscule themes, and associations of words and thoughts rather than fixed phrases. ἀοιδοί were masters of a special form of language, not jugglers of formulas.[16] Nevertheless the *Iliad* is stuffed with expressions that occur so frequently as to leave no doubt that they were formulas (cf. vol. 1 29–30), that is, groups of words that existed as groups before their utterance in the same way as a single word exists. Almost all reflect the linguistic habits that underlie the diction generally and became formulas as a result of repeated re-creation in accordance with those habits. In so far as this process is still going on in the *Iliad* 'formulicity' (A. B. Lord's term) is a matter of degree; the group of words that comes together each time they are used progressively coalesces into the word group that exists prior to its use. At that stage the formula has become a device for verbalizing a given thought in metrical form, a part of the singer's *vocabulary*; and just as words – most words – enter all manner of sentences and are grammatically modified accordingly, so formulas once formed are potentially subject to the same accidents (see §xv).

In a well developed tradition of heroic poetry many formulas, perhaps the majority, were acquired as formulas by each generation of singers. In some classes of formulas, nouns or personal names with decorative epithet, that is virtually certain (see §xiv). At 24.794, however, occurs (κατείβετο) δάκρυ παρειῶν, at *Od.* 4.198 and 223 (βαλέειν, etc.) δάκρυ παρειῶν. It may be that *Od.* 4.223 echoes 198, but the structure of the clauses, the location of the words, and the absence of any related expressions suggest that the appearance of the word-group in both epics is the result of the ubiquity of tears.

It is different with the expression ἄγχι παραστάς (4× *Il.*, 3× *Od.*). The greater frequency is encouraging but not conclusive, for 'standing nearby' is typical behaviour of comrades. However, the coherence of ἄγχι and παρίσταμαι persists in other parts of the verb: ἄγχι παρέστη, ἄγχι παρίστατο, ἄγχι παρισταμένη; and lastly there is a variant ἄγχι δ' ἄρα στάς, modified to take the connective, which seems to imply the prior existence of ἄγχι παραστάς.

[16] J. M. Foley, *Traditional Oral Epic* 155–7. Cf. Cicero, *Orator* 200.

The utility of formulas in an oral tradition is obvious, and published analyses of portions of the Homeric poems show high densities.[17] Early investigators, we can now see, tended to identify the inventory of formulas as the singer's primary resource and to exaggerate the control they exercised over his thought. 'He must have for his use word groups all made to fit his verse and tell what he has to tell' (Parry, *MHV* 270). Further research established the equal importance of having for his use the factors adduced in §§ii–vii and has questioned the controlling role of formulas. The key words, the nucleus of the sentence, have priority in localization; formulas accommodate to the length and shape of the hexameter what the poet wishes to say, and may be peripheral to the central thought.[18] Formulas thus often embody redundant elements and may themselves be dispensable complements to the nucleus of the sentence, like ὀξέϊ δουρί in such a sentence as 'A slew B *with his sharp spear*': δεδαϊγμένος ὀξέϊ χαλκῷ, 19.211 in the second half, but δεδαϊγμένος *tout court* in the same position, 19.203 and 19.319. The effect of the break between the cola is evident (cf. §ii *ad fin.*).

Very frequent formulas, those occurring, say, more than ten times, are not numerous and often owe their frequency to special circumstances, e.g. name–epithet formulas in the introductions to direct speech. Many occur only two or three times. That may be due to chance, or to the fact that the expression is still in the process of becoming a formula. But low frequencies raise the possibility that some genuine formulas appear in our texts only once. The ground is firm enough when an expression that occurs once in the *Iliad* recurs elsewhere in the early hexameter corpus. Such an expression either was not needed by the poet of the *Iliad* or was not near the surface of his mind: αἵματι καὶ λύθρῳ πεπαλαγμένον (6.268, 2× *Od.*); δι' αἰθέρος ἀτρυγέτοιο (17.425, 1× *HyDem*, 1× Hesiod); ξανθὴ Δημήτηρ (5.500, *HyDem*. 302); τελεσφόρον εἰς ἐνιαυτόν (19.32, 4× *Od.*, 1× Hesiod); ἡγήτορα λαῶν (20.383, 1× *HyDem*, 3× Hesiod); Φοῖβος ἀκερσεκόμης (20.39, 1× *HyAp*, 2× Hesiod).

For various reasons expressions that are unique in the whole corpus of early hexameter verse have been called formulas: νεοθηλέα ποίην (14.347–8, see n.), because it is brother to ἐριθηλέα ποίην in *HyHerm*; κελαινῇ λαίλαπι ἶσος (11.747), brother to ἐρεμνῇ λ. ἴ. (2×). There are other ways, however, to explain the genesis of these expressions.

There is a negative side to the use of formulas. They are inherently conservative; they make it easy to say what has been said before, and

---

[17] The most extensive is that of the whole of book 10 by G. Danek, *Dolonie* Anhang. The apparatus to N. J. Richardson's edition of *HyDem* also provides an elaborate formular analysis.

[18] E. Visser, *Homerische Versifikationstechnik. Versuch einer Rekonstruktion* (Frankfurt 1987), reversing the conventional opinion that formulas control thought. Visser has published a briefer account in English in *Würzb. Jahrb. f. d. Alt.* 14 (1988) 21–37.

difficult if only by contrast to say what is new (see 10.498n.). The evolution of culture and language makes them become obsolete, yet they are hard to replace (see §xvii). They are the right phrase in one context, but override a precise choice of language in another, so as to give a sense that is approximate (9.255n.), or even inappropriate (11.161n.). Metrically flawless in their primary shapes, their derivatives may be faulty: ἄφθιτον αἰεί > ἄφθιτα αἰεί with hiatus, μερόπων ἀνθρώπων > μέροπες ἄνθρωποι; sentence patterns bring them into juxtaposition and leave hiatus or short syllables uncorrected (see *MHV* 191–221). These accidents are not frequent: the *aristeia* of Agamemnon (11.91–168) is metrically flawless if a hiatus in ζώγρει, Ἀτρέος υἱέ and an observed digamma before ἄναξ are excused.

(ix) Types of formula

Formulas are simply groups of two or more words that are associated with each other; they are usually juxtaposed and syntactically linked, but neither condition is necessary: θοάων ... νηῶν or νεῶν ... θοάων (5×) is clearly formular, so is θυμὸς ἐνὶ στήθεσσι (35× *Il.*, 13× *Od.* – one of the most frequent formulas in the epic) where the prepositional phrase construes with the verb of the sentence. Formulas may thus arise among all grammatical categories of word. Strings of particles, lightly adapted from the formulas of vernacular speech, were noted in §iv and adverbial phrases (ἀσφαλὲς αἰεί, etc.) in §iii; the minimal statements of §v would harden into verb + object formulas. Homeric formulas parallel the formulas of vernacular speech: 'never-the-less' (particle string), 'break x's heart' (substitution system), 'serried ranks' (special epithet), 'arrant knave'/'fool'/'nonsense' (generic epithet).[19] In the epic there are more of them and they are, at least to begin with, related to metre.

Formulas of the simple kind, such as πῖπτε δὲ λαός, ὡπλίσσατο δεῖπνον, ἵμερος αἱρεῖ, ἕλε δ' ἄνδρα, ἀντίος ἔστη (11.85–95), come into being directly from the subject matter of the narrative. The hexameter, however, is a long verse, and consequently the versifier finds a certain amplitude of style, towards which he is already drawn as narrator, useful. Formulas that embody a redundant element come into existence then as part of the epic style. Of these there are two important kinds: doublets, which have received little attention, and noun–epithet formulas, which have been intensively studied.

Doublets: simple redundancy is common: ἡγήτορες ἠδὲ μέδοντες (9.17 etc.), ὑπέσχετο καὶ κατένευσεν (9.19), ἀπτολέμους τ' ... καὶ ἀναλκίδας (9.41); so are polar opposites: ἠμὲν νέοι ἠδὲ γέροντες (9.36). The nouns and

---

[19] Cf. P. Kiparsky, in *Oral Literature and the Formula*, eds. B. A. Stolz and R. S. Shannon (Ann Arbor 1976) 74–81.

adjectives connected by the ... τε ... τε pattern are usually quasi-synonyms: πόλεμόν τε μάχην τε, γενέην τε τόκον τε; or polar opposites: ἔργον τε ἔπος τε, ἀνδρῶν τε θεῶν τε. Verse-end formulas are extended to the caesura by quasi-synonyms: φόνον καὶ κῆρα μέλαιναν, θάνατος καὶ μοῖρα κραταιή. Verbs localized in the first half are reinforced by synonyms introduced by ἠδέ or οὐδέ and located in the fifth–sixth foot: ἀλλ' εὖ οἱ φάσθαι πυκινὸν ἔπος ἠδ' ὑποθέσθαι (11.788); ἔγχος δ' οὐ δύναμαι σχεῖν ἔμπεδον οὐδὲ μάχεσθαι (16.520).

Noun-epithet formulas incorporate some fully functional adjectives (πᾶς and πολύς the most obvious), but for the most part the word-group adds no information relevant to context that a single word would not convey. The redundant element may be the noun: ἡγήτορες ἄνδρες, σχέτλια ἔργα, πατρίδα γαῖαν, νηλέϊ θυμῷ (= 'pitilessly'), θνητῶν ἀνθρώπων; but in the characteristic noun–epithet formula it is the adjective. One such formula occurs in about one verse out of three.

No formula, unless it is in the vocative case, can be considered apart from the sentence in which it occurs. Most noun–epithet formulas are used as if they formed an element in a larger and looser whole: ἠέρι πολλῇ (6×), always with a part of καλύπτω; ξίφος ὀξύ (5×), always with ἐρύομαι; νώροπα χαλκόν, etc., (5×), always with a verb of dressing (δύομαι, εἴνυμαι, κορύσσομαι). In such expressions the techniques of formula, minimal statement, sentence pattern, and localization come together.

(x) Whole-line formulas, couplets, and runs

Complex formulas may themselves harden into fixed shapes. The thought expressed in a loosely worded form at 21.69–70 ἐγχείη ... ἐνὶ γαίῃ | ἔστη, ἱεμένη χροὸς ἄμεναι ἀνδρομέοιο is also expressed by a whole-verse formula: δοῦρα ... | ἐν γαίῃ ἵσταντο λιλαιόμενα χροὸς ἆσαι (2×). Such verses, occurring in the body of the narrative, are noted in the commentary.

Verses of introduction, transition, and conclusion naturally tend towards fixity: αὐτὰρ ἐπεὶ πόσιος καὶ ἐδητύος ἐξ ἔρον ἕντο (7× *Il.*, 14× *Od.*: for variants see Janko, *HHH* 130); ὡς οἱ μὲν μάρναντο δέμας πυρὸς (αἰθομένοιο) (5×); ὄφρα μὲν ἠὼς ἦν καὶ ἀέξετο ἱερὸν ἦμαρ (2× *Il.*, 1× *Od.*) 'When the day dawned ...' is expressed in the *Odyssey* by one of the most habitual of these formulas: ἦμος δ' ἠριγένεια φάνη ῥοδοδάκτυλος ἠώς (22×); the *Iliad* knows the line (2× in books 1 and 24) and uses the epithets in other verses, but is otherwise curiously uncertain over the expression of this thought: αὐτὰρ ἐπεί κε φανῇ καλὴ ῥοδοδάκτυλος ἠώς (1×), ἠὼς μὲν κροκόπεπλος ἐκίδνατο πᾶσαν ἐπ' αἶαν (2×), ἠὼς μὲν κροκόπεπλος ἀπ' Ὠκεανοῖο ῥοάων | ὄρνυθ' (1×), and a notable maverick: ἦμος δ' ἑωσφόρος εἶσι φόως ἐρέων ἐπὶ γαῖαν | ὅν τε μετὰ κροκόπεπλος ὑπεὶρ ἅλα κίδναται ἠώς, 23.226–7.

Formulas

For verses introducing speeches, see Parry, *MHV* 15–16, Edwards, *HSCP* 74 (1970) 1–36.

Transitions: ἄλλο δέ τοι ἐρέω, σὺ δ' ἐνὶ φρεσὶ βάλλεο σῇσι (7× *Il.*, 7× *Od.*), ἀλλ' ἄγε μοι τόδε εἰπὲ καὶ ἀτρεκέως κατάλεξον (4× *Il.*, 13× *Od.*).

Conclusions: ἂψ δ' ἑτάρων εἰς ἔθνος ἐχάζετο κῆρ' ἀλεείνων (6×), μάστιξεν δ' ἐλάαν· τὼ δ' οὐκ ἀέκοντε πετέσθην (3× *Il.*, 3× *Od.* + 2× with ἵππους for ἐλάαν), κεῖτο μέγας μεγαλωστί, λελασμένος ἱπποσυνάων (1× *Il.*, 1× *Od.*, but cf. 18.26–7 and n.).

Such formulas almost certainly belong to the tradition generally, but a few seem to have arisen within the context of the *Iliad*: φεύγωμεν (etc.)/ οἴχωνται σὺν νηυσὶ φίλην ἐς πατρίδα γαῖαν (5×), ἠτίμησας (etc.)· ἑλὼν γὰρ ἔχεις γέρας 4× (+ αὐτὸς ἀπούρας 3×).

Formal modes of address often occupy a whole verse: Ἀτρεΐδη κύδιστε, ἄναξ ἀνδρῶν Ἀγάμεμνον (8× *Il.*, 2× *Od.*, etc.). All major heroes in the poem – Aias, the Aiantes, Akhilleus, Diomedes, Hektor, Nestor, Odysseus – have such a formula, and so do the two sides: ὦ φίλοι, ἥρωες Δαναοί, θεράποντες Ἄρηος (4×), ὦ φίλοι, Ἀργείων ἡγήτορες ἠδὲ μέδοντες (9×), Τρῶες καὶ Λύκιοι καὶ Δάρδανοι ἀγχεμαχηταί (6×).

Formular couplets and runs of three verses or more are more problematical. The longer a formula the more likely it is to lose its cohesion and fall apart, yet when groups of two or three or six verses are repeated chance is an implausible explanation of how such runs of verses arise. It may be that a second occurrence is a deliberate echo of the first, or that it is an unconscious echo of the first, or that the coherence of the thought expressed leads to the same phrases coming to mind independently on each occasion, or that the group of verses exist as a block, a kind of super-formula.

Deliberate reference back to a previous passage, with the intention that the earlier passage should be recalled, is as indisputable in the *Iliad* as it is in any other work of literature of similar extent: the comments on the destruction of the Achaean wall at 12.1–33 recall the prophecy of its destruction at 7.443–63. If the passages are compared it will be seen that coincidence of thought is expressed by identical verses at two points: 7.449–50 ≅ 12.5–6 τεῖχος (ὃ) ἐτειχίσσαντο (ποιήσαντο) νεῶν ὕπερ, ἀμφὶ δὲ τάφρον | ἤλασαν, οὐδὲ θεοῖσι δόσαν κλειτὰς ἑκατόμβας; and 7.462–3 ≅ 12.31–2 αὖτις δ' ἠϊόνα μεγάλην ψαμάθοισι καλύψαι | . . . τεῖχος ἀμαλδύνηται (τεῖχος ἀμαλδύνας). Compare, for a possible unconscious echo, 7.323–6 = 9.92–5 αὐτὰρ ἐπεὶ πόσιος καὶ ἐδητύος ἐξ ἔρον ἔντο, | τοῖς ὁ γέρων πάμπρωτος ὑφαίνειν ἄρχετο μῆτιν, | Νέστωρ, οὗ καὶ πρόσθεν ἀρίστη φαίνετο βουλή· | ὅ σφιν ἐϋφρονέων ἀγορήσατο καὶ μετέειπεν . . . The significant fact here is noted by Kirk (on 7.323–6): 'The structure of the two scenes, whose purpose is to introduce an important new course of action, is similar.'

However, the scenes are by no means typical and further restrict their application by naming Nestor.

Runs occur as follows in the first hundred verses of book 11: 1–2 = *Od.* 5.1–2; 5–9 = 8.222–6; 11–14 = 2.451–4 (where ὦρσεν for ἔμβαλ'); 17–19 = 3.330–2 = 16.131–3 = 19.369–71; 41–3 = 3.336–8 = 16.137–9 (with variants); 47–9 = 12.77 + 84–5; 84–5 = 8.66–7; 97–8 = 12.185–6 = 20.399–400 (with variants in the first verse).

The variations found in typical scenes, even in those as regular as the sacrifice-meal and the arming, suggest that the cohesion of a run of verses is fragile. This observation is important, though disturbing, for the question of the stability of a poem and its constituent episodes in a truly oral milieu even in the mouth of the same ἀοιδός.

(xi) Ornamental epithets

Epithets are typical of most narrative styles.[20] What distinguishes their use in Homer is that their advantages to the story-teller are put to the service of the versifier. Inevitably it is the 'ornamental' epithet that makes the most conspicuous contribution both to amplitude and utility. Amplitude has its aesthetic advantages, but so has stark simplicity, especially at moments when words are inadequate, cf. bT at 22.61 'It is marvellous how he briefly brings this scene into view, using his words without superfluity. He doesn't say ὑψορόφους or δαιδαλέους θαλάμους or θύγατρας καλλικόμους or καλλισφύρους, but strips the disasters of epithets', a perceptive comment.

An 'ornamental' epithet is appropriate to the noun considered in isolation and to the themes to which the noun belongs. It completes and sharpens the idea expressed by the noun, just as similes sharpen a scene in the narrative. So much is evident; what it adds to the noun, however, in a particular verse is still controversial. Parry dared to affirm that it was no more than a touch of heroic colour; Vivante maintains that valuable meaning is always present.[21] Rather it is the case that relevance and redundancy are the ends of a spectrum: the epithet in a whole-verse formula with a highly predictable use will be semantically superfluous in a particular context, e.g. τὸν δ' αὖτε προσέειπεν ἄναξ ἀνδρῶν Ἀγαμέμνων (9.114 etc.), but significant in a less formalized context, e.g. Ἀτρείδης τε ἄναξ ἀνδρῶν καὶ δῖος Ἀχιλλεύς (1.7); an epithet that is neutral in most contexts acquires force when sense and context chime together: πεπνυμένος is the epithet of

---

[20] Bowra, *Heroic Poetry* 225–6; even when the medium is prose, K. O'Nolan, *CQ* 19 (1969) 1–19.
[21] Parry, *MHV* 118–72, P. Vivante, *The Epithet in Homer: a Study in Poetic Values* (New Haven 1982). Neither position gives enough weight to the historical factor (§xvii).

subordinate and youthful characters and appropriate generally, but appropriate specifically to Antilokhos (whom Menelaos has just called πρόσθεν πεπνυμένε) at 23.586; the raging Hektor at 11.295 is βροτολοιγῷ ἶσος Ἄρηι (4× elsewhere in conventional use), see also 9.255n., 19.408n., 20.497–8n. A clash of sense and context may have the same effect, as in the juxtaposition Πατρόκλοιο θανόντος ἀμύμονος 17.379, cf. 17.10. Yet a certain caution is necessary; in a line such as 9.625 ἄγριον ἐν στήθεσσι θέτο μεγαλήτορα θυμόν the use of the predicate ἄγριον shows how far μεγαλήτορα θυμόν is a single idea ('heroic heart' – heroes' hearts *ipso facto* are 'great-souled'). Outside the themes where it is at home there is a risk that context may contradict epithet. The surprising thing is that this happens so rarely: having just cursed Meleagros Althaie is still μητρὶ φίλη at 9.555; Nestor prays at 15.371, well before sunset, χεῖρ' ὀρέγων εἰς οὐρανὸν ἀστερόεντα; Nestor's horses, which he is about to describe as βάρδιστοι, are ὠκύποδες at 23.304.

(xii) Special and generic epithets

The ornamental epithets applied to persons fall into two classes, those that are confined to one deity, hero, or heroine, and those that are used apparently without discrimination of any member of his/her class. Usually it is deities or major heroes who have special designations; they are, so to speak, *sui generis*. This distinction is most conspicuous in the nominative case; if metrics permit, the special epithet (or a similar form) will be carried into the oblique cases: 'swift-footed Akhilleus' becomes ποδώκεα Πηλείωνα in the accusative case and ποδώκεος Αἰακίδαο in the genitive, but ἀμύμονα Πηλείωνα along with nine other named heroes and one heroic horse, and ἀμύμονος Αἰακίδαο with five others, if the initial vowel is required.

Without generic epithets it would be difficult to handle a cast as large as that of the *Iliad*. With a relatively small apparatus – Parry lists twenty epithets in the nominative case (*MHV* 89) – a literal army of minor or invented characters can be introduced into the cola and phrase patterns of the hexameter.

The distinction between special and generic is not always sharp. Agamemnon is ἄναξ ἀνδρῶν thirty-seven times, an appropriate description of his unique standing; but the poet's feeling for a link between epithet-phrase and special rank is not absolute and ἄναξ ἀνδρῶν is applied once to each of five other heroes.

Common nouns do not fall into classes to the same extent, so that special and generic lose much of their point as separate categories. Synonyms naturally share the same epithets, as far as metre and grammar allow: πτερόεντες ὀϊστοί – ἰὰ πτερόεντα, φάσγανον/ξίφος/ἄορ ὀξύ. There are also a few general categories: crops are 'honey-sweet' μελιηδέα καρπόν/οῖνον/ πυρόν, metallic objects are bright; otherwise different nouns are expanded in different ways. The epithets pick out some characteristic aspect of the denoted object, and that is not likely to be widely shared. All weapons are sharp, almost anything can be beautiful, but it is coincidental that ships and night are black, bones and barley white.

(xiii) Extension

Noun-epithet expressions are easily grouped into sets characterized by extension and economy. The number of expressions in a set constitutes its extension. In the accusative case (common nouns are most frequent in the accusative) the following expressions with juxtaposed ornamental epithet occur for 'wine': μέθυ ἡδύ (8× *Od.*), (ϝ)οῖνον ἐρυθρόν (3× *Od.*), αἴθοπα οἶνον (9× *Il.*, 11× *Od.*), αἴθοπα οἶνον ἐρυθρόν (1× *Od.*), μελιηδέα οῖνον (2× *Il.*, 4× *Od.*), εὐήνορα οῖνον (1× *Od.*), μελιηδέα οῖνον ἐρυθρόν (1× *Od.*), μελίφρονα οῖνον (2× *Il.*, 3× *Od.*), μελίφρονα οῖνον ἐρυθρόν (1×), οῖνον ἐΰφρονα (1× *Il.*), and οῖνον ἐριστάφυλον (2× *Od.*). The shape of each expression is related to the sentences and sentence patterns in which it occurs, and it is these, rather than the set itself, which are important for versification. Similar sets may be extracted from the text for many common nouns,[22] but it is also the case that many frequently used nouns have no such set of epithets, but enter the verse by other phrase and sentence patterns: σῖτος takes no ornamental epithets except γλυκερός in a whole-verse formula, οἶκος has none in the second half but a solitary πίονα οῖκον; bronze and iron have epithets, gold only a doubtfully formular τιμήεις and silver no epithets at all.

Parry's investigation of extension focused on name–epithet formulas. Common nouns have a relatively restricted number of verbs with which they construe whether as subject or object, and the verbs may not readily construe with different nouns. Kings and horses have few interests in common, and though their formulas are formed and used according to the same rules of poetical grammar it does not make much sense to group them together. However, the epic names kings but does not make a habit of naming horses. So on the one hand we have μώνυχες/ὠκέες ἵπποι, on the other κύδιμος ἥρως and *an open-ended set of personal names*, usually called a formula-type. The formula-type itself is a scholar's concept, an abstraction, but it had also some kind of reality for the singer: the larger formulas into which its members enter and the formular complements with which they

---

[22] The most complete collection is that of Paraskevaides (see n. 15), but see also Page, *HHI* 266–80.

construe are real enough. Every member of the genus 'god', 'hero', or whatever, must if possible furnish an expression to fit the larger formula. The effects are readily seen in speech-formulas.[23] τὸν δ᾽ ἠμείβετ᾽ ἔπειτα requires a half-verse subject phrase. That is no great problem, since personal names are often long and epithets may be cumulated; but what about the monosyllable Ζεύς? To fill the second half of the verse the ἀοιδοί paraphrased: πατὴρ ἀνδρῶν τε θεῶν τε and Ὀλύμπιος ἀστεροπητής. Ζεύς is awkward in another way; it begins with a double consonant. No masculine adjective in the nominative case can be placed before it without creating an inelegantly overlengthened syllable and in many cases an awkward grouping of consonantal sounds (-ος/-ης Ζ-, i.e. -s sd- or -s ds-): hence vocatives μητίετα and νεφεληγερέτα (this seems the best explanation of these forms) and even an accusative εὐρύοπα are pressed into service to complete the set. ἱππότα and ἱππηλάτα combine with names of heroes scanning – – and beginning with a consonant. True vocatives are also used: (προσέφης) Πατροκλέες ἱππεῦ, Εὔμαιε συβῶτα. All these turns of phrase are an essential part of the formular system, whatever artistic value they may also possess in a particular context. χρυσέη Ἀφροδίτη (22.470 and *HyAphr* 23) tolerates a hiatus to complete the goddess's set of formulas, but in this instance the nominative is not the primary form of the formula; 'golden Aphrodite' is so called nine times in the oblique cases.

(xiv) Economy

Economy implies that for each shape in a set of formulas there is normally only one expression. Economy of diction is probably specific to the ancient Greek epic tradition, and is so because the noun–epithet formula has been developed in Greek as an important element in the technique of versification. Economy is pervasive. The same epithet is used in all case-forms permitted by metre; the same idea runs through a formular set. Economy is evident also at the level of grammar, within the *Kunstsprache*, and to some extent at least at the thematic level. Dialect, archaic and artificial forms enter the *Kunstsprache* only where they differ from the corresponding Ionic forms, cf. vol. iv, 12–19; typical scenes have a fixed pattern.

Generally, the more reason there is to believe that an expression *is* a formula, the less likely it is to have a competitor. A formula comes ready-made, not as the product of some generative process. Where the latter operates, because a formula does not exist or does not come to mind, the results may not always be the same: εὐξέστῳ ἐνὶ δίφρῳ (and gen.) – εὐπλέκτῳ ἐ. δ., εὔτροχον ἅρμα (2× *Il.*) – εὔξοον ἅ. (1× *Il.*), (ἄττα) γεραιὲ

---

[23] Edwards. *CPh* 64 (1969) 81–7 and *HSCP* 74 (1970) 1–36.

διοτρεφές (3×) – γ. παλαιγενές (1×). Major formular sets often show this kind of superfluity among rarely used peripheral members but hardly ever among the frequently employed formulas at the core of the set. Some difficult examples remain, however: Διὸς θυγάτηρ Ἀφροδίτη – φιλομμειδὴς Ἀφροδίτη (see 3.424n. and 14.211–13n.), βοῶπις πότνια Ἥρη – θεὰ λευκώλενος Ἥρη,[24] Ἕκτορος ἱπποδάμοιο – Ἕκτορος ἀνδροφόνοιο (see 9.351n.).

Apparent breaches of economy occur when metrically equivalent formulas are appropriate to different contexts. In such cases economy is maintained within the same theme: ὄρεα νιφόεντα 3× – σκιόεντα 3× (see 13.754–5n.); perhaps μείλινον ἔγχος – χάλκεον ἔγχος (cf. E. Cosset, *REA* 85 (1983) 196–8), which clearly originally referred to the spear-shaft and the spear-head. μελίην εὔχαλκον (20.322) is specifically the spear of Akhilleus, not a duplicate of δολιχόσκιον ἔγχος (cf. R. Schmiel, *LCM* 9.3 (1984) 34–8). νώροπα/αἴθοπα χαλκόν etc. is armour being donned, νηλέϊ/ὀξέϊ χαλκῷ is a weapon being used. Meriones is πεπνυμένος in book 13 as subordinate to Idomeneus, but δουρικλυτός at 16.619 when he fights alone. ἄλκιμος υἱός is used after names in -εος and -ίου, but ἀγλαὸς υἱός after -ονος, -ορος (see 15.445–51n.).

Devices of modification or generation produce a duplicate expression: κρείων Ἐνοσίχθων 8× exists beside κλυτὸς Ἐννοσίγαιος 7×, because εὐρύ can be prefixed to the former (14.134–5n.); θῖνα θαλάσσης 11× at the verse-end is drawn back, extended with εὐρυπόροιο, and creates a duplicate of πολυφλοίσβοιο θαλάσσης; for μελιηδέος οἴνου – μέλανος οἴνοιο see §xvii. Occasionally a generic or derivative term replaces a special epithet without obvious reason: Πηληϊάδεω Ἀχιλῆος (8×) – μεγαθύμου Πηλεΐωνος (19.75); νηυσὶ θοῇσι – νηυσὶν ἐΐσης *Od.* 4.578.

Some apparent breaches result from substitution of an unusual epithet under contextual influence: ἅρμασι κολλητοῖσι (3×) – ἅ. δαιδαλέοισιν 17.448 (see note); Πουλυδάμας ἐγχέσπαλος (3×) – Π. πεπνυμένος 18.249; πόδας ὠκὺς Ἀχιλλεύς – μεγάθυμος Ἀ. (23.168; n.b. εἰς πόδας in the following line); νεφεληγερέτα Ζεύς (30×) – στεροπηγερέτα Ζ. (16.298), because the preceding word is νεφέλην. But how to explain φαεσίμβροτος ἠώς at 24.785 in place of ῥοδοδάκτυλος (27×) in a verse that otherwise repeats 6.175, unless it is to avoid the repetition of ῥοδοδάκτυλος at 24.788 (see n.)? Old formulas which have become unmetrical or unintelligible may survive in competition with more recent creations (see §xvii).

Diction apparently in flux: Ζηνὸς ἐριγδούπου (15.293); Ζ. ἐριβρεμέτεω (13.624); Ζ. ἐρισθενέος (Hesiod *Erga* 416). Expressions using Ζηνός and other parts of the stem Ζην- are unstable because that form of the stem is

---

[24] For attempts to relate the formulas to different contexts see Boedeker, *Aphrodite* 23, 30, W. Beck, *AJP* 107 (1986) 480–88.

analogical, of no great antiquity, and never made great inroads into the territory of the stem Δι-. But comparable instability may arise from the fact that the extension of a formula set is often achieved by the manipulation of a few associations of noun and epithet. Thus the set of formulas built up around the word σάκος is: σάκος μέγα τε στιβαρόν τε 5× (3× in a whole-verse formula), δεινόν σάκος ἑπταβόειον 2× (7.245 and 266), σάκος αἰόλον ἑπταβόειον 1×, σάκος ... ἑπταβόειον 1×, σάκος αἰόλον 1×, σάκος εὐρὺ παναίολον 1×, σάκος εὐρύ 1×, εὐρὺ ... σάκος 1×, σάκος ... τετραθέλυμνον 2×. (The formula φέρων σάκος ἠΰτε πύργον (3×) is exclusive to Telamonian Aias.) For the clustering of δεινόν σάκος ἑπταβόειον in book 7 see §xvi. For the two regular formulas, σάκος μέγα τε στιβαρόν τε and σάκος ... τετραθέλυμνον, the rule of economy operates and there is no other expression of the same metrical shape. The other expressions play with various arrangements of the three epithets ἑπταβόειον, αἰόλον, and εὐρύ, and not surprisingly where the diction is fluid threw up σάκος αἰόλον ἑπταβόειον, a duplicate to δεινόν σάκος ἑπταβόειον. In most formula sets, except for the 'hard' formulas in frequent use, this kind of fluidity is the norm, and the ability to handle it an essential part of the art of song.

(xv) Modification etc.[25]

Whatever the circumstances in which a formula comes into existence once it has done so the formular bond is hard to break. The word-group persists in spite of declension or conjugation, changed localization, expansion, or shortening. Even a change in grammatical case that does not affect word-order or shape means a change in the sentence patterns and/or complex formulas in which the formula is primarily employed. Graver accidents than these are survived: περικαλλέα δίφρον, both 'chair' and 'chariot', καλλίτριχες ἵπποι > καλλίτριχε ... ἵππω = 'chariot' (see 17.504–5n.), μένεα πνείοντες (attributive phrase) > μένος πνείοντες (participial phrase), εὐεργέα νῆα > νηῦς εὐεργής, πόντον ἐπ' ἰχθυόεντα > Ἑλλήσποντον ἐπ' ἰχθυόεντα, νήδυμος ὕπνος > ν. Ὕπνος personified. The formular link may even survive enjambment, the epithet slipping into the pattern of the run-over word: ἦτορ | ἄλκιμον, ἵππους | ὠκέας, ὦμον | δεξιόν, θυμῷ | πρόφρονι, etc.

A majority of formulas are restricted to a single colon of the verse by their length or metrics. Those whose shape would permit their location in two or more positions tend to follow the pattern of use of similarly shaped formulas whose position in the verse is fixed; most occurrences of formulas shaped

---

[25] See Hainsworth, *Flexibility* for an analysis of the use of noun–epithet formulas shaped —∪∪ — ∪ and ∪∪ — ∪.

⏑⏑–⏑⏑–⏑, for example, fall at the verse-end where formulas shaped ⏑⏑–⏑⏑–– must be located. Outside the sentence patterns that determine this distribution there is evidence of improvisation in an increased proportion of unique expressions; nevertheless large numbers of formulas that can be moved are moved: 29 out of 68 shaped ⏑⏑–⏑⏑–⏑ at the verse-end, 92 out of 163 shaped –⏑⏑–⏑ at the verse-end.

Moving a formula may often require its modification. Techniques here are mostly opportunist: δῖα θεάων > δῖα θεά, ἀλλὰ καὶ ἔμπης > ἀλλ' ἔμπης, κεῖτο τανυσθείς > κεῖτο ταθείς, ἔλπετο θυμός > θυμὸς ἐέλπετο. Verb-formulas add or drop prepositional prefixes. Noun–epithet formulas usually invert the order of words with or without further modification: ἤρα πολλήν > πολλὴν ἤρ' and ἤρα πουλύν, αἷμα κελαινόν > κελαινεφὲς αἷμα.

Adjustment to length without movement: ἐπιειμένος ἀλκήν > εἱμένος ἀλκήν, νηυσὶ θοῇσι > νήεσσι θοῇσι; to initial sound: ὤλεσε θυμόν > θυμὸν ὄλεσσε. Lengthening is otherwise achieved by adding a redundant element, epithet or synonym: δολιχόσκιον ἔγχος | βριθὺ μέγα στιβαρὸν κεκορυθμένον (16.801–2, an extreme case).

Splitting the formular word-group illustrates the close connexion between cola and phrase pattern. If an epithet fills the final colon, the noun easily floats free of it: δέπας . . . ἀμφικύπελλον, νέες . . . ἀμφιέλισσαι, ἀσπίδα . . . πάντοσ' ἐΐσην, usually to admit a verb; likewise if the epithet falls neatly between caesura and diaeresis: περικαλλέα . . . δίφρον, μεγαλήτορι . . . θυμῷ, χρυσάμπυκας . . . ἵππους; or with the noun brought back into the first half: ἔγχος . . . δολιχόσκιον, λώβην . . . θυμαλγέα, δῶρα . . . περικλυτά. Other cases do violence to phrase patterns and their relation to the cola: νῆες ⟨ἕποντο⟩ θοαί 2.619 with word-break between the shorts of the second foot.

(xvi) Clustering[26]

In every book of the *Iliad* there are a number of repeated lines which occur nowhere else in the poem. In book 11 we have αὐτὰρ ὁ τῶν ἄλλων ἐπεπωλεῖτο στίχας ἀνδρῶν | ἔγχεΐ τ' ἀορί τε μεγάλοισί τε χερμαδίοισιν (264–5 = 540–1), ἐς δίφρον δ' ἀνόρουσε, καὶ ἡνιόχῳ ἐπέτελλε | νηυσὶν ἐπὶ γλαφυρῇσιν ἐλαυνέμεν· ἤχθετο γὰρ κῆρ (273–4 = 399–400), ἤ, καὶ Πείσανδρον (Θυμβραῖον) μὲν ἀφ' ἵππων ὦσε χαμᾶζε (143 = 320), ἐς δ' ἄγε χειρὸς ἑλών, κατὰ δ' ἑδριάασθαι ἄνωγε (646 = 778). These repetitions occur in unrelated passages and are not the result of messages being repeated or commands executed. The verses incorporate formulas and are normally

---

[26] See Hainsworth, *Studies Palmer* 83–6, Janko, *Mnem.* 34 (1981) 251–64, F. X. Strasser, *Zu den Iterata der frühgriechischen Epik* (Königstein 1984) (cf. 17.395–7n.), C. Prato, *Miscellanea Filologica* (Genoa 1978) 77–89.

constructed; their context, battle, is the staple of the *Iliad*. The odd thing is that they recur after a short interval and do not recur again. Clustering – of verses, formulas, single words – is one of the phenomena of Homeric diction that neither Parry's model of formular composition nor its offshoots explain.

The obvious explanation is psychological; what the singer has sung remains for some time near the surface of his mind. (A curious echo over ninety lines occurs at 13.564 ὥς τε σκῶλος ... ἐπὶ γαίης and 13.654 ὥς τε σκώληξ ἐπὶ γαίῃ.) This is easily understood at the thematic level and may be illustrated by the iterated woundings and assaults of books 11 and 12. The repeated verses and runs are not much different, and clustering is apparent also at the level of the phrase (where the first instance may be taken as the product of phrase pattern or substitution): νυκτὰς ἴαυον (9.325, 470 only), εἰν ἑνὶ δίφρῳ ἐόντε (etc.) 11.103, 11.127; and 5.160, 5.609), πῖπτε κάρηνα (11.158 and 11.500), ὑπαὶ δέ τε κόμπος ὀδόντων (11.417, 12.149), ἐμῆς (θοῆς) ἀπὸ χειρὸς ἄκοντι (11.675, 12.306). Most striking, however, is clustering in the use of the formular stock: μεγακήτεϊ νηΐ (11.5, 11.600; and 8.222), κρατεροῖσιν ὀδοῦσι (11.114, 11.175; and 17.63), βροτολοιγῷ ἶσος Ἄρηϊ (11.295, 12.130, 13.802; and ἶσος Ἄρηϊ 11.604). πόδας ὠκὺς Ἀχιλλεύς occurs nineteen times between 1.58 and 19.198, the shorter ὠκὺς Ἀχιλλεύς first appears at 19.295 and then occurs beside the longer formula six times before the end of the poem.

There is evidence here that the stock of formulas, that is, the number of available formulas, fluctuates according to the themes and diction the singer has used in the immediate past. Maverick expressions often explicable by analogy but not explicable in the context of formular economy, perhaps reflect, if the text can be trusted, a temporary difficulty in retrieving the 'right' formula: Διΐ φίλε φαίδιμ' Ἀχιλλεῦ (21.216) – θεοῖς ἐπιείκελ' Ἀχιλλεῦ (6× *Il.*, 1× *Od.*), οὖλον Ἄρηα (5.717) – ὀξὺν Ἄρηα (6×), χαλκοκνήμιδες Ἀχαιοί (7.41) – μένεα πνείοντες Ἀχαιοί (3×), μοῖρα κακή (13.602) – μοῖρ' ὀλοή (2× *Il.*, 5× *Od.*), ὀϊζυροῦ πολέμοιο (3.112) – ὁμοιίου πολέμοιο (6× *Il.*, 2× *Od.*).

(xvii) Conservatism and replacement[27]

A formula has an immediate utility for the singer, but in the end it will betray him. The formula is a fixed element in a fluid medium, and being fixed it has lost the ability to evolve in step with linguistic and cultural

---

[27] See Hoekstra's monographs, *Modifications*, *Epic Verse before Homer* and *The Sub-Epic Stage of the Formulaic Tradition*, and on the question of obsolescence and replacement Hainsworth in Fenik, *Tradition* 41–50.

change. Where the changes are great they will render formulas unmetrical or unintelligible. Up to a point rough metre and obscure sense are tolerable in a song about a bygone age, but it would be unsafe to suppose that the poet of the *Iliad* was deliberately archaic. Here the expression ποδώκης εἶπετ' Ἀχιλλεύς (18.234) is instructive: ποδώκης (and ὠκύπους) have a markedly formular use, but it is not so formular as that of ποδάρκης which appears as an epithet only in the phrase ποδάρκης δῖος Ἀχιλλεύς (21×). When that formula was disrupted the poet abandoned archaism in favour of intelligibility and sang ποδώκης; when he recast the arming scene to honour Agamemnon the traditional σάκος became the contemporary ἀσπίς (11.32). Words like ποδάρκης and σάκος, aorists like ἆλτο and οὖτα, unmetrical formulas with obsolete case-endings like μέλανος οἴνοιο owe their continued existence to the conservatism, indeed to the inertia, of ἀοιδή. Clearly their time is borrowed. Between formulas the movable -ν and neglected digamma have become frequent; -ν can be used to repair the damage of a lost digamma, but generally formulas ignore and presumably antedate the phonetic developments of the mature Ionic dialect.

We may hypothesize that when a formula comes into existence its sense is vivid and apposite. That weakens in time by mere frequency of use, but as long as its elements remain part of the singer's regular vocabulary the formula is productive; it is moved, modified, expanded, and split to fit various sentence patterns, but within the themes to which it is appropriate. Some formulas reach a further stage and become restricted to certain sentence patterns or to certain sentences: θοῦρος is restricted to Ares, θοῦρις to ἀλκή, ἀσπίς, and αἰγίς; θούριδος ἀλκῆς (no variants) is something that one remembers, knows, or forgets; the *Iliad* used it 21× in those restricted contexts, seven of them in a whole-verse formula; the *Odyssey* remembered it only once (4.527). It is easy to understand how such a word may become a gloss, its original meaning scarcely understood (see Parry, *MHV* 240–50).

A gloss, supposing it is not simply tolerated, may prolong its life by being interpreted into something intelligible, or it may be replaced. The scholiasts, and probably the ἀοιδοί before them, were prepared to offer explanations for such words as αἰγίλιψ, ἀμφιέλισσα, γλαυκῶπις, ἐριούνιος, ἰόμωροι, μέροπες, μώνυχες, κτλ.; modern philologists have rarely been convinced. Occasionally the poet's interpretation may be glimpsed: in ἄχθος ἄροιτο at 20.247 the poet used ἄροιτο as if from ἀείρω not ἄρνυμαι; see 1.200 (and n.) for γλαυκῶπις and the gaze of Athene: at *Od.* 4.287–8 κρατερῇσι, separated from χερσί, interprets the formula χερσὶ στιβαρῇσι. The epithet of Athene, ἀγελείη, probably meant 'bringing booty' to the poet of 10.460 (Ἀθηναίη ληΐτιδι), but 'leading the host' to Hesiod (ἀγέστρατον, *Theog.* 925). The *Iliad* connects δαΐφρων with δάϊς, 'battle', the *Odyssey* with δαῆναι, 'learn'. ὠκύαλος is from ἅλλομαι (see 15.704–6n.), but is linked with ἅλς at *Od.* 8.111. Archaisms may be replaced even if understood: νηλέες ἦτορ > νηλέα θυμόν, ἀάατον Στυγὸς ὕδωρ > ἀμείλικτον Σ. ὕ. (*HyDem* 259); Διΐ φίλος (with archaic dative Διϝεί?) occurs 17× in the *Iliad* but is dropped in the *Odyssey*, *Hymns*, and Hesiod.

Personal names in -εύς on the evidence of Linear B tablets were popular in the Mycenaean epoch and are still well represented in the *Iliad*; alongside them are names with a more classical appearance, Antilokhos, Eurumakhos, Antinoos, Telemakhos, which must be placed in the first hemistich and require different sentence patterns: τὸν δ' αὖ(τ') name + epithet ἀντίον ηὔδα. The evolution of the Ionic dialect, especially the loss of digamma and the contraction of vowels, wreaked potential havoc on the formular diction; there are nineteen expressions scanned ⏑⏑ – ⏑⏑ – ⏑ which make use of the oblique cases of adjectives in -ης; forty-five adjectives in -ό(ϝ)εις or -ή(ϝ)εις used in the feminine or the oblique cases to fill the last colon became archaisms; basic parts of the formular diction based on neuter nouns like ἄλγεα, κήδεα, μήδεα, τεύχεα, etc., were threatened with obsolescence. Corresponding opportunities arose: new forms like (ἐσ)ήλατο, οὔτασε, χεύατο, are already in the text, but the advantage taken of the evolving dialect is still tentative in the *Iliad*: some contracted forms, Ἀχιλλεῖ, ἀγήρως, ἠοῦς; τεύχεα, θεοειδέα at the verse-end; connectives may be slipped in where they would not go before: θεὸς δ' ὣς τίετο δήμῳ, Χαρόποιό τ' ἄνακτος, τὸν δ' Ἑλένη. The differences observable in the diction of Hesiod and the *Hymns* – slight but sufficient with careful analysis to establish a relative chronology (Janko, *HHH*) – show that the *Kunstsprache* continued to undergo a gradual evolution.

A few formulas must be relatively new because they embody contractions or neglected digamma: Κρόνου πάϊς ἀγκυλομήτεω, μελιηδέος οἴνου, ὄφρ' εἴπω. μελιηδέος οἴνου (< the accusative μελιηδέα οἶνον) is replacing μέλανος οἴνοιο with its archaic genitive, lost digamma, and anomalous epithet, cf. Ἀπόλλωνος (ϝ)εκάτοιο and ἑκηβόλου Ἀπόλλωνος. Κρόνου πάϊς ἀγκυλομήτεω competes directly with πατὴρ ἀνδρῶν τε θεῶν τε (contrast 15.12 with 16.431) and has the advantage of a word-break at the bucolic diaeresis so that it can be shortened, cf. 2.319 and 6.139; even so πατὴρ ἀνδρῶν τε θεῶν τε is unchallenged in introductory and resumptive formulas.

The language and diction of the epic tradition was never static; it was always an amalgam of old and new, and the old was constantly being eroded. For this reason the heroic tradition by Homer's time could remember the Trojan war and preserve isolated details of its Mycenaean past, or of even earlier incarnations, but had lost touch with the real nature of Mycenaean culture and economy as it is now revealed to us. ἀοιδοί, guided by an infrastructure of habits in localization and sentence structure, could invent, improve, improvise, and expand their diction according to their competence as well as reproduce a traditional language, but their imagination could only feed on what was familiar to them, their own world. Formularity therefore potentially increased the power of expression of the gifted ἀοιδός, a power that the acquisition of the basic poetical diction had already enhanced. At its best the formular style can be read in the quarrel of book 1, in the discourses of book 9, and in that *tour de force* of battle narrative, 16.306–50.[28] A reading of such passages removes the lingering pejorative sense that clings to the word 'formular'. Yet there would be areas where formalization was strong, and these would limit the imagination of the ungifted ἀοιδός and give the impression that he never sought to express anything in word or tone or content that tradition did not supply. Such themes, like beaching or launching a ship in the *Iliad*, are like glosses, waiting for rejuvenation (cf. *Od.* 5.243–61 for a good ἀοιδός doing just that). Ossified language and concomitant ossified thought are the vices of formular composition, but they are vices that do not afflict its best exponents. In the *Iliad* variation on a theme is the norm, as in the confident and supremely competent descriptions of the individual combats during the Great Battle of books 11–17 (see 11.92–100nn.).

The *Iliad* is formular ('formular' in the broadest sense) throughout. Its formularity must be accepted, but it can now also begin to be appreciated as a mode of discourse that despite its formidable technicalities made possible the creation of one of the finest narrative styles in literature.[29]

[28] Kirk, *HOT* 74–81, discusses in detail several passages from this standpoint.
[29] For a comprehensive bibliography of the Homeric formula see M. W. Edwards, *Oral Tradition* 1 (1986) 171–230, and 3 (1988) 11–60.

2. The *Iliad* as heroic poetry

Comparison between Greek and other epic poetry has produced some of the most fruitful, though not necessarily correct, approaches to the Homeric poems. It is enough to mention Lachmann, Murray, and Parry in this connexion. Comparison is suggestive but can prove nothing, for the basic rule of all analogical reasoning has to be that like is compared with like. Yet the striking thing about the material discussed by H. M. and N. K. Chadwick (1932–40) and Bowra (1952) was how different all these poems and stories were. Bowra used nothing from Africa south of the Sahara or from modern India or Thailand, and tacitly assumed there was no heroic poetry from the New World. Since then the range of material cited by Finnegan (1977) and Hatto (1980–9) suggests that narrative verse is, or has been, universal; the mass of material has also become unwieldy, far more than it is reasonable to expect a single mind to know with the degree of intimacy that validates comparative study. On the broad front co-operative studies such as that directed by Hatto are necessary, while even the investigation of a narrowly defined topic, such as Foley's study (*Traditional Oral Epic*, 1990) of formulas in Greek, Slavic, and Old English epic (which led to the recognition of what is really fundamental in the composition of the verses) requires a profound knowledge of all three traditions. Consequently, unless students of Homer are exceptional polymaths they must rely on a selection of secondary sources; these, fortunately, are of high quality:

H. M. and N. K. Chadwick, *The Growth of Literature* I–III (Cambridge 1932–40)

C. M. Bowra, *Heroic Poetry* (London 1952)

J. de Vries, *Heroic Song and Heroic Legend* trans. B. J. Timmer (Oxford 1963), a popular account

N. K. Chadwick and V. M. Zhirmunsky, *Oral Epics of Central Asia* (Cambridge 1969), a revision of *The Growth of Literature* III 3–226

R. Finnegan, *Oral Poetry. Its Nature, Significance and Social Context* (Cambridge 1977)

F. J. Oinas, ed., *Heroic Epic and Saga: an Introduction to the World's Great Folk Epics* (Bloomington 1978)

A. T. Hatto, ed., *Traditions of Heroic and Epic Poetry* I–II (London 1980–9)
The journal *Oral Tradition* (Columbus 1986–)

The Chadwicks (III 697–903) and Hatto (II 145–306) provide digests of the material surveyed.

In view of the extensive use made of the South Slavic tradition since it was popularized by M. Parry it is worth mentioning:

M. Braun, *Das serbokroatische Heldenlied* (Göttingen 1961)
S. Koljević, *The Epic in the Making* (Oxford 1980)

and, as studies that apply the comparative method to Homer:

A. B. Lord, *Singer of Tales* (Cambridge, Mass., 1960)
B. C. Fenik, *Homer and the Nibelungenlied: Comparative Studies in Epic Style* (Cambridge, Mass., 1986)
J. M. Foley, *Traditional Oral Epic* (1990).

'Oral poetry' (for we are primarily concerned with oral or oral-derived poetry) is obviously a congeries, not a genre. In order to discuss so much material of diverse date, provenance, and character the obvious expedient is to draw a metaphorical line around that part of it that seems to promise results; and having done so it is well not to exclaim in wonder that the material does in fact exhibit the properties that were used to define it in the first place. The Chadwicks used ethos and social function for classification: (1) narrative poetry or saga (=prose narrative orally preserved) intended for entertainment; (2) poetry in semi-dramatic form; (3) gnomic poetry intended for instruction; (4) celebratory poetry (hymns, panegyrics); (5) personal poetry. There is much overlapping here, notably between narrative and dramatic form (cf. vol. II 29–30). Bowra used the concept of 'heroic poetry', a more narrowly defined portion of the Chadwicks' 'narrative poetry intended for entertainment'. But heroic poetry is not a concept analogous to that of, say, epic poetry in classical and modern literature. Epic poetry in those fields is a genre whose poets were self-consciously aware of the form that they were using, a form ultimately traceable to the Homeric epics. The similarities between Homer, Apollonius, Virgil, Tasso, Milton, and the rest are not fortuitous; the similarities between *Iliad, Gilgamesh, Beowulf, Roland, Digenis, Manas*, etc., are at best attributable to similar causes (orality, war, religion, etc.), not to any filiation. We can trace the evolution of the classical and neo-classical epic; we have to assume that the emergence, development, and maturity of traditions of heroic poetry were parallel.

There can be no necessary connexion between heroic poetry and, for example, techniques of composition, modes of performance, or the emergence of monumental epics. Other criteria for classification are equally valid. If the Homerist's purpose is to elucidate techniques of composition, then 'stichic verse' should be the area for investigation. Whatever the criteria the investigator is likely to be confronted with a continuum. There are no sharp distinctions between oral and literary (though that has been fiercely contested), between folktale and saga, between lyrical balladry and stichic narrative lays, between lays and epics, or even perhaps between traditional and non-traditional poems. Demodokos on the same occasion would sing of the sack of Troy and of a distinctly unheroic episode in the daily life of Olumpos. One can be heroic in the narrative boasts of E. and S. Africa, in all sorts of lyrical poems, in stichic verse epics thousands of lines long, and in prose stories too. The heroic ethos shades off into romance and folktale, stichic verses may be arranged into couplets and stanzas, or the verse may be so long that it breaks into two and the verse-end is overridden. In these circumstances comparison highlights the place on the continua occupied by a particular poem and by emphasizing how it differs from others deepens our understanding of it.

The Homeric poems rest on a tradition of singing

  (i) in a stichic but a quantitative metrical form,
  (ii) about the supposed events of a 'Heroic Age'

and embody

  (iii) a certain concept of heroism.

The questions put to the comparativist are: Where do the Homeric poems and the *Iliad* in particular stand in relation to the possibilities? In what respects do they stand out? What has their author done that others did not? It is sometimes useful to compare the *Iliad* with the rest of the Greek tradition (called here ἀοιδή); the two should not be uncritically identified.

(i) The verse and the singer

What counts as verse varies so greatly that comparison can only be made at a very general level. There is a count of syllables or morae and a verse-end; on that are imposed alternations of quantities or accents, patterns of assonance, alliteration, and stanzas. It is commonly said that the Greek hexameter is a difficult metre compared with the Serbo-Croat decasyllable (*deseterac*) or the seven-morae Kirghiz verse; it would be safer to say with respect to the trained singer that it posed different problems. The Greek singer had to master a special language that deviates sharply from any vernacular and a special poetic grammar, and the Old English *scop* faced a comparable task. The complexity of the special languages is indicative of the difficulty of the poetical form which would have confronted the singer if he had not acquired the means of overcoming it.

The technical point of these special speech forms was to enable the singer to give his thoughts expression in the appropriate verse-form with appropriate facility. The verse therefore shapes the form of the singer's thought. The length of the hexameter, twelve to seventeen syllables, encouraged a certain amplitude of style, a complex sentence structure with enjambment and subordination. The *deseterac* engendered a staccato antiphonic style: 'What is white in the green wood? | Is it snow? Is it swans? | If it were snow it would have melted; | swans would have flown away. | It is not snow, it is not swans; | it is the tent of Hasan Aga.' The two-part alliterative verse of Old English produced the unmistakable appositional style: 'Hnaef spoke then   the war-young king: | "This is not dawn from the east   nor is the dragon flying here, | nor of this hall   are the gables burning; | the enemy approach,   the birds cry, | grey wolf howls,   the war-beam resounds, | shield answers shaft."' The strict alternation of quantities in the hexameter, as always stricter in the last feet than in the first, must be responsible for the creation and preservation of the special language in Greek and for the accumulation of formulas. Formulas including runs of verses, dialect mixture, and linguistic archaism including the retention of glosses are widespread (Hatto, *Traditions* II 209–12), but the Greek *Kunstsprache* appears to stand at an extreme of complexity.

We can next ask what is entailed by the stichic form. We shall get no answers from Old French epic (which is composed in *laisses*, 'stanzas') defined by assonance, nor from Medieval German (which is again in stanzas). But one might get something from Anglo-Saxon, from Medieval and Modern Slavic, or from Turkic. What one gets is a strong implication that the stichic form goes with techniques by which the song, which is of course well rehearsed through previous performances, can be recreated in performance, of which the most obvious outward sign is a verbally fluid text. (Compare *HyHerm* 1–9 and *HyHom* 18.1–9, and see Finnegan, 76–80.) Deviant versions of songs and even maverick versions are easily collected in the field, as well as cases of very high stability.[1]

The *Odyssey* (1.325–44, 8.485–520) provides brief descriptions of the ἀοιδός in action. He is a *singer*, like the corresponding figures in all major traditions of heroic poetry, and accompanies himself on a lyre. It is almost certain that his chant remained unchanged from line to line, in spite of the high rhetoric of speeches or the speed and vigour of an *aristeia*. Modern examples (and a medieval French chant cited by D. J. A. Ross at Hatto, *Traditions* I 107) strike the ear as slow and musically unexciting. As for tone the adjectives λιγύς and λιγυρός are used, probably indicating that the ἀοιδός 'lifted up his voice' like a Hebrew prophet. Where performers recite without accompaniment this is, or is believed to be, a secondary development. A chant emphasizes the verse-end and has a normalizing effect on the sentence; there is, for example, very little enjambment in the Old French

---

[1] G. S. Kirk, *CQ* 10 (1960) 271–81 (=*HOT* 113–28), A. B. Lord, in *La poesia epica e la sua formazione*, edd. E. Cerulli et al. (Rome 1970) 13–28.

and Serbo-Croat traditions. The conjunction in Greek of singing and a relatively high frequency of enjambment deeply entrenched in its formulas and sentence patterns is unusual, and permits the Greek style a greater range of expression. How it was reconciled with the chant is of course unknown. Even if, as is sometimes reported,[2] the singer had several chants in his repertoire, it is hard to imagine how the powerful clashes of sense and rhythm at e.g. 9.336–43 could have been effectively rendered. Such passages seem, to our ear, to call for a histrionic talent like that of the rhapsode in Plato's *Ion* liberated from the levelling effect of singing.

The singer is primarily a performer not a poet. One occasionally comes across attempts to establish proprietorial rights (the Homeridai and Kreophuleioi may represent such attempts), but the repertoire is traditional and its ultimate authorship usually lost. Individual singers have thus as much but no more claim to fame than the practitioners of any other art, and are usually anonymous. The authority of the song lies elsewhere. In Siberia the singer and the shaman are one and the same; the singer tells the tale in the first person, and so questions about his (or, often, her) sources and veracity do not arise; the singer's knowledge is direct. The Greek singer began with an affectation of ignorance and called on the Muse, the daughter of Memory, to tell him the tale, cf. *Il* 2.484–6, but sang in the third person with minimal reference to himself. The first-person narrative of *Od.* 9–12 is subsumed in the third-person narrative of the epic and except in scale (a bold innovation) does not differ from the much shorter stories attributed to Glaukos and Nestor in the *Iliad*. The singer appealed to the Muses at intervals during the song, usually when access to special knowledge was required, e.g. the contingents of the Achaeans who went to Troy or the names of those slain by Agamemnon (see 11.218n.). Since the historicity of the setting of the *Iliad* is a question that engages the attention of Homerists (vol. II 36–50), it is worthwhile considering the implications of the appeal to the authority of the Muse. Serbo-Croat singers, for example, claim to have learned their songs from such and such a predecessor and rely on the tradition for their authority. That leads to faithfulness, at least as an ideal, and to criticism of singers who conflate and expand. For the Greek singer the legend is guaranteed by the Muse. He sets out to tell the tale κατὰ κόσμον (*Od.* 8.489), but the way is open for him to confuse his imagination with her instruction. Potentially the Muse is an alibi; she guarantees his fictions as facts (even his rewriting of the Meleagros-saga in

---

[2] 'Radlov tells us that the [Kirghiz] minstrel invariably employs two melodies, one executed in quick tempo, for the course of the action, the other in slow tempo and as a solemn recitative for the speeches' (Hatto, *Traditions* I 304–5).

book 9) and liberates his fancy.[3] Without the Muse there would be a quarrel of the chiefs, a short episode in the tale of Troy, but no *Iliad*.

In the *Odyssey* we meet also a familiar nexus of singer, patron, and audience; the ἀοιδός is a professional but not (at least in Demodokos' case) retained by a permanent patron; the occasion is the feast, the purpose entertainment; his status is relatively humble and the patron does not hesitate to interrupt. Professionalism in some degree is a necessary condition for the acquisition and practice of the skill and knowledge that a singer must possess. Most singers, real or represented in songs, are at least semi-professional (R. Finnegan, *Oral Poetry* (Cambridge 1977) 188–201); professionals may be itinerant or, if settled, the retainers of noble patrons; a genuine amateur, i.e. a patron of the first rank who can also sing, like Akhilleus at 9.186, or King Alfred among the Danes, is rare and the verisimilitude of such representations is called into question. In both cases the circumstances are exceptional, and of course Akhilleus is not giving a public performance. Semi-amateurs, like the thegn at Hrothgar's court or the *suta* of the *Mahābhārata*, are more in evidence. Sometimes the patron may be in effect a god. This is commonly the case in India (Smith, in Hatto, *Traditions* II 29–41), and turns performance into ritual with a corresponding attitude towards the text. The association of heroic figures with cult – Aias in Locris, Akhilleus at Elis (Paus. 6.23.3), Neoptolemos at Delphi (Pind. *N.* 7.44–7), Menelaos at Sparta – shows how readily a link between song and cult could arise. Nevertheless any connexion between ἀοιδή and religion was incidental; songs in the manner of the Homeric *Hymns* may have been sung *at* cult centres (cf. *HyAp* 165–73), but there is no evidence that they or an epic *Titanomachia* or the like were performed *as part of* cult; in Greece that was the business of the choral lyric. Typically, it was when the Homeric poems did become associated with cult, at the Panathenaea, that we first encounter anxiety about the integrity of the text.

Modern researchers stress the inadequacy of the written text to represent an art that properly exists only in performance and participation. Fortunately ἀοιδή is one of those traditions in which the audience did not physically participate. The audience dominated the performance but was not an active part of a ritual of which the performance was also a part. Its patrons felt no obligation to hear the singer out, but the effect of the song while they listened is described by the verb θέλγειν and the noun κηληθμός; everyone sat entranced in a state of 'silent exaltation' – as is reported of some African audiences. We lose less in reading the printed text of the *Iliad*, if it is read in the right mood, than might have been the case.

---

[3] M. Finkelberg, *AJP* III (1990) 291–303.

The vignettes of ἀοιδή in the *Odyssey*, there is no reason to doubt, describe circumstances in the background of the monumental epic. Where there is an individual patron, whether Danish kings, Kirghiz khans, West African chiefs, or Gaulish princelings, there is panegyric (Bowra, *HP* 412–17), though not to the exclusion of wider interests. The funeral feast, like that of Amphidamas to which Hesiod alludes (*Erga* 654–7), is another opportunity for praise poetry. Yet as the *Odyssey* describes it ἀοιδή praised no patron directly. The situation in which a patron (Odysseus) called for a song about *his own* exploits was not a contemporary situation. Praise was possible only indirectly, e.g. through the representation of ancestors, cf. the Neleids of Miletos and Nestor's heroic tales at *Il.* 7.132–56, 11.670–762. But the Neleids had to be content with an ancestor of secondary importance in the tradition taken as a whole, and the great heroes, Akhilleus and Odysseus, left no descendants in the Ionian world. Who then was the patron of the *Iliad*?

In the social system, for example, of the Germanic world patron (economic support) and audience (moral support) were separated. In Greece, at the time of the eighth century renaissance, they were not. The audience was the patron, and because some singers at least were not rooted in one spot (cf. *HyAp* 175) their potential audience was the whole community. The bT scholia made a good point when they said that the poet of the *Iliad* was φιλέλλην (e.g. at 10.13), the poet of the Ἕλληνες. The stories of a people, whether in a hundred lays or concentrated in a monumental epic, are the tale of the tribe. They are of immediate use for the inspiration of impetuous youth, and more generally they articulate the myths, beliefs, values, and hopes of the tribe that created them.[4] Wilamowitz thought that the tale of Troy reflected the struggle to colonize Aeolis; the Ionians perhaps saw in it a justification for their presence in western Asia. But the eclipse of the world in which Akhilleus and Odysseus had lived meant that the heroes could appeal to all Greeks. And they received their greatest literary promotion at the very time that a consciousness of Hellenic identity was beginning to establish itself.

(ii) The tradition

The secular subject matter of Phemios' and Demodokos' songs was highly predictable. It would be taken from a few cycles of stories. This restriction is not a primitive picture. Beside the tale of Thebes the *Iliad* itself alludes to stories about Calydon, Pylos, Centaurs, Herakles, and Bellerophon; the

---

[4] For this reason the communist administration in Kirghizia, it is said, endeavoured to suppress the Manas-cycle.

Odyssey, which defines the subjects of ἀοιδή as ἔργ' ἀνδρῶν τε θεῶν τε (*Od.* 1.338), adds the Argonauts. The ἔργ' ἀνδρῶν ('heroic poetry' in the modern idiom) range from austerely heroic lays (Nestor's tales) to romantically coloured adventures (Argonauts) and thinly heroized folktales (Bellerophon). All, however, are related as if they were historically true and were certainly believed to be true in a straightforward way. In most cases it is credible, even to us, that hard fact underlies many of them. The ἔργα θεῶν form for us a different genre, myth, but it is doubtful if singers for whom the divine world was an obvious reality could see any distinction.

True myth is not located in time, and heroic stories with an overtone of myth, like the Sumerian *Gilgamesh*, begin with the fairy-tale formula 'once upon a time . . .' Where the 'historical' mode prevails the stories are set in time and place. It would be well to speak of 'heroic' time and place, for it is far from clear that singers could relate the times and places of which they sang to the here and now. Places remain known and accessible, so that a tradition of song that remains *in situ* or in contact with the scene of its stories will preserve, or rather constantly renew, its geographical verisimilitude. That is how the *Iliad* is clear about the navigation of the northern Aegean (9.362–3), the visibility of Samothrace from the Trojan battlefield (13.11–14), the site of Troy (it must now be agreed), and the springs of Pınarbası (which the poet transferred to the neighbourhood of Troy, 22.147–52), and places around the coasts of the Hellespont and Troad. A temporary feature, like the Achaean encampment, was quickly forgotten and had to be located where the singers thought best (see vol. II 48–50). Typically, fine detail in the foreground, the oak of Zeus and the fig-tree, is fictional. The flood-plain of the lower Skamandros is flat, open, and dusty in summer, exactly what the Iliadic picture of battle required, so that there is no conflict between the terrain and the epic narrative. If there had been a conflict it is probable that the generic picture of battle would have prevailed over the geography, just as the defile at Roncesvalles was not allowed in the *geste* to cramp the tactics of Frankish knights. Where contact between place and tradition was broken by time or distance an air of verisimilitude must not be taken for knowledge. Heroic tales from the western Peloponnese preserved in the *Iliad* had only a general idea of the whereabouts of Pulos, and the *Odyssey* is none too sure about the location of Ithake. Thanks to allusions in late sources there is some reason to place the Heorot of *Beowulf* near the Danish town of Roskilde, but so far as the story goes it was merely somewhere in the land of the Geats, a tribe that had ceased to exist when the poem was created; and where was Ephure or Camelot? A remarkable and, it must be stressed, unusual perversion of geography is attested in the Old French cycle, the *Geste de Garin de Monglane*, whose central figure is identified with the liberator of Barcelona, Count

William of Toulouse but called Guillaume d'Orange in the *geste* and his exploits located in Languedoc. (Dümmler and Bethe, it will be recalled, wished to see a mainland origin for the earliest stories of the Trojan cycle, an idea revived for much of the Homeric onomasticon by A. Hoekstra, *Epic Verse before Homer* (Amsterdam 1981) 54–66.) Times and events are in a weaker position, for they are verifiable only so long as an independent memory persists. After that all depends on tradition, and tradition is not interested in the true story but in the best and most useful.

All the Greek stories had one thing in common: they were set on the further side of a deep political and social discontinuity, the collapse of the Mycenaean world and the subsequent migrations. Discontinuities of this kind set the present in contrast with the past and give rise to the theme οἷοι νῦν βροτοί εἰσι. Russian scholars connect the creation of the Kievan epic cycle to the destruction of the medieval kingdom by the Mongols in A.D. 1240 (a catastrophic discontinuity). Even without a clean historical break there can be a sense that a former age was different; Germans looked back from settled conditions to the Age of Migrations, the Franks to the age of Charlemagne and wars against the infidel. The necessary factor is a sense of difference which may or may not be tinged with nostalgia. There is nothing in the *Iliad* like 'These deeds were accomplished in the days of Sulejman the Magnificent. Goodly was Bosnia, and goodly were the times, and the sultan aided them well!' (*Wedding of Smailagić Meho, SCHS* III 246, cf. 79). Perhaps only in Greece was a bygone Heroic Age, formulated as such, a native idea (Hesiod, *Erga* 156–73). It is likely enough that the idea ultimately rested on some genuine qualities of the Mycenaean period, but essentially it was a construct of the singers who came afterwards. That is clear from Hesiod's description of the heroes as the men who died at Thebes and Troy, that is, the heroes were the protagonists in the two major cycles of the Greek heroic tradition. To emphasize the difference between then and now Hesiod called the heroes ἡμίθεοι (see 12.23n.). That idea ensured that there could be no heroic poetry about events later than the end of the Heroic Age; the events could not be 'mythologized'.[5]

Elsewhere Heroic Ages have been so named by modern scholars, but what is described is a by-product, as it was in Greece, of the tendency of heroic poetry to congeal into cycles, often (but not always) around a signal event. Perceived as a supreme effort of the greatest heroes, the event ensures that later generations cannot be equal to their predecessors

---

[5] See the interesting comments in the *Epitaphios* of [Demosthenes] (60.9) comparing contemporary achievements with the exploits of Theseus: '[contemporary deeds] which in point of merit are not inferior to any but, because they are nearer to our own time, have not yet assumed a mythical character nor been ranked in the class of heroic achievements' (οὕτω μεμυθολόγηται οὐδ' εἰς τὴν ἡρωϊκὴν ἐπανῆκται τάξιν).

and thus imposes a definite lower boundary to 'heroic time'. Observance of the boundary is meticulous in Greek, and perhaps only in Greek. A few sons of those who fought at Troy are named, but Telemakhos is a mere append- age of Odysseus and Orestes' sole heroic act is a tailpiece to the story of Agamemnon. The upper limit is apt to be more untidy because it depends on the success of the cycles in drawing ancient figures (like the greater Aias) into their compass.[6]

The theme οἷοι νῦν βροτοί εἰσι applies only to physical and spiritual strength; for material things – houses, ships, weapons – the normal assump- tion is that the age of heroes was much like the singer's. In this respect the *chanson de geste* and the *Iliad* are at opposite ends of the continuum. French feudalism of the twelfth century, chain mail, the couched lance, and the cavalry charge are projected onto the Carolingian age with no sense of anachronism, for it is hard to see that there has been change where there has been no marked discontinuity. In Greece, however, the end of the Heroic Age coincided with the beginning of the Iron Age, a development in technology that was not easily forgotten; so the heroes continued to use their bronze weapons. Chariots too impressed themselves on the collective memory, as they did too in India and Ireland. Generally, however, heroic poetry has little use for conscious archaism unless it touches the singers' sense of cultural or ethnic identity. Amerindians exclude reference to Euro- peans in their heroic world, Siberians to Russians, and Ionian singers to Dorian Greeks.

Where it can be verified the history of a heroic tale seems always to have begun with the celebration of contemporary or at least recent events. The best evidence for this is from Europe where the typology of the heroic poem has generally been realistic and where contemporary celebration has been recorded by historians and observed in practice. The Greek tradition is 'European' in being realistic and attached to real places, and this is the strongest comparative argument that some fragments of history lurk behind it. Elsewhere, especially in Asia, a tendency to raise the hero and his exploits to the supernatural plane has obscured whatever historical origins there may have been.

Moreover most heroic traditions are known only from relatively late stages in their history, when the events they purport to narrate lie beyond verification in a distant past. The fact that something seems to be strongly remembered is not a certificate that it happened in the way that it was told.

---

[6] In the South Slavic tradition a discontinuity, the battle of Kosovo, marks the *beginning* of a tense heroic period that lasted well into the nineteenth century. Earlier songs celebrate a relaxed and cheerful breed of hero, like Marko Kraljević. The reality of the Germanic Heroic Age, the principal subject of H. M. Chadwick's masterly study *The Heroic Age* (Cambridge 1912), has been doubted (Hatto, *Traditions* II 204).

Heroic song is not chronicle and the events related may have no historical importance provided they can be given dramatic interest and symbolic significance. The death of Roland did not change the course of history but a last stand with loyal vassals dying around their liege was a feudal ideal worthy of commemoration. If an event could not be given that sort of significance there would be little point in making a song about it. If a song was made about it shabby deeds became heroic and a trivial event, forgotten by historians, acquired cosmic significance.[7] From the very beginning then there will be deformation.

The primary source of deformation, familiar to historians, is 'ethnic truth'; an event must be what it ought to be. So the rearguard of Charlemagne's army was cut off by Saracens not by Basques, and the disaster was not due to rashness or accident but, like the defeat of Kosovo in the Serbian tradition, to treachery.

A kind of deformation to which heroic song is especially prone is that caused by the typology in terms of which the event is perceived and related. In a tradition of song most things are perceived generically; in the Germanic tradition a battle takes place in a confined space, the hall of Hrothgar in *Beowulf*, or that of Etzel (Attila) in the Nibelung story: in Greek, heroic action is often teamwork (the hunting of the Calydonian boar, the quest for the golden fleece, the attacks on Thebes and Troy); an assault on a fortification takes the form of a simultaneous attack on each of its gates, as in the Theban story or the Trojan attack on the Achaean camp in *Iliad* book 12.

The song itself is built up of episodes typical of its tradition (vol. II 15–27). There is an excellent instance of an *Iliupersis* analysed into its constituent themes in *Od.* 8.500–20, an analysis which has the advantage that it does not depend on the intuition of a modern theorist. The sack of Troy is there broken down into a sequence of council, *androktasia*, and *aristeia* assisted by a tutelar divinity. The obscure Finn episode in *Beowulf* (1068–1159) is essentially a similar summary. A council breaks down into a series of speeches, a battle into a series of combats, and so on, until minimal statements are reached (see pp. 12–13). At each stage the conception is generic. *Any* event can be seen in these terms, so that their application to a particular event is tantamount to fiction.

What these techniques of creating and preserving a song bring into the foreground is of no evidentiary value. The grains of truth, if any, lie in the background, in the event described, or (to be on the safe side) in the background of the event. It is easy to quote examples from less austerely

---

[7] The inclusion of the crucial phrase *et Hruodlandus Brittanniae limitis praefectus* is a matter of debate in the textual criticism of Egginhard's *Vita Karoli*. One must guard against the strong will to believe that exists in these matters.

realistic traditions than the Greek where the distinction between what has just been called foreground and background is obvious. The Chadwicks (II 318–19) cite a Slavic song about the second battle of Kosovo (A.D. 1448) in which one Sekula changes himself into a winged snake in order to fight the Turkish sultan and in that guise is shot by his own uncle. The Hungarian John Székély was present at the battle and was killed. Such a song, which differs only in degree from the fights of Akhilleus with Ethiopians and Amazons in the *Aithiopis*, illustrates Nilsson's comment that heroic songs 'start from a poetical remodelling of historic events which became more and more covered up by poetical motifs so that at last a few names only are recognizable as historical elements' (*HM* 44). But names too are an area where the distinction between foreground and background is useful: the Danish and Geatish kings who make up the background of *Beowulf* are historical, but the historicity of the hero himself is an open question. (His exploits are in the same class as Sekula's snake.) Discussing the personnel of *Smailagić Meho* (*SCHS* III 30–1), A. B. Lord distinguished two levels, the pashas on the historical level and the group of heroes on a more mythical level. The heroes are the local incarnations of figures in a ubiquitous story of marriage and succession. Similar reasoning applied to the *Chanson de Roland* would make it bad evidence for Roland's last stand against Saracens, questionable evidence (if we feel sceptical) for his presence at Roncesvalles, but good evidence for a campaign of Charlemagne across the Pyrenees, and excellent evidence for a conflict between the Frankish empire and the Muslims of Spain. In an extreme instance no nucleus of historical fact has been found in the Kirghiz epics (the *Manas* cycle), but they bear witness to the long struggle of the Kirghiz against Kalmuck inroads. An analogous approach to the *Iliad* would discount every statement in the poem but still accept it as evidence for Achaean raids on the Troad.

Where traditions are represented by many songs there is a natural tendency for songs to form groups around a particular hero or event. It helps the singer and his audience to find their way around the heroic world if there is some organizing factor. It is convenient, but premature at this stage, to speak of a 'cycle'. The Slavic Kosovo songs typify a group related by a common centre but each independent of the others. Such a 'cycle' is not the *disiecta membra* of an epic, but material waiting to be fused into an epic if conditions were right for such a development. In the Trojan cycle described in Proclus' *Chrestomathy* the kernel of the story of Troy has grown into a series of songs, each except the first presupposing the one before and together completing the grand episode called the Trojan war. Demodokos was presumed as a competent ἀοιδός to know it all, so that there was no need for Odysseus to ask if he could sing the 'Wooden Horse'. A singer would never have sung the whole story at a stretch. What he did was what Demodokos is said to have done and what the poets of the Homeric epics say they do – to take up the tale 'from some point'. This stage is well attested in some living traditions (Hatto, *Traditions* II 275–6), even to the extent that investigators have induced epics by eliciting the whole cycle from the singer *for the first time*.

A growing cycle is an open-ended string of episodes that draws in attractive figures and incidents from elsewhere. A classic example is the use of the murder of Siegfried in the *Nibelungenlied* to motivate the (historical) destruction of the Burgundians by a tribe of Huns, a tale that had already attracted into it, in defiance of history and chronology, such famous names as those of Theoderic and Attila. The catalogues of heroes who sailed in the *Argo*, hunted the Calydonian boar, and fought at Troy are obviously expanded, some of the intruders, like Telamonian Aias, scarcely disguised, others too famous to leave out but too brilliant to be in at the kill. When it was common knowledge that Jason secured the Fleece and Odysseus devised the Trojan Horse Herakles and Akhilleus could not be allowed to dominate the final act and usurp their glory; they must either leave or die.

The formation of a connected cycle exposes gaps and raises questions about the primary material: the birth or origin of the hero, his death and descendants, how he acquired associates and distinguishing characteristics, and so on. Is the story of the pursuit of Troilos by Akhilleus an *aition* for his epithet πόδας ὠκύς – or the origin of that description?[8] Kullmann's careful research into the content of the Trojan cycle (*Quellen* (1960)) has shown how much of it predates the *Iliad*, but it is clear from the description of the cycle by Proclus that parts of the *Cypria*, the *Nostoi*, and especially the *Telegony*, as they existed after Homer, are examples of this tendency to complete the story and arrange it around an outstanding poem or episode.[9]

(iii) The hero

'Heroic poetry' is a loose term, and heroes are correspondingly diverse. Folktales, hero tales, heroic lays, and romances are characterized by the dominance of certain viewpoints at the expense of, but not to the exclusion of others. Heroic poetry, in Bowra's classic description, 'works in conditions determined by special conceptions of manhood and honour. It cannot exist unless men believe that human beings are in themselves sufficient objects of interest and that their chief claim is the pursuit of honour through risk'

[8] There is a parallel in the invention of a story to explain *Cort Nes*, 'short-nosed', the soubriquet of Guillaume d'Orange in *Le Couronnement de Louis*, an invention because the epithet is known to be a misunderstanding of *Curb Nes*, 'hook-nosed' (M. de Riquer, *Les Chansons de geste françaises* trans. I. Cluzel (Paris 1957) 157–8).
[9] The Old French epic with some eighty poems is rich material for the study of cycles; a useful study is that of de Riquer (n. 8).

(*HP* 4–5). This formulation suits Akhilleus and the *Iliad* very well, but it allowed, as was necessary, for many types of hero and conceptions of heroism. The continuing advance of comparative studies has blurred the sharp distinction that Bowra perceived between the self-reliance of heroes in ancient and medieval European (and some Asian) epics and a heavy dependence on magic and shamanism elsewhere. Heroic poetry occupies that part of the spectrum of narrative poetry in which heroic qualities predominate. Within any one tradition the concept of heroism is described by its place along several axes.

(a) *Exemplary character*

Heroes have to be larger than life, but they must not be thought of, necessarily, as paragons of virtue even when they exert themselves for the public good. They are indeed exemplary to the extent that they embody what the audiences of heroic poems regarded with awe. (Indian epic has a hero Bhīsma, the Awesome.) That is their moral justification; their greatness gives them the right to exert their powers as they please. Heroes are seldom well-rounded personalities. Typically they embody one trait of character and, being supermen, embody it to excess, and the traits of character that heroes embody are by no means those that a well-ordered civilized society would unreservedly commend. As an old singer told Milman Parry, 'That heroism did not belong to us. The old heroes were worthy men, and hajduks (outlaws), they say; but we are not. Our people have come under discipline. Heroism has passed' (*SCHS* III 271). A hero who is explicitly insufferable is Gilgamesh. He is represented as so arrogant that his subjects prayed to be delivered from him. Agamemnon would have understood their attitude (see 1.176–81), for Akhilleus refused to act within the delicate web of personal relationships among the Achaean chiefs before Troy and nurtured a μῆνις that was οὐλομένη. Diomedes, who knew how to handle a difficult superior (9.32–49, cf. 4.412–18), is a morally more exemplary character. But before the discipline of civilization is imposed heroes deliver what is needful, and for that everything else must be forgiven them. Meanwhile in various degrees heroes embody violence, pride, cruelty, egotism, and sometimes other qualities that are in danger of becoming vices by excess. It is, of course, precisely these qualities that bring about the dramatic situations celebrated in heroic song.

(b) *Status*

The simplest way to exalt a hero is to give him status. In the Greek tradition he is an ἀριστεύς, and his status is justified by the suggestion that he enjoys a special relationship with Zeus; he is διογενής, διοτρεφής, and Διὶ

45

φίλος. In a few cases (Herakles, Akhilleus) the relationship is reinforced by immediate divine ancestry. In the narrative the heroes are represented as the only persons of consequence in their society; the productive classes are ignored. In the field the other ranks make up an anonymous λαός except when they are singled out for slaughter. Yet even then, for there is no credit in overcoming the unresistant, the poet of the *Iliad* will say τοὺς ἄρ' ὁ γ' ἡγεμόνας Δαναῶν ἕλεν (11.304) after listing the victims of an *androktasia*. To check a rout Odysseus appeals ἀγανοῖς ἐπέεσσι to the βασιλῆες and ἔξοχοι ἄνδρες, but uses the stick on the 'men of the people'. In the assembly only the ἀριστῆες speak, a custom enforced by blows on those who get above their station (2.265). After summoning an assembly of the whole host Akhilleus addressed himself solely to Agamemnon (19.56), Idaios the diplomatic herald added ἄλλοι ἀριστῆες Παναχαιῶν, but even at the lowest point of his demoralization Agamemnon could still ignore the rank and file and speak to Ἀργείων ἡγήτορες ἠδὲ μέδοντες (9.17). The ἀριστῆες then are the sole actors in the drama. Their position is assured in life and their memory in death.

This status is part of the background of the heroic tradition and presumably reflects some sort of social reality, though at a certain distance; the *Iliad*'s terminology of leadership is imprecise. Simpler societies that are innocent of hierarchy have heroes (leaders), but a genuinely lower class heroic character is probably always a product of special circumstances.[10]

Heroes may be kings, but a king who is a hero carries a heavy burden of symbolism that inhibits the application of many heroic themes to him. He and his line symbolize the continued existence of his people, and so, for example, the pathos of a gallant end must be denied him. Better to keep the king in the background and focus on a figure free of kingly responsibilities.

The idea of the king in the background, for whom, or in spite of whom, the hero fights is a powerful one and very common in any culture that incorporates the ranks of lord and vassal. In Old English epithets for heroes fall roughly into two classes, those meaning 'old, wise, or good' which are applied to kings, and those meaning 'bold, fierce, or strong' which are applied to warriors. Beowulf is held up as the ideal king (*Beowulf* 1380–2), cf. the Odyssean formula πατὴρ ὡς ἤπιος ἦεν (4×) and the implied description of Odysseus himself as ἀγανὸς καὶ ἤπιος at *Od.* 2.230 = 5.8. The king may be noble but distant, like Charlemagne in *Roland* and Hrothgar in *Beowulf*, or ungrateful or malevolent, like Louis in the *Guillaume*-cycle, Alphonso in the *Cid*, or Gunther in the *Nibelungenlied*. The idea seems to

---

[10] The Indian thug Ompurī is one example, cf. Hatto, *Traditions* 1 54. 'Robin Hood' figures lie on the margin of the heroic idea, or beyond it.

lurk in the portrayal of Agamemnon who is represented as blatantly unjust in his attitudes towards his colleagues, was prepared to abandon their common enterprise, and even rejoiced (*Od.* 8.76–8) at their disputes. Heroic poetry is often on the side of the vassal.

(c) Force and will

Heroes cannot *be*, they must *do*; courage in war, generosity in peace, not idle strength or wealth, are admired. The simplest form of heroism is the success-ful accomplishment of a mighty deed, seen most clearly when the hero is an isolated figure who does battle with monsters. Beowulf, Perseus, and Herakles are obvious examples.[11] Perhaps such heroes symbolize the success of the tribe over a hostile environment; at any rate they are common among peoples whose survival is precarious and it is typical of them that they win (Beowulf's last fight is an exception) and that their exploits are enhanced beyond reasonable probability. The point of these tales is the victory and the force exerted in winning it. Where the hero's antagonists are other humans there is more realism, more scope for victory in fair fight, and more risk of defeat. Even then he may fall with honour μέγα ῥέξας τι καὶ ἐσσομένοισι πυθέσθαι (22.305). The words are those of Hektor, the main exemplar of this idea in the Greek tradition. The hero's valiant end is characteristic of the Germanic concept of heroism.

Force comes to the fore in heroic poetry as the supernatural retreats into the background. The supernatural does not mean gods. Gods are part of the natural order; they personify causation, whether at the level of the principles that rule the world or at the level of hour-by-hour events. What heroic poetry *qua* heroic eschews is the sort of thing that pervades, for example, the Finnish tales that make up the *Kalevala*: magic. Magic is the natural order set aside. Väinämöinen rides over the water on a magic steed and builds a boat with magic words; Ilmarinen forges a talisman, the Sampo; Louhi creates plague and conceals the sun and moon.

The black art had an important role in the story of the Argonauts and has a foothold in the *Odyssey*, but only in the Wanderings; sorcery is *completely absent* from the action of the *Iliad*. (That can only partly be due to the fact that witchcraft is the province of females (Medea, Agamede, Circe).) It is not only that no spells are cast or even mooted, but there are not even such auxiliary aids to heroic success as invulnerable bodies and weapons that hit their target always and at vast distances. Invulnerability was not foreign to Greek heroic thought, but no one would guess from the *Iliad* and all the trouble about Akhilleus' armour that some said he had

---

[11] For the Saracens as collectively monsters in Roland see Hatto, *Traditions* II 245.

been spear-proofed in the waters of Styx, nor that Telamonian Aias was vulnerable only in the armpit. Special weapons that bear their own names fall short of magic ones but confer advantage on their wielders, by implication at least. Siegfried wielded Balmung; Roland, Oliver, and Charlemagne all christened their swords. Roland could not recognize defeat until his Durandel was shattered. The nearest the *Iliad* comes to a named weapon is the Πηλιὰς μελίη of Akhilleus, and it is significant that this is properly a thrusting spear that never left its owner's hand; one cannot have strong proprietorial feelings towards anything so easily lost as a missile weapon. But neither Akhilleus' spear nor Odysseus' bow, another weapon that only its owner could wield, appears to have any exceptional properties (cf. the fantasies detailed by Bowra, *HP* 149–54).

The hero then must epitomize force. Every major figure in the *Iliad* is given a rampage, an *aristeia*. A berserker is etymologically a frenzied Norse warrior, but battle frenzy (often illustrated by comparisons with ferocious animals, as in the *Iliad*) infects most heroes. Hektor's fury at 15.607–12 is a fine example, complete with blazing eyes and froth at the lips. Achaean warriors feel zest, χάρμη, and are inspired with μένος. Heroes who fight monsters or personify extreme violence use the club (Rainouart in Old French epic, Marko Kraljević, Bhīma). There is an obscure instance in the *Iliad*, Ereuthalion (7.141), in one of Nestor's reminiscences. The Herakles of realistic heroic poetry who fought at Pulos and Oikhalia used the bow, the hero of the labours the club.

Where a tradition presupposes a heroic class there can be a complication, for in a group where spheres of competence overlap each member must assert his right to membership by achieving his victory in competition with his fellows. The Greek tradition is unusual in explicitly putting equal weight on surpassing friends and defeating enemies (see 11.783n.).

The Greek tradition complicates the picture further by bracketing deeds with words; Akhilleus was taught μύθων τε ῥητῆρ' ἔμεναι πρηκτῆρά τε ἔργων (9.443), and was set off against a hero, Odysseus, who was a deviser as well as a doer. Odysseus is the outstanding instance of an unusual type of hero who retains in a realistic form the resourcefulness of the sorcerers and magicians of non-heroic narrative poetry.

The emphasis on physical force further reduces the possibilities for an active role for heroines in what are already represented as male-dominated societies. The secondary role, of course, may yet be important, e.g. the loyal wife of the absent hero (Penelope), or the actively supportive wife (Guiborc in the *Guillaume*-cycle, Kanıkey in *Manas*). To enter the story on the same level as the heroes heroines must either adopt masculine roles (Amazons), or excel in masculine skills (Atalante, Brunhild in the Nibelung story), or commit some awesome deed that would normally require a hero's hand and is or borders on the criminal (Klutaimestra, Kriemhild) – the moral ambiguity of heroines is even clearer than that of heroes.

There must be moral force to complement physical force, but this is a factor that requires scale for its full development. Tenacity, for example, is convincing in a Jason or an Odysseus, but is not really conveyed by the bald statement that the hero languished e.g. for *x* years in a Turkish prison. The moral stature of the hero is clearest when he confronts death. He risks death all the time, and in his noblest incarnations he chooses to die rather than live in the shadow, as he sees it, of disgrace. 'Men say he could have escaped, but he turned his horse to make a stand' is one of the themes of South Slavic heroic poetry. A refinement of this theme is to forewarn the hero of his danger, so that he chooses to enter the fight in the knowledge that he is doomed, like Akhilleus or the Serbian Tsar before Kosovo. Or, if the hero rejects advice and warning, realization comes at the moment of crisis, as it does to Roland and Hektor.

(d) Egotism and ἀεικέα ἔργα

Heroic qualities are morally ambiguous because they are excessive. Roland was too proud to summon aid; Akhilleus was too sensitive to insult to accept compensation and driven by that excessive sensitivity to abandon his own side. The *Iliad* regards this attitude sympathetically from the standpoint of Akhilleus, so that we do not immediately notice that the same sensitivity to slight inspired the treachery of Ganelon in the *Chanson de Roland* or that of Vuk Branković at Kosovo. Roland's heart was 'hard and proud' (verse 256); Akhilleus is rebellious, without pity (16.33), obdurate (9.678), impatient (19.199ff.), vindictive (22.395) and fractious (1.177); his terrible temper is οὐλομένη, not admirable but awesomely implacable.

The *Iliad* is more helpful than most epics in exposing the social foundation of heroism. Unless their heroism is pure pursuit of fame heroes are champions who fight for their people. To induce them to do so society punishes them with disgrace (22.104–7) or rewards them with honour (12.310–21). Fame is an aspect of honour; it may reach heaven and continue after the hero's death. Fame is a universal motive, but Greek is unusual in stressing its primacy. 'They choose one thing above all others,' said Heraclitus (fr. 29 Diels), 'immortal glory among mortals.' When other claims threaten to arise the heroes resolutely put them aside. Neither wife nor mother can sway the heroic mind; Hektor firmly dismisses Andromakhe (6.486ff.), Akhilleus Thetis (18.79ff.). 'Immovable once his decision is taken, deaf to appeals and persuasion, to reproof and threat, unterrified by physical violence, even by the ultimate violence of death itself, more stubborn as his isolation increases until he has no one to speak to but the unfeeling landscape, bitter at the disrespect and mockery the world levels at what it regards as failure, the hero prays for vengeance and curses his enemies as he welcomes the death that is the predictable end of his intransigence.'[12]

Excessive force is another area of moral ambiguity, though it is not easy to decide what is normal and what is excessive in a heroic milieu. Heroic poetry respects the hero's enemies unless it is infected by religious prejudice. The dramatic principle that the hero's antagonist must be worthy of him ensures the latter a fair deal up to the moment of his demise. At that point a competing dramatic principle takes over, the hero's triumph must by some means seize the imagination of the tale's audience. An awesome deed may be the answer. The actions of Kriemhild in hacking Hagen to death at the end of the *Nibelungenlied* or of Akhilleus in dragging Hektor (alive, some have thought, in an older tale) behind his chariot would lose their point as expressions of the lust for vengeance if they were not excessive. Bhīma – the name means 'terrible' – in Indian epic represents an extreme of violence, to such a degree that his allies have often to restrain him. 'Drawing his sharp sword with its excellent blade, and treading upon the throat of the writhing man, he cut open his breast as he lay on the ground, and drank his warm blood. Then, having quaffed and quaffed again, he looked up and spoke these words in his excessive fury: "Better than mother's milk ..."' (trans. Smith, in Hatto, *Traditions* I 57). No one in the *Iliad* indulges his taste for blood so literally, but the thought is not far away, cf. 4.35, 22.347, and the story of Thebes told how Tudeus devoured the brains of Melanippos.

There is no need to argue the artificiality and obvious hyperbole of this moral picture. There is nothing strange about the ability of literature to create a fictitious society to achieve its ends. No conscious effort is required; the development insensibly proceeds to a point where contact with underlying reality has become slight. *Quidquid delirant reges, plectuntur Achivi* – the behaviour of the heroes before Troy would tear apart society if there were not means, largely ignored in the *Iliad*, of restraining it. The behaviour of Akhilleus is indeed absurd, but it is the absurdity of excess and obsession and therefore not so absurd that we cannot comprehend it.

(iv) The Greek tradition and the *Iliad*

The *Iliad* is an epic with a wide vision but a sharp focus. It is concerned with the twin concepts, honour (τιμή) and glory (κλέος or κῦδος), that are the

---

[12] B. M. W. Knox, *The Heroic Temper: Studies in Sophoclean Tragedy* (Berkeley and Los Angeles 1964) 44.

driving force of a small group of men, the heroes. No one else is of serious consequence.[13]

The protagonists in the underlying story were not fighting in order to seek honour but to defend it, the Atreidai by recovering Helen, the Trojans by preserving their city. Others were at Troy because, as Hesiod explained, they were bound by their oath as Helen's suitors; Aineias joined in because he had been attacked by Akhilleus. Thus far we are in the world of heroic poetry, where the deeds of the heroes are celebrated and awkward questions are not asked. What an epic poem can do, or should do given its greater scale, is to explore as well as celebrate the ideology of heroism. Accordingly the *Iliad* turns its focus upon a hero the sole purpose of whose existence is the pursuit of glory. When the poem begins Akhilleus has no injury to avenge, no city or family to defend, but a knowledge that fate has assigned him a short life. He has therefore the strongest of motives for seeking fame and nothing to detract him from it. His ruthlessness is essential to his tragedy, but until the end it excludes two qualities that enter into the *Iliad*'s concept of true heroism, αἰδώς and ἔλεος (24.44). Outside the *Iliad* Akhilleus seems to have been a more sympathetic character, sparing suppliants and accepting ransoms, and within it the qualities he lacks are given to his *alter ego*, the kindly Patroklos, and sometimes even to his antagonist, Hektor (both of whom are also capable of violent action – see Kirk, *HOT* 50–1).

Stripped to its essence the creed of heroism is that the fame of great deeds defeats death. Loss of life is compensated by honour received and fame to come. Death is ultimately certain, for it is part of the μοῖρα of men; but what matters for the hero is that life is uncertain. A quiet, long life is not a realistic option, for ten thousand dooms of death stand over a man (12.326–7), so that the heroic course is to make a bid for fame and die, if it must be, having done some great deed. In simpler terms the ἀριστεύς has a duty; τὸν δὲ μάλα χρεὼ | ἑστάμεναι κρατερῶς (11.409–10) in the face of danger. Such a creed is not easy to live by in practice, for even ten thousand dooms of death do not amount to an absolute certainty; to save their lives Iliadic heroes call for aid, withdraw, and on occasion run away. But one hero could not look upon failure as a temporary setback; for him death – early death – was a certainty. He had traded life for honour (9.410–16), and his anger was all the deeper when the honour was not forthcoming. That is the uniqueness of Akhilleus.

---

[13] The world of the similes (and the Shield of Akhilleus) is a very different place or the same place from a very different viewpoint: there are no heroes and not many persons of rank. The *Odyssey* takes a more generous view of where moral worth may be found.

Where folktale and heroic poetry merge success may come to the hero relatively easily with the aid of superhuman endowments or special weapons. The cyclic epics and, especially, the *Argo* story contain many examples of these derogations from pure heroism: the flying sons of Boreas, the eyesight of Lunkeus, invulnerable heroes, impenetrable armour (probably), the talismanic bow of Philoktetes, numerous prophecies and oracles (seventeen are noted by Kullmann, *Quellen* 221) and exotic figures like Kuknos, Memnon, and Penthesileia who are not part of this world. In the *Iliad* heroes have only enhanced muscular power and strength of will.[14]

The tradition of the cyclic poems – and some asides in the *Odyssey* – undercut the creed of heroism by softening the horror of death. Heroes, however, are as great as the stakes are high; hence a widespread feeling, most conspicuous in the Germanic concept of heroism, that a hero is a tragic figure whose nature dooms him to an untimely death. The *Iliad* makes Herakles the supreme example of mortality: οὐδὲ γὰρ οὐδὲ βίη Ἡρακλῆος φύγε κῆρα | ὅς περ φίλτατος ἔσκε Διὶ Κρονίωνι ἄνακτι (18.117–18), the *Odyssey* in a *tour de force* of eschatology puts his εἴδωλον in Hades and his person (αὐτός) on Olumpos (*Od.* 11.601–3). Menelaos was promised an afterlife in Elysium (*Od.* 4.561–4), a privilege extended to heroes in general by Hesiod (*Erga* 167–73). Zeus immortalized Memnon, and Thetis removed Akhilleus from his pyre to the White Island in the *Aithiopis*. The *Cypria* granted immortality on alternate days to Kastor and Poludeukes. The *Telegony* devalued the motif by immortalizing all the survivors of his family after Odysseus' death. In the *Iliad* even a temporary resurrection by necromancy seems to be excluded; once the pyre has done its work there is no return (23.75–6). The price that must be paid for glory is thus clearly defined, without compromise. That is the uniqueness of the *Iliad*.

The slaying of Hektor was a great deed of war on a par with Akhilleus' victories over Penthesileia and Memnon. The *Aithiopis*, having told those exploits, went on to relate the death of Akhilleus, but as far as is known the poem did not bring its three major episodes into causal connexion. For articulation it relied on an external structure, balance and contrast. To some extent the *Iliad* does the same, most obviously in the balance in theme and detail of the first and last Books,[15] but the *Iliad* also has an inner logic and develops in the person of Akhilleus a causally connected nexus of ideas, those of glory, vengeance, foreknowledge, responsibility, and shame. (See introduction to book 9.) In the end Akhilleus cannot wreak a vengeance

---

[14] The suppression of magical elements is part of the *Iliad*'s avoidance of fantastic and romantic episodes, as critically set out by J. Griffin, *JHS* 97 (1977) 39–53.

[15] Whitman, *HHT* 257–84, explores the *Iliad*'s symmetries in detail. His analyses are not always convincing, but the principle is correct. See also N. J. Richardson in vol. VI, Introduction, ch. 1.

great enough to balance the shame he feels at the death of Patroklos. His mighty deed, his heroism, is insufficient to restore his honour and leads him to act 'like a raging lion that indulges its μεγάλη βίη and θυμὸς ἀγήνωρ' (24.41–2, see n. *ad loc.*). Like the dying Roland Akhilleus has his vision (and ours) widened as he makes peace with his soul. At first Roland cannot bear the thought that his sword will fall into another's hands – as in the *Iliad* the loss of weapons is the ultimate disgrace. Then he reflects that he holds the sword not for his own glory but for that of Charlemagne, finally that the sword, whose pommel contains holy relics, is a symbol of his faith. So Roland dies not cursing his conquerors in heroic style but as a Christian confessing his sins to God. That is the sort of vision an epic poet should have. With Priam kneeling before him Akhilleus too realizes that heroism is not enough. The conclusion of his dictum κάτθαν' ὁμῶς ὅ τ' ἀεργὸς ἀνὴρ ὅ τε πολλὰ ἑοργώς (9.320) is not that he should do more killing but that he should recognize that all men suffer the same troubles and the same end – that is, that he should shed tears for the nature of things. Accordingly he bows to the will of Zeus, who offers him a new honour (24.110) which victors and defeated can both share.

COMMENTARY

BOOK NINE

How the *Iliad* was created we shall never know. Even if the assumptions set out in the Introduction to volume 1 of this Commentary are accepted and we see in the poem the impact of an original genius on traditional sagas, an attempt to dissect the plot of the *Iliad* is no more likely to command assent than former attempts to dissect its text have been. But a commentator on book 9 cannot duck the question, and it behoves him to make his suppositions plain. The problem is that book 9 is well integrated into the idea of the *Iliad* but not so well integrated into its text. On an intellectual level the Book explores the moral stance that Akhilleus has adopted and is necessary for the understanding of his position and the dangers that it holds in store for him; on the other hand the role of Phoinix and the integrity of the Book have been questioned, and at the level of what is done and said on the field and in the camp the situation that the Book has created seems later to be overlooked, cf. 11.609n., 16.72–3, and 16.84–6.

An epic of Homeric quality must be a sequence of ideas as well as a sequence of events. At the level of the characters that the poet has created the epic ideas that Akhilleus embodies are those of glory, vengeance, foreknowledge, and responsibility. The first three are each traditional ideas: they are met with, for example, in loose combination in the fate of the sons of Antenor, Iphidamas and Koon, at 11.221–63. Agamemnon slays Iphidamas and loots his corpse (glory); Koon, grieved for his brother, attacks Agamemnon and wounds him (vengeance); to attack against such adverse odds is virtual foreknowledge of the ultimate result, Koon's death, but the explicit idea of divinely revealed foreknowledge appears a little later at 11.328–32.

The climax of the *Iliad* fittingly is a slaying: ἠράμεθα μέγα κῦδος· ἐπέφνομεν Ἕκτορα δῖον (22.393) is the fundamental idea of heroic poetry, but a mere slaying devoid of further overtones is not the stuff that a great epic is made of. Even as Akhilleus is made to utter those words he is made to remember that it is not only a glorious deed that he has performed, but an act of vengeance: τοῦ [Πατρόκλου] δ' οὐκ ἐπιλήσομαι (22.387). The idea of heroic glory is linked to that of heroic duty.

55

The duty of vengeance is always hazardous and supplied the *Iliad* with many moments of pathos; in the case of Akhilleus the pathos is refined into heroism by the foreknowledge granted him by Thetis that he lives under a conditional doom – if he slays Hektor he will quickly die himself (18.94–126). We should not underestimate the importance of this link. Yet it is directly mentioned only in book 18, a brilliant stroke, it is pleasant to conjecture, of the monumental composer, bringing into focus the traditional point that the hero was doomed to be short-lived and to die at Troy.

At the end of book 9 the Achaean leaders know where they stand: on their own. But to the action of the poem the Book contributes nothing, the situation on the ground being the same at the end as at the beginning: the Trojans on the plain, the Achaeans within their wall. What then does the Book add? It restores Akhilleus, who has been out of sight and mind from the end of book 1, to the focus of attention; it sharpens his characterization by showing him in contact with those nearest to him, as the encounters with Helen and Andromakhe do for Hektor (6.313–502); but the primary contribution of the Book is to the ethical plot of the *Iliad*. Without it the plot would be a familiar story of heroism. The young warrior accepts death as the price of heroic fame and duty. He admits to a mistake: it was his fault that Patroklos died, immediately for not being at Patroklos' side and more remotely for giving way to ἔρις (18.97–110). If what he said to Thetis were the sum of Akhilleus' responsibility, it would be easy to absolve him; he speaks under the stress of deep emotion, the quarrel with Agamemnon is too distant, and Patroklos had been reckless. For his mistakes he could have pleaded ἄτη; he had not acted with his eyes open.

The idea of the moral responsibility of Akhilleus was always latent in the story, but at some point, it is plausible to imagine, the monumental composer realized that an explicit error of moral judgement would form the keystone to his poem. It is the function of book 9 to make this clear. It was natural that Akhilleus should be made to relish the prospect of a chastened Agamemnon (11.608–10). So he made the prospect a reality and had Akhilleus reject the overtures of his friends. To achieve this end the poet had to confront a dilemma. As part of his motivation for the seizure of Briseis Agamemnon was given a reputation for greed, at least in Akhilleus' eyes (1.149); it would be easy therefore, maintaining the characterization of both heroes, to have Agamemnon make an offer which Akhilleus could stigmatize as mean and justifiably reject. On the other hand if Agamemnon is made to offer more than could be reasonably rejected on that score, on what understandable grounds could Akhilleus be made to reject it? There is strong evidence (see 640n.) that in a culture dominated by the ideas of honour and shame to reject compensation is to incur dishonour. Such an impression must here be avoided. The crucial passage is 379–87. Akhilleus is the best of the Achaeans, the greatest of heroes; in no way can he resign himself to the slightest disgrace. Let him therefore set on his honour an infinite value in material things. Of course it is an unreasonable and impractical position, but Akhilleus' soul is not the real world, and on his terms we can understand it. In book 9 therefore he is given a fair chance to extricate himself from the futile posture he had taken up in book 1, and refuses; he is then warned that his stance is wrong and dangerous, and takes no notice. His obstinacy on this occasion is in the classical sense an ἁμαρτία, and deepens his heroism with the idea of tragedy. Akhilleus is wrong but from an excess of rectitude. He rejects a fair offer, but does so from the highest heroic motives.

Book 9 is thus the key to the *Iliad*, and within book 9 the key is Phoinix' allegory of Ἄτη and the Λιταί (502–12). Neither is dispensable, but the way in which the episode has been worked into the Book and the Book into the poem has always seemed to give analytical critics their opportunity (see 182n., 11.609n., 16.72–3n.). To these genuine difficulties there is no easy answer from the unitarian standpoint. Reinhardt's hypothesis (*IuD* – pp. 212–23 discuss book 9, with a critical commentary at pp. 223–42) that the composition of our *Iliad* was a long-drawn-out process with repeated revision over many years rests on a persuasive premise: the poem cannot have been created in a moment of inspiration. It is in such places as book 9 that we have a glimpse into the workshop of Homer.

The design of the Book is simple and self-contained. A council, in active session at beginning and end, brackets the scene in Akhilleus' hut. Business there is transacted, not as in book 1 by debate, but by three long and two short discourses. The moral pressure on Akhilleus is intense, but the formality of the situation enables all to keep their tempers. The discourses and the revelations of character that they make are the Book. For their construction see nn. to 225, 307, 430, and Lohmann, *Reden* 213–277. As for their quality Leaf (who thought the Book intrusive) was deeply moved: 'alike in the vivid description of scene, in interplay of character and in the glowing rhetoric, the book is unsurpassed in Homer, perhaps in literature' (*The Iliad* i 371).

1–88 Demoralized by his defeat (as related in book 8) Agamemnon summons an assembly of the host and proposes withdrawal. Diomedes, to general applause, repudiates this pusillanimous suggestion, and Nestor after complimenting Diomedes' spirit outlines precautions for the night and hints at further measures

1–3 The resumptive formula ὡς οἱ μέν [sc. the Trojans] ... αὐτάρ (or δέ) makes a natural beginning to the Book, and makes it easy to imagine a pause in the singing, though not a long pause, between Books, for the ἀγορά of the Achaeans balances that of the Trojans (8.489–541). The same resumptive formula is used to introduce books 12, 16, 18, 20, 22, and 23; but it is a regular formula of transition between episodes, and implies nothing for the origin of the present division into books. [Plutarch], *Vita Hom.*, affirms that Aristarchus (i.e. a Hellenistic scholar, not necessarily Aristarchus himself) made the Book division. Indeed a Hellenistic date is very likely; see R. Pfeiffer, *History of Classical Scholarship* (Oxford 1968) 115–16. See also 11.848n. and Introduction to vol. VI 20–21.

1 φυλακὰς ἔχον: by the tomb of Ilos, according to 10.415, though the geography of that Book is idiosyncratic, see 10.428–31n., and the location of the tomb is never precisely conceived. Night has fallen (8.485–6), though very little notice is taken of the fact in the narrative, apart from a passing reference at 85.

2 With their usual precision the scholia (Arn/A bT and Arn/A on 14.10) seek to separate φόβος as ἡ μετὰ τοῦ δέους φυγή and φύζα as ἡ μετὰ φυγῆς δειλίασις, and suggest ἔκπληξις as the sense of φύζα here. 'Panic' is a suitably ambivalent rendering between the state of mind and its manifestation. The Achaeans of course are presently within the safety of their wall. — φόβου κρυόεντος: the correct form κρυόεις is here secure, as at 5.740, Hesiod, *Theog.* 936 and [Hesiod], *Aspis* 255. For the secondary form ὀκρυόεις, a creation (according to Leumann, *HW* 49–50) of Homer's predecessors, see 6.344n. and 64n. — The metaphor ἑταίρη recurs at 4.440–1 (ἔρις the sister and comrade of Ares).

3 βεβολήατο, as if from βολέω (only the medio-passive perfect is attested), is properly used metaphorically according to Aristarchus (Arn/A). βεβλήατο, read by Zenodotus 'and others', would imply physical wounds, cf. 9, and *Od.* 10.247, where βεβλημένος is read by many MSS for βεβολημένος.

4–8 The Book division conceals the contrast, clearly deliberate, between this simile of wind and storm and that of the calm night fourteen verses earlier that illustrates the Trojans' confident bivouac at 8.555–9. The oblique idiom 'as two winds stir up the sea', for 'as the sea is stirred up', is typical of Homeric similes.

Similes in general, like the narrative, are composed from the standpoint of an observer and comment upon external signs from which, of course, internal states of mind may be inferred. This simile therefore is unusual in that it comments on a metaphysical entity, the θυμός, which cannot be observed except in so far as a person may be aware of his own θυμός and, as here, of its palpitations. Storm similes, e.g. 11.297–8, 11.305–8, usually illustrate furious action.

4 The basic formula is prepositional, ἐπὶ πόντον ... ἰχθυόεντα (5× *Od.*) or πόντον ἐπ' ἰχθυόεντα (7× including variants, in several positions). The sea bred κήτεα that might attack a man (*Od.* 5.421, cf. the expression μεγακήτεα πόντον, *Od.* 3.158 and West's note *ad loc.*), and the heroes had a horror of drowning (*Od.* 5.308–12); even so 'abounding in fish' seems a innocent description of the sea, *pace* Householder and Nagy, who comment that 'the original selection of ἰχθυόεις was probably motivated not by a striving for fanciful descriptions of the sea, but rather by the implication of lurking danger' (F. Householder and G. Nagy, *Current Trends in Linguistics* 9 (1972) 768). Fish eats man in the heroic world, it is true, not vice versa, but in similes at least (as Aristarchus noted, Arn/A to 16.364) Homer drew on the world he knew and interpreted his diction accordingly. For fishing in a simile see 16.406–8 (and n.), 24.80–2, *Od.* 12.251–4.

5 Βορέης: the spondaic scansion (hence βορρᾶς in Allen's 'e' group of MSS) occurs also at 23.195 Βορέη καὶ Ζεφύρῳ. If the lengthening of the first syllable is not a metrical licence it is hard to say what articulation the epic orthography may represent, since -ρε- > -ρρ- is unknown in Ionic, cf. Βορῆς in Hdt., and a consonantalized ε (if such were possible) would not make position any more than the well attested consonantalized ι. συκέαι (*Od.* 7.116) is a phonetic, not a metrical parallel. Zephuros, cf. 4.423ff., is δυσαής at *Od.* 5.295, not a zephyr in the modern sense.

The winds mentioned blow from the north-west quadrant and therefore, if they blow from Thrace, strike the Asiatic coast and its offshore islands. Similar indications of the poet's geographical standpoint occur at 2.394ff., 4.422ff. (coasts beaten by winds from the south-west quadrant).

8 = 15.629.

9–78 The assembly (ἀγορή or ἀγών) is an important epic device for setting in motion a new action-sequence, cf. 1.54, 2.50 (the best instance), 7.345, 7.382, 8.489, 18.243, 19.40, 20.4, and Arend, *Scenen* 118–21. In the full sequence the assembly is summoned by heralds at the instance of one of the chiefs (Agamemnon, Akhilleus, Hektor, at 20.4 Zeus), the men sit, the convenor rises, takes the sceptre, and puts his proposal, other leaders may respond but not the rank and file, the army expresses its approval or has its approval taken for granted. The fuller the sequence, as usually the case in type-scenes, the more important the occasion, but departures from it imply exceptional circumstances: Thersites (2.212) is out of order, the standing Trojans at 18.246 signify their apprehension, the summons at 19.40 is by an impatient Akhilleus. Agamemnon sits at 19.77 because he is wounded.

9 This is a quasi-formular verse, cf. *Od.* 10.247 κῆρ ἄχεϊ μεγάλῳ βεβολημένος.

10 λιγύφθογγος is formular with κῆρυξ (4× *Il.*, 1× *Od.*), always in dat. plur. It is typical that no discomfort is felt when the epithet is immediately followed by the instruction μὴ βοᾶν (12).

11–12 κλήδην stands for ἐξονομακλήδην (22.415, *Od.* 4.278, 12.250, cf. πατρόθεν ἐκ γενεῆς 10.68), the usual etiquette in summoning the assembly. ἀγορήν denotes an assembly of the whole army or people, including

(19.42–5) supernumeraries as well as fighting men. At 17, Ἀργείων ἡγή-τορες ἠδὲ μέδοντες, Agamemnon ignores the λαός, but that is not unparalleled, cf. *Od.* 8.26 (Alkinoos to the Phaeacian assembly). The formula for addressing the rank and file is ὦ φίλοι, ἥρωες Δαναοί, θεράποντες Ἄρηος (4×) (cf. 17n.). αὐτὸς … πονεῖτο reflects Agamemnon's anxiety, as at 10.69–70. — There are four ἀγορά-scenes on the Achaean side in the *Iliad*, in books 1, 2, 9, and 19, discussed by Lohmann, *Reden* 214–27, who argues for a direct relation between them. It is assumed here that the relation is indirect, the poet having a pattern for such scenes which gives rise to the parallels in content and structure (cf. 12.61–79n.).

13–31 The scene is set with some repeated verses: 14–15 ≅ 16.3–4, 16 = the first hemistich of 18.323 + the second of 2.109, 18–25 = 2.111–18, 26–8 = 2.139–41, 29–31 = 9.693 + 695–6. As is usually the case in such passages there was omission and athetesis ἕνεκα τοῦ κατ' ἄλλους τόπους φέρεσθαι. Zenodotus (Arn/A) read μετὰ δ' Ἀργείοισιν ἔειπεν for the second hemistich of 14 and omitted the simile 14–15 and 23–5; 23–5 were also athetized by Aristophanes (Did/A) and Aristarchus (Arn/A), as being better at 2.116–18. For 26–31 Zenodotus read ἤτοι ὅ γ' ὣς εἰπὼν κατ' ἄρ' ἕζετο θυμὸν ἀχεύων· | τοῖσι δ' ἀνιστάμενος μετέφη κρατερὸς Διομήδης. Zenodotus normally sought a shorter text and was reputedly severe on repeated passages (τοιοῦτός ἐστιν ἐπὶ τῶν διφορουμένων (Arn/A on 23–5). Omission by Zenodotus followed by a more cautious athetesis on the part of Aristophanes and Aristarchus is a common pattern; nineteen instances in the *Iliad* are listed by Apthorp, *MS Evidence* 80.

14–15 These verses (simile of the fountain in the rock) = 16.3–4 (of Patroklos). Aristarchus countered Zenodotus' omission of the simile here with the argument that the simile was necessary for the amplification (αὔξησις) of Agamemnon's grief. (Aristarchus identified two functions of similes, αὔξησις and ἔμφασις, 'graphic effect', e.g. 11.297–8.) Acute distress at imminent disaster to the army causes floods of tears in both cases. No other connexion between the passages is made explicit and it is hard to imagine that an *audience* would make one, unless it were well trained in the nuances of the epic style. For the concept of the 'experienced audience' (the corollary of the 'well-rehearsed composer'), see M. M. Willcock, *AJP* 96 (1975) 107–10, and V. Leinieks, *Class. et Med.* 37 (1986) 5–20. For the similar difficulty presented by Agamemnon's words at 18–28 see n. *ad loc.* There *is* indeed a contrast between the tears of Agamemnon, who is concerned for his reputation, and those of Patroklos, which express his distress at others' sufferings, but that may do no more than illustrate the versatility of the epic's traditional diction and the diverse uses to which it may be put. — Agamemnon's tears are not unheroic in themselves, cf. bT to 1.349 ἕτοιμον τὸ ἡρωϊκὸν πρὸς δάκρυα and Odysseus' tears at *Od.* 5.82–4, 8.86,

8.521, and 16.191 (where see Hoekstra's note). Akhilleus' abuse of Patroklos' tears at 16.7–11 as 'girlish' reflects only his indignation that Patroklos should pity the Achaeans. Other notable weepers are Akhilleus himself (1.349), Telemakhos (*Od.* 2.81), Menelaos and company (*Od.* 4.183), and Odysseus (*Od.* 8.86, 8.522). There has been some temptation to take the blackness of the water as symbolic of Agamemnon's dark mood, e.g. Fränkel, *Gleichnisse* 21, but neither δνοφερός nor μελάνυδρος elsewhere have gloomy connotations. The spring water must run, or drip, down something to make a good analogue for tears, though Fränkel, *loc. cit.*, supposed that the rock symbolized the king's iron will beneath his tearful exterior, a gloss that will not work for the use of the image in book 16. (There are four other extended similes in the *Iliad* that are repeated, 5.782–3 = 7.256–7, 5.860–1 = 14.148–9, 6.506–11 = 15.263–8, 13.389–93 = 16.482–6, and one that is substantially repeated, 11.548–55 cf. 17.657–64. See also Edwards, vol. v 24. Such comparisons at least are probably traditional.)

15 αἰγίλιψ is an Iliadic gloss (also *h.Hom.* 19.4 but not in *Od.* or Hesiod), as an epithet always in the formula αἰγίλιπος πέτρης. The traditional explanation 'forsaken even by goats' is a pleasing fantasy; the root is seen in Lith. *lipti*, 'climbs', cf. the Hesychian glosses ἄλιψ· πέτρα, and λίψ· πέτρα ἀφ᾽ ἧς ὕδωρ στάζει. The poet probably understood the word to mean something like 'rocky', cf. the Ithacan toponym Αἰγίλιπα τρηχεῖαν mentioned in the Catalogue of Ships (2.633).

16 Homeric orators reinforced their words by the way they wielded the sceptre (cf. 3.216–20). Agamemnon must be presumed to take up the famous sceptre described at 2.101–8. He will do nothing with it, however, in this scene, so it is not mentioned.

17 = 2.79 (Nestor addressing a *Council*). At 2.110 (and 19.78), as bT note, Agamemnon took a broader view of his audience and said ὦ φίλοι ἥρωες Δαναοί, θεράποντες Ἄρηος in addressing the ἀγορή. The view expressed by bT, that only the leaders are now present, is unjustified.

18–28 = 2.111–18 + 139–41, see nn. *ad loc.* It is implausible to suppose that Agamemnon is represented as deliberately using the same words as he had used in the earlier fiasco, nor (in spite of the more appropriate circumstances) does the same result follow; this time the troops stand firm. As far as concerns Agamemnon therefore the repetition must be understood to be accidental. It is difficult, however, for the attentive hearer/reader to ignore the coincidence and accept that the repetition of the verses (presumably as part of a traditional characterization of a despondent leader or specifically of Agamemnon) is coincidental for the poet too. Yet the fact that it is easy to see irony in Agamemnon's now proposing in earnest what he had previously proposed in deceit should not obscure the points (1) that the text contains no signal that the previous passage is in mind (such a comment would have been appropriate at the beginning of Diomedes' speech at 32ff.), (2) that resounding silences concerning preceding events are more characteristic of the *Iliad* than the exploitation of backward reference, and (3) that the reuse of blocks of verses in widely different contexts is part of the Homeric technique of scene building. It does not follow that a passage cannot recall a previous context (see 34n.), only that such a recall may be read into the text at some risk of over-interpretation and should rest on thematic correspondence rather than verbal repetitions. Agamemnon will propose retreat for the third time at 14.65–81, where it will be Odysseus who leads the objectors. If a despondent Agamemnon is traditional, then for an educated audience the irony is not so much in the present passage as in book 2. bT wish to see in Agamemnon a regal character and defend his dubious actions; here they entertain the idea that this second proposal for retreat is a πεῖρα, like the first; that must be discounted, for lack of any hint in the text.

18 Ζεύς με ... ἄτη ἐνέδησε: Agamemnon was indeed deceived by Zeus with a dream at the beginning of book 2 and Zeus is responsible for his present plight, but Agamemnon does not know this and in his mouth the words are equivalent to his saying ἀασάμην, as he does at 116. It is possible that the reference may be more specific, to the prophecy of Anios of Delos, that Troy would be taken in the tenth year, cf. Lycophron 569–76, but see 20n.

19 σχέτλιος is not so much a moral characterization (but see on 2.112) as a protest at one whose behaviour is incomprehensibly perverse, cf. Aias' characterization of Akhilleus at 9.630. πρίν, the vulgate and preferable reading, is taken by Arn/A and bT to refer to the omens at Aulis, τότε (read by Aristarchus) to the dream of book 2.

20 = 2.113 = 2.288 = 5.716. This promise of success and safe return is variously attributed to Zeus, the army, and the goddesses Here and Athene, as if it had no place, or no recognized place, in the tradition. εὐτείχεον is an artificial form for εὐτειχέα (< εὐτειχής) and is confined to this repeated line and the formula Τροίην εὐτείχεον ἐξαλαπάξαι (2×). At 1.18–19, ὑμῖν ... ἐκπέρσαι Πριάμοιο πόλιν, εὖ δ᾽ οἴκαδ᾽ ἱκέσθαι, this formular verse is modified (note neglected ϝ- of οἴκαδ᾽) in order to accommodate the plural number. — ἀπονέεσθαι etc. are popular forms (20×) in spite of requiring an exceptional metrical lengthening of the first syllable, cf. Hoekstra, *Mnem.* 30 (1978) 15–23. Wyatt's comments on this form (*ML* 85–7) based on a hypothesized ἀ-πονέεσθαι, 'gain release from toil', are not persuasive.

21 Ζεύς ... κελεύει (like many references to the influence of Zeus) is readily taken as an inference from the general situation; T discern a specific reference to the thunderbolt of 8.133–6, but that is over-precise.

22 δυσκλέα (for δυσκλεέα, Chantraine, *GH* I 74): the point is naturally one that worries Agamemnon, cf. 4.178–82, 14.70, but the precise (or primary) cause of his shame is variously stated. It may be mere failure, or the vaunts of the Trojans, but the point is regularly made, as here, that many men have died for his sake; the same consideration weighed heavily with Hektor, see 22.99–107.

23 = 14.69 (and ≅ 13.226). For the athetesis and repetition of 23–5 (= 2.116–18) see 13–31n.

24 πολίων κάρηνα: the metaphor recalls the similar use of κρήδεμνα, 16.100, *Od.* 13.388, *HyDem* 151, though the nuance of desecration (explored at length by Nagler, *Spontaneity* 45–60) is lacking.

25–31 Six consecutive sentences each filling a whole verse is one of the longest such sequences in the *Iliad*, cf. 8.145–52, but the effect would be mitigated by the pause in recitation at 28 at the end of Agamemnon's speech. — The second hemistich is a useful tag (8×), variously introduced by τοῦ γάρ, ὅ τε, καὶ εὖ, ὅου, οὖ τε, and applied to Zeus, ἀλκή, an eagle, and the Cyclops.

26 This is a formular verse (6× *Il.* 2× *Od.*).

29 + 31 The basic formula is οἱ δ᾽ ἄρα πάντες ἀκὴν ἐγένοντο σιωπῇ (10× *Il.*, 6× *Od.*), followed (5× *Il.*, 2× *Od.*) by ὀψὲ δὲ δὴ μετέειπε, which is then variously expanded by such verses as 30 here, cf. 430ff., 693ff.

30 ἄνεῳ: see 3.84n. At *Od.* 23.93 the word is used, it may be by a solecism, with reference to a single woman.

31–49 In spite of the stress put on βουλή as a heroic accomplishment reasoned argument is seldom heard from speakers in the *Iliad*. Diomedes speaks in emotional terms but with this excuse, that Agamemnon's proposals deserve what they receive, scorn and rejection. In the response to similar proposals on his part at 14.64ff. the scornful reproaches were assigned to Odysseus (a senior counsellor) and the confident rejection to the younger man, Diomedes. Here Diomedes is given both roles in a strongly characterizing speech (cf. 697–709), the second (after Agamemnon's despondency) of several such delineations of personality hereabouts, cf. Nestor's softening response to Diomedes' strong language (57–64), and his oblique approach to the hitherto unmentionable topic of the quarrel with Akhilleus (96–113), Agamemnon's graceless appendix to his generosity (158–61), and the words of the four speakers in Akhilleus' hut – Ὀδυσσεὺς συνετός, πανοῦργος, θεραπευτικός· Ἀχιλλεὺς θυμικός, μεγαλόφρων· Φοῖνιξ ἠθικός, πρᾶος, παιδευτικός· Αἴας ἀνδρεῖος, σεμνός, μεγαλόφρων, ἁπλοῦς, δυσκίνητος, βαθύς (bT on 622). bT summarize Diomedes' credentials: he killed Hektor's charioteer (8.119–23), wounded Aphrodite (5.335–40), captured Aineias' horses (5.323–7), secured golden armour (6.234–6), alone responded to Idaios (7.400–2), alone withstood the thunderbolt (8.133–50), was last to flee (8.99–100), first to rally (8.253–5), and did not revile

Agamemnon (4.412–18) – add his wounding of Ares (5.855–63). Leaf takes ὀψέ at 31 to imply that Diomedes modestly waited for his seniors to speak first; rather what is implied is his self-confidence in speaking up when no others dared, cf. 696, and 7.399, 10.219. — The epithet phrase βοὴν ἀγαθός is generically applied to Telamonian Aias, Hektor and Polites but is the regular epithet in the third–fifth foot for Diomedes and Menelaos. The sense 'with powerful voice', like that of Stentor (see 5.785 and n.) alludes to the penetrating shout of a commanding officer urging on his men (ὁμοκλέω 16×) or summoning colleagues (e.g. 11.312, 11.461, cf. 12.337, 14.147), see further Griffin, *HLD* 37ff.

31 ὀψὲ δὲ δὴ μετέειπε is the formular (5× *Il.*, 2× *Od.*) response to perplexity in disturbing or embarrassing circumstances.

32 πρῶτα is imprecise. Diomedes appears to mean that he will begin with Agamemnon's foolish proposals (and proceed to the pusillanimity that the others have displayed by their prolonged silence). Diomedes speaks to Agamemnon in general terms, but his words are easily referred to the events of book 1 where Agamemnon, θέμις ... ἀγορῇ or no, could not abide the παρρησία of Akhilleus. For Diomedes' sensitivity towards his lack of senior status cf. 14.111–12 μή τι κότῳ ἀγάσησθε ἕκαστος | οὕνεκα δὴ γενεῆφι νεώτατός εἰμι μεθ' ὑμῖν.

33 Cf. 2.196 θυμὸς δὲ μέγας ἐστὶ διοτρεφέων βασιλήων. Agamemnon, being a king, must be presumed to be easily provoked by contradiction, cf. 1.78, 2.196. The *Odyssey* (2.230 = 5.8) suggests that a good king should be πρόφρων, ἀγανός, and ἤπιος, not χαλεπός; but the fact that the plea was made tells us something about traditional notions of regal character.

34 ἀλκὴν μέν μοι πρῶτον: the μέν is answered by the δέ of ταῦτα δὲ πάντα (35), but note the emphatic position and contrast of ἀλκὴν δέ (39). bT read πρῶτος (ἀντὶ τοῦ εἷς καὶ μόνος Τ), which sharpens the point – 'You criticized me first; don't object if I criticize you now.' Diomedes' allusion is to Agamemnon's ill-judged censure at 4.370ff. That the brave vassal is a better protector of society's values than his weak and ungrateful lord is a potent theme (latent in the Akhilleus story itself) and common in heroic poetry, see Introduction 46–7. It makes the exchange in book 4 more natural there and more easily recalled here. Odysseus had suffered similarly at Agamemnon's hands at 4.339ff. For subsequent reference to what appear at the time to be relatively unmemorable details cf. Hektor's recollection at 22.99–103 of Pouludamas' advice given at 18.254–83. The poet knows what he has sung, naturally, even though his thoughts seem normally to be directed forwards towards his immediate narrative goal.

35 Agamemnon did not in fact call Diomedes ἀπτόλεμος καὶ ἄναλκις in book 4, but it is easy to imagine that he did since the combination of the two terms (or of κακός and ἄναλκις) is evidently a traditional reproach

(5× *Il.*, 1× *Od.*). Diomedes also needs the contrast between ἄναλκις here and ἀλκή at 34 and 39 for his rhetoric. He is still concerned with this slur on his manhood at 14.126 in a discourse in many respects similar to this (see 14.110–12n.). — ταῦτα δὲ πάντα: 'to what extent I am ἀπτόλεμος καὶ ἄναλκις'.

36 ἠμὲν νέοι ἠδὲ γέροντες is the Iliadic formula (3×, and [Hesiod] fr. 75.13 M–W), the *Odyssey* has νέοι ἠδὲ παλαιοί (2×) without ἠμέν. γέροντες should be taken in a broad sense – Diomedes is alluding to an army in the field – as at 2.404 and 9.89, where the γέροντες include not only Nestor and Idomeneus but both Aiantes, Diomedes himself, and Odysseus. Zenodotus' text had ἡγήτορες ἠδὲ μέδοντες (Arn/A), one formula being substituted for another, cf. 12.230 and n.

37 διάνδιχα: 'in two ways' i.e. one thing and not another. The word is otherwise confined to the μερμηρίζειν formula (1.189, etc., 3×). ἀγκυλο-μήτεω: Kronos' cunning is not as much in evidence as his dexterity with a sickle; hence a derivation of the second element from ἀμάω has found favour, see *LfgrE* s.v. That supposes an original ἀγκυλ-αμήτης was re-interpreted (cf. Introduction 29) as a derivative of μῆτις.

38 The descent of Agamemnon's sceptre from Zeus is described at 2.101–8 (see n. *ad loc.*). It is here a symbol of something more than his kingship of Mycenae, though on what political relations, if any, lie behind τετιμῆσθαι περὶ πάντων the *Iliad* is scrupulously silent; see also 161n.

39 κράτος is 'authority', the right as well as the power to command. ἀλκή, 'valour', Diomedes implies, is its necessary condition. Other qualities might be suggested as the main part of κράτος, e.g. ἥβης ἄνθος (of Aineias, 13.484).

42–4 Diomedes calls Agamemnon's bluff. The thought and some of the language (εἰ ... τοι ... θυμὸς ἐπέσσυται) is, ironically, the same as that which Agamemnon had used to Akhilleus at 1.173, but θυμὸς ἐπέσσυται (etc.) is formular (4×). ὥς τε + infinitive: only here and at *Od.* 17.21 in the epic.

44 Like 416, q.v., this is an instance of the sort of verse that stands in light enjambment with its predecessor, supplies a verb, and is completed in the cumulative manner with unimportant but harmless detail. It is a common epic sentence pattern. If a verb can be readily understood, such a verse is in effect inorganic, and would be carefully scrutinized by the Alexandrian critics. Aristarchus athetized 44 (and 416) as being superfluous and weakening by verbosity the forthright effect of Diomedes' speech (Arn/A).

45 Optimism characterizes Diomedes, cf. his riposte to the failure of the embassy 697–709 and his retort at 14.110–32 to yet more of Agamemnon's despondency. He was also first to reject Trojan peace feelers at 7.400–2. He had of course led the battle in books 5 and 6, and Hektor expected him to be his main opponent when the fight was renewed (8.530–38). But Diomedes is alone in regarding the situation as a merely temporary setback; Nestor, Odysseus, Phoinix, Aias (by implication), and Menelaos (in book 10), all concur with Agamemnon's appreciation. His moral collapse, therefore, should not be scored too heavily against him.

46–7 εἰ (παρακελευστικόν) intensifies the imperative φευγόντων, cf. 262, and the common idiom εἰ δ' ἄγε.

48–9 The language recalls that of 7.30–1 (Apollo to Athene) μαχήσοντ' εἰς ὅ κε τέκμωρ | Ἰλίου εὕρωσιν, and the sentiment that of Akhilleus at 16.97–100. We are free to subsume the Argive λαός under Sthenelos and Diomedes. But the λαός is of so little consequence in the heroic tradition that it regularly slips out of view, cf. Herakles' taking of Oikhalia and (with Telamon) Troy, and Akhilleus' own proposal to take Troy with Patroklos (16.97–100) – his prayer on that occasion that all the rest on both sides perish is pure hyperbole. σὺν γὰρ θεῷ: the Achaeans believed that they had right on their side because of the crime of Paris, see Agamemnon's violent outburst at 6.55–60. Oracles at Aulis (2.308–19) and Delos had forecast their ultimate success. — εἰλήλουθμεν: the first person now includes all present. For the form cf. *Od.* 3.81 and Chantraine, *GH* 1 425. Although εἰλήλυθμεν would have long ū by position in Ionic metrics, the zero grade has been almost eliminated from the perfect conjugation in the epic (but ἀπελήλυθα 24.766 and 2× *Od.*). The initial long vowel εἰ- is the product of the normal treatment of antispastic (∪ − − ∪) words, and is regular at the verse-end (5.204 etc.).

50 = 7.403. For the form ἐπῖαχον see Chantraine, *GH* 1 140, 393. The forms transmitted with long ῑ (18× *Il.*, 2× *Od.*) are all 3rd person indicative and ignore the ϝ attested in the participle (with ῐ) and the compound αὐίαχος (13.41). An aorist is often required and always possible. Schulze, approved by Chantraine, *GH* 1 139–40, suggested that a root aorist ϝάχον (< σϝ-) lay behind these forms, how far behind it is impossible to say. They are practically confined to formular phrases.

52–78 For Nestor's tactical discourses see nn. to 2.360–8. Diomedes had begun impetuously and ended with hyperbole (cf. his reaction at 697–709 to the embassy's failure), but then these were vices of youth and Diomedes was the youngest of the Achaean leaders (14.112) and younger than any of Nestor's sons (57–8), cf. Akhilleus' hyperbole at 1.90 and his impetuosity at 19.199–214. The older and wiser man (Nestor here, Odysseus at 19.216ff.), brings him back to earth and the immediate requirements of the situation. Nestor's speech, like his contribution at 1.254–84, is a masterpiece in the tactful management of impetuous firebrands. Everything that Diomedes had said was quite beside the point (ἀτὰρ οὐ τέλος ἵκεο μύθων 56), but Nestor showers the speech with praise, excuses it, and then ignores it; what is needful is to secure the camp for the night (66–8) and some hard thinking about the situation (68–78).

52 On the form ἱππότα see 162n.

54 μετά + accusative in the sense 'among' (which must be the sense here) usually occurs with a collective noun or follows a verb of motion.

57–8 ἦ μὲν καὶ νέος ἐσσί: it is difficult to translate these words without making Nestor seem patronizing ('How young you are . . .', Fagles). ἦ μέν emphasizes the following assertion, 'You are a young man – there's no denying it – but you talk sense.' — Nestor is about seventy years of age, cf. 1.250–2 and n. — ὁπλότατος is an epic word = νεώτατος: a connexion with 'bearing arms' (ὅπλα) is generally accepted, though the use of the word in the feminine (2× *Il.*, 4× *Od.*) suggests that the connexion was no longer felt. The superlative formation is also probably secondary, see 14.267–70n. ὅπλα = 'arms' is a rare word in the epic (4× *Il.*, not in *Od.*), which uses ἔντεα or τεύχεα. — πεπνυμένα βάζεις, also at *Od.* 4.206, is probably formular. As an epithet πεπνυμένος is applied to subordinate or youthful characters who know their place. Nestor's point is that Diomedes has spoken to the Lord of Men frankly but as a young man should, not in the insolent and provocative manner favoured by Akhilleus in book 1. Nestor himself adopts the same diplomatic tone at 69 and 96ff. Agamemnon, in a neat touch of characterization, is mollified into generosity by this respect for protocol.

59 For the sense of βασιλεύς see 11.46n.

63–4 'Banished from tribe and home without the law . . .' The proverbial ring of the verses is unmistakable, hence πολέμου in 64 where ἔριδος would be more appropriate in this context. Phratries, hearth and θέμιστες are the hallmarks of a *community* to which the spirit of the contentious man is alien. Nestor's strong language recalls the curse of the Furies πῶς . . . ἐν Ἄργει δώματ' οἰκήσει πατρός; | ποίοισι βωμοῖς χρώμενος τοῖς δημίοις; | ποία δὲ χέρνιψ φρατέρων προσδέξεται; Aesch. *Eum.* 655–6, and the sentence passed by Draco on the criminal outcast (cf. Dem. 20.158). The verses are cited at Ar. *Pax* 1097, and elaborated with Ciceronian *copia* at *Phil.* 13.1. The key word in 64 is ἐπιδημίου; Nestor is cunningly forestalling (as Akhilleus did not in book 1) a violent reaction to his reasonable proposals, cf. his opening remarks below 96–103, and Diomedes' more perfunctory exordium 32–3. The gnome suits Nestor's age (cf. Arist. *Rhet.* 1395a for the appropriateness of proverbs to the elderly) and is a characteristic part of his rhetorical armament; he is, so to speak, the keeper of the Achaeans' conscience.

63 ἀφρήτωρ: a deprivation that comes from a world in which free men normally belonged to a phratry: 'an intrusion from [the poet's] own time', as A. Andrewes points out, *Hermes* 89 (1961) 132. See also 2.362–3n. The cumulation of negative words ἀφρήτωρ ἀθέμιστος ἀνέστιος is not a jingle (like ἄιστος ἄπυστος, *Od.* 1.242, or ἀγέλαστος ἄπαστος, *HyDem* 200),

67

but natural rhetoric, cf. Xen. *Cyr.* 7.5.53 ἄσιτος ἄποτος ἀναπόνιπτος, [Dem.] 25.52 ἄσπειστος ἀνίδρυτος ἄμεικτος, and for further examples Richardson on *HyDem* 200n., 19.344–9n. and 24.157–8n. — ἐκεῖνος, with ἐ-, is certain only here and at 11.653 in the *Iliad*. It is more frequent in the *Odyssey* (13×).

64 ἐπιδημίου ὀκρυόεντος: ὀκρυόεις is evidently synonymous with κρυόεις, 'chilling' (i.e. 'causing fear'), cf. κρυόεσσα 'Ιωκή (5.740), φόβου κρυόεντος (9.2 etc.), and πολέμῳ κρυόεντι (Hesiod, *Theog.* 936). The primary form of the present expression was doubtless ἐπιδημίοο κρυόεντος, which at some stage in the evolution of the *Kunstsprache* was wrongly divided, cf. Leumann, *HW* 49–50, under the influence of the bucolic diaeresis. ὀκρυόεις (2× *Il.*) is in neither case guaranteed, a fact that throws some doubt on Leumann's view that the false form antedated the epic. Primary -οο is plausibly assumed also at 2.325, 2.518, 5.21, 6.61 (= 7.120 = 13.788), 6.344 (see n.), 15.66 (= 21.104, 22.6), 22.313, *Od.* 1.70, 10.36, 10.60: see Monro, *HG* 83.

65–70 The ἀγορή must take some resolution, so Nestor is made to put forward two innocuous proposals, to prepare the evening meal and to post a picket outside the wall; but his real thoughts are elsewhere, to make overtures to Akhilleus. Note the consistent characterization of Agamemnon; if a proposal so humiliating to him were made in the open ἀγορή Agamemnon would return the sort of answer he gave in the assemblies in book 1 (1.24ff. and 101ff.). Nestor therefore proposes a private dinner for the γέροντες.

65–6 These verses (to ἐφοπλισόμεσθα) = 8.502–3 = *Od.* 12.291–2. To 'obey night' is apparently formular, cf. νυκτὶ πιθέσθαι 7.282 and 293.

66–7 Aristarchus (Arn/A) took λεξάσθων to be from λέγομαι, 'choose', and therefore changed φυλακτῆρες to the acc. to provide the verb with an object. κρινάσθων, as at *Od.* 8.36 in a not dissimilar context, would render that sense better. The vulgate requires λεξάσθων to be derived from *λέχομαι implied by λέξομαι, λέκτο, etc., i.e. 'lie down', 'bivouac', cf. 8.519.

67 See 8.213–14n. This verse with 87, κὰδ δὲ μέσον τάφρου καὶ τείχεος, is the clearest indication yet that the poet thinks of the trench as dug at some distance beyond the wall and not as being at the outer foot of the wall like the ditch or moat of a medieval castle or town-wall: 18.215, στῆ δ' ['Αχιλλεὺς] ἐπὶ τάφρον ἰὼν ἀπὸ τείχεος, envisages the same arrangement, and so, probably, does the difficult passage 8.213–16. Military advantage – keeping the enemy from the foot of the wall and increasing its effective height – and the convenience of building the wall from the material dug from the trench (cf. Thuc. 2.78) condemn the Homeric arrangement. See, however, 12.65–6n., the trench kept the Trojan chariotry at a respectful distance. The position of the wall and trench were originally conceived at 7.341 and 7.440 as adjacent (ἐγγύθι, ἐπ' αὐτῷ), but the picture has changed by 8.213–15 where the trench has become a sort of outer earthwork protecting a considerable *place d'armes* in front of the wall, a picture that is maintained from that point, cf. 10.126–7 with 194, 11.47ff., 12.85, 16.369, 18.215, and Lawrence, *Fortification* 279–88.

69–73 Nestor's elaborately rhetorical praise of Agamemnon is his tactful technique of preventing discord, cf. 1.277–81 and his praise of Agamemnon's offers at 9.164. This sort of tact is something in which Agamemnon is made to be remarkably deficient, as appears from 115ff, where he will expatiate at inordinate length about his gifts to Akhilleus but utter not one word of compliment – quite the reverse, see 158–61 – and that in spite of Nestor's proposal that they should appease Akhilleus with gifts *and words*. — βασιλεύτατος: see 161n. Agamemnon was φέρτερος, but also in a way that is never made clear enjoyed more τιμή (1.278). It was the latter point, which Nestor gracefully concedes, on which Agamemnon has been insisting and will go on doing so until the final catastrophe of book 17. — πλεῖαί τοι οἴνου κλισίαι, uttered here in complimentary tones, repeats the phrase structure of Thersites' jeer πλεῖαι τοι χαλκοῦ κλισίαι (2.226).

70 δαίνυ δαῖτα γέρουσιν: what Nestor really means is that Agamemnon should convene a βουλή of the chiefs, for council and refreshment often go together, cf. 2.402–40 (the fullest example).

72 The wine from Thrace would include the strong vintage of Ismaros (*Od.* 9.196–8, Archilochus fr. 2 West). The poet has overlooked the private supply from Lemnos enjoyed by the Atreidai, see 7.467–71 – but that, like many inessential details, was presumably invented to ornament the scene. — εὐρέα (4× *Il.*, 2× *Od.*): for this accusative form see Hoekstra, *Modifications* 112. The coincidence in the dat. sing. (εὐρέϊ πόντῳ) between the -ύς and -ής adjectival declensions made the analogy a relatively easy one.

73 πολέεσσι δ' ἀνάσσεις: Bentley's correction to πολέσιν δὲ ἀνάσσεις is a good instance of neglect of the principle that one should distinguish between the language of traditional formulas and the language of the singers who employed them. The insertion of connectives into formulas is a Homeric practice facilitated by the lapse of digamma, cf. πάντεσσι δ' ἀνάσσειν (1.288). πολέσιν with movable -ν is not an archaic form, cf. Hoekstra, *Modifications* 35, and is found in the *Iliad* only at 10.262. πολέεσσι ἀνάσσεις is not extant, but may be conjectured from πλεόνεσσι(ν) ἀνάσσει 1.281. The δέ of parataxis is compatible with various relations between clauses, including that which Aristarchus (Did/A) made explicit by reading πολέσιν γὰρ ἀνάσσεις.

74–5 Nestor modestly, or tactfully, leaves open the question whose advice will be best (so bT).

75 The construction of χρεώ with the acc. of those feeling the need is ungrammatical (unless we can understand ἱκάνεται or ἵκει, cf. 10.118 etc.) but regular, cf. 10.43, 11.606.

77 πύρα πολλά ... γηθήσειε seems to recall the well known simile at 8.555–9, culminating in the words γέγηθε δέ τε φρένα ποιμήν. The Trojan watchfires symbolize the peril of the Achaeans' present situation; they are mentioned again at 234 and 10.12.

81–84 Verse 82 ≅ 2.512, an elaborate formula common to the Catalogue of Ships and this book, on the implications of which see 2.512n. Beside the well-known Thrasumedes and Meriones we have five newcomers to the battlefield. Note that having introduced these heroes (except in the case of Iamenos, who is not mentioned again) the poet keeps them in mind. Askalaphos joined the front ranks before his accidental death at 13.518; Aphareus is killed by Aineias at 13.541, and Deïpuros by Helenos at 13.576: on these names see 13.478–9nn. Lukomedes appears at 12.366 and twice in other lists, 17.346 and 19.240. Some names at least have more to them than here appears: Askalaphos and Ialmenos were mentioned in the Catalogue (2.512) as leaders of the Orkhomenians, Aphareus is Καλητορίδης at 13.541 and is claimed by T as a nephew of Nestor, and Lukomedes was injured in the *Little Iliad* (fr. 13 Davies = Pausanias 10.25. 5). The mention of Thrasumedes draws attention to an absentee, Nestor's other son Antilokhos. He scored the first Achaean success, 4.457ff., and played a considerable role up to 6.32ff. and again from the beginning of book 13. In the interval he simply drops out of sight. See comment on Deïphobos, 12.94.

82 υἷας Ἄρηος is not an honorific epithet, as if it were plural of ὄζος Ἄρηος, but a true description, cf. 15.112.

88 Aristarchus' δόρπα ἕκαστος is the *lectio difficilior*, but may be a hypercorrection. There is no good reason to disturb the vulgate δόρπον; the singular is usual. Neglect of the ϝ- in ϝέκαστος is frequent in the *Iliad* (29×). Zenodotus' reading (Arn/A) in the final colon, δαῖτα θάλειαν, comes from 7.475.

89–181 Agamemnon entertains the leaders. After the meal Nestor reminds Agamemnon that his high-handed seizure of Briseis has brought about the present crisis and proposes that overtures be made to Akhilleus. In reply Agamemnon admits his mistake and names the price he is prepared to pay, but insists that Akhilleus must acknowledge his superior rank. Nestor welcomes Agamemnon's offers and proposes a deputation of chosen leaders to go to Akhilleus. Prayers and offerings for success are made

89 γέροντας: almost, in this context, 'counsellors'; so also at 2.53. The βουλή, naturally enough, is in name a Council of Elders, but it includes Diomedes and active fighting men.

90–2 A very perfunctory description of Agamemnon's entertainment (in

spite of its adumbration at 70ff.) in two and a half formular verses: with
90 cf. *Od.* 5.267 ἕν ... τίθει μενοεικέα πολλά; 91 = 221 = 24.627 (and 11×
Od.); 92 = 1.469 etc. 7× (and 14× *Od.*). The retardation that is so effective
at 199–222, the meal in Akhilleus' hut, would be out of place here, but the
meal cannot be overlooked because the sequence of themes surrounding the
council requires it: see Edwards, *TAPA* 105 (1975) 51–72. These three
verses correspond to the fine scene of sacrifice and feast at 2.402–31 (see
nn.). The mention must be brief lest the narrative should give an impression
of complacency instead of urgency, but mention there must be. The meal is
a matter of protocol and heavy with social symbolism (but see 12.310–
21n.). Oidipous cursed his sons in the *Thebais* (fr. 3 Davies) because they
did not give him the honourable cut of meat: see Griffin, *HLD* 14–15.

92–9 A run of verses (92–5 = 7.323–6) introduces Nestor's important
proposals. It is Nestor's habit to hold forth after dinner, cf. 2.432ff., 7.323ff.,
though not always so appositely as here. Verse 94 (= 7.325) is a formular
hint at Nestor's primary role as man of sense and moderation. In keeping
with this characterization Nestor is made to use at 96 the complimentary
whole-verse formula of address. Contrast the bare Ἀτρεΐδη (32) used by
Diomedes in his sharp response to Agamemnon and Nestor's own Τυδεΐδη
(53) in words of mild reproof. Nestor continues his compliments – ἐν σοὶ μὲν
λήξω, σέο δ' ἄρξομαι is the language in which the singers of hymns apostro-
phized a god – but in order to remind Agamemnon that kingship has its
duties, in this case to excel in βουλή.

99 It is Agamemnon's Zeus-given privilege to decide what is θέμις and
what is not. Nestor tactfully implies that Agamemnon's interpretation of his
rights in book 1 was, so to speak, *intra vires*, though others might complain
that he 'kept θέμις by his side' (cf. [Aesch.] *PV* 186): οὐ γὰρ εἶχον γραπτοὺς
νόμους, ἀλλὰ τὸ πᾶν ἦν ἐν τοῖς κρατοῦσιν (bT).

100–6 πέρι: i.e. 'more than the rest of us'. In 101 we may understand
ἔπος from the preceding verse as object of κρηῆναι (then ὅτ' ἄν = 'when-
ever'), or read ὅ τ' ἄν (= 'whatever') and make the clause the object. —
Verse 102: 'Credit will go to you for whatever he proposes' (Fagles). —
Verse 103 = 13.735. — Verse 106 ἐξέτι: 'ever since the time when', also at
Od. 8.245.

107 ἔβης κλισίηθεν ἀπούρας: 1.391 τὴν ... κλισίηθεν ἔβαν κήρυκες ἄγοντες
suggests that κλισίηθεν should be taken more closely with ἔβης than with
ἀπούρας. — In reporting the events of book 1 the *Iliad* regularly (here and
at 1.137, 1.185, 1.356, 2.240, 19.89) uses language (αὐτός) that naturally
implies personal action on Agamemnon's part, not action through agents.
The problem in the other passages lies in the use of αὐτός (on which see A.
Teffeteller, *CQ* 40 (1990) 16–20); here it lies in the verb ἔβης. The *participle*
ἰών (1.138, 22.123), like English 'go and do' may express indignation,

71

astonishment, or derision, not literal motion, but ἔβης is a different verb, in indicative mood, and qualified by κλισίηθεν. For whatever reason (see 1.185n.) Nestor's report is logically inconsistent with the narrative of book 1.

108–11 Nestor, who cannot refrain from saying 'I told you so', now condemns Agamemnon's actions in much plainer terms than he had used in his even-handed intervention in the quarrel at 1.254–84.

109 μεγαλήτορι θυμῷ: the combination of -ητορ and θυμός is probably no more incongruous than 'great-hearted soul' in English, but the stress is clearly on μεγαλο-. The epithet is (or can easily be understood to be) more than generically appropriate here (and with reference to Akhilleus at 255 and 675, cf. 496); so bT, who paraphrase with μεγαλοφροσύνη. By contrast, at 629 the poet can say without tautology that Akhilleus' μεγαλήτορα θυμόν is ἄγριον. 'Yielding to one's θυμός' implies a certain weakness of will, the opposite of ἴσχειν θυμόν (255) or δαμάζειν θυμόν (496), the course recommended to Akhilleus. For the turn of phrase cf. 10.122 (ὄκνῳ εἴκων), 10.238 (αἰδοῖ εἴκων).

110 φέριστος (and the more frequent φέρτατος) functions as a superlative of ἀγαθός but combined with the idea of *auctoritas*. At 1.280–1 φέρτατος (of Agamemnon) is contrasted with καρτερός (of Akhilleus). — περ intensifies the preceding adjective, so 'the very gods' (Leaf), cf. ταλάφρονά περ πολεμιστήν (13.300), 'the staunchest warrior'. (For uses of the particle περ in the epic see E. J. Bakker, *Linguistics and Formulas in Homer* (Amsterdam 1988) 67–106.)

111 On the metrics of this verse see 1.356n. The poet, doubtless unconsciously, gives to Nestor the same language as was used by Akhilleus in his complaint to Thetis (1.356). — ἠτίμησας acquires extra force from the immediately preceding ἀθάνατοί περ ἔτισαν.

112 The 1st plural πεπίθωμεν is natural enough for the subtle Nestor to use when he really means 'you, Agamemnon'; but it is also natural in the sense that all the Achaeans need Akhilleus and should make a collective approach to him. Such an approach would, like the approach made by Patroklos in book 16, be one that Akhilleus could not reasonably disdain. The poet is therefore careful to preclude it by the reaction assigned to Agamemnon.

113 'A soft answer turneth away wrath.' Nestor recommends an approach that Homeric society recognized as effective, cf. 23.586ff., Antilokhos' apology to Menelaos, which Menelaos, 23.602ff., immediately accepts, and among the anthropomorphic Olympians 1.582–3, where Hephaistos affirms that ἔπεα μαλακά will render Zeus ἵλαος forthwith; cf. also the argument of Phoinix at 496ff.: εὐχωλαὶ ἀγαναί will move even the gods. It is no wonder that the Achaeans find Akhilleus' attitude incomprehensible, and that the poet himself has some trouble in expressing it.

114–61 Agamemnon's response. The speech makes four points. First (115–18), Agamemnon admits that he had been overcome by ἄτη; second (119–40), he names ἀπερείσια ἄποινα, recompense for the seizure of Briseis; third (141–57), he specifies how he will in future honour Akhilleus; and fourth (158–61), he demands that Akhilleus for his part recognize Agamemnon's superiority in rank. The gifts immediately on offer are handed over and the oath taken at 19.243ff. in spite of Akhilleus' indifference to material honours after the death of Patroklos.

116 ἀασάμην: for recent bibliography on the concept of ἄτη see W. F. Wyatt, *AJP* 103 (1982) 247–76 and 19.85–138n. Wyatt's association of this verb with ἄω (< ἀάω), 'satiate', parallels the later conceptual association of ἄτη with κόρος. The language is characteristic of Agamemnon, cf. 19.78–144 where he dwells on ἄτη at length. Akhilleus avoids it, for the same reason as Agamemnon uses it, because it is exculpatory in a way that ἐκ φρένας εἵλετο Ζεύς (377) is not. Note the conjunction of ideas at 537 below ἢ λάθετ' ἢ οὐκ ἐνόησεν· ἀάσατο δὲ μέγα θυμῷ: Agamemnon may be understood to imply that, though he had in fact slighted Akhilleus and must make amends, he had not meant to do so and had not at the time realized what he was doing. There is a progression in Agamemnon's language. At 2.375–8 he has nothing to say about ἄτη but blames his quarrel with Akhilleus on Zeus and admits to starting it. Except at 16.805, ἄτη represents a verdict passed on a previous event; the disasters of book 8 have now shown that the quarrel was indubitably a mistake; it had not just postponed victory but put it in question. — ἀντί νυ πολλῶν κτλ.: 116–17 are an ingenious rearrangement of the elements of 97–8, typical of oral style. The effect is to make Agamemnon bitterly echo Nestor's opening compliments. Zeus had once honoured *him* with the sceptre, now he is honouring Akhilleus.

118 τοῦτον is of course Akhilleus. Agamemnon is made to deliver his whole speech without mentioning Akhilleus by name, doubtless a deliberate touch of characterization. At the reconciliation (if that is the right word) in book 19 Agamemnon is likewise made not to address Akhilleus directly.

119–20 ≅ 19.137–8 with the substitution of καί μευ φρένας ἐξέλετο Ζεύς for φρεσὶ λευγαλέῃσι πιθήσας. Agamemnon is presently in a chastened mood and takes a natural but fatal step. He reasonably takes the blame on himself but unreasonably excludes the others from the approach to Akhilleus. There is to be no collective gift-giving, as proposed in another context by Nestor at 10.212ff. The poet, of course, wishes to make the issue one between Akhilleus and Agamemnon only, so that Akhilleus can indignantly reject the offers without seeming worse than heroically unreasonable. — A curious plus-verse, 119a, is quoted by Athenaeus (11A) from Dioskourides, ἢ οἴνῳ μεθύων, ἤ μ' ἔβλαψαν θεοὶ αὐτοί; it was perhaps inspired by 1.225 οἰνοβαρές ... Wilamowitz was inclined to accept the verse on the assumption that the post-Homeric paradosis had suffered expurgation (*IuH* 66), on which it is sufficient to cite Wackernagel, *Untersuchungen* 224–9, for the limits of Homeric propriety, and Bolling, *External Evidence* 54–5, for the problems the assumption poses for the history of the transmission. This is a different point from that made at 11.100n. and 22.75n., that the poet of the *Iliad* himself brought to his work a certain attitude towards traditional heroic barbarities.

121–30 In negotiations with such a character as Akhilleus any number of things could go wrong, so Agamemnon makes sure that no one could criticize him for meanness and lists his gifts publicly. For other lists of gifts, which typify what is counted as wealth in the Homeric world, cf. 8.290–1 (tripod, horses, and concubine), 24.229–34 (clothing, gold, tripods, and cups), *Od.* 4.128–35 (bathtubs, tripods, gold, distaff, and work-basket), 8.392–3 (clothing and gold), 9.202–5 (gold, crater, wine), 24.274–7 (gold, crater, clothing), [Hesiod] frr. 197 M–W (women, goblets) and 200 M–W (bowl, tripod, gold). To the conventional items (gold and tripods) are added such extras as the donors may be thought to have handy, here horses (124) and slaves (128). It appears from 1.128, 1.213 that a reasonable recompense for mere loss, where donors and recipient stood on equal terms, was three- or fourfold. Priam, also in desperate circumstances, offered Akhilleus (in addition to a complete wardrobe and a special δέπας) no more than two tripods and four λέβητες. Agamemnon's offer therefore, as the circumstances require, is intended to be irresistible. This is important, for it must be clearly affirmed that Akhilleus has no material reason for his refusal. Moreover, by being regally overgenerous Agamemnon is asserting his status as βασιλεύτατος, a tender point with the King of Men. — δέκα χρυσοῖο τάλαντα: the weight of the Homeric talent (mentioned only as a measure of gold) is unknown, but hardly comparable to the classical standards (25.86 kg for the Euboeic, 37.8 kg for the Aeginetan talent). *Two* talents of gold were the fourth prize in the chariot race (23.269), less than a λέβης in mint condition. W. Ridgeway, *JHS* 8 (1878) 133, argued that the Homeric talent was equivalent in value to one ox.

122–32 These verses correspond in content, though with considerable variation in wording, to 19.243–8. In the latter passage the poet is speaking and must say 'They brought the tripods', etc.; here he allows Agamemnon to add to his gifts some complimentary descriptions: the horses are prize-winners, the gold will make Akhilleus rich, and the women are especially attractive. Agamemnon had a nice sense of material values (he was κερδαλεόφρων, 1.149).

124 πηγούς: 'εὐτραφεῖς', mentioned by bT (who prefer μέλανας) would fit all the epic occurrences. Hsch. has πηγόν· οἱ μὲν λευκόν, οἱ δὲ μέλαν, unhelpfully. ἀθλοφόρους, οἳ ἀέθλια ... ἄροντο: for the *schema etymologicum*, cf. 2.212–13. L. Ph. Rank, *Etymologiseering en verwante Verschijnselen bij*

Homerus (Assen 1951) 74–84, has a list of of similar expressions. Uncontracted ἀεθλοφόρος occurs at 22.22 and 22.162. The prizes are doubtless those offered at funeral games, like those of Patroklos or Akhilleus himself (*Od.* 24.87–92), cf. 22.164 ἀεθλοφόροι περὶ τέρματα μώνυχες ἵπποι | ῥίμφα μάλα τρωχῶσι. τὸ δὲ μέγα κεῖται ἄεθλον, | ἢ τρίπος ἠὲ γυνή, ἀνδρὸς κατατεθνηῶτος. There is no allusion in Homer to racing for prizes as a mere sport.

125 ἀλήϊος is strictly 'without booty' (Ion. ληΐη); its association with ἀκτήμων is quasi-formular, cf. 406–7, 5.613. πολυλήϊος (ἠδ' εὐλείμων) at [Hesiod] fr. 240.1 M–W, as if < λήϊον, 'crop', is a misunderstanding.

128–9 The operations of Akhilleus extended over Lesbos (129 = 271, 664), Skuros (668), Tenedos (11.625), Lurnessos (2.690, 19.60, 20.92, 20.191), Pedasos (20.92), and Thebe (1.366, 2.691). Skuros was held by the Dolopes in historical times, the rest lay in the Aeolic area (though within reasonable reach of a force based near Troy). For speculations based on the tradition of these raids see Bethe, *Homer: Dichtung und Sage* III (Leipzig 1927) 66–75. — In 128 Zenodotus read ἀμύμονας (clearly wrong before ἔργα), misled or encouraged by 23.263 γυναῖκα ... ἀμύμονα ἔργα ἰδυῖαν, about whose construction Arn/A were in despair. — ἕλεν αὐτός: cf. 329–33. All the booty in the Achaean camp seems to have been captured by Akhilleus, who is therefore now to be compensated with his own spoils.

130 Zenodotus (Arn/A to 638) wished to include Briseis among the seven women and read ἐξ ἑλόμην. The prefix ἐξ- was a dangerous temptation to ingenious exegesis, cf. 12.295.

132 κούρη Βρισῆος (2×, since 274 is a mere repetition of this verse) interprets Βρισηΐς, her usual designation (10×) as a patronymic parallel to Χρυσηΐς. Of this Briseus nothing was known or invented. 'Briseis' is little more than a label; she may once have been 'the woman of Brisa' (a place in Lesbos), though the *Iliad* associates her with Lurnessos, see 343 n., and the *Cypria* with Pedasos (fr. 21 Davies = Schol. T to 16.57). There were also nymphs called βρῖσαι in Keos and a Thracian tribe Brisae, see *RE* s.vv.

133–4 ≅ 19.176–7 which show the same variation in the second verse as appears at 276 below. Kirk (on 2.73–5) suggests that the custom (θέμις) probably refers to the taking of an oath in these circumstances; but that would make the verses put ἄνδρες and γυναῖκες (unless that expression is merely a polar expansion of ἄνθρωποι) on the same footing as legal personae, an unlikely eventuality, nor is there anywhere any implication that Briseis is expected to support Agamemnon's asseverations with her own oath; when Agamemnon takes the oath at 19.257ff. she is not even present. The 'way of men and women' therefore must be a gloss on the euphemisms εὐνῆς ἐπιβήμεναι and μιγῆναι, cf. Hebr. 'a man to come in unto us after the manner of all the earth' (Gen. 19.31). Agamemnon affirms in effect that if he had slept with Briseis he would only have been acting normally (and so irreproachably). It is part of his consistent characterization as βασιλεύτατος that he cannot admit any degree of culpability beyond that implied by ἀασάμην (116). This compares most unfavourably with the candour of Akhilleus, see 19.56–73 and nn.

133 τῆς εὐνῆς: τῆς is not the article but a demonstrative 'her' in reference to κούρη Βρισῆος in 132. εὐνῆς ἐπιβήμεναι: this euphemism occurs only here in the *Iliad* and in the repeated verse 275, but 5× in the Circe episode in the *Odyssey*. The doublet εὐνῆς ἐπιβήμεναι ἠδὲ μιγῆναι follows a common pattern 'verb/noun + at verse-end ἠδὲ (ἠδ') + quasi-synonymous verb/noun': there is a negative version of the pattern with οὐδὲ (οὐδ') for ἠδέ.

134 The rhythm, with a strong syntactical break at the end of the third foot, is very rare, cf. 5.580, 11.154, *Od.* 3.34, 5.234, 11.260, 11.266. For the relation of 134 and 276 see 264–99n.

138–9 εἰσελθών: i.e. having taken part in the sharing out. αὐτός: by virtue of the commander's privilege, cf. 11.703–4, as opposed to allocation by the λαός.

140 We do not need to be told why Helen was unavailable, but a plus-verse, 140a, τὴν γὰρ ἀπ' αὖτις ἐγὼ δώσω ξανθῷ Μενελάῳ, is reported by Aristonicus (Arn/A), an addition which he rightly characterizes as εὔηθες πάνυ.

141 οὖθαρ ἀρούρης: also at *HyDem* 450, a traditional metaphor for fertility.

142 Orestes is mentioned 6 times in the *Odyssey*, where the 'Atreidai-paradigm' is an important motif: see West, *Od.* vol. 1 16–17. This is the sole mention of Agamemnon's son in the *Iliad*. Like other important figures in the saga of Troy and its aftermath he is assumed to be familiar to the poet's audience and so to require no introduction.

143 τηλύγετος: 'late-born' i.e. 'cherished' is the conventional rendering, see 3.174–5n. and *HyDem* 164–5 where the word seems to be glossed as ὀψίγονος, πολυεύχετος, and ἀσπάσιος, used especially of an only child (or only son, as here), cf. the formula μοῦνον τηλύγετον (482 and *Od.* 16.19. The etymologies cited or implied by bT, Eust., and Hsch., which connect the first element with τῆλε and the second with the root of γίγνομαι and may go back to the fifth century (cf. Eur. *IT* 829), do violence to the root of the verb (*gen(e)*, *gnē*), see Chantraine, *Dict.* s. v. and 3.174–5n., see also 9.482n.

144 = 286: ἐνὶ μεγάρῳ εὐπήκτῳ, only in this repeated passage and at 2.661, is known also to *HyDem* (164) but not to the *Odyssey*. μέγαρον means 'a room' (usually a public or principal room but not apparently at *Od.* 11.374 and 18.198) and by extension, like 'hall', 'a house.' Its appropriation to the pillared halls of Late Helladic palatial complexes is a convenience of Mycenaean archaeology, on which see M. O. Knox, *CQ* 23 (1973) 1–21.

145 Homer does not mention an Iphigeneia or an Electra among the daughters of Agamemnon. It is likely enough that Iphianassa and Iphigeneia are variants of the same name, but the discrepancies from the later canonical version of Agamemnon's family soon began to trouble genealogists: the *Cypria* (fr. 15) made two persons out of Iphianassa–Iphigeneia and gave Agamemnon four daughters; [Hesiod] fr. 23a M–W mentions only two daughters, Iphimede and Electra; the lyric poet Xanthus (a predecessor of Stesichorus) made Electra a soubriquet of Laodike (because she was long unwed) according to Aelian, *Var. Hist.* 4.26. The Homeric names probably reflect an eastern or Ionian, as opposed to a western or mainland, tradition, cf. 11.15n.: the historical Agamemnon, king of Cyme, named his daughter Demodike (Arist. fr. 611 Rose), an evident reminiscence of the epic Laodike. Neither here nor elsewhere does Homer so much as hint at the dreadful events at Aulis before the war, though it does not follow that he was unaware of the legend.

146–8 Agamemnon remits the brideprice (ἀνάεδνον) and will throw in what is in effect, if not in name, a dowry. This seems to be a conflation of both ἕδνα systems. (On ἕδνα as brideprice, dowry, and indirect dowry see the account of A. M. Snodgrass, *JHS* 74 (1974) 114–25.) μείλια are properly 'soothing things', 'propitiatory gifts', like those listed at 122ff., but Agamemnon has now passed on from the subject of recompense to that of honour. — φίλην: 'as his dear one', sc. wife. There is no close parallel; at *Od.* 15.22, κουριδίοιο φίλοιο, κουρίδιος is taken to be the noun. A possessive use, which here would have to be stronger than that sometimes attributed to φίλος in such formulas as φίλον ἦτορ, should be discounted, see D. Robinson in *Owls to Athena. Essays on Classical Subjects for Sir Kenneth Dover*, ed. E. Craik (Oxford 1990) 97–108, with bibliography.

149–53 Agamemnon proposes to honour Akhilleus with a kingdom, as Menelaos on a less generous scale (μίαν πόλιν ἐξαλαπάξας *Od.* 4.174–80) wished to honour Odysseus as an especial friend. The seven cities of Pulos which Agamemnon generously proposes to bestow on Akhilleus were not listed in the Pylian entry in the Catalogue of Ships (see 2.591–602 and nn.). The suggestion of V. Burr, Νεῶν Κατάλογος, *Klio* Beiheft 49 (Leipzig 1944) 60–1, that these verses were 'transferred' from the Catalogue by the poet of book 9 should be discounted, see Page, *HHI* 165–6. The towns extend around the Messenian Gulf on either side of the modern Kalamai (= Φηραί) in, so far as the Catalogue goes, a neutral zone between the kingdoms of Nestor and Menelaos, see G. Jachmann, *Die homerische Schiffskatalog und die Ilias* (Köln 1958) 84, and R. Hope Simpson, *BSA* 61 (1966) 113–31. It is odd, but must be a mere coincidence of numbers, that the Mycenaean kingdom of Pulos was divided into a 'hither' and a 'further' province, the former having nine towns, as in the Pylian entry in the Catalogue, and the latter seven, see Ventris and Chadwick, *Documents*

142–5. Also odd is the expression νέαται Πύλου ἠμαθόεντος (≅11.712): 'Pulos' must here denote a region – it is not normal Homeric usage to use a toponym to mean 'the country ruled from ...,' (but cf. Ἄργος denoting the Peloponnese, 2.108 and n., and Ἀθῆναι Attica, 2.546); ἠμαθόεις is the epithet of Pulos the town almost certainly at *Od.* 1.93, 2.214 = 2.359, 11.459, and *HyAp* 393, 424, and most probably elsewhere (except 11.712 and *HyHerm* 398); νέατος (not connected etymologically with νέος) means 'at the bottom of', cf. νέαιρα, or 'at the edge of' – the latter sense is certain at 11.712 – but in order to comply with the political geography of either the Mycenaean or the Homeric Pulos the word must here signify 'just beyond the borders of'. The Alexandrians (Arn., Nic., Hrd/A) found the word difficult, and even toyed with the idea that νέαται could be a verb (<ναίω) in a formation parallel to the 3rd plural κέαται! It is a reasonable inference that lists such as these are not *ad hoc* compilations tailored to their specific context but exist for the poet as items in catalogues, cf. the rivers of the Troad, 12.20–22 and n., or the astronomical information, 18.486–9 ≅ *Od.* 5.272–5, and the difficulties of those passages. — Ἱρή is not the Ἱρή (or Εἶρα) of the Messenian wars (see Paus. 4.18–23), which was inland to the north of Messenia. (For Ἱρὴν ποιήεσσαν F. Kiechle, *Historia* 9 (1960) 62, prefers ἱρὴν Ποιήεσσαν.) The fourth town, Φηραί, recurs as Φηρή at 5.543 in the story of the sons of Diokles; since they 'followed the Argives to Troy τιμήν Ἀτρείδης ... ἀρνυμένω,' the poet may have thought Agamemnon had some claim to this region. Φηραί appears in the *Odyssey* (3.488 = 15.186), but without a note as to its political allegiance. — For the epithets ποιήεσσα, ζαθέαι, and ἀμπελόεσσα see vol. 1 173–7; βαθύλειμος and καλή do not occur with place-names in the Catalogue of Ships. — ἠμαθόεις (fem., but always in that form, never -εσσα) is special to Pulos. It is an exclusively epic word (except for the Cypriot toponym Ἀμαθοῦς) probably formed against ἠνεμόεις, the generic epithet of cities of that metrical shape, cf. West, on *Od.* 1.93.

154 = [Hesiod] fr. 240.3 M–W, with reference to Ἑλλοπίη (= Ἑλλοπία, another form of Ἑλλάς).

155 The royal δωτῖναι are nowhere defined but seem to go beyond the meat and drink mentioned by Sarpedon (12.311). Perhaps compare the levy of Alkinoos, ἡμεῖς δ᾽ αὖτε ἀγειρόμενοι κατὰ δῆμον | τισόμεθ᾽, *Od.* 13.14–15.

156 Elsewhere θέμιστες are clearly 'ordinances' or 'decisions' meted out by those who bear the symbol of authority, the σκῆπτρον, cf. 99 and the formula θεμιστοπόλων βασιλήων (etc.) 3× in *HyDem*. The difficulty is then to know what sense and construction to attribute to the epithet λιπαράς. Aristarchus seems to have taken it predicatively as 'prosperous' or 'pleasant', cf. ὑπ᾽ αὐτοῦ βασιλευόμενοι εἰρηνικῶς βιώσονται (Arn/A). But this does not seem very persuasive as the climax to a list of crudely material inducements. Modern lexica accordingly take θέμιστες as 'dues' (after Arn/ A, φόροι) and λιπαράς as 'rich', but quote no parallel after Homer for this use of θέμιστες: an expression on the enigmatic Cnossos tablet As 821 *e-ne-ka ti-mi-to* has been interpreted as = ἕνεκα θέμιστος. Shipp, *Studies* 267, compares Eng. 'customs', originally 'customary service due by feudal tenants to their lord' (*OED*). A feudal due would be a special sort of royal ordinance.

157–61 Odysseus reports only the first of these revealing verses, but that is damning enough. μεταλλήξαντι χόλοιο implies a condition: Akhilleus will get his presents if and when he fights. In other words Agamemnon's newfound love is strictly of the cupboard variety (a μῆτις, as Akhilleus says, 423), and implies no change of heart. Any suspicion that his offers mean otherwise is removed by the following verses. At 16.72–3 Akhilleus will say he would have routed the Trojans εἴ μοι κρείων Ἀγαμέμνων | ἤπια εἰδείη.

158 δμηθήτω: Zenodotus and Aristophanes read καμφθήτω (Did/AT), to avoid the repetition δμηθήτω … ἀδάμαστος. On the contrary ἀδάμαστος confirms δμηθήτω. κάμπτομαι is classical in the sense 'submit' (e.g. Plato, *Prot.* 320 B), which is not otherwise attested in Homer: for δάμνασθαι in that sense see e.g. 3.183. An alternative form of this verse, or a plus-verse 159a, is reported by Didymus (Did/AT), οὕνεκ' ἐπεί κε λάβῃσι πέλωρ (ἕλωρ (acc.) Nauck) ἔχει οὐδ' ἀνίησιν. As a designation of Hades πέλωρ is doubtful, being appropriate to the maimed (18.410), monstrous (*Od.* 12.87), or subhuman (*Od.* 9.428). For the cliché of the implacable Hades cf. Aesch. fr. 279 Mette, μόνος θεῶν γὰρ θάνατος οὐ δώρων ἐρᾷ | οὐδ' ἄν τι θύων οὐδ' ἐπισπένδων λάβοις, | οὐδ' ἐστὶ βωμός, οὐδὲ παιωνίζεται.

160–1 For the use of the noun βασιλεύς in Homer see 11.46. In what way Agamemnon is βασιλεύτερος *vis à vis* Akhilleus is perhaps explained by 1.281 φέρτερός ἐστίν, ἐπεὶ πλεόνεσσιν ἀνάσσει (which Thucydides took at face value, 1.9), cf. also *Od.* 15.533–6 where the family of Odysseus is βασιλεύτερον because its members are καρτεροί; but it would be natural to take βασιλεύτερος to mean that Agamemnon in some way outranked Akhilleus (as is generally implied), not merely that he could mobilize more ships and men. However, this aspect of the politics of the Heroic Age was unknown to the poet or at least not clarified by him. There was no reason why he should define it, for if he did the rights and wrongs of Akhilleus' dispute with Agamemnon would be defined also, and instead of a quarrel there would have been rebellion. In that case Agamemnon would have had, what he evidently lacks, sanctions. Instead we have an insoluble moral issue, the relative respect-worthiness of social eminence and martial excellence. Agamemnon's dignity seems sometimes to have a numinous foundation; cf. the references to his sceptre at 38 and especially at 99 where Nestor brackets his temporal power with a divine benediction. γενεῇ προγενέστερος

(161) must allude to this, with γενεή in the sense of 'ancestry' as at 11.786. That Akhilleus had been rude to an older man is not the point at issue; Agamemnon is being made to insist on those claims of rank which Akhilleus had pointedly flouted in the quarrel, see 1.185–7 ὄφρ' ἐΰ εἰδῇς | ὅσσον φέρτερός εἰμι σέθεν, στυγέῃ δὲ καὶ ἄλλος | Ἶσον ἐμοὶ φάσθαι καὶ ὁμοιωθήμεναι ἄντην. Having restored the situation that obtained before he diminished the τιμή of Akhilleus, he now demands the αἰδώς proper to that situation, cf. 4.401–2, 10.238–9, 15.129–31. In short Agamemnon makes no retreat on the moral front, but reserves to himself the rights of a βασιλεύτερος, whatever those were; one may compare the remarks of A. W. Kinglake about the 'respect' enjoyed by Lady Hester Stanhope in the Levant: 'Being "respected" amongst Orientals is not an empty or merely honorary distinction, but carries with it a clear right to take your neighbour's corn, his cattle, his eggs, and his honey, and almost anything that is his, except his wives' (*Eothen* ch. 8). Agamemnon's point is not tactful (tact is a virtue in which the King of Men is strikingly deficient) but is a real one. He too has his honour and status to consider in a world where authority does not exist unless it is seen to be exercised.

162 Γερήνιος ἱππότα Νέστωρ (25× *Il.*, 11× *Od.*): the first epithet is a puzzling gloss confined to Nestor (except for the v.l. γερήνιος ἱππότα Φοῖνιξ at 16.196). There was a place called Gerenia S.E. of Kalamaí which perplexed the erudite – 'Some people say Nestor was brought up in this city, others think he came here for refuge', Paus. 3.25.9; nor can the word be taken any more comprehensibly as a patronymic like Τελαμώνιος. A festival Γερήνια, attested at Miletos (Herondas 5.80), can only reflect the Pylian pretensions of Ionian Miletos. See further West on *Od.* 3.68. A metrically equivalent formula γέρων ἱππηλάτα Νέστωρ, modelled on γ. ἱ. Πηλεύς, is also found (*Od.* 3.436, 3.444). — ἱππότα: such forms, usually taken as secondary, are found as nominatives in some dialects, e.g. Boeotian, but are foreign to Ionic and Eastern Aeolic. They are thus to be taken as original vocatives retained in the nominative formulas either for euphony (e.g. μητίετα Ζεύς) or, as here, under metrical necessity. Νέστωρ (– – with initial consonant) is unexpectedly intractable in the second hemistich. Nestor's talents as a charioteer are noted at 4.301ff., 11.722ff., and 23.306ff. and 629ff., but in the *Iliad* the epithet is generic and amplifies the names of Oineus, Peleus, Phuleus, and Tudeus, cf. 432n.

164 Nestor's words certify (what no one could reasonably deny) that Agamemnon is not stinting his stores. From the standpoint of the Achaeans (and nowhere do they hint otherwise) Agamemnon has now honoured Akhilleus and fulfilled the last of his ally's conditions, ἵνα ... γνῶ δὲ καὶ Ἀτρείδης εὐρυκρείων Ἀγαμέμνων | ἣν ἄτην, ὅ τ' ἄριστον Ἀχαιῶν οὐδὲν ἔτισεν, 1.411–12. That δῶρα μέν has no answering δέ may be intended to draw attention to the fact that Agamemnon does not propose to accompany his gifts with prayers, but μέν *solitarium* is too regular to require such an inference.

165 Agamemnon spoke throughout in the first person as was fitting, since he had proceeded against Akhilleus αὐτὸς ἀπούρας (1.356, etc.). We are presumably to think of his offer as being relayed by his heralds. Nestor is now made to suggest an embassy of the highest rank. That honours Akhilleus, but it also widens the issue and potentially makes it one between him and the rest. So Odysseus can appeal to Akhilleus' pity for his comrades at 300–3, but Akhilleus can then make the point that Agamemnon dare not face him in person (372–3).

167 τοὺς ἂν ἐγὼ ἐπιόψομαι, οἱ δὲ πιθέσθων: it is easiest to take τούς as relative (as ἄν requires) and so δέ is 'apodotic'. The article is a referential pronoun, however, and as a relative should follow its antecedent, see Chantraine, *GH* II 167. ἐπιόψομαι, 'will choose', is a defective verb < *οπ- cf. Lat. *optare*. The same form, with the same sense, recurs at *Od.* 2.294, but is not confined to the epic. With respect to the construction, ἄν + future indicative, Leaf observes (on 5.212) 'There is no valid reason against regarding [the verb] as fut. indic. except that such a constr. is not Attic.' For other examples see Chantraine, *GH* II 223–4.

168–9 The poet does not explain why he chose Phoinix, Odysseus, and Aias as the Achaeans' emissaries, but it is not difficult to guess why the last two are designated. Diplomatic business in the *Iliad* is conducted by Odysseus alone (as in the return of Khruseis, 1.311) or by Odysseus and an appropriate or interested party (as with Menelaos in the formal demand for Helen mentioned at 3.205–6 and 11.139–40). We have been reminded of his oratorical talents at 3.221–4. Odysseus therefore is professionally well-qualified; however, the personalities attributed to Odysseus and Akhilleus do not encourage us to think of them as easy companions (in spite of the ἀγανοφροσύνη attributed to Odysseus by his mother, *Od.* 11.203), and it is appropriate that Akhilleus should be made to evince impatience (309ff.). Still, Odysseus is a φίλος ἀνήρ (197) to Akhilleus at this point and the obscure passage, *Od.* 8.73–82, probably invented for that occasion, which suggests an enmity between them, should not be pressed for the interpretation of this Book, see also 223n. Aias was not only ἄριστος (2.768, *Od.* 11.550–1) after Akhilleus himself and κήδιστος καὶ φίλτατος (9.642) to him, but also excelled in ἰδρείη (7.198) in his own estimation. Agamemnon thought him a possible alternative to Odysseus at 1.145. The *Iliad*, however, never makes a point of the fact that their genealogies make both Aias and Akhilleus grandsons of Aiakos and therefore cousins. (It is a question whether Homer knew that genealogy: the patronymic Αἰακίδης *always* refers to Akhilleus.) On the other hand Phoinix is an unknown quantity. If we knew as much about him as we do at the end of this book his inclusion could be seen as an attempt to coerce Akhilleus with the sort of moral pressure that a respected member of Peleus' household could exert. As it is, he has not been so much as mentioned up to this point. Apart from his admonition of Akhilleus at 496–605 he has a very minor role in the *Iliad* (16.196, 19.311, 23.360, with an allusion at 17.555) but received a mention in the *Cypria* (fr. 16 Davies = Paus. 10.26.4) where he is said to have bestowed the name Neoptolemos on the son of Akhilleus; D on 19.326 affirm that the recruiting officers who unmasked Akhilleus on Skuros included Phoinix as well as Odysseus and Nestor (frr. incert. loc. 4 Davies, not according to that editor from the *Cypria*). His introduction here as if he were as well-known a figure as Hektor (cf. 1.242 for *his* unheralded introduction), and a natural choice, is awkward – however appropriate he turns out to be. For his story see 434–95. He is now a dependant (ὀπάων 23.360) of the family of Peleus, lord of the Dolopes, and commander of the fourth regiment of Myrmidons (16.196). In spite of this he does not appear to reside with Akhilleus' contingents. It would indeed be necessary to mention Phoinix at this point and include him in the embassy only if he had some essential function to perform before his intervention at 434, e.g. to mollify an irate Akhilleus before the suppliants dared to present themselves. In the event, 192–3, the ambassadors felt no such inhibitions. The problems surrounding his introduction prompt the question, why Phoinix? To which the answer must be that the poet needs a character with strong moral leverage to put pressure on Akhilleus, but that the character best qualified to do so, Patroklos, is unavailable at this point, being held in reserve until book 16. (There is another Phoinix at 14.321. The name is probably from φοινός according to von Kamptz, *Personennamen* 143.)

πρώτιστα . . . ἡγησάσθω has been tendentiously interpreted at least since the time of Aristarchus to ease the difficulty of the dual verbs at 182ff., cf. Arn/A ὅτι ὁ Φοῖνιξ προέρχεται καὶ οὐ συμπρεσβεύει τοῖς περὶ τὸν Ὀδυσσέα ὥστε μὴ συγχεῖσθαι διὰ τῶν ἑξῆς τὰ δυϊκά. In 169 ἔπειτα was then taken in a strongly temporal sense. In a normal context ἡγεῖσθαι means 'lead' with a nuance of commanding or guiding. Neither specialized meaning is appropriate at this point, for Phoinix does not have the status to command Aias and Odysseus, nor does it make sense to have him show Akhilleus' friends the way to Akhilleus' quarters. In the present context ἡγεῖσθαι must be given its weakest sense, 'lead the way', so as to lend some dignity, perhaps, to the ambassadorial procession; the alternative is Higher Criticism or special pleading.

170 We should probably not ask to whom these heralds are attached. There are two of them because twoness and attendance are regularly conjoined, cf. the formula οὐκ οἶος, ἅμα τῷ γε δύω . . . (7× including variants).

bT opine that the heralds are there ἵνα δηλωσῇ ὅτι δημοσία ἡ πρεσβεία ἐστί, but it is hardly possible to distinguish what was δημόσιον and what was ἴδιον in the relations of the Achaean chiefs. Odysseus will bring in the sufferings of the other Achaeans, a public point, but Akhilleus will have none of it. A Greek Odios (or rather Hodios, heralds being great travellers and go-betweens) is otherwise unknown. (There is a Trojan ally Odios, leader of the Alizones, 2.856, 5.39.) For other appropriately named heralds see 17.322–6n. A Eurubates is Agamemnon's herald at 1.320, but has a *Doppelgänger*, Eurubates Ἰθακήσιος, in Odysseus' contingent at 2.184. Presumably it is the latter, or Eurubates in the latter capacity, that the poet here has in mind. It is interesting, whether as a traditional detail or as Odyssean knowledge of the *Iliad*, that Eurubates is mentioned, and his personal appearance described, at *Od.* 19.244–8. The presence of Talthubios, Agamemnon's usual herald, might in this delicate situation have appeared provocative. — ἐπέσθων is naturally taken as 3rd plural imperative, but could equally well be dual in view of the duals of 182ff.

171–6 These verses list the essentials of formal prayer, whether or not a sacrifice follows; for informal prayer cf. 5.114n. Washing the hands (ὕδωρ ἐπὶ χεῖρας ἔχευαν 174) is an essential preliminary, cf. 6.266–8 (Hektor speaking) χερσὶ δ' ἀνίπτοισιν Διὶ λείβειν αἴθοπα οἶνον | ἅζομαι· οὐδέ πη ἔστι κελαινεφέϊ Κρονίωνι | αἵματι καὶ λύθρῳ πεπαλαγμένον εὐχετάασθαι. The *Odyssey* but not the *Iliad* has a technical term χέρνιψ, 'lustral water', *Od.* 1.136 etc. εὐφημῆσαι denotes the ritual silence, the avoidance of ill-omened speech (βλασφημία, cf. Plato, *Leg.* 800A). A libation of wine or an offering of barley (οὐλόχυται) is then made and the prayer uttered, cf. 16.230–47 and Arend, *Scenen* 76–8.

171–2 The poet suppresses the Achaeans' prayer to Zeus. If that were a prayer for the success of the embassy, as it appears to be, then it would be difficult to avoid some such comment as ἕτερον μὲν δῶκε πατήρ, ἕτερον δ' ἀνένευσε (16.250, in response to Akhilleus' prayer for Patroklos). As it is, the reaction of Akhilleus is a shock, to the ambassadors certainly (430–1) and also to the audience. — εὐφημῆσαι has its ritual sense, 'keep silent', for *any* word in such circumstances might be ill-omened. ἐπ-ευφημεῖν (1.22, 1.376) has a quite a different meaning, 'to cry "εὖ" at something'.

173 ἐαδότα occurs only in this formular verse (= *Od.* 18.422). The -ᾱ- is presumably an Aeolism.

174–7 A short typical scene in heavily formular style: 174 ≅ *Od.* 1.146 etc. (3×), 175–6 = 1.470–1 and 3× *Od.*, 176–7 = *Od.* 7.183–4, 177 = *Od.* 3.342 etc. (6×); see 24.281–321, *Od.* 18.418–26 for a fuller account of the ritual. Prayer and libation (preceded by ritual washing) are the regular prelude to departure; the ambassadors are invoking a blessing on their enterprise. The movement from Agamemnon's quarters to those of Akhilleus is uncharacteristically rapid; speech is mentioned at three points (prayers to Zeus and Poseidon, Nestor's advice) but without *oratio recta*. — κήρυκες are the 'personal assistants' of the heroic world; they assist at the sacrifice and feast, summon to the assembly and act as envoys. The κοῦροι are free-born youths who are regularly pressed into this service, cf. 20.234 and T *ad loc.* This is a public occasion and waitresses (cf. Nestor's Hekamede 11.624 and the δμωαί at *Od.* 1.147 etc.) are out of place. — ἐπεστέψαντο is evidently 'fill to the brim', cf. 1.470n. and bT *ad loc.* ὑπὲρ τὸ χεῖλος ἐπλήρωσαν, ὡς δοκεῖν ἐστέφθαι τῷ ὑγρῷ. The metaphor was borrowed, or taken literally, by Virgil; see *Georg.* 2.528, *Aen.* 1.724, 3.525.

179–80 Why does the poet not relate Nestor's admonitions at length? A faintly cynical rehearsal of the kind of argument to which Akhilleus might respond would not be out of character, cf. Nestor's advice to his son Antilokhos at 23.306–48, but would be out of keeping with the scene in Akhilleus' hut, where it is important that the arguments seem seriously put and seriously rejected. Any anticipation of the scene would be fatal to its dramatic impact. Moreover Nestor is well aware of the influence that Patroklos can bring to bear, see 11.765–803, but if he were here to make it explicit, the issues (which for Akhilleus will be restricted in what follows to his personal dispute with Agamemnon) would be clouded. Patroklos is therefore kept in the background. None of the subsequent speakers is permitted so much as to allude to him, nor does the poet allow him to utter a word. Odysseus, it will be noted, is now cited as the principal emissary, a preparation for (or anticipation of) his intervention at 223. — δενδίλλων, 'glancing', is a *hapax legomenon* in Homer, taken up, like so many rare epic words, by Apollonius (3.281).

182–225 Accompanied by Phoinix and the heralds the ambassadors make their way along the shore to Akhilleus' quarters (on the right wing of the army), praying to Poseidon as they go. They enter Akhilleus' hut and are made welcome

Night, or at least dusk, had fallen at the end of book 8, so that the martial exercises of the Myrmidons (2.773–5) have ceased and the ambassadors can arrive unannounced. Conveniently they find Akhilleus within (see 186–7n.), for by the nature of their business they must make their appeal to him privately. The course of the narrative is complicated by the intersection of three types of visit-scene: delivery of a message, reception of a guest, and supplication. A messenger, having received instructions, proceeds directly to the recipient and repeats the message as far as possible verbatim. Only three other times in the epics does a messenger deliver a message to a residence: 1.327–44, 11.644–54, and *Od.* 5.43ff. These point to an initial coincidence between the messenger and hospitality scenes (see Arend, *Scenen*

34, 54), which may be broken down into (1) the journey is described; (2) the visitor arrives, with a description of the scene; (3) the visitor waits at the doors. If the visitor has the right standing, i.e. if he is not unwelcome (like Agamemnon's heralds at 1.327ff.), not an enemy (like Priam in 24), not a beggar (like Odysseus on Ithaca), he is then led within and seated. Odysseus and his party do not wait but enter without ceremony. That is the manner of suppliants, see 24.471–84 (Priam), *Od.* 7.134–45 (Odysseus), but suppliants must quickly make physical contact with their protector and Odysseus and Aias are not suppliants (see 501n.). Their action cannot be discourteous and may be explained with reference to 6.313–31, Hektor's visit to the house of Paris: a fellow citizen of equal rank need not stand on ceremony. A messenger would then immediately deliver his message (see 6.325, 11.647). From this point, however, the scene follows the pattern of the hospitality (and supplication) scene. The visitors are led within, seated, and given food and drink. Only then is the message delivered, at the point where it would have been appropriate in the hospitality scene for Akhilleus to enquire their business.

182 The appearance of the dual in this verse and at 183, 185, 192, 196, 197, and 198 (with a plural intervening at 186) is embarrassing, since with the addition of Phoinix the deputation has reached five in number; but no less odd is the disappearance of the dual after 198, for there can be no plausible reason why Akhilleus should receive his visitors in the dual and dismiss them (649) in the plural, nor why they should arrive in the dual and depart (657, 669) in the plural, especially when Akhilleus has subtracted Phoinix from their number. The principals, Odysseus and Aias, are no less a pair when they go than when they come. It would be prudent therefore, whatever assumptions are made about the textual integrity of this book, to concede that the duals in 182–98 are incidental, not integral, to the poet's conception of the embassy. For some reason he can say βάτην at 182, and under the influence of that use continue the dual for a dozen and a half verses. Why that number is possible in the first place is a question that may be answered in at least six ways. (1) The use is an abuse of grammar, the dual being treated in the *Kunstsprache* as interchangeable with the plural. This view is mentioned by D, and was presumably that of Zenodotus. It cannot be right in its simple form (but see (6) below); apart from some special cases (e.g. 5.487, 8.73–4 (see nn. *ad locc.*), *Od.* 8.35, 8.48) with special explanations, the plural may replace the dual where two are in question but not vice versa where the reference is to three or more. (The basic article is that of A. Debrunner, *Glotta* 15 (1927) 14–25). (2) The essence of the embassy is the pair, Odysseus and Aias: the rest are mere retinue, socially and grammatically invisible. This is intelligible, cf. Odysseus' approach to the Laestrygonians, ἄνδρε δύω κρίνας, τρίτατον κήρυχ' ἅμ' ὀπάσσας (*Od.* 10.102). Phoinix is certainly not in the same class as Aias and Odysseus, but it is a question whether his status can be reduced to that of the heralds, as A. Köhnken argues, *Glotta* 53 (1975) 25–36, and 56 (1978) 5–14, in response to A. Thornton, *ibid.* 1–4: he is ὀπάων of Peleus (23.360) and ἄναξ of the Dolopes (Δολόπεσσιν ἀνάσσων 484), worthy to rule beside Akhilleus (616), and he has a role, they have not. (3) Aristarchus (Arn/A on 168) therefore detached Phoinix from the embassy and sent him ahead. This strains the meaning of ἡγησάσθω at 168 and creates a new problem over Akhilleus' surprise at 193. (4) The embassy is conceived as two groups, Phoinix and the rest or the heralds and their principals, see R. Gordesiani, *Philologus* 124 (1980) 163–74. For this alleged usage, 5.487, 8.186, 23.413 and *HyAp* 456, 487, 501 are cited, but the embassy cannot easily be broken into any balanced pairs. (5) Nagy, *Best of the Achaeans* 50, 54–5, suggests that the dual at 182 refers to Aias and Odysseus, Phoinix having gone ahead, but that at 192 to Aias and Phoinix, the assertive Odysseus (cf. 223) having then taken the lead – as he is expressly stated to do on the return (657). Even for concise narrative that leaves too much unstated. C. Segal, *GRBS* 9 (1968) 104–5, refers the duals of 182–5 to the heralds and those of 192–8 to Aias and Odysseus. But the plural εὗρον (186) and the interlude 186–91 hardly justify the change of reference of the repeated τὼ δὲ βάτην. (6) The duals survive from an archetype in which they were grammatically appropriate. This seems the most promising line of attack, discreditable to the poet though it may appear. *Two* heralds were sent at 1.320ff. to take possession of Briseis with abundant use of the dual (including the expression βάτην παρὰ θῖνα 1.327), and two is a sensible number where a witness may be important, cf. Odysseus' defensive remarks at 688–9. That an embassy is a theme in the repertoire of Ionian minstrels cannot be demonstrated, but is suggested by 11.139–40, and if it were it would be reasonable to suppose that the dual would be part of its diction: note that the dual occurs at 9.689 and perhaps at 170 (ἐπέσθων) with specific reference to the heralds. (On the relation between 1.320ff. and 9.182ff. see C. Segal, *GRBS* 9 (1968) 101–114, Lohmann, *Reden* 227–31.) There is a recurrence of certain formulas: 1.322 ≅ 9.166, 1.327 ≅ 9.182, 1.328 = 9.185, but the important parallel is the pattern of the two scenes. Failure to adapt theme to context is observed in genuine oral poetry, when the generic (and traditional) form overrides the requirement of a specific context, but it is not a conspicuous characteristic of the Homeric poems. Where themes are confused, narrative illogicality is more likely to be the result, but for an example of grammatical confusion see 17.386–7 and nn. where a singular verb παλάσσετο is made to construe with no less than five plural subjects. Such confusion is either unnoticed by the audience or – and this would be the case with the Homeric epics – is quietly tolerated, for the acceptability of a text depends on its *auctoritas* as much as its intelligibility. There is some uncertainty about the dual verb in Homer (see 10.364n., 13.346n., and Hoekstra, *SES* 28), though nouns and pronouns seem to have given the poet little trouble (but see 5.487–8n.).

Solution (6) comes close to denying the integrity of the text, for it is but a short step from maintaining that the duals of 182–98 reflect an archetype to maintaining that the verses are an undigested fragment of an earlier or alternative embassy. It may be that there is an insight at this point into the mind of Homer at work, as he improves an embassy of two heralds (Agamemnon's first idea, it appears), to one with two major heroes besides, to one also including Phoinix – whose contribution alone advances the plot of the *Iliad*. The traditional position is less subtle and demands the excision of Phoinix and all allusions to him; see e.g. Leaf's introduction to his commentary to book 9 and Page's summary of the analysts' position in *HHI* 297–304. The excisions, however, cannot be performed with surgical neatness. The removal of Phoinix, moreover, obscures much of the *Iliad*'s moral force, see 502–12n. and introduction to this Book.

The conventions of iconography do not clearly reveal early understandings of the Πρεσβεία, see *Lex. Icon.* 'Achilleus' 437–65, Friis Johansen, *Iliad in Early Greek Art* 51–7. Some vases show Diomedes as if present but in an averted posture, to indicate his disapproval (cf. 697–703) of this approach to Akhilleus.

183 The assembled chiefs prayed to Zeus (implied at 172), now the emissaries pray to Poseidon alongside whose element they are walking and who is one of their stoutest allies on Olumpos. γαιήοχος (< γαιάϝοχος, *IG* v.i 213), probably because the ocean embraces and supports the earth, cf. Burkert, *Religion* 402. ἐννοσίγαιος should be capitalized; like Ἀμφιγυήεις, Κυλλοποδίων, Ἀργυρότοξος, Κυθερείη, the oblique reference avoids a metrically awkward divine name.

184 μεγάλας φρένας; i.e. 'proud' heart, like θυμὸν μέγαν at 496.

185 = 1.328. At 1.329 Akhilleus waited for Agamemnon's minions παρά τε κλισίη καὶ νηΐ μελαίνη, but the present scene contains no specific indication of Akhilleus' position. He is alone with Patroklos, unaware of the ambassadors' approach. If then he is within his κλισίη (as seems likely) there is a minor inconsistency between στὰν πρόσθ' αὐτοῖο (193) and προτέρω ἄγε δῖος Ἀχιλλεύς (199), explained by Edwards, *TAPA* 105 (1975) 64, as the result of blending of messenger and hospitality scenes.

186–7 τὸν δ' εὗρον (etc.) is formular at this point; visitors 'find' their host doing something, even if it is only sitting (ἥμενον, 1.330). The lyre Akhilleus plays would be like those represented on the monuments, see M. Wegner, *Arch. Hom.* υ 2–16. They have three to five strings. M. L. West,

JHS 101 (1981) 113–29, makes suggestions about the tuning and use in singing the hexameter verse. Like most of Akhilleus' property in the poem the lyre was loot, from Thebe like the horse Pedasos (16.152–4), cf. the prizes offered at the Funeral Games of Patroklos. Penelope's suitors played draughts (πεσσοί, *Od.* 1.107), and Athenian vase-painters depict Akhilleus and Aias thus amusing themselves; but the Iliadic Akhilleus is heroic and solitary even in his recreation. — The ζυγόν is the crossbar joining the two horns of the lyre, to which the pegs or other fittings that carried the strings were attached, cf. *Od.* 21.406–8.

189 The poet allows us to assume that Akhilleus' emotional turmoil, which was expressed by his retirement to the seashore νόσφι λιασθείς (1.349), has given way to tedium. He is singing to the lyre – but not just any song: Akhilleus the hero sings of the heroic deeds that he is no longer allowing himself to perform. — κλέα ἀνδρῶν, cf. 524, *Od.* 8.73 (and ἔργ' ἀνδρῶν τε θεῶν τε *Od.* 1.338), Hesiod, *Theog.* 100, is the Homeric expression for what is now called heroic poetry. As with many modern forms of the genre it was literally sung (ἀείδειν) accompanied by the singer on a stringed instrument. Akhilleus will be sitting, like Patroklos and like the archaic figurine illustrated at *Arch. Hom.* u plate 1a. An amateur singer, however, who is also a member of the patron class is not readily paralleled (see Introduction 37). κλέα + hiatus may represent κλέε(α), but κλέα was read e.g. by Apollonius 1.1 (κλέα φωτῶν); for the hyphaeresis cf. νηλέα, θεουδέα and Chantraine, *GH* i 74. Crespo prefers κλέᾱ, (< κλεῖᾱ by metathesis) with correption before ἀνδρῶν, see *Prosodia* 46–8 with bibliography. κλεῖα is extant at Hesiod, *Theog.* 100.

190 οἶος: the poet envisages the famous pair of heroes sitting alone together. Later (209), when it suits him, he adds Automedon and (658) ἕταροι and δμωαί.

191 δέγμενος ... ὅποτε λήξειεν: δέγμενος is clearly here a present participle, as the traditional accentuation suggests. For the formation, an athematic present conjugation, see 12.147n. Patroklos is simply listening to Akhilleus, perhaps with the implication that he would take up the song at the point where Akhilleus left off. There are many ways of performing heroic song, including the employment of two singers, but the only one described in Homer is that of the solo singer, *Od.* 1.325ff., 8.62ff., 8.499ff., 17.518ff. (The Muses, ἀμειβόμεναι ὀπὶ καλῇ (1.604, *Od.* 24.60), are, of course, a choir.) Solo singing is tiring and the singer pauses from time to time, cf. *Od.* 8.87 ἦ τοι ὅτε λήξειεν ἀείδων θεῖος ἀοιδός, and A. B. Lord, *TAPA* 67 (1936) 106–13.

192 The ambassadors enter (this is not stated but is implied by ὑπέασι μελάθρῳ at 204) unceremoniously, like Priam at 24.477, but with less excuse. If they had been paying a formal visit to a proper house they would have waited ἐν προθύροισι, like Nestor and Odysseus at 11.777, or Telemakhos and Peisistratos at *Od.* 4.20. In short the scene envisages a simple structure appropriate to an army in the field. When the κλισίη is described, however, at 24.448–56 it has grown to the plan and dimensions of a palace – ὑψηλή (but with a roof of thatch), with an αὐλή and massive door, an αἴθουσα (24.644) and a πρόδομος (24.673). At 16.231 (= 24.306) it has a ἕρκος. Yet even a κλισίη had doors, at which a polite visitor waited for attention, cf. Patroklos calling on Nestor (11.644).

193 Welcoming a guest is naturally governed by strict etiquette. The host rises, leads the guest within, seats him, and offers refreshment; finally it is permissible to mention the reason for the visit. (Details in Arend, *Scenen* 35–50.) ταφὼν δ' ἀνόρουσεν ∪ – – is formular in these circumstances, cf. 11.777, *Od.* 16.12; it implies little more than that the visitors were unexpected.

196–7 Greeting, an integral part of the arrival scene, has not given rise to much formular diction, except for parts of χαίρειν and δειδίσκεσθαι. Edwards, *TAPA* 105 (1975) 55, examines the scene. — δεικνύμενος: 'extending his hand to them in welcome' is perhaps how the poet understood the word, but the underlying root is that of δειδίσκομαι, 'pledge', not δείκνυμι, 'point at': see 4.4n. and Chantraine, *Dict.* s.v. δηδέχαται.

197–8 ἦ τι μάλα χρεώ 'indeed there is great need' – of what? Of help on the part of the Achaeans, or of company on the part of Akhilleus, or of welcome for the visitors? χρεώ is a word appropriate to the Achaeans' distress (e.g. 1.341, 9.75, 11.610). Leaf affirms that 'it is probably useless to attempt to produce from [this disconnected sentence] one connected logical whole', and Aristarchus seems to have agreed if the reading ἡμέτερόνδε for ἦ τι μάλα χρεώ reported by Did/A is his. ἦ τι μάλα χρεώ is a member of a formular set based on χρεώ (οὔ τι μ. χ., τὸν δὲ μ. χ., τῷ με μ. χ.) with modifications to accommodate pronouns (οὐδέ τί μιν χ., τίπτε δέ σε χ.). — σκυζομένῳ, 'being angry', is a strong word, usually used of divine wrath (4.23, 8.460, 8.483, 24.113). φίλτατοι: the dual φιλτάτω also has strong attestation. Akhilleus' greeting is effusive. There is small indication elsewhere that the three were particular friends (cf. 168–9, 641–2 and nn.).

200 πορφυρέοισιν: for the epithet cf. the amplified Odyssean verses ῥήγεα καλὰ | πορφύρε' ἐμβαλέειν, στορέσαι τ' ἐφύπερθε τάπητας (4.297–8 = 7.336–7). τάπητες are coverlets in Homer, thrown over furniture to sit on or lie under, not floor coverings to walk on. — κλισμοῖσι: the κλισμός, at any rate in the classical period, was a light chair without arms, less formal than the θρόνος but more comfortable than the δίφρος (a four-legged stool), cf. Richter, *Furniture* 33–7, figs. 160–97, S. Laser, *Arch. Hom.* P 34–56, and for ancient observations on Homeric furniture Athenaeus 192E. The heroes always sit to their meals in Homer (cf. 24.472 and Athenaeus 143E), even in the luxury of their palaces. The classical habit of reclining did not become customary until *c.* 600, on the evidence of Athenian vase-paintings, and then not universally.

201 The Achaeans brought some non-combatants with them to Troy (κυβερνῆται and ταμίαι are mentioned at 19.43–4, to whom we may add heralds), but oddly enough no menial servants for the present tasks: nor were Trojan prisoners pressed into this sort of service (Agamemnon's remarks at 2.127 were hypothetical, for an exception see 11.624n.). In Agamemnon's apparently grand establishment (it is nowhere described in detail) there were κήρυκες and κοῦροι (174–5) to act as waiters, but in this book Akhilleus' hut is represented as a modest shelter where self-service is the rule. Consequently Patroklos and Automedon (209) and even Akhilleus himself must do the jobs performed elsewhere by κοῦροι and, in the *Odyssey*, by δμωαί. It may be remarked that, though the heroes wash before prayers (174), in the *Iliad* they never wash before meals, a universal habit (assisted, however, by *female* domestics) in the *Odyssey*. Patroklos accepted his orders in silence, as he had done in delivering up Briseis (205 = 1.345), see 205n.

202–4 κρητῆρα: the poet attributes to the Heroic Age the drinking practice of his own and later times, although the Greek practice of diluting the wine is implied by Myc. *ka-ra-te-ra* MY Ue 611. Classical mixing bowls typically hold about three gallons (14 litres). — ζωρότερον: three parts water to one of wine are the unheroic proportions recommended by Hesiod, *Erga* 596 (see West's n. *ad loc.*). Athenaeus (426B–431B) cites various mixtures, none stronger than 1 : 1. (Which of Alcaeus' 1 : 2 mixture was the wine is disputed, see D. L. Page, *Sappho and Alcaeus* (Oxford 1955) 308.) The strength of wine that retained some sweetness (μέθυ ἡδύ, μελιηδέα οἶνον) after natural fermentation would give point to the dilution.

μελάθρῳ, 'roof-beam', 'roof', usually refers to a palatial dwelling, e.g. 2.414 (Priam's palace). The description of the hut in book 24 (see 192n.) and that of Eumaios' dwelling in *Od.* 14.5–10 show how the idea of a palace would override that of a cottage and credit a modest structure with an implausible architecture.

205 Patroklos makes no reply. bT make this a point of characterization, cf. their remark at 11.616, σιωπηλὸς ἀεὶ καὶ ἐνηὴς Πάτροκλος. His self-effacing and gentle nature (ἐνηείη, 17.670) is often praised by the exegetical scholia (bT at 1.307, 337, 345). Kindliness, like other co-operative virtues, is appropriate between friends, but there is no reason why it should be shown to enemies; Patroklos displays his mettle in book 16. In spite of his disapproval of Akhilleus' present attitude towards *his* friends, which surfaces at 16.29–35, respect for his superior in rank keeps Patroklos silent at this point. His silence is, of course, necessary if Akhilleus is to maintain his present stance.

206–21 The theme of the entertainment of guests takes over the narrative and requires Odysseus and his companions to eat, although they have already enjoyed a μενοεικέα δαῖτα in Agamemnon's hut (90–1) before setting out. Aristarchus was embarrassed at this supposed hint of heroic gluttony and thought of changing ἐξ ἔρον ἕντο (222) to ἂψ ἐπάσαντο, on which Didymus commented ἀλλ' ὁμῶς ὑπὸ περιττῆς εὐλαβείας οὐδὲν μετέθηκεν (Did/A). As Leaf observes, this does not show Aristarchus at his best. The present passage is the most elaborate description of a nonsacrificial meal in Homer, cf. 24.621–7 (Akhilleus' entertainment of Priam). Such retardation at a crucial moment is in the epic manner; further by incorporating such details as the personal attentions of Akhilleus the poet creates an atmosphere of amity that is soon to be cruelly betrayed. Aias makes this very point (640–2), that the claims of φιλία, renewed by this shared meal, have been ignored. As usual the meal scene is not expanded by the ornamentation of one of its components (as arming scenes are) but by piling up one element on another. Whole-verse sentences express each step, but not many of the elements of this exceptional scene are demonstrably formular (210 from καὶ ἀμφ' = 1.465, etc., 212 to ἑκάη ≅ 1.464, etc., with πῦρ for μῆρ', 216–17 = 24.625–6, with Automedon for Patroklos, 221 = 9.991, etc.). The standard scene (Arend, *Scenen* 68–70) is cast in the 3rd person plural, not in the singular as here, and is much more formalized in the *Odyssey* (six examples). — One result of the elaboration of the scene is the appearance of several *hapax legomena*: ἀνθρακιή, 'embers', ἐλεόν, 'side-table', θυηλαί, 'parts burnt as sacrifice', κρατευταί, 'fire-dogs', κρεῖον, 'carving dish'.

206 ἐν πυρὸς αὐγῇ is formular (2× *Od.*). The fire is as much for light as for heat, cf. *Od.* 19.64 of the fire in Odysseus' *megaron*, φόως ἔμεν ἠδὲ θέρεσθαι.

207–8 The νῶτον and the ῥάχις are the best cuts of the Homeric butcher, cf. 7.321 and n., *Od.* 4.65, 8.475, 14.437. At 217 (= 24.626, Akhilleus' entertainment of Priam) the hero must be understood to carve off a portion for each of his guests, as Odysseus did (νώτου ἀποπροταμών) for the singer Demodokos (*Od.* 8.475). — τεθαλυῖαν ἀλοιφῇ is by 'declension' of θαλέθοντες ἀλοιφῇ (2×), and well illustrates the equivalence of the perfective aspect of the verb and the -θ- formant, cf. Chantraine, *GH* 1, 326–7. τεθαλυῖαν ἀλοιφήν *Od.* 13.410 is another variant.

209 For Automedon see 16.145–8. He is third in the hierarchy of the Myrmidons and serves as Akhilleus' charioteer.

212 The verse is clearly derived from the whole-verse formula αὐτὰρ ἐπεὶ κατὰ μῆρ' ἐκάη καὶ σπλάγχνα πάσαντο (1.464, 2.427). The v.ll., ἐμαρήνατο, παύσατο δὲ φλόξ and πυρὸς ἄνθος, ἀπέπτατο δὲ φλόξ, are probably inspired by the slight awkwardness of κατακαίομαι with πῦρ (not the burned object) as subject, a construction that is more readily understood than paralleled. They bear some relation to 23.228, which repeats the expression παύσατο δὲ φλόξ. Arn/A derides the idea of πυρὸς ἄνθος in the variant preserved by Plutarch and scholia to [Aesch.] *PV* 7 (αὐτὰρ ἐπεὶ π. ἀ. ἀπέπτατο), and indeed the metaphor is out of place in these austerely factual verses.

214 Why should salt be θεῖος? διὰ τὸ ἄσηπτα τηρεῖν (T), or from its role in the ritual of hospitality (μέγαν ὅρκον ἅλας τε καὶ τράπεζαν, Archilochus fr. 173 West).

216 τραπέζῃ: that is, a small portable table, normally removed at the end of the meal, cf. 24.476 where, Akhilleus having just finished eating, ἔτι καὶ παρέκειτο τράπεζα, cf. S. Laser, *Hom. Arch* P, 56–68. Verses 216–17 = 24.625–6 (with Automedon).

218–19 ἀντίον ἷζεν ... τοίχου τοῦ ἑτέροιο: 'Achilleus wishes to be in a position to watch Odysseus' (Willcock, *Companion* 100). The station is usual for formal occasions, cf. 24.598 (Akhilleus and Priam). — 'Οδυσσῆος θείοιο: see 17.199–201n. and Hainsworth, *Od.* 5.11n.; the epic uses θείοιο as a generic epithet in the genitive case (with six different names, instead of δίοιο) especially at verse-end, as if the scansion were, or had been, ∪∪–∪. Obviously the sense is merely honorific.

220 This is the last mention of Patroklos till 620. For the point of his banishment from the narrative see 179n.

221–2 See 91–2n.

223 That Aias should prompt Phoinix is natural enough (why else had Phoinix been sent along if not to plead with Akhilleus?) but the intervention of Odysseus is given no motivation. The poet narrates as an observer and as a rule gives his audience no more clues to the inner life of his characters than an observer would normally have. Provided he makes his characters act and speak appropriately no one is troubled. So here if we care to ask what prompted Odysseus to intervene we may think, for example, that he could not bear to leave so delicate a piece of business as this to anyone but himself. The exegetical scholia (bT) suggest that Aias misunderstood the situation, being (they affirm) βραδὺς καὶ μεμψίμοιρος. The real reason is doubtless that the heroic tradition opposed Odysseus as the embodiment of μῆτις to Akhilleus as the embodiment of βίη, so that in the present clash of wills they are the natural protagonists for the poet to choose.

225–306 Discourse of Odysseus

The central section of the speech is a *Report* (264–99) and therefore repeats the words of Agamemnon (122–57) with such minor alterations as the change from 1st to 3rd person entails. However, the report of Agamemnon's proposals is inserted into a speech that for rhetorical method is the best conceived in Homer. It is a pity that the poet has not characterized the tone of this oration by an introductory formula (as, for example, is Odysseus' address to Nausikaa at *Od.* 6.148), but the reputation of Odysseus is such that we expect a κερδαλέος μῦθος. His speech indeed is the best organized of the four speakers; see the discussion by G. A. Kennedy, *Classical Rhetoric and its Christian and Secular Tradition from Ancient to Modern Times* (London 1980) 9–14.

Odysseus' approach is to identify the interests of Akhilleus with those of the Achaeans. He begins with a modest, low-key exordium, complimenting Akhilleus' gracious entertainment (225–8). He then contrasts the comforts of Akhilleus' hut with the dismal prospects confronting the Achaeans (228–31), with heavy stress on the alleged boasts of Hektor (232–46). This is put in clear, stark terms with no more hyperbole than rhetoric and circumstances demand. It is well calculated to arouse the interest and appetite of Akhilleus, and skilfully avoids bringing up the cause of his behaviour – the indefensible action of Agamemnon. Odysseus' proposition is put in two verses (247–8): 'Up, Akhilleus, save the Achaeans!' He then proceeds to argument: (1) if Akhilleus does not rescue his friends at this late hour there will be no second opportunity (249–51); (2) let him recall the wise words of his father on the evil of strife and put aside his anger (252–60); (3) Agamemnon will pay handsome immediate recompense with unheard-of honours to follow (260–99). Odysseus winds up with an appeal for pity for his own side and indignation against the other. If Akhilleus cannot bring himself to make up with Agamemnon, let him at least take pity on his devoted friends and seize the chance to fight the arrogant and insulting Hektor.

Nos rite coepturi ab Homero videmur (Quint. *Inst. Or.* 10.1.46) – the ancient view that Homer was a master not only of rhetoric but of rhetorical theory too finds its principal justification in this speech (and in those that follow, cf. [Plutarch], *Vita Hom.* 169–72). The exegetical scholia (bT) provide a rhetorical commentary on Odysseus' speech, probably derived (as their use of the term στάσις suggests) from the work of Telephus of Pergamum, Περὶ τῆς καθ' Ὅμηρον ῥητορικῆς, according to H. Schrader, *Hermes* 37 (1902) 530–81. Odysseus begins with what became the traditional orator's exordium, a *captatio benevolentiae*. The body of the speech then employs two στάσεις: (1) παρορμητική, i.e. Odysseus plays up (τραγῳδεῖν) the dire circumstances of the Achaeans; and (2) ἀλλοιωτική, i.e. Odysseus shifts the issue from Agamemnon to the peril of the army. After his brief introduction Odysseus sets out his case under four heads (κεφάλαια): (1) his *narratio* (διήγησις); Hektor and the victorious Trojans are about to burn the Achaean ships; it is Akhilleus' opportunity to win glory: (2) using the figure of ἠθοποιΐα, Odysseus seeks to render Akhilleus ἐπιεικής: (3) he rehearses the gifts: and (4) he appeals by every possible means (πανταχόθεν) to Akhilleus, ὑποσχέσει, δεήσει, ὠφελίμῳ, ἐλέῳ. Various subtleties are noted passim, e.g. the insinuation that the emissaries are from Agamemnon, 226 (they question the wisdom of introducing Agamemnon's name so soon, and wonder if it is not to suggest that the present dispute is a mere hiatus in a lasting φιλία); the flattery at 231; how *their* allies have not deserted the Trojans, 233; how Zeus too is angry with Agamemnon, 236; and how Akhilleus has forgotten, not disregarded, his father's injunction, 259; and the deferred mention of the gifts, avoiding τὸ αἰσχροκερδές, 260. In short, Odysseus presents a skilful argument, but its tone is cool and it lacks 'heart' (so Reinhardt, *IuD* 221–2), and so gets nowhere. Phoinix will strike a better emotional chord and win a grudging concession from Akhilleus, but Phoinix spoke from a position of moral advantage – he was like Patroklos in a manner kin to Akhilleus.

The speech is 82 verses long and could hardly have been made longer. It is unbalanced by the long report (44 verses) of Agamemnon's gifts and promises which is necessitated by epic convention, but if its general thrust is considered it is clear that Odysseus is not made to show much faith in the efficacy of either reason or bribery in dealing with Akhilleus, but appeals to his sense of pity and love of glory. In short the discourse is nicely fitted to the character of its hearer, and so to its speaker also: Akhilleus is like the young men in Aristotle's ethics – governed not by reason but by feeling, and especially by the fear of disrepute, cf. the attitude he displays towards Thetis at 18.79–126. Unfortunately for Odysseus, Akhilleus is about to be depicted as an unreasonable young man to whom glory now means nothing and who will seize on the very point that Odysseus was careful to omit, the real attitude of Agamemnon.

The scene in Akhilleus' hut, with Phoinix present, is attested in art from the second half of the seventh century, see Friis Johansen *Iliad in Early Greek Art* 51–7, 164–78.

224 Arn/A remarks on the absence of an explicit verb of speaking, but that did not prevent a minority of late medieval MSS adding 224a καί μιν φωνήσας ἔπεα πτερόεντα προσηύδα, cf. 10.191 and see Apthorp, *MS Evidence* 150–2 and vol. v 21 n. 7 for other examples of this tendency. – δείδεκτ' 'pledged'; for the form (δει- for δη-) see 4.4n. and *LfgrE* s.v. δηδέχαται. Odysseus is generous with his host's wine but apparently without breach of manners, cf. *Od.* 8.475–8, 13.57.

225 δαιτὸς μὲν ἐΐσης: noun and epithet are normally juxtaposed at the verse-end (8× *Il.*, 3× *Od.* including some MSS at 8.98). For the prothetic ἐ- see 11.61n. The feast is equal, i.e. equally shared, because it is one of the rituals by which the ἄριστοι affirm their status as a group of peers distinct from the community at large. ἐπιδευεῖς: it would be appropriate for

Odysseus to say 'Akhilleus, you have welcomed us in regal fashion ...'
therefore understand 'we' or 'people' as subject and ἐπιδευεῖς (nom. pl.) as
complement (so e.g. Ameis – Hentze). Some even proposed to read ἦμεν in
226 (Did/A). Not surprisingly, since antiquity this has been thought harshly
obscure. Lattimore's 'you' is presumably a slip. ἐπιδεύῃ, Aristarchus (Did,
Arn/A), and ἐπιδευής of some MSS would indeed refer to Akhilleus; but
could Odysseus begin by reminding his host of his relations with his enemy?
The expression depends in some way on the formulas οὐδέ τι θυμὸς ἐδεύετο
δαιτὸς ἐΐσης (5× *Il.*, 2× *Od.*) and οὐ ... βωμὸς ἐδεύετο δαιτὸς ἐΐσης (24.69).

228 δαίνυσθ(αι) is epexegetic infinitive, 'for us to dine on'. — ἐπηράτου:
ἐπήρατα Bentley, in order to save the ϝ- of ἔργα. ἔργον has a persistent ϝ-,
but its persistence is most evident inside formular word-groups (τάδε ἔργα,
λοίγια ἔργα, πολεμήϊα ἔργα, etc.); these account for about 65 occurrences
within the verse in the *Iliad*. There are 12 cases of neglected ϝ- and 14
of observed ϝ- where the metrics are not protected by formular usage;
ἐπηράτου may therefore stand.

230–1 These verses state the *divisio* of Odysseus' speech – 'the issue is
your fighting or our destruction'. Like many other such statements it is
careful to suppress the third option, 'to return home'. Akhilleus pointedly
advocates just that (417ff.). — σαώσεμεν (also at 19.401 and with -μεναι at
13.96) must be aorist, the so-called 'mixed aorist' or sigmatic aorist with
thematic endings. ἀπολέσθαι | νῆας: the possibility that Hektor might reach
(and burn) the ships is first mentioned at 8.182 and forms the goal towards
which the narrative wends its way until the firing of the ship of Protesilaos
at 16.112ff. Meanwhile reaching, saving, taking, or (the ultimate horror)
burning the ships is mentioned 35 times, running as a leitmotif through the
account of the Great Battle, see 241–2n.

233 = 6.111, where it is vocative. Τρῶες ὑπέρθυμοι: the Trojans have
certainly got their tails up, as happens usually to be the case where this
epithet is used (see 17.276n.), but the epithet, combined as it is 3× (or 2×,
see 11.564n.) with τηλεκλειτοί τ' ἐπίκουροι, where the second epithet must
be understood generically, cannot certainly be taken as a contextually
significant reference. — The epithets for the Trojans are examined by
J. Pinsent in Foxhall and Davies, *Trojan War* 141–62. Some they share with
the Achaeans (αἰχμηταί, μεγάθυμοι, φιλοπτόλεμοι); those special to the
Trojans (ἀγήνορες, ὑβρισταί, ὑπερηνορέοντες, ὑπέρθυμοι, ὑπερφίαλοι),
which may be shared with individual Achaeans, present them as high-
spirited to excess.

231 The metaphor δύσεαι ἀλκήν is formular, cf. 19.36, and is continued
in (ἐπι)ειμένος ἀλκήν (4× *Il.*, 2× *Od.*).

235 This verse (= 12.107, 12.126, 17.639) is a formular one and regularly preceded by οὐδ' ἔτι φασί (etc.), but the sense and construction of the

infinitives is variable (or misunderstood). Here the subject of σχήσεσθαι and ἐν . . . πεσέεσθαι can only be the Trojans, so that σχήσεσθαι must be passive in sense, 'be held back', and ἐν νηυσὶ μελαίνησιν πεσέεσθαι means not 'will die among the black ships' as in the similar expression at 11.824 (nor of course 'rush to get on board' as at 2.175), but 'will hurl themselves on', as at 13.742, πίπτειν serving regularly as the medio-passive of βάλλω. See 12.107n. The phrase ἐν νηυσὶ μελαίνησιν πεσέεσθαι (-ονται), 5×, incorporates the only use in the epic of the dative plural feminine of μέλας. The expression is formed by 'declension' (n.b. -σῖν) of ἐν νηυσὶ πολυκλήϊσι πέσωσι (-ωμεν, etc.) in order to accommodate the future tense, but has become formular (so A. Hoekstra, *Mnem.* 31 (1978) 9).

236–43 Odysseus is being persuasive, hence the heightened description of Zeus's interference and Hektor's threats and maniacal onslaught. Agamemnon's assessment of the situation, 10.43–52, coming as it does from that despondent leader, seems by contrast almost optimistic. Both heroes are right, as it happens, to blame Zeus for their reverses, but blaming Zeus for the untoward is almost a reflex action, see Hainsworth on *Od.* 5.304. With ἐνδέξια . . . ἀστράπτει (236–7) compare 2.353 ἀστράπτων ἐπιδέξι', ἐναίσιμα σήματα φαίνων.

239 λύσσα, (< λυκ-γα), describes the furious attack of a wolf (see similes, 4.471–2, 16.156–63, 16.352–5) or possibly the madness of a rabid dog, cf. κύνα λυσσητῆρα (8.299). Odysseus exaggerates; the narrative of book 8 did not go further than σθένεϊ βλεμεαίνων and a comparison to a guard-dog (8.337–42). All references to the λύσσα of Hektor (8.299, 9.239, 9.305, 13.53) are made by his enemies, but see the remarkable description of Hektor as berserker at 15.605–9.

241–2 Hektor had uttered this threat to burn the ships at 8.180–3, but Odysseus, of course, is putting words in Hektor's mouth for rhetorical effect. — στεῦται: 'promise' or, as here, 'threaten'. This and the imperfect στεῦτο are the only forms used of this epic verb (6× *Il.*, 2× *Od.*), see Leumann, *HW* 211. It is glossed with εὐχόμενος at 2.597. The author of *Od.* 11.584 (στεῦτο δὲ διψάων, the Tantalus episode) clearly misunderstood the word. It has disappeared from the vocabulary of Hesiod and the *Hymns.* κόρυμβος (plural κόρυμβα) = ἄφλαστον 15.717, the stern-post of a ship. For illustrations see D. H. F. Gray, *Arch. Hom.* G plates VI–XII. Hektor is imagined hacking them off as trophies.

244 αἰνῶς δείδοικα (δέδϝοικα) κατὰ φρένα μή . . . is formular (4×). αἰνῶς is frequent (19× *Il.*, 13× *Od.*) in this sense, cf. Engl. 'dreadfully'. The adverb is always αἰνῶς, not αἰνόν; conversely δεινόν is regular but δεινῶς is not found, so that αἰνός and δεινός are not metrical alternatives as are e.g. ἄλγος and κῆδος.

248 ἐρύεσθαι: 'rescue' preserves the ambiguity of the verb, which may be taken either as middle of (ϝ)ἐρύω, 'draw away', or as infinitive of ἐρύομαι, 'save', see 10.44n. and Leaf at 1.216. In the handling of these epic verbs the distinction is probably blurred in the poet's mind also. Here the construction with ὑπό, 'from under' suggests ϝερύεσθαι, the sense of the passage ἐρύεσθαι.

250 ἔστ' is for ἔσται according to Bekker, but the present is logical, 'there *will be* ἄχος because there *is* no μῆχος'. Odysseus ostensibly means the perils of the Achaeans, but the κακόν, the reader realizes, is the death of Patroklos, as at 11.604. — ἄκος εὑρεῖν gives a heavy rhythm usually avoided before a major sense-break at the diaeresis; it seems deliberate, for εὑρεῖν ἄκος is possible, perhaps to point up the punning contrast with ἄχος at the same point in 249.

251–8 Peleus' parting words to his son, with their obvious scope for pathetic irony, are mentioned several times in similar language to that used on this occasion, see 7.124–8, 11.786–9, 18.325–7. They *may* have been part of the tradition on which the *Cypria* drew, but they are too apposite to be other than virtually an example of what later rhetoricians called prosopopoeia, the orator's assumption of a convenient personality in whose name he affects to speak. Nestor, recalling the same occasion, appeals to *Patroklos* in similar terms at 11.786–9. At 18.326–7 Akhilleus recalls *his* last words to Menoitios in *oratio obliqua*. The Homeric style does not admit extensive use of indirect constructions (*Od.* 23.310–41 is the chief exception); nevertheless the direct quotation of Peleus' alleged words is emotively effective. The quotation is an oblique way of saying δάμασον θυμὸν μέγαν (496), words that at this juncture would be impolitic coming from Odysseus. — ὦ πέπον: Odysseus adopts a comradely or even avuncular tone. Nestor used the same expression to Patroklos, 11.765, again in the context of a father's parting words.

255 μεγαλήτορα θυμόν: see 109n. Observe that throughout the narrative of the quarrel between Akhilleus and Agamemnon the poet recognizes in addition to the account of loss and recompense an irrational and incalculable element, the θυμός of the injured party. Reason is of no avail unless the θυμός can be controlled (ἴσχειν 256, δαμάζειν 496) or mollified (ἰαίνειν 23.600). Agamemnon has balanced the account, but has left Odysseus with the task of trying to reach Akhilleus' θυμός. The best way to do this would be to add to the indispensable offers of recompense some words of excuse or explanation as Agamemnon does at 19.78–144 or as Antilokhos does more generously at 23.587–595, but Agamemnon has precluded this, the only approach that could conceivably be productive. — ἴσχειν: not 'keep', but 'keep in check', cf. ἐχέθυμος, 'continent', at *Od.* 8.320, the opposite of εἴκειν (109).

257 ληγέμεναι: the infinitive ending -μεναι (native only to the Aeolic dialect of Lesbos) is proper to athematic verbs and tenses. It is extended to thematic forms in 57 instances in the *Iliad*: 13× in books 1–8, 28× in 9–16 (of which 7× in 9, 6× in 10), and 18× in 17–24. The occurrences in book 9 are in six different verbs (the phraseology at 674 seems to depend on 347), and may be explained as an instance of clustering, the tendency for words and forms, having for whatever reason been used once, to remain at the surface of the poet's mind, see *Studies Palmer* (Innsbruck 1976) 83–6, and Introduction 27–8.

260 χόλον θυμαλγέα implies that his anger, not the cause of his anger, was the reason for Akhilleus' unhappiness. Akhilleus corrects Odysseus at 387 below – it is not his χόλος but his λώβη that is tormenting his soul.

264–99 = 122–57 (see nn.). Odysseus reports Agamemnon's words verbatim as far as the shift from 1st to 3rd person allows, with two exceptions:

127 ὅσσα μοι ἠνείκαντο ἀέθλια μώνυχες ἵπποι
269 ὅσσ' Ἀγαμέμνονος ἵπποι ἀέθλια ποσσὶν ἄροντο

and

134 ἤ θέμις ἀνθρώπων πέλει, ἀνδρῶν ἠδὲ γυναικῶν
276 ἤ θέμις ἐστίν, ἄναξ, ἤ τ' ἀνδρῶν ἤ τε γυναικῶν

In 269 ὅσσα οἱ ἠνείκαντο could certainly have stood but would have made the reference of οἱ formally unclear, the unnamed ἀνήρ being the subject of the whole sentence. θέμις in the sense of 'custom' is confined to the formula (ἤ) θέμις ἐστί (11× *Il.*, 8× *Od.*) except in 134 and *Od.* 24.286; at 276 (= 19.177) the formula reasserts itself with the aid of the voc. ἄναξ (for which cf. 9.33), impossible at 134. In a sense 134 presupposes 276, as 7.337–40 presuppose 7.436–9 (see nn.) and *Od.* 10.531–7 Circe's instructions at 11.44–50. Willcock, *AJP* 96 (1975) 107–9, plausibly argues that the 'prior' version existed in the poet's well-rehearsed mind rather than in a written or orally fixed text.

Odysseus' verbatim report is not so much a careful statement of the terms of a contract as the normal epic convention when orders, messages, etc. are delivered. Verbatim report is the usual practice in most traditions of heroic poetry, see Bowra, *HP* 254–8, J. Th. Kakridis, *Homer Revisited* (Lund 1971) 77–85. A. B. Lord in Wace and Stubbings, *Companion* 195, entertains the idea that the virtually exact repetition of such passages, as compared to the variation observed in most 'typical scenes', is due to normalization in transmission. Though not to be discounted, the material cited by Bowra makes the suggestion unnecessary.

270 ἔργα ἰδυίας: only in this verse does the paradosis transmit as a variant reading the reduced-grade feminine participle ἰδυῖα (elsewhere always εἰδυῖα, which is certain at 17.5). Bentley is responsible for the modern reading which preserves the digamma of ϝιδυῖα. Hoekstra (on *Od.* 13.417) and West (on *Od.* 1.428) are inclined to accept εἰδ- at least for the *Odyssey*. It is impossible to say in such a case which would prevail in the poet's time, the conservatism of the *Kunstsprache* or his vernacular speech.

300–6 Odysseus returns, by way of ring-composition, to his opening theme, the present peril. (Hektor is nearby cf. ἐγγὺς νηῶν 232, he is berserk cf. λύσσα 239.) He anticipates Akhilleus' reaction to their overtures. His loathing of Agamemnon may be beyond remedy; in that case let him ignore the King of Men and think of himself and his friends. As Sarpedon explained (12.310–28 and n.) heroism is a social and personal obligation that underpins the Homeric idea of kingship: the king protects the people, the people give him honour. Odysseus, of course, is speaking rhetorically: the Panakhaioi are not Akhilleus' subjects and Odysseus cannot claim that they have honoured him and so created an obligation on his part, only that they will do so (τείσουσ(ι), 303, future tense). But Odysseus' words bring to the surface the dilemma that now confronts Akhilleus: the conflict between his personal integrity (as he chooses to see it) and social obligation (see further 650–3n.). Nor can Odysseus at this point appeal to the most powerful obligations of comradeship, to avenge the death of a friend or assist him in mortal danger on the battlefield (cf. Glaukos' prayer to Apollo after Sarpedon's death, 16.514–26), for up to this point none of Akhilleus' fellow ἄριστοι (except the unimportant Tlepolemos, 5.655–9) have been killed or seriously injured. Nestor makes this plea through Patroklos at 11.660–5, after the front rank of the Achaeans has been decimated and, of course, it is made to be the decisive factor in Akhilleus' eventual return to the war.

300 κηρόθι μᾶλλον: though juxtaposed 2× *Il.*, 7× *Od.*, the words do not stand in grammatical concord and the formula is properly *Verb* (ἀπήχθετο, ἄχος ὀξὺ γενέσκετο, φίλει δέ ἑ, ἐχώσατο) κηρόθι μᾶλλον. The complement of μᾶλλον in such a formular phrase should be understood in general terms ('more than anyone') rather than a specific 'than one can forgive' (van Leeuwen, Leaf).

304–5 Hektor's bold advance offers Akhilleus the opportunity he had previously sought in vain, see 352–5, while Hektor kept open his line of retreat. — λύσσα: see 239n.

307–429 Discourse of Akhilleus

See Lohmann, *Reden* 236–45, for general discussion, and R. P. Martin, *The Language of Heroes: Speech and Performance in the Iliad* (Ithaca, N.Y. 1989), for close analysis. Akhilleus is the most eloquent, and also the most violent, speaker in the *Iliad* and his language has been the subject of much attention. He is presented to us as a powerful speaker whose skill is concealed by a free rhetorical style. P. Friedrich and J. Redfield, *Language* 54 (1978) 263–87 and 57 (1981) 901–3, characterize his speech as possessing a 'poetic directness' exemplified in detail and vividness; his style is abrupt and informal, employs more vocative expressions (including abusive terms), and freely uses emotive particles such as ἦ and δή and the attention-arresting νῦν δέ. J. Griffin, *JHS* 106 (1986) 52–7, describes the special vocabulary of Akhilleus' egotistical and declamatory rhetoric, e.g. αἱματόεις (metaphorical), ἀναιδείην ἐπιειμένος, δουρικτητή, εἰκοσάκις, ἐπισκύζομαι, ἐφυβρίζω, θυμαλγής, θυμαρής, κύνεος, λεϊστή, παριαύω, τρύζομαι. For the argument in general see H. Lloyd-Jones, *The Justice of Zeus* (Berkeley and Los Angeles 1971) 14–22. The speech is the longest stretch of continuous argument in the *Iliad*, for the longer discourses of Phoinix (434–605) and Nestor (11.656–803) contain long passages of narrative.

Bowra, *Tradition and Design* 18–19 puts Agamemnon's case (which he thinks *is* the case) very well: the offer is fair according to the *mores* of the Heroic Age, it absolves Agamemnon, its rejection will put Akhilleus in the wrong. On another occasion Akhilleus was willing to cool his animosity and accept a ransom for Hektor, among other reasons because it was οὐ ... ἀεικέα (24.594, where see Macleod's note). He must now argue therefore as his main point that Agamemnon is not absolved, but first he must deal with Odysseus' auxiliary arguments. Odysseus had rested his case on the twin carrots of κῦδος and τιμή and the spur of pity. Akhilleus, after a gracious exordium (308–11) disposes of the first two, but ignores the last, so leaving the way open for Phoinix' intervention. The poet represents Akhilleus as one who on his own (disingenuous) admission (18.105–6) is better at action than words, or, as bT have it, who is φιλότιμος, ἁπλοῦς, φιλαληθής, βαρύθυμος, and εἴρων, so it would be reasonable to expect his reply to be weak on logic and strong on emotion. This indeed is the case. He will speak his mind plainly (308–14). Odysseus had insinuated that the issue was between Akhilleus and a distressed Achaean army and that by inaction his friend was missing an opportunity for glory. Akhilleus quickly names the real enemy, Agamemnon, and retorts that he has tried action already, in the Troad and before Troy, and that doesn't bring honour either but humiliation (315–36). Warming to his theme the young orator narrows his argument from the general injustice of the world in order to draw out a telling parallel between his own treatment and the shame put on Menelaos by Paris (336–45), and winds up this part of his discourse with a malicious comparison of Agamemnon's present panic with Hektor's erstwhile timidity (346–55). Thus far Akhilleus has been brooding on the past and expounding the nature of his grievance (on which Odysseus had – prudently – been silent). He ignores the alleged admonitions of Peleus, to which there is no obvious retort at this point, and turning to the present offer of restored τιμή announces that Agamemnon can hold on to his loot, as a warning to anyone else who thinks of serving him; he himself is going home and Agamemnon can go and be hanged (356–77). No imaginable treasure could compensate Akhilleus for his grief. So Agamemnon can keep his gifts and his daughter too 'until he has repaid all the outrage' (378–91). So much for his presents' absolving Agamemnon's guilt. All this should probably be read as the grand gesture of a noble spirit to whom material things at this moment are of no account, but to unheroic minds the hyperbole of Akhilleus' language sounds the shrill note of wounded pride sharpened by the pettish insistence that follows (391–400) on his supposed humble station in life. Finally Akhilleus returns to his first point, but with a correction: then he had asked why he should risk his life for nothing, now he asks, since there is no equivalent for life, why he should risk it (indeed, why he should lose it) for all the treasures of Troy and Delphi. The lure of heroic glory at Troy had been a delusion; life itself was the better choice. So let the Achaeans think up some other plan (401–26). Phoinix, however, may come home with him (427–5). — The tenor of the discourse is what was later called 'ethical', balancing the evil mind of Agamemnon against the force of the emotional appeals just made to him.

Akhilleus' argument is too egotistical to have any practical validity. Phoinix will point out that in the real world there has to be appeasement. To say that no compensation can be sufficient is not practical; it is simply an emphatic way of saying 'no'. Rage, not calculation, is Akhilleus' motivation. He himself admits this at 646–8, cf. also 16.52–61, where Akhilleus is made to admit that though the pain continues the anger cannot last for ever.

Homeric eloquence rises here to its greatest heights as Akhilleus returns again and again to his contempt for Agamemnon and his outraged honour. These repetitions give the speech the so-called 'spiral' pattern (see Thalmann, *Conventions* 22–3), an emphatic form of ring-composition more characteristic of Hesiodic discourse. As always with great speeches there are many quotable turns of phrase: 'Hateful to me as the gates of hell ...' 'Whether a man does much or little ...', 'Do only the Atreidai love their wives?', 'Why must the Greeks and Trojans go to war?' It is important that these should be read in context. Akhilleus, the story demands, must refuse the Achaeans' pleas. He is made to say in effect, therefore, that he is sick of the whole business, but there is no need to take 'the whole business' to be more than the conduct of the Trojan War. Akhilleus is disillusioned, but he is disillusioned primarily with his place in the heroic scheme of things, having set an impossibly high value on his honour, see the comments of M. D. Reeve, *CQ* 23 (1973) 193–5. A. Parry, however, 'The language of Achilles', *TAPA* 87 (1956) 1–7 (= *Language and Background* 48–54), argues that Akhilleus' disillusion is with war itself, a disillusion shared by the poet and forming 'possibly the real plot of the second half of the *Iliad*'. In order to wrestle with the traditional ethos, however, Akhilleus must wrestle with the traditional language. His problem (i.e. that of the poet) is like that of Penelope seeking to redefine τὸ εὐκλεές (see 341n.), a problem that is exacerbated by, but not peculiar to, a formular diction. For criticism of Parry's argument see D. B. Claus, *TAPA* 105 (1975) 13–28, and P. Friedrich and J. M. Redfield, *Language* 54 (1978) 263–88: the Homeric language is not so fixed and unambiguous that it cannot evaluate what it describes, see 387n.

The disillusionment of Akhilleus is most clearly expressed in the passage 401–16, where Akhilleus is made to deny the heroic doctrine that glory outweighs life. This is perhaps a traditional point, for it recurs at *Od.* 11.488–91: the greatest hero can afford to question his role. No one takes up the point just as no one takes up the point of Akhilleus' immediate departure, probably because such manifest hyperboles could not be taken seriously; no one but Akhilleus *knew* that a long, inglorious life could be assured. At 12.322–8 Sarpedon too would not have fought if he had known he would live on, but since ten thousand dooms of death surrounded a mortal man the only thing he could be assured of was glory through valour.

For the relation of the speech to the general characterization of Akhilleus see Griffin, *HLD* 73–6, Edwards, *HPI* 222–4; for the language see Shipp, *Studies* 267–5. Shipp's comment is significant, 'The speech of Achilles is for the most part characterized by features that reflect contemporary Ionic, with lumps that make an older impression', that is to say, the speech is an original composition and does not depend as heavily as a battle scene on traditional themes and the traditional diction that goes with them.

308–14 Note the immediate characterization: Akhilleus is suspicious of Odysseus, although on this occasion he has faithfully conveyed the sense of the Achaean council. But there is also permanent characterization: Akhilleus is open, Odysseus indirect, cf. 644–55 where Akhilleus' attitude to Aias, a personality similar to his own, is noticeably warmer. Akhilleus' elaborate statement of his love of plain speaking seems to give it (*pace* Leaf and Von der Mühll) a specific implication beside its general reference. But it would be pointless to make Odysseus, the obvious candidate for a charge of duplicity, the sole target of Akhilleus' remarks: rather it is Agamemnon – Akhilleus had not heard Agamemnon's comparison of him to Hades (158), but we have, and 312 may be taken as a riposte to it. Agamemnon's generosity, Akhilleus implies already, is tainted by self-interest.

308 διογενὲς Λαερτιάδη ... is the regular whole-verse formula for Odysseus in the vocative case (7× *Il.*, 15× *Od.*). It has no special connotations for the speaker, beyond a certain formality (cf. 96n.), and is used indifferently by (in the *Iliad*) Agamemnon, Aias, Diomedes, Nestor, and the goddess Athene. Akhilleus keeps up the same formal, controlled tone in a series of end-stopped or very lightly enjambed verses (down to 320).

309 ἀπηλεγέως ἀποειπεῖν is an under-represented formula (also at *Od.* 1.373), to which the epic should have had frequent recourse. ἀπηλεγέως is 'forthrightly' (< ἀπό in a negative sense + ἀλεγ-ω).

311 Plato, *Hipp. Min.* 365A quotes 308–14, with trivial variations but without the inorganic v. 311. The dialogue also has κρανέω in 310 for φρονέω, attesting the antiquity of that v.l. κρανέω may well be right, the pleonasm with τετελεσμένον ἔσται adding solemnity to Akhilleus' words. τρύζω ('croak', like frogs (see Gow on Theocritus 7.139), an effective word) is mostly a Hellenistic poetic verb and is found only here in Homer, but in other respects the verse is unexceptional, and indeed makes an effective point. For Akhilleus' unpopularity cf. 16.203–6.

312 Hades has gates (because return is barred?) also at 5.646, 23.71, *Od.* 14.156 (= this verse), but not in *Od.* 11. The idea is probably very ancient, see Hoekstra on *Od.* 14.156, Kirk, *Myth* 191.

314 = 103 = 13.735. The sentiment 'I will tell you what I think is best' implies that the addressee's assessment of the situation is not the same as the speaker's. The premises of Odysseus' argument, we may guess already, are unacceptable to Akhilleus.

316–17 These verses embody the essence of Akhilleus' position. Instead of upholding the principle that holds his confederacy together, the equivalence of ἀρετή, κῦδος, τιμή, and γέρας, Agamemnon has dealt it a fatal blow. Odysseus' remarks are beside the point, because Akhilleus has decided that his loss of τιμή (which Zeus has effectively now restored to him) is a hurt that cannot be made good and that the κῦδος of victory is not worth fighting for. There is worse to come, of course, and then he will say τὰ μὲν ἄρ μοι Ὀλύμπιος ἐξετέλεσσεν. | ἀλλά τί μοι τῶν ἦδος, ἐπεὶ φίλος ὤλεθ᾽ ἑταῖρος (18.79–80). Akhilleus will never again, in the *Iliad*, go out to fight for glory, though he is happy enough to bask in it at the moment of victory, see 22.393–4.

316 Akhilleus' attitude towards the other leaders (the ἄλλους Δαναούς here) is not made clear. The envoys are φίλτατοι (198), yet in the quarrel scene in book 1, in spite of Agamemnon's threats against Aias and Odysseus (1.138), Akhilleus made no appeal to the solidarity of the other chiefs, and seems to have included them among his oppressors, cf. his wish at 1.410 ἵνα πάντες [Ἀχαιοί] ἐπαύρωνται βασιλῆος, and would have been happy to see them killed. Akhilleus, we must understand, is a hero who thinks big and for whom there are no shades of grey: he is rebuffed – the whole world is responsible, he is insulted – all honour is trash, his friend dies – his own life is worthless. In the end Priam will teach him that there is a better way.

318–20 The three whole-verse statements have each a proverbial ring. For the effect of such sequences of whole-verse sentences see Kirk, *YCS* 20 (1966) 124 = *HOT* 158–9. Akhilleus, we may imagine, controls his anger with difficulty and speaks with measured deliberation until his fury shatters any relation of sense to verse in 331ff. The connexion of thought between these gnomic lines (to 322) is imprecise and 320 has been thought interpolated as being irrelevant to the flow of Akhilleus' discourse (so Ameis–Hentze and Leaf). W. J. Verdenius, *REG* 73 (1960), argues that the connexion of thought lies in the ambiguity of μοῖρα, 'share' or 'fate', which enables Akhilleus to make two points. He says, with Agamemnon at the forefront of his mind, that the ἐσθλοί (including himself) receive the same honour as the κακοί (including Agamemnon), so why should he take the risk of trying to be ἐσθλός? Moreover both have the same measure of life, the ἀεργός and the πολλὰ ἐοργώς, so why try πολλὰ ἔρδειν? Akhilleus' early death is a keynote of the *Iliad*, cf. 1.352, 1.416, 1.505, 9.401ff., 17.407–9, 18.59–60, 24.85–6, and is latent here too. Bentley made the line innocuous (but a superfluous reiteration of 318–19) by emending κάτθαν' to λάγχαν'. In another context – the possibility of κῦδος – the idea of death as common to all could even be a spur to action (see Sarpedon's words at 12.322–8). For death the great leveller cf. Pind. *N.* 7.19–20, 30–1. — ὅ τ' ἀεργὸς ἀνὴρ κτλ.: 'Un des emplois où le sens de l'article est le plus évolué est celui où il désigne une catégorie générale', Chantraine, *GH* II 165; 13.278 is a close parallel.

319 This verse implies that for Akhilleus there is an ideal equation between κλέος/κῦδος and τιμή. In the real world that equation is a pretence, because distinctions in rank are not established by the achievement of fame and the possession of status *ipso facto* confers κῦδος, cf. 1.279. In a world where status was inherited along with the sceptre of kingship (2.100–8), it was hard even for an ἄριστος Ἀχαιῶν to be upwardly mobile.

323–4 Simile of the mother-bird and her chicks. Fully developed similes are part of the poet's commentary on the action of the epic and are rarely assigned to speakers, see 12.167–70n. and vol. v 39. Moulton, *Similes* 100, counts *c.* 50 *comparisons* made in speeches, 'most of them very brief', like 385 and 648 below. Akhilleus is given four of two verses or more. That is in keeping with his portrayal as a hero deeply concerned with his own heroism, for the simile is a device by which a speaker reflects on events from his own standpoint. But what in the mouth of the poet or a weak and helpless character would be a powerful instrument of pathos sounds a petulant note when it comes from the ἄριστος Ἀχαιῶν, cf. 385–9n. Parent-protecting-child similes are not infrequent, see 4.130–1, 5.554–8, 8.271, 12.167–70, 12.433–5, and 16.259–65, but (*pace* Moulton *loc. cit.*) this is not the point here: Akhilleus wishes to say that he is worn out in selfless unrewarded toil.

— μάστακ(α) would be 'mouthful', giving excellent sense and grammar, but the word is used in the *Odyssey* (4.287, 23.76) to mean 'mouth', and Plutarch (*Mor.* 80A) and the lexica so understand it here. In that case understand the dative μάστακ(ι) and an object for προφέρῃσι. κακῶς δ' ἄρα οἱ πέλει αὐτῇ is an aural echo of the (probably formular) expression κακοῦ δ' ἄρα οἱ πέλεν ἀρχή (11.604).

325–45 A fine rhetorical passage. As Akhilleus' passion rises the verses become enjambed, lightly at first, then more and more violently; strong breaks within the verse distort the normal arrangement of cola. As the verse, so to speak, loses its self-control, so does Akhilleus. (Note in contrast the reasonable tone of Odysseus' versification in the preceding speech.) These effects reach their peak in the striking series of rhetorical questions, 336–41, where Akhilleus' choler is at its most intense. Observe the heavy pauses in the second foot at 331, 332, 337, 338, 339, and 341, which like the diaereses at 333, 336, and 342 bring their clauses to an abrupt indignant close.

325–6 ἀΰπνους νυκτὰς ἴαυον: ἰαύω (cf. ἀ(F)έσκω, aor. ἄ(F)εσα) is 'pass the night' in sleep or wakefulness. ἰαύειν = ἐπαυλίζεσθαι (Arn/A at 19.71). The pleonastic combination with νύξ is formular (2× *Il.*, 1× *Od.*). — ἤματα αἱματόεντα is not formular, as is stressed by the placing of αἱματόεντα in a secondary position and not at the verse-end, and so draws attention to the easy (but surprisingly rare) metaphorical use of αἱματόεις, cf. πολέμοιο ... αἱματόεντος at 650 below (Akhilleus again speaking). There is another metaphorical use at 19.313 (see n. *ad loc.*).

327 μαρνάμενος ὀάρων ἕνεκα σφετεράων is explained by 328–31. The women, as part of the booty, are what the fighting is about, cf. 2.354–5, 4.238–9. σφετεράων is loosely used as a referential pronoun ('their', not 'their own') unless, as Leaf wished, we remove the comma at the end of 326 and read μαρναμένοις. The paradosis, however, is unanimous for μαρνάμενος.

330–3 These verses repeat the complaint made by Akhilleus during the quarrel scene, 1.165–8, that he did the work and Agamemnon kept the lion's share of booty at the distribution. Thersites, presumably with less justification, made the same point (2.225–34). πάντα ... Ἀγαμέμνονι δόσκον is a cutting rhetorical hyperbole that ignores both the role of the λαός in the allocation of prizes and the custom, as it doubtless was then as now, that prize money must be commensurate with rank. However, Akhilleus misses a trick; it is his own winnings (cf. 129) that he is now being offered as compensation.

333 In its allusions to the protocol of so important a matter as the distribution of booty the *Iliad* is curiously imprecise. At 1.127, 1.162, and 16.56 the 'Achaeans' are said to have assigned his prize to Akhilleus (cf. 11.627); a fuller description of the procedure is given at 11.703–5, ὁ γέρων

(Νηλεύς) ... | ἐξέλετ' ἄσπετα πολλά. τὰ δ' ἄλλ' ἐς δῆμον ἔδωκε | δαιτρεύειν, and at *Od.* 14.232–3, τῶν ἐξαιρεύμην μενοεικέα, πολλὰ δ' ὀπίσσω | λάγχανον. The latter practices would fit Agamemnon's alleged behaviour here, yet at 1.368 it is expressly stated that the υἶες Ἀχαιῶν assigned Khruseis to him, cf. *Od.* 7.10, where the Phaeacians assigned Eurumedousa to their king Alkinoos, and *Od.* 9.160, 9.550, where his companions assigned special prizes to Odysseus.

334 ἀριστήεσσι ... καὶ βασιλεῦσι: Homeric designations of rank are not precise and technical but express a vague contrast between 'leaders' with their θεράποντες and the rest. Akhilleus means men like himself, and completes the verse with a virtually synonymous word.

335–43 Akhilleus throws out a series of emphatic assertions and rhetorical questions that together make up a telling argument. 'Agamemnon has carried off my wife. But when Paris carried off Menelaos' wife he raised an army to recover her. He and his brother are not the only men to love their wives; I loved Briseis.' The train of thought is obscured partly by the staccato style in which Akhilleus gives vent to his anger, and partly by the intrusion of other thoughts into the argument: his present feelings towards Briseis, the reason why he is at Troy, and the idea of sexual continence. Akhilleus is saying, coherently but with some heat, that Agamemnon cannot have it both ways, or, as it is spelled out by AbT: Agamemnon was either wrong or silly; if seizing a woman was a trivial matter, he was silly to make war for Helen; if it was serious, he was wrong to seize Briseis (πρακτικὸς ὁ λόγος, δεικνὺς τὸν Ἀγαμέμνονα ἢ ἀσύνετον ἢ ἄδικον. εἰ μὲν γὰρ μικρὸν ἡγεῖται τὸ ἀδικηθῆναι περὶ γυναῖκα, πολεμεῖν οὐκ ἔδει περὶ Ἑλένης. ἀσύνετος οὖν ἐστι περὶ μικρᾶς αἰτίας πολεμεῖν. εἰ δὲ χαλεπὸν καὶ μέγα, πῶς ἅπερ παθὼν ὑπ' ἀλλοφύλων ἀγανακτεῖ, ταῦτα εἰς τοὺς φίλους ποιῶν οὐκ ἀδικεῖν νομιεῖ;)

336 ἄλοχον θυμαρέα is formular (*Od.* 232, [Hesiod] fr. 43a.20 M–W), but sounds a suitably pathetic (or self-pitying) note. As a description of Briseis ἄλοχος surprises, since the term normally denotes a wife (κουρίδιος is its regular epithet) and is contrasted with δούλη, 'concubine', at 3.409. Unfortunately, the argumentative point of ἄλοχος, to equate the emotional commitment of Akhilleus to that of Menelaos, is only too clear, cf. 343 and n. Never up to this point, nor afterwards, does anyone suggest that Agamemnon had wounded Akhilleus in his family honour. Adultery was beyond compensation – Penelope's suitors died for less. The specific term for a woman in Briseis' position is probably δούλη (see. *Od.* 4.12 for Menelaos' son ἐκ δούλης), but in spite of her significance in the story the status of this unhappy woman is undefined; she is never called a δμωή. The *Iliad* also knows the term παλλακίς (9.449, 9.452). — τῇ παριαύων | τερπέσθω is psychologically effective: what Akhilleus had loved he spurns when it has been soiled. At 343 he uses the past tense, φίλεον, of his feelings towards Briseis. Here as elsewhere Akhilleus is obsessed with his own humiliation. — The expression (γέρας) εἷλετ᾽, ἔχει δ᾽ ἄλοχον is clearly a variant of the formula ἑλὼν γὰρ ἔχει γέρας (3×). Nevertheless Leaf and some early commentators punctuated with a stop after εἷλετ᾽ and a comma after θυμαρέα. The sentence then translates 'He [Agamemnon] has an ἄλοχος of his own, let him be content with her.' But who then is the ἄλοχος? Briseis apart, Agamemnon has no named concubine in the camp at this moment, and to tell him to take his pleasure with Klutaimestra hundreds of miles away in Mycenae is too rhetorical to make an effective point. Allen's punctuation in the OCT, which is also that of Ameis–Hentze and Mazon and implied by the scholia (bT), is preferable. — The long -ᾱ- of θυμαρέα, beside θυμῆρες, *Od.* 10.362, is unexplained.

337–8 Akhilleus is asking 'Why are we here?' The implicit answer, for the sake of the argument, is that they are there to uphold the rights of Menelaos. He then sharpens the point and asks 'Why is Agamemnon here?', so as to bring out the falsity of Agamenon's position. — Impersonal δεῖ, 'there is need', does not express moral obligation in archaic literature (where χρή is used). The word occurs only here in the *Iliad* and not at all in the *Odyssey* or in Hesiod, but in a passage whose thought is untraditional that is no cause for surprise. Uncontracted -εε- from -εϝε- is usually maintained in the epic but has crept into the *Iliad* at 5.464 (υἱεῖς), 11.708 (πολεῖς), 11.611 (ἐρεῖο, if the reading is correct), and perhaps 9.612 (σύγχει, for which σύγχεε could be read); -εῖ- < -έϝει is attested only here and *Od.* 9.227, 9.470 (ἐπιπλεῖν).

339–41 The singular Ἀτρεΐδης in 339 must be Agamemnon in this context. Agamemnon gathered the host, but it was Menelaos who loved his wife, hence Ἀτρεΐδαι, plural, at 341. Akhilleus' argument would be even more effective if Agamemnon had been at Troy to recover *his* wife. But Agamemnon can have no complaint; he had identified his own honour with success at Troy, 2.114–15 = 9.21–2.

340 μερόπων ἀνθρώπων: the sense of μέροψ is unknown, see 1.250n. The formula, however, is not totally ossified, being declined into the nominative (18.288) and modified to provide the dat. plur. μερόπεσσι βροτοῖσιν (2.285).

341 Akhilleus attempts a 'persuasive definition', viz. to extend the application of ἐχέφρων into that of ἀγαθός so as to bring sexual relations within the province of heroic ἀρετή. But the underlying point is that Agamemnon has indulged his lust at another man's expense. The poet saw no conflict between Akhilleus' love for Briseis and his sleeping with Diomede this same night, see 664–5. Persuasive definitions are more frequent in the *Odyssey* where the heroic arrogance of the Suitors collides with the ethos of the epic, see Penelope's words at *Od.* 16.418ff. and 21.331ff., and those of Telemakhos at 2.48ff.

342 This is all that we hear from his own lips of Akhilleus' finer feelings towards Briseis; it is a pity that he should make this declaration, emphatic though it is, only in a context where his rhetoric requires her to be raised to the status of the ἄλοχοι of the Atreidai so that his loss may be equated with that of Menelaos. Now would have been the moment for Akhilleus to say κουριδίην ἄλοχον θήσειν, ἄξειν τ᾽ ἐνὶ νηυσὶν | ἐς Φθίην, δαίσειν δὲ γάμον μετὰ Μυρμιδόνεσσι (19.298–9), as Patroklos promised he would according to Briseis – but that is probably an *ad hoc* pathetic touch to round off her lament. Rhetorical though it is, Akhilleus' affirmation is at least an improvement on Agamemnon's inability to regard women as anything but objects to be returned undamaged or weighed out in sevens and scores (128–40). (Aias was no better, see 636–9.) Akhilleus' affection, however, was obliterated when he realized the awful consequences of his wrath; he wished Briseis had died at Lurnessos (19.59–60). — ἐχέφρων: in a broad sense the φρήν is the seat of reason, the θυμός that of passion. The expression ἀγαθὸς καὶ ἐχέφρων is virtually a contradiction in terms, for an Iliadic hero's primary trait is self-assertion, cf. 6.208 = 11.784 (ὑπείροχον ἔμμεναι ἄλλων). Akhilleus speaks *ad hominem* and *ad tempus*. Note that he condemns Agamemnon's arrogance, not his lust; the Homeric audience would have thought bizarre the idea that sexual continence might be part of the virtue of an ἀγαθός.

343 δουρικτητήν: from Lurnessos on one of Akhilleus' forays, according to 2.690. But 2.686–94 are an inorganic note to the Myrmidons' entry in the Catalogue of Ships, and Briseis' lament (19.291–6) names only the 'city of Munes'. The *Cypria* (fr. 21 Davies = T to 10.57) opted for Pedasos. See also 131n. Uncertainty on such a point reflects the tradition's total disregard for Briseis as a person: we do not even know her name, for 'Briseis' is a patronymic adjective in formation. At 16.57 Akhilleus uses the 1st person, κτεάτισσα, for his capture of Briseis, but it is noteworthy that the rules for the distribution of booty (it went into a 'pool', cf. 333n.) prevent him making a point of his being deprived of what he had *personally* seized as his prize of war.

345 Akhilleus scents a plot, as he does at 375 and 423–6, a plot not to make true amends but to get him to fight. There is no guarantee even (375) that having got his victory Agamemnon will pay up.

346–50 Akhilleus mocks Agamemnon's anxiety and precautions, see 674 and n.

348–55 Being an illustration of Agamemnon's desperate efforts ἀλεξέμεναι δήϊον πῦρ these lines do not advance Akhilleus' argument. They also presuppose the last scenes of book 7, where the building of the wall has been thought to create problems (see 7.327–43n.). Accordingly there is a possibility and (for some commentators) an advantage that they could be adjudged an interpolation. But this fine expression of Akhilleus' contempt for Agamemnon and heroic self-esteem cannot be rejected for the sake of a theory: see Page, *HHI* 338, who accepts the lines. The wall was Nestor's suggestion, but it is effective that Akhilleus' sarcasm attributes it to Agamemnon (note the singular verbs in 348–51). Akhilleus' disparagement is prophetic. The Achaeans hoped that their wall would prove ἄρρηκτον (14.56 = 68), but Hektor demolished the gate at 12.445ff.

349 Aristarchus' reading in the last colon, ἔκτοθι τάφρον, is intended to make it plainer that a space intervened between wall and trench.

351 The formulas for Hektor in the genitive, Ἕκτορος ἀνδροφόνοιο (10×) and Ἕ. ἱπποδάμοιο (5×) break the law of economy. ἱπποδάμοιο, used of eight characters, is clearly generic, while ἀνδροφόνοιο is virtually specific to Hektor (1× each of Ares and Lukoorgos). There is a tendency for Ἕ. ἀνδροφόνοιο to cluster (5× in books 16–18), but it is also possible to argue that the epithet has hubristic overtones and is assigned to contexts where such overtones, ironical or pathetic, are appropriate (so Sacks, *Traditional Phrase* 163–75).

352–5 Most of the fighting hitherto has been close to the walls of Troy. This is asserted by Here (disguised as Stentor) at 5.788–90, Poseidon (disguised as Kalkhas) at 13.105–6, and implied by the panic reaction of the Achaeans to Hektor's advance in book 8, and by the even more panic-stricken flight of the Trojans from the supposed return of Akhilleus in book 16 and his actual attack in 20. Bacchylides (13.110–20) recalled this evidently notorious point: πρὶν μὲν πολύπυργον | Ἰλίου θαητὸν ἄστυ | οὐ λεῖπον. Hektor (15.721) attributed the fact to the caution of the Trojan elders, a self-serving declaration we need not take seriously, cf. Von der Mühll, *Hypomnema* 236.

354 The Scaean gates are three times associated with the (nearby) oak-tree, see 5.692–3n. Hektor presumably stood in the gateway or before it to defend it, like Polupoites and Leonteus defending the Achaean camp at 12.131ff. On the gates of Troy see 3.145n. The Dardanian gate would be located somewhere in the S.E. quadrant of the enceinte (where indeed there are two gateways piercing the walls of Troy VI and VIIA), the Scaean gates might be anywhere where the contours of the site permitted an easy approach. Both gates are mentioned in formulas and their names are doubtless traditional, but it is too much to expect the town plan of Troy to have been so preserved. Scaean and Dardanian gates alike are thought of as leading towards the fighting. Aristarchus (Arn/A) envisaged one gate indifferently called Scaean or Dardanian. The oak-tree is twice (5.693, 7.60) said to belong to Zeus, like the famous oak at Dodona, but no special properties are attributed to it.

355 The incident when Hektor dared to face Akhilleus, if not rhetorical, is unknown. It could have figured in the *Cypria* in the first year of the war, before Achaeans and Trojans had taken each other's measure.

356–63 Akhilleus' announcement of his departure is a threat (and so described at 682). It should be taken as a hyperbolical sign of the speaker's fury, like his baffled attempt to name his price at 379–85. The threat is quickly modified in response to Phoinix at 618–19, and further modified in reply to Aias at 650–3. Akhilleus had climaxed his quarrel with Agamemnon with the same threat (1.169).

356 Why, if the paradosis can be relied on, should the poet sing ἔθελον πολεμίζειν Ἕκτορι δίῳ at 7.169 and ἐθέλω πολεμιζέμεν Ἕκτορι δίῳ here (as read by many MSS)? Probably πολεμιζέμεναι at 337 induced πολεμιζέμεν, or preserved it. Ἕκτορι δίῳ: bT (on 9.651) suggest the epithet was used to annoy the emissaries. That is unlikely; the formula occurs 26× in the accusative and 12× in the dative.

357–9 The participles ῥέξας and νηήσας, 'heap with', are in anacoluthon with ὄψεαι (πλεύσομαι or εἶμι would be expected); a dash at the end of 358 would be the better punctuation. The broken syntax is consonant with the hyperbole of Akhilleus' language. Verse 359 = 4.353, however, where the context is quite different and the syntax in order.

360 The expression Ἑλλήσποντον ἐπ' ἰχθυόεντα is obviously derived from the regular πόντον ἐπ' ἰχθυόεντα, see 9.4n. Formular usage is indifferent to the punning effect of such recombinations.

363–4 ἤματί κε τριτάτῳ: the distance is about 220 miles. For other navigational data for the Homeric Aegean see *Od.* 3.168–83. — ἐνθάδε ἔρρων is formular, cf. 8.239 and n.

365 χαλκὸν ἐρυθρόν (only here), whether specifically bronze or copper, evidently denotes the unworked material. The metrical duplicate νώροπα χαλκόν refers to bronze armour.

366 = 23.261, there with reference to the prizes that Akhilleus put up for the games of Patroklos. That Briseis turns out to be such a small proportion of Akhilleus' spoils of war underlines the fact that for him she is not a valuable property but a symbol of his honour. The verse is unbalanced in rhythm and not a true threefolder. Words of the metrics of γυναῖκας ($\cup - \cup$) are as handy at the verse-end as they are awkward in the rest of the verse, unless a trochee (ἠδέ or the like) can be contrived to precede. ἐΰζωνος and its virtual synonym βαθύζωνος (see 594n.) are loosely formular in the *Iliad* with γυνή, semantically related words, and feminine personal names: Ἶφις ἐΰζωνος, ἐΰζωνος παράκοιτις (1× each), βαθυζώνους τε γυναῖκας (2×, including the sole Odyssean instance of these epithets), and ἐϋζώνοιο γυναικός, γυναικὸς ἐΰζ., ἐΰζ. τιθήνης (1× each). It is in *HyDem* that the formulas appear: ἐΰζωνος (βαθύ-) Μετάνειρα etc. (5×), and βαθυζώνοιο θυγατρός (2×).

367 This is the only point where Briseis is said to be a present from Agamemnon, to make his offence seem the more heinous, cf. 333n. Akhilleus – or the poet – is carried away by his own rhetoric.

368 ἐφυβρίζων: ὕβρις is not a frequent Iliadic idea, only 1.203, 1.214, 11.695, 13.633, against 26× in the *Odyssey*.

372–3 Akhilleus reiterates some of the (probably formular) abuse he had employed in book 1. With αἰὲν ἀναιδείην ἐπιείμενος compare ἀναιδείην ἐπιείμενε (1.149), and with κύνεός περ ἐων 1.159 (κυνῶπα), 1.225 (κυνὸς ὄμματ᾽ ἔχων) and nn.

374 βουλαί and ἔργα are polar opposites; Akhilleus means 'no way at all'. With ἔργον understand συμπρήξω out of συμφράσσομαι. See also 357–9n.

375–8 The violent enjambments and short phrases admirably express Akhilleus' withering contempt, as Eust. saw (756.52). Verses with two major breaks of sense, like 376, are extremely rare in the *Iliad*, but there are three others in this book, 9.111, 9.197, 9.585.

376 ἅλις δέ οἱ: sc. ἐστι, that is, 'It is enough for him ⟨to have committed one offence⟩', cf. the idiom ἦ οὐχ ἅλις ὅττι …; 5.349, etc.

377 ἐκ γὰρ εὖ φρένας εἵλετο μητίετα Ζεύς is an expanded version of the formula (μευ) φρένας ἐξέλετο Ζεύς (2×). Agamemnon brackets it with ἀασάμην at 19.137. 'Zeus' is used, so to speak, generically; some god must have determined Agamemnon's actions, because, the heroes believe, nothing happens without some god, usually unidentifiable, causing it. Zeus himself is too often blamed unjustly when things go wrong (e.g. 12.164–6, and especially *Od.* 5.302–5, where the narrative has just described the action of *Poseidon*) for Akhilleus to mean what he says literally and specifically. In the narrative of the quarrel in book 1 Zeus is not so much as mentioned, but that did not prevent Agamemnon blaming Zeus for his folly at some length, 19.86ff. and n.

378–405 Akhilleus reaches, and dwells on, his retort to Agamemnon's generosity. The collision between the viewpoints of the two now emerges clearly. Agamemnon offered material recompense but no words of contrition; implicitly he has assimilated his seizure of Briseis to inadvertent damage to a piece of valuable property, which must be restored but which ought not to affect the personal relations of the two parties. For Akhilleus the material loss does not matter – he has plenty of other women (366); what mattered was that the seizure was an outrage that made the material compensation irrelevant. Akhilleus does not want compensation now (or not yet), even if Agamemnon could meet the highest conceivable demand. There is an ambiguity in the passage (see Page, *HHI* 308–9), which it is unnecessary and unwise to resolve, whether Akhilleus' present rejection of Agamemnon's offers reserves his claim to Briseis and the gifts or is a renunciation 'for ever, unconditionally' (Page, *loc. cit.*). Circumstances change and so do attitudes, cf. 16.49–100. What Akhilleus does want at this moment (if he is represented as wanting anything – all that is required for the purposes of the *Iliad* is that he should have a plausible reason for being obstinate) is concealed in 387 ἀπὸ πᾶσαν ἐμοὶ δόμεναι θυμαλγέα λώβην, 'pay me back my shame'. If that means 'undo what he has done', Akhilleus is demanding what is, of course, impossible and account must be taken of the view (see 307n.) that the traditional diction did not permit the clear expression of Akhilleus' thought, as if he were straitjacketed by traditional modes of thought and could not easily express a demand for a compensation that was not material. This is possible (cf. E. A. Havelock, 'Thoughtful Hesiod', *YCS* 20 (1966) 59–72, for another example, and 307n.). Subsequent comments in the *Iliad* (11.609ff. and 16.72–3, see nn.), if they presuppose the Embassy, may be taken to imply that in Akhilleus' view Agamemnon had not yet suffered a λώβη equal to that which he had inflicted (see 387n.). For the principle δράσαντα παθεῖν see 2.354–6.

378–87 No material compensation, however vast, can appease Akhilleus' injured soul. Akhilleus' words are an emphatic repudiation of Agamemnon's gifts, underlined by his repudiation of Agamemnon's daughter and the recognition of status implicit in that offer. But not only Akhilleus' words must be read, but also their tone and context. Akhilleus has a point to make about his θυμαλγέα λώβην (387) and does so with grandiose hyperbole. There is no contradiction on the emotional level with Akhilleus' satisfaction at 16.85–6 that the Achaeans would now οἱ περικαλλέα κούρην | ἄψ ἀπονάσσωσιν, ποτὶ δ᾽ ἀγλαὰ δῶρα πόρωσιν, for in his present indignation Akhilleus must be allowed to say more than he intends. Schadewaldt's point (*Iliasstudien* 130, which also discounts the rhetoric of the situation), that the present passage does not explicitly renounce a claim to Briseis, is sufficiently answered by Agamemnon's omission of her in his apology (19.140ff.), 'though the sequel shows that she was to be included' (so Page, *HHI* 331).

378 καρός: *hapax legomenon* and gen. sing. of an unknown noun, cf. καριμοίρους· τοὺς ἐν μηδεμιᾷ μοίρᾳ Hsch. Now usually associated with κείρω in the sense of 'chip', 'shaving'. αἴση: 'a portion', literally.

379–80 Akhilleus used the same asseveration in refusing Hektor ransom: οὐδ᾽ εἴ κεν δεκάκις τε καὶ εἰκοσινήριτ᾽ ἄποινα | στήσωσ᾽ ἐνθάδ᾽ ἄγοντες, ὑπόσχωνται δὲ καὶ ἄλλα ... (22.349–50), another hyperbolical resolution that he did not keep.

381–4 For Orkhomenos see 2.511n. Its grandeur, at its height in the thirteenth century B.C., is reflected in the fine ruined tholos-tomb, the 'Treasury of Minyas' ('one of the greatest wonders of Greece and the world', Paus. 9.38.2) with a side chamber like that of the 'Treasury of Atreus' at Mycenae. In conjunction with Orkhomenos 'Thebes' would naturally be taken as the well-known Boeotian Thebes (at this point of time, however, lying waste, cf. 2.505). If the line is traditional, as it may well be, the reference would certainly have been to the two Boeotian cities. Verses 382–4 are a 'most prosy interpolation' according to Leaf, but that comment is better applied to the amplified description at 383–4; 382 (= *Od.* 4.127) is effective here, Akhilleus saying in effect '... Thebes, and I don't mean Boeotian Thebes but the infinitely wealthier Thebes in Egypt'. The description of the Theban armies is indeed rhetorically otiose. Akhilleus is piling up a crescendo of exaggerations and descriptive digression is out of place; each οὐδ' εἰ ... or οὐδ' ὅσα ... must strike home before his hearers have recovered from the previous blast. — Why the Greeks called the Egyptian city Thebes is a mystery, none of the native names bearing any obvious resemblance (see A. L. Lloyd, *Herodotus Book ii* II (Leiden 1976) 12–13, for details, more briefly West on *Od.* 4.125–7). It is a question whether the city was ever walled, but the verses need not be supposed to reflect more than the reports that filtered down to Greek visitors to the Delta. In *Od.* the dominant image of Egypt is of its wealth (*Od.* 3.301, 4.229–30, and – it was worth raiding – 14.245ff.). Thebes was sacked by the Assyrians in 663 B.C., but the implications of that are uncertain, see W. Burkert, *WS* 89 (1976) 5–21, for the view that the verses reflect the revival of the city under the Ethiopian dynasty 715–663 B.C. Lorimer, *HM* 97–8, maintains the view that the verses preserve a memory of the glories of the New Kingdom.

383 ἀν' ἑκάστας: *sc.* πύλας. As Arn/A note, the *Iliad* does not use the singular πύλη.

385 Sand is such an obvious symbol for an incalculable number that it is striking it should be so rarely used for that purpose in Homer. ψάμαθος recurs at 2.800 where it is joined with φύλλα, the usual Homeric symbol for large numbers.

385, 388–90 Aristotle (*Rhet.* 1413a28) detected the strident sound of ὑπερβολαὶ μειρακιώδεις in these verses. As Bolling remarks, *External Evidence* 120, Aristotle intended to cite two quotations, not a text lacking 386–7. It is an epic idea that heroines should rival goddesses in skill and beauty, but it may have struck Aristotle as hubristic.

387 θυμαλγέα λώβην is a new point; it explains, psychologically at any rate, why Agamemnon's offers are ἐχθρά (378). Up to this point the injury to Akhilleus has been expressed by the words ἠτίμησεν· ἑλὼν γὰρ ἔχει γέρας, 1.356 = 1.507 = 2.240 ≅ 9.111, that is, in material terms. Now it is revealed that what really matters is Akhilleus' mental anguish, something that the Achaean chiefs had not thought of and cannot reach. The epic, it may be noted, has language for expressing regret at a wrongful act, it is to say ὡς ὄφελε, as Helen does at 3.173 and 6.345. Agamemnon had not said this. — Variants of θυμαλγέα λώβην are formular in the *Odyssey* (3×), but it remains true that in the *Iliad* what torments the soul is χόλος (3×) and what consumes it is ἔρις (5×). Akhilleus switches the source of his torment from his heart to its cause. λώβη expresses the construction put upon an action by the one that suffers from it, cf. 7.97–8 and the verb λωβάομαι at 1.232, and so complements αἴσχεα and ὀνείδεα ('reproaches'), which express the judgement and reactions of others. It hurts because the image a hero has of himself is that presented to him by his peers; Agamemnon's act and the others' acquiescence has reduced the 'best of the Achaeans' to a nonentity. — For the shape of the verse cf. 1.98 πρίν γ' ἀπὸ πατρὶ φίλῳ δόμεναι ἑλικώπιδα κούρην, but the comparison makes the obscurity of the present verse all the darker. Literally the meaning is 'pays me back all the heart-grieving outrage' (not, or not literally, 'pays me back *for* all the outrage', which is expressed by τίνειν λώβην, 11.142). Akhilleus appears to mean that he has 'paid' as it were a measure of humiliation to Agamemnon who must now 'pay' back an equivalent measure; Agamemnon at the moment is thoroughly alarmed, but he has not yet undergone the humiliation of total defeat. The objects of ἀποδίδωμι are normally material objects or such terms as ἀμοιβή, χρέος, ζημία, and ὄπις, and the subject is the avenger, e.g. Hesiod, *Theog.* 222 πρίν γ' ἀπὸ τῷ δώωσι [Κῆρες] κακὴν ὄπιν, ὅς τις ἁμάρτῃ. Neither Aias (628ff.), nor Odysseus (678–9), nor Diomedes (699–700) refer directly to this demand, but characterize the whole section (378–87) as obduracy. Comparative evidence of 'shame cultures' (e.g. Peristiany, *Honour and Shame* 193–241) makes it clear that in making amends both parties must save face; to insist on unconditional submission invites condemnation. It is likely therefore that the obscurity is intentional: if Akhilleus were to state his terms in clear language we should want a reason why the Achaeans did not meet them, or, alternatively, we should see that Akhilleus' terms were unacceptable to one of Agamemnon's rank and temper. As it is the clash of heroic wills continues, both sides locked into what Diomedes (700) calls ἀγηνορίη.

388 For the possible word-play οὐ γαμέω Ἀγαμέμνονος see vol. v 59.

392 βασιλεύτερος: a sneer at Agamemnon's obsession with rank, cf. 1.186, 1.281, and (though it has not been reported to Akhilleus) 9.161.

393–400 In order to underline his rejection of Agamemnon's material offers Akhilleus affirms that he will marry a woman of his own station and that the house of Peleus has wealth enough to satisfy him. This noble rhetoric stands in contrast with the materialism elsewhere attributed to the heroes, e.g. emphasis put on the κτήματα that Paris stole with Helen, 3.282ff., and on ξείνια in the *Odyssey*, 11.178, 13.40–2, 13.215–16, 24.283–6, and is indeed in contrast with Akhilleus' own concern for his lost γέρας.

394 γυναῖκα γαμέσσεται is the reading of all MSS and must represent the Hellenistic vulgate. The broken rhythm of the fourth foot ('Hermann's

Bridge') is exceptional (see Maas, *GM* 60, West, *GM* 37–8), and though the future middle of γαμέω does not occur elsewhere in the epic, it would be remarkable if γαμέσσομαι, for which there is no ready analogy, were the form; the normal future is γαμέω (388, 391). The middle voice is regularly used of the bride, and no parallel is quoted for the sense 'get one's child married'. Aristarchus' γε μάσσεται (Arn/A) is an elegant emendation, yet emendation it must be. μάσ-σ-ομαι is the future of μαίομαι (μασ-*y*-ομαι), 'search out'.

395 Akhilleus claims Hellas and Phthia as his ancestral home also at 2.683–4 (see n.). ἀν' Ἑλλάδα τε Φθίην τε is formular, cf. *Od.* 11.496, but the poet betrays some uncertainty over the political and geographical relations of the two regions and bequeathed controversy to his Hellenistic commentators, see Strabo 9.5.5–14. Phthie appears to designate the region to the south of Mt Othrys, some of it at least occupied by the domains of Protesilaos and Philoktetes; Φθῖοι (13.686 etc.) means the troops of those leaders, while Akhilleus' men are Μυρμιδόνες. Hellas was placed north of Mt Othrys by the authorities cited by Strabo at 9.5.6, but modern commentators place it south of the Spercheios adjacent to the kingdom of the lesser Aias (who ruled Πανέλληνες, 2.530). See HSL *Catalogue* 128–30. Hellas and Phthie are politically distinct at 447ff., yet Bathukles, a Myrmidon, lived in Hellas at 16.595.

396 οἵ τε πτολίεθρα ῥύονται is a unique phrase but as an expression of one aspect of the heroic role deserves to be formular. The complete hero, like Sarpedon at 12.310–28, displays his valour in protecting his dependants as well as in seeking fame. For Hektor as defender of Troy see 6.403, 22.507; the verb is (ἐ)ῥύομαι in both cases.

398–9 ἐπέσσυτο θυμὸς ἀγήνωρ is an expansion of the formula θυμὸς ἐπέσσυτο (3× *Il.*). γήμαντα: the accusative is undoubtedly right against the dative. The infinitive phrase tends to take the accusative case as its subject where the dative stands in the principal clause, see Chantraine, *GH* II 313.

401–3 Akhilleus indirectly adds another point – there is now no loot worth speaking of to be had anyway. The wealth of Priam had once exceeded that of anyone between Lesbos and Phrugie (24.544–5) but, according to Hektor at 17.221–6, it had been seriously depleted by the expense of bribing and feeding its allied defenders.

401 ψυχῆς: having asserted the impossibility of compensation Akhilleus explains why. He returns to the point he had made at 320: when he fights he puts his life on the line. But the stakes are not even: if a hero wins he receives honour (though Akhilleus doesn't receive even that); if he loses (and being ὠκύμορος he must lose sooner rather than later), he now points out, he loses his life; honour (= presents and precedence, cf. 12.310–20) may draw death's sting but is not an equivalent for life on any rational calculation. Only Akhilleus in his splendid isolation from the ties of family and community can make such a point. Hektor, for example, cannot opt for safe obscurity (6.441–6, 22.104–30) without incurring obloquy, for the heroic ethic must insist against reason that honour is indeed an equivalent for life.

403 = 22.156.

404–5 λάϊνος οὐδὸς ... Πυθοῖ: see Hainsworth, *Od.* 8.80n. The sole explicit reference to the oracle at Delphi in Homer is *Od.* 8.79–82, but the sacred site itself is of extreme antiquity: see P. Amandry, *La Mantique apollinienne à Delphes* (Paris 1950), and 2.519–23n. οὐδός would seem to imply the existence of a temple. For the epic's knowledge of holy places in mainland Greece see 16.234 (Dodona). Πυθών (2.519) or Πυθώ (*Od.* 8.80, 11.581) is the designation of the site both in the epic and the *Hymns*, save Δελφοί at *h.Hom.* 27.14. — ἀφήτορος puzzled the scholiasts (Arn/A) who are divided between ἀ-φη-, an allusion to the enigmatic speech of the oracle, and ἀφη-, 'let fly'. The Γλωσσογράφοι interpreted the word as 'socket' (στροφεύς), which Zenodotus accepted and proceeded to read νηοῦ for Φοίβου in 405 (Arn/A).

406–9 The end-stopped lines and consequent location of the contrasted words in the first foot, with the easy enjambment of 408–9, make a fine instance of natural eloquence, cf. vol. v 44.

409 ἀμείψεται ἕρκος ὀδόντων recurs in the *Odyssey* (10.328). The simple sense 'cross' is restricted to this phrase in the epic. The quaint phrase ἕρκος ὀδόντων is well entrenched in the diction (3× *Il.*, 7× *Od.*).

410–16 Akhilleus knows that his life will be short (and this knowledge, of course, redoubles the force of the heroic imperatives upon him), as is affirmed at 1.352, 1.417, 1.505, 18.95, 18.458, and 21.277; but this is the only point where Akhilleus is said to have a choice of destinies. (The closest parallel is that of Eukhenor, 13.663–70, see 13.658–9n.) The choice may have been part of the tradition of Akhilleus' birth but it seems more likely that it was invented here for its effectiveness as an argument, as Willcock, *HSCP* 81 (1977) 48–9 and *Commentary ad loc.*, suggests. There is an inconsistency with Patroklos' raising the matter at 16.36–7 and Akhilleus' denial that he had heard of any θεοπροπίη or message from Thetis (on which see 11.794–803n.). The usual point made is that Akhilleus *is* short-lived, therefore he has a claim to fame. But it is easy for him (or the poet) to reverse this argument and imply that renouncing fame even at this late date would entail long life. The *Odyssey* makes Akhilleus' ghost imply that he made the wrong choice – the worst conceivable kind of life, ἐπάρουρος ἐὼν θητευέμεν ἄλλῳ, is preferable to the best that Hades can offer (*Od.* 11.488–91). At

18.95–6 Thetis affirms that the doom of a short life will take effect as soon as (or, by implication, if) Hektor is slain. Plato blends that passage with the present, ['Αχιλλεύς] πεπυσμένος παρὰ τῆς μητρὸς ὡς ἀποθανοῖτο ἀποκτείνας Ἕκτορα, μὴ ποιήσας δὲ τοῦτο οἴκαδε ἐλθὼν γηραιὸς τελευτήσοι (*Symp.* 179ε). The tension between quest for glory and the emptiness of death is, of course, a theme of the whole *Iliad*. The idea that long life, *if only it could be assured*, might be preferable to glory recurs at 12.322–8 (Sarpedon to Glaukos), but as an impossible argument since it rests on a false premise.

411 κήρ is equated with μοῖρα by Hsch., κήρ· ἡ θανατηφόρος μοῖρα, i.e. κήρ is synonymous with μοῖρα where μοῖρα means or implies 'death', but κήρ never signifies (as μοῖρα can) 'the natural order'. The two terms share some epithets (ὀλοή, κακή), but μοῖρα is ineluctable (cf. μοῖραν δ' οὔ τινά φημι πεφυγμένον ἔμμεναι ἀνδρῶν 6.488), whereas κήρ' ἀλεείνων is a common formula. The usual etymology associates the words with κεραΐζω, 'ravage', but direct derivation from the root of κείρω, 'cut', is preferable, so that κήρ, μοῖρα (< μείρομαι), and δαίμων (probably < δαίομαι) represent the same semantic evolution at different stages: 'divide' > 'share' > 'fate' > 'death' > 'Death' (personified fate). See also 12.326n., Nilsson, *GgrR* 1 222–5.

413 κλέος ἄφθιτον ἔσται has frequently been compared with the semantically similar and etymologically identical expression in the Vedic hymns *śrávah ... ákṣitam* 1.9.7, cf. *ákṣiti śrávah* 1.40.4 etc., with the implication that the phrase is a fragment of an Indo-European heroic poetry: see M. Durante's list in R. Schmitt, *Indogermanische Dichtersprache* (Darmstadt 1968) 297–309. The words stand here as subject and predicate, but that may be a grammatical modification of a formula in which the epithet, though not decorative, is attributive, cf. the Delphic inscription *GDI* 1537, Ibycus fr. 1.47 Page, and Sappho fr. 44.4 L–P. The complete phrase, κλέος ἄφθιτον ἔσται, is an equivalent of the formular κλέος οὔποτ' ὀλεῖται (2× *Il.*, 1× *Od.*, *HyAp* 156, [Hesiod] fr. 70.7 M–W), and can readily be seen as an *ad hoc* creation from elements readily available to the poet, see M. Finkelberg, *CQ* 36 (1986) 1–5, with A. T. Edwards' correction, *CQ* 38 (1988) 25.

414 ἵκωμι was established in the printed texts by Wolf and has very little MS support; the paradosis, with remarkable unanimity, is the unmetrical ἵκωμαι. ἵκωμι, however, exchanges one anomaly for another – the ι of the active form ἵκω is long. οἴκαδ' + parts of ἱκέσθαι is formular (3× elsewhere in *Il.*, 5× *Od.*) and, again as οἴκαδ' ἵκωμαι, occurs at 393. ἵκωμαι, however, cannot stand here unless the following φίλην is emended to ἑήν (= ἐμήν, see 11.142n.) after Brugmann. The sense required of the verb is 'go', 'return', hence Nauck's ἵωμι, accepted by Leaf; but if this is a case of 'concordance corruption' the whole phrase οἴκαδ' ἵκωμαι may be intrusive. Wyatt, *ML*

33, moots the possibility here and at 5.256 (ἐᾷ as ∪∪) of a singer's slip, for which cf. A. B. Lord, *Singer of Tales* (Cambridge, Mass., 1960) 38, 44.

416 Athetized by Aristarchus (Arn/A) as being pleonastic and not read by Zenodotus (Did/AT). The verse gives a clearer construction to ἐπὶ δηρὸν δέ μοι αἰών in 415, as Aristarchus noted, and that would be a motive for its insertion, but see 44n.

420 χεῖρα ἑήν: for the hiatus before ἑήν cf. Ζεὺς δὲ ἑόν (1.533), ὅς τε ἑῆς (*Od.* 8.524). There is no initial digamma (ἑός < *sewos*), but the usage may well be affected by (ϝ)ός (< reduced-grade *swos*). The protective hand of Zeus is an easy metaphor, cf. 4.249, 5.433, 24.374, *Od.* 14.184, though more typical of Near Eastern thought than Greek. The formula is (αἴ κε) ὑπέρσχῃ χεῖρα Κρονίων (2×), but the conjugation of ὑπερέχειν results in a rather protean expression. The metaphorical uses of χείρ are examined by A. B. Gross, *Gymnasium* 77 (1970) 365–75.

422 The second hemistich of the verse = 4.323. There, however, γερόντων meant 'the old', here it implies 'counsellors'. The privilege is that of speaking freely (ἀποφάναι), cf. 33.

424 σαῷ < σαόῃ, subjunctive of σαόω, see LSJ s.v. σώζω. The MSS (and editors) are confused by the contraction, diectasis, and contamination of the form with the adjective σόος. The vulgate σόῃ (better σοῇ) may be retained, cf. 681.

425 ἥδε (μῆτις): perhaps the building of the wall, called a μῆτις at 7.324, but more likely the present approach to Akhilleus, also described as a μῆτις at 93.

426 ἀπομηνίσαντος: ἀπο- implies that the speaker will keep up his μῆνις *à l'outrance*, cf. ἀποθαυμάζω of *utter* amazement at *Od.* 6.49. The view that μῆνις, μηνίω itself connotes a 'lasting morally justified anger' (Frisk, Chantraine, *Dict.* s.v.) is questionable, see P. Considine, in *Studies Webster* 53–64, and should not be allowed to colour the understanding of the *Iliad*. The poet is happy to replace it from time to time with terms that have no moral connotation such as χώομαι (e.g. 107) or χόλος (e.g. 260). μῆνις is an archaism, used only for the anger of the gods and of Akhilleus, and doubtless implies an awe-inspiring and implacable passion, see C. Watkins, *Indo-European Studies* 3 (1977) 686–722, and J. S. Clay, *The Wrath of Athena* (Princeton 1983) 65 for other literature.

427 Phoinix commands the fourth regiment of the Myrmidons at 16.196 and ought (one supposes) to have had his quarters with his men. Even if his mention in book 16 reflects only the improvisation of an untraditional catalogue, his position as a dependant of the house of Peleus makes his quartering elsewhere in the Achaean army odd. Neither he nor his people, the Dolopes, are listed in the Catalogue of Ships.

428 = 691: φίλην ἐς πατρίδ' (also 12.16) is shortened from φ. ἐ. πατρίδα γαῖαν (16× *Il.*, 12× *Od.*) so as to accommodate the verb ἕπηται (ἕβησαν at 12.16).

430–605 Discourse of Phoinix: 'Akhilleus must be advised by his old friend and nurse. To reject suppliants is dangerous arrogance and probably counterproductive, as the story of Meleagros shows'

(The commentary on 430–605 assumes that the passage is integral to book 9. For the opposite view, which rests on partly on the duals at 182ff. and partly on the doctrines of 499–501 and 508–12, reinforced as usual with allegations of un-Homeric language and diction, see Page, *HHI* 297–304 and the literature there cited, and for the language Shipp, *Studies* 269–71.)

The conclusion of Akhilleus' discourse brings the plot of the *Iliad* to an impasse. The narrative goal set up by book 1 (1.408–12) has been reached: Agamemnon has acknowledged his ἄτη, and Akhilleus has refused to listen. His speech is described (by the poet) as κρατερός 'uncompromising', or 'brooking no contradiction', like Agamemnon's words to Khruses or to Akhilleus through Talthubios (1.25, 1.326), or Zeus's assertion of his superiority (8.29). Akhilleus will do nothing; there is nothing more the Achaeans can do. The ambassadors are silenced. Now that Nestor's plan has failed the only proposals the poet has left on the table are those of Agamemnon (to flee, 21–8) and Diomedes (to fight on alone, 45–9). It is therefore necessary at least to hint at a new narrative goal. This, for the plot of the *Iliad*, is the function of Phoinix' contribution to the debate. For Akhilleus had left one point unanswered, the appeal to his pity (301ff.), overshadowed as it was by his own self-pity. Phoinix takes this up, as will Patroklos at 16.21–35. In fact he discharges the role in the drama of this book which would be more naturally (but less dramatically and poetically, see 220n.) assigned to Akhilleus' friend. There are also parallels with Nestor's address to Patroklos at 11.656–803, on which see J. A. Rosner, *Phoenix* 30 (1976) 314–27, but it is likely that these arise from the fact that both discourses are pleas for intervention. Phoinix' speech is exceedingly long, a fact that indicates the urgency of the situation as perceived by the speaker, cf. 11.656–803n. His speech falls into three parts: his story (434–95), the allegory of the Litai (496–523), and the cautionary tale of Meleagros (524–605). The point of the first section is to establish Phoinix' credentials, for he is about to give Akhilleus, a superior figure, some moral advice, cf. Nestor's preliminary observations at 1.254ff. That done, Phoinix proceeds by insinuation to reproof and warning. His argument has a subtlety that would have been worthy of Odysseus but which would have sounded hypocritical on his lips. Until this night Akhilleus' obduracy had been completely justified, but now he was acting as if he were more than a god. For by taking the proper action (and the Achaeans *have* now taken the proper action towards Akhilleus) the anger even of the gods can be averted. Obduracy brings retribution from Zeus. Besides – and this is the point of the Meleagros paradigm – the enemy's victory may be more complete than was intended: Meleagros lost his gifts and had to fight just the same to save himself. None the less Phoinix' contribution, if not exactly 'a psychological and argumentative disaster' (Brenk), is without its intended effect; it does not move the action forward, as analytical scholars have emphasized by ejecting it. However, Akhilleus' only reply is a command to be silent (612), a confession that he is moved by Phoinix' argument and has no answer to it. It also motivates the weakening of Akhilleus' resolve to depart (619), as Plato astutely observed (*Hipp. Min.* 370), and this is necessary after his dramatic announcement at 356–61. Yet in a work of fiction the failure of the speech to stir Akhilleus into action is a hint that it is really addressed to us, the audience of the *Iliad*: it highlights the danger of Akhilleus' position from the moral standpoint and points the way to the tragedy that follows and the hero's realization through his own suffering what other values there are beside the κλέος that he has just rejected (see also 605n.).

A useful selection of the extensive literature on the scene is listed by F. E. Brenk, *Eranos* 84 (1986) 77–86, and R. Scodel, *AJP* 103 (1982) 128–36, and *CPh* 84 (1989) 91–9; see also Lohmann, *Reden* 245–76.

430–1 These verses constitute a formular couplet (῝Ως ἔφαθ', οἱ δ' ἄρα πάντες ... 10× *Il.*, 5× *Od.*, followed by μῦθον ἀγασσάμενοι· μάλα γὰρ ... 3× *Il.*). Verse 431 substitutes the more emphatic ἀπέειπεν for the ἀγόρευσεν of the other passages. κρατερῶς, indicating that the speech was an ἀπότομος ('unrelenting') λόγος (AbT), is the narrator's dispassionate comment. Aias will be much more forthright (628–38).

432 γέρων ἱππηλάτα (8× *Il.*, 2× *Od.*) is a generic epithet phrase used with Nestor, Oineus, Peleus, Phoinix, and (without γέρων) Tudeus, cf. 162n. Delebecque, *Cheval* 38, 164–5, notes that all these heroes are of the previous generation or won their spurs, so to speak, before the action of the *Iliad*, as if the epithet reflected an earlier mode of warfare. Horse epithets implying chariot driving (ἱππεύς, ἱππιοχάρμης, ἱππόδαμος, ἱπποκέλευθος, πλήξιππος), however, are common. γέρων provides a euphonic expansion of the epithet before the vowel of ἱππηλάτα, as μέγας before the consonants of κορυθαίολος and Τελαμώνιος.

433 δάκρυ' ἀναπρήσας (< ἀναπρήθω, 'let burst forth') is formular, cf. *Od.* 2.81. For heroic tears see 14n.

434 φαίδιμ' is the regular epithet with the vocative Ἀχιλλεῦ (5×), as also with the similarly scanned Ὀδυσσεῦ (5×).

For commentary on the diction of 434–41 see Introduction 3–4.

438–9 The sense of πέμπειν is slightly different in 438 from that in 439. Akhilleus was 'sent' to Agamemnon, Phoinix was 'made πομπός' to Akhilleus, i.e. as companion and mentor.

440 ὁμοίίου πολέμοιο: the original shape of the formula (6× *Il.*, 2× *Od.*) was doubtless ὁμοίίοο πτολέμοιο, see 9.64n., 13.358n. πτ-, unnecessary in the transmitted form, is preserved as a variant in all eight places. The metrics (see Wyatt, *ML* 174–8), formation, and sense of ὁμοίίος are matters of uncertainty: Hesiod, *Erga* 182, uses ὁμοίίος as an equivalent of ὁμοῖος, but the present formula requires a more specific sense, e.g. τὸ ὁμοίως συμβαῖνον (Ap. Soph. *Lex.* s.v.). That would suit the uses with γῆρας (4.315) and θάνατος (*Od.* 3.236), but is not especially appropriate to πόλεμος. Leaf on this passage suggested 'levelling', which is accepted after full discussion by Russo on *Od.* 18.264. Most authorities are inclined to separate ὁμοίίος and ὁμοῖος, in which case the original sense of ὁμοίίος is irrecoverable.

441 The Ionic genitive plural ἀγορέων is due to the use of the word in enjambment, cf. | καὶ πυλέων at 12.340. For another example of -έων in a modified formula (μελαινέων ἕρμ' ὀδυνάων) see 4.117n.

442 As educator of Akhilleus Phoinix here claims the role usually assigned to the centaur Kheiron, see R. von Scheliha, *Patroklos: Gedanken über Homers Dichtung und Gestalten* (Basel 1943) 222, and Kullmann, *Quellen* 371. Homer says, or has his characters say, what is appropriate at the moment. So Thetis, when about to lose her son, recalls how *she* had reared (τρέφειν) him (18.57). Kheiron would have been unacceptable to Homer in any case as tutor to the protagonist of his epic; for all his justice (11.832) Kheiron was a centaur, one of the mountain-dwelling φῆρες (1.268), whom Homer banishes to the sidelines of the *Iliad*.

444 ≃ 437, by ring-composition. φίλον τέκος: as a form of address the archaic τέκος (27×) is more usual in the *Iliad* than τέκνον (17×); in the *Odyssey* the reverse is true (τέκος 9×, τέκνον 21×).

447–77 The narrative of Phoinix' story is rather inconsequential, but that may be the result of the omission of explanatory details and general compression. The argument appears to run as follows: to the indignation of his wife Phoinix' father Amuntor brought home a concubine; ⟨in retaliation⟩ his mother urged Phoinix to anticipate his father's lust; he did so and ⟨in answer⟩ Phoinix' father cursed *him*; ⟨in response⟩ Phoinix [planned to murder him (458–61); and] resolved to leave home; at which the whole family of Amuntor imprisoned Phoinix in his father's house imploring him ⟨to remain? to restrain his parricidal urge?⟩, but after nine days he escaped. For the problem of 458–61 see n. *ad loc.*

447–8 These verses, with 478–9, draw a political and not merely a geographical distinction between Hellas, the kingdom of Amuntor, and Phthie, that of Peleus. Such a distinction is elsewhere ignored in the *Iliad*.

Phthie itself is a vague term, see 395n., 2.683–4n. and 13.685–8n. According to 10.266 Amuntor son of Ormenos, the original owner of the boar's tusk helmet, lived at Eleon (in Boeotia, according to the Catalogue, 2.500). This has seemed such confusion as to call in question the identity of these Amuntores, see bT to 10.266 (Aristarchus suspected they were different persons), Eust. 762, Strabo 9.5.18 (a good report of Hellenistic controversies), and RE s.v. 'Amyntor'. There was also an Ormenion in Thessaly (2.734), which would suit this passage well. Both Amuntor and Ormenos are good heroic names, the latter at least used freely (for Trojans at 8.274 and 12.187, for Eumaios' grandfather at *Od.* 18.414).

447–52 A comment on these verses is contained in Pap. vii (= Mus. Brit. 1605 c = Pack² 1188), see Pfeiffer, *Philol.* 92 (1937) 16–18, ὅπω]ς μισῇ τοῦ [γέροντος ἔρωτα. The motive attributed to Amuntor's wife, a demonstration of Phoinix' superior vigour, is probably misconceived, cf. the action of Absalom, 2 Samuel 16.21–3 with 20.3: the effect of Phoinix' action would be to alienate the γέρων not the παλλακίς. T reports a reading γέροντι, which suggests that some critics wished to understand the passage in the latter sense. For Amuntor's reaction cf. Genesis 35.22 with 49.4: as a result of seducing his father's concubine Reuben lost his right of primogeniture.

449 καλλικόμοιο is formular (1× *Od.*, 2× Hesiod) but under-represented. The complementary epithet ἠϋκόμοιο is remarkably more popular (15× *Il.*, 2× *Od.*, 11× Hesiod).

453 The first half of the verse was emended to τῇ οὐ πιθόμην †οὐδὲ ἔρεξα† (οὐδ' ἔρξα Cobet) by Sosiphanes (fourth century B.C.), a remarkably irresponsible bowdlerization, thought worthy of record by the exegetical scholia (A) and Eust. 363.9.

454 Amuntor calls on the Erinues because they are the guardians of oaths (Hesiod, *Erga* 803) and curses. In an oath the sanction of the goddesses is invoked on oneself, in a curse on another, see Burkert, *Religion* 200. They are associated on the one hand with μοῖρα (19.87) because they are the guardians of the natural order and punish those whose unnatural acts (whether speech by a horse (19.418) or disrespect for parents) have breached it, and on the other with Hades and Persephone because they live in the Underworld ('Ερέβεσφιν, 572) and perhaps have power to hound in death as well as life (see 3.278–9, 19.259–60 and nn.). The Erinues are a formidable sanction, but then keeping the oath and honouring parents are principles that are not easily enforced except by moral terrorism. — ἐπεκέκλετ(ο): by beating on the ground, see 568. One appealed to the Olympians standing and raising the arms. — 'Ερινῦς: an archaic acc. pl. in -ῦς (< -ύνς) of *u*-stems is common in the epic beside the secondary -ύας (ἐρινύας 21.412).

455 ἐφέσσεσθαι is future middle, 'that he should set on his knees' a grandson, cf 488 and *Od.* 16.443 (γούνασιν οἷσιν ἐφεσσάμενος). The v.l. γούνασ' ἐμοῖσιν is an obvious *facilior lectio*.

457 'Zeus under the earth' apparently = Plouton/Hades, a unique designation in Homer, but cf. Διὶ χθονίῳ, Hesiod, *Erga* 465, and for other references West's note *ad loc.*, and Nilsson, *GgrR* 1 376. Persephone is joined with Hades, as expected, in a similar context at 569.

458–61 These verses are absent from the MS tradition, the tradition of the scholia, and the late first- or early second-century glossary Pack² 1189, but are cited by Plutarch, *Mor.* 26 (and in part at *Mor.* 72B and *Vita Coriolani* 32). They owe their status in the printed vulgate to Wolf. Plutarch does not state his source for the verses, but alleges that Aristarchus removed (ἐξεῖλε) them. That seems to have been a rash inference on Plutarch's (or his source's) part from the absence of the verses from the vulgate. It would not be surprising, of course, if Aristarchus had been shocked, as Plutarch reports, at Phoinix' admission that it crossed his mind to murder his father, cf. 453n.; it is more surprising that he would have dared to set aside the paradosis and that his excision could have had such a subsequent effect. If the verses had stood in the early Hellenistic vulgate, Aristarchus would have athetized them and they would stand so stigmatized in our MSS. See Bolling, *External Evidence* 121, Apthorp, *MS Evidence* 91–9. This is a strong argument, for the evidence is slight that Aristarchus excised without diplomatic support. (It is possible that the 'shock' was not that of Aristarchus but that of earlier and more irresponsible transmitters of the Homeric text, for which see Janko, vol. IV 28.) The lines, however, are Homeric in style and language and motivate Phoinix' flight, cf. van der Valk, *Researches* II 483, 'Homer has to give a representation in which Phoinix is forced to leave his country and to take refuge with Peleus. To this end he invents a quarrel between Phoinix and his father. In ordinary circumstances we might have expected that Phoinix would have killed his father and fled from home. Homer, however, is loth to present facts which are very offensive. This time he has the more reason to be cautious, because Phoinix is Achilles' preceptor.'

464 ἕται are usually grouped with κασίγνητοι, cf. 6.239 (see n.), 16.456 (= 674), *Od.* 4.3, 15.273. The sense is imprecise; Hoekstra (on *Od.* 15.273) suggests that the formulas signify something like *cognati et socii* (who might all, of course, be *gentiles*). Chantraine, *Dict.* s.v., cites an extensive bibliography; see also 6.239n. The intentions and motivation of Amuntor's relatives, whose behaviour towards his property is reminiscent of that of Penelope's suitors, are unclear, especially if 458–61 are retained, but evidently coercive. One may perhaps compare the action of the Spartan ephors in blockading Pausanias in the temple of Athena until he was on the point of death (Thuc. 1.134), but what then would they be imploring (λισσόμενοι 465)

Phoinix to do? R. Carpenter, *Folktale, Fiction, and Saga in the Homeric Epics* (Berkeley and Los Angeles 1946) 170–2, recalls a story in Herodotus (7.197) about the family of Phrixos at Alos in Thessaly, whose eldest son was forbidden to enter the prytaneum on pain of never leaving except to be sacrificed, and how many had fled the country in consequence; but again what would be the point of λισσόμενοι?

466–9 = 23.166 (and ≃ Hesiod, *Erga* 795, fr. 198.11 M–W). For a briefer version of this list see *Od.* 9.45–6 ἔνθα δὲ πολλὸν μὲν μέθυ πίνετο, πολλὰ δὲ μῆλα | ἔσφαζον παρὰ θῖνα καὶ εἰλίποδας ἕλικας βοῦς. — ἕλικας βοῦς: 'crumpled kine', with or without 'swinging feet' is the regular formula (6× *Il.*, 8× *Od.* with variants). Some ancient commentators (see the evidence cited by Pfeiffer to Callimachus fr. 299 (= fr. 116 Hollis) suggested ἕλιξ = 'black', mainly to make sense of ἑλίκωψ, -ῶπις. 'Black' commended itself to Hellenistic poets, see A. S. F. Gow on Theocritus, *Id.* 25.127, and was accepted by Page (*HHI* 244–5) with reference to the epithet ἑλίκωπες. *HyHerm* 192 (βόας) κεράεσσιν ἑλικτάς doubtless paraphrases the sense as it was understood in the Late Archaic period. εἰλίποδας stands in contrast to ἀερσίποδες of horses (18.532).

467 θαλέθοντες ἀλοιφῇ is the nominative plural of τεθαλυῖαν ἀλοιφῇ 208 (see n.), also of pigs and pork. The suffix -θ- has stative or perfective force.

468 = 23.33. φλογὸς Ἡφαίστοιο: it is possible to take Ἡφαίστοιο as the god himself, as also at 17.88 and *Od.* 24.71, but at 2.426, σπλάγχνα … ὑπείρεχον Ἡφαίστοιο, Hephaistos simply represents fire, as Amphitrite (*Od.* 3.91) represents sea.

470 εἰνάνυχες: nine days (or nights) is a formular number, cf. 1.53, 24.664, 24.784.

478 εὐρυχόροιο: see 23.299n. and Hoekstra, *Od.* on 13.414. The epithet is most appropriately applied to towns (Mukalessos, Sikuon, Iolkos, Hupereie, Thebes, Sparta) but describes the district Elis at *Od.* 4.635. The importance of the χορός as a public religious ceremony is sufficient to explain the origin of the epithet. A conflation of its sense with εὐρύχωρος has been suspected, but is not certain before Pindar.

479–84 This part of Phoinix' story is parallel to that of the homicides Epeigeus (16.571–4), Patroklos (23.85–90), both of whom took refuge with Peleus, Tlepolemos (2.661–3), Lukophron (15.430–2), Medon (13.694–7 = 15.335–6), and the anonymous murderer of 24.480, cf. *Od.* 13.258–75 (a fictitious Cretan), 14.379–81 (an anonymous Aetolian), 15.272–8 (Theoklumenos), 23.118–20 (unnamed), Pausanias 7.3.3 (Promethos), and Peleus himself, exiled from Aigina for his part in the murder of Phokos (*Alkmaionis* fr. 1 Davies). These anecdotes of obligatory exiles clearly refer to a recognized practice of the archaic age, cf. R. R. Schlunk, *AJP* 97 (1976) 199–209. It was still known to Herodotus (1.35, Adrestos). One may compare the 'cities of refuge' of the Israelites (Joshua 20.1ff.). Alternatively the homicide might buy off the avengers (632–6).

479 ἐριβῶλαξ, 'with large clods', i.e. 'fertile', is a regular epithet of Phthie (2× and 1× ἐρίβωλος 363 above), but only here is the country said also to be 'mother of flocks'. ἐριβώλακα μητέρα μήλων etc. is probably formular (here and 11.222). At 1.155 the singer preferred βωτιανείρῃ for μητέρι μήλων. Did/AT at 11.222 attribute μητέρι θηρῶν to Zenodotus, but that is hardly congruous with ἐριβῶλαξ. There are no scholia to this verse. μ. μήλων is epithet of Phthie also at [Hesiod] fr. 211.1 M–W.

482 μοῦνον τηλύγετον is probably formular, cf. *Od.* 16.19, and so narrows the sense of τηλύγετος to something appropriate to an only son. There is no convincing etymology, cf. 143n.

483–4 Peleus treated Phoinix as Agamemnon proposed to treat Akhilleus (149–56), giving him a small kingdom. — ὤπασε λαόν (probably formular, cf. λαὸν ὄπασσε 18.452) does not imply a gift without strings: Phoinix thereby became ὀπάων of Peleus (cf. 23.360). For the relationship see 7.165n. and P. A. L. Greenhalgh, *BICS* 29 (1982) 81–90. The Dolopes, a hill tribe, are subsequently found to the east of Phthiotis and north of the Ainianes (with whom they are regularly linked, e.g. Hdt. 7.132, 185). They appear only here in Homer.

485–95 Phoinix speaks in the time-honoured manner of the aged retainer, fondly remembering the hero at an unheroic age, cf. Aesch. *Cho.* 750–60, or the Nurse in *Romeo and Juliet* Act I, Sc. 3. The effect of 492 πόλλ᾽ ἔπαθον καὶ πόλλ᾽ ἐμόγησα is comic, but the comedy quickly turns to the pathos of blighted hope: not for long will Akhilleus live to repay Phoinix' parental care. Where, it may be wondered, was Akhilleus' natural parent during his babyhood? Homer gives no answer, having exercised his authorial privilege to ignore the relations of Thetis with her mortal family. Tradition had it that she deserted Peleus during Akhilleus' infancy, leaving him to be reared, not as here by Phoinix, but by the centaur Kheiron, see Kullmann, *Quellen* 371, G. Schoek, *Ilias und Aithiopis* (Zürich 1961) 54.

485 τοσοῦτον is usually taken (e.g. by Leaf) to mean 'as big ⟨as you are now⟩' i.e. 'I reared you to manhood'; but the absence of any correlative to τοσοῦτον is awkward. Lohmann, *Reden* 249–50, having noted the parallel phraseology of 485 and 483 ([Πηλεὺς] μ᾽ ἀφνειὸν ἔθηκε), proposes to understand τοσοῦτον = ἀφνειόν and πολὺν λαὸν ἔχοντα, and to omit 484 to make the parallelism clearer. Phoinix would then be making a good point – 'As Peleus was to me, so am I to you.'

486 ἐκ θυμοῦ φιλέων: Phoinix echoes Akhilleus' language at 343 (his love for Briseis), but the text lacks any overt indication that the echo is deliberate or what the point would be if it were. ἐκ θυμοῦ φιλέειν does not recur.

488–9 See *Od.* 16.443–4 for a similar description of an infant set on the knee to be fed. Phoinix' role is that of a proud friend of the family, not that of a menial. In the Odyssean passage it is Odysseus himself who is represented as offering meat and wine to the infant Eurumakhos. — καθίσσας: the present is καθ-έζομαι/ίζω (< *sed-, *si-sd-) and the aor. indic. εἷσα, so that the orthography of the aor. participle should be καθ-έσ(σ)ας, but -εσσ- is pre-empted for parts of ἕννυμι and καθίζω is given the conjugation of a regular -ίζω verb.

490–1 There are no scholia to these verses although the amusing image of a slobbering infant might have been thought ἀπρεπές and more appropriate to the stylistic level of old comedy, cf. the vulgar image at Ar. *Nub.* 1380–5. Presumably the Alexandrians did not find it beneath the dignity they wished the epic genre to possess. In any case their objections were not to frank or brutal realism, of which there is plenty on the battlefield, but to acts or language that seemed to them to demean gods and major heroes. The scholiasts condemn, for example, the language of Agamemnon at 1.29–31 and that of Akhilleus at 1.225–33, they deplore his jealousy of Patroklos' success at 16.89–90 and the imputation to him of mercenary motives at 24.555–7; they dislike the idea that the gods might feel fear (1.396–406) or passion (14.153–353 and n.), and use violence (15.18–31). Mentions of grime, sweat, and blood pass without comment. One of Aristarchus' principles was that speech and character were harmonized in Homer (ἐν ἤθει λέγεται, e.g. Arn/A at 1.117), a view that would have protected Phoinix' reminiscence.

491 νηπιέη is for νηπιίη. On the formation see Chantraine, *Dict.*, and Schwyzer, *Gr. Gr.* 104. The word means 'the behaviour to be expected of a νήπιος': play at 15.363, folly at 20.411 and *Od.* 24.469. Hsch. glosses νηπύτιος with ἄφωνον, but see Chantraine, *Dict.* s.v. νήπιος; a connexion with (ϝ)έπος is impossible.

492 ≅ *Od.* 5.223 ≅ 8.155. Aristarchus here read πολλὰ πάθον καὶ πολλὰ μόγησα, moved perhaps by such variants of the formula as πολλὰ πάθοι (22.220), πολλὰ μογήσας etc. (2.690, 12× *Od.*), but more likely by his preference for the unaugmented forms, see Chantraine in P. Mazon, *Introduction à l'Iliade*, 2nd edn (Paris 1948) 133–4, for Aristarchus' views. See also 10.546n. The formula is associated with the travail of war, e.g. *Od.* 8.490, and may strike the reader as comic hyperbole for the sufferings of a male nurse; if so, it would be a happy chance, for the formular style must often proceed in an unusual passage by approximating the sense required with expressions proper to another context.

496 δαμάζειν is a powerful word appropriate for mastering violent heroic emotions; it recurs with the θυμός as its object at 18.133 = 19.66 and *Od.* 11.562. The θυμός is the seat of the passion to which Akhilleus has yielded, cf. J. N. Bremmer, *The Early Greek Concept of the Soul* (Princeton 1983) 54–6, with bibliography. The φρένες, of which Zeus deprives a man when he is misguided (e.g. 9.377), are the seat of reason.

497 στρεπτοὶ δέ τε καὶ θεοὶ αὐτοί has a proverbial ring. But Phoinix is suiting his doctrine to his argument. The gods could be relentless, cf. Aesch. *Ag.* 68–71 τελεῖται δ' ἐς τὸ πεπρωμένον· | οὔθ' ὑποκαίων οὔτ' ἐπιλείβων | οὔτε †δακρύων† ἀπύρων ἱερῶν | ὀργὰς ἀτενεῖς παραθέλξει. Akhilleus was slow to learn; at 24.40–1 Apollo complained that he did not have a νόημα | γναμπτὸν ἐνὶ στήθεσσι and therefore had no pity.

498 Plato cites the allegory of the Λιταί twelve times (four in *Hipp. Min.*). At *Rep.* 364D, he quotes 496–501 without 498, but there was no Alexandrian athetesis. Plato's citations are often made 'avec plus ou moins de complaisance' (J. Labarbe, *L'Homère de Platon* (Liège 1949)). Here the citation has λιστοί for στρεπτοί and θυσίαισι for θυέεσσι. — The verses make a point for Phoinix, to forestall any objection that Akhilleus might make on the grounds that forgiveness was a sign of weakness.

501 λισσόμενοι, for εὐχόμενοι 'praying', is not used elsewhere in the epic for the action of mortals approaching a god (though perhaps implied by πολύλλιστον δέ σ' ἱκάνω (σ' = the river god), *Od.* 5.445). Phoinix is laying the foundation for the allegory of the Λιταί and at the same time puts the action of the Achaeans in a wholly new light. Nestor (112) described their approach as persuasion, an offer of restitution made man to man; Odysseus modified that posture, appealing to Akhilleus' pity (302), but this is the first time that the Achaeans are implicitly said to have been 'imploring' Akhilleus. This is the language of supplication (1.502, 21.98), or at least of humble request, to which Agamemnon said he would not stoop at 1.173–4 and which Akhilleus anticipates with a certain relish at 11.609. It is one thing to reject an argument, quite another to refuse a suppliant, especially a suppliant bearing gifts; cf. Thornton, *Supplication* 111, and the parallel there cited. Phoinix is putting Akhilleus under strong moral pressure. λίσ-σεσθαι continues to be used both in the story of Meleagros (574, 581 (λιτάνευε), 585, 591) and in reference to the embassy itself (520, 698). Ominously, it was the word used on another occasion when ἀπερείσι' ἄποινα were on offer (1.13). — ὑπερβήῃ: the metaphorical sense of ὑπερβαίνειν is found only here in the epics. The related noun ὑπερβασίη, however, occurs 3× in each in reference to the breach of some norm of behaviour inspired by arrogance (see 3.107). The corresponding adjective is ὑπέρβιος (2× *Il.*, 7× *Od.*). Phoinix' doctrine is inevitable: if one believes that a god can be affronted, one must believe that an affronted god can be conciliated by sacrifice. So Apollo was angry at the treatment of his priest and was then propitiated with hecatombs (1.43–52, 1.447–74), see e.g. Thornton, *Supplication* 113–14, for the parallel with book 1. — ἁμάρτῃ in a metaphorical sense recurs in a religious context in the epic only at *Od.*

13.214, linguistically a very untraditional passage, see Hoekstra, *Od. ad loc.*,
but also at Hesiod, *Theog.* 222, with reference to παραιβασίαι.

502–12 The Λιταί: Phoinix produces an allegory (as we should call it),
a figure rarely employed in Greek epic, cf. 505n., because 'in Hesiod's time
it was not understood what abstractions are. They must be something; they
are invisible, imperishable, and have great influence over human affairs;
they must be gods' (West, *Theogony* 33). A rejected suppliant, like Khruses
in book 1, prayed to the god whom his rejection had dishonoured for
vengeance. The allegory, however, embellishes that natural and comprehensible action in a way that complicates the doctrine and its application
to the present case. A chain of action and reaction is begun by Ἄτη (505).
Ἄτη here has in personified form its usual Homeric sense of the spirit that
inspires an act of irrational folly (cf. ἀασάμην 116, of Agamemnon's behaviour in book 1); it is, so to speak, an inexplicable act of god (cf. the
formula φρένας ἐξέλετο Ζεύς, 2× *Il.* and several variants), but one that
produces unwelcome consequences. At 508 the allegory moves clearly into
the human sphere; the Λιταί represent an appeal addressed by the victim
of Ἄτη to the injured party. It is a moral duty to respect such an appeal; if
it is not respected, there will be trouble. Phoinix imagines the rejected Λιταί
as themselves praying to Zeus for vengeance. The vengeance again takes the
form of ἄτη (512) leading to disaster. ἄτη in Homer always implies disastrous consequences (see 511n.), and disaster (ἄτη in the classical sense) is
easily explicable as punishment. The idea that wickedness will be punished
is Homeric (e.g. 4.158–62, *Od.* 13.213–14), but ἄτη is applied elsewhere in
both epics to the crime not the punishment.

Phoinix' doctrine is tailored to his argument. Isolated, it is confused. Ἄτη
first acts spontaneously, then is sent by Zeus, and her victim would offer
restitution, not prayers, to the injured party. If the allegory is applied to
the present situation, it implies that the seizure of Briseis was the result of
ἄτη, that the offer of restitution is an appeal, and that the consequence of
rejection will be more ἄτη. Only the first of these implications is demonstrably true; the second is false, and the third is sustainable only by special
exegesis.

Since all events are subject to the Διὸς βουλή, and since the *Iliad* is more
than a chronicle of events, it is correct to see a moral connexion between
the temper of Akhilleus and his fate. In that sense the death of Patroklos
and his own πότμος ἑτοῖμος are a penalty brought upon him by his own
intransigence, not a morally neutral chain of causes and effects. The poet,
however, never suggests or makes Akhilleus suggest that subsequent events
were brought about by ἄτη overcoming him or that such ἄτη was itself
a penalty. The ἄτη ('loss of consciousness') that overcame Patroklos
(16.805) is irrelevant (but see Thornton, *Supplication* 135–6, 'Blind Madness

"follows" Achilles, and it does so by attacking his "substitute", his beloved friend Patroclus', *contra* Redfield, *Nature and Culture* 107, 'The crucial errors in Achilles' story are the errors of others – of Agamemnon, of Nestor, of Patroclus'). It should be borne in mind that the appeal to ἄτη is exculpatory. The poet does not wish to excuse Akhilleus and Akhilleus does not wish to excuse himself. He kills Hektor in the clear knowledge that his victory dooms him (see 18.95–6). That is heroism.

Whether Akhilleus' obduracy itself is caused by ἄτη is not in question here either. As an action with disastrous results it could no doubt be characterized as such, but neither Aias nor Diomedes does so characterize it, nor does Akhilleus in his brief comment on his relations with Agamemnon at 19.270–5.

502–3 The description of the Λιταί clearly must be pathetic, so that their being παραβλῶπες ὀφθαλμώ does not express suspicion (as παραβλέπω does in classical Greek) but apprehension and a sense of helplessness. For the form of words καὶ γάρ τε Λιταί εἰσι see West, *Works and Days* 142; it is characteristic of admonitory literature.

505 Ἄτη σθεναρή τε καὶ ἀρτίπος: cf. 19.91ff. πρέσβα Διὸς θυγάτηρ Ἄτη, ἣ πάντας ἀᾶται, | οὐλομένη. τῇ μέν θ' ἁπαλοὶ πόδες· οὐ γὰρ ἐπ' οὔδει | πίλναται, ἀλλ' ἄρα ἥ γε κατ' ἀνδρῶν κράατα βαίνει | βλάπτουσ' ἀνθρώπους.

Ἄτη is swift and strong because her victims are reckless. — οὕνεκα 'means "this I conclude from the fact that"', so H. Fränkel, *Early Greek Poetry and Philosophy*, transl. M. Hadas and J. Willis (Oxford 1975) 65, a hint that Phoinix himself should be understood as the author of this piece of allegorical theology.

511 The Λιταί have something in common with the Hesiodic Δίκη (*Erga* 256–62). When Δίκη is oppressed she complains to Zeus for vindication. Zeus is said to cause ἄτη generally at 19.270 and in specific instances (all false attributions) at 2.111, 8.237. 9.18, and 19.87; other gods mentioned are Moira and Erinus (19.87); Erinus alone (*Od.* 15.234); Aphrodite (*Od.* 4.261); Apollo (16.804–5). All these attributions (except the last, which is made by the poet) are made *post eventum*, and only when the speaker realizes that his mistake has led to unwelcome consequences (see 116n.). Phoinix reverses the thought and makes what is usually said as an explanation of what has happened into a prediction of what will happen. Since he is portraying the situation as a rejection of suppliants it is natural – and a powerful reinforcement of his argument – that he should name Zeus as the author of ἄτη.

515 Why γάρ? The reason is that implicit in Phoinix' appeal: '⟨You can accept my argument,⟩ for I should not be making it if Agamemnon were not now doing the right thing.' Leaf ('You may do so without disgrace') and Ameis – Hentze offer similar suggestions. This seems preferable to the suggestion of W. J. Verdenius, *REG* 73 (1960) 348, that Phoinix' thought slips imperceptibly from the respect due to a god from a hero to the respect due to a hero from other heroes (cf. 318–20n.).

517 For the sense of μῆνις see 426n.

519–23 This is the same argument as the one that Aias will put forward at 636–42; a decent request made by good friends and representatives of the army is being snubbed. For Akhilleus' differing responses see 643–55n.

523 Phoinix' remark that Akhilleus' anger had formerly been no matter of reproach implies that his dismissal of the illustrious ambassadors had made it just that. Hence the strong language of Aias at 629–32, 635–6 (ἄγριος, σχέτλιος, νηλής, ἀγήνωρ, ἄλληκτος, κακός), and Patroklos 16.29–35 (ἀμήχανος, νηλής, ἀπηνής).

524–605 The Meleagros story. A guide to the extensive bibliography on the story is given by F. Bömer, *P. Ovidius Naso, Metamorphosen viii–ix* (Heidelberg 1977) 94–8; the most important papers relevant to its use here are cited by Page, *HHI* 329; they include, E. Howald, *RhM* 73 (1924) 402–25, Kakridis, *Researches* 11–42, Schadewaldt, *Iliasstudien*, 139–42, W. Kraus, *WS* 63 (1948–9) 8–21, M. M. Willcock, *CQ* 14 (1964) 147, J. R. March, *BICS* Suppl. 49 (1987) 22–46, and S. C. R. Swain, *CQ* 38 (1988) 271–6. The principal ancient sources in addition to the present passage are [Hesiod] frr. 25 and 280 M–W, Bacchylides 5.94–154, Ovid, *Met.* 8.273–525, Paus. 10.31.3, and Apollod. 1.8.1–3

The story of Kaludon (linked with stories of Elis and Pulos) is one of the four cycles into which [Hesiod], *Catalogue of Women*, organized the population of the Heroic Age, the others being those of Iolkos, Thebes, and Troy, see West, *Catalogue* 137. The possession of this 'knowledge' was essential to the art of the ἀοιδός, and Homer clearly knows more than it suits him to bring into the *Iliad*: reference to other cycles is made also at 4.370ff., 5.395ff., 7.132ff., 11.670ff., 23.630ff., 23.679, and *Od.* 12.69ff.

The mythological paradigm is part of the Homeric rhetoric of persuasion, the speaker suggesting that the present situation is analogous to the one cited. The paradigm that Phoinix requires is that of a warrior who in anger scorned the appeals of his friends for aid. Phoinix cites the example of the Aetolian Meleagros. It is not the happiest of choices. Having just declared that even the gods are στρεπτοί (497) he cites the vindictiveness of Artemis over the sin of Oineus, cf. Bacchylides 5.94–104 χαλεπὸν | θεῶν παρατρέψαι νόον | ἄνδρεσσιν ἐπιχθονίοις. | καὶ γὰρ ἂν πλάξιππος Οἰνεύς | παῦσεν καλυκοστεφάνου | σεμνᾶς χόλον Ἀρτέμιδος λευκωλένου | λισσόμενος πολέων | τ' αἰγῶν θυσίαισι πατήρ | καὶ βοῶν φοινικονώτων· | ἀλλ' ἀνίκατον θεά | ἔσχεν χόλον. Moreover the end of the saga of Meleagros was the hero's death. The end of Meleagros, of course, was no part of Phoinix' parable, and he omits *all* direct reference to it as irrelevant (and indeed inimical) to

his purposes. The heroic days of Kaludon preceded the Trojan War by two
or three generations (see the genealogy 555–8n.); the Aitoloi are now led
by Thoas (2.638–42, where it is explained that the sons of Oineus were now
all dead). Phoinix begins his parable by setting the scene, how the Aitoloi
and the Kouretes were at war, in the succinct narrative style usual in
Homeric allusions to other sagas (529–49). The narrative at this point
is compressed, but perfectly clear.

Phoinix then explains (550–72) how Meleagros, after lording it over
the battlefield, had taken to his bed in wrath because, having killed his
mother's brother, he had been cursed by her. There is vagueness here.
Around whose city were the Aitoloi and Kouretes fighting? (See 552n.).
Who was Althaie's brother (the singular is used, 567) and how had
Meleagros come to kill him? How was her curse to operate? Why is
Alkuone/Kleopatre introduced at such length? Althaie's brothers are called
Iphiklos and Aphares by Bacchylides, Plexippus and Toxeus by Ovid,
Prothoos and Kometes by Pausanias, and Iphiklos, Plexippos, Poluphantes,
Phanes, and Eurupulos by Hrd/D. Such wide fluctuation indicates that no
canonical form of the story existed. In most accounts Meleagros had killed
his uncles in a dispute arising from the spoils of the Calydonian boar
(Bacchylides 5.127–35, Ovid, *Met.* 8.425–44). Althaie's response was to
seize the firebrand that represented Meleagros' life and throw it on the fire.
As it burned, Meleagros' strength ebbed away as he fought. The primitive
features of the story, the magical firebrand itself and the preference for
brothers over a son are warrant enough for a very ancient origin, see
Kakridis, *Researches* 14, 37 and Appendices i and iii, and for life-tokens as a
motif of folktale see S. Thompson, *Motif Index* E 765.1.2. However, the
question must be asked, though it cannot be answered, when the syncretism
of the folktale of the firebrand and the saga of Meleagros took place.
The association of firebrand and Meleagros first appears in Phrynichus'
Pleuroniae, then at Bacchylides 5.140–4, and Aesch. *Cho.* 602. For Kleopatre
see 561–3n.

Phoinix next proceeds to put the sting in the tale of his parable: offers
were made to Meleagros which he rejected until his house was under
bombardment (573–94). Then he had to fight, gifts or (as it happened) no
gifts. At this point of course Phoinix stops, though everyone would know
that Meleagros went out to his death, as Patroklos and soon Akhilleus
himself would do, and in each death Apollo would play a part.

Homer's version of the story is maverick in that it incorporates a 'wrath'.
Apollodorus cites it as an alternative (οἱ δέ φασι . . .), making no attempt
to blend it with the folktale. Did Homer invent his version? It is a thesis
strongly affirmed by Willcock, *CQ* 14 (1964) 141–54, that Homeric practice is to improve the fit of a paradigm by invented detail within the

traditional framework. In this case the poet will have shielded himself against criticism of his veracity by having Phoinix introduce his reminiscences with ἐπευθόμεθα (524). He will then have suppressed the firebrand, if it were already linked to Meleagros, but retained an echo of it in Althaie's curse. (The curse, of course, has no corresponding element on Akhilleus' side and is not itself a heroic motif.) He may also have introduced the name Κλεοπάτρη (561–3n.) and the ἑταῖροι of 585.

In the Hesiodic Ἠοῖαι (frr. 25.11–13, and 280 M–W), an exceedingly laconic notice, Meleagros is irresistible in the war with the Kouretes until he dies at the hands of Apollo, a heroic death similar to that of Akhilleus. The account in the *Minyas*, of which [Hesiod] fr. 25 M–W may be a fragment (so J. Schwartz, *Pseudo-Hesiodeia* (Leiden 1960) 28), stood in contrast to that of Althaie's curse, according to Paus. 10.31.3. It is unclear if or how the 'heroic' version of Meleagros' death can be reconciled with the folktale of the firebrand. Bacchylides has gone some way by slipping, not without awkwardness, from a quarrel over the boar's hide to full-scale war in which Meleagros unintentionally killed his uncles and died as he was looting a corpse. Further divination of the pre-Homeric tale is hampered by the fluctuations in the primary sources, see H. Bannert, *WS* 15 (1981) 69 n. 1, for the literature on the question, and for some speculations J. R. March, *BICS* Suppl. 49 (1987) 27–46. The extent of Homeric freedom in the use of a paradigm is most readily visible in the poet's telling of the Niobe story (24.602–20, with Macleod's note), but adjustment to improve the fit of the paradigm is not the same as inventing the very point which is to be invoked as a precedent, a point stressed by W. Kraus, *WS* 63 (1948–9) 8–21. Willcock, *Companion* 109, poses the alternatives: either the plot of the *Iliad* is modelled on a '*Meleagris*' or the parable on the *Iliad* – too stark a choice; the theme of anger – withdrawal – disaster – return informs both stories.

Like other digressions the Meleagros episode shows a higher density of 'late' or anomalous features in its language and diction in comparison with a similar passage of narrative. Page, *HHI* 327–9, and Shipp, *Studies* 270–2, list these; the more important of them are discussed below as they occur. Verbal parallels between the parable and narrative are examined by G. Nagy, *Best of the Achaeans* 100–6.

527 πάλαι, οὔ τι νέον γε suggests an ancient tale relative to the dramatic date of the *Iliad*, yet as the genealogies were regularized Meleagros lived only in the previous generation, see the stemma 558–8n. Phoinix (and the poet?) wishes to distance himself from affirming the historicity of the story.

529 Κουρῆτες: as a tribe the K. are known only in this context. Their town was Pleuron, about ten miles west of Kaludon. The name Κουρῆτες occurs by coincidence also in various Cretan rituals, see Burkert, *Religion*, 261–2, and at a later date in association with cults in Asia Minor. As a common noun with proparoxytone accent, κούρητες, the word means simply 'young warriors', 19.193 and n.

533–40 The verses express succinctly an article of popular religion: a disaster happens to the community; therefore a god has been offended; therefore the community's leaders have forgotten some ritual. The boar identifies Artemis as the offended deity, just as the plague in book 1 identified Apollo – and there too first thoughts turned to a ritual offence, εἴθ' εὐχωλῆς εἴθ' ἑκατόμβης (1.65).

533 Artemis' golden throne, like Iris' golden wings (8.398 = 11.185), is part of the aura of felicity that surrounds the gods. It is not just the luxury of the material, however, that is in question; gold is ἀγήραος, so to speak, and therefore ἀθάνατος, cf. Theogn. 451–2 τοῦ [χρυσοῦ] χροιῆς καθύπερθε μέλας οὐχ ἅπτεται ἰὸς | οὐδ' εὐρώς, αἰεὶ δ' ἄνθος ἔχει καθαρόν; Pind. fr. 222 Snell Διὸς παῖς ὁ χρυσός· κεῖνον οὐ σὴς οὐδὲ κίς [δάπτει].

535 δαίνυνθ', if pressed, provides the only instance in the epic of the gods being said to share the sacrificial meat of ordinary mortals – and presumably descending to earth to do so. The Aithiopes and Phaeacians who are so favoured (23.205, *Od.* 1.25, 7.201) do not belong to the real world, where it is the savour of the sacrifice that the gods appreciate. See Introduction of vol. II 9–12. In so laconic a reference, however, δαίνυσθαι may be taken in a very unspecific sense, 'partake of'.

537 ἢ λάθετ' ἢ οὐκ ἐνόησεν: in any case not a deliberate snub, not that the goddess cared about that. What mattered in the sphere of religion in the Archaic Age, as in the ascription of blame in the moral sphere, was the fact not the intention. The gods required the respect of mankind to complete their happiness. In Bacchylides (5.97–102) Oineus tried unsuccessfully with prayer and sacrifice to redeem his fault, but it would not do to make such a point in the present context. — Note that λανθάνεσθαι and οὐ νοεῖν explicate ἄασθαι. ἢ οὐκ: synizesis, cf. *Od.* 1.298.

538 δῖον γένος recurs at *HyDion* 2, where the meaning is clearly 'offspring of Zeus'. The phrase then stands in apposition to the subject ἥ, and δῖος (< διϝyος) bears its primary and precise sense.

539–40 Aristotle (*Hist. An.* 578a33) contaminated these verses with *Od.* 9.190–1, the description of the Cyclops, and read θρέψεν [a trivial substitution for ὦρσεν] ... οὐδὲ ἐῴκει | θηρί γε σιτοφάγῳ, ἀλλὰ ῥίῳ ὑλήεντι. Strabo (*apud* Eust. 252) cited the verses from Aristotle, thus creating the mirage of a genuine paradosis. — χλούνην: conjectures at the meaning of this obscure term are legion, see Chantraine, *Dict.* s.v., e.g. 'castrated' (Aristotle), 'solitary' (Eust. 772.59, citing Aristophanes Byz.), 'foaming' (schol. B).

540 ἔθων: only here and 16.260 (simile). On this word see Frisk, *GEW* s.v., with bibliography. 'Suo more', Leaf, but a link with εἴωθα is a popular rather than a scientific etymology. Arn/A and Hsch. cite a gloss βλάπτων, which was approved by Callimachus (fr. 55 Pfeiffer). ἀλωήν would then be the object of ἔθων, if one could be sure the poet more than half understood the word.

543–4 Meleagros' standing as a hero later elevated his parentage; he is firmly son of Oineus in the *Iliad*, but was attributed to Ares in [Hesiod] fr. 25.1ff. M–W, cf. the similar elevation of Bellerophon (son of Poseidon [Hesiod] fr. 43a.81 M–W, in defiance of 6.155). The many θηρήτορες that Meleagros recruited would have made a fine catalogue (see the list in Ovid, *Met.* 8.301–17) and would have included Atalante, to whom first blood was credited and to whom Meleagros awarded the spoils. Her omission from this succinct allusion is without special significance; she would not, for example, be parallel to Briseis as the cause of strife and her exotic character would clash with the low-key, realistic style of this summary.

546 πυρῆς ἐπέβησ᾽ ἀλεγεινῆς is evidently formular, cf. πυρῆς ἐπιβάντ᾽ ἀλεγεινῆς (4.99, see n.). The *Aithiopis*, with its many funerals, would have had more use for this area of diction.

551 κακῶς ἦν: for εἶναι construed with an adverb (a construction more familiar in Latin) see Chantraine, *GH* II 9.

552 The desire to make parallel the situations of Meleagros and Akhilleus has led to some lack of clarity. Kaludon was the city under siege (530–2), but the τεῖχος behind which the Kouretes were obliged to remain would naturally be the wall of their own city (Pleuron, but here unnamed), just as the Trojans did not dare to come out to face Akhilleus, cf. [Hesiod] fr. 25.13 M–W μαρνάμενος Κουρ[ῆσι περὶ Πλ]ε[υ]ρῶν[ι] μακεδνῇ. But the Kouretes are the aggressors (531–2) and should now be fighting around Kaludon, as they are below at 573. It is possible, in order to save the narrative, to imagine that the τεῖχος is the wall of the Kouretes' fortified encampment corresponding to the wall of the Achaeans' lately fortified camp, but nothing in the immediate context suggests it.

553–4 ἔδυ χόλος: the emotion as usual is conceived to originate outside the person and to 'enter' him or be 'put on', cf. 9.231 δύσεαι ἀλκήν. ἄλλων is a rather obvious oblique reference to Akhilleus, softened by νόον πύκα περ φρονεόντων.

555–8 The genealogies of the kings of Pleuron and Kaludon are intertwined, as shown in the two stemmata. (For other offspring of Oineus and Althaie see [Hesiod] fr. 25.14–17 M–W. The Aetolian saga (a sorry tale of intestine murder) included Oineus' slaying of his brothers, Agrios and Melas, sons of Porthaon (or Portheus, 14.115), and was linked to that of Herakles through H.'s marriage to Deianeira, sister to Meleagros.)

The names in both stemmata form part of the Kaludon – Elis – Pulos cycle in the Hesiodic catalogues and may have been consolidated into their genealogy in the first half of the eighth century, as argued by West, *Catalogue*

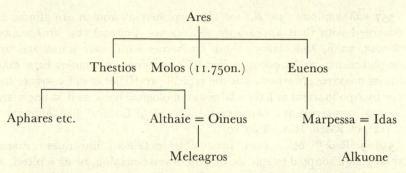

Ares

Thestios Molos (11.750n.) Euenos

Aphares etc. Althaie = Oineus Marpessa = Idas

Meleagros Alkuone

164ff. None of them (except Thersites, whose ancestry is carefully unstated at 2.212ff., and Diomedes) interlocks closely with the personnel of the Trojan saga and there is indecision as to which generations correspond. A pathetic comment in the Catalogue (2.641–2) implies that Meleagros might have commanded the Aitoloi at Troy, though as a contemporary of Herakles he should belong to the previous generation. Apollonius put both Idas and Meleagros among the Argonauts (*Arg.* 1.151, 1.190), and Stesichorus (fr. 179(ii) Davies Ἄθλα ἐπὶ Πελίᾳ) linked Meleagros with Amphiaraos. At 14.116 the sons of Portheus (Porthaon) are said to have resided in Pleuron *and* Kaludon.

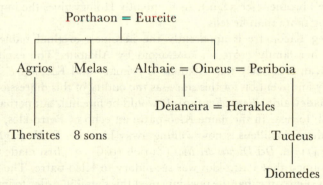

Porthaon = Eureite

Agrios Melas Althaie = Oineus = Periboia

Deianeira = Herakles

Thersites 8 sons Tudeus

Diomedes

555 μητρὶ φίλῃ: καθόλου τὸ φίλῃ· οὐ γὰρ ἦν αὐτῷ τότε φίλη ἡ μήτηρ (T), i.e. the formula is used in an inappropriate context, cf. Eriphule's 'dear' husband at *Od.* 11.327. Irony is easily understood in both cases (as also at 21.276), but is probably accidental. μητρὶ φίλῃ is formular (4× *Il.* 1× *Od.*). For the supposed weak possessive use of φίλος see D. Robinson in *Owls to Athens* (*Essays for Sir Kenneth Dover*) (Oxford 1990) 97–108, with a brief bibliography of Homeric φίλος.

556–65 Setting the scene for his parable in succinct style Phoinix now digresses (note the ring-form κεῖτο ... παρκατέλεκτο) and compresses his allusions to the point of obscurity.

557 καλλισφύρου (3× *Il.*, 1× *Od.*): epithets of women are almost all concerned with their appearance (βαθύζωνος, βαθύκολπος, ἐϋπλόκαμος, ἠΰκομος, καλή, λευκώλενος), those for heroes with their status and accomplishments. καλλίσφυρος excited bT's imagination: σημεῖόν ἐστιν συμμετρίας σώματος. Marpessa has the typical pre-Hellenic suffix -ησσα: her rape by Apollo seems to have a falsely etymological basis, as if < μάρπτειν. Εὐηνίνη: -ίνη serves as a patronymic suffix, 'd. of Euenos', like Ἀδρηστίνη (5.412), cf. Risch, *Wortbildung* 101.

558–9 Ἴδεώ θ᾽, ὅς ..., with 'irreducible' metathesis, illustrates vernacular language adapted to epic techniques of verse-making, being a blend, as it were, of Ἴδεω, ὅς ... (cf. Ἄλτεω, ὅς ..., 21.86), where -εω may be reduced to -α᾽, and e.g. Ἴδαν θ᾽, ὅς ... (cf. Αἰνείαν, ὅς ..., 11.58). The pattern of the verse, name with or without connective + relative clause, is formular.

559–61 Idas drew his bow against Apollo, not in a contest for a bride as 560 seems to imply but, according to Paus. 5.18.2 (description of the Chest of Kupselos), to defend his *wife* against the god's licentiousness. Idas was an important figure in heroic saga. He and his brother Lunkeus sailed on the *Argo* (Ap. Rhod. 1.152, etc.) and were slain in a quarrel over cattle by the Dioskouroi (*Cypria* fr. 13 Davies, Pind. *N.* 10.60–70). Idas' father was Aphareus, whose name (in the form Aphares) reappears as the name of Althaie's brother (see 524n.). As frequently Homer gives the impression of knowing more than he tells.

561–3 Kleopatre is apparently the heroine's original name replaced within her family (τότε ... καλέεσκον) by Alkuone. The explanation is whimsical; it is likely that Alkuone is primary and Kleopatre secondary, possibly an invention for this story, as the oddity of this digression suggests (so Schadewaldt, *Iliasstudien* 140). It would be fanciful, but perhaps not too fanciful, to hear in the name Kleo-patre an echo of Patro-klos, the friend with whom Akhilleus is now whiling away his time. E. Howald, *RhM* 73 (1924) 411, cf. *Der Dichter der Ilias* (Zurich 1946) 132, first made this point, but assumed that Patro-klos was secondary to Kleo-patre. The change of name is suggestive that the poet invented this detail in order to improve the fit of the parable.

563 οἶτον, 'fate', is barely sense but may stand in this very compressed and allusive passage (οἶκτον, 'plaintive wail', Leaf, but cf. ὄρνις, ἃ παρὰ πετρίνας πόντου δειράδας, ἀλκυών, ἔλεγον οἶτον [οἰκτρὸν Barnes] ἀείδεις Eur. *IT* 1089). What is meant is that Marpessa mourned as the ἀλκυών mourned for its mate. ἀλκυών is classically the name of the kingfisher, but that bird does not sing, plaintively or otherwise; in spite of ornithology a considerable mythology grew up around the bird, see Thompson, *A Glossary of Greek Birds* (Oxford 1936) 46–51.

565 ≅ 4.513. πέσσει, 'digest': Meleagros, like Akhilleus in the earlier passage, is clearly brooding on his wrongs and allowing them to fester in his mind (to use different metaphors). For the psychology cf. 1.81–2 εἴ περ γάρ τε χόλον γε καὶ αὐτῆμαρ καταπέψῃ | ἀλλά τε καὶ μετόπισθεν ἔχει κότον, ὄφρα τελέσσῃ, where, however, καταπέσσειν means 'stomach', i.e. 'choke back'.

567 This verse shows the 'abbreviated-reference style' (Kirk, *Songs* 164–9) at its most laconic with no mention of the occasion of the killing or the name of Meleagros' victim. Phoinix' point is that a hard heart is an imprudent heart: even so it seems odd to those familiar with the folktale version of the story that he does not mention at this point that the religious offence and its punishment led, as they did in book 1, to a dispute over spoils and its disastrous consequences. Homer would, of course, suppress the Amazon-like figure of Atalante to whom Meleagros wished to award the spoils of the boar to the vexation of his uncles.

568–9 Althaie beats the ground to attract the attention of the underworld gods, here called by their usual designations, Hades (= Ζεὺς καταχθόνιος, 457) and Persephone, cf. Here's similar action in a similar mood at *HyAp* 333. The Erinus answers Althaie's call because she is the agent of those gods (and of μοῖρα, 454–7n.). Persephone (it is usually she rather than Hades) and the Erinues are virtually identified in this context. So at 454–7 (an oddly similar incident) Amuntor called on the Erinues, and the underworld gods are said to have taken up his curse. In the symbolism of Hesiod (*Theog.* 183–5) the Erinues arose from the shed blood of Ouranos, the first victim of filial misconduct. For a mother's Erinues cf. 21.412, *Od.* 2.134–6, 11.279–80. Homer hints darkly at the Erinues' power to punish the dead as well as the living (19.259–60, cf. 3.278–9, an obscure passage, see n. *ad loc.*); at *HyDem.* 367–9 Hades predicts the chastisement of those who fail to appease Persephone. There is a natural reluctance on part of both poet and heroes to speak of Hades the god, except in the formula 'house of Hades', itself a euphemism: 20.61 ἄναξ ἐνέρων Ἀϊδωνεύς is the only reference in the narrative. The gods themselves are less inhibited, see 5.395, 8.367–8, 15.188. – ἀλοία: literally 'threshed' (cf. ἀλωή, 'threshing floor'), cf. ἵμασε *HyAp* 340 of Here performing a similar ritual act. The blows are repeated as the curse is intoned.

570 πρόχνυ καθεζομένη: i.e. kneeling. There is no single Homeric word for 'kneeling', since γουνάζομαι means 'entreat', so that the posture is expressed by ἕζομαι and ἵσταμαι with adverbs γνύξ (cf. 11.355), πρόχνυ, or ἐπὶ γοῦνα. πρόχνυ is clearly 'forward onto the knees', though the -χ- is unexplained. With (ἀπ)ὀλέσθαι (21.460, *Od.* 14.69), the sense is 'utterly'.

571 ἠεροφοῖτις: ἀήρ is the means by which gods and heroes are rendered unseen, e.g. 3.381, 11.752, 20.444, 21.597, or literally invisible, 21.549, *Od.* 7.41 and 140; ἠεροφοῖτις, 'that walks in darkness', may therefore imply 'coming unseen', αἱ ποιναὶ γὰρ ἀπροοράτως ἔρχονται (Arn/AbT), although the Erinues were accustomed to terrify their victims by their horrendous appearance. The Erinus 'that walks in darkness' (also 19.87) thus enhances her menace by the obscurity of her epithet. It is possible, though weak, that ἠερο- denotes simply the lower air, so that the Erinus is thought to fly, like a bird-daimon or Ate at 19.92–3. bT at 19.87, however, note a variant εἰαροπῶτις, 'blood-drinking' (cf. εἶαρ, 'blood', a Cypriot (i.e. Mycenaean?) word according to Hsch.), which may conceivably be the primary version of this formula before it became unintelligible and was reshaped. — Ἐρέβεσφιν: because the Erinues, like Hades and Persephone, dwell below ground, cf. 19.259–60 Ἐρινύες, αἵ θ' ὑπὸ γαῖαν | ἀνθρώπους τίνυνται. — The Erinus hearkened, as it should, to the parent's prayer and, since the action of such a being cannot be ineffective, the death of Meleagros is implied. Phoinix, of course, cannot mention it explicitly to Akhilleus, but an alert audience would notice that their return to battle sealed the fate of both heroes. For the Erinues supporting a mother against a son, see 21.412, *Od.* 2.135, 11.280.

574, 581, 585, 590 The suppliants – priests and elders, father, mother and sisters, comrades, wife – must represent an ascending intensity of moral pressure. Kakridis, *Researches* 20, pointed out that the scale: citizens, parents/brothers, husband/wife is a traditional scale of affection into which ἑταῖροι, who correspond to Odysseus and Aias, are inserted at the highest possible point before the successful petition of Kleopatre. Lohmann's thesis, *Reden* 258–63, is that the suppliants of the paradigm exactly mirror those of the embassy – Odysseus representing the army, Phoinix the father, Aias the comrades. Dramatic effect forms the pattern in each case. For those who knew the story of the *Iliad* (among whom must be included Homer's later audiences) there is irony in the fact that Kleopatre's plea succeeds, as will the different plea of Patroklos.

574 λίσσοντο γέροντες is probably formular and enters into a very similar sentence at 18.448–9 (where γέροντες includes Odysseus and Aias).

575 Arn/A allege that this line induced Sophocles to make the chorus of his *Meleager* priests. It is in fact not easy to guess what 'the noblest priests' are doing in this context, except as an exemplification of γέροντες.

577 πεδίον: Kaludon commands the coastal plain and lower valley of the Euenos river, see HSL *Catalogue* 109. ἐραννῆς: elsewhere αἰπεινή and πετρήεσσα are the epithets of Kàludon, a typical acropolis site.

578 For the τέμενος, the private estate of kings, see nn. to 12.313, 14.122–5, and 18.550–1. πεντηκοντόγυον: a very handsome offer. Alkinoos' fruit garden (ὄρχατος) at *Od.* 7.113, which seems to be identical with his τέμενος, was merely τετράγυος. bT, however, take the offer to be on the low side, in order to magnify what has been offered to Akhilleus. The γύη is a 'heroic' measure popular with the tragedians. Its actual extent is conjectural: in Hsch. the γύη is equated with the πλέθρον (*c.* 1,000 sq. yds), and at *Od.* 18.374 τετράγυος denotes the extent of a day's labour with the best oxen.

583 γουνούμενος: 'entreating' (Oineus is outside the doors), cf. γουνοῦμαι of Odysseus *standing* before Nausikaa (*Od.* 6.149).

584 κασίγνηται: there were four of them according to bT — Deianeira, Gorge, Poluxo, and Autonoe. μήτηρ: a slip, surely; in the circumstances Althaie's prayers could hardly have moved her son. A scholiast (b), however, noted that as an offending party Althaie is analogous to Agamemnon, but there is no hint that she ever repented of her action.

588–9 The fit of the parable is again made close: the city was on fire when Meleagros acted, just as Akhilleus was forced to act when the Trojans eventually fired a ship (16.122ff.).

593–4 A brief description of the horrors of a sack; cf., with further atrocities, Priam's vision of the sack of Troy (22.62–71).

594 βαθυζώνους describes the dress of archaic and classical times which allowed a fold of material (κόλπος) to hang over the girdle; the Mycenaean style was strikingly different, see Sp. Marinatos, *Arch. Hom.* A/B 25–31. βαθύκολπος (3× *Il.*) occurs in a formular verse referring to Trojan or Dardanian women, but that is hardly enough to establish a contrast between Greek and Asiatic fashions: see, however, West on *Od.* 3.154. — ἄλλοι is 'others' in the sense of 'strangers', as at 3.301. Zenodotus made the point clear by reading δήϊοι (Arn/A).

596 ἐδύσετο: a 'mixed' aorist, i.e. seeming to have the -σ- of the first aorist and the thematic conjugation of the second, see 11.16n.

598 εἴξας ᾧ θυμῷ: i.e. to the θυμός roused by the prospective fate of Kleopatre and the people of Kaludon at 595. It is, however, not very felicitous that the climax of the parable should be 'yielding to his θυμός' when the point of Phoinix' discourse is 'overcome your θυμός' (496).

600 Dodds, *Greeks and the Irrational* 11, points out that δαίμων, or an anonymous θεός, is a manner of speaking that the poet attributes to his characters, especially in the *Odyssey*, but very rarely uses himself (11.480 is an exception). This is in a sense realism. The poet believes and makes his characters believe that impulses emanate from without; as composer he 'knows' which god is responsible, but except in special circumstances his characters can only guess and are often content with a vague daimon or an unspecific god. A daimon is usually malevolent, e.g. 15.468 (see n.).

602 ἐπὶ δώρων: 'while the gifts still wait' (Fagles).

603 This verse picks up Odysseus' final promise at 302–3. ἶσον γάρ σε θεῷ: the necessary words τείσουσιν Ἀχαιοί force a reformulation of the traditional θεὸς ὥς formula.

605 τιμῆς is a contracted form of τιμή(ϝ)εις (τιμῆς, printed by some editors, is an incorrect orthography of the same form), cf. τιμῆντα (18.475), τεχνῆσσαι (*Od.* 7.110), so Arn/A. It is scarcely possible, in spite of the support of Aristarchus (Hrd/A), to construe τιμῆς as genitive of price, in spite of τιμῆς (genitive) in direct reference to this line at 608.

In its primary function as a model for Akhilleus to act upon the parable of Meleagros not only fails but is also encumbered with several superfluous features: the prominence of Kleopatre, her role in bringing pressure on Meleagros, and his implied death. The presence of these features helps to establish a secondary function of the paradigm by means of which the poet constructs a mirror of the action of his poem and communicates to his audience an interpretation of Akhilleus' μῆνις οὐλομένη.

606–19 Akhilleus replies with impatience to Phoinix' sermon. He acknowledges the moral pressure brought to bear on him and warns Phoinix to cease, but keeps the old man with him in case he should decide (now an open question) to return to Phthie

607 ≅ 17.561, see n. *ad loc.* The form ἄττα, always in the vocative, conveys affectionate regard. It is used 6× in *Od.* by Telemakhos in addressing old family servants. ἄττα is an old Indo-European expression surviving in Greek only in the epic (and reportedly in Thessalian, Eust. 777.54). Its function here is to define the tone of Akhilleus' words, which is otherwise obscured by the epic style. γεραιὲ διοτρεφές is formular (11.648 and 653).

608–9 Like much of Akhilleus' rhetoric, 'being honoured by the αἶσα of Zeus' is more impressive than clear. Taken with the preceding verse (οὔ τί με ταύτης | χρεὼ τιμῆς) the implication may be that Akhilleus now has no use for the earthbound conceptions of Agamemnon: 'he will risk all in the belief that nobility is not a mutual exchange of vain compliments among men whose lives are as evanescent as leaves, but an organic and inevitable part of the universe, independent of social contract' (Whitman, *HHT* 183). Agamemnon, however, made a similar and obviously petulant remark at 1.173–5, οὐδέ σ' ἔγωγε | λίσσομαι εἵνεκ' ἐμεῖο μένειν· πάρ' ἔμοιγε καὶ ἄλλοι | οἵ κέ με τιμήσουσι, μάλιστα δὲ μητίετα Ζεύς. — Akhilleus seems to recognize here that it is indeed his fate to remain and die at Troy, although he still speaks of the possibility of return to Phthie at 618–19.

609–10 ἀϋτμή is elsewhere (except at 10.89) associated with fire (8×, as if = 'hot blast') and once with the savour of roasted meat (*Od.* 12.369); the by-form ἀϋτμήν is used of wind (3×) and of the panting of a runner (23.765). It seems rather hyperbolical of Akhilleus to use the word, but there is no obvious alternative; πνοιή is equally associated with winds, and πνεῦμα is not part of the epic vocabulary.

612 Akhilleus is conscious that the rage in his heart will boil over at the smallest provocation. He shows a similar awareness at 24.568–70 that his respect for Priam is fragile.

615 The verse has a proverbial and 'Hesiodic' ring (cf. *Erga* 353–4 τὸν φιλέοντα φιλεῖν καὶ τῷ προσιόντι προσεῖναι | καὶ δόμεν ὅς κεν δῷ καὶ μὴ δόμεν ὅς κεν μὴ δῷ), but cannot be proverbial as it stands, for καλός is unusual in the epic as a moral term, cf. Adkins, *Merit and Responsibility* 43–4. Akhilleus adapts the sentiment to put Phoinix in his place.

617 λέξεο is the imperative of a 'mixed' aorist, a sigmatic stem conjugated with the thematic vowel; λέξο (24.650) is the corresponding athematic imperative.

618–19 These verses modify Akhilleus' previous threat (356–63) to depart in the morning. In fact no deliberation on the matter is reported, and Akhilleus' words may be taken as an indication of his continuing but slightly mellowed indignation.

620–68 Akhilleus signals Patroklos to prepare Phoinix' bed, then in a blunt and soldierly manner Aias suggests that he and Odysseus admit defeat. He is outraged at Akhilleus' failure to respond to their overtures. Aias' words strike a chord in Akhilleus' mind and he does not answer them directly but returns once again to Agamemnon's contempt. He is sufficiently moved, however, to overlook his intention to depart in the morning and make a concession: he will fight if Hektor reaches the huts and ships. Odysseus and Aias then depart. Akhilleus and his friends retire for the night

Aias' strong language is in keeping with the character most readers of the *Iliad* will attribute to him. He is big, cool, reliable, for the most part silent – this and 17.629–47 are his longest utterances in the *Iliad* – and it is tempting to imagine that his thoughts are as few as his words. His utterances however are very much to the point (see 17.626–55n.), as here. Aias' response to Akhilleus' complex personality is incomprehension, but his verdict, that Akhilleus suffers from ἀγηνορίη (635), is echoed by Diomedes (699) and later by Patroklos (16.29–35). The iterated statement, though in each case in character, is never contradicted either by another character or by the poet. One such judgement may be dismissed as characterization, but three look like an indirect authorial comment. At the least they reinforce the point made by Phoinix' parable and furnish a clue to the audience as to how they are to interpret the attitude so described; in short that Akhilleus from the best of motives has now put himself in the wrong.

620–3 Akhilleus avoids the discourtesy of an overt ἑτάροισιν ἰδὲ δμωῇσι κελεύειν (658) by discreetly signalling the empathetic Patroklos to give the visitors a broad hint. The subjects of μεδοίατο are Aias and Odysseus. The verses distort the regular retiring scene (Arend, *Scenen* 99–105) which follows at 658–68 (621 ≅ 659) by interposing an intermediary. (At 24.643 Akhilleus gives his orders directly.) This is because the emissaries must be got rid of – and have their final say.

ἦ is from *āg-t*, 'said', from the same root seen in Lat. *aio, ad-ag-ium*. The Iliadic formulas, not readily elicited from the concordances, are ἦ ῥ(α) ... δέ ... 4×, with change of subject, and without change of subject ἦ, καί ... 26× and ἦ ῥα, καί ... 30×.

622–3 The progressive enjambment in the speech introduction is unusual (but cf. τοῖσι δὲ Νέστωρ | ἡδυεπής ... 1.247–8), and has led to a recasting of the regular formula for Aias. — Τελαμωνιάδης: this patronymic is found only here and at 23.838. It implies an interpretation as well as a modification of the archaic Τελαμώνιος, 'le mot pouvant signifier l' «endurant»', Chantraine, *Dict*. s.v.

625–42 Aias' runover words and enjambed sentences give a powerful effect of his anger at Akhilleus' attitude, on which see Higbie, *Measure and Music* 118–20. The 'skewed sentence', i.e. one that begins in one verse and ends in the next with progressive or necessary enjambment, is an important aspect of Homeric style. In emotionally uncharged situations sentence and verse tend to coincide. By overriding this tendency the skewed sentence expresses the passion of speakers and, in battle scenes, the excitement of the poet.

624–36 Aias begins by ostensibly addressing Odysseus, but more and more as he proceeds his remarks are made for Akhilleus' ears, until he finally slips into the 2nd person in 636. Actual change of addressee in the course of a speech is marked as such, e.g. 7.361, 9.704, 11.819.

628–9 ἄγριον: an enduring aspect of Akhilleus' character, cf. Apollo's words at 24.41–5, ἄγρια οἶδεν ... ἔλεον μὲν ἀπώλεσεν, οὐδέ οἱ αἰδὼς | γίγνεται.

630 σχέτλιος: see 9.19n. Aias protests at Akhilleus' unreasonable behaviour. For him the values of the heroic world allow of no argument; they are friends under one roof, they have done the right thing, why can't Akhilleus? Aias' thought is similar to that of Odysseus at 256 and 301–3: acting like a friend to one's friends is the better course now that recompense has been made and by honouring Akhilleus the Achaeans have a claim in turn to his co-operation.

631 ἔξοχον: only in the formula ἔξοχον ἄλλων, otherwise ἔξοχα. The syntax is ambiguous, here and at 6.194, between adverb and adjective.

632 νηλής: more strong language, cf. 16.33, 16.204. Akhilleus is like a man who unreasonably insists on his pound of flesh.

632–6 Even for murder, apparently the worst crime Aias can think of, the victim's relatives accept compensation. There is another reference to this custom at 18.497–508 (see nn.). It was an option, of course, that in the world of the epic the relatives preferred not to take up, forcing the killer into exile.

636 δεξαμένῳ: the dative (instead of a genitive in agreement with τοῦ 635) is the well attested *lectio difficilior*. 'It is characteristic of Homer not to employ concord as a means of connecting distant words when other constructions are admissible' (Monro, *HG* 211).

637–9 Note that the agents now said to be responsible for the state of Akhilleus' θυμός are the gods. At 629 it was Akhilleus himself. Aias speaks in the usual way but loosely, since in so far as the gods have interfered at all it was to moderate Akhilleus' passion (1.194–218). Aias' failure to understand the θυμαλγὴς λώβη suffered by Akhilleus verges on the comic, as if the seizure of Briseis had been a mere theft. Whether Agamemnon seized one woman or the seven he now promised was all the same. In matters of honour it is the nature of the offence that counts; profit and loss do not come into it.

639 ἵλαος and ἱλάσκομαι are the *voces propriae* for expression of the gracious condescension of gods to mortals (so bT). Akhilleus is a man, divine mother notwithstanding, but being as it is supposed the indispensable saviour, happens to stand in the same relation to the helpless Achaeans as a god to a mortal. ἵλαος acknowledges that Akhilleus has the whip-hand and can grant his favour or not as he pleases, and insinuates, like Phoinix' language, that Akhilleus has suppliants before him, cf. ὑπωρόφιοι at 640 and the successful appeal of Odysseus to the Phaeacians from the hearth of Alkinoos (*Od.* 7.139ff.). Aias ends by being respectful as well as reproachful.

640 ὑπωρόφιοι: the reproach is clear. Aias is shocked that emissaries from the whole army, sincerely holding out the hand of friendship to Akhilleus, welcomed into his quarters, and entertained at his hearth, should have been snubbed. Comparative evidence makes it clear that where behaviour is controlled by honour the honour of both parties to a dispute must be preserved and that that is achieved by the injured party's acceptance of fair compensation. If he does not, he dishonours the other and incurs reproach himself, see Peristiany, *Honour and Shame* passim.

641 μέμαμεν expresses a powerful impulse: 'we are anxious to be' the best of friends.

643–55 Akhilleus' reply to Aias is couched in simple terms but conveys a terrible sense of resolve and continuing outrage. Aias said in effect 'I never thought you would treat your friends like this in your own house', and Akhilleus has no reply to that devastating comment. Accordingly he says 'Very well, I *shall* help you, but not yet.' His words closely correspond to what he will say at 16.49–63 in response to Patroklos' remonstrances. Thus in spite of his provocative language Aias is treated in a comradely manner which stands in contrast with Akhilleus' treatment of Phoinix. His response is the same in both cases, admitting the force of the argument but citing his feelings towards Agamemnon as an insuperable bar to action. Phoinix is treated to the imperative mood and a sharp reminder of his duty towards his patrons; the address to Aias follows the conciliatory pattern 'Yes ... But ... However ...', cf. Poseidon's reply to Iris, 15.206–17.

645–6 Aias' words were κατὰ θυμόν (i.e. Akhilleus' θυμός) but none the less unacceptable. If Akhilleus had intended to comply he would have said κατὰ μοῖραν, 'in accordance with what must be': κατὰ μοῖραν ἔειπες etc. (7× *Il.*, 12× *Od.*). Akhilleus recognizes the force of Aias' words but cannot budge because οἰδάνεται κραδίη χόλῳ. In a calmer mood, in a passage that echoes this one (16.49–55 – see n. and Lohmann, *Reden* 274–5) Akhilleus spoke of his αἰνὸν ἄχος rather than his χόλος; that permitted him to say τὰ μὲν προτετύχθαι ἐάσομεν (16.60), and relent a little. – Verse 645 was quoted by Plato, *Crat.* 428c, with contracted ἐείσω for ἐείσαο, thus illustrating the pressure on the text for assimilation to classical vernacular forms.

648 = 16.59. μετανάστης: a 'refugee', obliged to beg for his bread and abused by the more fortunate, would be a description more appropriate to Briseis than Akhilleus (as Rhianus, reading μετανάστιν, thought). Akhilleus speaks of his sufferings with his usual hyperbole. Patroklos, hovering in the background, would not have agreed that a μετανάστης was necessarily ἀτίμητος.

650–3 Akhilleus' words pick up Phoinix' argument that Meleagros had to fight when the battle reached his home (587–9). But indirectly Phoinix had shown the way out of Akhilleus' moral dilemma: if he has a *personal* reason for fighting he can save his friends while maintaining (or simply ignoring) his anger with Agamemnon. His words are appropriate to character and situation; Akhilleus misses his *métier* (cf. 189, 11.600), but cannot say so openly to present company, nor could Akhilleus make any concession less than the peril of his own huts and ships the occasion for his return. The distinction made between the Myrmidons and the Argives illuminates the limits of Akhilleus' sense of social obligation: it stops at the boundary of his own tribe. His statement 'I shall not think of war until ...' is the second affirmation that he will return to the war, more precise than that of Zeus (8.473–7, if genuine), and reads like a programmatic announcement, obliquely made through the mouth of a character. It is picked up by 16.61–3 – unless ἔφην there is taken with Arn/A to mean 'I thought' (διενοήθην), see n. *ad loc.* The poet reveals his intentions by stages; at 8.473–7 that Hektor will reach the ships, here that Hektor will burn them, at 11.792–801 that Patroklos will first take the field, and at 15.65 that Hektor will kill Patroklos. In each case the adumbration is embedded in detail which is appropriate at the time but falsified in the event, cf. 15.56–77n. The possibility that the Achaean ships themselves might be in danger was first adumbrated in book 8 (181 and four times subsequently). A previous battle by the ships may have figured in the *Cypria* when the Achaeans were repulsed from Teuthrania by Telephos, cf. Pind. *Ol.* 9.72 ὅτ' ἀλκᾶντας Δαναοὺς τρέψαις ἁλίαισιν πρύμναις Τήλεφος ἔμβαλεν. — In verse 653 the variant φλέξαι for σμῦξαι, noted by Aristonicus and Didymus, is old, being cited by Plato, *Hipp. Min.* 371C.

658–68 These verses cover the same ground at 24.643–8 + 673–6, *Od.* 4.294–305 and 7.335–47. In book 24 Akhilleus' hut is assimilated to a palace with αἴθουσα and/or πρόδομος before the μέγαρον. The host sleeps in the μέγαρον, the guest in the πρόδομος. Verisimilitude is better maintained in this passage, at the small cost of leaving the site of Phoinix' bed unspecified.

658 ≅ 24.643. Who are these δμωαί? Not, apparently, the concubines of 664–8 whose birth (see nn.) would exempt them from literal bedmaking. Prisoners presumably, like those on offer to Akhilleus, cf. 366 = 23.261 for the booty amassed on his raids. But it is possible that the poet has slipped into language appropriate to the heroic community at peace in its palaces, cf. the passing mention at *Od.* 5.199 of δμωαί in Kalupso's cave on Ogugie, see Hainsworth on *Od.* 5.264.

661 The formula for bed-making is a three-verse run 24.643–5 = *Od.* 4.297–9 = 7.336–8, which lists from the mattress upwards δέμνια, ῥήγεα, τάπητες, and χλαῖναι. *Od.* 10.352–3 adds λίς, 'smooth cloth' (not 'linen', see Heubeck, *Od. ad loc.*), spread under the ῥήγεα. The 'linen sheets' (λίνοιο λεπτὸν ἄωτον) of the present passage, which lists the coverings from the top downwards, imply a certain luxury – or misunderstand λίς.

663–5 An elaborated 'Retiring Scene' requires a note of an appropriate (or agreeable) bedfellow, cf. 1.611, *Od.* 3.403, 7.347, 23.295. We might have preferred a tormented Akhilleus tossing beneath his blankets for Briseis' sake as he did for Patroklos, cf. 24.3–6, but it may have been thought unheroic if Akhilleus' loss touched his heart as well as his honour, cf. 1.122n. In the *Aithiopis* Akhilleus was outraged at Thersites' suggestion that he had been emotionally involved with Penthesileia. Like Khruseis and Briseis, Diomede of Lesbos and Iphis of Skuros were prizes of war. Akhilleus' pillage of Lesbos is mentioned at 129 = 271 and perhaps implied at 24.544; it is not known to have been mentioned in the *Cypria*. In the *Cypria* and *Little Iliad* Akhilleus did not sack Skuros either (see Kullmann, *Quellen* 266), but called there on his return from the abortive attack on Teuthrania and married Lukomedes' daughter Deïdameia. As reported the cyclic poems did not suggest that Akhilleus used violence. Akhilleus' son (called Purrhos in the *Cypria*) is mentioned under the name Neoptolemos at 19.326–7 as living on Skuros, cf. *Od.* 11.506–9. None of this is to be reconciled with the story of Akhilleus' being hidden by Thetis among the daughters of Lukomedes and exposed by Odysseus. bT, assuming that Homer knew the romantic story, suggest that it was rejected for lacking heroic colour, cf. Introduction 52. The air of precise allusion here to stories of Akhilleus' raids may be deceptive. Verses 326–7 in book 19 seem to allude to the conventional story. Some escaped the difficulty by inventing a town Skuros in the Troad (Did, Arn/A).

663 μυχῷ κλισίης εὐπήκτου (= 24.675, note the irreducible genitive in -ου) adapts μυχῷ δόμου ὑψηλοῖο (1× *Il.*, 3× *Od.*) to the circumstances of the campaign; another adaptation is μυχῷ σπείους γλαφυροῖο (Kalupso's residence, *Od.* 5.226).

664–8 As usual among incidental characters the names are Greek and appear like the characters themselves to be invented *ad hoc* (a Trojan Phorbas appears at 14.490). None the less Diomede and Iphis inspired, along with Briseis, a famous painting by Polygnotus, see Paus. 10.25.2ff. For Akhilleus' raiding see Reinhardt, *IuD* 50–7. The fact that the women are named and the parentage of Diomede mentioned suggests that before their present degradation they were, like Khruseis and probably Briseis, persons of rank in their own communities. It should be counted against the Suitors of Penelope that they slept with menials. Enueus is unidentified – a Cretan, according to T. In 664 Zenodotus is reported (Arn/A) to have read Κάειρ' ἣν Λεσβόθεν ἦγε, which the scholia could not reconcile with classical Caria and derided accordingly.

669–713 After formalities of welcome Odysseus reports the failure of their overtures. The council is crushed by the news until roused by a resolute speech from Diomedes. He urges that the fight be renewed in the morning. All then return to their quarters for the night

669–709 The final scene of the book mirrors the opening council scene (ring-composition), even to introducing three speakers (Reinhardt, *IuD* 222). The linear narrative followed the ambassadors from the quarters of Agamemnon to those of Akhilleus, and now follows them back again. Action elsewhere, so to speak, ceased. If it had been appropriate to return to the council, e.g. to relate their forebodings, the poet would not have retraced his steps at this point but would have interrupted the confrontation with Akhilleus; but that would have been inept. What the council was doing or saying meanwhile is a question that does not arise. — Verse 669 = 7.313.

670–1 Courtesy requires Odysseus and Aias to be welcomed before they make their report, but the anxiety of the council is shown by their doing the honours on their feet. — υἷες Ἀχαιῶν (also 695) is a very frequent formula (53×). Its proper reference is shown by its alternant λαὸς Ἀχαιῶν (20×), i.e. the Achaean army, but all who can be in question here are the same γέροντες whom Agamemnon summoned at 89. As an expansion of an ethnic name υἶες + genitive of the ethnicon is restricted to this expression (and its derivative Τρώων καὶ Ἀχαιῶν υἶες ἄριστοι, *Od.* 24.38).

671 δειδέχατ᾽: 'pledged', for the spelling (-ει for -η-) see 4.4n. The text should not be corrected, however, for confusion of this verb with δείκνυμι is early, see 196n.

673–5 Agamemnon's short speech well expresses his anxiety; his question is 'Will Akhilleus fight?', and his gifts and daughter are forgotten.

673 = 10.544, and cf. *Od.* 12.184. Nestor is also μέγα κῦδος Ἀχαιῶν (4× *Il.*, 2× *Od.*). — πολύαινος: αἶνος is a 'tale', but are we to understand that Odysseus tells the tales, or that the tales are told of him? Odysseus is a diplomat here and a crafty schemer in the *Odyssey*, but it remains true generally that 'the epithets awarded Odysseus in the Iliad are supposed to relate only to the wanderings, and not to the "novelette" of the husband's homecoming' (U. Hölscher, in Fenik, *Tradition* 54). It is possible, of course, that the epithet has been reinterpreted, and shifted from the passive to the active sense.

674 Formular diction puts Agamemnon's anxious enquiry into the same language as Akhilleus used to taunt him, cf. (φραζέσθω) νήεσσιν ἀλεξέμεναι δήϊον πῦρ (347). — δήϊον πῦρ: as an epithet of πῦρ, δήϊος is scanned ∪∪ –; with other words or independently in the sense 'hostile', 'enemy', a dactylic scansion is usual. See Chantraine, *Dict.* s.v. for the implications. δήϊος is probably connected with δαίω, 'burn', at least secondarily. There are two formulas, δήϊον πῦρ (4×) and πυρὸς δηΐοιο (5×), found only in the *Iliad*.

677–92 Odysseus replies to Agamemnon's two questions in the usual reverse order: yes, Akhilleus is still full of wrath, and no, he will not help. Odysseus is made diplomatically to report Akhilleus' words indirectly; he thus avoids offensive language, e.g. ἐχθρὰ δέ μοι τοῦ δῶρα (378). This speech and that of Diomedes (697–9) are important for the light they shed on the speakers' reading of Akhilleus' mind. Odysseus affirms that his obduracy is to be taken seriously but implies that his (first) proposal to depart is a hyperbolical threat. Diomedes proposes to disregard it: Akhilleus, he asserts, will come round in his own time; meanwhile there is nothing anyone can do about it and trying only makes matters worse. The poet gives him the last word, implying that in the reading of Akhilleus' mind that he gives to Diomedes we have a correct assessment.

681 σόως is for σαόης (here σάως Aristarchus (Did/A)); it owes its vocalism to the adjective σόος, itself by diectasis of contracted σῶς (< σάϝος), cf. 424n.

682–3 These verses were obelized because Odysseus reports only the first decision of Akhilleus, 356–63, to return to Phthie in the morning, not the reversal of that hasty decision at 650–3 (see n.). — ἠπείλησε: note Odysseus' assessment of Akhilleus' words. Akhilleus has already uttered one empty threat (νῦν δ' εἶμι Φθίηνδ', 1.169), and no one takes this one seriously or remarks that Akhilleus is still there the following day. The essence of Akhilleus' position is that he will not help in the present crisis and that is what Odysseus reports (so bT), as if Akhilleus' words to Phoinix and Aias were irrelevant; moreover Akhilleus put an unacceptably humiliating condition on his co-operation: total Achaean catastrophe. See R. Scodel, *CPh* 84 (1989) 91–9. Reinhardt (*IuD* 240) suggested that ἅμ' ἠοῖ φαινομένηφι picked up the same phrase at 618 in Akhilleus' reply to Phoinix (which would support the argument for the integrity of the book), but it could equally well refer to ἦρι μάλα at 360 in Akhilleus' discourse.

683 The verse is a blend of νῆας ἅλαδ' ἑλκέμεν ἀμφιελίσσας (2.165 = 181) and νῆας ἐϋσσέλμους ἅλαδ' ἑλκέμεν (14.97, 14.106). νῆας ἐϋσσέλμους is strongly formular (10× *Il.*, 2× *Od.* + 4× nom.); ἀμφιέλισσαι, etc., in spite of the apparent antiquity of the word, occurs only 5× (+ 1× in a repeated verse) with archaic νῆες, -ας, from which it must be separated. Ionic forms νεός, -ες, -ας, gave the word a new vogue (3× *Il.*, but 10× *Od.*). σέλμα, first in Archilochus fr. 4 West and *h.Hom.* 7.47, like many technical expressions, is of disputed sense if precision is required: 'deck' or 'thwart'. Kurt, *Fachausdrücke* 124–6, inclines to the latter, see also D. H. F. Gray, *Arch. Hom.* G 94. ἀμφιέλισσαι is even more obscure (see *LfgrE* s.v.): the scholiasts suggest ἀμφοτέρωθεν ταῖς κώπαις ἐλαυνομένας (D on 2.165) or ἀμφοτέρωθεν στρεφόμεναι ὑπὸ κωπῶν (on *Od.* 6.264). Others prefer 'shaped in a ἕλιξ ("curve") on both sides (or both ends)', see Kurt, *Fachausdrücke* 39–41. ἕλιξ, however, means 'a spiral' not 'a curve'. If the adj. ἕλιξ can mean 'black' (see 12.293n.) yet another possibility arises.

685–7 Verse 685 is repeated verbatim from 418, hence the 2nd person δήετε; δήομεν, excluded by metre, would be more appropriate. For problems occasioned by change of number see West on *Od.* 4.578. δήειν serves as a future tense (= εὑρήσειν). Verses 686–7 revert to direct speech. The accusatives and infinitives of the indirect construction would require a drastic rephrasing of Akhilleus' words.

688–92 These verses were athetized by Aristophanes (Did/A) and Aristarchus (Arn/A) as being pedestrian and insulting to the witnesses. It is hard to follow their thinking; Odysseus' report made grim hearing and might well need confirmation, and he had to explain why Phoinix had gone but not come back. εἰπέμεν: the infinitive is consecutive, 'these men are here to tell', cf. 19.140.

689 πεπνυμένω ἄμφω is formular (3× *Il.*, 1× *Od.*) used in apposition to pairs of heralds or councillors (and improperly or ironically of two of Penelope's suitors at *Od.* 18.65). πεπνυμένος, from the same root as πινυτός according to Szemerényi, *Syncope in Greek and Indo-European* (Naples 1964) 71–8, commends one who knows how to behave towards his elders or betters, cf. 58 and n.

691–2 = 427–8 with change to the 3rd person.

694 Zenodotus (Did/AT) did not read this verse but, as usual, it was read but athetized by Aristophanes and Aristarchus. Their objection was that κρατερῶς described the manner of Akhilleus, not that of Odysseus: true, but the objection fails to take account of the habits of formular composition. The verse is repeated, with ἀγόρευσε for ἀπέειπεν, from 431. It is absent from the parallel run of verses 29–31 (29 = 693, 30–1 = 695–6), but that is without significance, for by no means could Agamemnon's defeatist manner at the beginning of the Book be described as speaking κρατερῶς. The same run, with 694 but without 695, recurs at 8.28–30, an instance of the way that these long formulas are adapted to their context. Verse 695 by repeating 30 emphasizes the utter failure of the Achaeans' initiative; they end the Book exactly where they began – but this is before Diomedes has spoken.

697–709 The characterization of Diomedes as a self-confident warrior (cf. his assumption that a flag of truce is sign of weakness, 7.400–2, and his boast at 48–9), a double in that respect of Akhilleus but keeping some sense of Agamemnon's rank, is well maintained in this short speech. Note the tact attributed to him in trying circumstances at 4.401ff. and his careful language at 32–41 above. λίσσεσθαι (698) and μυρία δῶρα (699) are bitter comments on the embassy and neatly expose the false situation into which Agamemnon's generosity has led him: the more he offers the less he negotiates from the position of a βασιλεύτερος.

699 ἀγήνωρ may be complimentary, a briefer synonym of μεγαλήτωρ, but here = ἄγαν ὑβριστικός (Arn/A). The implication is that Akhilleus has not heeded Phoinix' appeal δάμασον θυμὸν μέγαν (496), cf. Odysseus' words to the ghost of Aias δάμασον δὲ μένος καὶ ἀγήνορα θυμόν (*Od.* 11.562).

701–9 Diomedes' vigorous language is heavily formular: 701 ≅ *Od.* 14.183; in 703, the formula θυμὸς ἐνὶ στήθεσσιν ἀνώγῃ (3×) is drawn back by its enjambment from the verse-end position; 704 = 2.139 etc. (6× *Il.*, 2× *Od.*); 705, cf. τεταρπόμενός τε φίλον κῆρ (*Od.* 1.310); 706 = 19.161; 707 imperfectly recalls ἦμος δ' ἠριγένεια φάνη ῥοδοδάκτυλος Ἠώς (20× *Od.*, but only once previously (1.477) in *Il.*); 709, ἐνὶ (μετὰ) πρώτοισι μάχεσθαι etc. (6×).

709–9 Diomedes turns back to Agamemnon, as the singulars in 709 show, with a pointed remark. Agamemnon did not lead the battle that began at 4.446 – first blood went to Antilokhos – still less the fighting that began at 8.60; but he did not conduct the battle always from the safety of the rear either. He heads the list of victors at 5.38–83 (but not that at

6.5–36), and killed a companion of Aineias at 5.533–40, and fled with the rest at 8.78; not an impressive performance, although he was one of the three on whom it was hoped the lot would fall to fight Hektor in single combat (7.180). Diomedes reminds Agamemnon of his duty to lead, a challenge that the latter cannot decline. At the same time his words foreshadow Agamemnon's *aristeia* in book 11 – and create an expectation in the singer's audience.

710–3 The natural break in the narrative is marked by a few conventional verses, noting general assent, libation, departure, and retirement, cf. *Od.* 7.226–9. Verse 710 = 7.344, an adaptation (or the archetype) of . . . πάντες ἐπίαχον υἷες Ἀχαιῶν (50), or . . . πάντες ἐπευφήμησαν Ἀχαιοί (1.22); 711 = 51 = 7.404; 712 condenses the regular verses αὐτὰρ ἐπεὶ σπεῖσάν τε . . . (177 and 6× *Od.*) and . . . κακκείοντες ἔβαν κλισίηνδε (οἴκονδε) ἕκαστος (2× *Il.*, 4× *Od.*); 713 ≅ 7.482. They pour the libation to Hermes according to T, as the Phaeacians did (*Od.* 7.137), ὅτε μνησαίατο κοίτου.

The Book ends on a note of calm resolve, even of confidence. There is no more talk of evacuation; the Achaeans are going to fight again and do better. The opening of book 11, where Zeus stirs up the war and Agamemnon dons his most splendid fighting gear, would follow naturally. Nothing on the other hand prepares the ground for the sleeplessness and apprehension that dominate the first scenes of book 10.

BOOK TEN

In the scholia to book 10 two other versions of the Rhesos story are reported. First, a version attributed to Pindar (Arn/A and bT at 435) in which Rhesos comes to Troy, performs heroic deeds that so alarm Here that she sends Athene to despatch Diomedes and Odysseus by night to kill Rhesos as he sleeps. Second (Arn/A at 435), some said that an oracle had declared that if Rhesos and his horses once drank the water of Skamandros they would be invincible; accordingly he was killed by the two heroes the night he arrived before Troy. This second version was also known to Virgil (*Aen.* 1.472–3) and to Servius.

Rhesos' entry into the battle, the absence of Dolon, and the role of Here and Athene, point to versions of the story radically different until the denouement from that told in this Book. The Pindaric version is clearly an allomorph of the stories of Penthesileia, Memnon, and Eurupulus: a late arrival at Troy, an *aristeia*, and death. Those stories became a canonical part of the tale of Troy, that of Rhesos did not. The oracle version is basically a story of a conditional fate: if Rhesos drinks from Skamandros he will be victorious, just as Odysseus will be safe once he reaches the Phaeacians (*Od.* 5.288–9).

As to what version the poet of book 10 had before his mind, beyond the fact that Rhesos was slain by night by Diomedes and Odysseus, it is here unnecessary to speculate (see Fenik, *Iliad X and the Rhesus*). Some version he had, and that version he adapted for its present place in the *Iliad*. For although since antiquity opinion has been virtually universal among Homerists that the Book does not form part of the design of the *Iliad* (Shewan and van Leeuwen are the principal exceptions), the Book is not an *Einzellied*. Cf. Von der Mühll, *Hypomnema* 182–3.

However, to insert a substantial episode into a poem such as the *Iliad* is more difficult than some critics of the analytical school have assumed. The poet of the *Iliad* brought to the construction of his poem something of the outlook as well as the skills of his traditional art. In working out his design he began each episode as he began the poem itself 'from a certain point', presupposing what went before. He then proceeded to spin his tale in linear fashion. His mind was always directed forwards towards his next narrative goal. (That is why, unless it is germane to the episode he is telling, he does not expressly refer back to what has gone before.) Now to expand a paratactically constructed epic, such as the *Cypria* or the *Little Iliad* seem to have been, would hardly have been more difficult than to expand an *aristeia* with an additional duel; but such an expansion would be between, not within, the episodes. This is what made the task of the adaptor of the Rhesos-story so difficult. In conception the *Iliad* corresponds to one of the major episodes of the *Cypria*, not to the whole poem, as Aristotle saw long ago (*Poetics* 23). Expansion therefore has to be within the framework of the overall unity. The interpolated episode must begin from the situation reached at some point, and must necessarily then diverge from the main storyline. The trouble comes at the end; if a new situation has been created, there will be a hiatus; the original story, when resumed, will not presuppose the interpolation but what preceded it. That difficulty can be surmounted by making the expansion return to the same situation as obtained at its beginning, but that may not be easy either and if achieved may undercut whatever point the expansion ever had.

The opening lines of book 10 recall the way in which book 2 is joined to book 1; 'all retired to bed' (end of preceding Book), 'but X could not sleep' (opening lines of following Book). The junction with book 9 is smooth at the formal level, but not so smooth at the level of content. At the end of book 9 Diomedes recommended that they all have a good night's sleep (τὸ γὰρ μένος ἐστὶ καὶ ἀλκή, 706) and fight again, and all approved. At the beginning of book 10 we return to a state of mind that duplicates the situation at the beginning of book 9 and presupposes the Achaean disaster of book 8, Hektor's exploits in that Book, the Trojans and their allies encamped outside the city, and the danger to the ships. A mention of the ditch (194) presupposes its construction in book 7. Some minor details, e.g. the inspection of the watch, allude to arrangements made at the beginning of book 9 (79–84). All in all this is more allusion to preceding Books than the poet of the *Iliad* normally provides. There is no allusion, however, to the embassy to Akhilleus and its failure, not even where such an allusion would be natural and easy, e.g. at 18–20 and 43–5. But some attention is paid to time; the night was two-thirds gone when Odysseus and Diomedes set out (253), and that seems to take into account all that happened in book 9 as well as in the first 250 lines of book 10 since night fell at 8.485.

The new situation into which the story was introduced supplied a new motivation for the main action of the Book. Oracle and *aristeia* were impossible or beside the point, and were therefore dropped. Whether the poet invented, retained, or imported Dolon from another episode (Dictys of Crete 2.4.5 – for what it is worth – separated Dolon and Rhesos) seems to be an open question, but without an oracle or an *aristeia* Dolon is essential. How else were the Achaeans to know about Rhesos? And having learned of his arrival why should they kill him? Without the *aristeia* or the oracle there was no urgency. So the heroes were motivated by the prospect of κῦδος and a trophy. The death of Rhesos and twelve of his men, and the seizure of his horses, must be taken to restore the military situation with which the night began, so that when day dawns and a new sequence of themes begins it can follow book 10 as easily as book 9. The Achaeans are all spirit and resolution, and the poet looks forward to the construction of a great day of battle and, unhelpfully to his commentators, makes no explicit reference to any earlier Book.

Granted then that book 10 is adapted to its present place, there remain the questions by whom, at what time, and for what purpose the adaptation was made. Uniquely in the history of the Iliadic text there is external evidence in support of the analytical position: T to 10.1 φασὶ τὴν ῥαψωδίαν ὑφ᾽ Ὁμήρου ἰδίᾳ τετάχθαι καὶ μὴ εἶναι μέρος τῆς Ἰλιάδος, ὑπὸ δε Πεισιστράτου τετάχθαι εἰς τὴν Ἰλιάδα. Neither the date of the T scholia nor their sources are easy to establish, so it is impossible to say who first made this allegation and on what grounds. Written sources for sixth-century Athenian literary history are not earlier than the fourth century and not remarkable for their trustworthy colour ([Plato], *Hipparchus* 228B–229B, from a passage that maliciously contradicts the historical account of the Pisistratids). The scholium records a sensible inference that book 10 is a foreign body in the *Iliad*, together with a guess as to its provenance that was not unreasonable in the light of Hellenistic and later theories about the early history of the Homeric text.

The Athenians need not have had more than the assurances of a rhapsode for the authenticity of the Book, but what were the motives of the original adapter? Book 10 has been called 'a disaster stylistically, because of its folkloristic departures from normalcy; heroically, because of the disgraceful conduct exhibited by Odysseus and Diomedes; thematically, because it takes place in the dead of night; and structurally, because it leads to an Achaean victory' (Nagler, *Spontaneity* 136). One might add to the derelictions listed in that harsh verdict the 'philhellenism' of the Book, see 13–14n. Note also the analysis of van Thiel, *Ilias und Iliaden* 327–40, who conceives that the *Frühilias* had no *Doloneia* but an *Embassy* (of Odysseus and Aias), whereas the *Spätilias* put the *Embassy* at the beginning of what is now book 14 and inserted a *Doloneia* between the defeat of what is now book 8 and the initial victories of book 11. Van Thiel's analysis rests on an interpretation of repeated themes in the epic different from that assumed in this commentary, but the result throws light on one of the possible functions of books 9 and 10 – possible, because notoriously there is no allusion to the events of either Book in the ensuing battle. Having defeated the Achaeans in book 8 the poet should give them a plausible reason for renewed confidence to fight again the following day and do better. Book 9 does that in a subtle way, stripping away all extraneous aid and leaving the Achaeans (without

Akhilleus) to fight with the resolution of determined men 'with their backs to the wall and trusting in the justice of their cause' (cf. 9.49): book 10 in comparison is crudely simplistic; the Achaeans are given a cheap victory over unarmed and sleeping men.

In language and diction book 10 sends contradictory signals. Danek's careful examination (*Dolonie* 20–47) has established that the poet's handling of traditional language does not differ fundamentally from that of the *Iliad* proper. (Danek counts repeated phraseology at about 56% of the whole, which is about the Iliadic level.) Stylometric studies based on sentence-length and use of particles confirm that at this level book 10 is not distinguishable from the rest of the poem, see A. Q. Morton, *Literary Detection* (Edinburgh 1978) 158–64. At the surface, however, the differences are marked, pointing to an evolved form of the *Kunstsprache* more deeply penetrated by the contemporary vernacular, e.g. κ-perfects βεβίηκα, παρῴχηκα, aorist θήκατο; τ-stem χρωτός; ὁ ἡ τό as article; οὐδέν as adjective; and construction δείδω μὴ οὐ. Being exempted from the normalizing pressure of ordinary speech the *Kunstsprache* was always capable of creating anomalous formations, cf. 12.431n., but book 10 excels itself in this regard: ἀβροτάξομεν 65, ἀήθεσσον 493, ἐγρηγόρθασι 419, ἐγρηγορτί 182, εἴασεν 299, κράτεσφι 156, παραφθαίησι 346, σπεῖο 285, σφίσιν = ὑμῖν 398 (see nn. *ad locc.*). There is also much diction shared with the *Odyssey*, a feature book 10 shares with book 24: e.g. δόσις, φήμη, δόξα, δαίτη, εἴσθα, ἀωτέω, τοίσδεσσι, ἀδηκότες, ἀσάμινθος. 'Odyssean' verses and formulas are noted in the commentary as they occur. Before the use of traditional diction in heroic poetry was fully appreciated 'Odyssean' elements were taken as proof of the dependence of book 10 on the *Odyssey* rather than as evidence of a shared tradition. The Book has an exotic taste in vocabulary: ἀλαλύκτημαι, ἄφαλος, ἄλλοφος, δέελος, δραίνω, διοπτήρ -εύω, δυσωρέω, ἑκταδίη, ἐπιδιφριάς, καταῖτυξ, κτιδέη, ληῖτις, λυκέη, ὅπλα = 'arms', πῖλος, σαυρωτήρ, φύξις, which is only partly attributable to special subject matter. There is also a liking for unusual dress and equipment. Taken separately, as Shewan and Danek show, these points are of little weight; taken together they make up a body of evidence that the majority of critics have found persuasive, if not conclusive.

Special force was attached by Lohmann (*Reden* 143, cf. Danek, *Dolonie* 177–203) to the fact that the characteristic ring-forms and parallelisms of Homeric speeches were not typical of those in book 10, where a less formal style with short utterances is favoured – conversation mediated through the *Kunstsprache*. Likewise, though the themes employed by the poet of book 10 before the spies set out for the Trojan camp are Iliadic – the despair of Agamemnon, council of chiefs, Nestor having an idea, arming – the execution is idiosyncratic.

The commentary follows in general the approach of Danek (summary, *Dolonie* 230–4): the Rhesos-story was adapted for this place in the *Iliad* not long after the epic's composition by a poet familiar with the traditional art of ἀοιδή but not the poet of the *Iliad*.

Bibliography: F. Klingner, *Hermes* 75 (1940) 337–68 = *Studien zur griechischen und römischen Literatur* (Zürich 1964) 7–39; W. Jens, *Studium Generale* 8 (1955) 616–25; S. Laser, *Hermes* 86 (1958) 385–425; B. Fenik, *Iliad X and the Rhesos: the Myth*, Collection Latomus 73 (Brussels–Berchem 1964), followed by O. M. Davison, *Quaderni Urbinati* 30 (1979) 61–6; G. Danek, *Studien zur Dolonie* (Vienna 1988), with extensive literature.

The plan of book 10 is basically simple, but overwrought. It falls into almost exactly equal halves, 1–298 and 299–579, a deliberate balance that makes the first half slow and the second packed with incident. Verses 1–179, the 'Nyktegersia', bear some resemblance to the Epipolesis of book 4 in conception, the principal chiefs being visited in turn by Agamemnon and Nestor, see 1–179n. But it is not a mere list. There are many interlinking thoughts as we follow first Agamemnon and then Nestor through the camp. Menelaos and Diomedes are sent off in different directions but no details are related of their encounters. After inspecting the watch, the chiefs engage in council and decide to send out scouts to see if the Trojans intend to stay or retreat; Odysseus and Diomedes arm and set off (180–298). The Achaean council is balanced by a Trojan council which proposes an analogous scheme, to see if the Achaeans are staying put or evacuating their camp; Dolon, bribed with the offer of Akhilleus' horses, arms and sets out towards the Achaean camp (299–339). This plot requires the two scouting parties to meet, and so they do. There follows a sharp break, not only in the storyline but also in the tone of its telling. The despondency of the Achaeans is replaced by cool daring as they hear of the finest spoils ever likely to come anyone's way at Troy. The old Rhesos-story, the Thracian king's death in a night attack, follows and it is the Achaeans, not Dolon, who win a prize of horses. Balance rules book 10. Fenik's principle, that form makes content (*Homer and the Nibelungenlied* 34), is beautifully exemplified.

1–179 The Atreidai, sleepless and apprehensive, do the rounds of the camp and in a series of courteous exchanges awaken the chiefs in order to inspect the watch and concert their plans for the night

The passage makes a rather slow episode whose purpose is to introduce the night raid of Diomedes and Odysseus. The whole passage, like the rest of the Book (to 332 at least), is composed in a singularly prolix and leisurely style that belies the urgency of the situation, in contrast to the taut narrative at the beginning of book 9 and the tense atmosphere of crisis that it conveys;

but the episode is superficially well constructed and its coherence is enhanced by many cross-references within it:

3 Agamemnon cannot sleep – 25 neither can Menelaos – 116 Nestor suspects that Menelaos is slumbering;

18 Agamemnon decides to consult Nestor – 54 repeats his intention – 82 rouses Nestor;

37 Menelaos mentions sending out a spy – 204 Nestor proposes it;

53 Agamemnon proposes to rouse Aias and Idomeneus – 109 Nestor adds Diomedes, Odysseus, Meges and the other Aias – 148 Nestor rouses Diomedes and Odysseus – 179 Diomedes rouses Aias and Meges;

56 Agamemnon suggests to Menelaos inspecting the watch – 97 he suggests to Nestor the watch may be sleeping – 180 the watch are alert.

Beneath this superficial cohesion, however, the whole episode lacks a sense of direction. Agamemnon sets off to find Nestor and devise some plan to save the army (17–20); then his consultations expand to include Aias and Idomeneus (53); Nestor is roused to see if the watch are keeping proper guard (97–9); then Nestor tells Odysseus the issue is whether to flee or fight (146–7), but cites an undefined moment of crisis to Diomedes.

1–20 These verses make up a typical scene of reflection leading to decision, cf. Arend, *Scenen* 106–15. The key word μερμηρίζειν does not appear but lurks behind πολλὰ φρεσὶν ὁρμαίνοντα, a formula (2× *Il.*, 2× *Od.*) whose nominative case is πολλὰ φρεσὶ μερμηρίζων (*Od.* 1.427). The presence of the theme and the absence of μερμηρίζειν exemplify a difference between this Book's handling of traditional topics and that of the *Iliad*, which is more evident in its treatment of dressing and arming scenes. For detailed discussion see Danek, *Dolonie* 214–29.

1–4 As a transitional passage, verses 1–4 are closely parallel to 2.1–2 ἄλλοι μέν ῥα θεοί τε καὶ ἀνέρες ἱπποκορυσταὶ | εὗδον παννύχιοι, Δία δ' οὐκ ἔχε νήδυμος ὕπνος, cf. 24.677–9. A similar situation, but in different language, introduces book 24. As they stand, the verses serve to link this Book with book 9, which (712–13) ended with the retirement of the Achaean chiefs to bed. But the link is more apparent than real: the Achaeans retired in a resolute frame of mind after some rousing words from Diomedes, now they are all in as much despair and perplexity as at the beginning of book 9.

1–2 Aristotle (*Poet.* 1461a16) was misled by the similarity of the opening of book 2 to quote 2.1–2 where 10.1–2 were intended. He went on to transpose verses 12 and 13. Nothing about the text can be inferred from the philosopher's faulty recollection. Verse 13 is inorganic, and like many such verses has been ejected by austere modern critics on that ground.

2 = 24.678. δεδμημένοι ὕπνῳ is formular (5×). μαλακῷ: not very likely in the circumstances, but the oral style takes the slight inconsequence in its stride. Sleep, regardless of circumstances, is μαλακός, γλυκύς, or γλυκερός if qualified adjectivally.

3 Agamemnon reveals again his characteristic despondency, cf. 9.9ff., 14.65ff. Even when he had every reason for confidence he assumed in book 2 that the spirits of his men could only be raised by deceit.

5–9 The simile has incurred much criticism ('confused', 'unintelligible', 'pointless', 'turgid' (Leaf)). The thought behind a simile that compares Agamemnon's groans or the frequency of his groans (πυκίν', 9) to Zeus's lightning is indeed overstretched, to say the least. Fränkel, *Gleichnisse* 28–9, suggests that the comparison is between the impending disaster implied by a great king's distress and the calamities portended by lightning. That may stand as the first example of much strained thought and language in this Book. Much, however, turns on our estimate of the majesty of kings; bT find the comparison a noble one.

5 πόσις Ἥρης ἠϋκόμοιο is a unique expression which could have been avoided by using ἀστράπτῃσι as the subjunctive form + the usual formula πατὴρ ἀνδρῶν τε θεῶν τε. The prototype, ἐρίγδουπος πόσις Ἥρης (7×), normally used as an appositional phrase, is a paraphrase for Ζεύς at 16.88, and would also have been available after ἀστράπτῃσιν. In later epic the regular formula for Here in the genitive is Ἥρης χρυσοπεδίλου (*Od.* 11.604, Hesiod, *Theog.* 952, frr. 25.29, 229.9 M–W). Note the divergence of this Book from the *Odyssey* at this point. ἠΰκομος is reserved for mortals and minor divinities (Kalupso, Leto, Thetis) in older epic, but extended to Rhea and Demeter in *HyDem*.

8 'Or somewhere the mouth of piercing war' is a good epic metaphor (19.313, 20.359) but unexpected as an alternative to rain, hail, or snow as an effect of Zeus's lightning: a further instance of the pretentious usage of traditional language characteristic of this Book. However, at 17.548–9 war and bad weather are bracketed together as evils that Zeus might portend by a rainbow. Note also that a storm let loose by Zeus provides an image for the flight of the Trojans before Patroklos, 16.384–93. — στόμα is used classically to mean the fighting front of an army, e.g. Xen. *Anab.* 3.4.42, but that is not the point in the Homeric passages. War has jaws for the same reason that Death has jaws in English poetry: it devours. πευκεδανός, which must be derived from πεύκη, 'pine', occurs only here in archaic epic; it is supposed to mean 'piercing' (from the pine-needles) or 'bitter' (from the taste of the resin), cf. ἐχεπευκής, περιπευκής. πτολέμοιο ... πευκεδανοῖο is probably an 'improvement' on the banal π. ... λευγαλέοιο (13.97).

10 Zenodotus' reading φοβέοντο (Arn/A) for τρομέοντο gives φοβοῦμαι its classical sense. Aristarchus insisted that in Homer φοβοῦμαι and its cognates signified flight (see 9.2n.), but that doctrine may not be binding on this Book.

11–13 Though speaking of Agamemnon the poet considers the general situation. The armies are camped in sight of each other anticipating with diverse feelings the renewal of the battle at first light, like the English and French before Agincourt:

> Now entertain conjecture of a time
> When creeping murmur and the poring dark
> Fills the wide vessel of the universe.
> From camp to camp, through the foul womb of night,
> The hum of either army stilly sounds,
> That the fix'd sentinels almost receive
> The secret whispers of each other's watch:
> Fire answers fire, and through the paly flames
> Each battle sees the other's umber'd face ...
>
> (Shakespeare, *Henry V*, Act IV)

The simile 5–8 indirectly invites the audience to 'entertain conjecture ...', an important function of similes. Since we have not been told otherwise Agamemnon was thought by Aristarchus (Arn/A) to be tossing in (or by, cf. 74) his hut, from which he could not look out over the plain; such a challenge to critical ingenuity could not be declined, Agamemnon must be camped on elevated ground – ἐφ' ὑψοῦς ἡ βασιλικὴ σκηνή. — πυρὰ πολλά: the watchfires are those of the jubilant Trojans celebrating their success with drink and hecatombs, see 8.553–63. Ἰλιόθι πρό: cf. 8.561n.

13–14 This allusion to Trojan jollifications is the first of a series that give a characteristic colour to this Book, Trojan arrogance in victory set in contrast with the prudence and piety of the Achaeans. The contrast between the two sides, to the detriment of the Trojans, is more strongly marked than elsewhere in the *Iliad*. The flute and pipes, Arn/A note, do not occur in Achaean contexts (except in the Shield, 18.495). In the exegetical scholia (bT), but not in the A scholia, it is assumed that the poet is biased towards the Achaeans: ἀεὶ γὰρ φιλέλλην ὁ ποιητής is the comment here (and 17× elsewhere). The hostile bias of the bT scholia against the Trojans appears at 223 and 319 (the prudence of Diomedes versus the foolhardiness of Dolon), 277 (piety of the Achaeans versus the negligence of Dolon), 300 (cavalier behaviour of Hektor versus the courtesy of Agamemnon), 308 (Hektor's demand is excessive), 315 (Dolon's greed), 317 (his upbringing in a feminine atmosphere), 325 (his boastfulness), 436 (he curries favour). The bias exists elsewhere, notably in the portrayal of Hektor from book 12 onwards, but is usually tempered by the poet's humanity (so Mueller, *Iliad* 89–90). For the denigration of Hektor in bT see 12.231–50n., and for the portrayal of the Trojans generally see J. Pinsent in Foxhall and Davies, *Trojan War* 137–62, with the literature listed by de Jong, *Narrators* 250.

15 προθελύμνους is a term appropriate to the ravages of the boar on the forests of Kaludon (9.541). For the probable sense of -θέλυμνος ('surface') see Chantraine, *Dict.* s.v. The boar *levelled* the forest αὐτῆσι ῥίζησι: hence προθέλυμνος = 'by the roots' here. The word must be intended as an 'epicism' or it would be a frigid exaggeration even as an expression of Agamemnon's heroic grief. For further development of this epic word see 13.130–1n. For tearing out the hair as an expression of grief cf. 22.77–8 (Priam). ἕλκετο, unaugmented, is the form approved by Aristarchus, presumably to avoid the overlengthened syllable εἵλκ-. The paradosis augments in such cases, and so do Hellenistic poets, cf. εἵλκετο (Ap. Rhod. 1.533 etc.).

16 ὑψόθ' ἐόντι Διί: dative because Agamemnon is appealing to Zeus. The expression is unique, though ἥμενος ὕψι (20.155) is similar. The phrase is the second innovation in eleven verses in the diction for the Olympians, a normally very conservative area.

17–179 In essence this scene is a Catalogue with extended entries. The pattern here is (1) the hero rouses another, (2) addresses him, (3) he replies, (4) he dresses and arms; but there is some untidiness: the entries of Agamemnon and Menelaos are intertwined, that of Nestor develops into an extended conversation, finally (179) the pattern collapses into a bare statement. The whole passage is examined by B. Helwig, *Raum und Zeit* (Hildesheim 1964) 132–4.

17 = 2.5 etc. (3× *Il.*, 3× *Od.*, [Hesiod] fr. 209.1 M–W). There is a synonymous verse appropriate when a character has been debating with himself: ὧδε δέ οἱ φρονέοντι δοάσσατο κέρδιον εἶναι (3× *Il.*, 7× *Od.*).

18 Odysseus may be called πολύμητις and be renowned for his δόλοι and μήδεα πυκνά (3.202), but in the *Iliad* it is Nestor who is free with prudent advice, cf. 204.

19 τεκταίνετο: 'construct', 'put together'. The usual epic metaphor is to 'weave' a plan, ὑφαίνειν. μῆτιν ἀμύμονα (nominative at verse-end, *Od.* 9.414) is a 'beautiful i.e. effective plan' according to Amory Parry, *Blameless Aegisthus* 99–103. There is obviously no moral connotation in the present phrase. Nestor, of course, has already proposed one scheme in book 9, and that ended in fiasco. This Book, however, avoids any direct allusion to the events of the preceding Book subsequent to the appointment of the watch (9.80), cf. 106–7n. For a possible indirect allusion see 252 and n. When Agamemnon rouses Nestor he proposes nothing more than an inspection of the watch (96–101).

21–4 For a fuller, and in some respects more logical, dressing scene see 2.42–6. For male characters the scene is very simple, see Arend, *Scenen*

97–8, there being no complicated garb to itemize; women's dress is more elaborate, cf. 14.178–86. It is natural on going outdoors to put on something over the χιτών, e.g. the χλαῖνα of 133 or the φᾶρος of 2.43; the lion skin of 23 (cf. 177) betrays this Book's taste for exotic detail; we have a leopard skin at 29 and a wolf skin at 334; for possible symbolic nuances in this attire see 29n. and 334–5n. The sandals too (22 = 132 etc., 5× *Il.*, 8× *Od.*) are for outdoor wear. εἵλετο δ' ἔγχος: a hero is not fully dressed without some weapon; at 2.45, a whole-verse formula, Agamemnon took a sword. In this scene Menelaos, Nestor, and Diomedes are all said to take spears. The weapons are a badge of rank, or a claim to rank (cf. Telemakhos, *Od.* 2.10).

25 Save for Menelaos' surmise that Agamemnon is minded to spy out Trojan intentions (which shows the poet thinking ahead) the brothers' conversation is nugatory and prolix. Aristophanes and Aristarchus (Arn/A) athetized 51–2, without perceptible impact on the impression of verbose and none too careful composition: see nn. to 46 ἐπὶ φρένα θῆχ' ἱεροῖσιν, 48 ἐπ' ἤματι μητίσασθαι, 56 ἠδ' ἐπιτεῖλαι, 61 μύθῳ ἐπιτέλλεαι ἠδὲ κελεύεις, 68 πατρόθεν ἐκ γενεῆς.

26 ὕπνος ἐπὶ βλεφάροισι (cf. 187 ὕπνος ἀπὸ βλεφάροιιν) is formular in the *Odyssey* (6×), but not attested elsewhere in the *Iliad*. The metaphor of sleep 'sitting' upon a person's eyes recurs at 91–2 but is unique to this Book. Sleep is a sort of immaterial substance that is poured (the usual metaphor in both epics), falls, or is cast over the eyes.

26–8 The words – ostensibly those of the poet – πάθοιεν... ἕθεν εἵνεκα... πόλεμον θρασύν are a good instance of the oblique expression of a character's feelings (cf. de Jong, *Narrators* 118–22). Menelaos is always sensible how much he owes to others, Agamemnon how much others owe to him. The language here is like that concerning Helen at 3.126–8 (see n.) ἀέθλους... οὓς ἕθεν εἵνεκ' ἔπασχον, and expresses the same embarrassment. With 3.126ff. may be compared Helen's own words in a similar context, *Od.* 4.145–6 ὅτ' ἐμεῖο κυνώπιδος εἵνεκ' Ἀχαιοὶ | ἤλθεθ' ὑπὸ Τροίην...

27 πουλὺν ἐφ' ὑγρήν (also at *Od.* 4.709): πουλύν is used as a metrically convenient feminine 4×, without clear justification. θῆλυς, always feminine (8×), is a rather different case, since the gender need not be marked by a suffix when it is so to speak marked by the meaning. ὑγρήν, feminine after ἅλς or θάλασσα, is regularly used substantivally, (3× *Il.*, 4× *Od.*).

28 ≅ *Od.* 4.146. πόλεμον θρασύν: an unusual instance of an epithet transferred from the warriors to their trade; the expression, however, is formular, cf. 6.254.

29 παρδαλέη: Menelaos ὡς ἥττων παρδαλῆν ἐνδύει (bT), that is, it symbolizes his inferiority to Agamemnon, who (23) assumed the heroic garb of a lion skin. A poet who knew the *Iliad* well might find it appropriate to give Menelaos the same outfit as his rival – Paris wore a leopard skin at 3.17. μετάφρενον εὐρύ is unique, an easy thought but perhaps condensed from the formula μετάφρενον εὗρέε τ' ὤμω (2×).

30–1 στεφάνη (3×) is the rarest of Homeric words for the helmet, see D. H. F. Gray, *CQ* 41 (1947) 114–19 = *Language and Background* 60–5. The two initial consonants are metrically necessary in all three places. The preferred term for the helmet is κόρυς. — κεφαλῆφιν is dative singular, cf. 257, 261, 458, 496, *Od.* 20.94, a relatively late usage developed within the *Kunstsprache*. Mycenaean *-pi* is an instrumental plural (Ventris and Chadwick, *Documents* 83). κεφαλῆφιν is genitive and again singular at 11.350 and 16.762. Verses 30–1 resemble Hesiod, *Theog.* 578 στεφάνην χρυσέην κεφαλῆφιν ἔθηκε, but there the στεφάνη is Pandora's crown, not a (part of a) helmet. — θήκατο: the strong-grade θηκ- in the active plural and middle parts of τίθημι is relatively infrequent in the *Iliad* (5× and 8× *Od.*), and is nowhere formular. Two of the five occurrences are in book 24 (271, 795). For donning the helmet the traditional verse is κρατὶ δ' ἐπ' ἰφθίμῳ κυνέην εὔτυκτον ἔθηκεν (4×) with variant at 5.743 = 11.41, which reveals στεφάνην, κεφαλῆφι, θήκατο, and χαλκείην as innovatory in this context, cf. the handling of the μερμηρίζειν-scene, 4n.

32–3 Conventional praise of Agamemnon, cf. 1.78–9 (with κρατέει for ἤνασσε). θεὸς (δ') ὣς τίετο δήμῳ is formular (5× *Il.*, 1× *Od.*) Since ὣς is from σϝώς, the intrusion of δ' illustrates the increased flexibility of the epic diction as a result of the loss of ϝ-, see Hoekstra, *Modifications* 26–30. Two personages so honoured are priests, Dolopion (5.78) and Onetor (16.605), but the rest are warriors, so that the formula refers to the quality and quantity of the honour, not to its motivation.

34 τιθήμενον: for the -η- cf. τιθήμεναι (23.83, 23.247). Some metrical licence for the accommodation of τιθέμενον is necessary, but the usual lengthening of the first syllable has given way to the analogy of τί-θη-μι etc., cf. ἁήμενος (< ἄημι) at *Od.* 6.131. ἔντεα functions as a synonym of τεύχεα, e.g. in formulas with the epithets καλά and ποικίλα. Arn/A on 75, in accordance with the usual effort of ancient commentators to separate synonyms, limit ἔντεα to shield and helmet. The shield, as it happens, is the only piece of equipment donned about the shoulders with τίθημι as the verb, cf. 149, 15.479.

37 ἠθεῖε, see 6.518–19n., is a term of address between brothers or, in the form ἠθείη κεφαλή at 23.94, between men as close as brothers. Arn/A says it is appropriate for the younger man (or social inferior, cf. *Od.* 14.147).

38 ἐπίσκοπος in the sense of 'scout' is cited only from this verse and 342. The usual sense is 'guardian', e.g. 24.729. Aristarchus (Hdn/A) emended to κατάσκοπον, a more regular term. – αἰνῶς: see 9.244n.

39 μὴ οὐ with a verb of fearing: only here in *Il.*

41 Νύξ was a goddess (14.259, Hesiod, *Theog.* 123, and many early cosmogonies; see G. S. Kirk, J. E. Raven, M. Schofield, *The Presocratic Philosophers*, 2nd edn (Cambridge 1983) 19–24). The epithet ἀμβροσίη (4× *Il.*, including the variant at 2.57, 2× *Od.*) recognizes in the hours of darkness the numinous quality that brought about the deification, see West on *Od.* 4.429. J. Puhvel, *Zeitschr. f. vergleich. Sprachforschung* 73 (1956) 210, revives an ancient idea that links the 'ambrosial night' with sleep (cf. ἀμβρόσιος...ὕπνος, 2.19), taking ἀμβρόσιος as 'dispensing vital force'. Leaf records earlier speculations at 2.19n. This Book disposes of a duplicate formula, νύκτα δι' ὀρφναίην (83, 276, 386 (v.l. ἀμβροσίην), and as a v.l. at 142). νύκτα δι' ὀρφναίην is Odyssean (9.143, cf. *HyHerm* 578). The *Odyssey* has also νύκτα διὰ δνοφερήν (*Od.* 15.50). For an attempt to suit these epithets (best regarded as semantically redundant) to their contexts see Austin, *Archery* 71–3. θρασυκάρδιος: the second hemistich ≅ 13.343.

43 For χρεώ with acc. of the person in need see 9.75n. διοτρεφὲς ὦ Μενέλαε: cf. *Od.* 4.26, 4.561. The Iliadic formula is ὦ Μενέλαε διοτρεφές (7×).

44 ἐρύσσεται is future indicative with analogical -σσ- (Monro, *HG* 40–1, 63). ἐρύομαι (and ῥύομαι), 'save', must be distinguished from ἐρύω, 'drag away', though there is sometimes doubt, e.g. in the *rescue* of a corpse, which verb is in question (cf. 9.248n.). In Homer (ϝ)ἐρύω normally implies the diagamma, ἐρύομαι does not. A root *seru*, *srū*, cf. Lat. *servare*, used to be assumed (e.g. by LSJ and Leaf on 1.216), but this is questioned by Myc. *u-ru-to* PY An 657 = ϝρύντοι, 'are protecting', see Ventris and Chadwick, *Documents* 188–9, and Chantraine, *Dict.* s.v. ἔρυμαι. The absence of digamma would be explained if ἐ- were prothetic.

45 = 8.501 as that verse was read by Zenodotus.

46 Ἑκτόρεος here and Νεστόρεος (2.54, etc.), beside Ὀδυσῆϊος, appear to show Aeolic -ρ- > -ρε- (Risch, *Wortbildung* 131). Ἀγαμεμνόνεος (10.326, etc.) will then be a secondary extension of the formation. — ἐπιτιθέναι + dative φρενί, e.g. *Od.* 5.427, 21.1, is 'to implant a thought in someone else's mind'; here the active voice + accusative φρένα must signify 'apply one's own mind to', 'pay attention to'. The expression does not recur in the epic.

47 ἔκλυον αὐδήσαντος is formular, but in other occurrences agrees with a personal name; it is slightly misused here without noun or pronoun in agreement.

47–50 Agamemnon is astonished that a man of mortal parentage could have done such execution as Hektor did the preceding day. Divine ancestry is such an obvious way of accounting for a hero's superhuman strength that its haphazard attribution in the *Iliad* is worth noting. Of major figures only Aineias, Akhilleus, Sarpedon, and Rhesos had divine parents, and much good it did them. On the other hand insignificant characters like

Askalaphos and Ialmenos, captains of the watch (9.82) and the Myrmidon brigadier Eudoros (16.179) are given a god. Agamemnon's surprise betrays non-Iliadic and probably later thinking, when heroes had become ἡμίθεοι, cf. 12.23n. — μέρμερ(α) means deeds of war (8.453), especially slaughter, cf. 289 and 524. ἐπ' ἤματι: apparently = ἐφημέριος 'as his daily task'. The sense 'in one day', is possible (cf. 19.229). μητίσασθαι means 'plan and execute', like μήδεσθαι. In short, Agamemnon is made to concede to Hektor the βουλὴ κερδαλέη his own side lacks. αὔτως: 'by himself', without outside aid. θεᾶς: the epic uses the distinctive feminine forms in the formula δῖα θεάων and in places where, as here, it is necessary to distinguish goddesses from gods. The declension with -α- is an Aeolism, see Wathelet, *Traits éoliens* 354-5.

51-2 Aristophanes and Aristarchus felt with some justification that this pair of verses added nothing to the sense of 49–50, and accordingly athetized (Arn/A). Objection was also taken to the synonymy of δηθά and δολιχόν.

53 ≅ 112. Αἴαντα: Telamonian Aias, as 112 makes clear. Aristarchus read Αἴαντε according to Didymus (Did/A), presumably to make this line conform to the presence in the council of both Aiantes from 110 onwards. Didymus, however, was suspected of misreporting Aristarchus. The narrative follows Agamemnon till 130, and then switches to Nestor. Menelaos' errand and its accomplishment are simply assumed.

56-8 ἱερὸν τέλος: cf. 97, 180, and ἱεροὺς πυλαωρούς (24.681), ἱερὸς στρατός (*Od.* 24.81). ἱερὸν τέλος is interpreted as μέγα τάγμα by the Γλωσσογράφοι cited by Arn/A, cf. ἱερὸν ἰχθύν 16.407 and n. τέλος can mean 'duty', 'service' (e.g. 18.378), so that φυλάκων τέλος is a periphrasis for φύλακες. ἱερός compliments the dignity and importance of these sentinels, see P. Wulfing von Martitz, *Glotta* 38 (1960) 300, and 17.464–5n. This is another link with book 9; the sentinels were posted at the instance of Nestor (9.80–88). Agamemnon, as it subsequently transpires, means that the council of war is to be combined with an inspection of the watch, though it is not put very clearly. ἐπιτεῖλαι is vague for 'keep them on their toes', which is Agamemnon's present intention, cf. 97–9, 192–3. υἱός: Thrasumedes, cf. 9.81.

58 The arrangement of the sentence requires Meriones' description to fall after the feminine caesura, hence the word-order καὶ Ἰδομενῆος ὀπάων. Elsewhere the order is καὶ ὀπάων Ἰδομενῆος (7.165, 8.263, 17.258).

61-2 ἐπιτέλλεαι ἠδὲ κελεύεις: see 9.133n. — αὖθι μένω: i.e. where the sentinels are posted.

63 = (from αὖτις) 13.753, with a variant at 12.369.

65 ἀβροτάξομεν is aorist subjunctive and implies a present ἀβροτάζω. No other form is extant. The word is doubtless an epicism based on the Aeolism ἤμβροτον, etc., hence the smooth breathing. The omission of -μ-is parallel to ἁβρότη (14.78) beside ἀμβροσίη, in both cases metrically necessary.

67 φθέγγομαι (4× in this Book) is properly to 'speak up', as at 11.603 (Akhilleus summoning Patroklos) and 21.341 (φθέγξομαι ἰάχουσα). — ἐγρήγορθαι must be intended as the infinitive of the perfect middle with an ο-grade imported from the perfect active. There is an analogous plural imperative ἐγρήγορθε at 7.371 = 18.299, but that may represent a transformation of ἐγρήγορθι, an intransitive active form, see Chantraine *GH* i 429, and Wyatt, *ML* 111–13 and 419n. for a similar *monstrum* ἐγρηγόρθασι. The proparoxytone ('Aeolic') accent is certified by Herodian (Hrd/A).

68–9 πατρόθεν ἐκ γενεῆς: would this be formal courtesy or, like the patronymics of Russian, a claim to intimacy and friendship? It is difficult to disentangle an emotive use of patronymics from their obvious metrical utility. The usages at 87 ὦ Νέστορ Νηληϊάδη, 103 Ἀτρεΐδη κύδιστε, and 144 διογενὲς Λαερτιάδη are all parts of regular whole-verse formulas. κυδαίνων in any case implies the greatest courtesy, cf. Agamemnon's unwontedly apologetic tone towards Nestor at 96 and 120–5.

69–70 μηδὲ μεγαλίζεο θυμῷ: a nice touch of characterization; Agamemnon, of course, is normally very much inclined to stand on ceremony and would have summoned his allies by herald. Crisis, however, is a great leveller, as bT note at 9.12 (αὐτὸς δὲ ['Αγαμέμνων] μετὰ πρώτοισι πονεῖτο) on a similar occasion.

71 Agamemnon means that κακότης, 'sorry plight', generally is the lot assigned to mortals of which his present πόνος is an instance. But γεινομένοισι (aorist participle, with metrically lengthened first syllable) would be better – 'at the moment of our birth' with specific reference to the Atreidai (so Leaf). For Zeus's reputation as a hard master cf. the parable of his πίθοι (24.527ff.). Destiny in a general way was thought of as fixed at birth (γιγνομένοισι), so 20.127–8, 23.79, 24.209ff., *Od.* 7.196ff., Hesiod *Theog.* 218–19 ≅ 905–6. The agent in those passages is αἶσα or μοῖρα, not Zeus.

74 = 1.329. Nestor, like Odysseus at 151, seems to be sleeping outside (παρά) his κλισίη, ready for action. That is in keeping with the emergency but it is also convenient for the narrative, since it avoids the lengthy ceremonies of being welcomed by a host at home. In a rare lapse T (at 139) speaks of Agamemnon entering Nestor's hut. The situation is better stated at 151, Diomedes was ἐκτὸς ἀπὸ κλισίης.

75 Note the comfort of Nestor's bivouac, which bT attribute to his age, comparing Phoinix' bedding at 9.661 κώεά τε ῥῆγός τε λίνοιό τε λεπτὸν ἄωτον. That may well be right: the young Diomedes made do with ῥινὸν βοὸς ἀγραύλοιο (155 below).

75–8 The poet perhaps forgets the corslet in order to devote two and a half lines to Nestor's splendid belt. It must be by chance that no corslets at all are mentioned in this Book; the spies had good reason to be lightly armed. θωρήσσοιτο at the end of 78 is obviously used in a general sense.

79 ἐπέτρεπε: the intransitive sense 'give way to' (cf. Hdt. 3.36) occurs only here in the epic.

80–1 The rhythm of the verse justifies a comma after ἐπ' ἀγκῶνος, but with ἐπ' ἀγκῶνος κεφαλὴν ἐπαείρας compare ἐπ' ἀγκῶνος κεφαλὴν σχέθε, *Od.* 14.494. — ἐξερεείνετο μύθῳ is the only occurrence of this middle in the *Iliad* (4× *Od.*, including ἐρεείνετο μύθῳ, 17.305). For other metrically motivated middles, usually located before the bucolic diaeresis, see Meister, *Kunstsprache* 19–20.

83 = 24.363 (with ἀμβροσίην). νύκτα δι' ὀρφναίην (see 41n.) is read here but νύκτα δι' ἀμβροσίην in the parallel questions at 41 and 142. The variation may be fortuitous, but in view of the close proximity of the occurrences it suggests an unusual self-consciousness about repetitive diction.

84 Aristarchus thought the verse beside the point (ἄκαιρος) and linguistically incompetent, since a synonym of φύλαξ (οὖρος) was required whereas οὐρεύς = ἡμίονος. His answer of course was athetesis (Arn/A).

85 τίπτε δέ σε χρεώ is Odyssean (*Od.* 1.225, 4.312).

87 Agamemnon uses the full form of address in beginning his conversation with Nestor, in contrast to the familiar language which the Atreidai brothers used towards each other. Nestor replies with the same formality at 103; both then assume a warmer tone (ὦ γέρον 120, no vocative at 129).

88 γνώσεαι: the future tense functions as a polite imperative.

89 Agamemnon, like other men (e.g. Asios, 12.164–6, Odysseus, *Od.* 5.303–5), blames Zeus when things go wrong, a tendency that the god resented (*Od.* 1.32ff.).

89–90 = 9.609–10 (from εἰς ὅ κ' ἀϋτμή). ἀϋτμή is the hot breath (of life).

91 πλάζομαι is either 'I am distraught', cf. 2.132, or more likely 'I am wandering here because ...' For νήδυμος (< ἔχεν ἥδυμος etc. by false division according to Leumann, *HW* 44–5) see 2.1–2n. ἥδυμος, i.e. Ϝήδυμος, is attested as a v.l. in many places but is otherwise not found in the epic: ἥδυμος without Ϝ is first found at *HyHerm* 241, 449, and [Hesiod] fr. 330 M–W.

93–5 Agamemnon's symptoms of alarm, though not the language in which he expresses them, are like those of Andromakhe (22.452–5).

94 ἀλαλύκτημαι, 'be troubled', is *hapax legomenon* in the epic: an Ionic verb, the present ἀλυκτέω being attested in Hippocrates (*Mul.* 1.5), cf. ἀλυκτάζω, Hdt. 9.70.

95 The pomposity of Agamemnon's calling his own limbs φαίδιμα is an unintended consequence of the formular style, and so also must be the oxymoron of saying that φαίδιμα γυῖα shook. For the latter cf. τρόμος ἔλλαβε φαίδιμα γυῖα (8.452), where, however, the limbs are those of Here and Athene and the oxymoron is effective.

96 δραίνεις: δραίνω, 'be ready to act', is another Ionic word (cf. Hdt. 1.15), a doublet of δράω, found only here in the *Iliad*. Cf. ὀλιγοδρανέων.

97 The commanders of the φύλακες were named at 9.81–4; they included, though neither Agamemnon nor Nestor mentions it here, Nestor's son Thrasumedes. At 57 that was given as a reason for sending Nestor. Seven commanders were listed in book 9 and each commanded 100 κοῦροι. This large force is stationed beyond the wall but before the trench.

98 The similarity of this verse to *Od.* 12.281 has been used as a leading argument for the dependence of this Book on the *Odyssey* (so S. Laser, *Hermes* 86 (1958) 293–4), but could equally be attributed to the random effects of formular composition. — ἀδηκότες (or ἀδηκότες): this strange participle, always joined with καμάτῳ, clearly means in general terms 'overcome', cf. ὕπνῳ καὶ καμάτῳ ἀρημένος (*Od.* 6.2). It is found at *Od.* 12.281, *HyAp* 460, and no less than four times in this Book (here and 312 = 399, 471), a frequency that strikingly illustrates the author's linguistic taste. The derivation is disputed (< ἀϝαδέω according to *LfgrE*, which may be attested at *Od.* 1.134, cf. bT's gloss ἀηδισθέντες): see also Heubeck, *Odyssey* 12.281n. — ὕπνος in these contexts implies 'sleepiness' (= ἀγρυπνία, bT!).

100 ἧαται, here and elsewhere, is the preferred orthography in OCT. The MSS, with some fluctuation, offer ει as the reflex of original *ē* before the back vowels *o* and *a*, but η- before *e* or a consonant, hence ἧμαι (18.104 etc.) but εἷαται, here and 2.137 etc., see Chantraine, *GH* i 8–9. 'This looks like a bardic convention' (Janko, vol. iv 36), and should not be corrected.

101 'Nor do we know any way to prevent their being eager to fight during the night' – the μή-clause, originally an independent sentence, itself implies fear and the wish to avert the danger, and so is used with verbs like ὁράω and οἶδα in Homer as well as with verbs of fearing. The idea of a night attack is mooted only here in the *Iliad*. Otherwise night puts an end to all military operations. An ambush might be set by night (*Od.* 14.469ff.), but the *Iliad* will not admit such unheroic exploits.

104 θήν is similar to δή, but 'perhaps rather weaker in force' (Denniston, *Particles* 288).

106–7 The open condition, implying the possibility of Akhilleus reentering the fray, is unexpected when such a change of heart has just been ruled out of court. A remote condition 'Hektor would be in trouble if Akhilleus were to change his mind' would certainly be more appropriate, cf. 19 and n.

108 ἐγείρομεν is aorist subjunctive, 'let us arouse'. Odysseus is nearby, but Nestor does not relish the walk to Aias' distant quarters and puts his suggestion in the form of a wish, εἴ τις ... καλέσειεν (111).

110–12 The swift Aias is Aias son of Oileus: his perpetual epithet is determinative and distinguishes him from the other Aias; it is explained at 14.521–2 οὐ γάρ οἵ τις ὁμοῖος ἐπισπέσθαι ποσὶν ἦεν | ἀνδρῶν τρεσσάντων. The gallant son of Phuleus is Meges, Odysseus' neighbour in Doulikhion (or in Elis – there is some confusion over Meges' homeland, see 2.627–30n. and 13.685n.), a shadowy but not insignificant figure. Αἴαντα in 112 is the Telamonian Aias, ἀντίθεον being a purely decorative epithet. For the Achaean dispositions (with which the poet of this Book is clearly familiar) see 11.5–9n.; Nestor is in the centre next to Odysseus, Aias on the far left wing of the army, and next to him Idomeneus.

114–23 These verses are an interesting comment on the characterization of Menelaos in the *Iliad*: aware of his inferiority on the field but anxious to play his part, and overshadowed by his protective brother, see 240n. — The thrice repeated πονέεσθαι seems clumsy, but the epic style shows a certain indifference to such repetitions, cf. Hainsworth on *Od.* 7.116. For πονέεσθαι of the chore of convening a council cf. 2.409, 9.12; usually in the *Iliad* the reference is to the toil of the battlefield.

115 οὐδ' ἐπικεύσω is an under-represented formula in the *Iliad* (2×), but popular in the *Odyssey* (11×, with variants)

116 ὡς εὕδει: the construction puzzled Nicanor (Nic/A) who suggested an exclamatory ὡς. The syntax is analogous to that in which the suppressed antecedent of a relative pronoun has no clear construction in the principal clause, e.g. ὠκύμορος δή μοι, τέκος, ἔσσεαι, οἷ' ἀγορεύεις (18.95): 'I shall reproach Menelaos ⟨because I notice⟩ how he is asleep . . .' See Monro, *HG* 238.

118 = 11.610, probably a formular verse that is slightly misused in its present context. λισσόμενος is how Akhilleus would like to see Agamemnon (11.610); it by no means describes the actions of the Atreidai on this occasion.

123 ποτιδέγμενος ὁρμήν: a formula, cf. *Od.* 2.403. Agamemnon is patronizing, cf. 26–8n.; when he is not overshadowed Menelaos pulls his weight, e.g. 13.581ff., 13.601ff., 15.540ff., and 17.1ff. He volunteered for the night-raid, see 230 below, to the alarm of Agamemnon, but is consistently represented in the *Iliad* as conscious that others are better fighters than he, see 240n and 17.24–8n.

124 ἐμέο: this is the sole occurrence of the intermediate form in Homer (ἐμεῖο > ἐμέο > ἐμεῦ). σεο (23×), however, and ἑο (14×) are regular.

127 ἵνα γάρ: the combination is unexpected (see Chantraine, *GH* II 361, Monro, *HG* 318, Denniston, *Particles* 95), but similar to the use of γάρ after relatives, e.g. 12.344. The γάρ is, as it were, apodotic and indicates that the clause gives a reason or explanation.

130 Agamemnon now apparently accompanies Nestor (ἀλᾶσθε, plural, 141) to rouse Odysseus and Diomedes. Nestor, however, does all the talking until the council's decision is taken. With the departure of Menelaos in the opposite direction and the despatch of Diomedes for the Lesser Aias and Meges in prospect the storyline has become too complicated for traditional narrative techniques to handle easily. The poet extricates himself by ignoring Menelaos and Diomedes and sticking to Nestor.

133 ἀμφὶ δ' ἄρα χλαῖναν: cf. *Od.* 4.50 etc. (4×). φοινικόεσσαν: the proper epithet for a cloak (*Od.* 14.500, 21.118). The -νικ- syllable should be metrically long, cf. φοῖνιξ, φοίνικος, so that the word so spelled must be listed as one of the rare examples of metrical shortening. A contracted pronunciation φοινικοῦσσαν is never indicated for this class of adjectives in Homer (see, however, 12.283n. and *Od.* 7.107 (καιροσέων) with Chantraine's comment, *GH* 16). It is possible, of course, that the word was taken into the epic dialect in the form φοινίκϝεσσα, cf. the Mycenaean *pe-de-we-sa* i.e. πέδϝεσσα PY Ta 709, etc., where the syllabic signs *-de-we* indicate the absence of the linking vowel -o-.

134 διπλῆν: see 3.125–7n. ἐκταδίην is obscure (< ἐκ-τείνω?) but presumably indicates the blanket-like size of the cloak. οὔλη: wool is the normal material of the Homeric χλαῖνα, reasonably enough (2× in each epic). It may be used as a blanket (24.646, *Od.* 14.520). ἐπενήνοθε: for this strange epic verb, also found at 2.219 and *Od.* 8.365, 17.270, *HyAphr* 62, and (with prefix κατ-) *HyDem* 279, [Hesiod], *Aspis* 269, see 11.266n. A connexion with ἄνθος, which would permit a basic sense 'sprout up', is argued by J. M. Aitchison, *Glotta* 41 (1963) 271–8, but see also *LfgrE* s.v. and Wyatt, *ML* 116–17. The poet may not have understood the word so precisely, for it is odd to describe the nap of a woven garment as sprouting from it.

135 = 14.12, 15.482, a fragment of the standard arming scene, which the poet treats idiosyncratically, cf. 1–20n. ἀκαχμένον is clear enough in sense ('tipped', 'pointed') but of obscure derivation, see *LfgrE* s.v. Its equivalent at 11.43 in a secondary variant of this traditional verse is κεκορυθμένος.

137 Διῒ μῆτιν ἀτάλαντον: The formula is shown by its metrics to be an ancient element of the diction (< Διϝεὶ μῆτιν *sm̥*τάλαντον). It is probably used in this Book as an archaism, for like Διῒ φίλος (Διϝεὶ φίλος) it is absent from the *Odyssey*.

139 περὶ φρένας ἤλυθ' ἰωή: cf. *Od.* 17.261. Sound flows around the hearer in the epic. The closest verbal parallel, however, is *HyHerm* 421 ἐρατὴ δὲ διὰ φρένας ἤλυθ' ἰωή. In all these passages ἰωή is a sound, in the *Odyssey* and the *Hymn* the beguiling sound of music. Elsewhere in the *Iliad* (4.276, 11.308, 16.127) ἰωή (ϝιωή) refers to the force of wind or fire. Danek, *Dolonie* 91–7, takes the word for an archaism known to ἀοιδοί only from formulas and used by them, except here, with a defining genitive.

140–76 The short speeches that characterize the exchanges between Nestor and Odysseus and Diomedes give this section especially a realistic conversational tone. The feature is an important difference between this Book's use of direct speech and the more stylized structures of the *Iliad* proper. For Danek, *Dolonie* 177–203, the difference, taken with other differences in the handling of typical epic themes and topoi, is conclusive evidence that this Book was not created by the poet of the *Iliad*.

142 χρειὼ τόσον ἵκει: cf. *Od.* 2.28, 5.189.

145 = 16.22, likewise after a whole-verse vocative expression.

147 = 327. The verse is ejected by edd. (Leaf, Ameis–Hentze) as being interpolated from 327, where it is essential, in order to give ἐπέοικε in the preceding verse an unnecessary infinitive construction. However, the other councillors are given more or less plausible reasons for being summoned and Odysseus deserves a better reason for his disturbed rest than the ἄχος of 145. It is not of much consequence that the question of flight or fight has been resolved in book 9.

149 In what sense can a shield be ποικίλος? Presumably because it was blazoned or elaborately chased like that of Akhilleus (book 18), or heavily metallic like that of Agamemnon (11.32–40). In either case the polish of such a shield would nullify the alleged advantage of the special helmets (257–71). ποικίλος is evidently 'formular', a remnant of the frequent τεύχεα ποικίλα χαλκῷ. — Odysseus, implausibly, takes only a shield, as Diomedes at 178 takes only a spear. But the poet seems to remember these details when the two arm at 254–71 and provides both heroes with helmets, then Diomedes with sword and shield only, and Odysseus with bow and sword only.

150 τὸν δ' ἐκίχανον (not in *Od.*) is the verse-end equivalent of τὸν δ' εὗρον, etc., the usual formula (11× *Il.*, 1× *Od.*) that marks the beginning of a visit.

153 The σαυρωτήρ (only here) is the spike at the butt of the spear shaft rather than the butt (οὐρίαχος). The weapons depicted on the Warrior Vase from Mycenae illustrate the device.

153–4 χαλκὸς | λάμφ': a strikingly flexible formula, cf. χαλκὸς ... λάμπ' (11.44–5), χαλκῷ | λάμφ' (11.65–6), λάμπε δὲ χαλκῷ (12.463), λάμπετο χαλκῷ (20.156), χαλκὸς ἐλάμπετο (22.134), χαλκὸς ἔλαμπε (13.245 = 22.32). See Introduction 12–13. Verse 154 (to Διός) = 11.66. The formula, of course, is appropriate to the flash of polished bronze in bright sunlight, not to the present situation.

156 κράτεσφι: a *monstrum rhapsodicum*, formed by extracting a case-form -εσφι from archaic locative-instrumentals in -φι of *s*-stem nouns, e.g. ὄχεσφι, στήθεσφι, and attaching this to the innovated τ-stem κρατ-.

157 παρστάς: the form with παρ by apocope is rare – only here, against παραστάς 17× *Il.*, 9× *Od.* In the first hemistich the middle participle παριστάμενος is more convenient.

158 λὰξ ποδὶ κινήσας is formular and apparently not discourteous, cf. *Od.* 15.45 (Telemakhos rousing Peisistratos), where the scholia explain Nestor's behaviour here by reflecting that his age would prevent his stooping. 'Apparently the Alexandrians had no feeling for such a sign of rough camaraderie' (Hoekstra on *Od.* 15.45). — νείκεσέ τ' ἄντην: ironical, cf. *Od.* 8.158 for a malicious sense of the formula.

159 Aristarchus hesitated between ἔγρεο and ὄρσεο (Did/A). Eust. 519.32 cites a plus-verse, ὁ Νέστωρ τῷ Διομήδῃ πού [sc. in this passage] φησιν, "ἔγρεο, ... μή τίς τοι [καθ]εύδοντι μεταφρένῳ ἐν δόρυ πήξῃ" (≅ 8.95, which has φεύγοντι in mid-verse). But the verse has not wandered directly from book 8; it was the point of an indecent joke by Diogenes, who substituted εὕδοντι for φεύγοντι, a joke famous enough to find its way into the doxographies (see Diog. Laert. 6.53), whence it obtained this first small foothold in the text. ἀωτεῖς: an Odyssean word (10.548), glossed by Hsch. with ἀπανθίζειν, i.e. it was taken as a denominative of ἄωτος. Other conjectures in Frisk, *GEW* s.v.

160 ἀΐεις, an epic verb, is rather loosely used as 'realize' (properly 'perceive by hearing'). (Τρῶες) ἐπὶ θρωσμῷ πεδίοιο is formular, adapted from the whole-verse formula Τρῶες δ' αὖθ' ἑτέρωθεν ἐπὶ θρωσμῷ πεδίοιο (11.56 = 20.3, in both cases of the Trojans arming for battle after their bivouac outside the city). The θρωσμός ('rising ground') cannot be identified at the present day.

164 Diomedes affects to protest, not at being awakened by a kick, but at Nestor's indefatigable activity, cf. *Od.* 12.279–80 σχέτλιός εἰς, 'Οδυσεῦ· πέρι τοι μένος οὐδέ τι γυῖα | κάμνεις. σχέτλιος properly expresses exasperation at outrageous behaviour, cf. 2.112n., 9.19n. and AbT on this verse – ὁ ἄξια ἀγανακτήσεως πράσσων, but here of course the exasperation is a comic pretence. ἀμήχανος, 'impossible', at 167 continues Diomedes' humorous expostulation.

166 ἔπειτα: 'then' or 'therefore'. Ameis–Hentze cite 243 as a parallel. Or the poet adapted the very common ὃς (etc.) μὲν ἔπειτα (18× *Il.*, 20× *Od.*) at verse-end or verse-beginning.

168 Except in this verse Nestor is always given the formula τὸν δ' ἠμείβετ' ἔπειτα (8× *Il.*, 3× *Od.*) not its equivalent τὸν δ' αὖτε προσέειπε. There is no contextual explanation of this preference, which seems to imply a hardening of the sentence into a virtual whole-verse formula. It is significant that a usage persisting throughout the rest of the *Iliad* and in the *Odyssey* is not maintained in this Book.

169 = 23.626 (5× *Il.*, 3× *Od.*, with various vocatives). For the meaning of κατὰ μοῖραν see M. Finkelberg, *CPh* 82 (1987) 135–8; κατὰ μοῖραν, with long α, means 'in orderly succession', e.g. of troops (16.367), the linguistically more recent κατὰ μοῖραν, with short α, means 'rightly'. The formula κατὰ κόσμον shows a similar evolution.

170 παῖδες: only two of Nestor's sons are mentioned in the *Iliad*, Thrasumedes and Antilokhos. Thrasumedes is with the watch and Antilokhos is (in the *Iliad* proper) temporarily out of mind, see 9.81–4n.

173–4 ἐπὶ ξυροῦ: the first occurrence of what became a very common metaphor for crisis. As with scales (8.69 = 22.209, 12.433) the metaphor is from the uncertainty of balance. The construction of ἵσταται, which should be impersonal, ὄλεθρος, and the infinitive βιῶναι is curious, but the sense is perfectly clear.

177–8 These verses (from ἕσσατο) = 23–4. δέρμα λέοντος: heroic attire, cf. 23n.

180–253 Nestor calls for a volunteer to spy out Trojan intentions. Diomedes at once responds and calls for a companion. The other chiefs volunteer and, in order to spare Menelaos, Agamemnon tells Diomedes to make his own choice. He names Odysseus

180–2 The watch are on their toes. Their wakefulness is noted because 97–9 above had raised the possibility that they had all collapsed from exhaustion. — Verse 180 ≅ 3.209 (with Τρώεσσιν for φυλάκεσσιν). ἀγρομένοισιν, as if the pickets were at assembly, as the Trojans were at 3.209, is not very appropriate here, although the commanders are all found together. — ἐγρηγορτί: 'wakefully', a unique experiment; adverbs in -ί or -τι are properly formed against nominal stems.

183 δυσωρέω, 'keep painful watch', is a 'precious' linguistic invention, like Δύσπαρις (3.39, etc.), that found no imitators.

185 δι' ὄρεσφι: for -φι representing the genitive case see 11.350n. ὄρεσφι (7×) is found only in the *Iliad*, and there only in similes. The restriction is probably fortuitous; as a locative case, e.g. 11.474 ὄρεσφι (6×, of which 4× in similes) is not replaceable by ὄρεσσι, since the latter is restricted in the *Iliad* to the prepositional formula ἐν ὄρεσσι (except ἐπ' ἀκροπόλοισιν ὄρεσσιν 5.523). ὀρυμαγδός: as often the detail of the simile departs from the situation of the narrative. The Trojans are making the noise on this occasion, cf. 13.

187–8 The strange concord τῶν ... φυλασσομένοισι has a parallel at 14.139–41. The cumulative oral style does not encourage grammatical concord as a means of linking well-separated words if other constructions are possible.

190 A good example of the manipulation of formular diction. The basic formula is τὸν (etc.) δὲ ἰδὼν γήθησε + noun–epithet subject (2× *Il.*, 2× *Od.*) with a variant καὶ τὸν μὲν γήθησεν ἰδὼν + noun–epithet subject (2× *Il.*): this is condensed here in order to accommodate a co-ordinated phrase at the verse-end, cf. τὴν δ' Ὀδυσεὺς γήθησεν ἰδὼν καὶ μῦθον ἔειπε (*Od.* 22.207).

191 A minority of MSS rightly omit this verse, which serves merely to introduce an explicit verb of speaking, see 9.224n.

194–200 The sentinels, reasonably enough, are stationed on the inner side of the Achaeans' outer fortification, but why are the commanders made to cross the ditch into no-man's-land, not apparently to see matters for themselves, but (202) to confer? The notion of a 'council among the corpses' seems in keeping with the taste of this Book. At least it is hard to see what else can be made of the curious idea that no-man's-land was a good spot for a council of war or of the pretentious thought that καθαρός ground was at a premium after Hektor's exploits of the previous day. (Verse 199 = 8.491, see n. *ad loc.*, but there the situation is different; Hektor had withdrawn from the scene of slaughter to clear ground 'by the river' in order to convene a full ἀγορή.) The council's action here is not only implausible but, more importantly, it is pointless in the narrative of this Book. The scholia are at a loss, bT suggesting, for example, that the commanders' concern was not to disturb the sleeping army or, alternatively, to encourage the scouts by sharing their danger.

195 βουλήν must represent an accusative of the goal of motion, but that is strained – and unique – with καλέω. The construction is proper to verbs that imply reaching a point (Chantraine, *GH* II 45–6).

196–7 Nestor's son is Thrasumedes (see 9.81). Νέστορος υἱός (9× in the rest of the *Iliad*) is elsewhere Nestor's more distinguished son, Antilokhos, but there is here no ambiguity. After Meriones Thrasumedes is the most distinguished of the seven captains of the watch appointed at 9.79ff., and deserves a bigger role than the *Iliad* allows him. He saved his brother Antilokhos from attack at 16.321–4 and survived the war (*Od.* 3.39, etc.). The point of taking along Meriones and Thrasumedes to the council of war is transparent; they are to provide the scouts with suitable weapons (254–71).

199 = 8.491. In book 8 the space is that where Hektor convened the assembly of the Trojan army; here it is the furthest point of Hektor's advance. The Trojans naturally withdrew to a safe distance, but not too far – they are still μάλ' ἐγγύς (113, 221).

200 πιπτόντων: the present participle, 'falling', is odd where the perfect, 'fallen', is obviously required. The epic perfect participles are πεπτηώς (-ώτων) (3× *Od.*), and πεπτεῶτα (-ας) (21.503, *Od.* 22.384). πεπτεώτων or πεπτεότων would have been metrically possible, if they had been known to this poet. — ὄβριμος, a regular epithet of Hektor, is an archaic word of restricted usage (4× of Hektor, 5× of Ares, 13× of ἔγχος, and 1×, in the vocative, of Akhilleus), cf. ὀβριμοεργός 2×, and in *Od.* ὀβριμοπάτρη 2×. A free, archaizing use may be seen at 4.453, ὄβριμον ὕδωρ, in a simile, and 3× in *Od.* 9 of the boulder that the Cyclops used to block the exit from his cave.

201 περὶ νὺξ ἐκάλυψε: the result is the same, whether we understand

Hektor, the Argives, or the earth as object. νὺξ ἐκάλυψε is an Iliadic formula (6× in addition to this example) which is always used elsewhere metaphorically of the darkness of fainting or death covering the eyes (5.659 etc.). A modified form, νυκτὶ καλύψας (5.23), alludes to a device of divine rescue usually expressed by ἀήρ.

203 The preliminaries are now over and the story proper begun. It has taken the poet just twice as long to reach this point as was taken in book 9, where Nestor begins making his crucial proposal at verse 93.

204–10 As usual Nestor is made to come up with an idea, cf. 2.360–8 and nn. He proposes that spies creep up within earshot of the Trojan army or, more realistically, take prisoner a straggler. They are to find out whether the Trojans intend to pursue their advantage or withdraw. None of this is of any importance and is soon overtaken by events. All that is required here is a reason for Odysseus and Diomedes being out between the armies where they can meet the Trojan spy Dolon. Nestor's proposal has been derided as silly, but the appropriate question is whether it is plausible in the context of the heroic world: the idea of espionage such as Diomedes and Odysseus are to attempt was proposed by Dolon (325–7) and occurred also in the *Little Iliad*, fr. 2A Davies, where Nestor proposed that spies should creep up to the wall of Troy in order to listen to the Trojan women's assessments of the valour of the Achaean heroes. Plausibility aside, Nestor's suggestions are made curiously parallel to those of Hektor (308–12), on which see introduction to this Book. — Nestor's seven-verse sentence is of unusual complexity, with five levels of subordination, but its cumulative structure makes it easy to follow. OCT punctuates as a statement, which reduces Nestor's proposal to a hint. Leaf's question mark at the end of 210 is better: 'Would not some man trust his heart ...?'

204 The reinforcement of the possessive adjective ἑός by αὐτοῦ (only here in the *Iliad*) is Odyssean (1.409, 2.45, 16.197, 22.218).

207 φῆμιν: an Odyssean word (*Od.* 6.273, etc. (6×)).

211–12 The lack of connexion in the sentences ταῦτά κε and μέγα κεν is awkward, but ταῦτά τε (*pace* Leaf) hardly improves matters whether the ταῦτα-clause is made co-ordinate with ἕλοι (206) or πεπίθοιτο (204).

212–17 κλέος ... δόσις: as if fame and gifts were much the same thing; note the reversion to the ethic that Akhilleus has just repudiated. Nestor, however, unlike Agamemnon (see 9.114–61n.), stresses κλέος and subtly blends the two inducements that he dangles before his volunteers, and even the δόσις turns out to be the prestige of the feast. Like the other events of book 10 Nestor's generosity is, of course, forgotten in the sequel. — δόσις is Odyssean (4×).

212–13 ὑπουράνιον seems to contain the idea of the fame *being spread* over all mankind, hence ἐπί in πάντας ἐπ' ἀνθρώπους, cf. 24.202 for the same usage. For ὑπουράνιον κλέος εἴη cf. *Od.* 9.264; πάντας ἐπ' ἀνθρώπους is also Odyssean (3×).

214 νήεσσιν ἐπικρατέουσιν ἄριστοι: cf. *Od.* 1.245 = 16.122 = 19.130 with νήσοισιν for νήεσσιν. See Introduction 15 for 'substitution' as part of the technique of the formula. The collocation νηυσὶν ἐπικρατέως occurs at 16.67, but ἐπικρατέουσιν, 'bear rule over', is an odd verb with νήεσσιν as object.

215 τῶν πάντων is formular, cf. 12.24, 22.424, *Od.* 4.104, but the genitive is partitive only here in a barely logical construction with ἕκαστος.

216 θῆλυν is normal as a feminine form in the epic, cf. 27n. and 5.775–7n.

217 Partaking in the feast is a vital part of κλέος, cf. 2.402ff. and the formular verse 8.162 = 12.311 (τίειν) ἕδρη τε κρέασίν τε ἰδὲ πλείοις δεπάεσσι. Loss of this privilege was the worst fate that Andromakhe could envisage (at that moment) for Astuanax at 22.496–501. Leaf objects that the privilege of the feast is offering what the leaders enjoy already and that a single black sheep would not strain the resources of anyone present. The parallel with Theognis 239–40 (which Leaf discounts) should be noted: θοίνῃς δὲ καὶ εἰλαπίνῃσι παρέσσῃ | ἐν πάσαις, πολλῶν κείμενος ἐν στόμασιν. The scout's κλέος will live for ever on the lips of feasting heroes. If that is what the expression in this verse (a formula?) means, it is obscurely introduced at this point. — δαίτῃσι: this alternative to δαίς is otherwise Odyssean (5×).

219–32 Diomedes volunteers first, followed by most of the others. The list may be understood to signal the order in which the heroes signified their willingness, as the list at 7.161ff. certainly does. There Agamemnon led off, as duty required, followed by Diomedes, the two Aiantes again and (with Idomeneus) Meriones. Odysseus on both occasions is named last (as he is also, but in a different context, at 2.407). The roll of heroes at 7.161ff. added Eurupulos and Thoas and omitted Antilokhos; that at 8.261ff. incorporated Menelaos, substituted Teukros for Thoas, and omitted Odysseus. The core consists of the Atreidai (or one of them), the Aiantes, Diomedes, and, surprisingly, Meriones. The latter bears much the same relation to Idomeneus as Sthenelos does to Diomedes; he is ὀπάων and θεράπων to the older man but has an independent role also. For other lists of heroes see 7.161–8n.

222 bT seize the opportunity to compliment the prudence of Diomedes in asking for a companion, in contrast to the recklessness of Dolon in setting off alone.

224–5 For the dual divided into ὁ … ὁ … see on 3.209. σὺν δὲ δύ(ο): the archetype of such composita as σύντρεις. κέρδος and related terms (especially the comparative κέρδιον) imply the skilful assessment of a situation and getting the most out of it.

226 ≅ 23.590. βράσσων (< βράχ-γων) is an archaic comparative of βραχύς found only here in the epic corpus, and so to be taken as an archaism on the part of the composer. Arn/A toy with the idea of the participle of βράσσω, 'shake violently'. λεπτὴ δέ τε μῆτις = 23.590.

228–31 The fivefold anaphora of ἠθελέτην/ἤθελε is paralleled by the less emphatic τῷ δ' ἐπί/τοῖσι δ' ἐπ' in the list of volunteers at 7.163ff.

231–2 τλήμων ... ἐτόλμα: the couplet reads like a *schema etymologicum*, although this cannot be as τλήμων is usually understood (= πολύ-τλας or ὑπομενητικός (Arn/A)). For τλήμων = 'daring' see 21.430 and Theognis 196. Except for τλήμων in this book the epithets of Odysseus are the same in both epics, though more appropriate to the hero of the *Odyssey* than to an Iliadic fighting hero. — ὁ τλήμων Ὀδυσεύς is found only here and at 498, though similar language is used at 5.670 Ὀδυσεὺς ... τλήμονα θυμὸν ἔχων. For the article see 363n. — (κατα)δῦναι ὅμιλον is formular (6× *Il.*, 1× *Od.*) but elsewhere in the *Iliad* always of troops in the field. Aristarchus accordingly wished ὅμιλος to mean 'army' (Arn/A at 338 and 499), whereas here it signifies πλῆθος καὶ ἄθροισμα. Both the sharp observation and the excessively precise inference are characteristically Aristarchan. ὅμιλος takes its sense from its context, and is used at *Od.* 15.328, etc. of the company of Penelope's suitors.

234 ἐμῷ κεχαρισμένε θυμῷ: Agamemnon (who has no conspicuous affection for Diomedes, cf. 9.32ff.) uses a formular verse put more naturally into the mouth of Athene at 5.243 and 5.826. The hemistich occurs also at 11.608 and *Od.* 4.71.

236 φαινομένων: 'those who have come forward', 'the volunteers', is clearly what the poet wants, but his choice of word has puzzled commentators as to its precise sense, e.g. 'as they present themselves' (Leaf, Schadewaldt).

237–9 αἰδόμενος: in the heroic system of values αἰδώς denotes sensitivity to disapproval. It can therefore be a spur to action if the disapproved behaviour is e.g. cowardice, hence the cry αἰδώς, Ἀργεῖοι, κάκ' ἐλέγχεα, εἶδος ἀγητοί (5.787 = 8.228), or as here it can restrain a hero from showing disrespect, cf. *Od.* 3.24 αἰδὼς δ' αὖ νέον ἄνδρα γεραίτερον ἐξερέεσθαι (Telemakhos to 'Mentor'). Diomedes was a young man and sometimes at least (4.411–18, though not at 9.31–49) deferential towards seniority and rank. That a man can be χείρων but βασιλεύτερος is implicit in the wrath of Akhilleus, but as an *arcanum imperii* it is not usually so candidly revealed as it is here. — αἰδοῖ εἴκων < αἰδόϊ ϝείκων, ultimately that is, but preserved with hiatus by formular conservatism.

240 This verse was certainly missing from Zenodotus' text (Did/AT), and was probably athetized by his successors as violating heroic standards of courage. Modern taste would tend to think the text stronger if

Agamemnon's inner thoughts were implied rather than spelled out, but as a clarification of a speaker's motives for the benefit of the slow-witted the verse has many parallels, but is unusual in that ἔδεισεν δέ (δέ with the sense of γάρ, Denniston, *Particles* 169) does not mark a change of subject. αὖτις in 241 marks 242ff. as the second speech of Diomedes and has no bearing on the status of 240. — Menelaos, in spite of his inferiority as a fighting man (cf. μαλθακὸς αἰχμητής, 17.588 – Apollo's description), is sensible that the war is being fought for his sake (cf. the narrator's comment at 25–8 above) and cannot hang back on these perilous occasions, cf. his acceptance of Hektor's challenge, 7.94ff. Agamemnon reacted in the same way on that occasion too. Note also his reaction to Menelaos' wounding at 4.148ff., where his concern for Menelaos' safety was heightened (4.171–5) by his realization that his brother's death would deprive the war, in which his honour is implicit, of its *raison d'être*. Agamemnon's concern and the indirect manner in which he is made to express his wishes is a comic touch of characterization that should not be overlooked, cf. 61 (Menelaos' diffidence), 114 (Agamemnon having to do all the work), 123 (Menelaos' lack of initiative), 164 (Diomedes' mock-outrage). The *Odyssey* of course shows the same interest in the interactions of human personalities.

243 = *Od.* 1.65, a coincidence that has seemed significant to older commentators, see Von der Mühll, *Hypomnema* 187, and Danek, *Dolonie* 116–18. Diomedes' choice of Odysseus is eminently sensible but also thematic, the two being joined in several adventures before Troy: the slaying of Palamedes, the theft of the Palladium, the slaying of Philomelas, king of Lesbos (schol. to *Od.* 4.343), and at several points in the *Iliad*, 5.519, 8.91–2, 11.312, and 11.396. The two heroes complement each other in the tradition of the Cycle as they do in this Book; Odysseus is the planner, Diomedes the man of action. In the rest of the *Iliad* that characterization is still in germinal form. The reputation here bestowed on Odysseus alludes to his deeds in the tale of Troy as a whole. Thus far in the *Iliad* he had not been conspicuous in action, being given only a briefly told ἀνδροκτασία at 5.669–79. At 8.97 he ran with the foremost and abandoned Nestor. — Ὀδυσῆος | ἐγὼ θείοιο recasts the regular formula Ὀδυσσῆος θείοιο | (3× *Il.*).

244 κραδίη καὶ θυμὸς ἀγήνωρ may be taken together as a single idea 'his heart and gallant spirit ...' as at 220, 319, and 9.635, though it is possible to take ἀγήνωρ predicatively and parallel to πρόφρων. There is no ready parallel for the syntax of a redundant attributive adjective in a formula being modified to a predicative use.

245 φιλεῖ δέ ἑ Παλλὰς Ἀθήνη: Athene breathes μένος into Odysseus at 482, but to say that she loves him is to imply that he is lucky. Nestor in astonishment at the successful outcome of the raid uses the same language at 553. At 23.782–3 the defeated Aias (son of Oileus) complains that θεά ...

ἢ τὸ πάρος περ | μήτηρ ὡς 'Οδυσῆϊ παρίσταται ἠδ' ἐπαρήγει, but that is
true rather of the *Odyssey* and the Cycle than the *Iliad*, see M. W. M. Pope,
AJP 81 (1960) 113–35. — Παλλάς is the special epithet of Athene (26× *Il.*,
21× *Od.*) in the nominative and accusative cases. The link between epithet
and name is very tight, and the archaic epic does not use Παλλάς substantivally as a synonym or substitute for the divine name as, for example,
'Ενοσίχθων and 'Εννοσίγαιος are used for Poseidon. It was probably unintelligible to the poet: traditional etymologies, of which *P.Oxy.* 2260 retails a
sample, link it to the syllable παλλ- (παλλακή, πάλλειν – see 5.1n.), but an
equation with Semitic *ba'alat*, feminine of *ba'al*, 'mistress', cf. *a-ta-na-po-ti-ni-
ja* (= 'Αθάνα (or 'Αθάνας) πότνια) KN V 52 with πότνια = Παλλάς, must
be considered, for which see O. Carruba, *Atti del I Congresso di Micenologia*
(Rome 1968) 932–44. Janko (on 15.610–14) draws attention to Myc. *qa-ra₂*
(TH Of 37–8 – *qa-ra* at Knossos is a toponym).

247 περίοιδε νοῆσαι is probably formular, or an echo of a formula, cf.
οἶδε νοῆσαι (1.343 and n.), where, however, the amplification ἅμα πρόσσω
καὶ ὀπίσσω gives the sense of νοῆσαι its essential complement. The περι- is
intensifying, as at *Od.* 17.317 ἴχνεσι γὰρ περιήδη. There is a curious aural
perversion of the formula at *HyHerm* 208 παῖδα δ' ἔδοξα, φέριστε, σαφὲς δ'
οὐκ οἶδα, νοῆσαι.

249–50 Odysseus' modest disclaimer (by no means characteristic, cf. *Od.*
9.19–20) will stand in contrast with Dolon's boastfulness before the event
at 324–7.

251 ἄνεται: 'is completed', < ἄνϝω, so that the ἀ- is long in the epic
(except at 18.473), cf. φθάνω < φθάνϝω, against Attic φθᾰνω.

252 The proper form of the perfect of παρ-οίχομαι was disputed, the
scholars preferring -ωκ-. -ηκ- represents the assimilation of the vulgate to
the *koinē*. πλέων νύξ: cf. ἐγγύθι δ' ἠώς in 251. This point is probably part
of the adaptation of book 10 to its present place in the *Iliad*, for the whole
lengthy action of book 9 took place after nightfall, cf. 8.485–6. Here it
suggests no more than heroic impatience for action; in the other versions of
the Rhesos-story, especially in the oracle version (see introduction to this
Book) the same note of time would mean extreme urgency – if Rhesos
survived the night he would be invincible.

253 This verse was not read by Zenodotus (Did/A) and was athetized by
Aristophanes and Aristarchus (Did/AT, Arn/A) on the grounds that it was
unnecessary and prosaically precise (ὥσπερ ἀστρονόμου τινός). Aristarchus
also could find no other use of δύο as gen. or dat. in Homer (which is strictly
correct for δύο, but for δύω cf. 13.407 and *Od.* 10.515). (Homer has no form
δυοῖν.) Aristotle (*Poet.* 1461a25) quotes 252 as an ἀμφιβολία; in fact πλέων
might mean 'the great part of' as well as 'more than', though the genitive
of comparison τῶν δύο μοιράων requires the latter. Verse 253 is well

established in the paradosis, being attested in Pap. 98 and Pap. 211; it was also the subject of a πολυθρύλητον ζήτημα of depressing pedantry, how one-third of the night could be left when more than two-thirds had passed: Porphyry (149 Schrader) devoted more than six pages to this silly question. For the threefold division of the night hours cf. the curious Odyssean formula τρίχα νυκτός (*Od.* 12.312, 14.483).

254–98 The two heroes arm themselves for their dangerous mission, donning helmets of unusual design. With prayers to Athene and encouraged by an omen they set off through the night

For the normal arming scene see 3.330–8 and n. The poet uses none of the usual formulas and employs a new one twice, ἀμφὶ δέ οἱ κυνέην κεφαλῆφιν ἔθηκε (257 and 261). He is fond of κεφαλῆφιν (5×) which he uses as a locatival dative except at 458 (genitive). For -φιν see 11.350n. The second hemistich of 256 τὸ δ' ἐὸν παρὰ νηΐ λέλειπτο explains why Thrasumedes and Meriones, the captains of the watch, had to lend certain of their arms to the two scouts; but the text gives no explanation for the two special helmets. If this were a real situation it would be reasonable to suggest with bT that the usual bright metal helmet with nodding crest was inappropriate for spies who hoped to remain unseen, not to terrorize their foes with their panoply of war. This is reasoning that does not convincingly apply to the boar's tusks, nor to the σάκος (257) as usually conceived in Homer. It was known, however, to Virgil; Euryalus was betrayed by the glint of his helmet, *Aen.* 9.371–5. In fiction, if reasons are not given, it is probably because they are artistic reasons. The poet of this Book wished to introduce an interesting and exotic object, cf. 23n. The Trojan spy Dolon (335) took a leather helmet also, though again there is no comment by the poet.

254 ὅπλοισιν: ὅπλα has the general sense of 'gear'. With specific reference to warlike gear it recurs only at 272, 18.614 (Shield of Akhilleus) and 19.21, cf. also ὁπλίζοντο (8.55). The word is common in the *Odyssey* (13×), especially in the sense of 'ship's gear', 'rope'.

256–61 The borrowed weapons complement those the heroes brought to the council. At 149 Odysseus took only a shield and at 178 Diomedes only a spear.

258 It is clear that κυνέη can imply 'leather' generally rather than 'dog-skin' specifically. None the less Aristarchus (Arn/A) objected to κυνέην ... ταυρείην. — ἄφαλον: 'without φάλοι'. φάλοι appear to be, at least originally, the metal plates forming the outer protective covering of the helmet, see J. Borchhardt, *Arch. Hom.* E 72–4, and cf. the epithets ἀμφίφαλος and τετράφαλος. — ἄλλοφον: the double -λλ-, which has no etymological justification, is by analogy with such forms as ἔλλαβε. — καταῖτυξ: a strange term for a strange object. καταῖτυξ is a *hapax legomenon* which bT interpret

Figure 1. The boar's tusk helmet. From H.-G. Buchholz, *Arch. Hom.* E pl. 1a.

etymologically as a compound of κατά and the root of τεύχω, the helmet being so called because it lacked height, having no crest. It is clear that the scholiasts had nothing before them but the text. Bechtel, *Lexilogus zu Homer* (Halle 1914) 187, having accepted Schulze's hypothesis that λόφος was a Carian loan-word, conjectured the same source for καταῖτυξ.

260 Meriones used the bow in battle at 13.650 and in the archery contest at the funeral games of Patroklos at 23.870–81. At other times, as second in command to Idomeneus (see 13.249–50n.), he fights in the normal way with the spear. T remembered that Meriones was a Cretan and that the classical Cretans were great archers. A more important question is why a bow should be thought a useful weapon for a spy to have. T supposed that Odysseus could have shot from the darkness at men illuminated by the firelight. Rather the poet wanted variety, a spear for Diomedes and, with a glance at the *Odyssey*, a bow for Odysseus, just as he provided the spies with two different helmets.

261–5 The boar's tusk helmet (see fig. 1). To W. Reichel (see *Über homerische Waffen* (2nd edn Vienna 1901) 102) is owed the distinction of recognizing the significance of the ivory fragments turned up by nineteenth-century excavators of Mycenaean sites. The boar's tusk helmet was chiefly current during the LHI and LHII periods but fell out of fashion during LHIIIA (sixteenth–fifteenth century B.C.), so Lorimer, *HM* 212–19, see also J. Borchhardt, *Homerische Helme* (Mainz 1972) 18–37, 47–52. The tell-tale boar's ivory plaques, however, are found in later contexts, as late as a

Sub-Minoan grave at Knossos (*JHS Archaeological Reports 1982–3* 53). There is no doubt – and the fact is remarkable enough – that a piece of bronze-age equipment is referred to, but it is questionable whether the verses themselves could be survivals from the bronze age, their language being in no respect exceptionally archaic. (Note κεφαλῆφιν (261) with singular -φι(ν), ῥινοῦ (262) not -οιο, πόλεσιν (262) with movable -ν making position.) A plaque showing a warrior wearing a boar's tusk helmet was included in a late eighth-century foundation deposit on Delos, see *CAH*[3], plates to vols. I and II 124 (c); the poet, however, is aware not only of the appearance of the helmet but also of its construction, as if he were familiar with an actual specimen more or less intact. (He could hardly have emulated Reichel by reconstructing the object from its loose pieces.) Vase-painters (see 454n.) had no clue, but give both heroes broad-brimmed travellers' hats (πέτασοι), which were also made of felt like the foundation of Odysseus' helmet. — ἱμᾶσιν | ἐντέτατο στερεῶς: it was formed within of 'thongs tightly strained', cf. 5.727–8 of the construction of Here's chariot; but it is hard to imagine what kind of reinforcement to the felt is here being described. ἔχον: intransitive – 'led'. ἔνθα καὶ ἔνθα means, to judge from the representations, that the curve of the tusks was reversed in alternate rows,

$$))) \ldots \text{ then } (((\ldots $$

In spite of its distinctive appearance the formular diction preserved no epithets commemorating this style of helmet. If such had existed and had become unintelligible, it is likely they would have been replaced.

(For signs that the formular system for the helmet had been – or was being – reconstructed at the time of the *Iliad*'s composition see D. H. F. Gray, *CQ* 41 (1947) 118–19 = *Language and Background* 64–5.) If the lion skin of Diomedes (177) and the wolf skin of Dolon (334) symbolize the spirits of those characters, the tusks of the boar should do the same for Odysseus. After the lion the boar is indeed the most frequent symbol of heroic courage in similes, a beast οὗ τε μέγιστος | θυμὸς ἐνὶ στήθεσσι περὶ σθένεϊ βλεμεαίνει (17.21–2).

265 All helmets, as Arn/A point out, were doubtless lined for a comfortable fit, and it is only to complete the full description that the point is here mentioned. According to Arn/A the verse was taken *ad hominem* and started the iconographic tradition of representing Odysseus wearing the πιλίον.

266–70 It is common epic practice to identify an object by its history, see 2.101–8 (Agamemnon's sceptre), 7.137–49 (Ereuthalion's armour), 11.19–23 (Agamemnon's corslet), 15.529–34 (Meges' corslet), 16.140–4 (Akhilleus' spear), 17.194–7 (Akhilleus' armour), 24.234–7 (Priam's goblet), *Od.* 4.125–7 (Helen's work-basket), and 21.31–3 (Odysseus' bow).

266 ἐξ Ἐλεῶνος Ἀμύντορος Ὀρμενίδαο: the poet keeps the generations straight (Amuntor was father of Phoinix who was nurse to Akhilleus, and Autolukos therefore Amuntor's contemporary), but his geography is suspicious, see 9.447–8n. Eleon is in Boeotia (2.500). Kuthera, lying between Crete and Laconia, was a place of some importance in the second millennium B.C. (see 15.429–35n. for details). It is unclear why the helmet travelled in the first place to Kuthera (it had to go somewhere), but having got there it is reasonable that it should pass to Meriones in Crete. Valuable gear tended to circulate about the heroic world through the institution of the ξεινήϊον: see West on *Od.* 1.311–13, and for the custom in Homeric times J. N. Coldstream in R. Hägg (ed.), *The Greek Renaissance of the Eighth Century BC* (Stockholm 1983) 201–7. Normally it is a host who so honours a guest, as at *Od.* 1.311, etc., but some presents arrived unsolicited from afar, e.g. Agamemnon's corslet (11.20). For the combination of gift and heirloom cf. the corslet of Meges (15.529–34). The efficiency of ξενίη as a mechanism for the distribution of valuable objects throughout the heroic world may be remarked, cf. Finley, *World* 58–164, with the corrections of J. T. Hooker, *BICS* 36 (1989) 79–90.

267 If the helmet had to be stolen there could be no better candidate for the theft than Autolukos (maternal grandfather of Odysseus, as it happens, though it would be ungracious to mention it at this point), cf. ὃς ἀνθρώπους ἐκέκαστο | κλεπτοσύνῃ (*Od.* 19.395–6). — πυκινὸν δόμον is formular (2× *Il.*, 3× *Od.*), but would be appropriate to Mycenaean Eleon, see 2.500n. ἀντιτορήσας: the *modus operandi* of the Greek housebreaker (τοιχώρυχος) implies accessible mud-brick construction, not the stone lower courses of the Mycenaean palatial style.

268 Amphidamas is the weak link in the helmet's travels in contrast to its origin and final destination; he is otherwise unknown.

269 Molos, father of Meriones (13.249), was son of Deukalion and half-brother of Idomeneus. Molos, like much of the Cretan onomasticon, is a name with Lycian connexions. Μολος, Μολης, Μωλης are among the commonest Lycian names (von Kamptz, *Personennamen* 353); Greeks would connect it with μολεῖν.

270 φορῆναι: an infinitive of *verba contracta* in -ήμεναι is attested for φορέω and seven other verbs, cf. Chantraine, *GH* I 306. The type is not attested in the Aeolic dialects and is best regarded as a recent creation within the *Kunstsprache*. A parallel formation using the Ionic infinitive -ναι with the athematic stem -η- would be an easy analogy with the infinitive in -ήμεναι but is found (4×) only with this verb.

271 Odysseus dons the helmet. He is now equipped with helmet, shield (149), bow, and sword. Diomedes is similarly equipped, but with spear (178) instead of bow. The shield is of doubtful utility for their present enterprise, and probably has been carried over from the conventional arming scene. Odysseus would have difficulty in managing bow and shield at the same time, not to mention racing after the fleet-footed Dolon. Dolon, who took a bow and javelin (333–5), dispensed with a shield. None of the three wears a full corslet, but Diomedes and Dolon wear lion or wolf skins.

273 λιπέτην κατ᾽ αὐτόθι: i.e. κατ(ά) is to be construed *in tmesi* with λιπέτην, cf. 21.201 κατ᾽ αὐτόθι λεῖπεν, and 17.535, 24.470 κατ᾽ αὖθι λίπεν, but in this Book καταυτόθι may already be felt as a single word, as in Ap. Rhod. 2.16, 4.916, and 4.1409.

274–5 ἐρωδιός is the name of several long-legged birds, here clearly a night-heron, a bird of good omen (bT and Plutarch, *Mor.* 405D) and a symbol of Athene on coins of Corinth and Ambracia. πελλόν in 275 (for Παλλάς), an over-clever suggestion of Zopyrus, also denotes a species of heron and would stand here as epithet to ἐρωδιόν. The invisibility of the bird in the darkness makes its sound more numinous. It is of no consequence that soon there was light enough to aim a spear at Dolon (372).

275 Athene is the goddess of success and so, apart from her patronage of the Achaeans, the appropriate deity to send the omen. Her activity in the *Iliad* is threefold: (1) to instill μένος or give other assistance, (2) to give advice, and (3) as patroness of craftsmanship. The most frequent recipients of her aid are Akhilleus, Diomedes, and Odysseus (3 times only), never Agamemnon, either of the two Aiantes, Nestor (at Troy), Idomeneus, or any Trojan. She distributes advice with the same partiality. As patroness of craftsmanship, however, she is unbiased – twice in similes, once on Olumpos, twice in connexion with Trojans. In this Book, as argued by M. W. M. Pope, *AJP* 81 (1960) 113–35, she is even-handed in her favours to the two heroes. — Omens are relatively frequent in the *Iliad* (eagles 8.247, 12.201, 13.821, 24.315; rainbows 11.27, 17.547; thunder 11.45, lightning 10.5, unlucky words 18.272), but like this heron they are usually sent by the god or, as we should say, are chance events. The business of the οἰωνιστής or οἰωνοπόλος was to interpret such signs, not to seek them. Only at 24.310 is a sign requested (by Priam) in the *Iliad*, but cf. *Od.* 3.173, 20.97ff.

275–6 The cry in the night of the invisible bird is an imaginative touch. Athene intervenes at the right psychological moment as the heroes move out into the darkness. She is present here but impalpable, breathes μένος into Diomedes at 482, and speaks, unseen, at 509. The Iliadic conception of divine intervention at this level is more concrete, the god appearing openly or disguised or literally acting upon events.

278–9 Odysseus' prayer is made in regular form: a mention of the goddess's titles and former aid, then the special request; but it is also similar verbally to that uttered by Diomedes at 5.115–20. Verse 278 = 5.115 (to τέκος), 280 ≅ 5.117. Diomedes' prayer at 284–94 follows the same formula. It is not easy to think of an alternative approach, cf. 'O God, our help in

ages past . . .' — αἰγιόχοιο Διὸς τέκος is independently formular (4× *Il.*, 2×
Od., always vocative). For the aegis, Zeus' magical weapon, see 2.446–51n.
and J. T. Hooker, *IF* 84 (1979) 113–15. Although the aegis was made for
Zeus by Hephaistos (15.310) it is Athene who makes the most use of it
(2.447, 5.738, 18.204, 21.400, *Od.* 22.297). Verse 278–9 (το παρίστασαι) ≅
Od. 13.300–1, where Athene is speaking to Odysseus and the sentence is
recast into the 1st person.

279–80 οὐδέ σε λήθω | κινύμενος is unclear. 'Nor am I forgotten as I go
my ways' (Lattimore) is probably too general. In 279 the πόνοι of Odysseus
must be the toil of war, so that κινύμενος should be something like 'as I
rouse myself for action', cf. 4.281, etc. Danek renders 'Ich entgehe deiner
Aufmerksamkeit nicht, wann immer ich mich (zu einer Tat) in Bewegung
setze' (*Dolonie* 124), and compares *Od.* 13.393–4 οὐδέ με λήσεις | ὁππότε
κεν δὴ ταῦτα πενώμεθα . . ., κινύμενος here corresponding to the temporal
sentence in the Odyssean verse.

282 Both heroes already have in mind some heroic deed (μέγα ἔργον 282,
μέρμερα . . . ἔργα 289, like those of Tudeus) beyond the scouting expedition
for which they had volunteered.

284 Ἀτρυτώνη is restricted to the formula κλῦθί μευ, αἰγιόχοιο Διὸς τέκος,
Ἀτρυτώνη (4× *Il.*, 2× *Od.*) and this derivative, which is modified so that
Diomedes as second speaker can say καὶ ἐμεῖο. The conventional rendering
'Unwearied', as if < ἄτρυτος (τρύειν) + -ώνη probably satisfied the poet
but does not please modern philologists (see *LfgrE* s.v.). The original sense,
as with so many divine epithets, is now lost beyond recovery.

285 σπεῖο represents the imperative of the root aorist ἐ-σπ-όμην, ἕσπεο
(< σε-σπ-όμην) the indicative of a reduplicated aorist. There is no explanation for the lengthening of σπέο to σπεῖο, except as an arbitrary licence,
unless the analogy of αἰδεῖο (αἰδέομαι) ~ αἴδεο (αἴδομαι) suggested itself, cf.
Wyatt, *ML* 136–7.

285–90 For Tudeus' exploits at Thebes see also 4.370–98 and 5.802–8.
The μέρμερα ἔργα (289) are his massacre of all but one of fifty κοῦροι who
lay in ambush for him. The poet of course already intends that this part of
Diomedes' prayer will be fulfilled. The employment of the Tudeus-story on
three separate occasions allows some insight into the technique of use of
such paradigms. In book 4 Agamemnon permits himself to enlarge on
the (supposed) role of his subjects, the Mycenaeans, as if the house of
Tudeus owed him aid in return. Athene comments in book 5 on the
assistance she rendered Tudeus in spite of his disregarding her advice.
(These are both hortatory paradigms with emphasis on Tudeus' exploits.)
Diomedes here omits the athletic contests provoked by Tudeus and stresses
Athene's aid in the ambush – a hazard that he and Odysseus might well
soon encounter.

287 The pause at the Asopos river is mentioned at 4.383. (λίπε) χαλκοχίτωνας Ἀχαιούς: the regular formula is Ἀχαιῶν χαλκοχιτώνων. Declension into the accusative case is no significance in itself; what is remarkable is that the genitive is an exceptionally firmly fixed expression (22× *Il.*, 2× *Od.*), which only here shows any modification. The poet could have said λίπ᾽ Ἀχαιούς χαλκοχίτωνας, keeping the word order of the primary formula; that he did not do so is probably a response to the localization of case-forms of Ἀχαιοί (∪ − −), except in a few fixed formulas, at the verse-end. The epithet itself, in the nominative case, is transferred to the Ἐπειοί at 11.694. A literal bronze χιτών (like the Dendra cuirass, *Arch. Hom.* E pl. VII?) would be an uncomfortable garment, and was perhaps misunderstood in the later stages of the epic tradition, whence the gloss χαλκεοθωρήκων (4.448 = 8.62 and nn.). In all three allusions to the Theban saga the Thebans are called Καδμεῖοι or Καδμείωνες, their attackers Ἀχαιοί, as if the war of the Seven had been a national enterprise.

290 ≅ *Od.* 13.391 which has πότνα θεά for δῖα θεά and ἐπαρήγοις for παρέστης. — πρόφρασσα, also at 21.500 and 3× *Od.*, is an epic feminine of πρόφρων (which also serves as a feminine, e.g. at 244). The formation is analogical after archaic feminines in -ασσα of ντ-stems.

291 παρίστάο, imperative, is preserved by Zenodotus, Aristarchus (Arn/A), and αἱ πλείους (i.e. the majority of the 'better' texts), and is supported by μάρναο 15.475. All the medieval MSS have παρίστασο, the Attic and Koine form and, *pace* van der Valk, *Textual Criticism of the Odyssey* (Leiden 1949) 165, clearly intrusive. — καὶ πόρε κῦδος (Zenodotus, Arn/A), in place of καί με φύλασσε, is not a Homeric expression. The vulgate is confirmed by παρίσταμαι ἠδὲ φυλάσσω (*Od.* 13.301) and παρίσταται ἠδ᾽ ἐπαρήγει (23.783).

292–4 (= *Od.* 3.382–4): the vow is one of the formulas of prayer. Since the narrative of the night's events ends before daybreak there is no notice of Diomedes' having fulfilled his promise to the goddess. — ἦνιν is used only in this formula; for the probable meaning 'yearling' see Frisk, *GEW* and Chantraine, *Dict.* s.v. The properispomenon accentuation was approved by Herodian in spite of the anomalous metrics in the fourth foot which that accentuation implies. The toleration of a short syllable (-ῐν) in the unstressed part of the foot is more typical of the first foot (West, *GM* 39). The suffix was probably originally in long ῑ.

294 χρυσὸν κέρασιν περιχεύας is evidently a memory of ancient practice. περιχεύειν is to *spread* gold leaf over an object. The poet of *Od.* 3.432–8 affects to describe the gilding process, but has no real knowledge of it and represents the smith, in a highly inaccurate manner, as using a hammer to apply the gold leaf, see D. H. F. Gray, *JHS* 74 (1954) 12–13.

297 The lion is the epic's favourite beast for illustrating the heroic temper, with 40 instances in the *Iliad* and a further seven in the *Odyssey*. See 12.299–306n.

298 An effective verse – and the archetype of many purple passages, e.g. Xen. *Ages.* 2.14. The polysyndeton is traditional (cf. 1.177 = 5.891 αἰεὶ γάρ τοι ἔρις τε φίλη πόλεμοί τε μάχαι τε, and its echo at *Od.* 8.248, and 11.163–4 ἔκ τε κονίης | ἔκ τ᾽ ἀνδροκτασίης ἔκ θ᾽ αἵματος ἔκ τε κυδοιμοῦ), and the verse itself is probably so, for the second hemistich is used again (and misunderstood) at 23.806.

299–331 The Trojans too are in council: in return for the promise of the horses of Akhilleus Dolon volunteers to spy out the Achaean intentions

The Trojan scene mirrors that before the Achaean camp exactly, except that Hektor's call for volunteers elicits only one response; but it is much shorter, as is usually the case when two parties go through the same sequence of actions, cf. 333–7n. The speed of the narrative now quickens as we move towards the Book's climax.

299 εἴασεν has an anomalous short ᾰ, another linguistic experiment, probably after such alternative forms as ἠτίμασα (<ἀτιμάζω) beside ἠτίμησα.

302 = 2.55. πυκινὴν ἀρτύνετο βουλήν: for the phrase see 2.55n. It is in order here where Hektor has a 'shrewd plan' to put forward. ἀρτύνετο βουλήν implies speaking, so that direct speech follows without further introduction. At 2.55 Zenodotus' text worked in a verb of speaking, but no divergence is noted here. πυκινός (πυκνός), which qualifies δόμος, θάλαμος, λέχος, στίξ, φάλαγξ, and χλαῖνα, as well as βουλή, μήδεα, and μῆτις, means 'well constructed', 'well knit', literally or metaphorically. πυκινὰς φρένας (14.294) makes a bridge between the two uses.

304 ≅ Hesiod, *Erga* 370. The hemistich μισθὸς δέ ... is Odyssean (*Od,* 18.358). ἄρκιος is properly 'reliable', see 2.393n., but seems here to be associated with ἀρκεῖν, 'be sufficient'.

306 ἄριστοι ἔωσιν is the reading of Aristarchus for the vulgate ἀριστεύωσιν. Aristarchus believed, surely unnecessarily, that ἀριστεύειν should be limited to human excellence. Zenodotus had a different verse (= 323, with αὐτούς for δωσέμεν), which would make Hektor promise the horses of Akhilleus at this point. It is better that that suggestion should come from Dolon. Aristophanes' reading, καλούς, οἱ φορέουσιν ..., looks like an 'improvement' on that of Zenodotus.

308 Cf. 8.507–12. A minor inconsistency, Hektor had there ordered bonfires (ὥς κεν ... σέλας εἰς οὐρανὸν ἵκη) to illuminate an Achaean embarkation, if one were attempted.

309 = 396. The formula νῆες θοαί (4× *Il.*) replaces γλαφυραὶ νέες (4×

in book 2) where it is not necessary to lengthen the syllable that precedes it. Ship-formulas make up the most extensive system built on a single noun in the epic; for details see B. Alexanderson, *Eranos* 68 (1970) 1–46.

311 = 398. φύξις, 'flight', occurs only in this Book, in these verses and at 447. From the root φυγ- the normal epic words are φυγή or φύζα.

312 ἀδηκότες: see 98n.

314–18 The sentence structure ἦν δέ τις ... ὅς δή τοι ... ὅς ῥα τότε ... is exactly paralleled by *Od.* 20.287–91; it elaborates the formula used to introduce new characters in battle scenes, ἦν δέ τις ... followed by a single relative or δέ-clause (5.9, etc.).

314 Δόλων, 'Sneaky', is an obviously invented name, created for this episode and alien to the primary forms of the Rhesos-saga, see B. Fenik, *Iliad X and the Rhesos* (Brussels–Berchem 1964) 17. The coining of appropriate names such as this (which do not figure prominently among the victims of battle) was part of the singers' art, see H. Mühlestein, *SMEA* 9 (1969) 67–94 (= *Homerische Namenstudien* (Frankfurt 1987) 28–55). ὀνοματοθετικὸς ὁ ποιητής is the comment of Didymus (Did/A to 12.342).

315 κήρυκος θείοιο: for θείοιο see 9.218n. The sense of the epithet is not strongly felt, or not taken literally, but heralds have a better claim to it than most, being Διὸς ἄγγελοι ἠδὲ καὶ ἀνδρῶν (1.334). Talthubios is a θεῖον κήρυκα at 4.192. — πολύχρυσος πολύχαλκος is apparently formular, cf. 18.289 (of Troy, acc. sing.), and for the jingle πολύρρηνες πολυβοῦται (9.154 = 9.296). The mention of Dolon's wealth looks forward to his attempt to offer ransom (378–81).

316 The sense of εἶδος μὲν ἔην κακός is one of the 'problems' cited in Arist. *Poet.* 25 1461a: how could Dolon run fast if he were deformed? The solution was to understand the phrase, rightly, as meaning 'ugly'. But why should Dolon be ugly? Because, like Thersites 2.216–19, he is intended to be despised. His outrageous boast that he will slip through the Achaean army as far as Agamemnon's ship and his ridiculous claim to the arms and horses of Akhilleus (322–3) have the same effect. For Dolon's appearance on vases see Friis Johansen, *Iliad in Early Greek Art* 70–5, and the commentary in Wathelet, *Dictionnaire* 437–41; the wolf skin (334) was an attractive motif. — ποδώκης: it is remarkable that this epithet is otherwise strictly confined in the singular to Akhilleus, for whom it provides the oblique cases of ποδάρκης. As such, and as an epithet of horses in the plural it seems to imply exceptional speed. If so, it is inappropriate (and anti-traditional) in its application to Dolon.

317 In other contexts the remark that Dolon was an only son would certainly be pathetic: his death would leave his house ἄκουρος (or ἄπαις, Hdt. 5.48) in spite of his five sisters, cf. *Od.* 7.64. But such comments are usually made at a warrior's death (cf. 11.241, 11.329, etc.), and there is no return to this point when Dolon is killed at 454. Willcock therefore is probably right to take 317 with 316 as characterization and to put the stress on κασιγνήτῃσιν: Dolon is a sissy (so T). — Zenodotus read κασιγνήτοισι, for which he was derided by Arn/A as if he had intended a masculine form; Zenodotus in fact accepted the post-Homeric usage in which κασίγνητος can be feminine, cf. his ἀθανάτοισι, feminine, at 7.32. Word-break between the short syllables of the fourth foot ('Hermann's Bridge', see West, *GM* 37–8) is strikingly rare in Homer. Leaf cites 23.760, *Od.* 1.241, 4.684, 18.140; the vulgate at 9.394 would be another instance.

320 ἔκ τε πυθέσθαι rather abruptly terminates Dolon's response, though the sense is easily completed from 309–12.

321–3 For the symbolism of sceptres in Homer see 2.109n. Akhilleus actually swore *by* his sceptre at 1.234, though it more usually embodies or symbolizes the power by which the oath is taken. The sceptre is itself a numinous object; as here it was raised up πᾶσι θεοῖσι at 7.412 to confirm an oath. τό, also at 7.412, is half-way between demonstrative and article, = 'the sceptre he was holding' (Leaf's suggestion that τό means the sceptre Dolon was holding as speaker is contradicted by the scene in book 7). Observe the over-confidence of the Trojans (already noted by Arn/A and T and Eust. 808.40) and the contrast set up with the cautious prudence of the Achaeans and the undemanding self-sacrifice of their volunteers. Dolon's request for the spoils of Akhilleus is a fatuous piece of vainglory which foreshadows, if not his ludicrous cowardice (374–6), then certainly the failure of his expedition, see 402–4n. and 17.75–81n. It is a deliberate irony of course that in the event it is not the horses of Akhilleus but those of Rhesos that become booty. Akhilleus' chariot like that of Agamemnon (4.226) has merely formular decoration: ποικίλα χαλκῷ, formular with τεύχεα (4×) and ἅρματα (3× and *HyAphr* 13). Contrast that of Diomedes χρυσῷ πεπυκασμένα κασσιτέρῳ τε (23.503), and the even more splendid vehicle of Rhesos himself, which χρυσῷ τε καὶ ἀργύρῳ εὖ ἤσκηται (438).

323 ≅ 2.770 (with ἵπποι for δωσέμεν and imperf. φορέεσκον). ποδώκεα, a reading known to Aristarchus, is found in many MSS in place of ἀμύμονα. Aristarchus objected to ποδώκεα as inappropriate in the context of riding a chariot, an insufficient reason for ejecting it since the formular style would easily tolerate the minor inappropriateness. ποδώκεα (-εϊ) occurs 12× with Πηλεΐωνα (-ι), and ἀμύμονα without a preceding preposition 5×; in three places the initial vowel of ἀμύμονα is metrically necessary, here and at 22.278 it is admitted by the movable -ν at the end of the preceding verb. The Homeric usage of these two formulas is normally to leave off the -ν from the verb and employ the formula with the initial consonant, cf. 8.474, 13.113, 16.281, 18.267, 20.27, 22.193; but in this Book normal practice is an unsure guide and an echo of 2.770 very probable.

324 οὐχ ἅλιος σκοπός ... οὐδ' ἀπὸ δόξης: ἀπὸ δόξης is 'contrary to expectation', as at *Od.* 11.344 (preceded by ἀπὸ σκοποῦ!), the only occurrences of δόξα in Homer. ἅλιος usually qualifies words or missiles and only here is applied to a person (but ἅλιον στρατόν at 4.179). Possibly an aural echo of the epic word ἀλαοσκοπίη. The formular system οὐχ ἅλιος (etc.) σκοπὸς/ἔπος/ὁδὸς ἔσσομαι (etc.) recurs in book 24 and *Od.* 2 (2× in each).

325–6 Dolon does not explain how he proposes to negotiate the ditch and wall (of which this Book is aware, 194), but nothing should be made of it; he has to promise something to Hektor on the lines of penetrating the Achaean camp, and the promise he makes balances the proposals of Nestor (204–10), to creep up and overhear the enemy's talk. — For the formation of the adjective Ἀγαμεμνονέην see 46n.

327 This verse repeats Nestor's words at 147.

329–31 Hektor's ready acquiescence in Dolon's ridiculous demands underlines Trojan arrogance in anticipated victory, cf. 13n. For the formula of the oath see Arend, *Scenen* 122–3. ἴστω (4× *Il.*, 5× *Od.*) is the normal – and probably very ancient – language of an oath, calling the god to 'bear witness', cf. μάρτυροι ἔστε in the very elaborate expression used at 3.276ff. The verb (< *weid-*, *wid-*) retains its primary force of 'seeing', cf. Boeotian Ϝίστορες, 'witnesses', *IG* vii 1779. Zeus is the god by whom mortals always swear in Homer, though other deities may be added for extra solemnity. ἐρίγδουπος πόσις Ἥρης (4× *Il.*, 3× *Od.*) is not a periphrasis for Zeus (except at 16.88), like πατὴρ ἀνδρῶν τε θεῶν τε, but an appositional phrase used especially in oaths and prayers.

330 μὴ ... ἐποχήσεται: the grammatical construction, μή + indicative, in oaths is regular (but inexplicable according to Goodwin, *Syntax* 270), cf. ἴστω ... μὴ ... πημαίνει (15.36–42); ἴστω ... μὴ ... ἐπένεικα (19.258–61). (These examples show that ἐποχήσεται is not aorist subjunctive.) Classical examples appear to be restricted to Aristophanes (*Lys.* 917, etc.).

331 διαμπερές: apparently = 'for ever', as at *Od.* 8.245, 10.88. ἀγλαϊεῖσθαι: 'will pride yourself upon', perhaps implying the pride that precedes a fall, as at 18.133. For the ambiguous nuance cf. the sneer κέρα ἀγλαέ (11.385).

332–468 Dolon equips himself and sets off towards the ships. The two Achaeans hear his approach and slip aside. They cut off his retreat and take him prisoner. Under interrogation Dolon reveals the arrival, apparently that very night, of Rhesos with his Thracians and some magnificent pieces of prospective booty: golden armour, a gold and silver chariot, and a team of snow-white horses. Without hesitation the two Achaeans kill Dolon and change their target to the new arrivals

333–7 A truncated arming and departure scene. Epic practice, where both sides go through the same set sequence of action, is to give a full narrative for the first and a passing reference for the second, cf. 11.15–46 (Achaeans and Agamemnon, 32 verses) but 56–60 (Trojans, 5 verses). Dolon takes no corslet and neither sword nor shield, cf. 257ff. At 459 he has a bow, here omitted.

334–5 Dolon dons a wolf skin as a sort of cloak or camouflage. In [Eur.] *Rhesus* Dolon is made to have the grotesque idea of disguising himself as a wolf and creeping up to the ships on all fours (*Rhesus* 208–13). — κτιδέην: for *ἰκτιδέην (< ἴκτις, 'marten,'). κτίς in Hsch. is a ghost-word 'imaginé pour les besoins d'explication' (Chantraine, *Dict.* s.v. ἴκτις). ἰκτιδέην could be read here but not at 458. On the loss of ἰ- by the misunderstanding of a rare epic word see Leumann, *HW* 53–4. It is a question whether any symbolism should be read into Dolon's wolf and weasel skins. Fenik, *Iliad X and the Rhesus* 60, roundly discounts a possibility that opens the door to wide-ranging anthropological speculation, but see 29n. Reinhardt on the other hand, *IuD* 247, recognizes that something of the character of the lion, leopard, boar, wolf, and weasel rubs off on the wearers of their skins, cf. bT (at verse 23) Δόλωνα δὲ ὡς δειλὸν καὶ λαθρίδιον πρᾶξιν ὁρμῶντα λυκῆν [ἐνδύει]. The weasel too was of evil reputation.

336–40 bT note the effect of the foreshadowing; it creates suspense to know that Dolon is going to his doom. The focus of the narrative, however, at once switches to the two Achaeans and we follow events through their eyes, except for a brief digression at 515–25. One result is that from this point the Trojan council is forgotten.

338 The expression 'ὅμιλος of men and horses' is a paraphrase, using the formulas of the battle scene, for 'camp', the horses being tethered to their chariots beside the men, cf. 470ff. There is in fact no epic word to express encampment. The Achaeans' camp, called ναύσταθμον by Aristarchus, is expressed by 'the ships' or 'the ships and huts'.

340 διογενὴς Ὀδυσεύς: only here in the *Iliad* (*Od.* 5×). Διομήδεα δὲ προσέειπεν seems an odd half-verse with which to introduce direct speech but recurs at 8.138. The oddity is rather that the introductory sentence begins in the preceding verse with consequent enjambment, cf. 9.622–3.

343 This is the sole allusion in the *Iliad* to the unsavoury (and of course unheroic) practice of scavenging loot on a battlefield. One may compare the unpleasant aspects of the real world that slip out in similes, e.g. the enslavement of a woman at *Od.* 8.523–30. In the heat of battle at 6.66–71 Nestor urges the Achaeans to press on, not stopping to strip their victims (similarly Hektor to the Trojans at 15.347), ἔπειτα δὲ καὶ τὰ [the ἔναρα] ἕκηλοι | νεκροὺς ἂμ πεδίον συλήσετε τεθνηῶτας. But those were fighting men returning to the scene of their victory; here Dolon is suspected of furtively despoiling the corpses (of both sides?) by night.

344 ἐῶμεν: ἐῶ- must be scanned as one syllable, for which see 5.255–6n. μιν is delayed; it should form part of the particle string at the beginning of the sentence. πεδίοιο is the usual genitive of the ground covered, as in the formula διέπρησσον πεδίοιο (3×).

346 παραφθαίησι (or -ησι): a notorious *monstrum rhapsodicum*. The optative apparently is intended. The formation contaminates the vernacular optative -αίη with the epic subjunctive -ησι (-ῃσι), an experiment that was not repeated. Cf. κράτεσφι (156 and n.). Leaf and Willcock print παραφθάνησι, as read by a few MSS.

347 στρατόφι: only here, but the termination is paralleled by χαλκόφι at 11.351. προτιειλεῖν: 'force him against' the ships, as it were into a trap. The infinitive stands for the singular imperative, as is shown by ἔγχει ἐπαΐσσων. Diomedes had a spear, Odysseus a bow.

349–50 Some ancient texts inserted an additional verse at this point: ἐν μέντοι τῇ Ἀριστοφάνους καὶ ἄλλαις ἑτέρως ἐφέρετο "ὡς ἔφατ', οὐδ' ἀπίθησε βοὴν ἀγαθὸς Διομήδης | ἐλθόντες δ' ἑκάτερθε παρὲξ ὁδοῦ ἐν νεκύεσσι | κλινθήτην" (Did/A). For the dual φωνήσαντε, the cause of the trouble, Didymus compared 21.298, but the grammatical concord (agreement with the dual subject of κλινθήτην when the reference is to one of those subjects) requires no defence, cf. 224 and 24.412–3. The oral style has a speaker's attitude towards grammar.

351–2 ἐπὶ οὖρα ... ἡμιόνων: Aristarchus complimented the poet's knowledge of agriculture: φασὶ γὰρ οἱ ἔμπειροι ὡς μὲν τῇ πρώτῃ τῆς γῆς ἐργασίᾳ βοῶν δεῖ σχολαιοτέρων ὄντων καὶ γενναιοτέρων ὡς ἂν βαθεῖα γένηται ἡ τομή, ἐν δὲ νειῷ ἤδη προεσχισμένῳ χρήσιμον τὸ τῶν ὀρέων γένος μᾶλλον ὡς ὀξύτερον (Arn/A). The image recurs at *Od.* 8.124–5.

Homer uses no measures of distance such as must have been in vernacular use (e.g. fingers, feet, cubits) except the πέλεθρον (21.407, *Od.* 11.577), but makes imprecise and imaginative comparisons (see W. C. Scott, *The Oral Nature of the Homeric Simile* (Leiden 1974) 20–4), some of which at least appear to be traditional – 'as far as a spear cast' (2× *Il.*), 'as far as a man shouting can make himself heard' (4× *Od.*), cf. 15.358–61n. The οὖρον is either a distance appropriate for mules ploughing a standard plot in a given time, or the distance by which mules would outpace oxen, as Aristarchus thought. The former seems more likely, see Hainsworth at *Od.* 8.124–5.

353 The language of this quasi-simile and those at 13.703–7 and *Od.* 13.31–4 (πηκτὸν ἄροτρον, βόε οἴνοπε, νειόν) is clearly related, though without any necessary implication that that is true of the passages themselves. — ἑλκέμεναι νειοῖο: the genitive must be taken in a local sense (cf. ἕλκησιν πεδίοιο, 23.518), presumably after the common πεδίοιο θέειν/διώκειν etc., though possibly by misinterpretation of a verse like 18.547 νειοῖο βαθείης τέλσον ἀρούρης (so Leumann, *HW* 190 n.), where the genitive depends on τέλσον. — For πηκτός see West, *Works and Days* on *Erga* 433. It represents a jointed plough as opposed to one in which the share and the beam are in one piece, see the illustrations in *Arch. Hom.* H 48 and pls. i and ii (W. von Schiering). προφερής occurs in the epic only here and in three Odyssean passages, always in the comparative or superlative forms. Hesiod (*Theog.* 79, 361) has the superlative twice.

354–5 δοῦπον ἀκούσας: only here in the *Iliad* (4× *Od.*). — ἔλπετο could be merely 'expected', but 'hoped' would be more in keeping with Dolon's characterization.

357 δουρηνεκές: 'a spear-carrying distance', a *hapax legomenon*, but a familiar idea, for which the *Iliad* proper has a formula, ὅσον τ' ἐπὶ δουρὸς ἐρωή (2×).

358 Odysseus was a contender in the footrace (23.755), but Dolon was fast (ποδώκης, 316) and kept his distance till he almost reached the Achaean lines.

360–64 Odysseus and Diomedes are likened to hounds, an infrequent but respectable comparison, cf. 8.337–42 (Hektor) and 22.188–93 (Akhilleus). For the symbolism of the Homeric dog see Redfield, *Nature and Culture* 193–9 and 1.225n. Greek draws no linguistic distinction between the hound, a noble creature (feminine in classical Greek, description in Xen. *Cyn.* 3–4) to which heroes in their pride may be compared, and the scavenging mongrel cur implied by the use of κύων as a term of abuse or insult, cf. 1.225n.

361–2 The mood and tense of ἐπείγετον must be indicative and present with the primary dual ending -τον; διώκετον, however, at 364 is imperfect. In the latter case διωκέτην would be metrically impossible. The grammarians' dogma, that the 2nd person dual of the historic tenses had -τον, -σθον, the 3rd person -την, -σθην, is correct historically (cf. Skt *-tăm, -tām*), but poorly maintained in Greek, see 13.346–8n. and Monro, *HG* 6. The epic tended to generalize -τον, -σθον, Attic -την, -σθην. Leaf asserts that in similes the leading verb should be in the subjunctive, the following in the indicative after δέ τε, a grammatical nicety for which this poet had no feeling. — μεμηκώς, 'shrieking' in terror, is a typical elaboration of the simile. Dolon was scared, but not that scared.

363 There is a v.l. ἠδὲ πτολίπορθος Ὀδυσσεύς, omitting the article (so also at 2.278). ὁ πτολίπορθος, with the article, is necessary in the three Odyssean occurrences of the formula. For the article in formulas in this book cf. ὁ τλήμων Ὀδυσσεύς (231, 498), ὁ κρατερὸς Διομήδης (536).

366 μένος ἔμβαλ': ἔμβαλε is probably an innovation for ὦρσε in this formula, cf. 11.11n.

368 The last colon = 22.207. The δεύτερος ἐλθών got no credit, of course, much less the τρίτος, cf. Patroklos' dying jeer at Hektor, 16.850.

373 εὖξου (only here) so accented is from a form εὖξος. εὐξοῦ could be read with Bechtel (*Die Vocalcontraction bei Homer* (Halle 1908) 98), but cf.

χείμαρρος beside χειμάρροος. ἐΰξοος is not used elsewhere as an epithet of δόρυ.

375 ≅ *Aspis* 404. βαμβαίνων: 'stuttering', an onomatopoeic word rather than a reduplicated form of βαίνω ('staggering'). — ἄραβος is a strong word for chattering teeth; the verb ἀραβέω is confined in Homer to the clatter of armour, but is used of the teeth by [Hesiod], *Aspis* 249, and by Hellenistic poets. Elsewhere the *Iliad* prefers κόμπος (11.417 = 12.149).

376 χλωρὸς ὑπαὶ δείους: elsewhere only at 15.4 (with χλωροί), but probably a modernized descendant of an old formula χλωρὸς ὑπὸ δϝέεος. The common χλωρὸν δέος (10×), with transferred epithet, would then be secondary.

378–81 Dolon's plea is typical, cf. 6.46ff. and 11.131 (379–81 ≅ 6.48–50 ≅ 11.133–5); typical also, but on the battlefield, is its brutal rejection. Convention permitted Trojans and Achaeans to recognize each other, cf. 447, and Dolon should have appealed to his captors by name. Verse 378 corresponds to two verses in the other scenes: ζώγρει, Ἀτρέος υἱέ, σὺ δ' ἄξια δέξαι ἄποινα· | πολλὰ δ' ἐν ἀφνειοῦ πατρὸς (Ἀντιμάχοιο δόμοις) κειμήλια κεῖται (6.46–7, 11.131–2). The poet's difficulty in adapting these verses (the other passages are appeals to a single captor) would have been to accommodate two vocatives in the first verse while bringing up the idea of ransom at the same time. His recasting of δέξαι ἄποινα gave ἐγὼν ἐμὲ λύσομαι, a slightly inaccurate expression.

379 πολύκμητος: iron is so described because it was worked by hammering, not cast like bronze. For iron as a precious metal cf. 23.826–35.

380 Aeolic ὕμμιν, transmitted by most MSS for the normal (and metrically possible) ὑμῖν, is odd and unexplained, unless it is used as an epicism. The movable -ν makes position in the dat. plur. of the personal pronouns only here.

383 Cf. 17.201, where Zeus neatly converts this negative command into a pathetic statement as he watches Hektor don the armour of Akhilleus. Odysseus' reassurance of the wretched Dolon seems at first reading a pleasant return to the conventions of war that prevailed before the opening of the *Iliad*, when Akhilleus habitually took prisoners and allowed them to be ransomed (11.104–6, 21.100–2). But of course it is Odysseus who speaks and he is trying to extract information. Beside the prospect of booty that Dolon imprudently reveals his ransom will not be worth collecting.

384 The whole verse is Odyssean (13×). καὶ ἀτρεκέως κατάλεξον (-ω) occurs 4× in this Book and twice in book 24. The verb occurs also at 9.262 and 38× in the *Odyssey*. The skewed distribution reflects not only the subject matter of the poems but also the semantic evolution of καταλέγω from 'recount' to 'tell'. καταλέγω refers primarily to the passing on of information point by point; see M. Finkelberg, *CPh* 82 (1987) 135–8.

385-6 ≅ 82-3 (Nestor disturbed by Agamemnon).

387 = 343, and was athetized by Aristophanes and Aristarchus for that reason (Arn/A); they also objected that since Dolon had almost reached the Achaean sentinels he would have run past the corpses.

391 παρὲκ νόον 'outside and beyond' sense and reason, 'stupidly'; a formular expression, cf. 20.133, *HyAphr* 36. ἄτησιν: for the plural cf. 9.115. The association with Hektor as subject is a little odd, but for the active use of the verb ἀάω with a personal subject cf. *Od.* 10.68 ἄασαν μ' ἕταροι. The usual employment of the verb is in the middle or passive with the agent (a god?) left vague.

392 Πηλεΐωνος | ἀγαυοῦ: a unique expression which, however, retains the regular placing of the genitive ἀγαυοῦ between the caesura and bucolic diaeresis, see 11.1n.

394 As an epithet of night θοή (6×, 2× in this book and 2× in 24; not in *Od.*) is unexpected; perhaps because darkness falls rapidly in the relatively low latitudes of Greece (Did/A on 12.463). A mechanical transference of the epithet from the formula θοὴν ἐπὶ νῆα μέλαιναν (also dative with παρά, σύν, 7×) is not to be ruled out.

395-9 ≅ 308-12 with grammatical adjustments. ἀνδρῶν δυσμενέων corresponds to νηῶν ὠκυπόρων at 308, but in the event Dolon has not reached the ships and adjusts his language accordingly.

397-9 These verses were athetized by Aristophanes and Aristarchus (Arn/A), presumably because of the syntactical difficulties that attracted comment from later scholiasts (Nemesion and Apion, see Nickau, *Zenodotos* 260-3). — Verse 398 βουλεύουσι μετὰ σφίσιν: OCT's text is that of Aristarchus and a few late MSS and conforms best to Homeric practice: with this reading Dolon repeats Hector's exact words from 311 and gives σφίσιν its correct sense as a 3rd person pronoun. Unfortunately neither consideration carries its usual weight in this Book and Aristarchus may be suspected of correcting the vulgate. Most MSS have the verbs in the 2nd person plural optative, βουλεύοιτε ... ἐθέλοιτε, as if Dolon adapted his words to the fact that he was now addressing Achaeans, as he did in 395. The optative is possible in an indirect question (Chantraine, *GH* II 224), though awkward after the indicative φυλάσσονται in the co-ordinate clause, but σφίσιν would then have to serve as a 2nd person pronoun, a use found in Hellenistic epic (e.g. Ap. Rhod. 2.1278) but without parallel in Homer, see Chantraine, *GH* I 274-5, and for the 'general' use of the adjective ἑός, ὅς 11.142n. In talking to Dolon about his compatriots Odysseus uses the 3rd person (409-11) not the 2nd.

399 ἀδηκότες: see 98n.

402-4 = 17.76-8: a short run of verses, used in the latter passage by the Kikonian Mentes to censure Hektor's ambition to acquire these immortal steeds. Zeus (17.443–49) is made to regret bestowing them on a mortal, even a mortal so highly favoured as Peleus. Odysseus shows incredulous amusement (ἐπιμειδήσας, 400) at Dolon's ridiculous request.

406–11 Odysseus prefixes an enquiry about Trojan dispositions and then repeats the spies' orders (409–11 = 208–10). The former are natural and harmless at this point but immediately turn out to be of vital importance for the story. Dolon is never given an opportunity to reveal Trojan intentions. Verses 409–11 were accordingly athetized (Arn/A). Those verses are in an indirect construction, as it were after κατάλεξον (405), which awkwardly follows the direct questions of 406–8. Leaf cites *Od.* 1.170–1 as a parallel.

408 Aristarchus read δαί here and at *Od.* 1.225, 24.299. δαί is a colloquialism, found in Euripides (at least 8×), Aristophanes (45×) and Plato (10×), but not admitted to formal prose: see Denniston, *Particles* 262–3. The epic admits some forms from the low stylistic register (e.g. ἄττα, τέττα), but the role of δαί, which is never necessary and always useful for the circumvention of some metrical or grammatical oddity, suggests that it is a conjecture: see further H. Erbse, *Beiträge zum Verständnis der Odyssee* (Berlin 1972) 212–13.

409–11 = 208–10, and were athetized for that reason.

415–17 θείου παρὰ σήματι Ἴλου: for the geography of the Trojan plain see 11.166n. Ilos was eponymous founder of Troy (Ilios) and grandfather of Priam. His tomb is one of the permanent Iliadic landmarks, unlike the tomb of Aisuetes, 2.793, which seems invented for the occasion. Obviously Ilos' tomb was not near the surf (φλοῖσβος, see 416n.), but the poet seems to have in mind the picture of the Trojan and allied dispositions outlined in 427–31, which began πρὸς ἁλός. — θείου: cf. 9.218n., but the expression here is like none of those cited in that note. There is no traditional pattern for a genitive name with separated epithet in these positions, where both epithet and name have the contracted genitive in -ου. φυλακάς is attracted into the case of the relative of which it is antecedent, an unusual idiom in the epic. ἥρως: the unqualified vocative in the sixth foot in mid-speech is otiose and rare, cf. 1.86 (Κάλχαν), and 2.761 (Μοῦσα), both, however, in clauses beginning in the fourth or fifth foot. κεκριμένη: 'chosen', 'picked out' for guard duty.

416 νόσφιν ἀπὸ φλοίσβου: the three other uses of the simple noun in the *Iliad* (5.322, 5.469, and 20.377) refer to battle, a situation from which a hero or his corpse is to be extricated. The common rendering 'din', hence '(roar of the) surf' here, is rejected by Danek (*Dolonie* 146–7) on the grounds that the word is a metaphor whose primary sense is no longer recoverable. In that case the poet here is using the expression as a genuine cliché and with an imperfect grasp of its true sense.

418–20 According to Leaf ὅσσαι μὲν Τρώων πυρὸς ἐσχάραι is equivalent to ἐφέστιοι ὅσσοι ἔασι at 2.125, i.e. true Trojans as opposed to allies. ἐσχάραι is not a natural word for watchfires, but cf. 8.562–3 πὰρ δὲ ἑκάστῳ (πυρί) | ἥατο πεντήκοντα, to which it is tempting to refer this obscure expression. The μέν is answered by ἀτάρ in 420, the δ' of 419 being apodotic.

419 ἐγρηγόρθασι, cf. 67n., a notorious *monstrum*. Such forms arise from false analogies and would usually be rejected by vernacular dialects; within the *Kunstsprache*, however, such misbegotten formations could find acceptance as poeticisms, cf. 12.431n. (ἐρράδατο). For a 'θ-perfect' cf. βεβρώθοις (4.35) and such forms as βέβριθα and γέγηθα; see also Wyatt, *ML* 111. φυλασσέμεναι: see 9.257n. The use of the -μεναι form here is doubtless brought about by the previous occurrences of the same word at 312 and 399.

420 πολύκλητοι: the Trojan allies are 'summoned from many places'. The same epithet occurs as a predicate at 4.438 (see n.). There is an aural similarity to other epithets of the allies, e.g. (τηλε-)κλειτοί (v.l. τηλέκλητοι), for which the poet used πολύκλητοι as a metrical variant.

422 The point appears to be that, though their allies may enjoy a carefree sleep, the Trojans have everything at stake and therefore will keep a good watch. The wives and children of losers are, of course, the victors' prize of war, a bait held out before his men by Nestor (2.354–6) and feared by Hektor (6.448–63). As the staple of eve-of-action rhetoric (cf. Thuc. 5.69), the thought of hearth and home naturally heartens the Trojans (15.494–9) and could even encourage the Achaeans (15.662–6).

428–31 The Trojan order of battle extends from a point 'on the side towards the sea' (πρός with genitive, cf. νήσοισι πρὸς Ἤλιδος at *Od.* 21.347), presumably the Hellespont, to a point 'on the side towards Thumbre'. Thumbre, or rather the temple of Thymbraean Apollo, was known to the epic tradition from the stories of the deaths of Troilos and Akhilleus himself. Classical Thumbre was on the Skamandros 50 stades from Ilium (Strabo 13.1.35). The Trojan dispositions therefore lie roughly on a north–south line, as if the poet of this passage held the view of those modern investigators (among whom Dörpfeld) that the Achaean ναύσταθμον lay at Beşika Bay opposite Tenedos, on which see M. Korfmann in M. J. Mellink (ed.), *Troy and the Trojan War* (Bryn Mawr 1986) 6–13, or rather as Hestiaia of Alexandria Troas (*apud* Strabo 13.1.36) supposed, that in heroic times the sea formed a bay extending southward between Sigeion and Rhoiteion, so that the Achaean camp lay not to the north of Troy but to the west. As part of her argument Hestiaia also held that Priam's Troy was sited at the 'Village of the Ilians' 30 stades east of Hisarlik, so as to leave space for the ships and battlefield. For the actual topography in prehistoric times see G. Rapp and J. A. Gifford (edd.), *Troy: the Archaeological Geography*

(Princeton 1982), and vol. II 48–50. The list of Trojan allies tallies with that of the 'middle distant' allies named in the Trojan Catalogue (Pelasgoi, Musoi, Phruges, Meiones, Kares, Lukioi, and Paiones, 2.840–77) but for obvious reasons deletes the Thracians (and with them the Kikones); instead of the more distant Halizones and Paphlagones the present list has Leleges and Kaukones. Both the latter are known to the *Iliad* (Leleges 20.96 and 21.86, Kaukones 20.329), but not to the direct paradosis of the Catalogue (see 2.853–5n.). Leleges and Kaukones, or their names, as well as Pelasgoi, are attested also on the Greek mainland.

428 For the Παίονες ἀγκυλότοξοι see 2.848–50n. The epithet presupposes the formula ἄγκυλα τόξα (2× *Il.*, 1× *Od.*). The poet follows the tradition of the Catalogue rather than the main body of the *Iliad* which prefers generic ἱπποκορυσταί as the epithet. However, he wanted that epithet for Μῄονες at 431, a tribe strange to the heroic tradition.

431 There is a Ἱππόμαχος at 12.189, but an *epithet* ἱππόμαχος would be *hapax legomenon* if the OCT's Φρύγες ἱππόμαχοι, from Aristarchus and Allen's '**h**' family of MSS, is accepted here. No reason is given for Aristarchus' reading; however, the plural ἱππόδαμοι, the reading of the vulgate, is otherwise restricted to the Trojans, as Aristarchus may well have observed. Arn/A notes that the Trojans and Phrygians are not confounded in Homer.

433–41 In his terror, we may imagine, Dolon reveals more than he was asked (so Dio Chrysostom 55.14). This is the turning-point of the Book. At the report of Rhesos' splendid horses all thought for their original mission disappears from the two Achaeans' minds.

434 The Thracians are introduced as if this was their first appearance at Troy. They were of course cited among the allies in the Trojan Catalogue (2.844–5) and appear several times in books 4 and 5, but then these 'original' Thracians drop out of sight and play no role in the Great Battle of books 11–17; neither, of course, do the survivors of Rhesos' contingent. — ἔσχατοι: a superlative in sense but not in formation (< ἔξ-κατος).

435 For the scholia to this verse and the amplification of the Rhesos story they contain see introduction to this Book. — Ῥῆσος appears to be a genuine Thracian name < *rēg-*, 'king'; any connexion with the river Ῥῆσος (12.20) is problematical. If the name, or word, is genuinely Thracian the question arises how the poet had come to know it; perhaps through Ionian attempts at colonization in the region in the early seventh century. Typically, his cousin Ἱπποκόων (518) is given an excellent Greek name. βασιλεύς in the sense 'king' is a relatively recent usage, but one that is already well established in the *Iliad*, see 11.46n. Ἠϊονῆος: cf. Ἠϊών, the town at the mouth of the Strymon river. Other authorities call his father Strymon; he had a divine mother, a Muse. There is an Achaean Eioneus at 7.11.

436–41 The horses are mentioned first as being the most valuable part of the prospective loot. Chariots in Homer are not valued highly; none of those driven by mortals is highly wrought or decorated (except at 23.503), least of all with gold and silver, and consequently none is specifically seized as plunder. In the event Diomedes and Odysseus abandon the chariot (but see 498ff. nn.). For Here's exotic chariot, all gold, silver, bronze, and steel, see 5.722–31 and nn., and for golden armour cf. 6.236, 11.25, and, of course, the armour made for Akhilleus (18.475, 612).

437 The nominatives could be exclamatory, but are more likely to be an instance of 'speakers' grammar', cf. 349–50n.

439 Golden armour is an 'extravagant conceit so far as mortals are concerned' (Kirk, 6.234–6n.), though that would not trouble the author of this Book. If anything real is meant, we must think of gold decoration, like that on Agamemnon's corslet (11.25). — (τεύχεα) πελώρια, θαῦμα ἰδέσθαι recurs at 18.83 as a description of the (original) arms of Akhilleus. πελώρια: the nouns πέλωρ and πέλωρον denote something frightening, e.g. a Gorgon (5.741); πελώριος should therefore be 'dread', and that suits its application to Ares and his spear and to Hades. None of the Iliadic usages require a connotation of size, but that is certainly present in the *Odyssey*, e.g. *Od.* 11.594 (the stone of Sisuphos). As an epithet of magnificent armour one may compare the colloquialism 'stunning'.

440–1 The sentence pattern οὔ τι καταθνητοῖσιν ἔοικεν ... ἀλλ' ἀθανάτοισι θεοῖσιν recurs exactly at *HyAp* 464–5.

442 πελάσσετον is dual of the future. 'You shall despatch me to the ships' is a possible utterance for Dolon, a confident statement from a prisoner who thinks he has bought himself out of trouble, which he immediately modifies as being too hopeful.

444 πειρηθῆτον is the only instance in the epic of the subjunctive of the aorist passive dual. The epic form would be πειρηθήετον, cf. παροτήετον at *Od.* 18.183.

447 Dolon did not reveal his name at 378–81, as he easily could have done, but what his audience knows an epic poet may let his characters know too. Dolon has been exceedingly helpful throughout his interrogation and his captors did not need to use verbal or physical violence to make him talk. His summary execution in cold blood therefore comes as something of a shock, especially since the poet has no comment by way of explanation or excuse but makes Odysseus immediately offer the ἔναρα βροτόεντα (528) to Athene. The force of Diomedes' argument at 449–51 is nullified by the custom of ransom and the release of prisoners to which stories of Isos and Antiphos (11.101ff) and Lukaon (21.34ff.) bear witness. The sons of the Trojan aristocracy or of Priam himself had rights, perhaps, that were denied to Dolon, the son of a herald (315). There is an ambiguity in the poet of the *Iliad*'s attitude towards extreme violence (see Segal, *Mutilation* 9–17), but that is violence between fighting men; we need not weep over the demise of the humble and unwarlike Dolon. His death was quick, and in an episode where torture would have been applied or threatened in any culture that condoned its practice there is no hint of it.

450 εἶσθα, 2nd person sing. future for εἶ, occurs also at *Od.* 19.69 and 20.179. Against the drawing of any hasty conclusion Shewan observed (*Lay of Dolon* 66) that the 2nd person sing. of εἶμι did not occur in the other twenty-three books of the *Iliad*.

454 At some point, either now or when he was first taken, Dolon fell to his knees; he now reaches up to touch Diomedes' chin in a powerful gesture of supplication, cf. 1.501 (Thetis to Zeus, a full description). He does this with the right hand while grasping the knees of his captor with the left (cf. 1.501–2), cf. J. P. Gould, *JHS* 93 (1973) 74–82. Diomedes is quick to execute the would-be suppliant before he can make physical contact, cf. 6.61–5, where Menelaus is careful to break contact before Adrestos is slain. There are no successful suppliants on the battlefield in the narrative of the *Iliad*; the poem also ignores the role of Zeus as protector of suppliants. The omission is probably deliberate, in order to heighten the stakes for which the heroes play. The scene of Dolon's death attracted the interest of vase painters and other artists from the late seventh century onwards, see Friis Johansen, *Iliad in Early Greek Art* 74–5, 160–4, Wathelet, *Dictionnaire* 439–41, though in what context they knew the story is uncertain.

456 The latter half of the verse = 14.466, *Aspis* 419, in each case of decapitation. A similar expression πρὸς δ' ἄμφω ῥῆξε τένοντε occurs at 5.307, but with reference to a wound in the hip caused by a stone. Not for the squeamish are Salih Ugljanin's comments on decapitation in hand-to-hand combat: '*Salih*: Three fingers of hair above the nape of the neck. Then it jumps off like a cap. *Parry*: Does it jump far? *Salih*: Yes, it will jump five metres' (Lord (ed.), *SCHS* I 641).

457 = *Od,* 22.329. The v.l. φθεγγομένη (in agreement with a feminine κάρη) would imply the severed head still pleading, a bizarre and gruesome thought, typical enough of this poet. Articulate speech is not in question in the Odyssean passage, and need not be foisted onto this.

460 Ἀθηναίη ληΐτιδι occurs only here; the epithet is probably a gloss on the ambiguous epithet ἀγελείη (6× *Il.*, 3× *Od.*), on which see 4.128n.

462 τοῖσδεσσι (or -εσι): found 5× in the *Odyssey* but only here in the *Iliad*. The double declension (τωνδέων and τοῖσδεσι) occurs in Lesbian Aeolic among the vernaculars.

463 ἐπιδωσόμεθ', 'we shall call to witness', cf. 22.254, is Aristarchus' reading for ἐπιβωσόμεθ', 'we shall call out for aid', of the paradosis. The MS reading is supported by *Od.* 1.378 = 2.143 θεοὺς ἐπιβώσομαι αἰὲν ἐόντας.

For the contraction -βω- (< -βοη-) see 12.337. Odysseus and Diomedes have finished the easy part of their business and have set themselves the more dangerous task of attacking the Thracians. Odysseus naturally calls on Athene for safe conduct (πέμψον, 464).

466 δέελον δ' ἐπὶ σῆμά τ' ἔθηκε is virtually unintelligible but must conceal the sense that Odysseus put some mark on the tamarisk so that they could pick up the spoils on their return. Hsch. has a gloss δέελος· δεσμός, ἅμμα, which almost certainly recalls an attempt to interpret this passage: δέελον would then be a noun ('bundle' of something) co-ordinated with σῆμα. Arn/A take δέελον as an uncontracted form of δῆλον, which would give good sense were it not for the τ'. δέελον could be a deliberate archaism based on εὐδείελος (3× *Od.*) and τ' may be ejected despite the unusual hiatus that would follow. Either that, or the verse has been the victim of deep and very early corruption.

467 ἐριθηλέας ὄζους looks as though it should be formular, cf. τανυήκεας ὄζους 16.768, but both are unique expressions. Hesiod has δάφνης ἐριθηλέος ὄζον (*Theog.* 30).

469–502 The Achaeans surprise the Thracians sleeping. Diomedes slays Rhesos and twelve other Thracians while Odysseus makes off with the horses

For a scene with such graphic possibilities the death of Rhesos is poorly represented in classical vase-painting, there being no certain examples in Attic black and red figure, but cf. 454n. Virgil included the scene among his decorations of the temple of Juno at Carthage, *Aen.* 1.469–73.

471 ἀδηκότες: see 98n.

473 τριστοιχί: 'in three rows', only here in the epic (and Hesiod, *Theog.* 727), but the formation is impeccable. δίζυγες ἵπποι: only in the phrase παρὰ δέ σφιν ἑκάστῳ δ. ἵ. (2× *Il.*) The horses are a matched pair, ready to be yoked. The epithet is thus contextually significant, a 'marked' form, and not a formular equivalent of the 'free' form, μώνυχες ἵπποι, that immediately follows.

475 ἐξ ἐπιδιφριάδος: *hapax legomenon*, but evidently the breastwork or the chariot rail, like ἄντυξ, see the many drawings in *Arch. Hom.* F 42–69 (J. Wiesner). It is not necessary to state what every ancient reader would assume, that the horses were unyoked for the night (cf. 8.543–4, and see 498ff. with nn.). πυμάτης is difficult to understand precisely (the rail at the back of the chariot?), and may have been influenced by the use of πυμάτη with ἄντυξ as part of a shield (6.118, 18.608). The ἄντυξ of a chariot was the natural place to fasten the reins, cf. the formula ἐξ ἄντυγος ἡνία τείνας (2× *Il.*). ἱμᾶσι: as a specific term in connexion with horses ἱμάς means a whiplash (23.363), but it has a wide application and here presumably means the reins (ἥνια, the specific term for reins, would be metrically impossible in the dative).

476 δεῖξεν has no precise parallel as an introduction to direct speech, but followed by οὗτος ... οὗτοι ... is tantamount to 'pointed out with these words', cf. ἐπιτέλλειν at 9.252, 11.785, and δέχεσθαι at 9.224 (with n.). Similar is προίει at 12.342 = 'sent off ⟨with these words⟩'. There is no record of any attempt to interpolate a verb of speaking (cf. 302 for a similarly implied verb).

478 πιφαύσκε: the long quantity of the ι has no etymological justification. It is short at 202, long again at 502. The *Odyssey* has short ι throughout and the only other place in the *Iliad* where it is long is 18.500. The word should mean 'reveal' (root φαϝ-, as in φά(ϝ)ος), but its use in contexts of speaking and with μῦθος or ἔπος as object suggests that it was equated with φάσκω, cf. 18.500n.

480–1 The expression ἀλλὰ λύ' ἵππους recurs at *Od.* 4.35. λύειν in this context normally means 'to release from the yoke', as it does in the Odyssean occurrence, not to release from their tether. μελήσουσιν δ' ἐμοὶ ἵπποι: also at 5.228.

483–4 = 21.20–1 (Akhilleus slaughtering the Trojans in the river), with τύπτε for κτεῖνε, and followed as here by a simile. Verse 483 is also Odyssean, cf. *Od.* 22.308 (with τύπτον), 24.184 (with κτεῖνον). ἀεικής is probably to be taken generally; the groans of the dying were not a pleasant sound. Groaning is not in itself shameful or unheroic, cf. the formula βαρέα στενάχοντα of wounded men (4× *Il.*).

485 The Homeric lion is never hunted for sport by martial princes (like the kings of Assyria) but pursued as a species of dangerous vermin by shepherds and villagers. Lion similes therefore associate themselves in the first instance with the agrarian scenes of other similes (discussion in Shipp, *Studies* 213–15); but they are most safely regarded as a literary 'improvement' on those realistic pictures of peasant life.

First place in eighth-century art is taken by the horse; in the seventh century by the lion, sometimes alone, sometimes striking down his prey or engaged in not unequal combat with man. The lion is, of course, a natural being, not like the sphinx or griffin or chimaera; and there were lions in Thrace in the fifth century (Hdt. 7.125). But I do not suppose that any Greek went there to study their habits and anatomy; detailed comparisons of drawing show beyond doubt that the models for the lions in early Greek art were found in the area of neo-Hittite culture. The lions of Homeric similes may also have been of similar remote origin. For, vigorous and lifelike as it is, one thing is lacking to the Homeric lion: it is never heard to roar. The roar would be an awesome thing to hear as the lion prowled round a sheep-fold or put to flight its hunters, and a splendid point of comparison with the heroes (cf. the mighty roars of Stentor (5.786) and Akhilleus (18.217) and the formula βοὴν ἀγαθός). It follows that Homer had never heard a lion, but had his knowledge of them at second hand from somewhere farther east [than Ionia] where they were hunted. (T. J. Dunbabin, *The Greeks and their Eastern Neighbours* (London 1957) 46)

See also S. R. West on *Od.* 4.335. The lion was, of course, also familiar to Mycenaean art. Lions, it is said, do not roar when actually attacking prey, as is the case in many similes, but the point holds, that while the behaviour of e.g. the boar is described in some detail a striking aspect of the lion is ignored. See, however, vol. v 36 n. 42, and for other zoological inaccuracies 13.198–200n. There is a monograph on the Homeric lion: Annie Schnapp-Gourbeillon, *Lions, héros, masques: les représentations de l'animal chez Homère* (Paris 1981). — ἀσημάντοισι: the negligence of herdsmen is a not infrequent motif of similes, cf. 5.139, 15.632, 16.354.

488 Twelve victims is a modest but realistic total for this exploit and a pleasant contrast with the natural tendency of epic poetry to enhance the achievements of heroes. Akhilleus' massacre ἐπιστροφάδην at 21.17–33, which went on until his arm was tired, choked the river. Twelve casualties would make no impact on the 50,000 Trojans and allies encamped on the plain (8.562–3, where Zenodotus' text would give 500,000). Perhaps we are to imagine the twelve victims were Rhesos' θεράποντες and ὀπάονες, but the important matter, both militarily and poetically, is the slaying of Rhesos himself. Twelve is the Homeric code for a clean sweep, cf. G. Germain, *Homère et le mystique des nombres* (Paris 1954) 17–18.

490 It might be thought more natural, as well as more dignified, to draw the corpses aside by lifting them under the arms, but dragging by the foot is the Homeric norm, with six other instances. No well-formed system of formulas, however, was developed for the topos, see Introduction p. 13. The repetition of Ὀδυσεύς after Ὀδυσσεύς at 488 seems clumsy but is readily paralleled, see Hainsworth on *Od.* 7.116.

493 ἀήθεσσον γὰρ ἔτ' αὐτῶν: the ambiguity of which Leaf complains, subject and pronoun being either the horses or the heroes, is formal only. The poet's point is a good one: the horses, nervous animals, would shy at the unaccustomed sight of Diomedes' handiwork. ἀήθεσσον is easily interpreted (< ἀήθης, 'unused to') but the formation, another linguistic experiment, is unparalleled. As an exotic form and a Homeric *hapax legomenon* it attracted the attention of Hellenistic poets, e.g. Ap. Rhod. 4.38. Eust. 820.21 found the construction with the genitive strange.

496–7 ἀσθμαίνειν in Homer describes the breathing of those about to expire, cf. 521 below and 21.182 of the disembowelled Asteropaios, but it can refer to the panting of one under heavy exertion, cf. 16.109 of Aias, and could reasonably be used of the effects of a nightmare. Diomedes slew him as he dreamt and the γάρ-clause explains ἀσθμαίνοντα. Now the trouble begins. Of whom, or what, was Rhesos dreaming? One cannot dream of X in the epic style if X is not thought to be objectively present in some form or manner. At 23.68ff. Akhilleus is asleep and the shade of Patroklos στῆ ... ὑπὲρ κεφαλῆς and addressed him, and at *Od.* 6.15ff. Athene similarly addressed Nausikaa. In the latter case especially we should say that what was being described was a dream. It seems not impossible therefore that in placing Οἰνεΐδαο πάϊς (i.e. Diomedes, grandson of Oineus) in apposition to ὄναρ the poet wished to signify that 'Diomedes' appeared to Rhesos in a prophetic dream. If so, the expression is not only concise to the point of obscurity, but leads besides to an intolerable confusion of 'Diomedes' (a spectre) with the real Diomedes. When he steps outside the traditional diction (or outside traditional themes, cf. 513) the poet has some trouble in finding clear expression of his thought.

It would be a rhetorically much more powerful thought if ἀσθμαίνοντα could be taken proleptically 'from the gasping corpse' (cf. Virg. *Aen.* 9.332–3 *truncumque reliquit* | *sanguine singultantem*), and κακὸν ὄναρ as a bitter oxymoron; the bad dream *was* Diomedes, sword in hand, not *of* Diomedes: a neat twist, if it could be safely attributed to this poet (see 497n.).

496 κεφαλῆφιν ἐπέστη: the usual position of a substantified dream, cf. 2.20–1n. The expression adapts the formula στῆ δ' ἄρ' ὑπὲρ κεφαλῆς (2× *Il.*, 2× *Od.*).

497 This verse was missing from the texts of Zenodotus and Aristophanes (Did/A), but was athetized (and so read) by Aristarchus (Arn/A). The banal (εὐτελής) explanation of Rhesos' 'dream' undercuts the irony of κακὸν ὄναρ, but see 240n. Fault has been found with the syntax, the accusative of extent (τὴν νύκτα) being out of place, with the metrics, the digamma of (ϝ)Οἰνεΐδαο being neglected, and with the introduction of Athene, μᾶλλον γὰρ διὰ τὴν Δόλωνος ἀπαγγελίαν, as the scholiast pedantically put it.

498ff. λύε: i.e. from the ἐπιδιφριάς of 475. Odysseus had then to rope the horses (we must assume they were unbridled for the night) and drive them clear. He does not bother with the chariot-whip. Diomedes wonders whether to drag or carry off the chariot (decorated with gold and silver, 438), or to carry on killing. While he ponders this question, Athene prompts him to get out while he can. So far so good. The two heroes should have taken both horses and chariot as their loot in poetic justice, because Dolon asked for the horses *and chariot* of Akhilleus (322). But did they do so? Without further action noted, Diomedes ἵππων ἐπεβήσετο (513). The plural ἵπποι can denote the vehicle drawn by the horses and regularly does so, e.g. 11.94, 109, 143, 179 in Agamemnon's *aristeia*, and in construction with parts of ἐπι-, ἀπο-, and καταβαίνειν alternates with unambiguous terms for the chariot, δίφρος and ὄχεα. Odysseus then whips the pair into motion (513–14) and the formula τοὶ δ' ἐπέτοντο (5× including minor variants, elsewhere always of a yoked team) describes their gallop towards the ships. This is the language of a hero mounting his chariot to withdraw from action. Similar language is used when the heroes pause to recover the arms of Dolon: Odysseus halts the horses (527), Diomedes leaps down and then again ἐπεβήσετο ἵππων (529), and one of the two, it is unclear which, again whips up the pair. The hemistich τὼ δ' οὐκ ἀέκοντε πετέσθην, which describes their gallop at this point (530), is the normal formula for chariot-driving (7× *Il.*, 3× *Od.*). Thus far the heroes do indeed seem to be driving Rhesos' chariot. But then no mention is made of this splendid vehicle, although the dedication of the wretched Dolon's armour is specially noted (570–1). That we must imagine the heroes' harnessing the horses to the chariot would imply an improbable ellipse after the detail of 498–502. Therefore the heroes do not take the chariot; they were after all in a hurry, and yoking a team of horses was not a simple operation, see 24.268–77. If they seem at times to do so that is because the diction available to the poet does not include formulas for horse-riding as opposed to horse-driving. He slips into the use, *faute de mieux*, of language that is a close but inexact approximation to the idea he wishes to express. Delebecque supposes that the use of chariot diction is deliberate, to gloss over the fact that in this episode the anachronism of riding is allowed to show more plainly than is usual in epic narrative: 'dans cet épisode l'auteur manifeste à des signes déjà remarqués non seulement des connaissances sûres, mais un véritable sens de cheval; on est donc bien obligé de croire qu'il a deliberément cultivé les obscurités semées comme à plaisir dans l'épisode, si exact en général et si coloré', *Cheval* 80. For riding in the Mycenaean and Archaic periods see J. Wiesner, *Arch. Hom.* F 114–24; the skill was certainly known though not so frequently represented in art as that of chariot-driving. For horse-riding in Homer see 15.679–84n. and Greenhalgh, *Early Greek Warfare* 40–1, 53–6. In the epic (apart from this ambiguous passage) it is mentioned only in similes, as Aristarchus noted (Arn/A at 15.679). Here Arn/A and bT are much exercised by the thought that σὺν δ' ἤειρεν (499) means that the two horses were ridden off *roped together*. It is hardly believable that the poet intended any such thing; he has Odysseus rope the horses together so that the hero can lead them off with one hand free to use his bow as a whip. (For another example of the way in which traditional language imposes traditional thought see E. A. Havelock, *YCS* 20 (1966) 61–72.) [Eur.] *Rhesus* 783 and the scholia understand the passage to refer to horse-riding. Shewan, *Lay of Dolon* 274–8, argues for chariot-driving; Leaf, like many who have delved into the question, changed his mind and opted for riding in the second edition of his commentary.

498–502 In a few well-conceived lines the poet tells how Odysseus secured the horses. The hero wastes no time doing so and forgets the whip lying in the chariot. Controlling the horses with his bow he signals Diomedes with a whistle.

499 σὺν δ' ἤειρεν: Odysseus roped the horses together, like the expert rider at 15.680, πίσυρας συναείρεται ἵππους. This is not the same as yoking the horses to a chariot. For ἀείρειν of harnessing an animal cf. παρήορος, 'a tracehorse'; it is, as it were, hung onto the chariot, as Schulze, *QE* 420, explained the metaphor.

500 τόξῳ: the poet presumably has in mind a longish 'self' bow, or are we to imagine him using the loose bowstring as a whiplash? That is unlikely.

502 ῥοίζησεν: 'hiss' (of a snake, Ap. Rhod. 4.129). πιφαύσκων: see 478n. A complement must be supplied, 'indicating' ⟨that he had the horses⟩.

503–79 Prompted by Athene Diomedes and Odysseus make good their escape, while Apollo alerts Rhesos' cousin, Hippokoon. The two Achaeans arrive home safely with their loot, collecting the arms of Dolon en route. Welcomed by their friends the heroes dispose of the booty, bathe, and dine.

Athene is the goddess of doing the right thing at the right time, cf. *Od.* 5.427 (Odysseus would have been torn to shreds if Athene had not prompted him to seize a rock). Since Diomedes and Odysseus withdraw just before the Thracians take alarm, therefore in poetical language a deity must have warned them. The goddess is apparently invisible – she is recognized by her voice – but in this passage of rapid narrative it is not necessary for the poet to say so, still less to involve himself in the kind of explanation given for Akhilleus' second thoughts at 1.193ff. (see nn. *ad loc.*): οἴῳ φαινομένη· τῶν δ' ἄλλων οὔ τις ὁρᾶτο (1.198). Athene and Apollo are here interfering with the action in the very way forbidden to the other gods by Zeus at 8.5–17. The prominence of Athene in this Book (13 mentions) suggests that the presence of the gods ignores that injunction and is not an inadvertence, as Athene's intervention at 15.668–73 appears to be (see n.).

503–7 For the μερμηρίζειν-scene see Arend, *Scenen* 106. After the statement of a problem the formula ἥδε ... ἀρίστη φαίνετο βουλή follows, or if alternatives are stated ὧδε ... δοάσσατο κέρδιον εἶναι. If, as here, deliberation is overtaken by events, the formula is ἧος ὁ ταῦθ' ὥρμαινε. — The disjunction is marked by ἤ (504) and ἤ (506); the ἤ of 505 joins ἐξερύοι and ἐκφέροι.

505 The poet does not comment on Diomedes' thought of literally carrying off the chariot, so the verse is good evidence for the lightness of the chariots (racing vehicles?) known to the poet. An exaggeration of heroic strength would have prompted a mention of the οἷοι νῦν βροτοί εἰσι motif.

506 ≅ 5.673 (with Λυκίων for Θρηκῶν).

507–13 Athene intervenes as if she had been present throughout. At 1.194–6, in other respects a similar scene, Athene had to be prompted by Here (a passage that Zenodotus omitted) before descending to earth and addressing the hero. In neither case did the goddess reveal her identity directly, but she took no precautions to conceal it either. In the present case Diomedes and Odysseus are alone and there is no plausible disguise the goddess could assume. As usual Athene's intervention poses a problem for the understanding of human motivation in the epic. For the poet Athene is not a fiction, and we must assume that the action he attributes to her is the sort of thing that he believed happened in the Heroic Age. On the other hand in a realistic narrative it must be possible to interpret the intervention of the goddess in realistic terms, e.g. that Diomedes felt he had done a good night's work and ought to get out while he could. The problem is well examined by A. Lesky, *Sitz. Heidelberger Akad. d. Wiss., Phil.-Hist. Klasse*, (1961) 4. Divine monitions are a limiting case of the tendency of the epic to externalize the workings of the mind, see 1.193–4n. Iliadic gods regularly are said to take away a man's wits or fill him with courage, but the gods as source of sudden thoughts, brilliant or silly notions, fits of forgetfulness, etc., is a typically Odyssean topos, see vol. IV 3–4.

507–8 ἦος ὁ ταῦθ' ὅρμαινε κατὰ φρένα καὶ κατὰ θυμόν is a formula of transition (4× *Il.*, 3× *Od.*), followed four times by τόφρα δέ. The replacement of the last colon here by τόφρα δ' Ἀθήνη is unexceptionable but by drawing back the apodotic δ' entails the modification of the formular verse 508 – ἐγγύθεν ἱσταμένη (medial at 15.710 and 17.582) for ἀγχοῦ δ' ἱσταμένη προσέφη ... OCT reads ἦος as the conjunction wherever metre permits, here as a correction for ἕως μέν of the vulgate: probably a hyper-correction, since the metathesis ηο > εω certainly antedates the *Iliad*, cf. Hainsworth, *Od.* 5.123n.

512 = 2.182 and (to ξυνέηκε) 15.442. A voice out of the darkness could be nothing else but the voice of the goddess, but the epic implies that the speech of the undisguised Olympians was recognizable as divine. The *Odyssey* has a formula θεοῖς ἐναλίγκιος αὐδήν (2×), and both epics use the word ὀμφή for a divine utterance, on which see J. S. Clay, *Hermes* 102 (1974) 129–36.

513 ἐπεβήσετο (also at 529) is a 'mixed' aorist, see 11.16n.

515–22 The heroes have a narrow escape, the inevitable climax of this story-pattern. Nevertheless, for a god, the intervention of Apollo is remarkably too little and too late, but we should not be too hard on the god; Hippokoon was awakened to the scene of horror – by what? Nothing is said to happen in the epic by chance. The answer to such a question therefore is that some external (or externalized) agent has acted – if nothing else, then a god. The god is necessary here because for the purposes of the story the Thracians were encamped ἔσχατοι ἄλλων, well away from the wakeful Trojans around the tomb of Ilos.

515 οὐδ' ἀλαοσκοπιὴν εἶχ(ε) is formular (3× *Il.*, 1× *Od.*, Hesiod, *Theog.* 466), and awkwardly applied here to the tardy Apollo. Aristarchus (Arn/A) may have preferred to write ἀλαὸς σκοπιήν; Zenodotus read ἀλαὸν σκοπιήν; both are feeble turns of phrase beside the fine epic compound.

518 Note the obviously Greek name of Hippokoon. The second element, however, is moribund in Greek nomenclature, see Chantraine, *Dict.* s.v. κοέω, and Risch, *Wortbildung* 27, so that the name is probably taken from a traditional stock or story rather than invented. A Hippokoon, brother of Tundareos, was killed by Herakles at Sparta (Alcman fr. 1 Page).

520–2 Zenodotus' text is reported to have exchanged the second hemistich of 520, ὅθ' ἔστασαν ὠκέες ἵπποι, and that of 522, φίλον τ' ὀνόμηνεν ἑταῖρον, and placed 521 after 522 (Arn/A). That is simply mechanical confusion, either in Zenodotus' text or in the transmission of his reading. Bolling, *External Evidence* 128, points out that ὤμωξεν τ' ἄρ' ἔπειτα (522) should introduce direct speech and hypothesizes that in an independent Lay of Dolon a lament for Rhesos may have followed. That would be inappropriate in the present context (so bT).

522 = 23.178 = 24.591. φίλον τ' ὀνόμηνεν ἑταῖρον is pathetically applied to a comrade already dead.

523–5 Hektor's council, like Agamemnon's in book 9, must be imagined to wait for the return of Dolon. This three-verse report of the Trojan reaction to Rhesos' death therefore is excessively laconic. If Hektor did not shed a tear for Dolon, whose death he could infer from the carnage of the Thracians, he could at least have been made to utter a few words over the body of his latest ally. One can only assume that the focus of the poet is so firmly set on his two heroes that he is blind to the other side.

523 The second hemistich is formular, at least in derivation, cf. ἐν ἄσπετον ὦρσε κυδοιμόν (18.218), and ἐν δὲ κυδοιμόν | ὦρσε (11.52).

525 κοῖλος is from κόϝιλος. The shape of the uncontracted form is entrenched in the series of ship-formulas. The contracted form, however, was familiar to the poet of the *Odyssey* (| κοῖλον ἐς αἰγιαλόν *Od.* 22.385), and may be understood everywhere.

527–30 There are a number of formulas relating to the harnessing and unharnessing of horses based on ὑπὸ ζυγὸν ἄγειν and ὑπὸ ζυγοῦ λύειν, none of which are used here. However, as Edwards observes (19.392–5n.), there is no type-scene for these frequent actions, although a full account is given at 24.265–80. (In arming scenes the focus is on the hero and mention of the duties of his charioteer might be out of place.) For the resulting obscurities see 498ff. n.

528 ἔναρα: 'spoils', an old epic word restricted (except at 13.268) to the formula ἔναρα βροτόεντα (8× *Il.*, not in *Od.*, but revived at [Hes.] *Aspis* 367). The derivatives ἐναίρω and (ἐξ)ἐναρίζω enjoy a freer use. For this poet ἔναρα was probably an epicism; he used it again at 570.

530–1 = 11.519–20, where the second verse refers to Greek horses. It is nonsense that Rhesos' animals should have any wish to reach the Greek ships, and the verse should be omitted as an instance of post-aristarchean 'concordance interpolation'. It is in fact not read in some good MSS. To take φίλον as φίλον to Diomedes would be, as Leaf says, pointless. 'Concordance interpolation', where not a deliberate attempt to 'improve' the text, is analogous to 'formular override' (see Introduction 18) at the transmission stage of the text; the mind of the copyist focuses on a familiar passage more sharply than on that before his eyes. It is possible, of course, that the composer himself sometimes fell victim to this accident. The two verses in book 11 refer to a chariot, and taken in isolation 526–31 would certainly be taken to describe a pause in a chariot ride, although there would be some uncertainty who is driver (Odysseus at 527, Diomedes perhaps at 530). μάστιξεν is formular and imprecise; as riders they had left the whip behind (500).

532 ἄϊε (with ᾱ-), read also at 21.388, looks like an Atticism. ἤϊον is not found except as Zenodotus' reading at *Od.* 2.42.

534 = *Od.* 4.140, and for that reason was not read here by Zenodotus (T). There is no note of any later athetesis.

537 ὧδ' is certainly 'hither', as at 18.392 (πρόμολ' ὧδε). Aristarchus doubted this use, but he overlooked a few passages, having only his memory to check his text. ἐλασαίατο: the middle voice is appropriate to driving home booty, cf. 11.674.

540 (to ἔπος) = *Od.* 16.11.

543-4 ≅ 9.672–3, with the formula for Agamemnon in place of that for Nestor.

544-53 Nestor admires the horses. Nothing is said of the fact that the heroes have exceeded their orders and have learned nothing about Trojan intentions for the morning. That sort of discipline was a Roman invention. What counted for the Achaeans, after the spoils, was the doing of a mighty deed of war. — For λάβετον (545) Zenodotus read the Attic λαβέτην Arn/A), see 361–2n.

546 Zenodotus read σφῶϊ, which is nom. or acc. dual of the 2nd person pronoun (cf. 552) and, as Arn/A remark, will not construe. Zenodotus perhaps took it for the dat. (σφῶϊν, 4.341 etc.). σφῶε, i.e. the pair of horses, is dual of the 3rd person. The scholia imply a reading σφῶ' ἔπορεν, but in accordance with his normal preference Aristarchus removed the augment, cf. 9.492n.

547 For αἰνῶς, 'terribly', emphasizing parts of ἔοικα see 3.158n., where the Odyssean character of the usage is noted; but cf. Richardson on 24.198. With a stop at the end of 546 ἐοικότες must be taken as an absolute, virtually exclamatory use of the nominative case, as if = 'Like rays of the sun ⟨they are⟩!'; cf. *Od.* 11.606–8 ὁ δ' [Herakles] ἐρεμνῇ νυκτὶ ἐοικώς, γυμνὸν τόξον ἔχων καὶ ἐπὶ νευρῆφιν ὀιστὸν | δεινὸν παπταίνων, αἰὲν βαλέοντι ἐοικώς, 'like one about to shoot ⟨he was⟩!' Or to illustrate his excitement Nestor is given the grammar of a speaker, as if the horses, the object of his attention, had been the subject of his opening words.

548–9 Nestor speaks the truth about his presence on the battlefield, but his contribution was limited to exhortation, e.g. 6.66–71, and was sometimes embarrassing, e.g. 8.80ff., when he had to be rescued by Diomedes. His hardihood eventually brought about the death of his son Antilokhos (Pind. *P.* 6.28–36). He was out again in book 11, but then remained by the ships ὀτρύνων πόλεμόνδε μελαινάων ἀπὸ νηῶν (17.383).

549 γέρων περ ἐὼν πολεμιστής: περ, although enclitic, seems to form a group with the participle, so that there is no caesura between the short syllables of the fourth foot, cf. λιγύς περ ἐὼν ἀγορητής (2×), θοός περ ἐὼν πολεμιστής (2×), πάρος περ ἐὼν ἐλεεινός (*Od.* 19.253).

552 = 7.280, of Aias and Hektor.

559 ἄνακτ': 'master'. The generalized sense of ἄναξ is paralleled, again of horses, at 16.371 and 16.507 λίπον ἅρματ' ἀνάκτων, where the neglect of ϝ- indicates a relatively late usage. ἀγαθὸς Διομήδης, shortened from βοὴν ἀγαθὸς Διομήδης (21×) occurs only here. The shortening is paralleled by ἀγαθὸν Μενέλαον at 4.181 (βοὴν ἀγαθὸς Μενέλαος, 21×).

560 πάντας ἀρίστους (8× *Il.*, 4× *Od.*) is used casually and is unconfirmed by the account of the killing, but see 488n.

561 Odysseus means the thirteenth besides Rhesos, but τρισκαιδέκατον is awkwardly repeated from 495. The heroes' score was fourteen dead if Dolon is included, hence the v.l. τετρακαιδέκατον reported by Arn/A.

564 The Achaean chiefs were waiting outside the camp, so Odysseus (who had dismounted at 541) must now drive the horses over the ditch. How and where is unstated. The singular διήλασε with μώνυχας ἵππους is the language of chariot-driving again.

566 κλισίην εὔτυκτον with ἱκάνω is formular, cf. 13.240, but the epithet properly belongs to the helmet (κυνέη, 3× *Il.*, 2× *Od.*).

567–8 Diomedes apparently appropriates the horses, of which nothing further is heard, not even in the chariot race of book 23. ἐϋτμήτοισιν ἱμᾶσι is formular (also 21.30) and generated the acc. ἱμάντας ἐϋτμήτους (23.684) but is otherwise isolated. Odysseus had no horses at Troy, and so no stall or manger, cf. 11.488n.

569 πυρὸν ἔδοντες, cf. *Od.* 19.536 (ἔδουσι). The epithet μελιηδέα is borrowed from the formulas for wine, similarly μελίφρονα πυρόν (8.188). πυρός is wheat, in the *Odyssey* ground for the suitors (*Od.* 20.107–9), in the *Iliad* the food of horses (8.188).

570–1 νηΐ πάρα πρύμνῃ must be Odysseus' ship, drawn up on the beach with the stern towards the land. ἱρόν may be a sacrifice, or the sacrifice vowed by Diomedes at 292, which is otherwise forgotten, but it is more likely that the arms, which Odysseus has already offered to Athene at 460, are themselves the ἱρόν. Dedications, ἀναθήματα, are not part of the religious practice of the Heroic Age, but were known to Homer (see 7.81–3) and *a fortiori* to this poet. — ἔναρα: see 528n.

572–5 The heroes bathe in the sea, partly in order to cool off after their exertions (575). After that they enjoy the pleasure of the (hot) bath as if preparing for a feast. There is more than a suspicion of 'thematic override' from this point to the end of the Book, see 576–9n., as the heroes are indulged in the amenities of an Odyssean palace wholly out of place in their κλισίαι along the shore.

573 λόφος in the epic usually denotes the mane of a horse or the crest of a helmet. It is an odd word for the back of a man's neck and oddly placed between the shins and thighs.

574 ἱδρῶ πολλόν: primarily doubtless ἱδρόα if the expression is formular, cf. ἠῶ δῖαν for ἠόα δ., at the verse-end; see Meister, *Kunstsprache* 7. The contraction is not necessarily post-Homeric; conservatism preserves the use of these expressions in spite of awkwardness brought about by linguistic evolution, cf. 11.1n., see Introduction 28–30.

575 Wackernagel, *Untersuchungen* 146, denounced χρῶτ(α) as an Atticism and proof of interpolation. The τ-stem, however, occurs at *Od.* 18.172, 18.179 and at Hesiod, *Erga* 556; it may be assumed to be a neologism of the vernacular making a tentative entry into *Kunstsprache*, where the old (originally s-stem) forms χρόα etc. were well entrenched.

576–9 Four formular verses round off the book: 576 = *Od.* 4.48, 17.87; 577 = *Od.* 6.96 (with χρισάμεναι), from the regular bathing scene, cf. Arend, *Scenen* 124–6. The notice of the bath and meal is almost absurdly laconic and omits the heating of the water and the female assistant, see West on *Od.* 3.464ff. Familiarity prevented the poet reflecting that bathtubs (usually heavy ceramic fixtures, archaeologically) were an improbable amenity for an army on campaign; likewise that the δεῖπνον was Diomedes' second and Odysseus' third repast this night. Since the heroes have already bathed in the sea the point of the tub must be that it provided a hot bath, as is certainly the case at *Od.* 8.450 and 10.361, and fresh water to remove the sea-salt. — ἐΰξέστας, the regular epithet (3×), suggests the possibility of wooden tubs (S. Laser, *Arch. Hom.* s 139). — After the mention of so much detail one misses a note of the retirement to bed, as at 9.658ff., unless the scholiast's suggestion (Arn/A) is accepted that the δεῖπνον was really the ἄριστον and taken just before dawn. The next Book begins abruptly at sunrise.

576 ἀσάμινθος occurs only here in the *Iliad*, though a bathtub is implied at 22.442–4, where Andromakhe is preparing θερμὰ λόετρα against

Hektor's return from battle, and perhaps also in Nestor's comfortable quarters at 14.6–7. ἀσάμινθος is clearly a word of non-Greek provenance (note the intervocalic -σ- and the suffix -νθ-) but is attested on a Knossos sealing KN Ws 8497; it is the normal term in the *Odyssey* (10×) for this amenity.

577 λίπ(α): always in *Il.* (3×) and once in *Od.* occurs with parts of ἀλείφειν, a jingle rather than an etymology, cf. τέτρατον ἦμαρ ... τετέλεστο ... πέμπτῳ πέμπ' ... *Od.* 5.262–3.

578 The libation is part of the ritual of drinking and sometimes a formality, the god(s) being unspecified. That the two heroes here give thanks to Athene for their success and safe return is a graceful note on which to end the Book.

BOOK ELEVEN

The previous day of fighting (book 8) ended with the Achaeans forced back to their ships. Their appeal to Akhilleus was unavailing, but Agamemnon had been shamed (see 9.707ff.) into leading them back into the fray. A splendid arming scene heralds Agamemnon's initial success; after heavy fighting the Achaeans rout the Trojans and drive them back to the city. But this effort is doomed to failure, and the poet must already have in mind the superb 'epic moment' to which he works his way at the conclusion of book 12 when, spears in hand, Hektor burst through the gates of the Achaean wall. He has already hinted at this at 9.650–3:

οὐ γὰρ πρὶν πολέμοιο μεδήσομαι αἱματόεντος,
πρίν γ' υἱὸν Πριάμοιο δαΐφρονος, Ἕκτορα δῖον,
Μυρμιδόνων ἐπί τε κλισίας καὶ νῆας ἱκέσθαι
κτείνοντ' Ἀργείους, κατά τε σμῦξαι πυρὶ νῆας.

That does not come to pass in fact until we reach another fine moment at the end of the fifteenth book when Hektor cries "οἴσετε πῦρ" and lays hold of the ship of Protesilaos; for the Great Battle of the central Books of the *Iliad* is related in two roughly parallel episodes, 11–12 and 13–15, each beginning with Achaean success and ending in Achaean disaster. The repeated pattern is part of the poet's technique for increasing the amplitude of the narrative, but it affords him also (as b to 13.1 notice) the opportunity to embroider his tale (ποικιλία) as well as augment it. The moments of great visual imagination and dramatic power with which the two episodes culminate are narrative foci, which in oral traditions of heroic poetry the singer can bear in mind and around which he can weave a sequence of appropriate themes.

Despite his early success therefore Agamemnon is soon wounded and the tide rapidly turns. Diomedes, Odysseus, Makhaon, and Eurupulos are wounded in succession as the Achaeans, their retreat covered by Aias, are forced back to their starting-point. bT attribute this order of narration, victory before defeat, to the pro-Greek bias of the poet. On any account, however, the bias is subtle and the effect here is rather to show that, without Akhilleus and against the malign influence of Zeus, the best efforts of the Achaeans cannot prevail.

The first part of the book (1–283) should be compared for its content with the entry into battle of Patroklos in 16.130–418. It is evident from that carefully composed passage that the present episode omits several regular themes. (For the repertoire see Krischer, *Konventionen* 23.) There is no council or assembly, though the theme αἴ κέν πως θωρήξομεν υἷας Ἀχαιῶν (2.83), is much more to the point here than in book 2 (the council had convened the previous night and its natural omission here carries with it the omission of the sacrifice); no meal is taken, as was noted before the previous day's fighting (8.53) and despite the labouring of this point at 19.154ff.; there is no harangue or prayer; a catalogue of the Trojan leaders is given (56–61) but not of the Achaeans. In the fighting itself there is no use made of the theme ἀνὴρ ἕλεν ἄνδρα, the exploits of those seconding the leading hero, and no major duel leading to a signal victory or a divine rescue. Speeches are kept short: in the battle section, 67–180, 211–595, there are 18 speeches with an average length of just over five lines.

The immediate cause of this thematic concision is that the Book (i.e. the narrative of this phase of the battle) covers more ground, from the ships to Troy and back, than any other and is packed with more incidents of consequence: three major warriors (or five, if Makhaon and Eurupulos are promoted into that category) are removed from the scene. One effect is to make the *aristeia* of Agamemnon, 91ff., seem unsupported and premature. In that respect it parallels the assault of Akhilleus in book 20. But Akhilleus had his reasons for impetuosity. Here we gain an impression that Agamemnon's attack has something of the reckless fury of a desperate man. We are not surprised in that case when the poet reveals that the immediate goal of his narrative (at 79 and more clearly at 191ff.) contradicts the expectations of the theme and that Agamemnon is doomed to ignominy and defeat. The further goal, the defence of the Achaean wall, was set up at 7.337ff. and will occupy books 12–15. The poet hastens towards those Trojan successes and makes them militarily plausible by decimating the Achaean front ranks.

The climax of Agamemnon's *aristeia* is followed by a counter-*aristeia* of Hektor, briefly told (284–309). The pattern of the Book then settles into the theme of a fighting retreat culminating in the disablement of the hero: Diomedes 310–400, Odysseus 401–88, Aias and Makhaon 489–574, Eurupulos 575–95. This is interwoven with the successes of Paris as archer. Finally, by a neat linking to the episodes of Makhaon and Eurupulos, the narrative picks up again the story of Akhilleus and foreshadows the entry of Patroklos into the battle (596–848).

The parallelism between the several episodes of this Book exemplifies, perhaps more clearly than any similar passage of the *Iliad*, the epic art of constructing the story of a battle: the setting up of narrative goals and the amplification of a major episode (the Achaean retreat) by repeating the substance of lesser episodes within it (see Fenik, *Homer and the Nibelungenlied*

5–21). In view of the formularity of the epic at other levels the economical explanation of the tendency to reuse (but also of course to recast) material is that it is part of the art of oral heroic poetry that the Homeric epic inherited. Repetition, however, continues to be a major criterion in the school of analytical criticism. H. van Thiel, for example (*Iliaden und Ilias* (Stuttgart 1982)), assigns the first part of Agamemnon's *aristeia* and the wounding of Odysseus to the 'Frühilias', the woundings of Agamemnon and the other leaders to the 'Spätilias', and the episode of Zeus and Iris to a poem on the Achaean Wall which supplied also the episodes of Asios and Hektor in book 12, on which see the comments of M. M. Willcock at *JHS* 104 (1984) 188–90.

The successive presentation of Agamemnon, Diomedes, Odysseus, and Aias throws the characterization of these heroes into relief, see Fenik, *Tradition* 74–7. Agamemnon is vengeful and brutal, Diomedes gallant but mercurial, Odysseus clear-thinking and realistic, Aias ever-reliable and stubborn in adversity.

1–66 The new day dawns and Zeus despatches Strife to stir up the Achaeans. Agamemnon's magnificent armour is described. The Achaeans then march out from their new fortifications. On the other side the Trojans, spurred on by Hektor, advance to meet them

1–14 The function of this introductory passage is to effect a brisk transition from the preceding book (whichever that was) to this and to introduce in a fitting manner a new sequence of events. For Eris cf. 4.440–1, 20.48, and for the Homeric usage of the term (basically = 'rivalry') see J. C. Hogan, *Grazer Beiträge* 10 (1981) 21–53. Dawn is a natural starting-point for a new episode, cf. 2.48, 8.1, 19.1, though the habit of using dawn and nightfall (or rather retirement to bed) to articulate the narrative is more evident in the *Odyssey*, e.g. 2.1, 3.1, 5.1, 6.48, 7.1, 15.56, 16.1–2, 17.1, where there are more days of action. This dawn marks the fifth day of action since the second Book and the twenty-fifth since the beginning of the *Iliad*. It is introduced in this elaborate way because it heralds, as both sides believe, the day of decision and has been carefully marked as such by previous references: 8.470-2, 8.525, 8.565, 9.240. The day will prove to be the longest in the epic, for the sun does not set upon the fighting until 18.239. The decorated style of the whole passage and the allegory of Eris underline the importance of the following narrative and add an ominous touch: the bright dawn heralds a black day.

1–2 For dawn-formulas, with which the poet is generously supplied, see nn. to 2.48-9.; there is a list of references in G. M. Calhoun, *Univ. Cal. Publ. in Class. Phil.* (1933) 17. Verses 1–2 = *Od.* 5.1–2 where they mark the starting-point of the *Odyssey* proper: here they mark the Achaeans' final attempt to master the Trojans in fair fight without Akhilleus, there being no gods to cloud the issue as there were in books 5 and 6. Verse 2 = 19.2. — ἀγαυοῦ Τιθωνοῖο: the three spondees which end the verse, if that is what the poet sang, are not chosen for their rhythmical effect. The verse is formular and as such had to be accepted. The gen. sing. ἀγαυοῦ, however, uniquely among the case-forms of ἀγαυός is invariably found in the third–fourth foot in archaic epic (except at Hesiod fr. 141.7 M–W) and must have been fixed in that position in the form ἀγαυόο so as to give an elegant and normal dactyl in the fourth foot, cf. the similar location of the genitive μεγαθύμου (31×). ἀγαυός is probably an Aeolism (note the -αυ- diphthong < -αϝ-): ἀγητός is the Ionic form. Τιθωνοῖο: for his pedigree see 20.237 and the stemma at vol. v 316. He was a scion of the Trojan royal house and father of Memnon, Akhilleus' last great opponent, but that is irrelevant to the dawn-formula: we are not to suppose that this dawn is biased against the Achaeans. His miserable immortality is first attested at *HyAphr* 218–38, and Mimnermus fr. 4 West. Like others of his dynasty (see 13.171–3n.) Tithonos may have a genuinely Anatolian name, cf. τιτώ· ἠώς, αὔριον (Hsch.), and Τιτώ, 'dawn goddess' (Callimachus, fr. 21.3 Pfeiffer, Lycophron 941).

3 Zeus now begins to implement his threat at 8.740–2 to wreak even worse destruction on the Achaeans, but as usual the will of Zeus is accomplished by a devious route; catastrophe will be preceded by victory. The Olympian gods have been banished from the battlefield by Zeus's edict at 8.10–17, which he reaffirmed to a rebellious Here and Athene at 8.399–408, cf. 73–9 below. Eris, of course, is not a god in the same sense, not a person but a personification; however, the poet seems aware that he has undercut his picture of the battle and inserts a comment, see 74–5 and n. Since it takes two to make a quarrel Eris' actions are often more impartial than her present intervention. See further 4.440-1n.

4 πολέμοιο τέρας: what Eris held in her hands it is impossible to say and perhaps was never precisely conceived (Arn/A mentions ἀστραπή, ξίφος, λαμπάς). Like her war-shout it is the more awesome for being vague. Athene's aegis, decorated with various allegories including Eris, is called a Διὸς τέρας at 5.742, and at 2.450–2 was used to urge on the Achaeans. (The aegis was primarily a means of causing stupefaction and panic, cf. 15.320–2, *Od.* 22.297–8.) In the parallel scene at 8.220–6 Agamemnon waved πορφύρεον μέγα φᾶρος. As Fenik remarks, *TBS* 78, this looks like a small typical scene.

5–9 =8.222–6, where it was Agamemnon who did the shouting. Whatever it describes, the Catalogue of Ships does not describe the order of the ships drawn up on the Trojan shore, in spite of Αἴας ... στῆσε .. ἵν᾽

Ἀθηναίων ἵσταντο φάλαγγες at 2.557–8 (see n.). J. Cuillandre, *La Droite et la gauche* 23–34, has worked out the order of battle of the principal Achaean contingents generally implied in the *Iliad* in so far as there is a consistent picture (see also 13.681n.):

Left				Centre					Right			
Aias	Idom-	Mene-	Agam-	Nes-	Odys-	Euru-	Diom-	Aias	Meges	Menes-	Podar-	Akhil-
s.of	eneus	laos	emnon	tor	seus	pulos	edes	s.of		theus	kes	leus
Telamon								Oïleus				

In spite of the memorable position of his ship Telamonian Aias is (apparently) brigaded next to Odysseus at 3.225 and between Idomeneus and Nestor at 4.273. The two Aiantes also are often made to act in concert. In the ναύσταθμον itself some contingents in the centre were probably thought to be quartered behind others (15.653 and n.), the whole protected by a semicircular rampart (14.31–2, 14.75). In the normal order of battle the two best πρόμαχοι are stationed on the wings, the right wing, as so often, being the place of greatest honour. The left wing is only apparently weaker, for the contingents of Idomeneus (80 ships), Menelaos (60), Agamemnon (100), and Nestor (90) are among the largest. Agamemnon's offensive develops on the left and in the centre, so that when it fails it is there that the casualties, Odysseus, Eurupulos, and Diomedes, are sustained; Menelaos (463), Idomeneus, and Nestor are also involved (510ff.), but Aias has to be summoned (463ff.). In the absence of Akhilleus the right wing fails to distinguish itself. Verses 5–9 = 8.222–6 and 11–14 (from μέγα σθένος) ≅ 2.451–4, arousing suspicion of secondary composition, see e.g. Von der Mühll, *Hypomnema* 190, Reinhardt, *IuD* 178.

5 μεγακήτεϊ νηΐ: 'au flancs profonds', Chantraine s.v. κῆτος, though that sense is not easily derived from a word appropriate to the deep sea (*Od.* 3.158) and its denizens (κήτεα, e.g. the dolphin, 21.22 etc.). F. Bechtel, *Lexilogus zu Homer* (Halle 1914) 194, suspected a word κῆτος, 'hollow'.

6 γεγωνέμεν is an explanatory infinitive, 'so as to call.'

11–12 ≅ 14.151–2: σθένος ἔμβαλ' ἑκάστῳ: the ϝ- of ἕκαστος is widely neglected, but the prototype of the formula is extant at 2.451 σθένος ὦρσε(ν) ἑκάστῳ. This is an instance of Hoekstra's category 'archaic constituent replaced by a familiar form' (*Modifications* 53).

12–14 = 2.452–4. As is so often the case with repeated runs of verses the Alexandrians suspected interpolation. Zenodotus omitted 13–14 (Arn/A, Did/T); they were read, but athetized, by Aristophanes and Aristarchus, on the ground that the verses belonged in book 2. The alternative of returning home, which is very apposite in book 2, has not been mentioned since the beginning of book 9 and is indeed gratuitously introduced at this point.

15–46 Agamemnon arms for battle. Armour is an outward, visible symbol of heroism and the description of the hero's splendid war-harness is endemic in heroic poetry, e.g.:

> The emir does not wish to waste time. He puts on a byrnie whose flaps are yellow with varnish, laces on his helm which is decorated with precious stones set in gold and then he girds on his sword on his left side. In his pride he has found a name for it. Because of Charles' sword of which he had heard tell he has had his sword called Précieuse. That was his war cry in a pitched battle and he made his knights shout it. He hangs a great broad shield of his about his neck; the boss is of gold and it is bordered with crystal. The belt of it is made of good silken cloth embroidered with circles. He grasps his lance and he calls it Maltet. The shaft of it was as thick as a club and the iron head of it alone would be as much as a mule could carry.
>
> (*Chanson de Roland* 3140–54)

> He [Ðulić] put on his green coat. All its seams were finished with golden braid. On his head he placed his fine fez; about the fez he wound a Tripolitan sash, and about it his golden plumed headdress. All the plumes were of gold. Then he adjusted his vest and breastplate and girded on his studded arms belt. In the belt were two small golden pistols. At his right side was his flint box of gold, and from his left side he hung his curved sabre. Then he drew on his officer's pantaloons and pulled over them his boots and long socks.
>
> ('The Captivity of Ðulić Ibrahim', *SCHS* I, 105.)

See generally J. I. Armstrong, *AJP* 79 (1958) 337–54, Arend, *Scenen* 92–95, and nn. to 3.330–8. In the epic the amplification marks the importance of the occasion: this is Agamemnon's decisive effort. The four great arming scenes of the *Iliad* (3.330–8, 16.130ff., 19.364ff., and the present passage) name the same arms (greaves, corslet, sword, shield, helmet, spear(s), always in that order) but skilfully vary the elaboration. The *Odyssey* has no arming scene as such, but Melanthios brings the Suitors shields, spears, and helmets, *Od.* 22.144–5; [Hesiod], *Aspis* 122–38, has a similar scene with reuse of the old formulas but places the shield (a hoplite shield?) last – for which there are artistic reasons in that poem – and Alcaeus fr. 140 L–P lists helmets, greaves, corslets, shields, swords, ζώματα, and κυπάσσιδες (see D. L. Page, *Sappho and Alcaeus* (Oxford 1955) 209–23). The disreputable Paris (3.330ff.) is given the basic gear with minimal detail; here the emphasis is on Agamemnon's magnificent corslet and shield with a brief comment on the gold and silver fittings of his sword. His greaves and helmet make do with conventional (but in the latter case cumulated) description. Armour was extremely valuable (nine oxen for a workaday bronze outfit, 6.236, or a hundred oxen for the de luxe model in gold, *ibid.*); its smooth surfaces invited ostentatious decoration to express (as here) the status and vanity of the wearer, cf. the corslet of Asteropaios (23.560–2). It seems also to possess a special symbolism for the Homeric warrior. Its seizure took precedence over tactical military considerations or personal safety, as if victory were not complete without the spoils of war. The important pieces for that purpose are helmet, shield, corslet and spear, cf. the lists at 13.264–5 and 19.359–61. Special armour is noted at 6.235, 7.136, 8.191, 17.194, and of course 18.478ff.

15 The narrative plunges immediately into the arming scene without any notice of sacrifice, prayer, or meal, as in books 2 and 19 (the entry into battle of the Myrmidons in book 16 is in response to an emergency, but even there space is found for Akhilleus' prayer to Zeus). If the poet had intended his hearers to suppose that Agamemnon had omitted those crucial precautions he would have said as much; even so the tempo of the narrative leaves an indelible sense of Agamemnon's impatience. Ἀτρείδης: this is Agamemnon's great moment and a note on his royal ancestry would not have been inappropriate, but this has already been given when he stood before the assembly at 2.100ff. The Homeric poems know (or mention) only Pelops, Atreus, and Thuestes in earlier generations of the Pelopidae, and only Menelaos and Aigisthos in Agamemnon's; there is no mention of Pleisthenes, whom the *Cypria* (fr. 10 Davies) and mainland and western poets from Hesiod (fr. 194 M–W) and Stesichorus (fr. 219 Davies) onwards insert at unspecific points into the genealogy. It is possible that these allusions preserve the remnants of a memory of the Pelopidae at Mycenae lost from the main Ionian tradition. Pleisthenes was made brother or half-brother of Atreus by schol. Pind. *Ol.* 1.144 and inserted between Atreus and Agamemnon by schol. Eur. *Or.* 4. See Fraenkel's note to Aesch. *Ag.* 1569 for further references.

16 ἐδύσετο: the conjugation of sigmatic aorists with the thematic vowel is an epic type confined to a few verbs, chiefly δύομαι, βαίνω, and compounds, see Chantraine, *GH* I 416–17. The paradosis has often introduced -σα- forms in spite of ancient grammatical opinion that identified the formation as an imperfect. See further West on *Od.* 1.330, Hainsworth on *Od.* 5.194, 6.321 and the literature there cited.

17–19 = 3.330–2 = 16.131–3 = 19.369–71. Apparently the greaves, though often of metal in the Late Helladic (LH) period (and at 7.41, 18.613, 21.592) did not lend themselves to detailed description, at least no attempt is made to elaborate their mention beyond the two-verse formula 17–18. Nor were they worth looting, in spite of their silver clasps. For a full account see H. W. Catling, *Arch. Hom.* E 143–61. The obsolescence of the tower shield made it necessary to protect the lower legs which could not be covered by the smaller shields of the later Mycenaean and Dark Age periods. Missiles appear especially to have been feared, cf. Alcaeus fr. 357.6 L–P ἄρκος ἰσχύρω βέλεος, Aesch. *Th.* 676 αἰχμῆς καὶ πέτρων προβλήματα, see also 377 (wounding of Diomedes).

20 The archaeological evidence for the corslet is discussed by H. W. Catling, *Arch. Hom.* E 74–118. LH examples are mostly plate-corslets, those of the Iron Age (before the advent of the hoplite panoply) are, to judge from the iconography, leather jerkins. Such a masterpiece of craftsmanship as Agamemnon's cuirass must have a history, but the point, if any, of assigning to it a Cypriot origin is unclear, unless it is to imply that the fame of Agamemnon had reached the ends of the earth. The scholia (bT) have nothing plausible to report. This is the only reference to Cyprus in the *Iliad*. The island, however, was part of the heroic world with seven mentions in the *Odyssey* and the major *Homeric Hymns*, and provided Aphrodite with her epithets Κύπρις and Κυπρογένεια. It was colonized by Teukros after the Trojan war, and the poet may have heard of the wealth of the kings of archaic Salamis, now revealed by the excavation of their tombs: see V. Karageorghis, *Excavations in the Necropolis of Salamis* I–IV (Nicosia 1967–71). Kinures is cited as an example of wealth at Tyrtaeus fr. 12.6 West and Pind. *N.* 8.18, and was later celebrated as founder of the cult of Aphrodite at Paphos. For ξεινήϊα see 10.266n., and for another cuirass with a history 15.530–4.

21 πεύθετο γὰρ Κύπρονδε: 'in Cyprus' or even 'from Cyprus' in the English idiom. The adlative form is used because the report travelled *to* Cyprus to its recipient, see 4.455n. and 16.515.

24–8 The οἶμοι must be bands or strips of material, probably inlaid or otherwise fastened as decoration to the main material of the corslet. Unfortunately the text gives no indication how these bands were arranged, whether vertically or horizontally, in blocks, irregularly, or in some re-peated sequence. Three different materials, in quantities of 10, 12, and 20, cannot be arranged in any sort of repeated pattern if the materials must alternate. If, however, two bands of the same material may be juxtaposed, then GGTT KKTT GGTT KKTT GGTT KK TTGG TTKK TTGG TTKK TTGG is possible (G = gold, T = tin, K = kuanos; grouped in fours here to clarify the pattern). Two blocks of 21 bands (GT KT GT ... TG TK TG) would equally be possible. Lorimer, *HM* 208, thinks of a scale corslet, Willcock of a θώρηξ with breast- and back-plates. These are pleas-ing patterns and suggest that the numbers of οἶμοι are not arbitrary choices but conceivably describe an object that the composer of the verses had seen and examined. On the other hand the object in the text may (like the shield described at 32–40) be a composite or be elaborated imaginatively. Corslets with some sort of horizontal banding are indicated by the Linear

B ideogram 162 ▤, but the snakes better suit the fashion of the orientalizing period. Catling, *Arch. Hom.* E 79, suggests that this corslet was parade armour not fighting gear, but Homer knows no such distinction, cf. Glaukos' golden armour (6.236) and Nestor's golden shield (8.192–3).

24 μέλανος κυάνοιο: for the tint cf. μείλανι πόντῳ (24.79), but μέλας denoted any dark colour, especially that of blood, αἷμα μέλαν etc. (11×); see R. Halleux, *SMEA* 9 (1969) 47–66. κύανος (< Hitt. *kuwanna-* or a related Anatolian dialect) denotes various decorative substances – the natural mineral lapis lazuli, its imitation in glass paste, or the blue–black alloy known as niello. See Edwards, vol. V 203 and F. Eckstein, *Arch. Hom.* L 40–1. Niello, which was used on the daggers from the Shaft Graves at Mycenae, is perhaps most likely in the decoration of a breastplate, see D. H. F. Gray, *JHS* 74 (1954) 1–15, or E. Vermeule, *Greece in the Bronze Age* (Chicago 1964) 98–9.

25 κασσιτέροιο: tin decorated the cuirass of Asteropaios (23.561); tin, unalloyed, was used in Akhilleus' armour, 18.474, 18.565, 18.574, 18.613, and elsewhere, contrary to normal metallurgical practice. It is probably adduced as a precious metal and a mark of luxury, like the gold.

26 Snakes, here depicted on the breastplate (also on the shield-strap as if they had some special symbolism for Agamemnon), are more than ornamental, cf. [Hesiod], *Aspis* 161–2 ἐν δ' ὀφίων κεφαλαὶ δεινῶν ἔσαν, οὔ τι φατειῶν, | δώδεκα, καὶ φοβέεσκον ἐπὶ χθονὶ φῦλ' ἀνθρώπων (cf. *Aspis* 144 in C. F. Russo's edition). The countryman in the simile at 3.33–6 recoils at the sight of a snake, ὦχρός τέ μιν εἷλε παρειάς.

27–8 A τέρας is a divine interference with the course of nature such as to cause encouragement or dismay, e.g. an omen (2.324), or the thunder which Zeus may send in response to prayer (15.379, *Od.* 3.173): or here perhaps just to cause astonishment and fear. The rainbow is a τέρας ἤ πολέμοιο | ἤ καὶ χειμῶνος at 17.548–9. μερόπων: a notorious gloss, see 1.250n.

29–31 On the Homeric sword see S. Foltiny, *Arch. Hom.* E 235–74. Agamemnon takes a sword that has gold rivets in defiance of the formula φάσγανον/ξίφος ἀργυρόηλον (9× *Il.*, 4× *Od.*) applied to his weapon at 2.45, on which see nn. *ad loc.* Gold-plated rivets are well attested throughout the LH period (Lorimer, *HM* 273), and may conceivably have been known to the poet; but the value of the metal primarily reflects the importance of the occasion (as Aristarchus (Arn/A) noted), or the luxury of the article (cf. the epithet χρυσάορος and Nestor's cup, 633 below). Agamemnon, as the poet's audience would know (and would not savour the full effect of book 1 if they did not), was immensely rich, king πολυχρύσοιο Μυκήνης. For the relation of the expressions βάλετο ξίφος and ξίφος ἀργυρόηλον see Introduction 9. The formular verse with ἀργυρόηλον is followed by χάλκεον, αὐτὰρ ἔπειτα σάκος ... (3.335, 16.136, 19.373). As Shipp remarks (*Studies* 278), the dropping of ἀργυρόηλον in favour of the gold studs has resulted in the shield verse (32) being completely recast. ἀορτήρεσσιν: not the baldric itself (τελαμών) but, according to Hsch., οἱ κρίκοι τῆς θήκης, the metal rings by which the scabbard was clipped to the leather.

29, 34, 39 οἱ: the use of ἑ, οὑ, οἱ with reference to things is unusual, but cf. 1.236, 9.419, 21.586, 24.452.

32-9 The shield of Agamemnon. There is a discussion by H. Borchhardt in *Arch. Hom.* ε 50-6 with a line-drawing of the Gorgon-shield from Carchemish first published by C. L. Woolley, *Carchemish* II (London 1921) pl. 24. In conception Agamemnon's shield is similar to the aegis of Athene at 5.738-42, αἰγίδα ... δεινήν, ἣν περὶ μὲν πάντῃ φόβος ἐστεφάνωται· | ἐν δ' Ἔρις, ἐν δ' Ἀλκή, ἐξ δὲ κρυόεσσα Ἰωκή, | ἐν δέ τε Γοργείη κεφαλὴ δεινοῖο πελώρου, | δεινή τε σμερδνή τε, Διὸς τέρας αἰγιόχοιο. The shield of Herakles was even more horrific, *Aspis* 144-67. This aspect probably reflects the latest models known to the poet and is combined with features familiar to him from traditional descriptions: tin and κύανος are Mycenaean, bosses are known from the late Bronze Age, the κύκλοι from Dark Age practice. It is not clear how, or if, a central boss of κύανος can be combined with the Gorgon's head, and the verb ἐστεφάνωτο does not help matters (see 36-7n). This is the only arming scene in which the shield is denoted by ἀσπίς not σάκος; see D. H. F. Gray, *CQ* 41 (1947) 113-14, 119-21, and Whallon, *Formula, Character, and Context* 36-54, for the usage of these two terms.

32 ἀσπίς, the commoner term in the narrative, 95× against σάκος 76×, is the vernacular word that replaces σάκος when the formular verse is abandoned. ἀμφιβρότην is taken from the formula in the gen. sing. ἀσπίδος ἀμφιβρότης (3× *Il.*). The strict sense 'covering a man on both sides' is not applicable to the round, bossed, shield, and the epic must have taken it in a generalized way to mean 'protecting the warrior', see the literature cited in *LfrgE* s.v. Even so the epithet is giving way to the modernism εὔκυκλος. If ἀμφῐβρότη is an archaism the short ι before βρ and the implied sense of βροτός = ἀνήρ raise the possibility that an unintelligible term has been reinterpreted, cf. Myc. *a-pi-qo-to*, 'round' (?), PY Ta 642. For -βρ- < -mr- (cf. τερψίμβροτος) see M. Lejeune, *Phonétique historique du mycénien et du grec ancien* (Paris 1972) 307, and for the view that ἀμφῐβρότη reflects Myc. *amphimr̥tā* see Janko vol. IV 11. The metrical effect of r̥ is suspected in compounds of βροτός (ἀβρότη, ἀβροτάξομεν < -mr̥tós), formulas (δειλοῖσῐ βροτοῖσι), and in compounds of ἀνήρ (ἀνδροτῆτα, ἀνδρεϊφόντη < anr̥-, cf. Myc. *a-no-qo-ta* KN Da 1289, etc.). πολυδαίδαλον: usually of the corslet (4×), only here of the shield, but a fitting anticipation of the following description. θοῦριν (with ἀσπίδα 20.162, αἰγίδα 15.308) is unexpected as epithet of something naturally to be thought of as defensive equipment. Agamemnon's shield is clearly intended to terrorize, but by its visual impact not by its being used to beat an opponent to the ground.

33 The κύκλοι δέκα χάλκεοι remain obscure, see 13.406–7n., but probably refer to the appearance of the face. K. Fittschen, *Arch. Hom.* N, gives several illustrations of early votives (reproduced in vol. v 204–6) with decoration arranged in concentric bands. At 20.275–6, however, the implication is that the materials of a shield thinned out towards the edge, leaving only two κύκλοι, but a shield with ten layers of bronze at the centre is hardly possible outside the heroic world.

35 λευκοί: a reading λευκοῖ᾽ (gen. sing.) was known to the scholia (Hrd/A) and is read by Leaf. If the early stages of the transmission had understood the genitive the paradosis would have been λευκοῦ. Elided -οιο is attested in the paradosis of the lyric poets but not in the Homeric vulgate; it should not be introduced (Allen's λίνοι᾽ at 5.487 is unnecessary).

36–7 These verses have been ejected, e.g. by Lorimer, *HM* 190–1, on the grounds that the Gorgoneion and its supporters are incompatible with the bosses of 34–5, for which 36–7 are a graphic alternative. The Gorgon is known from the eighth century (Hampe, *Frühe griechische Sagenbilder* (Athens 1936) 63, pl. 42) though not attested as part of the ornament of a shield until the mid-seventh century. For monumental parallels to Agamemnon's shield see vol. v 203–4 and K. Fittschen, *Arch. Hom.* N 7–10; the most striking is that from the Idaean cave now in the Herakleion museum (reproduced as a line-drawing *locc. cit.*) A blazon can inspire terror as well as identify the bearer (Odysseus, however, was satisfied with a dolphin according to Stesichorus (fr. 225 Page)). Agamemnon's blazon lacks the symbolic character of those attributed by Aeschylus to some of the shields borne by the Seven (*Th.* 466, storming of a city; 539, the Sphinx, πόλεως ὄνειδος; 642, Justice). The narrative does not return to the shield's fearsome aspect, but the Gorgon's head makes two other appearances in the *Iliad* at 5.741 and 8.349 (where Hektor's fierce look is compared to it) and one in the *Odyssey* at 11.634. Lorimer notes (*HM* 190) that in seventh- and sixth-century art the Gorgon is frequently the blazon of Akhilleus and in the sixth century that of Aias. The Gorgon is common also in the fifth century (Ar. *Ach.* 574, 964, *Lys.* 560, cf. *Lex. Icon.* s.v. 'Gorgo'). — ἐπί ... ἐστεφάνωτο 'was set like a wreath'; the image appears to be that of snakes (the Gorgon's hair) encircling the boss, cf. T. Worthen, *Glotta* 66 (1988) 3–4. στεφανόομαι (only in the perfect tenses in the epic) is usually clarified by περί or ἀμφί except at 18.485 (see n.). Snakes regularly enhance the horrific appearance of Gorgons, but the mention of them is here reserved for the cuirass (26) and the shield-strap (39). βλοσυρῶπις: apparently 'of horrid aspect', though the epic uses the simplex βλοσυρός in the sense 'shaggy', e.g. 7.212. The *Aspis* poet has the first clear use of the word as a synonym of ὁλοός (see Russo's note on *Aspis* 147). Leumann, *HW* 141–8, would regard βλοσυρῶπις as primary and, taking the first element as an Aeolism (< *g^wltur*-), connects it with Lat. *vultur* to give a sense 'vulture-eyed' or 'vulture-headed'. The accentuation, according to Schwyzer, *Gr. Gr.* 1 463 n. 5, should be paroxytone, βλοσυρῶπις, the final syllable being long.

37 περί: understand 'were depicted' from ἐστεφάνωτο in 36. Δεῖμος and Φόβος are paired also at 4.440 (where see n.), 15.119, Hesiod, *Theog.* 934, and *Aspis* 195. Reasonably enough, *Theog.* makes the pair sons of Ares. Φόβος was represented as a figure with a lion's head in the depiction of Agamemnon's shield on the Chest of Kupselos (see 248–63n.), Paus. 5.19.4, see Friis Johansen, *Iliad in Early Greek Art* 70.

38–90 With Agamemnon's silver τελαμών (i.e. with decoration in silver) compare the golden one of Herakles at *Od.* 11.609–12, decorated with ἄρκτοι τ' ἀγρότεροί τε σύες χαροποί τε λέοντες, | ὑσμῖναί τε μάχαι τε φόνοι τ' ἀνδροκτασίαι τε. Akhilleus' shield-strap was silvered (18.480), the decoration being unspecified.

39 The snakes are numinous – and ominous, see 2.308–19. They reinforced the image of Tuphon on the shield of Tudeus (Aesch. *Th.* 495).

40 ἀμφιστρεφέες (read by Aristarchus, Did/AT): 'turned in all directions'; ἀμφι- is awkward with the numeral τρεῖς, but the picture, one head facing upward, the others to right and left, is clear enough. The vulgate ἀμφιστεφέες is no easier and may be influenced by ἐστεφάνωτο in 35, but we may imagine the three heads in the same arrangement forming a sort of crown.

41 = 5.743 (see n.): κυνέη is the less frequent of the two common words for 'helmet' (κόρυς 46×, κυνέη 28×) and must originally have meant 'dog skin', though the special properties of such leather are not reported. Various bronze attachments are noted including probably the φάλοι implied by the epithet ἀμφίφαλος – probably metal plates, four in number according to the epithet τετράφαλον (12.384, 22.315). The other epithet τετραφάληρος is obscure, though it had meaning for the poet who sang of φάλαρ' εὐποίητα at 16.106 (see n.). The grandiose obscure epithets (only in this repeated verse) suited the helmet of the goddess Athene in book 5, and add a mysterious and menacing dimension to Agamemnon's equipment. Homeric helmets are discussed by Lorimer, *HM* 237–45, D. H. F. Gray, *CQ* 41 (1947) 109–21 (= *Language and Background* 55–67), and J. Borchhardt, *Arch. Hom.* ε 57–74. In Alcaeus' list of armour (fr. 357 L–P) the κυνία (Lesbian = κυνέη) is clearly metallic, as were the greaves.

42 The nodding plume, cf. the famous passage 6.466ff., was a characteristic enhancement of the warrior's fearsome appearance from the earliest representations to the close of the Geometric period. The crest of the later 'Corinthian' helmet was a much stiffer adornment.

43 A unique verse, surprisingly, but cf. 3.18, 16.139. The concord of plural and dual in ἄλκιμα δοῦρε is a strong indication of a secondary usage, cf. ὄσσε φαεινά 13.435, a mid-verse variant of the verse-end formula ὄσσε φαεινώ. The verse εἵλετο δ' ἄλκιμα δοῦρε δύω κεκορυθμένα χαλκῷ | ὀξέα is adapted from the verse describing the thrusting-spear εἵλετο δ' ἄλκιμον ἔγχος ἀκαχμένον ὀξέϊ χαλκῷ (15.482). The two spears are for throwing, and describe the equipment of the Iron Age or even that of the Late Geometric period when warriors armed with two spears become a frequent element in iconography. It is characteristic of oral poetry that it tends to substitute the familiar (i.e. what is contemporary with the poet or within the memory of his audience) for the archaic but does not do so systematically. Agamemnon will use a single thrusting-spear in his *aristeia*, see 95–8n. κεκορυθμένος (< κόρυς), properly 'helmeted', replaces the archaic ἀκαχμένος; the sense 'tipped' is confined to this verse and its congener (3.18), with an ambiguous use at 16.802.

44–5 The gleam of the armour is a good omen; its absence is a portent of death, cf. T. Krischer, *Konventionen* 36. αὐτόφι (6× *Il.* only, always in fourth foot) supplies a convenient dactylic form for the genitive and dative plurals of αὐτός; the reference is to the δοῦρε of 43. ἐπὶ ... ἐγδούπησαν: only here of thunder (which must be meant). Thunder, elsewhere the prerogative of Zeus and expressed by κτυπεῖν, is a favourable omen, cf. 8.170, 15.377, 17.595, *Od.* 21.413, heralding victory. (At 8.75–7 it is the σέλας not the thunder that cows the Achaeans.) Agamemnon's entry into battle must have some divine accompaniment, but Zeus for the moment favours his enemies and he must make do with a distant rumble from the goddesses on Olumpos.

46 ≅ 7.180 (and πολυχρύσοιο Μυκήνης at *Od.* 3.305). The wealth of Mycenae and its dynasty was proverbial long before modern archaeological discoveries, cf. Hesiod fr. 203 M–W ἀλκὴν μὲν γὰρ ἔδωκεν Ὀλύμπιος Αἰακίδησι, | νοῦν δ' Ἀμυθαονίδαις, πλοῦτον δ' ἔπορ' Ἀτρεΐδησι. (The sons of Amuthaon were Melampous and Bias, cousins of Nestor.) The tholos tombs at Mycenae (and Orchomenos) were known in late antiquity as θησαυροί (Paus. 2.16.5), but it is uncertain when that erroneous identification was first made. πολυχρύσοιο Μυχήνης is presumably an old formula created when the wealth of Mycenae existed or was remembered, but its combination with βασιλῆα is not traditional. βασιλεύς denotes a person of rank in the epic but otherwise is imprecise: for the extensive bibliography on the term see *LfgrE* s.v. Where it is least vague, e.g. in the description of the polity of the Phaeacians at *Od.* 8.390–1 (see Hainsworth, *Od. ad loc.* and pp. 342–3), a βασιλεύς is a nobleman of consequence but is outranked by the monarch. For βασιλεύς, 'chief' (*qa-si-re-u*), in Linear B texts see Ventris and Chadwick, *Documents* 121, 409. βασιλεύς is a common word in the epic (over 100×), but makes only three noun–epithet formulas: διοτρεφέες βασιλῆες, etc. (12×), θείου β., etc. (3× in *Od.*), and ὑπερμενέων β., etc. (3×). Contrast the behaviour of ἄναξ, on which see Ruijgh, *L'Elément achéen* 112–16. Only in this verse is βασιλεύς used to express 'king of such and such a place'.

47–55 A very truncated notice of the remaining themes of the 'entering battle' sequence: the parade and the charge. The poet apparently regards the deployment of an army as something so familiar that he can afford to be allusive. Concision as so often has led to obscurity, mainly because there is no indication when or how the army crossed the defensive ditch which is before the poet's mind for the first and only time in this Book. An army about to advance would not fall in with a barrier intended to be impassable for chariots in front, so that the poet must think of the army forming up before it, i.e. on the plain with the ditch at their backs; ἐπὶ τάφρῳ therefore at 48 and 51 refers to the outer side of the ditch. The men are in position before the chariots, for reasons that are left to the imagination, e.g. because of congestion at the gates of the camp or the crossings of the ditch. (For the gates see introduction to book 12.) αὐτοί at 49 are the fighting men (as opposed to the ἡνίοχοι) who advance with their chariots *at the rear*. Nestor's shock-tactics (4.297ff.) naturally stationed the chariots in the van and are not in question here. – πρυλέες: also at 5.744 (see n.), 12.77, 15.517, 21.90, a word of uncertain meaning, πρόμαχοι according to an old suggestion of Hermann's, 'en masse' in later poets, perhaps 'on foot' here and at 12.77, as Arn/A suggests and as Eustathius (893.32) thought on the strength of the word's occurrence in Cretan; not, as LSJ s.v. propose, common soldiers 'opp. to chiefs fighting from chariots', at least not here. (The πρυλέες have a ἡγεμών at 15.517.) Verses 47–8 = 12.84–5, where ἐπὶ τάφρῳ refers to the outer side of the ditch. The ἱππῆες at 52 are then those in charge of the chariots, the ἡνίοχοι. Verses 48–9 are repeated with grammatical changes to introduce the imperative mood at 12.76–7, but there it is Pouludamas recommending these same tactics to the Trojans.

50 The noise of the Achaean advance seems to be an inadvertence; cf. 3.8–9, 4.429–31. ἠῶθι πρό: here and 2× *Od.*; for the shape of the formula cf. Ἰλιόθι πρό (3× *Il.*, 1× *Od.*) and the isolated οὐρανόθι πρό 3.3. The syntax is unclear (from an archetype Ἰλίοο πρό?), cf. 3.3n.

51–2 μετεκίαθον: the chariotry follow in the approved manner at a short distance. μετεκίαθον (with ῑ by metrical lengthening) is an obsolescent verb (5× *Il.*, 1× *Od.*, not in Hesiod) beside the simplex (ἐ)κίον. Both forms are aorists. The root is evidently *kiH- with laryngeal, cf. the factitive κῑνέω. The proper function of the -θ- suffix is to indicate 'que l'aboutissement de l'action est envisagé' (Chantraine, *GH* I 326), a function most evident at 16.685 Τρῶας καὶ Λυκίους μετεκίαθε.

53–4 The symbolism of the bloody rain is obvious, cf. the bloody rain-drops at 16.459–61, *Aspis* 384.

55 = 1.3 but with κεφαλάς for ψυχάς, see 1.3n. Surprisingly, only the Genavensis (s. xiii) suggests the possibility of reading ψυχάς here, and that in suprascript. κεφαλάς was evidently read by Apollonius Rhodius at 1.3 and must have been read here, but it is odd none the less that it should be used unnecessarily and by metonymy for the ψυχή, the life-force. ἴφθιμος is not formular with either ψυχή or κεφαλή, so that the coincidence with the proemium is not an accidental result of formulas coming together to make a verse: nor is there any reason beyond the repetition here in question for supposing the verse is a whole-verse formula. It is therefore possible that the echo is the result of the poet's mind running on the same thoughts: the wrath of Akhilleus was to cause a fearsome massacre, now Zeus is going to bring it about.

56–61 The Trojans, camped overnight on the plain, arm for battle. The scene is expressed in its barest form but incorporates none the less a succinct catalogue of leaders. It is necessary because the epic narrative of events must not omit 'what happened', but nowhere in the *Iliad* are the Trojans given the full arming sequence. Absent from this setting out for war is the striking idea present in books 2–4: the silence and discipline of the Achaeans in contrast with the clamorous polyglot host that fought for Troy, see 3.2–14n.

56 A formular verse (= 20.3). Τρῶες δ' αὖθ' ἑτέρωθεν is also formular in its own right (3×). It is quite uncertain to what geographical feature, if any, the 'rise' in the plain refers.

57–60 Only the Trojan and Dardanian leaders are mentioned. They constitute (except for Polubos, only here) a canonical list who reappear among the commanders in the assault on the Achaean wall in book 12. All the names are, or could be, Greek, although it is likely that Αἰνείας is of alien origin. (The etymology (< αἰνὸν ἄχος) given at *HyAphr* 198–9 is clearly of the popular kind.)

57 Πουλυδάμαντα: see 12.60n. Like Deiphobos (see 12.94n.) he is part of the personnel of the second half of the *Iliad*. Pouludamas, son of the Trojan elder Panthoos (3.146), is an important figure who will soon establish his role as wise adviser to Hektor.

58 Cf. 10.33n. θεὸς ὣς τίετο δήμῳ: 5× *Il.*, 1× *Od.*; this occurrence and *Od.* 14.205 are the only instances that preserve the original prosody (< σϜός). δήμῳ is subsumed in the 'essential idea' of the formula, so that it is possible to add another dative, Τρωσί, which formally duplicates the construction of δήμῳ. Hoekstra (on *Od.* 14.205) notes that the poet thought the sense (for which see 12.310–14) needed explanation.

59–60 Of these sons of Antenor, valiant enough to fight in the front rank, Polubos is otherwise unknown, Akamas has an entry in the Trojan Catalogue (2.823, see n. *ad loc.*), leads a battalion at 12.100, and is slain – if that is the same Akamas – at 16.342, but Agenor in spite of his commonplace name is much the most distinguished, with thirteen mentions in the *Iliad*. He was slain by Neoptolemos in the *Little Iliad* (fr. 15 Davies = Paus. 10.27.1). Two other sons of Antenor appear in this book, 221ff. The Antenorids are elsewhere often associated with Aineias, but have only a peripheral role in the *Iliad*, not commensurate with their rank and dignity, see Espermann, *Antenor, Theano, Antenoriden*. Antenor himself is of the generation of Priam, too old for war, and appears as the leader of the Trojan peace party. His politics avail him little in the *Iliad*, where seven of his sons are killed.

61 πάντοσ' ἐΐσην: as an epithet of the ship ἐΐση appears to mean 'well-balanced', a quality that would also be useful in a shield, but the addition of the adverb πάντοσε makes the sense primarily 'round', like εὔκυκλος. The prothetic ἐ- of ἐΐσην is found only in the feminine of ἴσος (except for an Hesychian gloss ἔϊσον· ἀγαθόν) and may have arisen within the tradition of the *Kunstsprache* by false division of this formula (< πάντοσε Ϝίσην). The Mycenaean dialect has *wi-so-wo-pa-na* (PY Sh 740), where ϜισϜο- seems a certain transcription, but also an obscure *e-wi-su-zo-ko* (KN Se 965, etc.), which may represent ἐϜισϜ-.

62–73 The compression of the narrative of the Trojan deployment followed by the truncated account of the first stages of the battle brings four similes together in less than a dozen lines. The brevity of the second (66) and third (72) make an effect very different from the 'majestic prologue' (Leaf) beginning at 2.455 (see nn.). The comparison with wolves (72) especially craves extension if it is not to seem pointless.

62–6 This short scene expresses in concise form the Trojan advance to battle. κελεύων (65) suggests comparison with the commander's harangue, e.g. 16.200–9. The simile of the star, which illustrates the gleam of armour at 5.5–8, 19.381, and 22.26–31, is unusually applied to Hektor's appearance and disappearance. At 22.30 the star is a κακὸν σῆμα, as at 62 it is οὔλιος, 'full of menace', like Hektor's advance.

62 οὔλιος ἀστήρ is supposed to mean Sirius, whose baleful effects are described by Hesiod (*Erga.* 586ff.). But all astronomical and meteorological phenomena are potentially menacing, cf. Sirius again at 22.26ff., and the lightning that heralds the intervention of Idomeneus at 13.242. Ap. Rhod. 4.1629–30, ἀστὴρ αὔλιος, 'star that bids the shepherd fold', i.e. the planet Venus, may allude to an ancient v.l. noted by Arn/A.

64–5 Hektor's movement from front ranks to back and then to the front again is typical, see Fenik, *TBS* 80. Athene does the same at 20.48–50 and Ares at 20.51–3, also using their voice. Rarely in the poetry of war is it so freely admitted that leaders may have a problem in persuading the κακοί to fight, cf. 408, 4.299.

65–6 To say that the hero 'shone with bronze' is a variant, here and at

12.463 (Hektor again), of the literal expression 'the bronze shone' with nominative χαλκός as at 44–5 and 10.153–4 (see n. there for other variants of this formula). πᾶς δ' ἄρα χαλκῷ is a formular word-group in its own right, cf. π. δ' ἄ. χ. | σμερδαλέῳ κεκάλυφθ' (13.191–2). The comparison of the flash of metal to lightning is used also at 13.242ff. and 14.386.

66 ≅ 10.154 (to Διός). For the conjunction of στεροπή and Διός αἰγιόχοιο see 15.18–31n. and 15.308–11n., where the suggestion is made that the aegis was primitively the thunderbolt.

67–91 The mutual slaughter of the two armies, watched by Zeus and Eris, leads to an Achaean break-through

In an epic poem, a poem about heroes, the narrative of a battle must be told from the standpoint of the men wielding the weapons; but that can only be done, when thousands of men are involved, by ruthless selectivity. The unselected warriors are not thought of as doing nothing, they are simply not thought of. In this Book there is abridgement as well as selection. The abbreviated style is imposed by the very full content of this Book, but since joining battle is a regular sequence of themes the poem's audience would easily understand the picture the poet intended to draw. In books 4–5 and 16 the focus of the narrative progressively shortens, passing from the general view of the field, through the exploits of a list of heroes, to the career of one hero and culminating in a duel between two major figures (16.295–507 is the clearest example); here the preliminaries are cut out and we proceed at once to Agamemnon's *aristeia*. The Iliadic battle then is a work of art. In it the naming of names is of prime poetical importance, and this is exploited so as to bring a semblance of order to an inherently disorderly event. The basic device is to divide the combatants into πρόμαχοι and πληθύς. The latter is marshalled (φάλαγγες, 90) on a broad front, so that the battle has a right and left wing (see 5n.). The men engage with missiles (84–5), or may come hand to hand (4.446–51), or both (8.60–7), or may leave matters to the πρόμαχοι. The formations are not tight or static; if broken they can rally and reform, they permit the movements of officers, the use of chariots, the advance of the πρόμαχοι, the pillage of their victims, and their retreat εἰς ἔθνος ἑταίρων. The πρόμαχοι include the great heroes, obviously, but others also, for it can be said of a reckless warrior that he θῦνε διὰ προμάχων (342, etc., 3×). This does not seem historically improbable, except perhaps for the chariots. In the ideology of epic warfare the decisive role is played by the πρόμαχοι and among them by the great heroes in justification of their status (cf. 12.310–16 and nn.); in its practice the desire for spoils and κῦδος appears a dominant motivation. For a careful discussion of the Homeric battle see Latacz, *Kampfdarstellung* 31–95. H. van Wees, *CQ* 38 (1988) 1–24, provides a useful discussion of earlier views and bibliography. The general conclusion is that the poet has a clear enough general picture of the course of battle and commanded a technique adequate for its description. Yet it is a battle of heroes (only they are militarily significant, according to Odysseus, 2.200–3), and it must be borne in mind that ἀοιδοί not only preserved old tactics (chariots, tower shields) in old formulas but incorporated the old tactics into newer systems of formulas. To the extent that this took place (which remains unexplored) there is confusion already in the detailed presentation of battle. For the general picture Latacz compares the action before Syracuse described by Thucydides (6.69–70).

67–9 General descriptions of the fighting are regularly ornamented by similes, cf. 67–9, 72–3, 86–9. For the Homeric harvest-field see W. Richter, *Arch. Hom.* H 119–21 and the description of reaping at 18.550–6. There is some confusion in the thought behind the present comparison. Each army cut down the other, so the poet must combine the idea of reaping with that of two sides. He pictures two teams of reapers working from opposite ends of a field (ἐναντίοι ἀλλήλοισι, 67) to represent the Trojans and Achaeans, but the crop must also at the same time represent the Trojans for the Achaeans and the Achaeans for the Trojans, cf. Fränkel, *Gleichnisse* 41. As at 18.550–60 the fine crop belongs to a landlord, a μάκαρ here, a βασιλεύς in book 18. The metaphor of 'mowing down' an enemy is surprisingly rare in Greek (19.221–4, Soph. fr. 625 and then Ap. Rhod. 3.1187, 3.1382 – where the victims had been *sown*), probably because Greeks fought most of the time with the spear rather than with slashing weapons. Occupying as it does an almost programmatic position in the book this simile sets the tone of the following narrative. In books 3–8 there had been included glimpses of the conventions of war (duels, truces, burial of the slain), of its chivalrous side (Diomedes and Glaukos), even of its humorous aspects (the panics of Aphrodite and Ares); in book 10 war brought fame and profit and little risk. All that now disappears. Vultures not burial await the dead. There is a horrendous list of casualties, in quantity on the Trojan side, in quality on the Achaean. The brutal slayings of Agamemnon are followed by the nasty incapacitating wounds of the leading Achaeans. This is *guerre à l'outrance*, πόλεμος πολύδακρυς not μάχη κυδιάνειρα.

70–1 = 16.770–1, and 85 = 16.778 (with similarities in the adjacent verses). The situations are much the same. In book 16 the battle has reached an impasse over the body of Kebriones. The same pattern, presumably traditional, asserts itself: both sides are locked in battle ... simile ... As long as ... so long did the missiles fly ... but when ...

72 Neither army will give ground. ἴσας κεφαλὰς ἔχεν, 'held their heads on a line' (Lattimore), 'locked them head to head' (Fagles), is one of those expressions whose force is evident but which defy rational analysis.

The vulgate reading ἔχον would require ὑσμίνη to be emended into the dative.

73–83 The poet reminds his audience of the state of the conflict on Olumpos. Other summaries of the politics of Olumpos, e.g. 13.345–60 and 15.592–604, explicitly adumbrate the course of events, and this reminder of the watchful eye of Zeus is more than a hint that Agamemnon's offensive will fail. The point is made repeatedly (cf. 11.300, 12.37, 12.174, 12.255, 12.437, and 3× in book 15), as if to explain the paradox of this day of Trojan victory. Reinhardt (*IuD* 253) notes the 'demonic' rule that every Achaean success in the *Iliad* up to the return of Akhilleus to the war leads finally to disaster. The gods were confined to Olumpos by Zeus's edict at 8.10–17. Their absence is maintained consistently (except in book 10, and see 438n.) until the intervention of Poseidon at 13.34. This deprives the poet of some useful motifs: no one prays for divine aid, no one is divinely rescued from danger or inspired with μένος, no fog is shed over the combatants, but the most consequential absence is that of Athene from the Achaean side: Athene is the concomitant of success, and her absence here, like her absence in book 16, dooms the Achaean efforts to failure.

73–5 These verses are a naive comment on, or explanation of, the poet's allegory of Eris with which he introduced this day of conflict. Eris is a personification as we should say, a rhetorical abstraction, and from this point the poet forgets her, but for his audience at least she is a daimon and therefore formally contravenes Zeus's confinement of the gods to Olumpos.

75–6 ἔκηλος (properly 'not involved in', < ἑκάς, but usually ≅ οὔ τιν' ἔχειν πόνον, cf. *Od.* 13.423) is not a permanent epithet of the gods, although it would well describe their condition, cf. ῥεῖα ζώοντες (1× *Il.*, 2× *Od.*). The word is here merely the complement of οὐ πάρεσαν; the gods are 'not involved' but by no means 'at their ease'. σφοῖσιν: for the vulgate οἷσιν, which should imply a singular reference, see 142n.

78–83 The usual pattern of omission (Zenodotus) and athetesis (Aristophanes and Aristarchus (Did/AT, Arn/A)) makes its appearance. The objections were partly pedantic ('all' the gods could not include the pro-Trojan party), partly sensitive to the situation and the conventions of the *Iliad* (Zeus prefers to superintend the battle from Ida but is currently on Olumpos), partly ideological (the gods should not be represented as angry with Zeus). Hellenistic criticism is often over-precise, cf. 17.545–6 and n. What the gods found objectionable, of course, was that Zeus was keeping control of events to himself. Exasperated at the interference of Here and Athene Zeus had taken up his station on Ida (80–3 echo 8.47–52), to enjoy the view of the fray. He had then withdrawn to Olumpos (8.438), whence he returns at 11.182–4 οὐρανόθεν καταβάς; the only objectionable verses are therefore 82–3 (≅ 8.51–2). Some note of where Zeus took his station would also be expected, if he is already watching the battle. Zeus here watches the battle as if it were a theatrical performance, cf. Griffin, *HLD* 175–82, where other passages are cited. The gods take delight in a spectacle in whose perils they have, and can have, no share, like the landsman in Lucretius watching a shipwreck (2.1–4, cf. 5–6 *suave etiam belli certamina magna tueri | per campos instructa tua sine parte pericli*), but with a sort of awed fascination at the zest of the heroes for strife and suffering.

81 γαίω is a by-form of γάνυμαι only found in the formula κύδεϊ γαίων (4× *Il.* only), which is used (always preceded by καθέζετο) of Zeus and those, like Briareus (1.405) and Ares (5.906), who bask in his reflected glory.

83 ὀλλύντας τ' ὀλλυμένους τε: other examples of *polyptoton* are cited by Edwards, vol v 59, cf. 13.131n. The figure often expresses reciprocity.

84–5 The transition from one incident to the next is marked, as so often, by a formular 'run' (here 84–5 = 8.66–7, in both places followed by ἦμος δέ ...); 84 = *Od.* 9.56 and 85 = 16.778. The *Iliad* divides the day into three parts (21.111), so that ἠώς may be understood to mean 'before the heat of the day'. The action of 11.91–16.779 (when 'Ἥλιος μετενίσετο βουλυτόνδε) then takes place during the μέσον ἦμαρ, always supposing that the narrative prospect before the poet's mind at this point extends in detail so far ahead and incorporates a nicely calculated time scheme. The battle turned at noon at 8.68, and again (in a note similar to the simile 86–9) when the sun was sinking βουλυτόνδε at 16.779. — ἱερὸν ἦμαρ: bT suggest that morning is sacred because it is the time of sacrifice, which clearly will not do, for night (κνέφας ἱερόν, 11.194 = 15.455) is also 'holy'. Natural phenomena, of course, are controlled by gods, cf. ἀμβροσίη νύξ (10.41) etc. see P. Wülfing-von Martitz, *Glotta* 38 (1959–60) 272–307, esp. 292ff.

86 δεῖπνον, which may denote any meal, is evidently the woodcutters' morning repast (= ἄριστον Arn/A, in the epic only at 24.124 and *Od.* 16.2). It probably marks the end of the first third of the day. δόρπον, read by Zenodotus and a few MSS, is the evening meal and wrong here – but cf. *HyDem* 128–9 for an equation of δεῖπνον and δόρπον. The closest parallel to this way of marking the time of day is *Od.* 12.439–41 ἦμος δ' ἐπὶ δόρπον ἀνὴρ ἀγορῆθεν ἀνέστη.

89 = *HyAp* 461 (with σίτοιο γλυκεροῖο).

90 Δαναοὶ ῥήξαντο φάλαγγας: it is necessary to keep this picture in mind until Agamemnon is wounded, 248ff. The Trojans are routed and Agamemnon leaps in to cut down the fugitives. The φάλαγγες and στίχες (91) are the ranks of the army. They must not be thought of necessarily as close-packed, for missile weapons are used and bold warriors may break ranks. Moreover if the order is shattered as here it can reform (284ff.); the closely marshalled classical phalanx deployed more spears along its front but once committed to action sacrificed the possibility of manoeuvre (cf. Thuc. 5.71–2) and could not rally if broken.

91–283 As the Trojans flee Agamemnon launches a ferocious attack and slays eight named Trojans with great brutality. Hektor does not oppose him, having been warned by Zeus through Iris to hold back until Agamemnon is disabled and withdraws. Agamemnon's last victim, Koon, maddened by the death of his brother, wounds the king in the arm before he is killed. Agamemnon keeps the field for a time, but at last is overcome by pain and is driven off to the ships

In broad terms – and in some details – Agamemnon's onslaught is told in similar fashion to that of Akhilleus at 20.353–21.135. Hektor is kept out of sight by divine agency; the Achaean executes a massacre; his pursuit of the routed Trojans is compared to forest fire; the rout is described; the hero's hands drip blood (169 = 20.503); the massacre is then resumed.

The form of the narrative and particularly its balance will best be apprehended by a schematic summary:

	84–91	Prefatory general description, with a quasi-simile.
	91–100	Agamemnon slays Bienor and Oïleus. They are not identified. The manner of Bienor's death is unspecified, Oïleus is speared through the head.
	101–21	Agamemnon slays the brothers Isos and Antiphos.
		102–4: they are identified as sons of Priam.
		104–6: brief anecdote.
		Isos is speared, Antiphos killed with the sword.
		113–19: simile.
	122–47	Agamemnon slays the brothers Peisandros and Hippolokhos.
		123–5: they are identified by a brief anecdote.
		126–47: they are petrified and surrender but Agamemnon spears Peisandros and decapitates Hippolokhos with his sword
	148–62	General description, with simile.
A	163–4	Zeus keeps Hektor out of trouble.
	165–80	More general description, with simile.
BX	181–210	Zeus, through Iris, warns Hektor to keep away until Agamemnon is wounded and withdraws. Hektor will then have victory.
	211–16	Trojan rally.
	216–63	Resumed *aristeia* (216–17, ἐν δ' Ἀγαμέμνων | πρῶτος ὄρουσ' = 91–2).
		Agamemnon slays Iphidamas and Koon. The slayings are

231

linked since Iphidamas and Koon are brothers, but are related as separate episodes within ring-composition (221 ~
261).

221–47   Iphidamas.
    221–30: he is identified by an anecdote.
    232–3: Agamemnon's spear misses.
    234–40: Iphidamas hits but does not injure Agamemnon.
    240: Agamemnon kills him with the sword.
    241–45: pathetic observations on his death.
C   248–63   Koon.
    248–50: he is briefly identified.
    251–3: he wounds Agamemnon in the arm.
    254–60: Agamemnon spears Koon.
D   264–83   Agamemnon withdraws.
    269–72: simile.
Y   284ff.   Hektor's counter-attack.

The alternation of general description and particular incident is typical
of Homeric narrative technique. The exegetical scholia (who are familiar
with the point that events may be parallel but narration must be linear)
call it προανακεφαλαίωσις; bT comment on 90ff. ἐν κεφαλαίοις εἶπεν ὡς
ἀνήρηνται [*sc.* Bienor and Oïleus], τὸ πῶς ἐπάγει κατὰ μέρος. The poet's
remark on one reason for Agamemnon's success, Hektor's absence (A), is
developed into a foreshadowing of the termination of his *aristeia* (B), and of
Hektor's success (X). The former is fulfilled at C–D, the latter leads at Y
into the next sequence of themes. The exegetical scholia comment frequently upon such linking trains of thought (προαναφώνησις, πρόληψις,
προοικονομία) in which they perceive the poet's grand design formed and
finished before any verse was composed. For the technique of the anecdote
see C. R. Beye, *The Iliad, the Odyssey, and the Epic Tradition* (London 1968)
94–6.

The second part of Agamemnon's *aristeia* is short-weight in content since
he is given only one straight slaying before being wounded, against six in
the earlier episodes, but the space allocated is not grossly disparate (the
latter half of the *aristeia* with its ancillary general descriptions has 70 verses
against 101 in the former).

91–147 First part of the *aristeia* of Agamemnon. In three brisk fights the
king attacks men mounted in chariots and despatches three pairs of minor
Trojans. The intention is doubtless to stress the ferocity of the hero's onslaught. That does credit to the μένος of the King of Men, but it is not so
gallant as it may appear: the Trojans are mounted in order to flee, not to
fight at an advantage. On very few occasions in the *Iliad* is anyone said to

fight from a chariot (5.13, 8.118ff., 11.531ff., 15.386 and 16.377ff.), cf. Snodgrass, *Early Greek Armour and Weapons* (Edinburgh 1964) 260 n. 26, to which add the equivocal description of Euphorbos' tactics (16.809ff.). See also 150–3n.

The repeated theme of men killed in pairs imposes some order on a narrative that might otherwise be as chaotic as the battle itself; it is used also of Diomedes' exploits at 5.9ff., 144ff., 148ff. 152ff., 159ff. (a remarkable series), and of Diomedes and Odysseus (themselves fighting as a pair) later in this book (328ff.). Most of the pairs are brothers, a fact that increases the moments of pathos and motivates the hopeless attempts of the second brother to avenge the first and stand up to a mighty hero. The repetition of the themes is part of the poet's technique, but the way in which they are elaborated is part of his art: the three episodes form a crescendo marked by increasing length ($9\frac{1}{2}$, 21, and 27 verses respectively) and savagery. This is more artful composition than is observed at some other points, e.g. 16.173–97, 18.478–613, 23.262–897, *Od.* books 9–10, where the poet begins at length and speeds up as he proceeds. S. E. Bassett, *TAPA* 6 (1934) 47–69, is disparaging of Agamemnon's prowess. Agamemnon's victims are not indeed fighting men of the first rank, but the same may be said of the slain in any *aristeia*. The first pair, Bienor and Oïleus, are nonentities who enter the *Iliad* only here. None the less the details of his end give Oïleus at least a fragment of individuality; he dared to stand his ground. The second and third pairs are persons of more consequence and potentially more formidable antagonists, being represented as sons respectively of Priam and his counsellor Antimakhos, but only Antiphos is mentioned elsewhere, see 101–21n. The fact is that few men with a life outside the scene of their death are slain in the *Iliad*, and very few, so far as we can tell, who have a life outside the poem. The inference is that scenes such as Agamemnon's *aristeia* are *ad hoc* fictions: the King of Men must be given his moment of glory in a narrative of Iliadic scale, but the tradition named for him no memorable opponent. It is not therefore surprising that all eight of Agamemnon's victims in this Book have Greek names; over two-thirds of the 340-odd Trojans and allies mentioned in the *Iliad* are given such names.

These deaths are related in a strikingly detached style which is graphic but minimizes the horrors of hand-to-hand combat. An *aristeia*, of course, must be read from the standpoint of the ἀριστεύς, and so might easily be tainted with sadism. The objective style avoids that danger, but at the risk of seeming to lack sympathy. Note therefore the use of anecdote (104–6), simile (113–19), and direct speech (131–5) which momentarily turn attention from the ἀριστεύς to his victims. bT rightly find pathos in these episodes.

92 πρῶτος: the common pattern of battle description narrows the focus first to a series of slayings by different heroes. It is natural to begin such a section with πρῶτος, cf. 4.457, 5.38, 6.5, 13.170, 16.284. Here there is no space for the exploits of a second or third warrior (see 67–91n.), and the poet plunges forthwith into Agamemnon's *aristeia*. πρῶτος has point, however; Agamemnon is impetuous; he also jumps in first at 5.38 and 7.162.

92–100 Slaying of Bienor and Oïleus. Aristarchus (Arn/A) read the Attic form Βιάνορα, for an unknown reason. Oïleus is the name of the lesser Aias' parent and an odd choice for a minor Trojan: it is unlikely that the Ionian singer recognized that 'Οϊλεύς represented Fιλεύς ([Hesiod] fr. 235 M–W etc., see 12.365n.) and connected it with (F)Ιλιος. The 'O- is necessarily vocalic in at least 13 of the 21 Iliadic occurrences of 'Οϊλεύς and 'Οϊλιάδης. Both this Oïleus and Bienor are otherwise unknown to the archaic epic and their choice here seems arbitrary. Oïleus is the charioteer, not because of his epithet πλήξιππος (a generic epithet used of Pelops and two other *fighting* men in the *Iliad*), but because the regular sequence is to slay the fighting man first and his driver second, e.g. 6.12ff. Oïleus, however, shows more spirit than most ἡνίοχοι, who in present circumstances are paralysed with fear, e.g. Asios' driver at 13.394ff. and Thestor at 16.401ff. Note that even these minor figures are thought to have a chariot at hand.

The battle scenes are the stock scenes of the *Iliad* and presumably an indispensable and ancient part of heroic poetry, see Introduction to vol. ii, ch. 2, and Mueller, *Iliad* 78–83. Fenik, *TBS passim* (pp. 78–114 deal with book 11), has supplied a masterly analysis of their thematic content which it would be otiose to reproduce in detail. It may, however, be useful to analyse the diction of 92–100 as an example of the way in which such scenes are constructed at the formula level (ciphers refer to Iliadic occurrences):

92 πρῶτος ὄρουσ(ε): also 11.217 (note the tendency to repeat a phrase after a short interval).
ἕλε δ' (or ἕλον) ἄνδρα: 3×.
∪ – ∪∪ ποιμένα (-ι) λαῶν: 6×.

93 αὐτόν, ἔπειτα δ': only here, in spite of the hero's so frequently pouncing without delay on his next victim.
∪ – – – πλήξιππον: also at 4.327.

94 ἤτοι ὅ γ': 7×.
ἐξ ἵππων κατεπάλμενος: only here, but cf. ἐπάλμενος 6× before the diaeresis, and ἐξ (καθ', ἀφ') ἵππων ἆλτο 4×.
ἀντίος ἔστη: the plural ἀντίοι ἔσταν occurs at 1.535 and 4× with ἐναντίοι.

95 ἰθὺς μεμαῶτα (-ι): 3×.
μετώπιον ὀξεῖ δουρί: cf. μετώπιον ὀξέϊ λᾶϊ 16.739: ὀξέϊ δουρί 10× always at verse-end.

96 νύξ(ε): 9× with elision in the initial position.

χαλκοβάρεια: 2× at verse-end; the rest of 96 is unique.

97–8 (from ἐγκέφαλος) = 12.185–6 = 20.399–400.

– ∪∪– δέ at verse-end: 10×.

99 τοὺς μὲν λίπεν αὖθι: only here, but cf. τοὺς (τὴν) λίπεν αὐτοῦ 3×.

ἄναξ ἀνδρῶν Ἀγαμέμνων: 36×.

100 στήθεσι παμφαίνοντας: cf. τεύχεσι παμφαίνων 2×.

περίδυσε χιτῶνας: cf. the formula ἔνδυνε περὶ στήθεσσι χιτῶνα 2×.

These scenes are by no means solidly formular: if they were, the sense of masterly versatility in the handling of essentially monotonous material would be lost. At the same time each verse contains, and most verses are made up of, diction adapted from formulas.

94 κατεπάλμενος: καταπαλμένος Hsch., which may have been read by some Hellenistic texts, if *Anth. Pal.* 9.326 (Leonidas) καταπαλμένον ὕδωρ depends on it. See nn. on κατεπᾶλτο at 19.351. The form must be understood as κατ-επ-άλ-μενος, athematic aorist of (κατ-εφ-)ἅλλομαι, with psilosis, the athematic forms being unknown to those responsible for the orthography of the vulgate, cf. vol. v 35.

95–6 ὀξέϊ δουρὶ | νύξ᾽: Agamemnon now wields a thrusting-spear in spite of his taking two (throwing) spears at his arming (11.43). The confusion is not unique, cf. 3.361 (Menelaos rushes in with the sword after *one* spear-cast) with 379, and 22.273 (the great spear of Peleus is *thrown*) with 326 (Hector is wounded by a *thrust*), cf. 11.420ff. The verbs of close combat are ἐλαύνειν, ἐρείδειν, νύσσειν, ὀρέγεσθαι, οὐτάζειν, (ἐμ-)πηγνύναι, πλήσσειν, ὠθεῖν, those of missile-throwing ἀκοντίζειν, βάλλειν, (ἐφ-, προ-)ιέναι, χεύειν, with little overlap between them. — Shattering head-wounds are frequent enough (4.460, 6.10, 8.85 (a horse), 12.185, 12.384, 16.347, 16.740, 17.297 (with extra detail), 20.399) to be obviously part of the typology of battle; see Thornton, *Supplication* 95–100. Verses 97–6 ≅ 12.185–6 ≅ 20.399–400. At 3.300 the pouring out of sacrificial wine reminds the witnesses of spilled brains. Agamemnon used excessive force, but then so did Akhilleus at 20.395ff. Friedrich, *Verwundung* 52, notes that Agamemnon's killings tend towards the gruesome character assigned to the exploits of second-rank warriors, cf. his slayings of Deikoon (5.533ff.) and Hippolokhos (11.145ff.). Agamemnon is especially savage with the sword (a slashing weapon), see his treatment of Peisandros (146), but only here is the dramatic effect of his spear-thrust described. The Homeric spear does not inflict a neat puncture but an extensive wound; at 16.322–5 a spear-thrust shears off an arm. It is not necessary for the poet always to state in rapid narrative that such injuries were fatal, see 108, 144, 321, 338–9, 421, etc., and Mueller, *Iliad* 86–9.

96 στεφάνη could mean the rim of the headgear rather than the whole helmet here and at 7.12 (but not at 10.30), but probably serves as a synonym (with metrically useful στ-) for πήληξ (so D. H. F. Gray, *CQ* 41 (1947) 116 = *Language and Background* 62, *contra* Lorimer, *HM* 243, preferring 'rim').

97–8 The whole phrase ἐγκέφαλος δὲ | ἔνδον ἅπας πεπάλακτο is formular (3× in the vulgate, but see 12.183–6n., with 11.535 = 20.500 as a variant). The brain was not 'spattered all about', for the injury was ἔνδον, probably within the helmet, cf. Friedrich, *Verwundung* 46–7. A similar injury is more lucidly described (and in detail) at 17.295–8 where the brain is said to gush from the wound. Apollonius Rhodius is reported to have excised 98 and read ἐγκέφαλόνδε in 97, construing it with the preceding ἦλθε. The Alexandrians suspected repeated groups of verses but rarely resorted to excision if that necessitated emendation of the verse retained.

100 The obscurity of this verse lies in the verb περίδυσε. Leaf insists, with justification from classical usage, that without an indication of removal δύω should mean 'put on'; but if περίδυσε is right the only possible sense is that Agamemnon stripped the corpses, cf. Antiphon 2.2.5 and later authors for this sense. The authors of the banal v.l. ἐπεὶ κλυτὰ τεύχε' ἀπηύρα saw what was required but could not extract the sense needed from the paradosis. Aristarchus (bT) swallowed the camel but strained at the gnat, supposing that στήθεσι παμφαίνοντας could be separated from τούς and construed with χιτῶνας (which he took to mean 'armour'). What Agamemnon inflicts on these minor foes is what he prayed to inflict on Hektor, Ἑκτόρεον δὲ χιτῶνα περὶ στήθεσσι δαΐξαι (2.416). See G. Murray, *The Rise of the Greek Epic*, 4th edn (Oxford 1934) 127–8, on this and 22.75n. στήθεσι παμφαίνοντας: behind the superficially objective phrase is a pathetic oxymoron; in life a warrior was τεύχεσι παμφαίνων (6.513, 19.398). Nicanor (T) detected a further pathetic touch: the phrase showed their youth. J. Griffin, *CQ* 26 (1976) 161–87, shows how these seemingly cool comments by the poet link up with passages of undoubted pathos.

101–21 Slaying of Isos and Antiphos. Isos makes no other appearance, but this Antiphos has a brief moment of glory at 4.489–93. Agamemnon, fighting on foot, kills them both in their chariot: an unusual feat, achieved also by Akhilleus at 20.484ff., and by Diomedes at 5.159–60 and (but for the intervention of a god) at 5.9ff. This, and the fact that his victims are sons of Priam (as are Diomedes' victims at 5.159–60), redounds to Agamemnon's glory. Schadewaldt, *Iliasstudien* 47, discusses the scene and its momentary flashes of pathos.

101 Ἴσος is presumably < Ϝίσϝος like the adjective ἴσος, so that the ῥ' is a metrical stopgap. Ἄντιφος is a shortened name < Ἀντίφονος (who appears, oddly enough, as one of Priam's sons at 24.250). For the brother pairs see Reinhardt, *IuD* 252, and C. Trypanis on related pairs of warriors, *RhM* 106 (1963) 289–97. There is also an Achaean Antiphos (2.678 etc.).

102 νόθον καὶ γνήσιον: the poet makes a Greek evaluation of Priam's polygamous household. Isos has to be νόθος because the canon of Hekabe's children (the γνήσιοι) could not be arbitrarily extended. Trojan νόθοι are quite common: Demokoon 4.499, Doruklos 11.490, Medesikaste 13.173 and Kebriones 16.738. Like Kebriones, the bastard Isos plays the inferior role as charioteer. Priam's νόθοι are listed by Apollodorus 3.12.5 and Hyginus 90. On the Achaean side both Aiantes had νόθοι half-brothers, Teukros and Medon.

104–6 The fate of Isos and Antiphos – capture while engaged on some peaceful pursuit, ransom, and subsequent death on the battlefield – is parallel to that of another of Priam's sons, Lukaon (21.34ff.), with the difference that the perfunctory telling here is there expanded into a passage of remarkable pathos. Aineias narrowly escaped the same fate (20.90–4). In spite of their rank the ἄριστοι perform their own chores, just as their womenfolk do their own housework, so distant is the Heroic Age from the palatial culture of the LH period. ὤ (104) is accusative dual, a tricky form for the transmission of the text, see Allen's app. crit. in OCT. Oddly, Zenodotus failed to recognize the dual (understand ποιμαίνοντ(ε), not ποιμαίνοντ(α) in 106), the reason being, with reference to ὤ in 104, that he did not recognize the significance of the archaic orthography O and added ν to make the acc. sing. (γεγραμμένου τοῦ ο ὑπ' ἀρχαϊκῆς σημασίας ἀντὶ τοῦ ω, προσθεὶς τὸ ν, Arn/A). μόσχοισι λύγοισι: μόσχος, 'shoot', is a generic noun to which the specific term λύγος, 'willow', or the like, is added in apposition.

111 For Agamemnon's special animus against everything Trojan see 6.55ff. The detail that Agamemnon recognized his victims does not imply that he would otherwise have taken them prisoner: prisoners are not taken on the Iliadic battlefield (except, for an evil purpose, at 21.26ff.). But it adds a note of vindictiveness to Agamemnon's execution of his feeble opponents which the poet brings out sharply in the next scene. Meanwhile he turns his attention to the victims.

112 εἶδεν < ἐϝιδε; the first syllable is elsewhere resolvable except at 19.292.

113–19 Simile of the lion, the fawns, and the hind. The lion naturally represents ferocity just as the deer does timidity. The exploit of this dastardly lion adds little to our appreciation of Agamemnon's prowess, cf. the lion's attack on unguarded sheep at 10.485–6 which illustrates Diomedes' slaying of sleeping men. Attention then shifts to the hind and by doing so raises obliquely the question why Hektor was not there at the brothers' moment of need, a point to which the poet returns at 163. For the moment it is sufficient to say that the entire Trojan army is in full flight. — This is the first of a series of seven lion similes or short comparisons in this Book, a cumulation that reflects the ferocity of the fighting. Other Books with large numbers of lion similes are 5 with five and 17 with six. See also 10.485n., 12.299–306n. Verse 114 ≅ 175 = 17.63. Krischer, *Konventionen* 36–75, comprehensively examines the use of similes in Iliadic *aristeiai*.

118–19 διὰ δρυμὰ πυκνὰ καὶ ὕλην is formular, cf. *Od.* 10.150. κραταιοῦ is back-formation from the feminine κραταιή, only here and 13.345 in the *Iliad* and 2× *Od.*

120 No one could help Priam's sons, a frequent pathetic comment. When the fated moment is at hand nothing can avail a man, cf. 5.53, 6.16, 15.450, 17.242, not even a divine mother (21.110).

122–47 Slaying of Peisandros and Hippolokhos. Πείσανδρος is a stock name: it is used for an opponent of Menelaos at 13.601ff. (see n. *ad loc.* for the implications of this coincidence in the victims of the Atreidai) and for a Myrmidon commander at 16.193. Hippolokhos is used in the pedigree of the Lycian royal house (6.197), but not elsewhere. The father of these brothers, Antimakhos, would have appeared in the *Cypria*, but the poet takes care to motivate Agamemnon's cruelty by an explicit allusion to his offences (123ff., 139ff.). Stripped of that elaboration the scene is identical even to the inclusion of a lion simile with the slaying of Ekhemmon and Khromios by Diomedes at 5.159ff. Another son of Antimakhos, Hippomakhos, is killed at 12.189.

122–7 The syntax of this long sentence wanders through a long relative clause with subordinate participial and appositional phrases before losing itself at the end of 125. It is then resumed as if the preceding relative clause had been a principal sentence. This is how we speak, and how an oral poet sings.

123–5 The brief anecdote about Antimakhos prepares the way for his sons' inadvertent mention of their parent (they are the only victims to do so) and Agamemnon's violent reaction. Zenodotus read κακόφρονος for δαΐφρονος here and at 138 according to Did/A, perhaps supposing that δαΐφρων (a regular generic epithet) as too complimentary for the wicked Antimakhos. — μάλιστα is best taken with οὐκ εἴασκε. δεδεγμένος: Homeric usage elsewhere requires the sense 'expect', 'await' which must also be understood here.

124 Paris' bribery *may* have been mentioned in the *Cypria*, but it is too obvious an explanation for irrational behaviour for there to be any need of the authority of tradition for this little anecdote. Agamemnon will cite, or invent, a much more serious charge against Antimakhos (138–41). — ἀγλαὰ δῶρα: formular epithets are usually complimentary of what they describe, nor does the poet feel any need to change or abandon them if 'noble' (φαίδιμος) limbs tremble or 'splendid' gifts prove fatal. If he thought about it he probably relished the contrast between the superficial brilliance of the heroic world and its underlying futility and waste.

127–8 ὁμοῦ δ' ἔχον ὠκέας ἵππους seems to be explained by the following verse, as γάρ suggests. The driver has lost control of the chariot and the fighting man is helping him regain it (so Did/A), but the plural σφεας when the charioteer is meant is unexpected.

128–9 The spear-fodder are petrified at the hero's approach, cf. Thestor before Patroklos at 16.403, Alkathoos before Idomeneus at 13.434.

129 ἐναντίον ὦρτο λέων ὥς | recurs at 20.164 with Akhilleus as subject, but there the short comparison is extended by runover epithet and relative clauses into a nine-verse simile. A long simile at this point would upset the balance of these short scenes.

130–5 The appeal for quarter was made in similar words to Menelaos (131–5 ≅ 6.46–50, cf. 10.378–81), who was willing to give it ear: Agamemnon, then and now, is made of sterner stuff and displays an unrelenting animus against everything Trojan. For the expression of the theme see 10.378-81n. Akhilleus, before the opening of the *Iliad*, had been willing to take prisoners, but in the *Iliad* itself no appeal for mercy is admitted, cf. 6.46, 10.378, 16.330, 20.463, 21.74ff.

130 An oddly spondaic verse, especially if we read Ἀτρείδης as three syllables with Arn/A. γουναζέσθην: 'entreat', introducing direct speech without any further verb of speaking. But nothing prevents us imagining the two Trojans also *kneeling* to make their supplication.

131 = 6.46, where Ἀτρέος υἱέ denotes Menelaos, a neat example of formular economy.

133 This is a formular verse (3× *Il.*, 1× *Od.*).

137 ἀμείλικτον δ' ὄπ' ἄκουσαν is formular, cf. 21.98 (Akhilleus to Lukaon), but is here neatly opposed to the even more formular μειλιχίοις ἐπέεσσι (4× *Il.*, 14× *Od.*, including variants). Note the neglected digamma of ϝόπα. These are the sole verses that introduce direct speech with a verb of hearing not speaking, i.e. from the standpoint of the addressee. No less than seven of Agamemnon's 46 speeches in the *Iliad* are introduced as 'stern' or 'pitiless'. 'Implacable' (ἀμείλικτος) excellently characterizes Agamemnon, who here practises the ruthless slaughter of suppliants he preached at Menelaos at 6.55–60.

139–40 Menelaos' and Odysseus' embassy is mentioned at 3.205–24 and was related in the *Cypria*. This would also have been the occasion of Paris' bribery (124). Kullmann, *Quellen* 277, accepts the embassy story as pre-Iliadic, but supposes, very plausibly, that the *sons* of Antimakhos are a Homeric invention. It is needless to ask how Agamemnon knew of

239

Antimakhos' treachery, if the inherited guilt of Antimakhos' sons is not a convenient fiction to justify their treatment: the characters are permitted to know what the audience knows – at least in incidental references. What Agamemnon says here about Antimakhos is not wholly consistent with his allegation at 125.

140 ἀγγελίην: 'a famous if overrated problem' (Kirk on 3.206), but ἀγγελίην is clearly an internal accusative here, as at 4.384, cf. ἐξεσίην ἐλθόντι (24.235). For Aristarchus' view, which cannot be accepted, that there was an epic noun ἀγγελίης, 'messenger', see Leumann, *HW* 168–70. The 'problem' arises in five places besides the present: 3.206, 4.384, 13.252, 15.640, Hesiod, *Theog.* 781 (see nn. *ad locc.*).

142 τοῦ: Zenodotus read οὗ as 2nd person reflexive adjective. The v.l. σφοῦ is a correction to avoid the apparent use of ὅς with a plural reference (which is found in Zen.'s reading at 3.244). As ἑ, ὅς, ἑός passed out of vernacular use their abuse in the *Kunstsprache* increased: Hesiod has the adjective as a plural at *Erga* 58 and *Theog.* 71, ἑ is plural at *HyAphr* 267, and Hellenistic poets use the forms indifferently as to person and number. Since Brugmann's examination of the subject, *Ein Problem der homerischen Textkritik und der vergleichenden Sprachwissenschaft* (Leipzig 1876), it has been generally conceded that the 'general' use of the adjective (not the pronoun) was Homeric, see Monro, *HG* 221–4, Leaf I 559–65, Chantraine, *GH* I 273–5. Brugmann's Iliadic examples are as follows:

ἑός/ὅς = ἐμός 6.221, 7.153, 19.322, and probably 9.414, 19.331
= σός 1.393, 14,249, 15.138, 19.342, 21.412, 24.422, 24.550, and probably 1.297, 2.33, 2.70, 4.39, 5.259, 9.611, 10.237, 14.221, 14.264, 16.36, 16.444, 16.851, 18.463, 19.29, 19.174, 20.310, 21.94, 24.310
= ὑμέτερος 11.142
= σφός 3.244, 18.231, and probably 11.76

There are up to 39 cases in *Od*. In most instances, however, the text is in doubt, Zen. and a substantial number of MSS attesting the 'general' use, Aristarchus eliminating it. There is no need to follow Brugmann in supposing that the 'general' use continues an Indo-European situation: the usage of the pronoun and the emergence of σφός and the other personal adjectives point to the restriction of the root *sw-* in Greek to the 3rd person sing. The question then is whether or how far a secondary 'general' use which had established itself in the pre-Aristarchan text had already established itself in the Homeric form of the *Kunstsprache*. It is impossible to deny that this may have been the case. — λώβην: always protective of his brother Agamemnon uses one of the strongest terms in the heroic vocabulary, one that Akhilleus had used for an unforgivable injury (9.387).

143-7 The slaying follows the normal pattern for two victims despatched in quick succession: the first is speared, the second killed with the sword, cf. also 5.835. Verse 143 = 320 (with Θυμβραῖον for Πείσανδρον).

144 ὕπτιος: i.e. ἀπὸ τῆς πληγῆς (Arn/A), the victim falls back under the force of the blow, a common effect (11x). Aristarchus was interested in the effects of wounds. οὔδει ἐρείσθη, 'was forced to the ground', is the vulgate both here and at 12.192. Aristarchus preferred οὖδας ἔρεισε in both places, though not apparently at 7.145. ἐρεισθείς at 22.225, the only other occurrence of the aorist passive in the *Iliad*, means 'leaning on', a sense that Aristarchus may have understood (and found unacceptable) here.

146 It has often been noted, e.g. by Friedrich, *Verwundung* 61, that Agamemnon is the most wantonly violent in battle of all the Achaeans. So here Hippolokhos receives the sort of treatment reserved for treacherous slaves in the *Odyssey* (22.475-7). Heads are cut off elsewhere in the *Iliad* (11.261, 13.202, 14.496) but not arms, see generally Segal, *Mutilation*. A. Severyns, *Homère* III (Bruxelles 1948) 109-15, has a list of these unpleasant scenes. They are usually expressive of fury inspiring an act of vengeance, but Agamemnon's present cause of anger is rather remote. Nevertheless it should not be thought that the poet's descriptions necessarily have a hostile edge; the King of Men must be terrible in his valour, see Introduction 50.

147 At 13.202-4 Aias (son of Oïleus) takes off a head and sends it spinning (σφαιρηδὸν ἑλιξάμενος), but it is not so easy to imagine Hippolokhos' reduction to a headless and armless trunk as sending him rolling without further action on Agamemnon's part. Arn/A explains ὅλμον as κοῖλος λίθος: that cannot be right, since a stone mortar does not resemble a decapitated trunk. At Hesiod, *Erga* 423, ὅλμος is a *wooden* mortar 'three feet high', see West's n. *ad loc.*, used for pounding grain. That would be a tree-trunk with the centre hollowed out to a suitable depth, and is clearly the object here in mind. Actual decapitations, as opposed to threats, are confined to books 10-14, cf. 10.456n. Agamemnon perpetrates another at 261, the only warrior on either side to do so.

148-80 Agamemnon pursues the routed Trojans towards the city. Two scenes of general description, each ornamented by a simile (155-7 and 172-6), are separated by the comment that Hektor has been withdrawn from the battle by Zeus. The comment not only answers the naive question why Hektor was not opposing Agamemnon's rampage but adumbrates the course of the narrative in the next scene. The poet is looking ahead and, as it turns out, hastening towards his goal. — The description of the rout is a *mélange* of typical details, cf. for example 16.364-93.

150-3 These verses have been suspected in modern times, e.g. as a 'hoplite interpolation' by Lorimer, *HM* 325, for the use of ἱππεῖς ('charioteers') in the supposed sense of cavalry, because of the clumsy parenthesis 151–2 and the similarity to the comment at 178–9, cf. van Thiel, *Ilias und Iliaden* 347–8. Leaf on 151 appears to envisage the use of chariotry (or cavalry) *en masse* for pursuit, cf. 289n. and 754ff., but the rhetoric of the passage precludes a literal interpretation of the verse. For chariot tactics see Lorimer, *loc. cit.*, and 4.297–300n. In the Ionian hinterland they continued in use long after Homer's day, see Sappho fr. 16.19–20 L–P καὶ Λύδων ἄρματα καὶ πανόπλοις | πεσδομάχεντας. — ἱππεῖς (the new Attic and *koinē* orthography for ἱππῆς): the monosyllabic scansion of the oblique cases of the -εύς noun is rare, cf. 4.384, 15.339 (acc. sing.), 23.792 (dat. sing.), see Chantraine, *GH* I 223, but is necessitated by the *polyptota* of 150–1, unless recourse is had to emendation (ἱππῆες δ' ἱππῆας, ὑπὸ σφισι δ' Lehrs and Brandreth; ἱππῆες is read by many MSS). δηϊόωντες refers back to πεζοί and ἱππεῖς.

155–9 The fire, which advances on a broad front, would seem to provide a better simile for the attack of the whole army, not just that of Agamemnon, but cf. in this Book 297–8 (Hektor attacks 'like a whirlwind'), and 305–9 (Hektor is 'like a thunderstorm'). As usual these natural phenomena are adduced as instances of sheer force. εἰλυφόων, 'rolling along', is the main point of the simile. A similar comparison, using εἰλυφάζω (the sole occurrences of these variants of εἰλύω) is used at 20.490–3.

155 ἀξύλῳ: Hellenistic (Arn/Did/A) ingenuity made three attempts to understand this *hapax legomenon*: (1) = πολύξυλος, with intensifying ἀ-; (2) = θρυώδης, 'rushy', as if the reference were to undergrowth; and (3) = ἀφ' ἧς οὐδεὶς ἐξυλίσατο, comparing the Hesiodic ἀξυλίη (fr. 314 M–W). *LfgrE* prefers the intensive ἀ-, and points out that ξύλον in the *Iliad* is dead, inflammable wood. πῦρ ἀΐδηλον is the formula for 'fire' used before the caesura; it does not compete with θεσπιδαὲς πῦρ, a formula formed according to a pattern prevalent in the last colon, to which it is confined.

160 The empty chariots are a pathetic but formular detail of the Homeric battlefield, cf. 15.453 (with κροτέοντες for κροτάλιζον). — κροτάλιζον is used as a quasi-synonym of κροτέω (κρόταλα are castanets) to provide ∪∪–∪ in the imperfect. ἀνὰ πτολέμοιο γεφύρας, 'up and down the battlefield', is formular (πτολέμοιο γεφύρας 5×) and rather imprecise. γέφυρα, a word of uncertain etymology (perhaps Semitic *gb*, 'raised up', see J. T. Hooker, *Current Issues in Linguistic Theory* 11 (1979) 387–98), certainly means 'embankment' in a simile at 5.88, and conceivably the formula could have originally signified military earthworks (as at 8.553?). The suggestion of T at 4.371 τὰς διόδους τῶν φαλάγγων seems to be a shrewd guess.

161–2 ποθέοντες: for the attachment of horses to charioteer cf. 5.230–4, 17.426–40. ἀμύμονας, whatever it means ('handsome' according to Amory Parry, *Blameless Aegisthus*), is formular in this position but inappropriate in its immediate context, see Introduction 21–2. Vultures and wives recur together in this Book at 395, and vultures again at 453–4. At this point, in the mouth of the poet, the conjunction is pathetic, at 395 (Diomedes speaking) it expresses the grim humour of the heat of battle.

163 Three combats described in some detail are about par for the course in an *aristeia*: Diomedes has four (5.144–65) but not related at the same length, Patroklos three (16.399–414) followed by a long list without annotation. This then is the moment when a leading Trojan (Aineias in book 5, Sarpedon in book 16) should 'notice' what is happening and intervene. Only Hektor, the Trojan leader, is possible as the opponent of the Achaeans' King of Men. If Hektor opposed Agamemnon and wounded him there would be a nice irony – Agamemnon humiliatingly fails where Akhilleus triumphantly succeeds. But the poet does not like to humiliate the Achaeans, cf. the way in which he arranges the death of Patroklos, and has Agamemnon, and later Odysseus (434–9), wounded by Trojans whom they can immediately slay. It is therefore necessary to insert the note (163–4) that Hektor was not present to 'notice' Agamemnon's rampage because Zeus (whose inscrutable will explains everything) has removed him from the battle. Note that this brief statement of the theme is presently followed by its restatement in a highly elaborated form, see 181–210n.

163–4 The polysyndeton is a deliberate trope to draw a picture of the rout, cf. ἂμ φόνον, ἂν νέκυας, διά τ᾽ ἔντεα καὶ μέλαν αἷμα (10.298). κονίης: Greek warfare was typically a summertime activity (the *Iliad* seems to assume the summer season) and dust was its natural concomitant. At 17.645ff. the murk (ἀήρ) was such that Aias could not see the ships from his place on the battlefield.

165 σφεδανόν = σφόδρα, 'vehemently'.

166 Ἴλου σῆμα: Ilos was son of Tros and father of Laomedon, 20.231ff. His tomb, the fig-tree (167), the oak (170), and the 'rise' (θρωσμός, 10.160, etc.) are the permanent landmarks of the *Iliad*'s geography of the Trojan plain, cf. 10.415, 11.372 (Ilos' tomb); 6.433, 22.145 (the fig-tree); 5.693, etc. (the oak, near the Scaean gates (6.237, 9.354)). The fig-tree was near the city, the tomb in the middle of the plain according to Nic/A, cf. 6.433n. The Catalogue of Ships uses a different system, see nn. to 2.793, 2.811–15. Another landmark, Kallikolone near the Simoeis river, is mentioned only at 20.53 and 151. — It is unclear what monuments may have existed in the Skamandros valley while the tradition of the Trojan war was developing, see Cook, *Troad* 159–65 and n. to 2.813–14. Most of the tumuli visible today appear to have been erected during the archaic period, but at least one – Beşik Tepe – is prehistoric. That may have inspired the mention of the σῆμα, but except in the most general terms the epic geography of the Troad is clearly a poetical construction. See 22.145n. on the location of the fig-tree. How the ford of Skamandros (14.433 = 21.1 = 24.692) fits into this geography is unclear (see 498–9n.); it nowhere impedes the advance and retreat of the armies.

168 κεκληγώς, an Ionic, or Ionicized, form, is the reading of the paradosis everywhere for the nominative singular of this perfect participle. OCT correct to the Aeolic κεκλήγων after the plural κεκλήγοντες. κεκληγώς was retained here in early impressions of OCT 3rd edn, and survives in the sixteenth impression (1990) at 17.88 and *Od.* 12.408, apparently by inadvertence. On the principle that where possible singers approximated the *Kunstsprache* to their vernacular the paradosis may be retained (see 16.430n.). For the plural form in -οντες see 12.125n.

169 λύθρος is a typical result of battle, cf. 6.268, but 169 ≅ 20.503, a verse that concludes an exceptionally savage *aristeia* (ten victims) by Akhilleus. Both that and the present passage incorporate forest-fire similes in order to complete the impression of indiscriminate slaughter. ἄαπτους is mostly reserved for Akhilleus' hands. T. Eide, *Symbolae Osloenses* 111 (1986) 18, observes that of the epithets for the hand 'παχύς and στιβαρός (add κρατερός) are used of the hand acting, while βαρύς, θρασύς and ἄαπτος are emotionally laden and denote the hand primarily as a harmful instrument'. ἄαπτος is from ἄϝεπτος by contraction and subsequent diectasis, i.e. 'inexpressibly strong' (so *LfgrE* s.v.), but the poet probably associated this obsolete word (only found in the formula χεῖρες ἄαπτοι and variants) with ἅπτομαι. See also 12.166n.

170 For the gates and oak-tree see 9.354n.

173–7 The simile continues the picture of Agamemnon's battle-rage drawn at 113–5 and combines two points: a lion terrifies a herd of cattle and brutally kills one of them. With 172–3 cf. 15.323–4, then 176–7 = 17.63–4, another lion simile; 18.583 ἔγκατα καὶ μέλαν αἷμα λαφύσσετον is a variant of 177. νυκτὸς ἀμολγῷ: an Iliadic formula (4×, all similes, and *Od.* 4.841). The etymological connexion with ἀμέλγω, 'milk', is inescapable, so that the expression ought to refer to morning (22.28, as the mention of Sirius shows) or evening twilight (22.317); elsewhere, as here, 'at dead of night' seems to be the sense, in which case the etymological sense of ἀμολγῷ has been lost. See 22.28n. and Shipp, *Studies* 192, citing (from Kretschmer) usages in modern Greek dialects and concluding that the formula is an archaism, imperfectly understood.

175 See 113–19n. For the lion's tactics cf. 5.161 and many representations in art, listed in *Arch. Hom.* J 21–30.

178 That Agamemnon kills the hindmost (easy victims?) has no especial significance; the same verse is used of Hektor at 8.342.

179–80 The scholia (Did/A, Arn/A) are mutilated but clearly affirm that Zenodotus omitted these two verses and probably that Aristophanes athetized them as contradicting 160 (where the chariots were already empty: now, 179, they are still manned) or as belonging in book 16 (180 = 16.699 (with Πατρόκλου for Ἀτρεΐδεω)). Aristarchus was content to athetize 180 only. For the reading see Bolling, *External Evidence* 130–1.

181–210 Zeus installs himself on Mt Ida and instructs Iris to descend to the battlefield and tell Hektor to avoid fighting until he sees Agamemnon wounded. This short Olympian scene takes up the brief anticipation of the narrative at 163–4. The passage is thus not only a coda to the preceding scene giving a repeated sequence: Description – Simile – Hektor, but sets up a new narrative goal, the termination of Agamemnon's offensive. The whole passage 148–64 + 165–217 is an extreme example of the epic practice of introducing a motif in relatively brief terms and then repeating it with greater elaboration, cf. 21.211–26 (Skamandros protests to Akhilleus) + 240–83 (Skamandros nearly drowns Akhilleus), *Od.* 8.62–103 (Odysseus weeps at Demodokos' first song) and 8.469–586 (he weeps again at Demodokos' second song). Other examples of the 'anticipatory doublet' (which seem to give a glimpse of the oral composer at work) are cited by M. W. Edwards in *Homer: Beyond Oral Poetry*, ed. Bremer (Amsterdam 1987) 50–1 and vol. v 19–20.

183 At 8.47–8 Zeus had a precinct on Ida, cf. Cook, *Troad* 257–8, but the highest peak of the region is probably chosen as a fitting vantage point for the mightiest of the gods. At 8.48 (see n.) and three other places the peak is called Γάργαρον. For Zeus's movements see 78–83n. The lesser gods preferred to watch the battle from ringside seats, the wall of Herakles or the brow of Kallikolone (20.149–52). Zeus exerts his influence at 336 and 544. His presence as a spectator is a device of 'focalization' whereby the poet may seek to direct his audience's reaction to the narrative. — πιδηέσσης: only here in archaic epic, but cf. πολυπίδακα (-ος) (8× *Il.*, 3× *HyAphr*). Strabo 13.1.43, specifically linked πολυπῖδαξ with the rivers Skamandros, Granikos, and Aisepos (cf. 12.21) whose sources all lay within twenty stadia of each other.

184 The thunderbolt is a permanent attribute of Zeus, like Hermes' staff (*HyHerm* 528–32) or Poseidon's trident (12.27); it does not create an expectation that Zeus is about to use it. The special epithets of gods and heroes are the aural equivalents of these pieces of equipment.

185 = 8.398, the only places in Homer where a deity is said to be winged. Iris is also ἀελλόπος at 8.409. Lorimer, *HM* 474, notes the reluctance of the earliest Greek art to welcome oriental winged monsters. As in book 8 Iris is conveniently present when Zeus requires her.

186 βάσκ' ἴθι: cf. βῆ/βὰν δ' ἴμεν/ἴμεναι for the redundancy. βάσκ' ἴθι forms a complex formula with Ἶρι ταχεῖα (4×), and occurs only twice (2.8, 24.336) outside it. Although the formation of the word is impeccable (< $g^w\eta$-skō, cf. Skt *gácchati*), the singular imperative is the only form attested in the epic and only in the *Iliad*. Hipponax (fr. 92 West) cites the word as Lydian, cf. Hsch. βάσκε πικρολέα· πλησίον ἐξεθόαζε, Λυδιστί, but it is more likely to be an obsolete word surviving in a formula than an intrusion of a foreign word into the *Kunstsprache*.

189–90 Apollo's advice to Hektor at 20.376–8 was more explicit: μηκέτι πάμπαν Ἀχιλλῆϊ προμάχιζε, | ἀλλὰ κατὰ πληθύν τε καὶ ἐκ φλοίσβοιο δέδεξο, | μή πώς σ' ἠὲ βάλῃ ἠὲ σχεδὸν ἄορι τύψῃ. The essential point is μὴ προμάχιζε, for that is what the hero would naturally do in order to check a victorious opponent, e.g. Aineias at 5.166ff., or Sarpedon at 16.419ff.

192–4 The verses are a fair summary of Zeus's plan to fulfil Thetis' request to 'Give the Trojans victory until the Achaeans honour my son' (1.509–10), but when they are repeated to Hektor at 207–9 they take on the opacity that always shrouds the will of god. What is to follow Hektor's reaching the ships? Something more significant than nightfall, surely. Hektor can imagine that he will burn the ships (see 15.719–20), *we* can guess that it means the re-entry of Akhilleus into the war. The poet puts it plainly at 13.348–50 οὐδέ τι πάμπαν | ἤθελε λαὸν ὀλέσθαι Ἀχαιϊκὸν Ἰλιόθι πρό, | ἀλλὰ Θέτιν κύδαινε καὶ υἱέα καρτερόθυμον. At 17.441–55 (193–4 = 17.454–5) Zeus remembers that his promise did not include the capture of Akhilleus' horses.

193–4 = 17.454–5. The day, already half spent at 84, does not end until 18.239, and then only with the assistance of Here. κνέφας is ἱερόν only in this repeated line; perhaps cf. ἀμβροσίη as an epithet of νύξ, and 84–5n.

195–9 Iris' descent to earth is closely paralleled by Apollo's descent in similar circumstances at 15.236–43 (see nn.). — Verse 196 (to ὀρέων) = 15.237, 197 = 15.239, 199 ≅ 15.243. Ἴλιον ἱρήν, usually preceded by προτί, is strongly formular (15× *Il.*, 2× *Od.*). προτί, the observed digamma, and the Aeolic form of the epithet, all point to a very old formula. The epithet does not appear to imply any special sanctity, or if it does it does not inhibit hostile attack, cf. 1.366–7 'We went to Thebe, holy city of Eetion, and sacked it.'

198 = 4.366. (see n.). Hektor, it is clear, is standing in his chariot. ἄρματα recalls the Myc. *a-mo-ta* (KN So 437 etc.), 'wheels', being so identified by an ideogram, see Ventris and Chadwick, *Documents* 371–2. κολλητοῖσι, 'fastened (with glue, studs, or whatever)', is marginally more appropriate to spoked wheels than to the wicker bodywork of a chariot. But there is little doubt that ἔν θ' ἵπποισι καὶ ἄρμασι κολλητοῖσι, like 'horse and cart', is a unitary idea. The formula allows a variation in sense (see Introduction 26), for ἵπποισι and ἄρμασι κολλητοῖσι are conjoined also at 23.286 where ἵπποισι = 'horses'.

199 Divinities prefer to disguise themselves when they appear to men, e.g. Poseidon at 13.43ff., 216ff.; but Apollo, on the same duty as Iris here, does not conceal himself from Hektor at 15.243ff. On that occasion Hektor remarked on the epiphany, and it is odd that he does not do so here, or make any direct response to Iris. We may understand that on such occasions the deity is visible, or audible, to the hero alone (as is stated explicitly at 1.198), and are therefore free to assume, if we wish, that the poet presents the hero's decision in colourful theological language as the result of prompting from without. Covering a retreat is a hazardous operation, as 310ff. show: Hektor has decided to bide his time.

200–1 = 7.47. υἷε: the short scansion of the first syllable is frequent. Διὶ μῆτιν ἀτάλαντε: the formula (see 10.137n.) is properly associated with Odysseus (4×), for whom it defines an important aspect of character: for Hektor it is an ornamental compliment, and not especially appropriate in view of his portrayal with increasing emphasis in books 11–18 as over-confident, in contrast to the prudent Pouludamas. Verse 201 ≅ *Od.* 4.829. τεῖν = σοι, only here in *Il.* but 4× in *Od.*

202–9 ≅ 187–94. In accordance with the normal epic convention Iris repeats her instructions to Hektor verbatim and neatly changes the 3rd persons of Zeus's directive into the 2nd except in 204, where ἀναχωρείτω (199) is turned into ὑπόεικε μάχης.

210–15 The poet is not yet ready to shift his interest from Agamemnon, but must note Hektor's response to Iris' instructions, and does so in an abbreviated style with a few formular verses. Verse 210 is simply the resumptive verse after direct speech; it is followed by a four-verse run (211–14 = 5.494–7 and 6.103–6), and another formular verse (215 = 12.415).

214–16 The battle enters a new phase. After their rout the Trojans rally (ἐλελίχθησαν) and form a front (ἀρτύνθη δὲ μάχη); for the tactic see 310–11n. A short passage of general description of the σταδίη ὑσμίνη, cf. 15.312–17, would be expected to follow, but the poet is sparing of such comments in this Book and proceeds at once to the continuation of Agamemnon's *aristeia*.

216–84 Resumed *aristeia* of Agamemnon. He slays Iphidamas, a son of Antenor, and a young man of great hopes. In revenge Koon, brother of Iphidamas, wounds Agamemnon, who then slays him. His wound eventually overcomes Agamemnon and he withdraws from the battle.

The appeal to the Muses at 218 (= 2.484, 14.508, 16.112), and especially the use of πρῶτος at 219, may seem to presage a feat of memory on the part of the poet, as it does at 2.484 and 14.508, and therefore a lengthy list of slayings by the King of Men. The Muse gives the singer authority and certifies the accuracy of the list, see M. Finkelberg, *AJP* 111 (1990) 291–6). At 16.112, however, the appeal to the Muses marks a crisis point (how Hektor fired the ships). So here Agamemnon's irresistible march to the Scaean gates is to be halted. As bT put it ἐπὶ τοῖς μεγίστοις τὰς Μούσας καλεῖ ὡς ἐρῶν τι καινότερον· αἱ γὰρ τοιαῦται ἀκμαιοτέρας ποιοῦσι τὰς προσοχὰς τοῖς ἀκροαταῖς, see also W. W. Minton, *TAPA* 91 (1960) 292–309. The poet has set the narrative a goal, the wounding of Agamemnon, and hastens to it, allowing Agamemnon only one regular slaying before he is wounded by Koon. His opponents are sons of Antenor, a detail doubtless suggested by the sons of Antimakhos in the preceding *aristeia*. For the good Antenor as host of Odysseus and Menelaos stands in sharpest contrast to the base Antimakhos.

The whole episode of Agamemnon's last fights and wounding should be compared with the wounding of Odysseus at 426–71; the details are different, but the thread of the story is identical: the hero kills a Trojan, the Trojan's brother wounds the hero, the hero kills the second Trojan, finally the hero withdraws. Fenik's remarks (*TBS* 9) on a subsequent passage are worth quoting here:

> the poet composed by describing certain basic, recurrent situations with which he associated certain details. These details in turn group themselves along certain general structural lines – i.e. they form patterns. But this does not happen according to any unalterable or fixed system. The structural framework of all the patterns is variable at almost any given point, although a majority of identifying details is always present in an one example. Both the repetitiveness and the elasticity of the system are demonstrated by the fact that although the battle narrative is composed almost entirely of repeated elements of all kinds, no two battle scenes, large or small, are wholly alike.

For the formular character of 218–63 see Espermann, *Antenor, Theano, Antenoriden* 119–29, who counts 21 verses substantially repeated elsewhere.

218–21 Within the epic the poet's appeals to the Muses follow a certain pattern. A question, directly or indirectly, is put to the goddesses, and answered in a sentence that often (though not here) echoes the wording of the question, see 2.761–2 with 768, 14.508–10 with 511. The appeal therefore is for information, not inspiration, cf. P. Murray, *JHS* 101 (1981) 87–100, and de Jong, *Narrators* 45–53 (with bibliography). The form is common to Hesiod, *Theog.* 114–16, 965–9, 1021–2 with fr. 1 M–W, and betrays a certain self-consciousness in the narrator. The Muse reveals to him the 'facts' of the story which the singer then transmits, with commentary, to his audience. Only 1.1 (ἄειδε, θεά) seems to suggest that the singer is a mere mouthpiece of the Muse, who is the real author of the poem: a form that is best taken as a simplification of the usual relationship of singer and Muse; see, however, A. Lenz, *Das Proöm des frühgriechischen Epos* (Bonn 1980) 27. The author of 12.176 ἀργαλέον δέ με ταῦτα θεὸν ὣς πάντ᾽ ἀγορεῦσαι drew a distinction between himself and the god/muse, cf. 2.485–92. We may say that the Muse is a symbol of the singer's special 'knowledge' and skill, but for him, of course, she is real enough. For the effect of a belief in the Muses on the poet's use of the heroic tradition see Introduction 36.

221 The poet answers the implicit question of 218–20 with a fine three-folder verse. By making Agamemnon's next victim a son of Antenor the poet gives him a certain status, cf. 91–147n. Ἰφιδάμας appears only in this episode which, however, enjoyed a certain fame: the fight over his body was represented on the Chest of Kupselos (Paus. 5.19.4). His exploit is recalled at 19.53. The episode is a skilful deployment of typical details, cf. the analysis in Strasburger, *Kämpfer* 71–2, but the overall effect is one of great pathos. For the frequent names in -δάμας, 'subduer', see 10.269n. Ten of Antenor's progeny have Greek (or Hellenized) names: Ἀγήνωρ, Ἀκάμας, Ἀρχέλοχος, Δημολέων, Ἑλικάων, Ἰφιδάμας, Κόων, Λαοδάμας, Λαόδοκος and Πόλυβος. The eleventh is Πήδαιος, to be linked with the local toponym Πήδαιον (13.172). The contrast with the indigenous names of the family of Aineias (Ἀγχίσης, Κάπυς, Ἀσσάρακος) is remarkable.

222 μητέρι μήλων: see on 9.479. Zenodotus' μητέρι θηρῶν (Did/A) borrows the epithet of Ida (14.283, 15.151). He probably thought that Thrace was wild country.

224–6 τίκτε (ἔτικτε in the vulgate) is regular in this position (9× *Il.*, 4× *Od.*) and in the sense 'beget', of the father (10×), a use confined in classical Greek to the higher poetical genres. Homer does not use γεννᾶν. Θεανώ: see 5.70n., 6.298n. and Espermann, *Antenor, Theano, Antenoriden* 35–49. She was priestess of Athene in Troy. The implied genealogy is shown in the stemma – so that Iphidamas was in fact married to his aunt, an unusual alliance; but the poet is building up the pathos of Iphidamas' death by emphasizing his hopes and promise, cf. the fates of Protesilaos (2.698–709), Imbrios (13.170–81), Othruoneus (13.361–73), Alkathoos (13.424–44), Huperenor (17.34–40), and see Griffin, *HLD* 131–4. Diomedes also married his aunt (Aigialeia, daughter of Adrastos, 5.412).

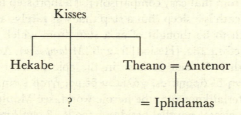

225–6 Verse 225 = [Hesiod] fr. 205.2 M–W (with πολυηράτου for ἐρικυδέος. Verse 226 = 6.192 (king of Lycia and Bellerophon). Willcock takes the imperfects κατέρυκε and δίδου as conative, which is effective here but not in book 6.

227 μετὰ κλέος ... Ἀχαιῶν: objective genitive, 'in pursuit of glory over the Achaeans.'

229 Περκώτη was a place on the southern side of the Hellespont between

Abudos and Lampsakos, according to Strabo (13.1.20). It was listed in the Trojan Catalogue, 2.835, and is mentioned again at 15.548.

230 πεζὸς ἐών: apparently a typical detail, cf. Pandaros' abandonment of his horses, 5.192ff. (230 ≅ 5.204).

231 ἀντίον ἦλθεν: because the Trojans have rallied, and Antenor's sons must behave in a manner worthy of their father.

232–40 A typical minor duel related in whole-verse formulas; the sequence A misses B, B strikes A ineffectively, A kills B is invariable, see Fenik, *TBS* 6–7. Verse 232 = 13.604, etc. (5×); 233 = 13.605; 235 = 17.48.

234 'Hit him in the ζώνη beneath the θώρηξ but failed to penetrate the ζωστήρ.' We may take ζώνη with Leaf to mean 'waist', as at 2.479 (ἴκελος) Ἄρει ζώνην, but there is no reason why the word should not be synonymous with ζωστήρ, since hits κατὰ ζωστῆρα are usual enough (3× elsewhere). Agamemnon is now wearing the sort of equipment envisaged at 4.187 = 4.216 (see nn.), a short breastplate with a belt (to carry the μίτρη if worn) below it. But what the ζωστήρ was and how it was worn is unclear, cf. H. Brandenburg, *Arch. Hom.* E 119–22. παναίολος is its regular epithet (4×).

238 εὐρὺ κρείων Ἀγαμέμνων: the name–epithet expression (expanded from κρείων Ἀγαμέμνων 30×) is of unusual length and owes its existence to the long, complex formula (ἥρως) Ἀτρείδης εὐρὺ κρείων Ἀγαμέμνων (10×).

239 λίς, 'lion', occurs 4× (and once in the accusative, 11.480) in the *Iliad*, and then not until [Hesiod], *Aspis* 172. Three occurrences are in the phrase ὥς τε λὶς (ἠϋγένειος), an old formula of comparison with an archaic noun and an ancient prosody. If the word is of Semitic origin (Hebr. *lyš*), it strictly means 'old lion', cf. Isaiah 30.6.

241 χάλκεον ὕπνον: Sleep is the brother of Death at 16.672 and Hesiod, *Theog.* 212. From that easy comparison it is a short step to saying euphemistically that death is a sleep (but a step that was rarely taken before religion allowed death to be thought of as a state from which there could be an awakening), cf. 14.482, [Hesiod] fr. 278 (*Melampodia*), Aesch. *Ag.* 1451. The sleep of death is brazen because in the epic at least it is unbreakable, cf. 2.490 φωνὴ δ' ἄρρηκτος, χάλκεον δέ μοι ἦτορ ἐνείη, bronze being the toughest material known to the heroic world, see Moulton, *CPh* 74 (1979) 279–93. The closest parallel besides 2.490 is 18.222 ὄπα χάλκεον. χάλκεος Ἄρης is too close to χαλκοχίτων to be certainly metaphorical. χάλκεος οὐρανός and similar expressions probably describe a literal part of the Homeric cosmos, the firmament of heaven.

242–3 The formular hyperbaton is an unusual result of the additive style, ἀστοῖσιν ἀρήγων amplifying πεσών and κουριδίης the now separated ἀλόχου. The jerky structure lends itself to a pathetic rendering on the reciter's part. bT note the pathetic colour of the verses in contrast to the factual tone of the preceding narrative, i.e. from 229. Homeric pathos normally resides in the description of the warrior's death or his circumstances, so with the runover word κουριδίης in 243. For the detail given here cf. the death of Hippothoos (17.300–3). The disappointed hopes of the slain are an unusual variant on the frequent motif of the bereaved wife, parent, or child. (Other frequent motifs are a death far from home, the impotence of friends to help, the fate of the body, and the youth of those killed.) Here οἰκτρός sounds a rare 'empathetic' note (so T at 243), an intrusion of the poet into his narrative that is more characteristic of Virgil. It is noteworthy that this is the only use of οἰκτρός of a person in Homer. ἀστοῖσιν: a strangely rare word in Homer in view of the frequency of ἄστυ, but 'fellow citizens' is the specialized sense also at *Od.* 13.192, the sole other occurrence in Homer. The heroes of course fight primarily for themselves even if their honour is involved in defence of others. πολλὰ δ' ἔδωκε: for the custom of brideprice see 9.146n.

244–5 χίλι(α) and the relative τά slip into the neuter gender, cf. 5.140 and n., as if the multiple object, αἶγας + ὄϊς, merged into the idea of μῆλα, *vel sim.* Comments, like similes, reveal the preoccupations of the poet's world, a rural world in which oxen, goats, and sheep are kept properly distinct, cf. 696–7. ἄ-σπε-τα is 'in-effa-ble' i.e. 'countless'.

246 ἐξενάριξε: stripping the corpse is part of the ritual of battle, enhancing the κῦδος of the victor by inflicting additional ὄνειδος on the victim and his friends. But it was notoriously dangerous: in this Book Diomedes, 368–78, and Eurupulos, 580–4, are wounded in the same circumstances.

248–63 Koon's success and death. Koon reacts to Iphidamas' death as a brother should and tries to avenge him despite the odds and rescue the corpse. Vengeance and rescue were another dangerous part of the warrior's duty, the subject of the first fight in the *Iliad*, 4.463ff., and of many other incidents, e.g. 428ff., 5.20, 14.476, 16.319, 20.419, cf. H. van. Wees, *CQ* 38 (1988) 6; similarly of more distant relatives at 13.463, 15.422 and 15.553. As explained at 4.463–9, the action of seizing the body exposed the warrior's πλευρά.

248 ὡς οὖν: 'In Homer οὖν almost invariably follows ἐπεί or ὡς in a subordinate temporal clause ...' (Denniston, *Particles* 416). For the name Koon (< κοέω) cf. Δηΐ-, Δημο-, Ἱππο-κόων 4.499 (see n.) and von Kamptz, *Personennamen* 263.

249–50 Koon is blinded by grief, literally and metaphorically, like Hektor at the death of *his* brother Poludoros (20.419–21), and 'blindly' takes on the unequal combat. For the expression πένθος ὀφθαλμοὺς ἐκάλυψε cf. the overtly metaphorical ἄχεος νεφέλη ἐκάλυψε μέλαινα (17.591).

251 στῆ δ' εὐρὰξ σὺν δουρὶ λαθών: a formular posture cf. 15.541, where the absolute use of λαθών shows that it is part of the essential idea. Hrd/A connects εὐράξ with εὐρύς (which could only be by analogy with other adverbs in -άξ and -ίξ) and paraphrases as ἐκ πλαγίου, that is 'to one side of Agamemnon'. But the posture must be that of Koon; he turned 'sideways' to minimize the target he presented.

252–3 It is not clear what was Agamemnon's posture when he sustained his wound: he was last seen (247) bearing off Iphidamas' armour. Diomedes (368) and Eurupulos (581) are wounded while actually stripping the corpse, a more dangerous moment and a motif established by the death of Elephenor at 4.463–9, see 248–63n. χεῖρα μέσην is clearly the forearm, the left (if one must be precise) since Agamemnon was still able to wield his spear.

254 When Diomedes was wounded in book 5 he immediately prayed to Athene to be granted vengeance (5.114ff.). Agamemnon omits that formality, as does Odysseus at 439ff., and carries on fighting. Having banished the gods from the battlefield, the poet may bear in mind that such a prayer would be pointless (though its futility could be turned into a pathetic touch), but the chief reason for the omission of such digressive ornaments is the general compression of the narrative in this Book, on which see 1n.

256 ἔχων ἀνεμοτρεφὲς ἔγχος: ἀνεμοτρεφής is an Iliadic word, cf. 15.625. It is not clear why Agamemnon's spear should be distinguished in this way, nor indeed what the metaphor implies. Arn/A and T mention ἰσχυρός, εὔτονος, εὐκίνητος, and κοῦφος: *LfgrE* prefers the first, citing Seneca, *Prov.* 4.16, *non est arbor solida nec fortis, nisi in quam frequens ventus incursat*. There is no compelling metrical reason for the use of an epithet with initial vowel, cf. ἔχων δολιχόσκιον ἔ. (6.44, 21.139).

258 ἕλκε ποδός: undignified (as certainly at *Od.* 18.101 – Odysseus disposing of Iros) but regular, cf. 4.463, 10.490, 13.383, 14.477, 16.763, 17.289, 18.155, 18.537, 21.120. The action, whether needing both hands or not, was likely as here to impede the handling of the shield and expose the rescuer to attack.

260 = 4.469, where see n. ξυστῷ: this term for the spear is clustered (5×) in books 11–15. χαλκήρης is an epic and poetical word except in Mycenaean, cf. [e]-ke-a ka-ka-re-a KN R 1815 (= Ventris and Chadwick, *Documents* 263). It is possible that some old formulas retained the word, but the epic applies it freely to spears, arrows, helmets, and shields.

262–3 The laconic statement of the two brothers' death is strangely affecting, cf. 5.559–60, 16.325–6 for similar brief statements of this pathetic motif.

263 The deaths of Iphidamas and Koon conclude Agamemnon's *aristeia*. In summary the king slew eight named Trojans and numerous nameless ones (178), and inflicted wounds to the back, head (2), breast (2), neck (3), and one unspecified, and received a wound in the arm. His weapon is

Location	Result	Weapon				Total
		Stone	Sword	Spear	Arrow	
Head	Fatal	4	8	17	2	31
	Not fatal	1	0	0	0	1
	Uncertain	0	0	0	0	0
Neck	Fatal	1	4	8	0	13
	Not fatal	0	0	1	0	1
	Uncertain	1	0	0	1	2
Trunk	Fatal	1	4	59	3	67
	Not fatal	1	0	5	3	9
	Uncertain	0	0	3	0	3
Arms	Fatal	1	1	0	0	2
	Not fatal	0	0	6	1	7
	Uncertain	0	0	1	0	1
Legs	Fatal	1	0	0	0	1
	Not fatal	2	0	3	2	7
	Uncertain	0	0	3	0	3
Total		13	17	106	12	148

the spear 4×, the sword 3×, and unspecified 1×. The general statistics for Homeric wounds are as shown in the table (after H. Frölich, *Die Militärmedizin Homers* (Stuttgart 1879).

The spear, it is clear, is *the* weapon; recourse is had to the sword when no spear is available or to give the *coup de grâce*. The injuries immediately inflicted are plausibly described, but the poetical image of war represents these injuries, for the most part, as immediately fatal. The disquieting picture of a battlefield strewn with wounded, or of men lingering in agony until they were carried off by septicaemia or gangrene is thus avoided.

264–6 In spite of his arm's being run through Agamemnon does not feel his wound in the heat of battle: at least that is how we (and Lucretius 3.642ff.) would put it. For Homer the explanation is put in physical terms, a wound does not incapacitate so long as it bleeds, cf. the wounded deer, 474ff. It is odd that this aspect of hand-to-hand fighting should enter the *Iliad* only in this incident. ἐπεπωλεῖτο στίχας ἀνδρῶν recalls 4.231, etc., but here the ranks along which Agamemnon passes weapons in hand, are those of the Trojan army.

264–5 = 540–1: stone-throwing is not unheroic, for special purposes (12.445), or when nothing better is to hand, but it is not easy to picture

Agamemnon holding his spear (or putting it down) while throwing stones. Lorimer, *HM* 273, notes that the line implies a single (thrusting) spear, since Agamemnon has no missiles but stones. Stone-throwing later devolved on the γυμνῆτες, Tyrtaeus fr. 11.35–6 West. μεγάλοισί τε χερμαδίοισι: the diminutive force of the suffix -ίον is no longer present, cf. μάλα μέγα θηρίον (*Od.* 10.171), μέγα τειχίον (*Od.* 16.165, where see Hoekstra on *Od.* 16.434). Genuinely diminutive forms are avoided by the epic.

265–89 These verses, together with 284–9, 678–92, 12.127–31, 12.190–8, are contained in pap. 432 (P. Hamburg 153, dated to the latter half of third century B.C.) which was not available to OCT. In this section there are at least nine plus-verses, 266a–d, 266y–z, 272a, and 280a–b; 281–3 are omitted; see S. R. West, *Ptolemaic Papyri* 91–103, with literature. Variant readings are noted below. Such papyri as this show the difficulty, and the necessity, of the work of the Alexandrian scholars. Here the extra verses, which defy restoration, would have added something to Agamemnon's exploits before his ignominious departure.

266 ἀνήνοθεν is generally taken to be the same verb as (ἐπ)ενήνοθε 10.134, etc. In that case we assume a haplology, ἀν⟨εν⟩ήνοθε, with Frisk, *GEW* 1 517. The subject of (ἐπ-, κατ-, ἀν-)ήνοθε is variously hair, a savour, oil, dust, and here blood. If a connexion with ἄνθος is sustainable a sense 'sprout', 'spring up', > 'well up', could be posited for the present and 'be risen over', > 'lie upon', 'cover', for the perfective forms. But we cannot be certain that the singer had a clear idea of the sense and form of this epic verb. The poet of the Ares-and-Aphrodite episode (*Od.* 8.365) certainly misused the verb of the anointing oil of the gods, oil that covered their bodies but did not well up from within; the same may be said of the dust at [Hesiod], *Aspis* 269. In the present passage the anomalous formation does not inspire confidence in a precise usage; in fact an imperfect sense 'while the blood was welling up from his wound' best fits the context. Wyatt, *ML* 116–18, discusses this strange word, with bibliography.

Pap. 432 reads κελαινε]φὲς ἐξ ὠτειλῆς. However supplemented (e.g. ὄφρ' ἔτ' ἀνήνοθεν αἷμα ... Bolling, ὄφρα δ' ἀνήνοθεν αἷμα ... West) the sense will not differ much from the paradosis. The remains of six plus-verses follow.

268 δῦνον was obscure to Hellenistic readers and the schol. (bT) comment on it (τὴν εἰς βάθος χωρήσασαν ἀλγηδόνα ἐσήμανεν). τεῖρον (and τεῖρεν in 272) of pap. 432 is a response to the difficulty.

269–72 The image of the woman in labour is a unique and memorable simile which, coming at this point, is eloquent testimony to the range and humanity of the poet's imagination. The immediate point of the simile is to affirm that Agamemnon's body is racked with pain, but there is an inescapable irony at several levels in the comparison. The great effort of the King of Men ends with his being rushed off to his surgeons like a woman to her accouchement – but like a woman none the less. At a deeper level the poet understands the zest for battle (in a way that Virgil, for example, did not), but is not so carried away by admiration for it that he cannot equate the self-sought sufferings of the ἄριστοι, about which they make so much fuss (9.315–31, *Od.* 4.240–8, 8.489–90), with the pains of others' everyday existence. Note, however, that Agamemnon (and still less those gallant men, Diomedes and Odysseus, later) does not cry out or groan, unlike the Trojan Deiphobos in similar circumstances (13.538).

270–2 Pap. 432 here provides striking testimony to the deterioration of the Homeric text in the hands of Hellenistic booksellers: προιᾶσι, an Atticism, for προιεῖσι; χαλεπάς for πικράς, a random slip; and ὀξεῖ' ὀδύνη for ὀξεῖ(αι) ὀδύναι, to avoid the unusual elision.

270 μογοστόκοι Εἰλείθυιαι is formular, cf. 16.187. The first syllable of the divine name is modified by metrical lengthening. The Myc. (*e-re-u-ti-ja* KN Gg 705 etc.) and Doric dialects have -ευ- in the second syllable, suggesting a connexion with ἐλεύσομαι, ἤλυθον, as if the woman awaited the *onset* of her pains, or cried to her '*that comes* in need' (LSJ). But these goddesses are probably pre-Greek. Frisk, *GEW* s.v. cites an extensive bibliography. They are the daughters of Here (271) because she presides over marriage. μογοστόκος means 'causing birth-pangs' by some ill-defined process whereby the literal force of τόκος colours the sense of μόγος. μόγος (e.g. 4.27) does not normally mean 'labour' in the obstetric sense and other compounds of -τόκος do not lose their connexion with the literal force of τίκτω. In *HyAp* 91ff., where a distinction had to be made, Eileithuia brought on the birth not the pains, cf. 16.187–8, 19.119.

272 Ring-composition, the usual mode for inserting a simile into the narrative, requires the repetition of ὀξεῖαι ὀδύναι (268), which in its turn has entailed the unique elision of nom. plur., -αι. After 272 Pap. 432, in order to amplify Agamemnon's agonies, has a plus-verse [πολλ]άς ἐκ κεφαλῆς [προθελύμνους ἕλκετο χαίτας, cf. 10.15, though the restoration πολλ]άς is short for the space.

273–4 = 399–400, possibly formular. Woundings, to which the couplet is appropriate, are not typical of the fighting in other Books of the *Iliad*. Evacuation by chariot forms a sort of refrain in this Book cf. 399–400, 487–8, 519–20, rounding off each episode, and Reinhardt, *IuD* 254.

275–6 = 586–7 = 17.247–8. The first verse is strongly formular (6×). διαπρύσιον, 'with penetrating voice', is clearly a derivative of the common epic preposition διαπρό, but the precise connexion is uncertain. The -υ- has been considered an Aeolism.

277 Pap. 432 and a few MSS read περ νῦν ('you at least'), for μὲν νῦν. νηυσὶν ἀμύνετε: the battle has moved close to the walls of Troy (181), so that Agamemnon's orders are premature; they anticipate the débâcle that follows Hektor's counter-attack. If the words are well-chosen they are an eloquent comment on Agamemnon's morale and egotism: he sees his great offensive as an operation of defence and despairs at its first check.

278 φύλοπιν ἀργαλέην is a unique expression, though hardly more than a variant of φύλοπις αἰνή, etc. (11×). Pap. 432 reads φυλόπιδος κρατερῆς, which is slightly more familiar (1× in each epic). If the genitive is not a mere slip something must have replaced ποντοπόροισι in 277 to give it construction (καὶ μνήσασθε Merkelbach, λοίγια ἔργα or λυγρὸν ὄλεθρον West).

280–1 These verses expand the formular verse μάστιξεν δ' ἵππους (or ἐλάαν)· τὼ δ' οὐκ ἀέκοντε πετέσθην (10×). For chariot as ambulance cf. 399 (Diomedes), 488 (Odysseus), 517 (Makhaon); Eurupulos had to walk (σκάζων, 811). The Trojans had the same practice (13.538 = 14.430, 13.657).

Pap. 432 replaces 281–3 with

μάστιγι ῥαδινῇ τὼ [δὲ πλ]ηγῆς ἀΐοντες
[ῥί]μφα ἔφ[ερον βασιλῆα θο]ὰς ἐπὶ νῆας Ἀχαι[ῶν (suppl. Merkelbach).

The paragraph could well have ended with the common tag τὼ δ' οὐκ ἀέκοντε πετέσθην at 281, and West, *Ptolemaic Papyri* 98, suggests independent expansion of the brief notice of Agamemnon's retreat. Or the interpolator may have shied at the two synizeses, ἄφρεον and στήθεα at 282 in the vulgate. The synizeses are paralleled separately of course (Shipp, *Studies* 155, 181), but not in conjunction. That could as easily be a sign of improvisation as of rhapsodic expansion. Emendations are unconvincing, since other anomalies are introduced. The idea of the horses' bellies being soiled with dust does not recur (at 23.502 it is the driver, not the horses, who suffers this hazard of high-speed charioteering). ἄφρεον: the subject is the horses, with στήθεα as acc. of respect. — This is the moment Hektor has been waiting for, and he immediately launches a counter-attack.

284–309 Hektor sees Agamemnon withdraw and encourages his men. The Trojans rally and a short aristeia *of Hektor follows*

The expression of the themes is extremely succinct, the *aristeia* itself being reduced to a list of names, but the essential elements are all present: the harangue, the general scene (with similes), and the itemized exploits, cf. Krischer, *Konventionen* 75–84. The multiplication of the similes is not unusual at the beginning of a major episode in the narrative, cf. 2.87ff., 4.422ff., but here the two similes 292–3 and 297–8 are very brief and perfunctory. The general pattern in the *Iliad* is that the battle swings back and forth and *aristeia* balances *aristeia*. It is now Hektor's turn and the tale of his exploits should balance those of Agamemnon, but the focus of attention in this book is the Achaeans, and the story of Hektor's attack will be told from their viewpoint. Accordingly Hektor's *aristeia* is compressed to minimal dimensions. To compensate, as it were, for his scale, and to assert Hektor's furious rampage, it is ornamented by three similes: 292–3 (dogs), 297–8, 305–8 (storms). The rally is a regular feature of the Iliadic battle, cf. 8.173ff., 15.484ff. and Fenik, *TBS* 90, and important for the manner in which it is conceived. It is a war of movement (except when specifically described as σταδίη ὑσμίνη) with copious use of missile weapons. Note the themes of the surrounded warrior (401ff.) and the fighting retreat (544ff.).

284 νόσφι: νόσφιν[in pap. 432. ἐόντα should probably be supplied. Aristarchus disliked νόσφι κιόντα elsewhere (τὸ κιόντα κατάχρησις, according to T at 14.440).

285–90 285–7 = 15.485–7. Hektor's call on the face of it is for a chariot charge (the tactics recommended by Nestor at 4.297–309, see nn. *ad loc.*), but it should be observed that the Achaeans are now in retreat so that the situation is like that at 15.343ff.; Hektor is calling for a pursuit, cf. 754ff. The use of massed chariotry for shock in the manner of some Levantine armies of the second millennium b.c. seems to be hinted at below (502–3, 15.352–4), but in none of these cases is there any allusion to an actual clash of chariotry (see 150n. above). The *Iliad* has no allusion to the use of chariots to bring archers into action as frequently depicted on Egyptian monuments. For individuals fighting from chariots see Fenik, *TBS* 11. Generally, the epic's idea of the use of chariots, for flight, pursuit, and transport of leaders, is consistent (see Latacz, *Kampfdarstellung* 216–23), though it is usually thought to be an unrealistic reminiscence of the Mycenaean age. Yet instruments of war may be valued for their majesty and terror, in literature as in fact, as much as for their effectiveness. Greenhalgh, *Warfare* 50–63, argues that the military role of the heroic chariot belongs to the mounted horse of the Geometric period. The chariots depicted in the art of the Geometric period were used merely as a means of transport according to G. Ahlberg, *Fighting on Land and Sea in Greek Geometric Art* (Stockholm 1971) 55.

286 A formular statement (6×) of the Trojan army's composition. The Dardanians, led by Aineias, are the Trojans' neighbours, see 2.819–20n. But who are the Λύκιοι? In spite of the distinguished leadership of Sarpedon and Glaukos it seems invidious to single out the men of classical Lycia for sole mention among Hektor's many allies, though the poet may well have so understood the verse in view of Τρωσί τε καὶ Λυκίοισι in 285. Yet at 8.173, 13.150, and 17.184 the verse picks up a previous Τρώεσσι *tout court*; it is possible that its original reference was to the northern Λύκιοι around the river Aisepos, cf. 4.89–91 and 5.171–3. There is another formula −∪∪−

Τρῶες καὶ Δάρδανοι ἠδ' ἐπίκουροι (4×) that gives a more generous acknowledgement to Hektor's auxiliaries. In any event Hektor speaks in
formulas: Lycians should imply Sarpedon and Dardanians Aineias, but in
this book neither puts in an appearance. Pap. 432 reads Δάρδ]ανοι ἠδ'
ἐπίκουροι, probably κέκλυτέ μευ, Τρῶες καὶ Δάρδ]ανοι ἠδ' ἐπίκουροι (3.456
etc. 4×).

288–9 Hektor speaks as he did at 8.173ff., and will do at 15.486ff.,
proclaiming when the tide has turned that Zeus is on his side. He could
hardly tell his men otherwise, and on neither of the other occasions did he
have the assurance that the visit of Iris has given him here. ὥριστος: a
temporary distinction, cf. the description of Diomedes during his *aristeia*
(5.414, 5.839).

290 ἰφθίμων Δαναῶν is a unique expression, cf. Ἀργείων Δαναῶν (*Od.*
8.578). Δαναοί does not enter noun–epithet formulas (except ἥρωες Δαναοί
5×, in a whole-verse formula).

292–3 The simile of the hounds and their quarry sounds the keynote of
the narrative from this point: the Achaeans for all their individual courage
are hunted beasts, see Moulton, *Similes* 45–9. At 12.41–8 we have the same
combination of hounds, hunters, boar, and lion, but the points of reference
are reversed (such is the versatility of the poet's handling of traditional
details) and Hektor has become the lion that scatters the dogs. There are ten
boar similes in the *Iliad*, six of them in books 11–13 with another cluster in
books 16–17. Three times the comparison is with a boar or lion. Except at
16.823–6 (where a lion forces a boar from a spring of water and kills it) the
scene is an encounter between boar(s) and hunters with their hounds. The
boar is the attacker in five instances, pursued or cornered in four. The men
form a κολοσυρτός (12.147, 13.472), the boar gnashes its teeth (κόμπος
ὀδόντων, 11.417, 12.149), whets its tusks (θήγειν ὀδόντας, 11.416, 13.474),
and charges with a sideswipe of the tusk (12.148). As here the men come
out of these encounters with rather less credit than their hounds.

293 συῒ καπρίῳ illustrates a common epic turn of phrase, cf. βοῦς ...
ταῦρος (2.480), δρυτόμος ἀνήρ (11.86), αἰπόλοι ἄνδρες (2.474), etc. The
combination permits the poet to turn the short comparison συῒ εἴκελος
ἀλκήν (4.253) into a full simile at 17.281–2 συῒ εἴκελος ἀλκήν | καπρίῳ,
ὅς ...

295 Πρῑαμίδης: the lengthening of the first syllable is hard to explain
except as a metrical licence in accordance with Schulze's rule (*QE* 8) that in
a sequence of three or more shorts the syllable under ictus is treated as long.
Wyatt, *ML* 154, cites no convincing analogies that might persuade singers
that the quantity was ambiguous, nor is the influence of Aeolic Πέρραμος
(unknown to the epic) convincing. However established, the rhythm of
Πρῑαμίδης was extended to other patronymics where the long vowel contrasts

with a short in the personal name (list in Wyatt, *ML* 186). Πριαμίδης etc. is normally Hektor (25×), but not exclusively, see 490n.

297 ὑπεραέϊ ἶσος ἀέλλη: such images of violent destruction are freely applied to Hektor, cf. 305–9 (λαῖλαψ), 13.137–42 (a boulder).

299 A whole-verse formula (= 5.703, 16.692, with a shortened variant at 8.273) employed in each case to introduce a bare list of victims. The effect in arresting the attention of an audience and directing it to what follows is like that of an appeal to the Muses at 218. De Jong in fact goes so far as to suggest that the question is addressed to the Muses (*Narrators* 49–50). 'Hektor' in the personalized narrative of the *Iliad* represents the Trojan army, as 'Agamemnon' represented the Achaeans at 91ff.

300 = 8.216 = 19.204, cf. 12.174 = 15.596. Thetis' request (1.521) was that Zeus should Τρώεσσιν ἀρήγειν. In heroic narrative the anonymous Τρῶες must be translated into a particular hero. Hence from the moment, at the beginning of book 8, when Zeus bestirs himself to implement his promise, his activity is described as 'giving κῦδος to Hektor.'

301–3 Hektor's victims seem to be a random list, but in some cases bring with them certain associations. Dolops son of Klutos has a double, a Trojan Dolops son of Lampos (whose brother was Klutios) at 15.525 (see n.). There is a Trojan Opheltios at 6.20, and a Suitor Agelaos at *Od.* 20.321 etc. An Opheltes appeared in the Theban saga, and the name is known also in Cypriot. The impression is that these lists are drawn from a stock of heroic names rather than invented *ex nihilo*. Aisumnos on the other hand has, for an Achaean, a very Asiatic name meaning 'prince' or the like, see 13.427–33n. But an Ionian poet could not be expected to know this; αἰσυμνήτης (*Od.* 8.258, and with suffix -τήρ, *Il.* 24.347) is a common title of civic officers in the area of Ionia. Agelaos certainly and Opheltes probably occur as men's names in Mycenaean texts, see Ventris and Chadwick, *Documents* 104–5, who cite 58 names thought certainly to be common to the tablets and the epic; more than twenty are names assigned to Trojans or their allies, for the poet of the *Iliad*, like the poet of *Roland*, had a stock of traditional foreign names that was too limited for the scale of his narrative. — Bare lists such as this occur at 5.677–8 (eight victims), 5.705–7 (six), 8.274–6 (eight), 16.415–17 (nine), 16.694–6 (nine), 21.209–10, and by various victors 14.511–16 (eight); 15.329–42 (eight) is similar but with minimal added anecdote. Hektor's performance therefore is impressive and made more so by the addition (305) of an anonymous πληθύς.

304–5 Note that the slain are said to be ἡγεμόνες and that the πληθύς do not receive even a token named representative. The ostensible reason for silence is practical, cf. 2.488ff. οὐδ᾽ εἴ μοι δέκα μὲν γλῶσσαι ..., but the truest cause is doubtless the social focus of the *Iliad*. The deaths of leaders stand for the massacre of the λαός.

305–8 The poet's thought runs on Hektor's whirlwind attack and repeats with amplification the image of the preceding simile (297–8), adding repetition to ferocity. The clouds and waves make an image of something happening in succession, cf. the wave simile at 4.422–6 where ἐπασσύτερον makes the image clear. πυκνά at 309 adds the idea of *quick* succession (for this sense see 454n.). Notos, the South Wind, brings the clouds which Zephuros blows away. ἀργεστής is 'the cleanser', see Frisk, *GEW* s.v., and West on Hesiod, *Theog.* 379, where ἀργεστής is epithet of Zephuros.

307 τρόφι κῦμα is a unique expression which provides the metrically necessary two initial consonants. It is derived from the formular κύματά τε τροφόεντα (15.621, *Od.* 3.290 (v.l. κύματά τε τροφέοντο)).

310–400 Counter-attack of Odysseus and Diomedes. The two Achaeans fight as a pair and slay several Trojans. Finally Diomedes injures Hektor with a spear-cast to his helmet. Hektor retreats, to Diomedes' jeers. Diomedes is then wounded in the foot by Paris with an arrow and is forced to withdraw to the ships

Hektor's eventual retreat winds up the episode of battle that began at 284 and balanced the *aristeia* of Agamemnon, but in order to extricate himself, so to speak, the poet brings on two major Achaean characters, whose entry begins a new sequence of battle themes. Hektor's career and its climax also establishes the pattern that controls the narrative in the remainder of this Book: the wounding of a hero at the climax of his *aristeia*, cf. 376 (Diomedes), 437 (Odysseus), 506 (Makhaon), 583 (Eurupulos). Odysseus and Diomedes are regularly conjoined in the Trojan saga (murder of Palamedes, night raid in book 10, theft of the Palladion), although Diomedes is not seconded by Odysseus during his great *aristeia* in book 5.

310–11 Hektor's victories will take him straight to the ships. The trench and wall whose opportune construction at what turned out to be the last possible moment was related in such detail at 7.337–43 and 435–41 to be an ἄρρηκτον εἶλαρ (14.68) exist for the great battle described in book 12 and seem here to be ignored. There are passing allusions in the interim including a neat sarcasm on the lips of Akhilleus (9.349–50) and an obscure reference at 11.48, 11.51. Verses 310–11 could be taken as a hyperbole, but 823–4 omit the new fortifications even more explicitly: οὐκέτι ... ἄλκαρ Ἀχαιῶν | ἔσσεται. The Achaeans, it must now be assumed, are in retreat and threatened with a rout (λοιγός, 'ruin'), but the narrative is focused to an unusual degree on the major figures and obscures the shift of the battle from the Scaean gates (170) to the Achaean camp (12.4). Diomedes' call to Odysseus may be compared with the tactics of Thoas (15.294–99): the ἄριστοι form a front beside the great leaders while the πληθύς withdraw behind their defences. The leaders must withdraw as they fight, as Aias does (544ff.), or they will find themselves isolated like Odysseus at 401. Since the Achaeans have rallied the losses now fall on the Trojans, whose second-rank warriors confront the Achaean ἄριστοι, but the poet reveals a certain reluctance to kill Achaeans (only 61 named casualties in the *Iliad* against 208 Trojans and allies (see 15.405–591n.)). No named Achaean falls in the rest of this Book. The poet's pity, however, is impartial.

310 The verse of transition is apparently formular (= 8.130).

311 πέσον: 'fall dead', a necessary but oddly rare sense of πίπτω. Aristarchus, on 15.63, even denied that it was Homeric.

312 The call for aid is a typical detail. As it happens Diomedes had called for Odysseus' aid at 8.93 and got no response. As usual there is no recollection of the previous incident.

313 τί παθόντε is usually thought to be an Attic idiom, being well attested in that familiar dialect; but it is better to take it (like πέπον in 314) as a mark of informality. It recurs at *Od.* 24.106.

314 For the imperative form ἵστασο see 10.291n. ἔλεγχος: an unbearable reproach, cf. 22.100 where Hektor will fight Akhilleus sooner than suffer ἐλεγχείη. The Achaeans are now fighting to save their ships – Odysseus' words are rather alarmist; at an earlier stage the unbearable disgrace had been to return empty-handed (2.119ff., 284ff.).

315 The Trojans' reaching the ships is the goal set up for the narrative of the middle *Iliad* in book 8, see 8.180–2n. and 9.230–1n. The possibility of this disaster is mentioned 35 times before the ship of Protesilaos is fired at 16.122. κορυθαίολος Ἕκτωρ: the epithet is not 'shaking the helmet' (LSJ and others) but 'with flashing helmet' according to Page, *HHI* 248–51. κορυθαίολος is restricted to Hektor (and Ares (20.38, see n.)) and is of very fixed use – always juxtaposed except at 22.471 – and perhaps was not of very clear meaning to the poet. Note its absence from the famous scene at 6.466ff. It may be glossed by another epithet of Hektor, χαλκοκορυστής (9× in acc. and dat.); αἰόλος is used of armour at 5.295, but usually means, or may mean, 'moving quickly', cf. 12.167n.

317 Pap. 60 (which is usually prone to random omission of verses and omits e.g. 313) prefixes Diomedes' short speech with a formal verse of address, διογενὲς Λαερτιάδη, πολυμήχαν' Ὀδυσσεῦ (= 2.173 etc.), and adds the same verse before Diomedes' even more laconic remarks at 347–8, as if every utterance should be introduced by the vocative case.

319 βόλεται: the conjugation as a root verb βολ- (cf. *Od.* 1.234, 16.387) as opposed to the suffixed βουλ- (probably < βολσ-) is generally attributed to Arcadian among the classical dialects. The presence of Arcado-Cypriot and Mycenaean words and forms in the epic implies at least the antiquity of its linguistic tradition, although the relation of this 'Achaean' component (in the sense used by C. J. Ruijgh in *L'Élément achéen*) to the Ionic remains obscure. Ruijgh, *op. cit.* 111–67, discusses the Arcado-Cypriot element in the epic vocabulary. It includes such basic epic words as αἶσα, ἄναξ, δατέομαι, δέπας, δῶμα, and ἦμαρ. Our ignorance of the early stages in the formation of the Attic–Ionic dialect should prevent an easy assumption that the cradle of the epic tradition must be sought in the Mycenaean Peloponnese. βόλ-, for example, is also attested in the Ionic of Euboea.

320ff. The Trojans are in their chariots to hasten the pursuit, cf. 754–61. The two Achaeans fight as a pair, like Menelaos and Antilokhos at 5.576ff., and continue the pattern set by Agamemnon's *aristeia* by slaying men in pairs. Two heroes, not being fighting man and charioteer, do not act together to attack a single opponent; that would not be heroic.

320 Θυμβραῖον: cf. Θύμβρη (10.430), a town on the Skamandros. This is Thumbraios' sole appearance.

322 The θεράπων performs the duties of an inferior; he attends his principal in the field especially as charioteer, receives guests, serves food and wine, assists at sacrifice, and acts as messenger. His civilian duties thus overlap those of the κῆρυξ, cf. 1.321 where Talthubios and Eurubates are described as κήρυκε καὶ θεράποντε. The θεράπων, however, is not a man of the people. He might have wealthy parents (24.398); Patroklos could be so described (16.653), and θεράπων Ἰδομενῆος is a formular description of Meriones (6×). Μολίονα: the name may be identical with Myc. *mo-ri-wo* PY Cn 1287. -ίων is not primarily a patronymic suffix, cf. Hsch. μολίονες· μαχεταί. A Molos was father of the Greek Meriones (10.269–70, 13.249). For more famous Moliones see 710 and 750 below and nn.

324–5 The simile of boars and hounds again, cf. 292–3, only this time the boars are the aggressors.

327 φεύγοντες is transitive with Ἕκτορα δῖον as object. The hyperbaton is unusual, but cf. 242–3.

328–34 The sons of Merops are not invented for this episode and are of more consequence than their demise seems to imply. They are named in the Trojan Catalogue (2.830) as Adrestos and Amphios of *Apaisos*, commanders of a Hellespontine contingent (329–32 = 2.831–4). Their subsequent history in the Iliad is curiously confused, as if the tradition about them was real but half-forgotten: an Adrestos is killed at 6.63–5, and another at 16.694, see n. to 2.830, while an Amphios of *Paisos* is slain by Diomedes at 5.612 (see nn. *ad loc.*). The names Amphios and Adrestos echo those of the Theban cycle (Amphiaraos and Adrastos), a further complication, cf. 13.663–70 and n. It is odd that the two brothers are not named more specifically, perhaps as Strasburger suggests, *Kämpfer* 26, because the focus of interest in the incident is the plight of the father not the fate of the sons. Seers and priests are popular as fathers of the slain, their disregarded warnings, or failures to give warning, being a ready source of pathos, cf. 5.148ff., 13.663ff. Merops of Perkote (actually of Adresteia in the Trojan

Catalogue – both are towns on the Hellespont) caught the attention of Hellenistic poet-scholars, probably because of the puzzles over his sons: he comes into Apollonius' poem, *Arg.* 1.975.

334 κεκαδών: this active form, a reduplicated second aorist, clearly means 'deprive'. The middle (κεκάδοντο 4.497 = 15.574) means 'withdraw'.

335 Ἱππόδαμος and Ὑπείροχος are epic adjectives elevated into proper names to provide a victory for Odysseus. Ὑπείροχον: the Trojans are typically ὑπέρθυμοι (7× *Il.*), and since they are the sinners who provoked the war, it is likely that a pejorative nuance, not to be overstressed, clings to the name, see J. Pinsent in Foxhall and Davies, *Trojan War* 147–8. Other Trojan names with a touch of arrogance are Hupeiron 5.144, Arkheptolemos (Zenodotus read 'Erasiptolemos') 8.128, Huperenor 14.516, Hupsenor 5.76 (a second Hupsenor, however, is an Achaean, 13.411).

336 μάχην ἐτάνυσσε: The general idea of 'stress' is clear enough though the image is difficult to understand precisely, as if in*tens*ity were expressed by ex*tens*ion, cf. the simile at 17.389–93 (stretching a hide) in close proximity to Ζεὺς ... ἐτάνυσσε κακὸν πόνον. See also 13.358–60n. and 17.400–1n. The metaphor is frequent in the central Books of the *Iliad* (13.359, 14.389, 16.662, 17.401), and must be related in some way to the enigmatic formula ὀλέθρου πείρατ' ἐφῆπται (ἵκηαι), 'fasten the bonds of destruction', on which see 6.143n. Verse 336 is a variant, with subject and active verb, of 12.436 = 15.413 ἐπὶ ἶσα μάχη τέτατο πτόλεμός τε.

337–61 Parts of these verses are contained in *P.Oxy.* 3827. At 344a the papyrus has a hitherto unattested plus-verse ending ὀνόσαιτ]ο μετελθών (cf. 13.127) unknown to the general paradosis.

337 ἐξ Ἴδης καθορῶν: specifically from the Γάργαρον ἄκρον 8.48 (see n. for the identification of the peak). In the poet's imagination Ida commanded a truly magnificent view – Thrace, Mysia, the lands of the Hippemolgoi and Abioi (13.4–7 and n.).

338 Agastrophos is known only from this episode.

340 Compare Idomeneus' lucky escape by chariot at 17.605–25. Agastrophos' tactical error in being separated from his transport is portentously described as ἀάσατο δὲ μέγα θυμῷ, as if it were an offence against god or morality, but the phrase is formular (= 9.537).

342 = 20.412, cf. 5.250. θῦνε διὰ προμάχων: a common but hazardous tactic, cf. 5.249–50 where Diomedes is warned against it. The warrior, one supposes, watched for his opportunity just out of spear-shot, and then darted forward to hurl his weapon before nimbly retreating: it called for ποδῶν ἀρετήν (20.411). Agastrophos' folly was compounded by the negligence of his charioteer; contrast 13.384–6 where Asios fought with his horses breathing down his neck. Note that the pathetic touch, bravado followed by nemesis, is built into the formular diction of the *Iliad*.

343–5 ≅ 5.590–1, 596. As often the repeated verses point to a parallelism between the scenes, but not to a genetic relationship (but see nn. to 5.590–5): in book 5 a pair of Achaeans, Menelaos and Antilokhos, have scored successes, Hektor rushes to the scene, Diomedes shudders at his approach. The situation is thematic (cf. Fenik, *TBS* 64) and the three verses themselves are strongly formular: ὀξὺ νόησε 8× (2× with Ἕκτωρ), κατὰ στίχας 6×, ὦρτο δ' ἐπ' αὐτούς etc. 3×, | κεκλήγων 3×, – – ∪ (verb) φάλαγγες | 7×, τὸν δὲ ἰδών 12×, βοὴν ἀγαθὸς Διομήδης 21×. In the event Diomedes' apprehension is not justified. There is a tension in the *Iliad* between the philhellenism of the poet (cf. 10.13–4n.) and the plot of the poem, which requires an Achaean defeat. The prowess of Hektor is therefore emphasized by statements such as the present, but the premise (1.242) that without Akhilleus the rest would be helpless before Hektor is not borne out by the narrative. Tlepolemos fell to Sarpedon and Patroklos to the intervention of Apollo. In fact no leading Achaean is killed or even wounded by Hektor in fair fight.

344 κεκλήγων: the Aeolic participle should not be restored in the nominative case, see 168 n. The paradosis is everywhere κεκληγώς.

345 Diomedes is an Akhilleus-like character with redeeming features: insubordinate at 9.32ff., unafraid to attack gods (with divine permission) in 5, over-confident at 9.48–9, unabashed at Akhilleus' refusal to help (9.697ff.), he is modest before Agamemnon (4.412ff.), and here shudders at the approach of Hektor but having resolved to stand his ground fells him easily enough and then sinks to abuse; later he sneers at Paris' success (οὐκ ἀλέγω, 389) and a moment afterwards leaps in agony onto his chariot. Odysseus in contrast shows the steadiness that comes with age. Since Hektor is plainly inferior to Aias in the duel in book 7 and by implication at least to Agamemnon in this Book, it is clear that the Trojan front rank (Hektor, Aineias, Sarpedon, and from book 13 onward Deiphobos and Pouludamas) is conceived to be no match in the field for the leading Achaeans. At 7.162–68 Agamemnon, Diomedes, both Aiantes, Idomeneus, Meriones, Eurupulos, Thoas, and Odysseus are listed as willing to challenge Hektor, but some of them perhaps had succumbed to Nestor's moral blackmail, for the prayer of the Achaeans (7.175–80) was that Aias (*sc.* the Telamonian), Diomedes, or Agamemnon himself should draw the lot to fight the Trojan.

347 πῆμα κυλίνδεται (cf. 17.99, 17.688, *Od.* 2.163, 8.81): for the origin of the metaphor cf. κῦμα κυλίνδει (*Od.* 1.162, etc.).

348 = 22.231 ('Deiphobos' speaking to Hektor).

349–67 The poet seems momentarily to lose his sureness of touch. At 5.166ff. and 20.419ff. a Trojan counter-attacks an Achaean, is repulsed, and is rescued by a god. (For a detailed comparison see Fenik, *TBS* 93–5.) In books 5 and 20 the typical details combine to produce a clear picture; here the poet cannot use the motif of divine rescue, because the gods have been banished from the battlefield, and he is obliged to have Hektor withdraw unhindered after being stunned and only then collapse, while Diomedes instead of attacking with the sword is made to give Hektor respite (an unparalleled detail) by retrieving his spear, and then to abuse him for his (Hektor's) good fortune. Diomedes is made to avoid Hektor at 5.596–606 and encounters him only here. The poet has a problem in constructing narratives of great battles in which the protagonists cannot meet, or cannot meet decisively, because their roles are determined by the tradition of the Trojan story. So the duels of books 3 and 7 must be aborted, Hektor must not meet Agamemnon and must escape from Diomedes here and from Aias (14.409ff.), and Aineias from Diomedes (5.311ff.) and from Akhilleus (20.79ff.). As one of these rare encounters the fight of Hektor and Diomedes attracted the interest of vase-painters, see Friis Johansen, *Iliad in Early Greek Art* 219, 269.

349–50 A formular couplet (7×).

350 τιτυσκόμενος κεφαλῆφιν: -φι in Mycenaean Greek is mainly an instrumental plural ending in the declension of *a*- and consonant-stem nouns, but its loss as a regular case-form from the later dialects has permitted its metrically convenient spread within the *Kunstsprache* to the singular and to genitival and locatival usages. Since the epic can express 'place at which' both by the locatival dative and by the locatival (partitive) genitive it is often unclear what is the grammatical equivalence of -φι. τιτύσκομαι, of course, normally construes with the genitive. G. P. Shipp's excellent study of Homeric -φι, *Studies in the Language of Homer*, 1st edn (Cambridge 1953) 1–17, did not have the benefit of the Mycenaean decipherment and his inference from Homeric usage that the termination was primarily a singular and appropriate to consonant stems must be corrected, see his *Essays in Mycenaean and Homeric Greek* (Melbourne 1961) 29–41. χαλκόφι in 351 is clearly singular and genitive. There are a few examples of -φι as a case-ending in the *o*-stem declension in Mycenaean (Cnossos) but this extension of the suffix is mainly the achievement of the *Kunstsprache*. The range of usage is well set out by Meister, *Kunstsprache* 135–46. The *Iliad* has no instances of -όφι extracted from the *o*-stem and extended to consonant stems (4× in *Od.*).

353 Saying that the helmet was a gift of Apollo is a way of affirming the excellent quality of its materials and workmanship, cf. 7.146 where Areithoos is given his armour by Ares, see M. M. Willcock, *BICS* 17 (1970) 1–10. The provenance of Pandaros' bow (2.827 gift of Apollo, but 4.105–11 built by Pandaros himself) is a strong indication that no literal gift is intended by this idiom. Teukros' bow was also a gift of Apollo (15.441). τρίπτυχος: only here. One layer would be leather (Lorimer, *HM* 342) or felt, like the boar's tusk helmet (10.265). τρυφάλεια ... αὐλῶπις: cf. 5.182, 13.530, 16.795 and see 5.182n. and 13.132n.

354 ἀπέλεθρον: i.e. λίαν, ἀμέτρως (T); in strict sense probably 'without turning', π(ἐ)λεθρον denoting the limit of an area of ploughland (*LfgrE*), cf. 5.245n.

355–6 ≅ 5.309–10 (where the couplet is neatly extended back into the preceding verse: αὐτὰρ ὁ γ' ἥρως | ἔστη γνὺξ ἐριπών ...). Verse 356 was omitted by Zenodotus (Did/A) and athetized by his successors ὅτι ἐν ἄλλῳ τόπῳ ὀρθῶς κεῖται (Arn/A), a common but inadequate justification for athetesis. Hektor, the scholia point out, has not been badly hurt on this occasion. For the use of στῆ with γνύξ see 9.570n., and for the posture ('kneeling *up*' as we might say) see 5.309–10n.

357–60 Diomedes rushes forward to recover his spear, thus giving Hektor a chance to recover – a hero normally draws his sword in these circumstances and goes in for the kill. The relation of this scene to other narrow escapes of Hektor is a good test of critical method. The escape of Hektor at 14.423ff. (by being surrounded by his companions) or at 20.443ff. (by action of Apollo) is more typical of the Homeric battlefield; is the present scene then a (clumsy) transfer of a specific scene, e.g. 20.443ff., from its proper place, or a (less than perfect) adaptation of a type-scene? See van Thiel, *Ilias und Iliaden* 354–5, and Fenik, *TBS* 92–5. Von der Mühll, *Hypomnema* 195, conjectures that the poet wished to give Diomedes a victory over Hektor like those of Aias and Akhilleus. A duel of sorts seems to be foreshadowed by Hektor's words (whatever they were – see nn. *ad loc.*) at 8.532–8.

358 καταείσατο, 'sped down', is properly from (Ϝ)ίεμαι, though after the loss of initial digamma confusion with εἶμι set in, most clearly at 24.462 (εἴσομαι = 'I shall go'). The -ει- may be a true diphthong, cf. Skt *véti*, 'pursue', and see Chantraine, *GH* I 293.

362–7 (= 20.449–54): apparently a formular jeer, neatly used by Akhilleus in book 20, where Apollo did in fact rescue Hektor. The lines are defended in their present position by Ø. Andersen, *Symbolae Osloenses* Suppl. 25 (1978) 136–7, and Fenik, *TBS* 94–5. The attribution of bad luck to the interference of a god seldom rests on knowledge – Akhilleus did not see Apollo – and here Diomedes reasonably blames the principal divine ally of the Trojans. It is unnecessary to see any echo of the fact that Hektor's protective helmet was a 'gift of Apollo' (353). Observe the superiority that Diomedes displays over Hektor in this episode, cf. 345n. Nevertheless he will not have a second chance to meet Hektor. κύον here (as at 8.423, 21.481, 22.345, cf. *Od.* 22.35) is mere abuse without serious imputation of supposedly canine characteristics (shamelessness, greed, and lewdness, cf. 1.225n.).

365 For θήν see 10.104n. It has much the same function as δή, though perhaps not so emphatic.

368 Παιονίδην: Agastrophos, wounded if not slain at 338–9. ἐξενάριξεν: the sense of the imperfect is 'proceeded to …' – to do what? ἐξεναρίζειν is properly to strip the ἔναρα, 'spoils', from the body of a slain enemy, though it can also incorporate the act of slaying as well as despoiling, as at 335. The primary sense fits best here; Diomedes will be wounded, like many another, as he drops his guard in seizing a trophy.

369–83 In this case the archery of Paris scores the point, so that there is a thematic correspondence with the exploits of Teukros on the Achaean side (8.266ff., 12.387ff., 15.442ff.). Keeping to his usual practice, however, the poet does not give the Trojan a formal *aristeia* of successively narrated successes, contrast 8.266ff., but reuses the motif of the deadly archer to shape the narrative in the episodes of Makhaon (505ff.) and Eurupulos (581ff.). Paris fights in the open, protected only by his distance from the spearmen. Only the Greek Aias is regularly thought of as wielding the σάκος ἠΰτε πύργον, and so the poet cannot reuse the fine image of the archer (who cannot effectively manage his own shield) crouching behind the great body-shield, see 8.266–72. This is the only place in the *Iliad* where an arrow wound is sustained in the foot, but unfortunately too little is known of the greatest of Paris' exploits, the fatal wounding of Akhilleus in the ankle at the Scaean gates (in the Trojan Cycle that occurred in the *Aithiopis*) for a useful thematic comparison to be made. His injury has been taken to symbolize the fact that Diomedes has up to this point played the role of Akhilleus but cannot in the end replace him (so Kullmann, *GRBS* 25 (1984) 307–23). The similar, though not identical, location of the wound, however, is the main point of similarity; in other respects the briefly told wounding of Glaukos by Teukros (12.387–91) has as good a claim to be conceived after the death of Akhilleus, for Glaukos is hit while storming a wall. Fenik, adducing the earlier wounding of Diomedes (5.95–113), maintains with some justice that on the evidence of the *Iliad* these injuries are composites of typical details, not derivatives of a single archetype, see *TBS* 234–5. In the absence of titulature, representations in art of a hero wounded in the foot are more likely to depict Akhilleus than Diomedes; some possible examples are listed in the *Lexicon Iconographicum* s.v. 'Diomedes' 112–14.

369 The verse, from Ἀλέξανδρος, is formular (6×). Ἀλέξανδρος: for the name see 3.16n. Ἑλένης: an initial digamma is attested in inscriptions from Sparta, *SEG* xxvi 458, but the frequent lengthening of a naturally short syllable before the caesura prevents this verse being cited for a Homeric Ϝελένη. Both epics imply Ἑ- by regularly eliding vowels before it (29× in OCT out of 58 occurrences).

371–2 For the tomb of Ilos see 166n. The battle has now swung back towards the Achaean ships. Grave-mounds in Homer are memorials without any numinous aura; consequently they are treated casually as convenient landmarks (23.331), watchtowers (2.793), or fighting posts. Verse 372 expands Ἴλου ... παλαιοῦ Δαρδανίδαο (166) with a rearrangement of the epithets. δημογέροντος, 'elder of the people', is therefore not a traditional description of Ilos, an ancestor of the royal line of Troy, for whom it would be inappropriate if strictly interpreted.

373–5 The lines expand the formular phrase (καὶ) αἴνυτο τεύχε' ἀπ' ὤμων (11.580, 13.550) with some resulting awkwardness: παναίολον is construed with θώρηκα *pace* Lattimore, cf. the formula ζωστῆρα παναίολον (4.215, 11.236); ἀσπίδα τ' ὤμων is unparalleled.

375ff. There is a striking lack of any cross-reference to Diomedes' previous injury from an arrow. In 5.95ff. he was hit by Pandaros, but prayed at once to Athene and was healed. Except in the case of Menelaos' narrow escape at 4.134–40, the Homeric arrow will not penetrate defensive armour, cf. 12.401 where Teukros' arrow is stopped by the shield-strap and leaves Sarpedon uninjured, and 13.586–7. The archer must therefore aim at, or luckily hit, some part of his target that is (cf. 12.389) γυμνωθείς. (Diomedes was stooping over his victim.) So it is the *right* shoulder, exposed by the shield, that is hit (5.98, 11.507), or the *right* thigh (11.583). Other spots are the waist (4.134), the breast (8.303, 8.313), the arm (unspecified, but hardly the shield-arm, 12.389), and the back of the neck (15.451). Vase-painters, however, often depict arrow wounds in the lower leg, see Lorimer, *BSA* 42 (1947) figs. 7, 9, 11.

375 πῆχυν: some fitment at the centre of the bow-stave is intended by which the bow was held and the arrow guided, cf. *Od.* 21.419 (ὀϊστὸν) ἐπὶ πήχει ἑλὼν ἕλκεν νευρὴν γλυφίδας τε.

376 ≅ 5.18 = 16.480 (from 2nd foot). βάλεν construes with ταρσόν in the following verse – 'let fly ... and hit'.

377 διὰ δ' ἀμπερές: an unusual tmesis of the adverb διαμπερές, cf. ἐκ δ' ὀνομακλήδην (*Od.* 4.278).

379 καὶ εὐχόμενος ἔπος ηὔδα is formular (6×) but is elsewhere always used of an Achaean boasting over a *dead* Trojan. The fact that this phrase is used of Paris when Diomedes is not dead underlines the vanity of his self-congratulation. The victor's boast and the disparaging response make up a typical motif, see Fenik, *TBS* 32, and Sacks, *Traditional Phrase*, 12.

380 βέβληαι: the scansion is probably as a dactyl, with the -η- shortened.

385–95 Diomedes' words are an eloquent expression of the aristocratic spearman's contempt for those who fight at distance (and often anonymously) with the bow. The sentiment is characteristic of the *Iliad*, where among the heroes of some (relatively modest) distinction only Pandaros, Paris, Teukros, and sometimes Meriones fight with the bow. Pandaros explained it by his lack of a chariot (5.201–5). The attitude of the *Odyssey*, e.g. at 8.215ff. is much more indulgent. The issue rumbled on, see e.g. Archilochus fr. 3 West, Eur. *Her.* 151–203. The lance- and sword-wielding Franks cultivated a similar attitude; in *Roland* missiles generally and not just arrows are contemptible weapons used by a cowardly enemy who dare not come to close quarters with Roland and Turpin (*Roland* 2152ff.)

385 κέρᾳ ἀγλαέ: κέρα(α) was also read, without effect on the sense. Aristarchus (Arn/A) and the Lexica affirm that if κέρᾳς were taken as a reference to the bow the gibe τοξότα would be otiose, and therefore take κέρᾳς to denote a style of hairdressing, εἰς κέρατος τρόπον ἀνεπλέκοντο οἱ ἀρχαῖοι. The possibility of this interpretation is confirmed by the term κεροπλαστής in Archilochus fr. 117 West and by the monuments, see S. Marinatos, *Arch. Hom.* B 12–13. The Homeric use of κέρᾳς is unhelpful, being always for the object 'horn' or the material, not for anything made from it or similar to it. Aristotle (T) paraphrased ὦ τῷ τόξῳ σεμνυνόμενε. Paris, however, was a fop (3.17).

388 αὔτως is 'like this', see 17.448–50n.

391–3 Diomedes' grim gloating over the weeping widow and desecrated corpse is calculated to make Paris *and the audience* shudder. Heroes are awesome in their threats as in their deeds. ἄλλως ... ὀξὺ βέλος πέλεται: Leaf compares 20.99 ἄλλως τοῦ γ' ἰθὺ βέλος πέτετ', where ἰθύ must be predicative, to suggest that ὀξύ is predicative here. ὀξὺ βέλος is formular with attributive adjective, cf. 845 and βέλος ὀξύ (2×), and may be so construed here. πέτεται would be easier, but there is no v.l. ἀκήριον, i.e. 'lifeless' (<κῆρ, 'heart'). Aristarchus' conjecture (Did/A), ἄνδρα for αἶψα, is intended to provide an object for τίθησι.

396ff. Odysseus' defence of the disabled Diomedes is a variant of the type-scene in which a hero defends a corpse. The defence and retrieval of Patroklos' body in book 17 is the most elaborate example in the *Iliad*, but the most famous was the defence of the body of Akhilleus himself in the *Aithiopis*. For the argument that this scene is derived from that in the *Aithiopis* (e.g. W. Schadewaldt, *Von Homers Welt und Werk* (Stuttgart 1959) 170, and Kullmann, *Quellen* 326–7) it is sufficient to refer to Fenik, *TBS* 236–7.

401–88 Odysseus is isolated but after reminding himself of his heroic duty stands his ground. He slays several Trojans including Kharops. Sokos, brother of Kharops, succeeds in wounding Odysseus. Hard-pressed by the Trojans, Odysseus calls for help. Menelaos hears his cries and brings Aias to his rescue. The latter holds off the Trojans while Menelaos leads Odysseus away

The scale of narration, to balance the woundings of Agamemnon and Diomedes, is full, with prefatory monologue and preliminary *aristeia*.

401 T, who is alert to such matters, stresses that the poet piles on the agony of the Achaean reverse by emphasizing the peril of Odysseus ὥστε ἐκ παντὸς συνέχει τὸν ἀκροατήν. (For the empathy of the Greek audience see, for example, Plato, *Ion* 535.) Reinhardt, *IuD* 107, discusses these situations, for which there is a formula, ἔνθα κε λοιγὸς ἔην ...

403 This is the standard formula that introduces monologues (7× + 4× in *Od.*), and illustrates again the tendency of the epic to represent what goes on in the mind (as we should say) as a dialogue between the person and a personified entity (so Dodds, *Greeks and the Irrational* 16), cf. 12.292–307n. The monologue, as a device to reveal a character's motivation at a critical juncture, has a curious distribution in the *Iliad*. There are none until this point, two in this Book, cf. 404ff., and ten in books 17–22. The situation in which Odysseus finds himself, the lone warrior in peril, is a common one, and the scatter is unexplained. The monologue 'Shall I stand and fight or withdraw?' is a type-scene and therefore the hero always resolves to stand his ground, cf. 21.553–70, 22.98–130 (the exception is Menelaos, 17.90–105), see Fenik, *TBS* 96–8, 163–4, and S. Scully, *TAPA* 114 (1984) 11–27. The monologue is followed by a simile of animals pitted against men and, except in book 22, by the hero's escape. — ὀχθήσας: 'perplexed'.

405–6 ῥίγιον, literally 'more chilly' (as at *Od.* 17.191) is regularly metaphorical, as is the verb ῥιγόω. Odysseus shudders at the prospect confronting him. Punctuation after μοῦνος (note the emphatic runover position) should be light; the flight of the others is part of Odysseus' fears.

407–10 Odysseus puts to himself a moral argument: the ἄριστος *qua* ἄριστος has a duty to stand and fight. Poseidon put the matter similarly to the laggard chiefs at 13.116–19:

> ὑμεῖς δ' οὐκέτι καλὰ μεθίετε θούριδος ἀλκῆς
> πάντες ἄριστοι ἐόντες ἀνὰ στρατόν. οὐδ' ἂν ἔγωγε
> ἀνδρὶ μαχεσσαίμην ὅς τις πολέμοιο μεθείη
> λυγρὸς ἐών· ὑμῖν δὲ νεμεσσῶμαι περὶ κῆρι.

Cf. the words of Hektor to Andromakhe at 6.441–6, and contrast the practical argument of Sarpedon at 12.322–28. Verse 407 = 17.97 etc. (5×). Verse 407 is the standard verse with which the hero dismisses his doubts.

410 Note the fatalistic touch characteristic of the *Iliad*, cf. 430–3, 12.328, and most pathetically 21.111–13 (Akhilleus to Lukaon). ἔβλητ(ο): this middle form is always used in a passive sense. For the sentiment 'kill or be killed' cf. 12.172. The aorists are gnomic.

411–12 = 17.106–7 less the filler ἀσπιστάων; in both passages the situation is then illustrated by a simile. For ἧος see 10.507n. Verse 412 = 4.221.

413 The second half-verse is obscure. Aristarchus (Arn/A) took πῆμα to be that which the Trojans were bringing on Odysseus now that he was μετὰ σφίσι, but that is rather far-fetched. The πῆμα is rather the Trojans' own who found their intended victim too hot to handle (so bT), as the following simile makes clear. Zenodotus read μετὰ σφίσι, πῆμα δὲ ἔλσαν, which at least gives the right sense.

414–18 A boar simile, cf. 5.780ff., 12.146ff., 13.471–5, and 17.281ff., also [Hesiod], *Aspis* 386–91 (a fine description with details unknown to the *Iliad*). The boar is a good figure for truculent counter-aggression when under attack, as the lion represents primary aggression.

419 Διὶ φίλος is one of the *Iliad*'s most frequent generic epithets (17×), though only here and at 473 applied to Odysseus. It is remarkable that the word is absent from the *Odyssey*, the *Hymns*, and the Hesiodic corpus (including *Aspis*).

420–7 When a warrior is hard pressed by superior numbers he retreats until he is received into the ranks of his own side, cf. the retreat of Aias (563–74). It is therefore unusual that Odysseus stands his ground and engages in a small *aristeia* culminating in a minor duel. He does not retreat till 461.

422 Θόωνα: there are two other Trojans named Thoon, 5.152 and 12.140 cf. 13.545, both slain. Ἔννομον: too much attention should not be paid to the personnel in these uncommented lists of slain. An Ἔννομος οἰωνιστής, for example, alive at 17.218, was commander of the Mysians at 2.858–60 where he is expressly stated to have been killed by Akhilleus 'at the river' (though he is not mentioned in books 20–1). Several MSS, including B, read Ὄρμενον, probably by contamination with 12.187 αὐτὰρ ἔπειτα Πύλωνα καὶ Ὄρμενον ἐξενάριξεν ∼ αὐτὰρ ἔπειτα Θόωνα καὶ Ὄρμενον ἐξενάριξεν.

423 ≅ 20.401 with Ἱπποδάμαντα for Χερσιδάμαντα, as if the jingle – δάμαντα ... ἀΐξαντα stuck in the poet's subconscious mind. Χερσιδάμαντα: only here.

424 πρότμησιν: ancient commentators were generally agreed that this rare word denoted the belly or even the ὀσφῦς, 'crotch' (where Homeric decency forbade anyone to be wounded, according to T); for that location cf. Tyrtaeus fr. 10.25 West. The exception was the doctor Phylotimos who took the word to mean the neck (Arn/A).

425 ἀγοστῷ: 'with crooked hand' (?), only in the extended formula ὁ δ' ἐν κονίῃσι πεσὼν ἕλε γαῖαν ἀγοστῷ (5× *Il.* of which this is the first occurrence, not in *Od.* or the Hesiodic corpus, in neither of which would there be much use for it). The precise sense and the etymology are uncertain.

426–7 Kharops and his brother Sokos ('Strong', probably, cf. 20.72) appear only in this episode. Another son of Hippasos (or a Hippasos), one Hupsenor, is killed at 13.411. There are many such minor links between books 11, 12, and 13, indicating that these books of battle narrative form some kind of internal unit within the *Iliad*. A Hippasos also begat the Paeonian Apisaon (17.348), on whom see 577–95n. Kharops is one of those

Trojans who bear a Mycenaean name, see 301–3n. The vase-painter who attributed the death of Kharops (defended by Hippolokhos, cf. 122) to Diomedes had forgotten his *Iliad* (*Lex. Icon.* 'Diomedes' 19).

427 εὐηφενέος: εὐηγενέος is read or implied by some MSS (including Pap. 59) and is unnecessarily emended after 23.81, see nn. *ad loc.* The -η- can only be an analogical intrusion (after μοιρηγενής, etc.?), but the word is genuine enough, being attested at *HyAphr* 229, as a personal name in late fifth-century Eretria (*IG* xII Suppl. 588), and in Hellenistic literature. Other three-word verses are 2.706, 15.678, *Od.* 10.137; they seem accidental rather than for special effect.

429 καί μιν πρὸς μῦθον ἔειπε: verbal exchanges between the combatants are common before, during, and after duels, but they follow no fixed pattern. There is no parallel, as it happens, to the victor making two speeches, as here, 441–5 and 450–5.

430–3 Sokos' banal words stem from a common heroic standpoint, best known from the noble words of Sarpedon at 12.322–8 and those of Hektor at 16.859–61 (433 ≅ 16.861). Moira may have decreed, but for all a man usually knows what happens seems like a matter of chance; therefore let him fight and fight well, fate does not always favour the big battalions. — δόλων ἆτ᾽ ἠδὲ πόνοιο is very much a generic description of the epic personality of Odysseus. It has no justification in the present context, except in so far as an uncomplimentary expression is wanted, and very little in the *Iliad* as a whole; it fits Odysseus' record in the Cycle, however, as well as in the *Odyssey* (where, oddly enough, δόλων ἆτ᾽ occurs but once, 13.293). πόνος is specifically the toil of battle in the *Iliad*, see 15.235n. The polite form of address to Odysseus is διογενὲς Λαερτιάδη, πολυμήχαν᾽ Ὀδυσσεῦ (9.308 etc.)

433 ≅ 12.250 ≅ 16.861.

434–6 These verses (from κατ᾽ ἀσπίδα) constitute a short formular run (= 3.356–8 = 7.250–2, with a variant at 4.135–6). Inevitably such runs fit some contexts better than others, and all uses of this scene have attracted criticism, see Murray, *Rise* 155–7 and nn. to 3.355–60 and 4.135–6. In the present case the situation, however, seems clear: Sokos (one may imagine) aimed at the centre of Odysseus' shield, consequently the spear, after piercing the shield, ploughed through his θώρηξ on his left side inflicting a flesh wound. πολυδαίδαλου is readily understood of chased or inlaid metal, on the analogy of medieval armour, but the implication is uncertain, see n. to 4.135–6. δῑά: the lengthening occurs also in the similar (and probably derivative) expression διὰ μὲν ἂρ ζωστῆρος (4.135). Shipp, *Studies* 28, is clearly correct to see a rhetorical purpose in the location of the preposition at the head of the verse and sentence. Further justification for the quantity of the ι is hard to find, unless it be by aural contamination with the adjective δῖα (so Wyatt, *ML* 215–17).

437–8 Athene's action in warding off a fatal blow is typical, cf. 4.127–9, but her mention at this point is a momentary lapse (or *façon de parler*). Zeus can incline the course of the battle from the summit of Ida, but the lesser gods must be physically present in order to exert their power. Athene, along with the other gods, has been banished from the battlefield, cf. 75ff.

437 Aristarchus' χροός (Did/A) is almost unintelligible, as Erbse observes, and ignores the digamma of Ϝέργαθεν (= 'cut off,' cf. 5.147 and n.).

438 ἔγκασι: a heteroclite form, according to Leumann, *HW* 158 n. 1, from an adjective *ἔγκατος parallel to ἔσχατος (10.434n.); but there is no trace of singular ἔγκατον before Hellenistic times. This is the only time the word is used in the *Iliad* for human guts, in place of ἔντερα (5× between 13.507 and 20.420).

439 τέλος: 'the spear did not come to a fatal end', even with the support of Aristarchus and the χαριέστεραι, is an unhappy expression and has very slender MS attestation. βέλος as subject of ἦλθεν was read by Zenodotus and the vulgate, and causes no difficulty except for those like Aristarchus who suppose that βέλος must denote a missile weapon (Sokos appears to have thrust at Odysseus), cf. οὐκ ἐν καιρίῳ ὀξὺ πάγη βέλος 4.185, and van der Valk, *Researches* II 11.

441 If Sokos used a thrusting weapon, as 434ff. seem to envisage, then he is now almost disarmed. Odysseus seems to realize his advantage, and at 446 Sokos loses his nerve and tries to escape. ἆ δείλ' expresses genuine commiseration at 816 but here is clearly offensively patronizing, cf. 17.199–201n.

443–5 = 5.652–4 (with a variation in the first hemistich of 653, Sarpedon speaking), a formular threat. Verse 445 = 16.625. For κλυτόπωλος as an epithet of Hades, see Nilsson, *GgrR* 425, who accepts the suggestion that in one concept of Hades the god appeared with his chariot to carry off the souls of the dying, cf. the rape of Persephone. In the epic of course the soul makes its way to the underworld without assistance. Generally in Greek religion the horse is associated with Poseidon, cf. Burkert, *Religion* 138.

447–8 = 8.258–9.

450–5 These verses explain why it was so important to recover the corpses of the slain. After the chivalrous proposals of Hektor that the victor take the armour but release the body of the slain for decent burial (7.76–91) Odysseus' boast sounds a mean, unpleasant note. Dogs and vultures are the fate of the common soldiers (1.4–5, 2.393, 4.237, 8.379), but this is the first time in the *Iliad* that a named victim is threatened with them. Henceforth, however, the tension of the narrative rises and there is a crescendo of atrocity, see Segal, *Mutilation*. For similar unpleasant boasts cf. 391–5, and 15.349, 21.122, 22.335. None apparently were actually put into effect.

454 ἐρύουσι: the tense is future, cf. 15.351n. ὠμησταὶ ἐρύουσι is formular, but the subject may be vultures, as here, or dogs, as at 22.66. – As an epithet of wings πυκνά would be expected to mean 'with dense ⟨feathers⟩', cf. δρυμά πυκνά at 118 and other uses of thickets and foliage. πτερά πυκνά is a formula (3× and as πυκινά πτερά, *Od.* 5.53), and may be used loosely in the present context, for the action of a bird 'flinging its densely feathered wings' about a corpse is hardly comprehensible. πυκνά may be understood here as 'fast beating', as certainly at Sappho fr. 1.11 L–P πύκνα δίννεντες πτέρα. The vulture seizes the carrion and to help it tear the beakful loose flaps its wings. It would be possible in principle to segment the expression as περὶ πτερὰ | πυκνὰ βαλόντες (for such persistence of the words and form of a formula in spite of radically different syntax cf. μενοεικέα· πολλὰ δ' at *Od.* 14.232). But πυκνά as an adverb is restricted in the *Iliad* to the formula πυκνὰ μάλα στενάχων (-οντα) 2×.

455 The reading of OCT, αὐτὰρ ἔμ', εἴ κε θάνω, is that of Aristarchus (Did/A), for αὐτὰρ ἐπεί κε θάνω; it entails the correction of the vulgate κτεριοῦσί με (γε Aristarchus). The emphatic ἔμ(ε) is attractive, but γε is pointless; the paradosis may surely stand.

458 οἱ: Zenodotus (Did/A) read οὗ, so as to give a clearer construction to the isolated participle σπασθέντος. οὗ, however, confirms the paradosis since τοῦ would be the correct epic pronoun. ἀνέσσυτο is a more violent word than that used of Diomedes' wound at 5.113 (ἀνηκόντιζε). We must understand a serious wound in spite of the bold face Odysseus put upon it.

459–88 The second part of Odysseus' gallant stand closely follows the pattern of the first:

A Odysseus decides to make a stand, 401–10.
B Simile of a boar set upon by dogs, 414–20.
C He is wounded by Sokos, 420–58.
A′ Odysseus calls for help, 459–73.
B′ Simile of wounded deer set upon by jackals, 474–84.
C′ He is rescued by Aias, 485–8.

460 = 13.332.

462 It is natural for the man in peril to call for help, cf. 13.477, 17.120, but the thrice repeated cry is untypical. The picture drawn at 401–2 is still valid: Odysseus is isolated (470) and thoroughly alarmed. Odysseus possessed a μεγάλην ὄπα (3.221), being βοὴν ἀγαθός in fact if not in formular diction.

465 Aias is the natural choice for Menelaos' appeal: he was the best warrior of the Achaean front rank after Akhilleus (2.768, 17.279–80), and outstanding in defence.

466 ἵκετ' ἀϋτή (OCT, for ἵκετο φωνή) is Aristarchus' reading, which he preferred (Did/A) because it echoed ἤϋσε at 462.

470 The short vowel of μονωθείς (< μονϝ-) surprises, cf. μουνωθέντα (*Od.*

15.386), μούνωσε (*Od.* 16.117). The short vowel is characteristic of West Ionic (Euboean) and Attic, but is usually admitted into the epic only under metrical necessity.

471 ≅ 17.690 (from μεγάλη and with τέτυκται).

473–84 This picture of a wounded man at bay has no precise parallel in the *Iliad*, where the concept of heroic action is mostly focused on the victorious advance. (Contrast with this the ideal of the fight to the finish in a narrow place that characterizes Germanic and Old French epic.) The rescue of the hero, however, is readily modelled on the motif of the recovery of a corpse: one hero holds off the enemy while his friends drag the body away. In fact the present scene is a miniature of the action of book 17, the recovery of Patroklos' body, where Menelaos and Aias again have a principal role. The situation that preceded Odysseus' wounding reasserts itself, but the position of Odysseus is represented as more desperate.

474 The resumptive verse after the simile (483) has Τρῶες ἕπον, which, as Leaf says, almost guarantees the correction of ἕπονθ' to ἕπον here. The active form, ἀμφιέπω or ἀμφέπω, 'crowd round', is usual in the epic, but corrections that assume archaisms (here Ϝως) are often over-corrections, see Hoekstra, *Modifications* 54, 63.

474–81 This long and complex simile illustrates the movement of the action before it and after it (note the repeated διέτρεσσαν, 481 and 486). Odysseus is the wounded deer set upon by jackals who are then dispersed by the arrival of a lion (Aias). As usual the details are not to be over-interpreted: Odysseus is retreating but he is not deer-like, nor do the Trojans inflict any further harm on him, and still less does Aias set about *him*, see Moulton, *Similes* 46, and for similar anticipatory similes 15.271–6n. bT warn against the generalization of the comparison; Odysseus is not like a deer in spirit, a point that should be borne in mind when Aias is likened to a donkey at 558 below.

476–8 The idea that a wound, if not fatal, is not immediately felt echoes the effect of Agamemnon's wound (264–8). So here Odysseus fights on despite his injury.

479–81 For the behaviour of this lion in stealing the jackals' prey see on 3.23–7; there is a pair of thievish lions at 13.198–200. Verses 480–1 of the simile anticipate the action that follows at 483–4.

480 It is hard to attach any appropriate sense to Zenodotus' ἐν νέμεϊ γλαφυρῷ, but *Od.* 12.305 has ἐν λιμένι γλαφυρῷ, which appears to mean a harbour with a narrow entrance and a sheltered interior. For σκιερῷ cf. ἄλσος ὑπὸ σκιερόν (*Od.* 20.278). λῖν: 'lion', see 239n. — δαίμων: see 9.600n. Although a simile is an utterance of the poet himself not a character in the epic, it is an appeal to the experience of the audience and therefore adopts the imprecise language (δαίμων not a named god) of the unprivileged observer. Some god sends the lion but one can only guess which god.

482 δαΐφρονα ποικιλομήτην: here and 5× *Od*. As a generic epithet of heroes δαΐφρων must bear the sense 'war-minded' and be derived from δαΐς, but it is clear that in the *Odyssey* the word has been reinterpreted and associated with δαῆναι: see nn. to 5.181, and West's discussion at *Od*. 1.48–9n. It is possible that 'prudent' was the sense understood here to complement ποικιλομήτην, but we can never be sure of the exact nuances of epithets that appear only as formular attributes.

485 = 7.219 = 17.128. φέρων σάκος ἠΰτε πύργον: see 7.219n., and 15.645–8. for other reminiscences of the 'tower-shield'. Aias is the only hero consistently associated with this cumbrous protection, a fact that has encouraged much speculation about the antiquity of stories about him, see Page, *HHI* 232–5. It is a moot point whether the formula originally meant that the shield looked like a tower or that Aias fought from behind it as one would from a πύργος. The poet can cite some of the tactics appropriate to the tower-shield and apparently understands them, e.g. in the protection of archers, 8.266–72 (perhaps contemporary oriental practice, but cf. the Lion Hunt dagger blade from Shaft Grave IV, Lorimer, *HM* 140 fig. 1), and that understanding was sufficient to prevent σάκος and ἀσπίς falling together as synonyms, although confusion between the two is frequent. See also 526–7n. The expression φέρων σάκος (as opposed e.g. to νωμῆσαι βῶν, 7.238) may be more significant than it seems; there is an epithet φερεσσακής at [Hesiod], *Aspis* 13. σάκος and ἀσπίς are not wholly interchangeable: Akhilleus and Aias have the σάκος, their opponents, Hektor and Aineias, the ἀσπίς, see Whallon, *Formula, Character, and Context* 49–54, for this bias in the use of the terms. — Some MSS add a plus-verse 485a χάλκεον ἑπταβόειον ὅ οἱ Τύχιος κάμε τεύχων (= 7.220), a typical example of 'concordance interpolation'. No elaboration of Aias' equipment is needed here.

487–8 Odysseus' is a disabling wound. It is mentioned again at the same places as Diomedes' (661 = 16.26, 14.29 = 380, 19.48–9) but, again like that of Diomedes, is forgotten in the Funeral Games of book 23.

488 The chariot is clearly that of Menelaos. bT explain that being an islander Odysseus had no chariot, cf. *Od*. 4.605–8. Aias, another islander, never mounts a chariot either.

489–595 Aias covers the withdrawal of Odysseus and slays several Trojans. Meanwhile Hektor has moved 'towards the left', where Paris wounds Makhaon with an arrow. Nestor takes Makhaon back to the ships. Hektor continues to do execution and Zeus forces Aias to retreat. Eurupulos endeavours to second his efforts but is shot by Paris. Finally Aias makes it back to the main Achaean forces

The episode repeats many of the themes used in those preceding: rally and temporary success, retreat under pressure, the menace of Hektor, Paris' archery. To keep the episode parallel with that of Diomedes, 369ff., would call for the wounding of Aias, but poetical necessity – the shape of the narrative to 595 – preserves him. The response to the wounding of Makhaon adumbrates the final scene of the Book, a conversation by the ships. Diomedes and Odysseus were left to make their own way home so that the narrative could remain on the field of battle. Having thus set up his immediate prospect the poet describes Aias' withdrawal in general terms, refusing to be sidetracked into a prolonged *androktasia*. To emphasize the Trojan pressure he gives Paris a final success, the wounding of Eurupolos. As is to be expected the details of Aias' stand and subsequent retreat are typical, see Fenik, *TBS* 105–13.

489 Aias, to 543, is given what appear to be the preliminaries to a normal aggressive *aristeia*. He slays three Trojans and rages like a river in flood, as does the rampant Diomedes at 5.87–92; Hektor avoids him. But the Achaeans are making a fighting retreat and Aias is the hero of defence. His characteristic role reasserts itself from 544. Δόρυκλος: only here, another of Priam's νόθοι, for whom see 102n. It is surprising that the patronymic Πριαμίδης (25× of Hektor) should be given to this nonentity, but cf. 3.356 (Paris, the verse = 7.250 of Hektor!), 4.490 (Antiphos), 6.76 and 13.586 (Helenos), 13.157 (Deiphobos), 20.87 (Lukaon), 20.407 (Poludoros).

490–1 There is some irony in the names of Aias' remaining victims: Πυλάρτης is an epithet of Hades (8.367, 13.415) and Πάνδοκος, 'receiver of all', would be equally appropriate. Λύσ-ανδρος and Πύρ-ασος are self-explanatory. Πύρασος was a place in Thessaly at 2.690; a Πυλάρτης was killed by Patroklos at 16.696.

492–3 Note the similar comparison of the triumphant Diomedes to a torrent in flood at 5.87–92. Damage is the prime point of comparison, but the noise of a flood is as impressive as its destructiveness, cf. the similes at 4.452–5, 16.389–92, 17.263–5, and note κλονέων at 496. Similes such as this almost compel vizualization (ἐνάργεια, ἔμφασις – of the battle as well as the flood), cf. bT at 4.130: 'you can hear the sound of the two rivers'.

493 κατ' ὄρεσφιν: κατά shows that -φι(ν) must here serve as genitive case, see 10.185n.

494 ≅ [Hesiod], *Aspis* 376 but with the usual epithet ὑψίκομοι (as at 23.118). δρῦς ἀζαλέας: the epithet ('dry') is unexpected in this context, for the fact that the timber is dead or shrivelled is pointless. It is possible that the epithet is formular in related contexts or that the phrase means 'brushwood' (in either case cf. ὕλης ἀζαλέης, *Od.* 9.234); but we surely should think of trees uprooted by the torrent. Aristarchus (Arn/A) was puzzled and thought of timber left on the banks by loggers, for which see 4.487 and n.

496 φαίδιμος (5×) is the regular epithet of the Telamonian Aias for this shape and position. The formulas for the two Aiantes are normally kept distinct. The lesser Aias is Ὀϊλῆος ταχὺς Αἴας (7× + 2 variants) only, except at 23.779 where he usurps φαίδιμος from the formular system of his namesake.

497–520 These verses interrupt the main thread of the narrative to look briefly at another part of the battlefield (still, however, within the range of Paris' bow), and for that reason have been widely condemned, see Von der Mühll, *Hypomnema* 197–8, and van Thiel, *Ilias und Iliaden* 367–8. The episode serves, however, through the wounding of Makhaon to anticipate and motivate the important encounter between Nestor and Patroklos.

497 Why is Hektor not opposing Aias? Not this time because Zeus has warned him off, but because he has somehow wandered from the point where he attacked Diomedes and Odysseus (the centre, see 5–9n.) to the edge of the battlefield opposite Nestor and Idomeneus (501), and 'on the left by Skamandros' (498–9). At the present day, that would have to be the Trojan left, but the course of the Skamandros in the *Iliad* is notoriously unclear. T roundly affirm that Skamandros flowed to the left of the camp, i.e. further up the Hellespont, see Cuillandre, *La Droite et la gauche* 64, 99. The presence of Nestor and Idomeneus confirms that it is the left of the Achaean army that is in question here. There is a ford over the river (14.433 (see n.) = 21.1 = 24.692), though no one is said in as many words to cross it when moving between Troy and the Achaean camp. Indeed at 21.3–8 Akhilleus splits the Trojan army, drives some towards the scene of today's action and forces the rest into the river, i.e. for one going southward from the sea the city is towards the left and the river to the right, as is the case at the present day. It may be asked, where does the narrator station himself, as it were, to view the plain of Troy? The gods may sit on Samothrace behind the Achaeans (13.12), or on Ida behind the Trojans (8.47), but the poet's station seems to be with the Achaeans where the detail matters (so that right and left in reference to the battle mean the Achaean right and left, see 13.675n.) or more generally in their ranks, whence no overall view of the armies and their disposition is possible. The poet's picture of the scene may be momentarily confused, for there is something formular about movement ἐπ' ἀριστερά, the 'normal orientation when there is movement from one part of the battlefield to another' (Fenik, *TBS* 41); see also 5.355n., or Hektor's position is simply a graphic detail without military significance. He must be absent from the focus of the narrative here because the poet is entering upon a new thematic structure, the Rebuke Pattern, on which see Fenik, *TBS* 49–52. At 521 Kebriones draws Hektor's attention to Aias' attack.

501 Idomeneus is getting on in years (cf. μεσαιπόλιος, 13.361) and is fitly associated with Nestor. He has made sporadic appearances earlier, but his great moment is yet to come, at 13.210ff. Nestor's activity on the battlefield is strictly hortatory and on this occasion the poet quickly sends him back to the ships. At 5.37–94 the Achaean front rank included, besides Agamemnon and Diomedes, Idomeneus, Menelaos, Meriones, Meges, and Eurupulos (who is soon eliminated, 581–91); at 16.307–50 Patroklos (not in question here), Antilokhos and Thrasumedes, the lesser Aias, Peneleos, Meriones, and Idomeneus. The impression then that Achaean fortunes now depend on the efforts of two superannuated heroes is not strictly true, dramatically effective as it is.

502–37 Pap. 8, the first 'wild' papyrus to be published, has five plus-verses: 504a]voι περ, 509a]χη ἕλοιντο, 513a]voιo, 514a]αλλους, and 519a ὥς ο[. However supplemented they can only have degraded the text, nor is ἕλοιντο (for-οἴατο) an acceptable Homeric form. The pap. omits one verse, 530, q.v. For a full account of its readings, see West, *Ptolemaic Papyri* 103–7. — ὁμίλει (= ἐμάχετο) caught the attention of Aristarchus (Arn/A). Such ironical euphemisms are common: ὀαριστύς (13.291, 17.228), 'warm welcome', 'salvo.'

503 ἔγχεΐ θ' ἱπποσύνῃ τε seems after μέρμερα ῥέζων to express a single idea (unlike 16.809 where it is joined with πόδεσσι), as if Hektor were fighting with his spear from his chariot. What μέρμερα ἔργα could he perform in the ordinary way from his chariot? νέων φάλαγγας, 'the ranks of the young men', is a natural expression but does not recur; its uniqueness must have prompted Aristarchus and his followers to read νεῶν, 'of the ships'. Hektor, however, as yet is nowhere near the ships.

506 παῦσεν ἀριστεύοντα: the idea is formular, cf. παῦσε δὲ χάρμης (2×), but the phrase recurs only at [Hesiod] fr. 33a.23 M–W. Μαχάονα: see 4.193–4n. He was son of Asklepios and brother of Podaleirios, and like him an ἰητρός as well as a warrior. In Homer he is a general practitioner, later poets made Makhaon the surgeon, cf. ἰοὺς ἐκτάμνειν 515, and Podaleirios the pharmacist (φάρμακα πάσσειν), see *Iliupersis* fr. 1 Davies = bT here. It is perhaps for that reason that Podaleirios has a very minor role in the *Iliad*. Makhaon was slain by Eurupulos (son of Telephos), *Little Iliad* fr. 7 Davies.

507 τριγλώχινι (also at 5.393 with ὀϊστῷ) describes a triangular arrowhead (the so-called 'Scythian' type).

509 μετακλινθέντος: the literal use of the simple verb is seen at 19.223–4 ἐπὴν κλίνῃσι τάλαντα | Ζεύς. In Homeric Greek the battle 'is inclined back', the ebb and flow of battle (to use the English metaphor) being compared to the beam of a balance as it moves up and down.

510 Idomeneus has not been heard of since book 8 (263) and will not appear again until 13.210, where he escorts an injured comrade, unnamed, to his hut, after which he plays a major role. His introduction in book 13 reads like an imperfect recollection of this episode.

514 πολλῶν ἀντάξιος: cf. ἀντί νυ πολλῶν (9.116), with the same sense, for the ease with which such composita are created.

515 This harmless verse was missing from Zenodotus' edition and was athetized by Aristarchus and Aristophanes (Did/A). It diminished the doctor's profession, it was alleged, by restricting its scope. In another context the precise scholarship of the Alexandrians might have suggested that the poet made the outstanding instance of the surgeon's skill (ἰοὺς ἐκτάμνειν) stand for the whole. Plato cites 514 without 515 three times (*Symp.* 214b, *Pol.* 297e, *Leg.* 730d), but it cannot be inferred that 515 did not stand in his texts. ἐκτάμνειν (cf. 829) reflects the use of the ἰὸς τριγλώχις (507n.) with its spreading barbs: Iliadic practice, however, is usually to *pull* out the arrow (5.112 and 4.213, 11.397), implying a simple pointed or two-barbed arrowhead. Patroklos, however, used the μάχαιρα to extract an arrow from Eurupulos' thigh at 844–5.

516 Γερήνιος ἱππότα Νέστωρ (also at 655 below): for the epithets see 9.162n.

519–20 Verse 519 is formular (3× *Il.*; with ἐλάαν for ἵππους 3× *Il.*, 3× *Od.*). Verse 520 is an inorganic one. The formular hemistich τὼ δ' οὐκ ἀέκοντε πετέσθην (7× *Il.*, 3× *Od.*) requires no following complement and receives one only here, where the most that could be said against 520 would be that it is otiose, and at 10.531, where it is much less apposite.

From this point to the end of the Book the narrative skilfully maintains its unbroken temporal flow without the awkwardness that may result from the narration of simultaneous events as if they were sequential ('Zieliński's Law'): Nestor departs for the ships; the fighting continues, culminating in the wounding of Eurupulos. Verses 521–95 constitute a sort of parenthesis, a device to fill the time while Nestor is rushing Makhaon back to the ships, cf. bT to 3.2 and Schadewaldt, *Iliasstudien* 77. Obvious parallels are 6.119–236, where Diomedes meets Glaukos while Hektor returns to Troy, and 17.702–61, where the fighting is described as Antilokhos runs to tell Akhilleus of the disaster to Patroklos. Akhilleus notes the arrival of Nestor (599), and despatches Patroklos to him; on his return Patroklos encounters Eurupulos (809), whose painful retreat on foot takes place during Nestor's long homily.

521 Κεβριόνης, a bastard son of Priam (cf. 102n.), was promoted Hektor's driver (παρβεβαώς 522) at 8.318–19 after the death of Archeptolemos. Hektor's charioteers played a hazardous role, and Kebriones was himself killed by Patroklos at 16.737. The name is North West Anatolian, the root Κεβρ- appearing in many place, river and tribal names in that area, see e.g. Strabo 13.1.3.

524 The edge of the battle is by the Skamandros, see 497n.

526–7 Kebriones recognizes Aias' shield. The armour of Diomedes (5.182) and Akhilleus (16.40–2) was also distinctive. It is not clear, however, what was special for Kebriones about Aias' gear: the formula σάκος εὐρύ (3× *Il.*, 1× *Od.*) is applied to the shields of Antilokhos (13.552), Menelaos (13.608), and Laertes (*Od.* 22.184), as well as that of Aias (17.132), and therefore cannot have a specific reference to the famous σάκος ἠΰτε πύργον of Aias (485n.), which would be tall rather than wide. Yet the 'broad shield' of Aias was felt to be characteristic of him; his son by Tekmessa was named Eurusakes. It must be remembered that the poet is unlikely ever to have seen a tower-shield or a representation of one, and probably thought of a big shield, such as Aias (an impressive figure – πελώριος, 3.166 etc.) wielded to protect Teukros at 8.267ff., as a broad shield. When the poet described its manufacture at 7.219–23 he omitted to mention its shape or decoration. Convention usually permitted warriors on the opposite side to be recognized directly, and no reference is made to blazons such as those attributed to Agamemnon's equipment at 11.26–40. The shield is said to be worn across the shoulders because (whatever type was in the poet's mind) it was carried on a baldric. For the epithets of Homeric shields and the types they may represent see D. H. F. Gray, *CQ* 41 (1947) 109 (= *Language and Background* 55), Whallon, *Formula, Character and Context* 34–54, or Trümpy, *Fachausdrücke* 30–1.

528–30 Where was the fiercest fight, on the left or around Odysseus? The expression ἔνθα μάλιστα … βοὴ δ' ἄσβεστος ὄρωρεν(=499–500) draws attention to the minor contradiction between the two scenes, a trivial example of 'thematic override' by which the generic concept of the battle takes precedence over a particular context.

529 ἱππῆες πεζοί τε: cf. πεζοί θ' ἱππῆές τε (2.810, *Od.* 24.70), a loose formular group. The mention of ἱππῆες in 52 and 151 keeps that element of the army at the front of the oral composer's mind. Pap. 8 has κοῦροί τ[ε ἱππῆές τε …, a trivialization, but must, or should, have ended the verse with a finite verb (προφέρονται van Leeuwen), since 530 is missing from its text. ἔριδα προβαλόντες: for the metaphor cf. ἔριδα προφέρονται (3.7). προβάλλω (for προφέρω) suits the violent tone of the present episode.

530 ἀλλήλους ὀλέκουσι recurs at 18.172 but at the verse-end; βοὴ δ' ἄσβεστος ὀρώρει is a formular half-verse (5×). Bolling (*Evidence* 134) and others, disliking this mode of composition, preferred the shorter text of Pap. 8. In fact Kebriones' mention of the noise of battle in his speech neatly picks up its mention in the narrative at 500.

533 = 17.458.

534–7 ≅ 20.499–502: clear ground was hardly come by on the Homeric battlefield, cf. 8.491 = 10.199. Commentators, e.g. Schadewaldt, *Iliasstudien* 7–8, generally regard the context of the run as better in book 20, *contra* van der Valk, *Researches* II 457–8. There has been enough slaughter in this Book to justify this grim picture.

534 This verse, together with 16.774 πολλὰ δὲ χερμάδια μεγάλ' ἀσπίδας ἐστυφέλιξαν, is the source according to Leumann of the ghost-word (ἀ)σπιδής, 'plain', see 754n.

538–9 ἐν δὲ κυδοιμὸν | ἧκε κακόν = 52–3 (with ὧρσε, Zeus as subject). μίνυνθα δὲ χάζετο δουρός, 'withdrew from the spear for (only) a short time', is a curious expression, variously understood – 'did not give way when he had thrown his spear but followed it up at once' (Monro), perhaps 'lost no time in joining the fight'. For the litotes cf. 16.736, where οὐδὲ δὴν χάζετο φωτός means 'attacked him forthwith'.

540–1 = 264–5 (Agamemnon, after his wounding). The verses describe the appropriate behaviour of a commander who, for whatever reason, is not actually fighting, whether the wounded Agamemnon or the cautious Hektor.

542 For all its elaborate introduction Hektor's intervention changes the situation not a whit. The duel in book 7 has shown that he is no match in fair fight for Aias, and therefore the two must not be allowed to meet. Aias' retreat, however, must continue and is therefore attributed to the action of Zeus.

543–74 *Aias at bay.* Aias' retreat here is described in the same heroic terms as that of book 17. The scene repeats with greater ornamentation the picture of Odysseus at bay drawn at 473ff.: a powerful and vivid episode, but only if Aias is understood to fight on the same terms as other men. There was a story (see Arn/A on 14.402) that Aias, like Akhilleus, was invulnerable save in one spot, in Aias' case the neck. This kind of fantasy, beloved by the Cyclic poets (see Griffin, *JHS* 97 (1977) 39–53), is austerely excluded from the *Iliad*.

543 This verse has no support in the medieval paradosis but is cited with slight variations by Arist. *Rhet.* 1387a35, Plutarch, *Mor.* 24c, and [Plutarch], *Vit. Hom.* 2.132. It is ignored by the scholia. Plutarch's text lacked 541 (= 265), but that verse is attested here in two papyri (Pap. 25 and Pap. 60) and by the medieval paradosis. Verse 542 would not be missed either by the modern reader, but the Homeric audience would want to know how it was that the leading attacker (Hektor) did not come face to face with the leading defender (Aias), cf. 163–4n. The interpolated verse 543 then was intended to explain why Hektor avoided Aias, but the iterative νεμέσασχ' and the optative μάχοιτο cannot refer to this single incident.

544 The formula ἐν φόβον ὧρσε (3×) usually implies flight, the outward manifestation of fear. 'Flight' is rather strong for Aias' reluctant retreat, in his own time, ὀλίγον γόνυ γουνὸς ἀμείβων (547), but retreating he is, so that the formula used with less than usual precision is not ἐν φόβον ὧρσε here but στῆ δὲ ταφών in 545.

545 ὄπιθεν δὲ σάκος βάλεν: this phrase (like the fate of Periphetes, 15.645–7) must be a fragment of the poetry of tower-shield warfare. No round-shield bearer would expose his unprotected lower limbs in this manner. With the tower-shield its wearer could turn his back on the enemy, being protected from neck to ankle, cf. 6.117 ἀμφὶ δέ μιν σφυρὰ τύπτε καὶ αὐχένα δέρμα κελαινόν. Leaf compares the elliptical expression μετὰ νῶτα βαλών at 8.94, which describes the action of a fleeing man. Spearmen with the tower-shield slung across their backs are depicted on the lion-hunt dagger-blades from the shaft-graves, though they are there advancing not retreating and we cannot be dogmatic about the conventions of the drawing.

546–7 θηρί evidently means a lion, as at 119 and 15.633. The expression θηρὶ ἐοικώς seems to anticipate, or to suggest, the extended simile that follows at 548ff. — ἐντροπαλιζόμενος: Menelaos used the same tactic, shield unspecified, during his retreat at 17.108–15. παπτήνας (546), cf. παπταίνων (17.115). The situation both here and in book 17 leads to a lion simile.

548–57 Zenodotus omitted the lion simile, probably out of his hostility to repetition. Arn/A guess that he thought the lion incompatible with the ass simile that follows, and make the obvious reply that two aspects of Aias' defence are illustrated. The common factor is Aias' tenacity under attack, although in the simile the attacker is the lion. — This simile is the fifth in a series (see 292ff., 324ff., 414ff., 474ff.) which pit single wild beasts against packs of dogs and men: an indication of the way in which the poet conceives the battle. The Achaean πρόμαχοι are being pressed hard by the Trojan λαός. The image continues into book 12 (12.41ff., 12.146ff., 12.299ff.). The simile is substantially repeated in book 17 (548 ≅ 17.657, 550–5 = 17.659–65) where it is used to illustrate the retreat of Menelaos from the defence of Patroklos' body; for repeated similes see 9.14–15n., and Moulton, *Similes* 94 – the implication, of course, is that such comparisons at least are traditional.

549 = 15.272, but there the men and hounds are pursuing a stag or wild goat. Aristarchus (Did/A) read ἐσσεύοντο here but -αντο at 15.272 (see n.), perhaps for lack of a concordance (but see van der Valk, *Researches* II 172); -οντο is the vulgate in both places. Leaf, retaining the vulgate, takes it as a thematic aorist. A timeless present or aorist indicative, or a subjunctive, is expected in a simile. ἀγροιῶται = ἀγρόται (*Od.* 16.218) *metri gratia*, cf. Risch, *Wortbildung* 35. It becomes a term of abuse in the mouth of the suitor Antinoos (*Od.* 21.85), like βουγάϊος (13.824).

550–5 πῖαρ is certainly neuter but can hardly be an adjective after βοῶν. At *Od.* 9.135, πῖαρ ὑπ' οὖδας, the syntax is ambivalent, but a noun is required here: πῖαρ = 'fat (i.e. choicest) one or part'. πάννυχοι (for παννύχιοι) occurs only here and in the parallel passage in book 17.

555–6 τετιηότι and τετιημένος illustrate the nice distinction in sense between the intransitive perfect active (which will admit but does not require a causative agent) and the perfect passive (of which the question ὑπὸ τίνος can always in principle be asked). The variation is rather pointless, for the epic style would not object to the repetition of the formula τετιηότι θυμῷ.

558–62 The simile of the ass in the cornfield is unparalleled, but like many other topics used once only is clearly drawn from daily life. It may not, however, be 'original'; there was a proverb ὄνος βαδίζεις εἰς ἄχυρα τραγημάτων (Philemon fr. 188). Heroes are normally compared to 'noble' animals, lions, boars, or stallions, whose courage is easily imputed to the hero even if it is not the point of comparison. Ideas of Aias' characterization have not been helped by the contrast drawn between him and Odysseus – in the poems of the Cycle, not in the *Iliad* – as if Aias symbolized brute unthinking brawn in opposition to the other's sharpness and subtlety. The Iliadic Aias was characterized by ἰδρείη (7.198), at least in his own estimation, and Hektor recognized his πινυτή (7.289). Hektor's jeer at 13.824 Αἶαν ἁμαρτοεπές, βουγάϊε, is mere abuse. Here the point of the simile is that Aias shrugs off the Trojan attacks and retreats only when he is ready to do so. It implies tenacity not stupidity, or even obstinacy, and so illustrates Aias' *forte*, the αὐτοσταδίη, in which he did not yield even to Akhilleus (see Idomeneus' comment, 13.321–25). The eventual departure of the ass foreshadows the eventual escape of Aias from his present predicament. In general, Homeric similes, being drawn from the concrete world of nature, maintain the same observer's style as the narrative. They do not directly affirm permanent ethical traits. bT have an elaborate note on this comparison (cited by Edwards, vol. v 30).

This the fifteenth and last simile of the Book. Similes find typical slots in the pattern of battle narrative of which they form the characteristic ποικιλία (see 62n., 67–9n.). The character of the narrative changes shortly, at 596, from the ferocity of the battlefield to the leisurely discourse of Nestor and Patroklos, and with the change ornamentation by simile drops out.

559 ἐάγη: the long -ᾱ- is hard to explain, see *LfgrE* s.v. ἄγνυμι and Wyatt, *ML* 78–9. Confusion with the perfect stem seen in ἔαγα (Hesiod, *Erga.* 534) is possible, though (κατ)έηγα is the usual Ionic form.

564–74 With this picture of Aias fending off the Trojans compare the retreat of Antilokhos at 13.551–9. The details are similar: the ineffective bombardment with spears and the tactic of alternate retreat and turning to fight (cf. Fenik, *TBS* 98). The diction of the two passages, however, has nothing in common.

564 ≅ 6.111 = 9.233 (see n.). The reading πολυηγερέες (for τηλεκλειτοί) is due to Aristarchus (Did/AT). πολυηγερέες, a *hapax legomenon*, is apposite here, though that does not guarantee that it is right. The formular verse, with τηλεκλειτοί, is in the vocative case.

571–4 = 15.314–17 but with ἄλλα μὲν ἐν χροῖ πῆγνυτ' ἀρηϊθόων αἰζηῶν for 572. There is a variant χρόα καλόν – the regular formula (14× including a variant χρόα κάλλιμον) – in both places but the direction of corruption is obvious and χρόα λευκόν (not found outside this repeated couplet) must be retained. One is surprised to read that the skin of the quintessentially masculine Aias was white after so many battle-weary days under the Trojan sun; when Odysseus was beautified by Athene he became μελαγχροιής (*Od.* 16.175). Mycenaean fresco-painters and archaic and classical vase-painters maintained a convention that female flesh was white (cf. the epithet λευκώλενος of Here and mortal women and the πήχεε λευκώ of Aphrodite at 5.314) but male flesh was brown. Presumably here the flesh is light in contrast to something perceived as dark, perhaps the 'black' blood for which the missiles thirsted (λιλαιόμενα). See further Russo on *Od.* 18.196.

572 πάγεν: a leather shield, such as is often envisaged where the poet is not describing a de luxe article faced with bronze, would indeed be prone to catch and hold javelins that struck it. Note the absence of glancing blows to the Homeric shield; the pathos of an 'accidental death', like that of Kebriones at 16.733ff., results from a spear missing its target.

574 = 15.317; the singular has γαίῃ ἐνεστήρικτο for ἐν γαίῃ ἵσταντο at 21.168, with a variant at 21.70. λιλαιόμενα χροὸς ἆσαι is a formular but effective personification, cf. 12.18n., 13.444n. W. B. Stanford, *Greek Metaphor* 138–9, lists similar personifications, see also vol. v 51. Aristotle liked the figure as being a major aspect of poetical genius, see *Poet.* 1459a4, *Rhet.* 1411b31. It is a question, however, whether the personification is a rhetorical fancy of the poet or an animistic aspect of popular speech; in a world where wind (5.524), rivers (12.18), fire (23.177, etc.), the sun (*Od.* 10.160), are said to have μένος, weapons may easily share the μένος of the hands that hurl them. The personification of weapons in Homer, however, if it is such, does not extend to their being given names, as the sword Durandel in *Roland*, presumably because the principal weapon, the spear, is thrown and easily lost: significantly the nearest thing to a named weapon in the *Iliad*, the Πηλιὰς μελίη of Akhilleus, is a thrusting spear.

575–95 Paris' third victim. Eurupulos, leader of a Thessalian contingent (2.734–7), rushes forward to help Aias but is immediately wounded and forced to withdraw. With this scene, which balances that of Makhaon, 504ff., the long sequence of battle scenes is completed. When it is resumed in book 12 the Achaeans are back where they started, behind their wall and ditch. The final stages of the retreat as the army crowds into the camp are not described. The poet can imagine such a scene, even down to pathetic detail ('Is X safe? Has Y been slain?'), cf. 21.606–11, 22.46–8, but in spite of its evident possibilities nowhere gives it full treatment. This is surprising, for Greek heroic warfare is waged for the most part about a besieged town and would, it may be supposed, have developed the appropriate themes and diction.

575–6 This Eurupulos is a person of some consequence, one of Helen's suitors indeed (Apollod. 1.131). In the first clashes of the *Iliad* he slew Hupsenor (5.76–83), and is mentioned in books 6, 7, 8, and 10. Patroklos treats him with respect (814ff.) and acts as his surgeon. The poet would have known another Eurupulos, son of Telephos and last of the Trojan allies, who enjoyed an *aristeia* in the *Little Iliad*.

577–95 A heavily formular passage: 577 ≅ 4.496, etc. (3×); 578–9 ≅ 17.348–9 with Ἱππασίδην for Φαυσιάδην (17.348–9, with another Apisaon, in their turn ≅ 13.411–12 which have Ὑψήνορα for Ἀπισάονα: a good instance of the poet's juggling with his onomastic resources). The primary name is probably Apisaon son of Hippasos, for Hippasos was a king of Sikuon and Apesas was a mountain near Nemea (Paus. 2.13.2; Hesiod, *Theog.* 331); see the discussion in Hoekstra, *Epic Verse before Homer* 63–4. Once more the poet allows a glimpse into the vast quantity of 'knowledge' preserved by the tradition of heroic poetry. — Verse 585 = 3.32, etc. (7×). The answering verse (στῆ δὲ μεταστρεφθείς, ἐπεὶ ἵκετο ἔθνος ἑταίρων, 595 = 15.591 = 17.114) is not so strongly formular: 586–7 = 17.247–8 (see 275–6n. above): 589–91, cf. 18.306–8 οὔ μιν ἔγωγε | φεύξομαι ἐκ πολέμοιο δυσηχέος, ἀλλά μιν ἄντην | στήσομαι; 593 = 13.488.

578–9 Apisaon's being run through the liver is a routine part of the pornography of wounds, though not so nasty as the death of Tros (20.469–71), whose liver fell out through his wound. The problem of protecting the abdomen, where in reality any wound was likely to mean a lingering and unpleasant death, without immobilizing the waist was never solved by Greek armourers. For the singularly uncomfortable μίτρη, a Cretan invention, see H. Brandenburg, *Arch. Hom.* E 119–43 with plates x and xi. The name Apisaon is used only in these two incidents. Phausios may be < φαϝ-, 'bright', *pace* Watlelet, *Dictionnaire* ii 1046. The combination of un-Hellenic names in two generations would be unusual, but cf. Axulos and Teuthras at 6.13, Hurtios and Gurtios at 14.511.

580–4 Once again a hero exposes himself to attack in order to plunder a corpse, cf. the wounding of Diomedes, 375ff. and n. As usual in these circumstances the injury is to the right side of the body.

590 πολέμοιο δυσηχέος (7× *Il.* only): war was a noisy business in the epic, but the use of the epithet with θάνατος (3×) suggests that the singers associated it with ἄχος, 'grief'. Add δυσηχής therefore to the other negative but formular evaluations of the principal heroic activity: αἱματόεις, ἀργαλέος, δακρυόεις, δυσηλεγής, κακός, λευγαλέος, ὀϊζυρός, πολύδακρυς, στυγερός, and φθισήνωρ.

592–5 Eurupulos advanced towards Aias' isolated position (577), killed

Apisaon, and was then wounded. He withdrew within the defensive 'hedgehog' of his companions. Aias followed, shield doubtless over his shoulders and therefore facing the Achaeans (τῶν ἀντίος, 594). Received into their ranks he then turned to face the enemy (595). At this point we leave the battlefield until the beginning of book 12.

593–4 σάκε' ὤμοισι κλίναντες | δούρατ' ἀνασχόμενοι: what is this posture? See 22.4n., and Leaf *ad locc.* The context requires it to be some sort of defensive formation to cover the wounded Eurupulos and into whose protection Aias can withdraw, but it is difficult to imagine a satisfactory posture for a man 'leaning his shield on his shoulders' while 'holding up his spear (or spears)'. Perhaps he held a spear in each hand, letting the shield hang by its strap. It has been thought that σάκε' ὤμοισι κλίναντες may mean that the lower edges of these (tower?) shields rested on the ground (Lorimer, *HM* 188). — Verse 593 = 13.488 and (from σάκε') 22.4. δούρατ' ἀνασχόμενοι is also formular (3×).

596–617 Not without a feeling of satisfaction, mixed with curiosity, Akhilleus observes the wounded brought back to the ships. He sends Patroklos to investigate

It is the poet's practice, in those battle Books from which Akhilleus is absent, to remind his audience as he does here of the hero's reputation and brooding presence, cf. 2.241, 4.512, 5.788, 6.414ff., 7.113, 8.225, etc.

596 (= 13.673, 18.1, and without αἰθομένοιο 17.366): a formular verse marking a transition to a new episode. Fire is the type of something that, like war, rages (19× *Il.*, 1× *Od.*).

597 Nestor left the battlefield at 520. Νηλήϊαι ἵπποι: Homeric horses, unlike those of most later Greek poetry, are usually masculine where the gender is clear. Mares are specifically so designated (θήλειαι, 2.767, 5.269, 11.680, 20.222, cf. 23.376), or given feminine forms of their epithets (ὠκειάων, 4.500, 7.15, 7.240). Nestor's steeds are curiously epicene, masculine at 8.81, 8.104, feminine at 8.113 and here, masculine again at 23.310, for no rational purpose. It is pure surmise that a feminine ἵπποι has replaced a descendant of the Myc. *i-qi-ja* (so Lee, *BICS* 6 (1959) 8–17).

598 ἱδρῶσαι: a rare contraction, cf. ἱδρώουσα (11.119); ζῶντος (1.88) is the nearest other analogue. Meister, *Kunstsprache* 90–2 discusses these forms.

599 τὸν δὲ ἰδὼν ἐνόησε seems prolix but results from the interplay of formulas: τὸν δὲ ἰδὼν ∪∪–∪ (9×) + ἐνόησε (23× in that position).

600 Akhilleus chooses a point of vantage to survey the field. The ships are drawn up on the beach stern first according to normal practice, see Hoekstra, *Od.* 13.114–15n. Thus when Hektor reaches the ships (which is not till 15.704) it is the stern of the ship of Protesilaos that he seizes. It is a nice touch that Akhilleus should be watching the battle with interest, as if he cannot bear to be altogether absent from his *métier* (so bT here), but the point can be overstressed. The poet is motivating the despatch of Patroklos and his meeting with Nestor. Akhilleus had felt no need to survey the field personally during the events of 2–8 and when his ignorance of the career and death of Patroklos becomes an important motif then he is kept at ground level (18.3). μεγακήτεϊ: for the epithet see 5n.

601 πόνον αἰπύν (2× *Il.* in OCT, see 17.364–5n.): the metaphorical sense of αἰπύς (literally 'steep') is evidently 'hard to overcome' or, in the common αἰπὺς ὄλεθρος, 'impossible to overcome'. For the literal and figurative uses of this word see *LfgrE* s.v. The figurative usage has spread to a number of other dissyllabic nouns, φόνος, χόλος, and (in Hesiod) δόλος, with which it makes a metrically convenient unit.

602 In formular use προσέειπε would be followed by direct speech. The habit is broken here (and nowhere else) partly by the intrusion of the participial clause φθεγξάμενος παρὰ νῆος, and partly by the fact that Akhilleus could be made to say little more than 'Come here'. The *Iliad* avoids very short passages of direct speech. Patroklos' response at 606 is the only instance of a single verse of direct speech before 18.182.

604 ἔκμολεν ἶσος Ἄρηϊ describes a dramatic entry, as if Patroklos had heard a summons to arms. ἶσος Ἄρηϊ is a compliment otherwise (except at 12.130, see n.) reserved for Akhilleus at 20.46 and Hektor at 11.295 and 13.802, cf. ἶσος Ἐνυαλίῳ (22.132, of Akhilleus), and ἀτάλαντος Ἄρηϊ (8.215, 17.72, of Hektor). The phrase is a reminder that Patroklos is not only the gentlest of the heroes but also a warrior of the first class. κακοῦ ... ἀρχή: the poet likes to notice the ἀρχή of something cf. 5.63, 22.116, *Od.* 8.81, but as a reflection on the past course of events. Here he is looking forward, but looking forward a remarkably long way (cf. 10.336n., 11.163n.) and making a precise foreshadowing of events in book 16 some 3,000 verses ahead (προῳκονόμησε τοῦτο ὁ ποιητής, but just enough to whet the appetite, as Arn/A and bT observe). The despatch of Patroklos is, of course, a pathetic touch which is underlined by Nestor's appeal at 796ff. that Patroklos might be permitted to aid the Achaeans if Akhilleus will not; but, like so many of the poet's skilful touches, it has also a technical function in setting up a narrative goal; it is a corollary of this that the intervening material, brilliantly told as it is, is an Aristotelian ἐπεισόδιον or, in modern parlance, a 'retardation'.

605 Having mentioned Patroklos as Akhilleus' ἑταῖρος at 602 the poet now mentions his father Menoitios. This could well be read as a discreet introduction of a new character, had not the patronymic Μενοιτιάδης made its appearance without further explanation at 1.307 (where see n.). But it should be borne in mind that in a poem of the *Iliad*'s probable provenance there is no such thing as a new character, even if that character was created by the poet, as some have thought (see vol. IV 313). As the product of an oral tradition the *Iliad*-story as we have it was not sung to an audience who had never heard it before and needed explanations of its personnel; it is the product of many singings, each a rehearsal for the next. Menoitios is called Ἄκτορος υἱός at 785, 16.14. This Aktor is probably the son of Murmidon noted by [Hesiod] fr. 10a.101 M–W; Pind. *Ol.* 9.70 adds his wife Aigina. Since *she* was mother of Aiakos, grandfather of Akhilleus, it would follow that Akhilleus and Patroklos were kin. [Hesiod] (fr. 212a M–W = Eust. 112.44–5) actually made Menoitios a brother of Peleus, if reported correctly. If Homer knew this genealogy in any form he is careful to suppress it. Cf. 2.558n. for the Catalogue's treatment of Aias and Telamon.

606 For χρεώ with acc. of the person in need see 9.75n. The correption of -εω- after synizesis is harsh, especially towards the verse-end.

608–15 Nestor's opening remarks at 656–68 provide a gloss to Akhilleus' words. Nestor makes a distinction between ὀλοφύρεσθαι (which Akhilleus' present enquiry implies) and κήδεσθαι or ἐλεαίρειν (which mean 'show pity' by some positive action rather than 'feel pity'). An appeal had been made to Akhilleus' pity by Odysseus at 9.301–3 without effect, and Aias had commented on his hardness of heart at 9.628–38, as Patroklos will do again at 16.29–35; we should not see therefore in Akhilleus' curiosity the first stirrings of some concern for the effects of his anger on his friends. On the contrary the opening verses of the speech sound a distinctly vindictive note, and it is appropriate that they should; the more Akhilleus is perceived as concerned solely with his own honour the greater will be felt the shock of remorse at the disaster to Patroklos which that selfish concern brings about.

608 τῷ ἐμῷ κεχαρισμένε θυμῷ, cf. 19.287, is a comradely form of address, cf. 5.243 (Sthenelos to Diomedes), 5.826 (Athene to Diomedes), *Od.* 4.71 (Telemakhos to Peisistratos), and was so understood by Virgil, *Aen.* 12.142 *animo gratissima [carissima* PRb] *nostro* (Juno to Juturna). See 786n. for relations between Akhilleus and Patroklos. Note the trivial expansion of the formula by the prefixed article. μοι . . . πλεῖστον κεχαρισμένε θυμῷ at 19.287 is a more violent modification of the same formula.

609 Cf. 16.72–3 εἴ μοι κρείων Ἀγαμέμνων | ἤπια εἰδείη. These two passages cannot be reconciled with a previous appeal to Akhilleus such as we have in book 9, except by rather forced argument, e.g. that the content of a scene is always relevant only to its immediate context and may ignore what is to come and what has been, or that 'This phraseology admittedly ignores book 9 and its attempt at conciliation, but in my opinion it might be explicable either as a pardonable oversight by a single poet or even as a deliberate neglect by Achilles of offers which were unaccompanied by any frank admission of Agamemnon's high-handedness' (Kirk, *Songs*

214). On that argument Akhilleus should now be anticipating what he received after a fashion in book 19, a public acknowledgement by Agamemnon of his ἄτη (cf. 1. 411–12 and 9.372–3 – where Agamemnon is taunted for acting by proxy); yet Akhilleus says nothing here about frank admissions on Agamemnon's part, Agamemnon being not so much as mentioned. περὶ γούνατα στῆναι λισσομένους, it may be said, implies a more humble posture than that assumed by Odysseus and Aias in book 9 (see 9.501n.), but the lack of it did not form there any part of Akhilleus' complaint. The verses therefore remain a strong indication that the Embassy is among the latest of the ideas and episodes built into the *Iliad* whose contribution to the poem is here and in book 16 overridden by an older concept of a vengeful Akhilleus; they do not of themselves, of course, indicate when or at whose hands the evolution of the tale of Akhilleus took that form. See introduction to book 9 and 2.51–2nn. for the methodology adopted in this commentary in the face of such inconsistencies, and also Page, *HHI* 305–6, and Schadewaldt, *Iliasstudien* 81. The thesis that in oral or oral-derived composition the poet habitually looks forward to the next narrative goal (cf. introduction to book 10) explains silences with respect to preceding events, but not contradictions.

610 = 10.118 where see n.

611–15 Patroklos is now given the role of messenger. He has previously performed humble tasks for Akhilleus, having acted as server (9.201ff.), officiant (9.219), and major-domo (9.658). These were normally the tasks of κήρυκες, cf. *Od.* 7.178 (server), *Il.* 12.351 (messenger). Patroklos is, in comparison with Akhilleus, remarkably lacking in heroic self-assertiveness. Even so his being assigned these humble roles seems to reflect the poet's desire to bring him by any means to his audience's attention as Akhilleus' ἑταῖρος before his debut as warrior in book 16.

611 Contraction in the classical verb always affects the personal ending, but epic forms in which the termination is unaffected and contraction of the root and thematic vowels takes place are attested, cf. αἰδεῖο (< αἰδέ-ε-ο, 24.503), μυθεῖαι (*Od.* 8.180), νεῖαι (*Od.* 11.114, 12.141, < -ε-ε-αι); so here ἔρειο *sic*, for ἐρεῖο < ἐρέ-ε-ο, with the same form of the root as ἐρέονται (8.445, etc.).

615 παρήϊξαν: we should not enquire by what gate Agamemnon, Diomedes, and Odysseus entered the camp, for up to this point the scene of the narrative has been the battlefield, not the camp. Akhilleus is assumed to be in ignorance of their fate – he first hears of it at 16.23ff. The wounded Makhaon, however, was driven past (παρ-) Akhilleus' quarters, which were on the Achaean extreme right, a detail that is necessary to motivate Akhilleus' interest. With the shift of the narrative to the camp the detail of the Achaean retreat becomes clearer. At 12.118 it is stated that the Achaeans retreated within their fortifications by a gate νηῶν ἐπ' ἀριστερά.

617 Patroklos runs off towards the centre of the Achaean encampment. He does not start his return journey until 15.405. Many of the intervening events, especially in book 12, though narrated in the usual linear fashion, may be understood as simultaneous if Patroklos' absence seems unduly prolonged. In the plan of the *Iliad*, of course, it is essential for the returning Patroklos to bring news dire enough to motivate the events of book 16.

618–69 Patroklos finds Nestor taking refreshment after his return from the battle-field and delivers his message. Nestor reports the disasters that have just occurred. All this, however, is preliminary to Nestor's making an oblique appeal to Akhilleus

The passage, down to 654, illustrates the epic's characteristic love for the detail of the heroic world: the unyoked horses, the slave woman and her story, Nestor's refreshment, his special cup. Length, however (αὔξησις as the scholiasts say), is correlated with significance in Homer. The reason, therefore, why the love of detail is indulged at this point is that it is part of the important scene between Nestor and Patroklos in which the fatal intervention of the latter is adumbrated.

619–21 For a fuller scene of unyoking and stabling see *Od.* 4.39–42; the horses are fed and the chariot carefully stowed.

620 Eurumedon is named as Nestor's charioteer at 8.114 also. Agamemnon's charioteer was another Eurumedon (4.228). It is not clear why the name was suitable for that profession, but cf. Automedon, Akhilleus' charioteer. The simplex μέδων means 'ruling', but could conceivably have been interpreted as 'driving' *vel sim.*, cf. Lat. *rego* for a similar development in the reverse direction. The etymological dictionaries are unhelpful.

621 ἱδρῶ ἀπεψύχοντο χιτώνων clearly means that Eurupulos, despite his injury, and Nestor dried off their sweat-soaked clothing in the sea-breeze. The same verb is used of washing off sweat at 21.561.

623 On the κλισμός and other Homeric chairs see West on *Od.* 1.130, Richter, *Furniture* 13, and for ancient attempts to differentiate them Athenaeus 192E (δίφρος, κλισμός, θρόνος, in ascending order of grandeur). Having seated himself on a κλισμός here Nestor arises from a θρόνος at 645. Such sets of quasi-synonyms are regularly used to denote the same object (see Introduction 13–14).

624 κυκειῶ: see 638–41n. Hekamede, like other women in the *Iliad*, is represented as a prize of war. Her name was perhaps suggested by her role in preparing the restorative κυκειών, cf. Ἀγαμήδην, ἣ τόσα φάρμακα ἤδη ... 740–1, or may come from heroic tales of Akhilleus' raids; but her father Arsinoos bears a name with possible Messenian connexions, cf. the nymph Ἀρσινόη of Messene, Paus. 4.31.6 (< ἄρδειν, 'to make wet', + νοά 'spring'), as if the present context put the poet in mind of Pylian traditions. For a female as οἰνοχόος, a service usually performed by κοῦροι, one may compare Hebe among the gods (4.2ff.). Hekamede reappears at 14.6 preparing a hot bath for Makhaon.

625 Another note of Akhilleus' raids on the satellite towns of Troy, see 9.328–9. Tenedos, however, was the Achaeans' rendezvous on their way to Troy in the *Cypria*. Tenedos' roles as host and victim are by no means incompatible, for Akhilleus' forays are a reminder that heroic war was the pursuit of plunder, not a calculated strategy. (In another strand of tradition Lemnos figured as the Achaeans' staging post, see 2.718–22, 8.230n.)

628–9 τράπεζαν: Greek tables were low, light, and portable. For Homeric furniture in general see 9.200n. The decoration is reminiscent of that listed on the Pylos Ta series of tablets, see Ventris and Chadwick, *Documents* 332–5.

630 A metal κάνεον ('bowl' therefore or 'basin' rather than 'basket') is attested also at *Od.* 10.355. 'An onion' (κρόμυον) 'as seasoning for the drink' is an unexplained complication of the recipe for the κυκειών. This incidental onion is one of the few mentions of vegetables in the *Iliad*, see W. Richter, *Arch. Hom.* H 123–7. Meat is the food for heroes (and for gentlemen – Pepys and Woodforde, for example, on the evidence of their diaries, dined almost exclusively on flesh). Athenaeus (24F–25E) discusses the Homeric diet.

631 ἀλφίτου ἱεροῦ ἀκτήν is probably formular, recurring at *Od.* 2.355, 14.429 without ἱεροῦ. ἀλφίτου is genitive of ἄλφιτα; there is no singular ἄλφιτον, but ἀλφίτων would be unmetrical. Shipp, *Studies* 191, aptly points to the correspondence of παλύνας ἀλφίτου ἀκτῇ (*Od.* 14.429) to ἄλφιτα λευκὰ πάλυνε (*ibid.* 77). Hesiod had naturally more use for ἀκτή; his principal formula is Δημήτερος ἱερὸν ἀκτήν (3× Hesiod *Erga*) – whence the v.l. ἱερόν here – or more briefly Δημήτερος ἀκτήν (2× *Il.*, *Erga* 32, *Aspis* 290). Outside these formulas (apart from a few imitations) the word is unknown, and must be an epic fossil. The sense 'meal' suggested a connexion with ἄγνυμι to the D scholia (but that is Ϝάγνυμι); *LfgrE* compares Skt *aś-nā-ti*, 'eat'.

632–5 The description of Nestor's famous cup, see G. Bruns, *Arch. Hom.* G 42–3, Lorimer, *HM* 328–35. The word δέπας is apparently of Anatolian origin, cf. Hitt. *tapišana-*. Commentators' conceptions of the vessel change as archaeological material accumulates, see E. Vermeule, *Greece in the Bronze Age* (Chicago 1964) 309–11. The doves recall the well-known gold cup from the fourth shaft-grave at Mycenae, but that is probably a libation vessel and the birds that decorate its handles are falcons (so S. Marinatos, *Festschrift*

B. *Schweitzer* (Stuttgart 1954) 11–12), see also Webster, *Mycenae to Homer* 33, 112, A. Heubeck, *Die homerische Frage* (Darmstadt 1974) 222; and four handles are represented on Linear B ideograms depicting a vessel called *di-pa*, discussed by Ventris and Chadwick, *Documents* 326–7. The δύω πυθμένες may refer to a double or false bottom as found in many household pots from Crete (so Webster, *op. cit.* 112), but are usually taken either as 'supports' to the handles as in the cup from Mycenae, or as legs, cf. 18.375, where πυθμήν denotes the leg of a tripod. The Ischia skyphos (e.g. L. H. Jeffery, *The Local Scripts of Archaic Greece* (Oxford 1961) 235, pl. 47), though describing itself as 'Nestor's', sheds no light on the shape of the Homeric cup. Aristarchus (ex A) was much exercised by this vessel, explaining the πυθμένες as οὐχ ἕτερον ἐξ ἑτέρου ἀλλ' ἑκατέρωθεν and the handles as arranged in pairs on opposite sides, a convenient setting for lifting and drinking. Special cups appear also at 16.225–8 (Akhilleus) and 24.234–5 (Priam), where the introduction of such treasures serves to mark the gravity or solemnity of the moment. The elaborate description, like the anecdote of Pandaros' bow (4.105–11), could as easily be understood to imply that the cup is invented for this episode as that it was a well-known object (*contra* Kullmann, *Quellen* 257).

633 χρυσείοις ἥλοισι πεπαρμένον (= 1.246, where the phrase is applied to Akhilleus' staff): gold rivets signify a luxurious object, but not so luxurious as the gold cups wielded by gods (4.3, 24.101) or favoured mortals (6.220, 23.196, 24.285, and 5× *Od.*).

635 νεμέθοντο, 'were feeding', is *hapax legomenon* like the noun νέμος (480), from which it is evidently derived by means of the -εθ- suffix on the pattern e.g. of φάος > φαέθω.

636–7 In spite of the excitements of books 12–13 Nestor is still drinking at 14.1. The strength of the ancient hero's elbow is surprising. Schol. (Arn/A) sensibly takes it as a conventional compliment, τοῦτο τῶν ἐπαίνων λεγομένων Νέστορός ἐστι, which is better than Leaf's suggestion that 637 is intrusive from 24.456. The motif 'only X could do something' is applied, more reasonably, to Akhilleus' equipment, his horses (10.404 etc.), his spear (19.389), and his door-bar (24.456). It is more understandable that a hero should have a cup reserved for his sole use, as does Akhilleus at 16.225.

638–41 This interesting *potage* has long attracted puzzlement and censure, cf. Plato, *Rep.* 405E (φλεγματώδης, so also Porphyry 1.167.11), 'stimulating porridge' (Leaf). But it is not an aberration; the *Odyssey* knows the same concoction (*Od.* 10.234–5), cf. frumenty or furmity, 'a mixture of corn in the grain, flour, milk, raisins, currants, and what not' to which alcohol was added for a consideration (Hardy, *The Mayor of Casterbridge*, ch. 1). κυκεών was also the designation of the sacred potion drunk by the initiates at Eleusis, see Richardson, *The Homeric Hymn to Demeter* (Oxford 1974)

344–8, with further bibliography; it was also supposed to have medicinal virtues. Schol. b describes the mixture as τροφὴν ἅμα καὶ πότον ἔχων and suitable for the weary, which adds nothing to the present context. The aphrodisiac potency of the Ischia skyphos (632–5n.) is unhelpful. At 642 the mixture is said to quench thirst.

638 ἐϊκυῖα θεῆσι (3× *Il.*, 1× *Od.*, [Hesiod] fr. 185.23 M–W). Hekamede is in good company, the formula being used of Briseis, Nausicaa, and Kastianeira (minor wife of Priam). The epic accurately preserves the weak gradation of the feminine participle (ἐϊκ- < ϝεϝικ-) against the strong grade of the masculine/neuter (ἐοικ- < ϝεϝοικ-).

639 οἴνῳ Πραμνείῳ (also at *Od.* 10.235): see W. Richter, *Arch. Hom.* H 129–30. Πράμνειος ought to designate the provenance of the wine, but no place Pramnos, *vel sim.*, is known, unless we accept Crates' (DT) assertion that there was a mountain Πράμνη on Icaria. Other conjectures are noted by Athenaeus, 30c, ε. The term occurs later, in Hippocrates and the comic poets, but as a designation of quality. The scholiast (T on 624) says red wine.

645 The θρόνος is a luxurious piece of camp furniture otherwise found only in Akhilleus' grand quarters in book 24. It appears properly to denote a heavy chair fitted with arms and a high back (Richter, *Furniture* 13–33). Iliadic references are elsewhere to the thrones in the palaces of gods. φαεινοῦ implies the decoration noted at 18.422 and frequently in the *Odyssey*. Here Nestor rises from the same chair that was called a κλισμός (strictly a light chair without arms) at 623. The choice of words is partly governed by the interaction of formulas and sentence-pattern; both ἐπὶ κλισμοῖσι κάθιζον (623, also *Od.* 17.90) and ἀπὸ (ὑπὸ) θρόνου ὦρτο (ἇλτο) (3× *Il.*, 1× *Od.*) are formular.

646 =778: the constituents of the verse are formular: χειρὸς ἑλών etc. (8× *Il.*, 4× *Od.*), κατὰ δ' (καὶ) ἑδριάασθαι ἄνωγε (also *Od.* 3.35, *HyDem* 191), but probably not the whole verse. It is absent from normal scenes of welcome, e.g. 9.192ff., 18.388ff.

647–54 Patroklos recognizes the wounded man and proposes to leave at once, but he is caught between a peremptory Akhilleus and a garrulous Nestor. Vainly he lays the foundation for a quick departure by declining a seat (cf. 6.360, Hektor and Helen) and delivering a heightened description of Akhilleus' heroic temper – a rare Iliadic example of κωμῳδία ἠθολογουμένη, as [Longinus], *De Sublimitate* 9.15, termed a typically Odyssean quality. — Makhaon remained with Nestor during the following scene (he is still there at 14.1–8), but is ignored by the speakers even when the presence of a wounded man would have served Nestor's argument at 762ff. He has served his purpose in motivating Patroklos' visit. Epic narrative focuses not only on each scene in turn but on the essence of the scene, here on the moral pressure Nestor applies to his visitor. Patroklos comments on the paradox of the wounded doctor at 833–6 but fails to include him in his report to Akhilleus at 16.23–9

649 νεμεσητός: αἰδοῖος is associated with δεινός when the person described is of superior rank, real or implied: 3.172 (Helen of Priam), 18.394 (Hephaistos of Thetis), and 2× *Od.* in ambiguous contexts. Between equals the formula is αἰδοῖός τε φίλος τε (7× with variants). Patroklos uses a unique combination and a unique sense of νεμεσητός in which the suffix -τός is active (or neutral) in force: he means that Akhilleus' prickly pride is 'apt to take umbrage' if Patroklos is sent on an urgent errand and then spends time in social courtesies. (The common νεμεσσητός is passive and means 'that towards which one feels νέμεσις'.)

653–4 For Akhilleus' ungovernable temper see 24.582–6 (where he reflects that he might be unable to restrain himself should Priam make a false move).

653 ἐκεῖνος (for κεῖνος) is a 'recent' form with a poor representation in the Homeric text, see Janko, *HHH* 237–8.

656–803 This is the longest of Nestor's admonitory discourses. It is true that 'logorrhoea' is (in Greek) a symptom of senility and that Patroklos is anxious to get away, and that the combination of the two is not without a trace of humour, but this is overridden by the paradoxical epic principle (described by N. Austin, *GRBS* 7 (1966) 295–312) that the more urgent an action the more it is held up by discourse and description. Nestor's garrulity was also attested in the *Cypria*: Νέστωρ δὲ ἐν παρεκβάσει διηγεῖται αὐτῷ [Μενελάῳ] ὡς Ἐπωπεὺς φθείρας τὴν Λυκούργου θυγατέρα ἐξεπορθήθη, καὶ τὰ περὶ Οἰδίπουν καὶ τὴν Ἡρακλέους μανίαν καὶ τὰ περὶ Θησέα καὶ Ἀριάδνην (Proclus, *Chrestomathia*).

656 ὀλοφύρεται: Nestor is made to take Akhilleus' interest for concern. Akhilleus had not allowed any word of pity to escape his lips (608–15), but the psychology is plausible. We are being invited to see him as a man willing himself not to do what in his heart he desires to do – fight. We thus see him in a better light than the wilful obstinacy of book 9 and are prepared for his concession in book 16 in sending Patroklos to the war.

658–62 + 794–803 These passages form the essence of Nestor's admonition. Usually message and report follow each other closely in the text and this example is exceptional in that Patroklos does not deliver Nestor's suggestion until 16.23–7 + 36–45.

659–62 = 16.24–27 whence 662, the notice of Eurupulos' disablement, has clearly intruded. Leaf rightly brackets the verse, which is omitted by many MSS; Nestor left the field with Makhaon before Eurupulos was wounded. Note the distinction maintained between βάλλω of missile weapons (Diomedes, see 368ff.) and οὐτάω of the spear (Odysseus, see 434ff.).

666–8 Nestor means 'Surely Akhilleus is not going to wait until the last possible moment?' and his words are therefore unconsciously ironical, for that is exactly what Akhilleus intends to do (see 9.650–3). After the digression on the war in Elis Nestor will suggest that Patroklos take up the fight, another irony, for that is what Zeus intends shall happen. πυρὸς δηΐοιο θέρηται is formular, cf. 6.331.

668 ἐπισχερώ: the sense 'in turn' is evident in the Homeric passages (here and 18.68, 23.125) and later usage, but it is odd that all three Homeric occurrences are in proximity to the word ἀκτή or, as here, to the idea of the sea-shore, as if there were some connexion at least in the poet's mind with σχερός, cf. Janko, *Glotta* 57 (1579) 20–3.

669 (= *Od.* 11.394, 21.283, *HyAphr* 238) ἐνὶ γναμπτοῖσι μέλεσσι: the epithet should denote a generic aspect of limbs, that is, it should refer to the action of the joints; it is true, however, that all occurrences of the formula are in contexts where age, or ageing, is in question (24.359 of Priam, see n., *Od.* 11.394 of Agamemnon's ghost, 13.398, 13.430 of Odysseus as beggar) as if 'bent' were the sense understood.

670–762 The Pylian epic. In the hope that Patroklos may be moved to defend the ships Nestor relates a heroic exploit from his younger days in which, in spite of his youth and against his father's wishes, he went to war and defeated the champions of the Epeans

The basic paper is F. Bölte, *RhM* 83 (1934) 319–47, see also Von der Mühll, *Hypomnema* 200. The details of the fighting, etc., are typical, see Fenik, *TBS* 113–14., but in this condensed narrative are mentioned without elaboration. Nestor's reminiscences have, from his standpoint, two purposes. First, to use an incident from his heroic youth in order to insist on his credentials and the value of his words, so as not to seem to 'twitter like a cicada', like the Trojan elders at 3.151; second, indirectly to admonish or exhort. The crucial lines therefore are 716ff., the eagerness of the Pylians to fight and Nestor's insistence, in spite of his father's dissuasion, on being their leader; Patroklos should overcome Akhilleus' opposition and insist on leading the eager Myrmidons to war.

Nestor prefixes his tale with a digression on the causes of the conflict between the Epeioi and the Pylians. It began with that most heroic of exploits, a cattle raid (671–84) executed in the interests of rough justice, for the Epeioi had taken advantage of Pylian weakness to renege on their debts (685–707). The scene thus set, Nestor describes, how

1. the Epeioi attacked Thruoessa in retaliation for Nestor's raid (707–13),
2. Nestor insisted on leading the Pylians to the rescue (714–21),
3. Nestor won a famous victory (722–61).

For a similar tale see 7.132ff. (7.123–60nn.), and for peaceable relations with the Epeioi 23.629–42. It has been plausibly thought (e.g. by Kirk, *Songs* 22) that the petty international relations implicit in Nestor's tales are more likely to recall disturbed post-Mycenaean conditions than the conflicts of the highly organized states revealed by the Linear B tablets. They are, however, of the same genre as many other hero-tales, e.g. of Herakles against Eurutos, and of Idas and Lunkeus against Castor and Poludeukes. See also 690n. Willcock, *CQ* 58 (1964) 141–54, has argued that these stories, or some of them, are *autoschediasmata*, invented for the occasion. The mention of Ereuthalion at 4.319, however, anticipating his story at 7.136ff., militates against the inclusion of the Pylian epic in that class, though the general situation, the bad faith of the Epeioi and the fight with the Molione, could in principle be modelled on the story of the death of the twins at the hands of Herakles (see Pind. *Ol.* 10.24–38). The story is here assumed to be a fragment of genuinely traditional material.

The geography and chronology of the tale is presented with unusual clarity (for narrative topoi see nn.):

Day 1. Nestor seizes cattle, etc.
Night 1. (ἐννύχιοι, 683) The booty is driven down to Pulos.
Day 2. The booty is divided.
(Night 2. No action.)
Day 3. (τρίτῳ ἤματι, 707) The Epeioi attack Thruoessa (= Θρύον Ἀλφειοῖο πόρον, 2.592).
Night 3. (ἔννυχος, 716) The news reaches Pulos. The Pylians at once set out.
Day 4. The Pylians march via the R. Minueios to the Alpheios where they take their evening meal (δόρπον, 730).
Night 4. The Pylians bivouac under arms (731).
Day 5. The battle. The Epeioi are harried as far as Bouprasion.

There are two difficulties here (1) the location of Pulos, and (2) the pursuit to Bouprasion. It is twice implied that 'Pulos' is a day's (or night's) march from the Epean territory. It follows that this 'Pulos' cannot be the Messenian Pulos, which lies more than a hundred miles away at Epano Englianos, unless the poet's sources were much more incoherent about the geography of the western Peloponnese than appears to be the case. A Pulos at modern Kakovatos in Triphylia about twenty miles south of the Alpheios would fit the tale much better. (The exegetic scholia to 726 speak of an 'Arcadian Pulos' 130 stades from the Alpheios.) Nestor's reminiscences are of course extraneous to the action of the *Iliad* and evidently draw on different source material; they are not the best evidence for the location of 'Pulos' in the main narrative of either Homeric epic. See 2.591–4n., Strabo

8.3.7, and for modern discussion HSL *Catalogue* 82–90 and S. R. West on *Od.* 3.4ff. Strabo, who argued for the northern Pulos, noted the former existence of a Messenian Pulos under Mt Aigaleon (8.4.1). Triphylia was once the country of the Kaukones (*Od.* 3.366), who, however, do not enter Nestor's narrative.

The Olenian Rock and the Hill of Alesion are listed in the Catalogue (2.615–17) but their location is unknown. Bouprasion, however, whether town or region (see 756–7n.) lies in north-western Elis well to the north of the Alpheios. Its mention here introduces a single note of incoherence into an otherwise remarkably plausible narrative.

The story clearly belongs to the same cycle as 7.132–57 (how Nestor slew the Goliath Ereuthalion, μήκιστον καὶ κάρτιστον ἄνδρα) and 23.629–42 (how Nestor carried off prizes at the funeral games of the Epean Amarunkeus). The existence of a corpus of Pylian heroic poetry would go some way, as Bölte argues, towards explaining the prominence of Nestor in the *Iliad*. As examples of pure heroic poetry celebrating what could well be historical events these tales represent one extreme of the subject matter of ἀοιδή, as the lightly heroized folktale of Bellerophon (6.152–95) represents the other.

The ethos of the tale – raiding, battle, booty and its division – is like that of the background to the *Iliad* itself and similar to that of Odysseus' raid on the Kikones (*Od.* 9.39–61), and the stories told to Eumaios (*Od.* 14.199–359), and Penelope (*Od.* 19.172–307). Those stories, however, interweave the theme of ἀτασθαλίη with that of heroic action, in contrast to the triumphalism of Nestor's narrative. In both cases of course the theme is suited to the context and purpose of the tale. The triumphant tone depends on statements of fact, for Nestor tells his tale generally in the same manner as the narrator of the *Iliad*. Like the poet he knows what the gods did (714–15, 721, 753 – contrast *Od.* 12.389), and unlike speakers in the *Iliad* he avoids subjective language except in the short passage (689–95) describing the plight of the Pylians and the aggression of the Epeans, n.b. παῦροι, ἐκάκωσε, ὑπερηφανέοντες, ὑβρίζοντες, ἀτάσθαλα.

670 = 7.157, 23.629, *Od.* 14.468, cf. also 4.313, all in the *Iliad* spoken by or with reference to Nestor.

671–707 The background to Nestor's exploit. bT (at 671) come close to recognizing the principle of ring-composition: the poet states the main facts (671–689), then goes back to the causes (690–702). He then returns at 703–7 to the Pylian booty.

671 Ἠλείοισι: the country, Ἦλις, is mentioned at 2.615 and 5× in the *Odyssey*, but this is the only point in the *Iliad* where this tribe (the Ϝαλεῖοι in their own dialect) is mentioned. The epic consistently ignores the digamma, see 686n. In the epic the inhabitants of the north-western

Peloponnesos are the Ἐπειοί (2.619), as indeed the Pylians' enemies are called at 688, etc. There was a story that after the Trojan war the Aetolian Oxulos occupied the country and expelled or absorbed the Epeans (Strabo 8.3.33, Paus. 5.4.1–3).

672 Itumoneus, like Ereuthalion in another of Nestor's tales (7.136), is known only from this reference.

673 δῖα is the standard epithet for Elis (3× *Il.* in this episode, 3× *Od.*), but is almost certainly generic with any place-name of appropriate metrics, cf. Λακεδαίμονα δῖαν (3× *Od.*).

674 ῥύσια are pledges seized as surety for repayments, or simply booty seized in reprisal. It is odd that that a term so appropriate to a principal diversion of the heroic world should occur only here in the epic. The offence for which this freebooting of Nestor's was retaliation is told at 698ff.

677 ἤλιθα πολλήν is Odyssean (4×) except for this one occurrence.

678 βοῶν ἀγέλαι καὶ πώεα οἰῶν, with variants, is formular (2× *Il.*, 2× *Od.*). The hiatus between πώεα and οἰῶν suggests that it is secondary to the singular βοῶν ἀγέλην καὶ πῶυ μέγ' οἰῶν (696, 15.323 and *Od.* 12.299). Hesiod, *Erga* 786, substituted μήλων for οἰῶν to smooth the rhythm.

683 γεγήθει δὲ φρένα + subject is a formula (cf. *HyDem.* 232) whose present tense (in similes) is γέγηθε δέ τε φρένα – – (2× *Il.* + 3× with synonyms of γέγηθα, 1× *Od.*). The νεώτεροι, according to Arn/A, disagreed with the *Iliad*'s allusion to Neleus and affirmed that he was slain by Herakles at the sack of Pulos, cf. 690.

684–92 Parts of these verses are contained in Pap. 432 (see 265n.).

685 ≅ 12.306 (with θοῆς for ἐμῆς).

686 χρεῖος ὀφείλετ': χρῆος would be the etymological spelling; -ει-, preferred by Aristophanes and almost universal in the paradosis, represents a close articulation of the first vowel in hiatus that was probably traditional among rhapsodes. χρέος (*Od.* 8.353 etc.) is the Ionic form. Aristarchus here wrote χρέως ὠφείλετο (Arn/A), oddly, but cf. his preference for χρείως at *Od.* 3.367 where there are no metrical consequences. Pap. 432 reads ὀφέλλετ', the Aeolic form of the verb that prevails against the Ionic ὀφείλω where the verb means 'ought' rather than 'owe' and in the paradosis of the *Odyssey* at 3.367 and 21.17. With remarkable unanimity the MSS give ὀφείλ- in 686 and 698; at 688 they are divided and already Aristarchus had to insist on ὀφείλ-, though his reasons unfortunately are not recorded. Shipp, *Studies* 84–5 and L. R. Palmer in Wace and Stubbings, *Companion* 106, draw far-reaching conclusions about the history of the Iliadic text from the orthographic variation. However, the localization of ὀφείλ- in the Pylian episode loses much of its significance from the absence of allusion elsewhere in the *Iliad* to the payment of debts. The visible difference therefore is not between the Pylian episode and the *Iliad*, but between the orthographic traditions of the *Iliad* versus those of the *Odyssey*. If the primitive text had ΟΦΕΛ- either spelling could have been derived from it. — The χρεῖος may well have arisen in the first place from an Epean βοηλασίη, cf. the χρεῖος of *Od*. 21.16–19 Ὀδυσσεὺς | ἦλθε μετὰ χρεῖος, τό ῥά οἱ πᾶς δῆμος ὄφελλε· | μῆλα γὰρ ἐξ Ἰθάκης Μεσσήνιοι ἄνδρες ἄειραν | νηυσὶ πολυκλήϊσι τριηκόσι' ἠδὲ νομῆας. The weak caesura in the fourth foot, ὀφείλετ' | ἐν Ἤλιδι δίη, surprises, and may reflect a prototype -ετο Fάλιδι δίη. Note, however, that of eleven occurrences of the place-name and its ethnic in Homer none observe the digamma and nine clearly neglect it.

688 δαίτρευον: an Odyssean word (2×) but in the sense of dividing the portions at a feast. — The Ἐπειοί, the primitive inhabitants of Elis (Pind. *Ol*. 9.54), were a tribe that did not survive the Heroic Age. Pap. viii (= Pack², 1194, cited by Erbse, III 118–21), which contains a commentary on 11.677–754, asserts that ἐν Ἤλιδι οἱ ἀ[γρωτ?]αι Ἐπειοι λέγονται – a hitherto unknown doctrine and clearly untenable.

690 Herakles' attack on Pulos. It is conceivable that Herakles is here not so much the mythical hero as a symbol of the Dorian onslaught on the Peloponnese, cf. Kirk, *Songs*, 22. If so the Homeric turn of phrase soon became part of the Herakles story: he fought Poseidon's son Neleus at Pulos and Poseidon came to the rescue cf. [Hesiod] fr. 33(a).23ff. M–W, *Aspis* 355–65, Pind. *Ol*. 9.29–35. The wounding of Ares and Here by Herakles (5.392–402, see nn. *ad loc*.) was brought into connexion with this adventure by the D-scholia. The scholia record many conjectures about Herakles' motivation in making this attack, all more ingenious than persuasive. — βίη Ἡρακληείη: for this formula-type see 2.658–60n. The type is still productive (or revived?) in the Hesiodic corpus (11× for Herakles, β. [Ἠλεκτρυονείη fr. 135.7 M–W, β. Σθενέλοιο fr. 190.9). ἐλθὼν ... βίη Ἡρακληείη, with masculine participle, is an easy *constructio ad sensum*, and a useful certification that the formula is indeed the equivalent of a name–epithet phrase.

691 Pap. 432 reads ...]δεκα[..., which is too close to part of κατὰ δ' ἔκταθεν to warrant any inference.

692–3 The names of Nestor's brothers are listed at [Hesiod] fr. 33(a). 9–12 M–W, and in an almost wholly discrepant list by bT; three only are named in the Nekyia at *Od*. 11.286. None are otherwise known to legend.

693 λιπόμην: passive sense, as at *Od*. 8.125 etc.

694–5 ταῦθ' is adverbial, 'at this', if ὑπερηφανέοντες is intransitive. ὑπερηφανέοντες is 'arrogant' or the like. The word is a *hapax legomenon* and susceptible only to difficult and complicated etymology. Connexions have been suggested with φαίνομαι, κατ-ήφων, and ἄφενος, see Chantraine, *Dict*. s.v. ὑβρίζειν (only here in *Il*.) is a common verb in the *Odyssey* (7×), a poem that has more use for the concept; the noun ὕβρις, however, is Iliadic

(2×), as is ὑβριστής (13.633). The ὕβρις of the Epeans is Augeias' greed and mistreatment of Neleus' charioteer.

696–7 τρῑηκόσι'(α): the irregular prosody suggests the derivative nature of the verse, cf. *Od.* 21.18–19 μῆλα ... τρῑηκόσι' ἠδὲ νομῆας. The formula is thus proper to flocks of sheep and should be taken here as an explication of πῶϋ μέγα in 696. A reference to both ἀγέλην βοῶν and πῶϋ οἰῶν so as to mean 'three hundred beasts' would be the only place in Homer where sheep and cattle were counted together, an unnatural calculation for any pastoralist, cf. 244–5n.

699–700 This and the controversial passage 8.185 are the sole allusions in the *Iliad* to four-horsed chariots (the singular ἐλατῆρ' at 702 shows that one chariot is meant here). Aristarchus (Arn/A) and Pap. viii (see 688n.) note the anachronism. But Nestor's booty were ἀθλοφόροι (on the contracted vowel see 9.124n.), i.e. yoked for racing not for war. In this context μετ' ἄεθλα, unless it is anachronistic, seems to imply some precursors of the classical Olympic games (reputedly founded in 776 B.C.). Paus. 5.8.7 alleges that chariot racing was introduced in Ol. 25. Prize-giving for sports is restricted in the epic to funeral games. For Pylian participation in such games in Elis see 23.630, the games of Amarunkeus. Those, however, are not the subject of the present passage, for Nestor himself took part.

701 Augeias borrows ἄναξ ἀνδρῶν as his epithet from the formula system of Agamemnon, as do the metrically similar Aineias, Ankhises, Euphetes, and Eumelos, all once only. ἄναξ ἐνέρων Ἀϊδωνεύς (20.61) is another variant. These incipient generic uses of the epithet indicate that whatever specific force it may have had as a description of Agamemnon's status is no longer understood by the poet. Augeias was brother of Aktor (cf. 750n.) and father of Phuleus whose son Meges was now fighting alongside Nestor. Phuleus, however, had no love for his father, see 2.627–30 and n. For his daughter Agamede see 740n. The epic has no reference to the famous stables or their cleansing. For his stinginess cf. Pind. *Ol.* 10.28–30; he refused to pay Herakles for clearing the dung.

703 ἐπέων implies that in a less summary narrative of these events Augeias added insult to injury. He can hardly be supposed to have sent the charioteer home without some message for Neleus. 'Noun + ἠδὲ καί + noun' is a regular phrase pattern (8× in *Il.*) but the words that enter it are not for that reason themselves formular; ἔργων, which consistently preserves its digamma in the nominative and accusative cases within formulas, has here its Ionic vernacular form without digamma.

704–5 There is a certain confusion (doubtless also in practice) between forcible restitution of debt and simple pillage: Neleus is entitled to his four horses or their value and takes it, the δῆμος then makes assignments in language appropriate to the distribution of booty (705 ≅ *Od.* 9.42 (the loot of Ismaros), 9.549). Zenodotus (Did/AT) omitted 705, an explanatory expansion on 704, and Aristarchus (Arn/A) condemned the verse. The objection, in addition to the repetition of the verse, was to the unfairness of an equal distribution among varied creditors. If the line is retained, the important principle of 'fair share of booty' will have been embodied in a formula. ἴσης: *sc.* μοίρης or αἴσης.

706 διείπομεν is imperfect of διέπω, 'were dealing with' the matter.

709, 725 πανσυδίη (cf. σεύω): 'with all speed' satisfies the Homeric occurrences. The sense 'in full force' is not attested before Xenophon (*HG* 4.4.9 and *Ages.* 2.19). Μολίονε: see 750n.

710 παῖδ᾽ ἔτ᾽ ἐόντ᾽: this chronological note, together with the statement that the Molione were not *yet* furious warriors (and so almost fell victim to the youthful Nestor, 750–2) hints at the existence of a cycle of heroic tales with its focus on the western Peloponnese. More of its personnel are listed at 23.634ff.

711, 722 ἔστι δέ τις: the formula for setting a scene, cf. 2.811, *Od.* 3.293, 4.844, not, however, exclusively a Greek verse-formula, for Latin and Sanskrit have a similar idiom. Θρυόεσσα: called Θρύον in the Catalogue (2.592). θρύον is a species of rush, flourishing presumably at the foot of the αἰπεῖα κολώνη (formular, cf. 2.811).

712 νεάτη here must mean 'furthest' in the sense 'just within the boundaries' of Pulos, cf. 9.153 and n. ἠμαθόεις: see 9.153n. The -όεις form is used for both masculine and feminine genders.

714 μετεκίαθον is properly 'go after' and is misused with πεδίον. What Nestor probably means is that the Epeans scoured the country in search of plunder or to destroy crops, after the manner of Greek invading armies.

715 = 18.167.

717–20 A rather compressed statement. By concealing his horses and stressing his inexperience Neleus understandably tries to keep his sole surviving heir safe, a consideration that could not affect Nestor's heroic mind. So Nestor went to war without a chariot but still somehow counting himself among the ἱππεῖς at 724. In the course of the fighting he captured the horses and chariot of Moulios (738–44).

722 The ποταμὸς Μινυήϊος, otherwise unheard-of, must be a minor stream. A contrast is implied with the ἱερὸς ῥόος of the mighty Alpheios (726). 'Minyan' is the epithet of Orchomenos in Boeotia, the home of Nestor's mother Chloris, but it is impossible to recover what implication, if any, the name may have.

723 Arene is mentioned in the Catalogue (2.591) immediately after Pulos itself. It was situated in Triphylia at classical Samikon, see map 1, vol. 1 189. Ἠῶ (or ἠῶ, the personification is doubtful) (7× *Il.*, 17× *Od.*)

can always be resolved into a dactylic scansion, and obviously reflects prototypes ἠόα δῖαν, ἠόα μίμνειν, etc.

724 ἔθνεα πεζῶν looks like a useful phrase that is not repeated. ἔθνος in the epic is a generic collective noun, a 'body' of men, a 'swarm' of bees, a 'herd' of swine, etc.

726 ἔνδιοι, i.e. at noon, cf. *Od.* 4.450 (Proteus emerged from the sea for his siesta ἔνδιος) and Hsch. ἔνδια· μεσημβρία.

727–61 The narrative slips into an elaborate ring-form centred on Nestor's encounter with the Molione (750–2), see vol. v 47.

727–30 Note the Pylian piety, cf. 753 and 761. The Pylians are about to cross their frontier, so that διαβατήρια are in order (cf. Thuc. 5.54 and 116). The δόρπον, of course, is part of the sacrificial ritual. In the fifth century διαβατήρια were at least partly divinatory, an aspect of sacrifice not known to Homer. – Διὶ ... ὑπερμενεῖ with correption of the final syllable, a light modification of the traditional Διὶ ... ὑπερμενέϊ (3×), marks another intrusion of the Ionic vernacular into the traditional diction. Verse 730 = 7.380 (a doubtfully genuine verse) ≅ 18.298. ἐν τελέεσσι must be 'in their companies/ranks', cf. 10.56, 470.

735 Arn/A try to draw a distinction between the language of the poet and the language he gives to Nestor; the poet's language is to say that the heavenly bodies rise from Ocean. That is not the whole truth; dawn spreads 'over the sea' at 23.227, and 'over the whole earth' at 8.1 ≅ 24.695. The scholia are right to look for characterization by language in direct speech (cf. 9.307n.) but are unlikely to find it where the direct speech is also narrative, cf. 747n. — The intransitive use of ὑπερέσχεθε, 'held himself over', has a parallel only at *Od.* 13.93 (ὑπερέσχε, of a star).

738 Μούλιος has namesakes at 16.696, 20.472 (both Trojans), and at *Od.* 18.423 (a herald). The first syllable is apparently lengthened for metrical reasons, cf. μόλος, 'battle', but the etymology is disputed, see 10.269n.

739–40 These verses resemble 13.428–9. The hand of the eldest daughter is presumably more prestigious than that of her sisters.

740 Agamede, 'Very Intelligent', bears a significant name. As Perimede she was linked with Circe and Medea by Theocritus (*Id.* 2.14–15, cf. Prop. 2.4.7). Magic is a female speciality, incompatible with the masculine ideal of heroism. Agamede's reputation as a witch may be taken with Odyssean allusions to Ephyre, if that is the Elean Ephyre, see 15.531n. and West's note to *Od.* 1.257ff. Ephyre was a source of arrow-poison (*Od.* 2.328–9). Odysseus' host there was Ilos son of Mermeros ('Pernicious', another significant name), son of another famous witch, Medea.

742 ≅ *Od.* 13.267 (with κατιόντα). χαλκήρεϊ δουρί (also acc. plur.): see 260n.

744–5 μεγάθυμοι ... ἔτρεσαν: not a contradiction. The epithet, generic in the sense that it may be applied to any tribe of men, is used also in a genuinely generic way, to describe the true character of the Epeioi which, as it happens, their flight does not display at this instant.

746 ≅ 16.292 (with κτείνας for ἱππήων).

747 λαίλαπι ἴσος (2×, with epithet ἐρεμνῇ) is formular and, as Arn/A note, belongs to the narrative language of the poet, cf. 735n. There is characterization in 747ff., but it lies in the old man's enthusiastic recollection of his youthful prowess.

748 πεντήκοντα (15× *Il.*, 9× *Od.*) is Homer's standard large number.

750 Kteatos and Eurutos, the Ἀκτορίωνε, were nominally sons of Aktor (brother of Augeias, according to Eust. 303.5), their real father (751) being Poseidon. Μολίονε – the combination of two patronymics is most unusual – alludes to their descent on the mother's side, cf. Arn/A (ἡ διπλῆ) ὅτι ἐντεῦθεν Ἡσίοδος Ἄκτορος κατ' ἐπίκλησιν καὶ Μολιόνης αὐτοὺς γεγενεαλόγηκεν, γόνῳ δὲ Ποσειδῶνος (= [Hesiod] fr. 17b M–W). Molos, a member of the Aetolian royal house (see 9.555–8n.) was their maternal grandfather. C. J. Ruijgh, *REG* 80 (1967) 15, suggests that Molione was their name as a pair, Kteatos and Eurutos their names as individuals. They were twins (δίδυμοι), a fact that gave them an advantage at chariotry (23.641–2). One drove while the other whipped, and so beat Nestor at the funeral games of Amarunkeus. As early as the Hesiodic catalogues they were Siamese twins, and Aristarchus assumed that Homer also so conceived them, cf. Arn/A to 23.641 Ἀρίσταρχος δὲ "διδύμους" ἀκούει οὐχ οὕτως ὡς ἡμεῖς ἐν τῇ συνηθείᾳ νοοῦμεν, οἷοι ἦσαν καὶ οἱ Διόσκοροι, ἀλλὰ τοὺς διφυεῖς [δύο ἔχοντας σώματα], Ἡσιόδῳ μάρτυρι χρώμενος [καὶ τοὺς συμπεφυκότας ἀλλήλοις] (= [Hesiod] fr. 18 M–W), and this conception was maintained later, e.g. Ibycus fr. 285 Davies ἰσοκέφαλοι ἐνίγυιοι . This aspect of their physique is not mentioned directly by Homer, perhaps because it seemed inhuman. See also 2.620–1n. and 23.638–42n. They have been identified with the double figures represented in late eighth-century vase-painting, see K. Fittschen, *Untersuchungen zum Beginn der Sagendarstellung bei den Griechen* (Berlin 1969) 70–5, and *LfgrE* s.v. Ἀκτορίων. Their sons, Amphimakhos and Thalpios, were now fighting alongside Nestor at Troy. Aktor, 'leader', is a good heroic name, borne by two other ancient heroes (sons of Murmidon and Deion – see West, *Catalogue* 61, 68) and by four Iliadic personages (see 2.513–15n., where it is observed that different forms of patronymic, -ίδης, -ίων, and genitive + υἱός, distinguish their sons). — ἀλάπαξα is a neat hyperbole for Nestor's 'overthrow' of the formidable pair; the verb usually means to 'sack' a town or 'rout' an army.

751 κρείων is epithet of (or noun in apposition to) six different characters. As participle of an obsolete verb it is twelve times expanded with εὐρύ to make a formula for Agamemnon but only here is it so expanded as an epithet of Poseidon. For κρείων of a god, cf. the title of Zeus ὕπατε κρειόντων (8.31, 3× *Od.*).

752 The Molione must escape on this occasion, for tradition assigned their slaying to Herakles (Pind. *Ol.* 10.25–8); their preservation is explained with a typical theme (a hero is rescued by a god) and a typical detail (they are shrouded in mist).

754 σπιδέος: *hapax legomenon*, hence the attempt by Ptol. Asc. and others to read δι᾽ ἀσπιδέος (explained as 'shield-like' i.e. 'round', or 'covered in shields'. bT explain *σπιδής as 'vast' or 'rugged'. LSJ prefer the former, comparing the related forms σπίδιον, σπιδνός, σπίζω.

756–7 Bouprasion is probably a district, see 2.615–17n. and Strabo 8.3.8, with a settlement of the same name. — Verse 756 contains no fewer than nine labial stops. The only other verse in the *Iliad* to contain so many is 13.158, describing Deiphobos *prancing* forward. The sound of the verse, it may be unconsciously, echoes that of Nestor's chariot ride. (Statistics of the frequencies of the vowels and consonants in Homer are given by D. W. Packard, *TAPA* 106 (1974) 239–60. See also vol. v, 57.) πολυπύρου: the epithet is probably merely complimentary. Elis is indeed a fertile region by Greek standards, but the most formular use of the word is with Δουλίχιον (3× *Od.*), an island of uncertain identity, for which the most productive candidate is said to be at best 'fertile in parts' (see vol. 1 182–3). The Olenian rock, if classical Olenos had anything to do with it, would lie on the coast within the entrance to the Corinthian Gulf, with the hill of Alesion to the south of it. On these locations see HSL *Catalogue* 98–9.

759 Ἀχαιοί was used as a term for the speaker's party in stories of Tudeus at 4.384, 5.803, and 10.286, and contrasted with Καδμεῖοι. That may reflect a genuine distinction, but the use of Ἀχαιοί here must be a slip, or rather an instance of formular override, cf. αὐτὰρ Ἀχαιοί 9× elsewhere in the *Iliad*. Πύλιοι is the term used at 687, 724, 753, and placed in direct contrast to Ἐπειοί at 737.

762–803 Nestor urges Patroklos to use his influence with Akhilleus, either to display his ἀρετή again in person or to send Patroklos back to the fight

As usual Nestor's is the voice of compromise and reason. He now proceeds in the same manner as Phoinix in book 9, reminding Patroklos of their meeting when he and Odysseus had come to Phthie to raise troops for the Trojan war, and thereby reinforcing his right now to put moral pressure on Patroklos and through him on Akhilleus by putting them in mind of their fathers' parting words. It is typically Nestor who comes up with a plan of action which he urges another to implement, cf. 9.179–81, 10.204–17.

762 εἴ ποτ' ἔον γε is pathetic, a verbal sigh over the loss of something, cf.
3.180, 24.426. Nestor's youth is so long past that he can scarcely believe in
it. The phrase is formular (3× *Il.*, 3× *Od.*, with one variant without γε) but
in the 3rd person (ἔην) except here. The prevalence of the 3rd person and
the rarity of the thematic 1st person ἔον (an artificial form) led the vulgate
to adopt ἔην here also, but ἔον is virtually guaranteed by its sole other
occurrence outside this verse, ὡς ποτ' ἔον (23.643).

763 οἷος picks up μετ' ἀνδράσι from 762. Prowess in Nestor's world
is not a private virtue; it must be displayed publicly and for public purposes.
Nestor immediately corrects himself: Akhilleus will not reap any profit at
all, but will shed tears when it is too late.

765 ≅ 9.252.

766 = 9.253 = 9.439. Menoitios, conveniently for this story, is living in
Phthie, whither he had fled with Patroklos τυτθὸν ἐόντα, after the latter's
precocious slaying of a playmate (23.85). There is uncertainty, however,
about the home and family of Patroklos. He is from Locris according to
18.324–7 and 23.85–6, but the Hesiodic catalogue makes Menoitios a
brother of Peleus (fr. 212a M–W = Eust. 112.44), see vol. IV 313 and 605n.

767–85 These verses were athetized by Aristophanes and Aristarchus
(Did/Arn/A) on grounds of pedestrian composition and the inconsistency
between them and 9.254–8; his arguments are challenged by bT. Peleus'
valediction varies according to the wishes of the speaker recalling it. Inconsistency between a statement and a previous statement, each being apposite
in its context, is not infrequent, cf. 5.508ff. with 455–9; 15.721ff. with
5.788ff., 9.352ff., and 13.105–6; 16.50–1 with 9.410ff.; 21.229ff. with
15.231–2. The inference is, or should be, that such statements are figments,
part of the poet's 'ornamentation' of the episode on which he is engaged, on
which see M. M. Willcock, *HSCP* 81 (1977) 46–7. For a possible illustration
of the scene on a vase from Olynthos see Stella G. Miller, *AJA* 90 (1986)
164.

770 Ἀχαιΐδα borrows the epithet of Ἑλλάδα καλλιγύναικα (2.683, 9.447)
at 3.75 (=3.258), or here that of χθόνα, etc. (13× *Il.*, 3× *Od.*).

771–81 These verses form a condensed visit-scene, cf. Arend, *Scenen* 35
and for more leisurely accounts *Od.* 3.1–68, 4.1–70. The host is sacrificing
or feasting, the strangers wait without, they are welcomed, seated, and
offered food, lastly they state their business, cf. 9.193n.

777 ≅ 9.193 (see n.).

778 = 646.

780 ≅ *Od.* 5.201 (τάρπησαν). The regular formula, with πόσιος καὶ
ἐδητύος ἐξ ἔρον ἕντο , would not conjugate into the 1st person.

782 A father's admonition is a typical motif, cf. 5.197, 6.207. It could be
varied by citing not what the respected parent had said but what he would

say if he knew how badly he was being let down, cf. 7.125 ἦ κε μέγ' οἰμώξειε [Πηλεύς] ...

784 = 6.208 (Hippolokhos' injunction to Glaukos).

785 For Aktor, father of Menoitios (so also at 16.14), see 605n.

786–9 For the effective use of direct quotation see 9.251–8 n. Here the pressure is on Patroklos and the important words are not those of Peleus (which are reduced to a formular verse in an indirect construction) but those of Menoitios.

786 γενεῇ ... ὑπέρτερος: an important note for the relationship of Akhilleus and Patroklos (rightly interpreted by Xen. *Symp.* 8.31). Arn/A cite Archilochus (fr. 38 West) for ὑπέρτερος = νεώτερος (which would make the μέν ... δέ ... rather pointless) but proceed to argue, rightly, that Akhilleus was ὑπέρτερος in that his ancestry was divine; Patroklos was the elder, but the autobiographical passage 23.85–90 makes it clear that he was the elder by a few years only. That was inconvenient to those who wished to interpret the bonds of heroic friendship *in malam partem*, whether like Phaidros in Plato's *Symposium* (180A) Akhilleus is made the ἐρώμενος (and said, wrongly, to be νεώτερος πολύ), or like Aeschylus in his lost play *Myrmidons* they made the obviously inferior Patroklos the παιδικά of Akhilleus (and so gave Homer the lie). In book 9, verses 666–8 assert, rather pointedly, the virility of Patroklos. He had been made θεράπων to Akhilleus, having fled to Peleus to avoid the consequences of homicide, cf. the story of Phoinix, 9.447–91, hence his generally obliging behaviour towards his friend. It would have hardly have been fitting to portray Akhilleus in the passive role of the ἐρώμενος, but there is in any case no overt allusion to homosexual love in either Homeric epic, on which matter see Aeschines, *In Timarchum* 141–50, and among modern contributions Stella G. Miller, *AJA* 90 (1986) 165–7 (*contra* S. Levin, *TAPA* 80 (1949) 43–6, and W. M. Clarke, *Hermes* 106 (1978) 381–96), and the full discussion by D. M. Halperin, *One Hundred Years of Homosexuality and Other Essays on Greek Love* (New York 1990) 87–93. The silence is apparently deliberate, as the discreet allusions to Ganumedes 5.266 and 20.231–5 suggest: see also 16.97n. with schol. *ad loc.*, and B. Sergent, *Homosexuality in Greek Myth*, trans. Goldhammer (London 1987) 250–8. Apollonius appears to have taken the discretion as epic regard for τὸ πρέπον and was careful never to affirm explicitly that Herakles and Hulas were lovers, *Arg.* 1.1240–72, 1344–50 (at 1.131–2 Hulas is ἐσθλὸς ὀπάων | πρωθήβης).

788–12.8 Pap. 5 (second century B.C.), a slovenly text with many orthographic slips, contains the ends of verses 788–809 and 837–12.8, and the beginnings of 810–34. There are plus-verses at 795a and b, 804a, 805a, 807a, 827a, b, and c, and 840a.

790–1 In the event, at 16.21ff., Patroklos made no use of this tactfully indirect argument, nor of anything that could be fairly described as παραί-φασις (793). Nestor moots two possibilities, either Akhilleus will fight personally or he will despatch Patroklos to the battle as he does in book 16, without any indication being given at this point which, if either, will come to pass. This is therefore a good example of Schadewaldt's 'Ungenauigkeit' (*Iliasstudien* 110, 140); the action of the poem is foreshadowed but partially and ambiguously. Verse 790 = 9.259.

792–3 = 15.403–4 (with ὀρίνω for ὀρίναις); Patroklos will be speaking to Eurupulos. The use of the vague σὺν δαίμονι (almost = 'with luck', 'if all goes well') may suggest that Nestor is doubtful of success, see Erbse, *Funktion der Götter* 266. δαίμων expresses the driving force of events where no more specific and approachable agency can be named, cf. 15.461–5n. and Burkert, *Religion* 180.

793 (= 15.404) παρειπών: the ᾱ is long by position (< παρ-ϝειπών). The word is picked up by παραί-φασις. ἑταίρου is significant; this παραίφα-σις is well-intended, not like that with which Here arms herself at 14.217, ἥ τ' ἔκλεψε νόον πύκα περ φρονεόντων.

794–803 ≅ 16.36–45 with grammatical changes. In the latter passage Patroklos is pleading with Akhilleus to be allowed to enter the fight. Zenodotus 'cancelled' (περιέγραψεν) 794–5 (Arn/A) and possibly all ten verses, see Bolling, *External Evidence* 136–7, and Nickau, *Zenodotos* 82–97, for that scholar's objection to repeated passages. Aristarchus athetized 802–3 on the grounds that the Trojans were at this moment neither exhausted nor among the ships, as is the case at 16.44–5. That shows his characteristic over-precision, though 'concordance interpolation' between repeated verse-groups is a widespread feature of Homeric textual history. Verses 799–801 = 18.199–201 also but with σ' ὑποδείσαντες for σε τῷ εἴσκοντες.

796–803 A piece of direct tactical advice, typical of Nestor (cf. 2.360–8n.), but here with an unusual overtone of tragic irony: he would be sending Patroklos to his death. It is characteristic of the portrayal of Nestor that he is made to come up with a potentially acceptable compromise: Akhilleus will keep up his μῆνις but send out a surrogate, and the Achaeans will get not their supreme champion but the next best thing.

797 φόως, 'light of salvation', is a traditional metaphor (797 ≅ 8.282, 16.39).

798–9 For men being unrecognizable in armour, see 3.166n. The Homeric helmet may have cheek-pieces (cf. the formula κυνέης διὰ χαλκοπαρῄου, 3×), but there is no evidence that it covered the face as completely as did the broad cheek-pieces and nose-guards of classical and later times. Therefore Patroklos' wearing of Akhilleus' armour is not so much a matter of *suppressio veri* as of *suggestio falsi*; what the Trojans would recognize would be the devices on the shield and the ornamentation of the breastplate, cf. 19–40. Shields might also be distinctively coloured, cf. Δηΐφοβον ... λευκάσπιδα (22.294). In the narrative itself heroes have no difficulty in recognizing each other.

799 εἴσκοντες, with prothetic ἐ-, has good authority here (including Aristarchus (Hrd/A) and Pap. 59), though Allen prints ἴσκοντες (*wik-sk-*) at 16.41 in the parallel passage and ἴσκουσα at *Od.* 4.279. ἐΐσκω is normally trisyllabic.

801 This is a whole-verse formula (= 16.43 = 18.201).

804–41 Patroklos runs back towards Akhilleus' quarters. On the way he meets another casualty, Eurupulos, and gives him aid

806–7 The 'place of assembly' is near the ships of Odysseus because that was more or less the centre of the Greek encampment, see 11.5–7n. θέμις is evidently 'assembly', θέμιστες being what such a body endorsed, cf. *Od.* 9.112 where the Kuklopes are said to have neither ἀγοραί nor θέμιστες.

806 'Οδυσσῆος θείοιο: for the epithet, regular with names scanning ∪ – – –, see 9.218n.

808 ἦην is supported here by almost the whole body of MSS, but is otherwise an Odyssean form (3×). It may be regarded as an 'augmented' form of ἔην when that form of the 3rd singular, of whatever provenance, became established, see E. Tagliaferro, *Helikon* 19 (1979) 340–51.

811 σκάζων: 'limping', because he had been shot in the thigh (581–4). δὲ νότιος : initial nasal consonants make position, if need be, whether they represent an original *sm-*, *sn-* or not. The etymology of νότος is unclear. The practice of Aristophanes (but not of Aristarchus) was to write the initial consonant double in such cases. Early papyri, including Pap. 5 here, follow Aristophanes' practice.

813 κελάρυζε: 'gushed' or 'poured', like the sea-water from Odysseus' head at *Od.* 5.323. In fact the arrow-head and broken shaft were still impaled in Eurupulos' thigh.

815 Pap. 5 provides a good instance of 'formular' corruption, i.e. the substitution of one more or less synonymous formula for another. The papyrus reads ἐν τ' ἄρα [οἱ] φῦ χειρὶ ἔπος τ' ἔφατ' ἔκ τ' ὀνόμαζε[ν (6× *Il.*, 5× *Od.*).

816–18 Patroklos sighs aloud. The Achaeans are suffering what they had just now been inflicting; they are dying far from hearth and home, like Iphidamas whom Agamemnon slew at 241–5, their bodies abandoned to the dogs, just as Odysseus threatened to leave Sokos to the vultures at 453–4.

819–20 The vocative phrase Εὐρύπυλ' ἥρως occurs only here and at

838; it is paralleled by Τηλέμαχ' ἥρως at *Od.* 4.312. Nominative ἥρως preceded by a dactylic name, however, is an established formula type: Ἄσιος/Λήϊτος/Μούλιος/Πείροος/Φαίδιμος ἥρως. πελώριος is generic, being used of Aias, Akhilleus, Hektor, Periphas, and indirectly of Agamemnon, but is very much to the point here.

822 The pattern of the verse is that used for a name scanned $-\cup\cup-$ followed by epithet (δουρικλυτός, πεπνυμένος, etc.), the epithet being here replaced by a word appropriate to context, the participle βεβλημένος. A substantial part of the paradosis has πεπνυμένος here, although in the *Iliad* that epithet is kept for councillors (Antenor 3.203, Pouludamas 18.249), young men (Antilokhos 23.586), subordinate warriors (Meriones 13.254, 266), and heralds (7.276 etc.). βεβλημένος is almost a special epithet for Eurupulos in this neighbourhood (592, 809, 12.2).

824 For the sense of ἐν νηυσὶ ... πεσέονται, here 'die beside the ships', see 9.235n. The Achaeans are clearly the subject. Aristarchus (Arn/A) wished to understand Τρῶες, perhaps for consistency with the other occurrences. There is, however, no difficulty in a formula's being flexible in its meaning as well as its shape.

825–6 = 16.23–4.

829ff. On the treatment of wounds, see 4.218–19n. Eurupulos evidently does not fear poison, for Patroklos is invited merely to wash the wound not to suck it, as Makhaon did that of Menelaos in book 4. For ἔκταμ' see 844n.

831–2 The poet alludes without further explanation to a well-known corpus of 'knowledge', the saga of Akhilleus, beginning with (or indeed before) his birth and education. In the *Iliad* Kheiron is always an instructor of heroes, supplying φάρμακα as here to Makhaon at 4.219 and the famous spear to Peleus in a similar verse at 16.143. This passing reference to his teaching Akhilleus accords with legend ([Hesiod] fr. 204.87–9 M–W, Pind. *Pyth.* 6.21–3, *N.* 3.43–53), but implicitly contradicts Phoinix' story at 9.485–95 – which was almost certainly an *ad hoc* invention. It is not clear why he should be δικαιότατος unless it be in contrast with the hubristic disposition of the other Centaurs. — προτί appears to construe with the genitive Ἀχιλῆος (so Leaf), a rare usage; equally rare is the use of προτί where πρός could stand. προτί occurs in the vernacular dialects (in the form πορτί) only in Central Cretan and in the epic tradition only in *Iliad* and *Odyssey*, not in Hesiod or the *Hymns*. The complex usage of πρός, ποτί, προτί is examined by W. F. Wyatt, *SMEA* 19 (1978) 89–123: generally πρός is the free form, π(ρ)οτί restricted to traditional phraseology. — Zenodotus read δεδάασθαι for δεδιδάχθαι: an attractive reading, but the paradosis (including Pap. 5) is unanimous against him.

833–6 Eurupulos uses a speaker's grammar, first stating his subject ('As for the surgeons ...'), then slipping into an indirect statement (τὸν μὲν ...

ὀΐομαι), then back to direct speech (ὁ δ' ... in apposition to ἰητροί in 833).

833 For Podaleirios, son of Asklepios and brother of Makhaon, see 4.193–4n.

835–7 Pap. 5 (contrary to the statement in OCT's *app. crit.*) has at least two and perhaps as many as four plus-verses at this point, see West, *Ptolemaic Papyri* 117. West suggests that 16.517–19 (ἕλκος μὲν γὰρ ἔχω ...) and 16.523–4 ("ἄναξ, τόδε ... ἕλκος ἄκεσσαι") would make a satisfactory interpolation after the digression about Kheiron.

841 In spite of Akhilleus' uncertain temper (649) and his own haste the kindly Patroklos stops to aid Eurupulos. Akhilleus, we know, is resolved not to act until the Trojans are among the ships and will not accede at this moment to a request relayed from Nestor. Patroklos must therefore be delayed until the Trojans have broken into the Achaean camp. The injuries to Makhaon and Eurupulus and the actions of Aias, Nestor, Akhilleus, and Patroklos from 489 to the end of the Book are neatly dovetailed:

> Fighting on the plain. Makhaon wounded.
> Nestor sets off for the ships with Makhaon.
> Aias continues fighting while Nestor is driving back.
> Eurupulos is wounded and goes back to the ships on foot.
> Akhilleus sees Nestor arrive with a wounded man (Makhaon) and sends Patroklos to find out his identity.
> Patroklos goes to Nestor's quarters, where he is detained for a time while Eurupulos staggers home.
> Patroklos, returning to Akhilleus, meets Eurupulos arriving at the ships.

οὐδ' ὥς περ ... τειρομένοιο: οὐδ' ὥς followed by participle + περ normally means 'even in such and such circumstances ...' or 'in spite of being ...', e.g. 721 above. Here the participle ('exhausted as you are') gives the reason for Patroklos' action, and the introductory particles, which do not recur together in the *Iliad*, mean little more than 'nevertheless'.

842–8 A succinct notice of the treatment of Eurupulos' wound rounds off the book, see S. Laser, *Arch. Hom* s 106–8, who remarks on the omission of bandaging (cf. 13.599–600). The medication is continued at 15.393–5. When the poet-narrator reports the execution of a command he may do so in the same words with only trivial grammatical adjustments (e.g. 11.512–13 ≅ 517–18), sometimes with condensation, but usually as here with some additional detail. — Note the practical character of Patroklos' treatment of the wound in contrast with that received by the injured Odysseus at *Od.* 19.457–8 ἐπαοιδῇ δ' αἷμα ... ἔσχεθον. The Homeric doctor did not deal in cautery and the knife (except to remove a barbed arrow-head) but in pain-killers; he was πολυφάρμακος (16.28, cf. 4.190, 15.394). For the bibli-ography of Homeric medicine see A. H. M. Kerkhoff, *Janus* 62 (1975) 43–9, and Laser, *Arch. Hom.* s. bT make heavy weather of the fact that Patroklos should providentially happen to have the bitter root by him, as if they were commenting on an action report. As appropriate roots they suggest *Achillea* ('woundwort') or, more obscurely, *Aristolochia*, a herb used in the relief of birth-pangs. On these φάρμακα see Pliny, *NH* 25.42–4 and 95–7, or Dioscorides 3.4 and 4.36.

844 The μάχαιρα is carried by the hero but not as a weapon, at least it is never said to be used as such. At 3.271–2 = 19.252–3 it is used to sever the sacrificial hair from a victim. Distinguish this implement therefore from that denoted by the synonyms ξίφος, ἄορ, and φάσγανον (μάχαιρα = παραξιφίδιον, Arn/A). The arrow is imagined to have penetrated deeply into the muscles of the thigh; either it could not be pulled out (the shaft had broken, 584) or its extraction would cause the barbs to lacerate the flesh or leave the arrow-head embedded. The μάχαιρα makes a clean cut and avoids the arteries. — Patroklos is still treating Eurupulos when this thread of the narrative is picked up at 15.390, see nn. there for the poet's handling of his narrative as a sequence of episodes and the apparent delay that follows in the movements of Nestor and Patroklos. In book 16 (25–9) Patroklos tells Akhilleus that the surgeons are attending to the casualties and does not mention his own services.

848 Four papyri from the third century B.C. bridge a Book division: *Il.* Pap. 5 (11–12), Pap. 12 (22–3), *Od.* Pap. 31 (9–10), Pap. 146 (21–2); but Pap. 5 is the only one with the left margin intact. There is no para-graphos or any mark at all of the Book division, nor did any of the other papyri leave, for example, additional space. The implications, which in any case are obscure, are discussed by West, *Ptolemaic Papyri* 20–5.

BOOK TWELVE

The twelfth Book contains some of the most celebrated scenes in the *Iliad*: Hektor's riposte to Pouludamas at 231–50, Sarpedon's address to Glaukos at 310–28, and Hektor's breaking through the gates at 445–66, as well as some notable narrative scenes such as the Trojan storming party at 256–64. The Book also contains some of the finest Iliadic similes, the snowflakes of 278–86 and the lion of 299–306. However, these undoubted qualities of execution exist within one of the most weakly constructed Books of the *Iliad*. Yet all should have been clear: at 88–104 the Trojans divide themselves into five battalions; the attacks of each, thought of as simultaneous but narrated in sequence, should then have followed. The plan would have been simple, easy to handle, and above all clear. In fact, after the assault of Asios the storyline loses itself and only partially recovers with the attacks of Sarpedon and Hektor. For Leaf and other analysts the immediate solution was easy: the catalogue at 88ff. was the work of that author who 'so often interpolated into the speeches of Nestor untimely displays of tactical erudition'. Surgery of that kind, however, does little to remove the impression that the shape and detail of the Achaean fortress has not been worked out in the *Iliad* so well as the geography of the main battlefield.

In the scholia to the *Iliad* there are traces of an old controversy about the number of gates to the Achaean fortress. Nowhere indeed are we told clearly how many gates the poet imagined. Aristarchus wrote a monograph, Περὶ τοῦ ναυστάθμου, in which he argued that there was only one gate. As part of that argument he had to athetize lines 175–80. Those are rather pointless lines, but they do contain a reference to ἄλλαι πύλαι, i.e. at least two more besides the one under attack. Elsewhere references to unspecific πύλαι could be as easily understood to mean *the* gate, the single gate, as several; for the *Iliad*, as Aristarchus noted (Arn/A at 9.383), does not use πύλη in the singular.

How plausible is Aristarchus' suggestion in the narrative, supposing that he has not fallen into a historicist fallacy and attributed to the poet more precision than was ever intended? If there is a single gate, the question arises: where was it? bT to 7.339 provide the most detailed note: μία μὲν ἦν ἱππήλατος ἐπὶ τὸ ἀριστερὸν τοῦ ναυστάθμου πρὸς τὸ Ῥοίτειον (similarly Arn/A on 12.118). Verses 118–19 do indeed state that Asios proceeded νηῶν ἐπ' ἀριστερά where the Achaeans were still pouring into the camp. From his standpoint, however, 'left' would mean the Achaean right where

313

Akhilleus had his station. That is consistent with the narrative of 11.613–15, where the wounded are driven past Akhilleus to reach their quarters, and consistent with Asios' meeting the Lapithai, one of the Thessalian contingents (see 175–8n.). But a single gate on the extreme left (or right) of the camp is unconvincing as a sole means of access, even if (as the scholia propose) that was the sole ἱππήλατος gate and other πυλίδες were provided. And would the poet make the Trojans attack the very sector behind which the Myrmidons were waiting?

After the repulse of Asios the narrative moves to Hektor. While (ὄφρα 195) the Lapithai were doing execution, Hektor's troops were waiting at the ditch (199) while their officers pondered on an omen. The attack is led in the first instance by Hektor and Pouludamas but presently they drop out of sight and the attack is made by the Trojans generally not by Hektor personally. But where is Hektor? He *could* be waiting to take over the attack after Asios' failure. But if that were so he would first have to deal with the victorious Lapithai. As it is they disappear from the narrative completely. And at this point Hektor's troops do not make an attack on a gate. Their aim is to breach the *wall* – ῥήγνυσθαι μέγα τεῖχος – and that is intended literally because how they proposed to do it is described in detail with plentiful use of technical terms (251–64). Their attack then is made on a different sector from that assaulted by Asios (see 443n.).

Then at lines 290–414 Sarpedon and Glaukos enter the battle. They attack and partially breach the *wall* (397–9). They do so at a specific point, the πύργος defended by Menestheus (332). In the Greek order of battle Menestheus is stationed on the centre right next to the Thessalians under Podarkes. The Aiantes, who had been resisting Hektor at 265ff., must move to his aid, so that Sarpedon's attack is on yet another sector. Hektor then makes a final effort, presumably on the sector which the movement of the Aiantes has weakened. The Trojans make for the *wall*, but Hektor seizes a chance to burst open a *gate* (436–71). This gate is not on the Achaean left, for the fighting in book 13 takes place distant from the quarters of Idomeneus which were on the Achaean left (13.210ff.) and Hektor is said to be fighting νηυσὶν ἐν μέσσῃσιν at 13.312.

This obscurity about the gate, unimportant in itself, is indicative of the ambiguity of the narrative line. The brigading of the Trojans and their allies into five divisions foreshadows a typology like that of the attack on Thebes by the Seven; five gates and five assaults – simultaneous but narrated sequentially (bT to 12.1 recognize this technique). For three hundred verses the narrative seems to follow this pattern: 118–94 Asios with the third division; 195–289 Hektor with the first division; 290–429 Sarpedon and Glaukos with the fifth division. What has happened to the divisions of Paris and Aineias, and why is Hektor's first assault not kept for the climax? But with the failure of Asios' attack the whole typology of the fighting becomes assimilated to the pattern of fighting on the open plain before Troy. Familiar motifs are employed: a hero encourages another, a warrior summons another to his aid, general descriptions with similes. There is a short *aristeia* of the Lapithai (182–94). The poet then puts in a long general description of the Trojan attack and Achaean defence (251–89). Sarpedon encourages Glaukos (cf. the conversation of Aineias and Pandaros, 5.166–238); Teukros incapacitates Glaukos with an arrow and nearly wounds Sarpedon (cf. Paris' exploits in book 11). Paris and Aineias drop out completely. And with the disappearance of the five divisions the narrative follows the convenience of the moment and there disappears also any idea of their attacking separate gates.

The most awkward matter is the fact that Paris and Aineias are formally introduced and then given nothing to do. Nor is their absence explained. This is the most striking example in the *Iliad* of a major pattern of narrative broken off before it is completed, but cf. 14.402 where πρῶτος should mark the beginning of an *aristeia*, or the council (14.27–134), which foreshadows the entry into battle of the wounded leaders, an effective scene that fails to materialize. At the risk of invoking a universal panacea it is possible that the stresses of oral composition have upset the poet's designs. (An accident of rhapsodic transmission of the text would be equally possible and equally hypothetical.) The twelfth Book is a well defined episode, clearly marked off from the preceding and following episodes, but it is a short Book, only 471 lines, and impressive as its content is it is overshadowed and truncated by the climax of the fifteenth Book which the composer must simultaneously keep in mind. Its culmination is the tremendous epic moment of Hektor standing in the open gate, a moment *towards which the poet is hastening* from the moment when he brought the Trojans up to the Achaean trench.

For further discussion of the structure of the Book see Fenik, *Homer and the Nibelungenlied* 12–34, and for recent, analytical views of the fighting at the Wall van Thiel, *Ilias und Iliaden* 33–50. Van Thiel posits a 'Mauergedicht' which provided much material for what is now books 12–15.

The episodes themselves form a succession of imaginative *tours de force* that depict the scene in heightened heroic colours – one did not in life attack a gate in a chariot, pull down a wall with a wrench of the arm, or shatter a gate with a stone held in one hand – but the underlying narrative is realistic, though the tactics described do not reflect a high level of sophistication in siege warfare. Attackers and defenders make use of their normal weapons; there are no siege engines, not even a simple battering ram, and no thought is given to filling the Achaean ditch or heaping up a siege mound against the wall. This then is an improvised assault, and within the limits set by such an operation of war both sides conduct themselves like competent armies. No gods intervene to smooth the way, as Apollo does at 15.360–6, so the Trojans must try to carry the wall by weight of numbers or breach it with crowbars, while the Achaeans man the battlements and reinforce a threatened sector.

The Homeric picture may be compared with the account of a historical attack on a palisaded fort, the defence of Le Puiset, a motte-and-bailey castle, against the forces of Louis the Fat in A.D. 1111 as related by Abbot Suger, an eyewitness. The attack moved through six stages.

First, the rebel count, Hugo, sought to fight off the royalists outside his defences, cf. the tactics of the Lapithai (124ff.). When that failed he manned his ramparts to use the advantage of height. The royalists launched a general attack and forced the defenders inside their fortifications. A furious exchange of missiles followed with arrows falling like a shower of rain, cf. 151ff., with some use of larger missiles, cf. the μύλακες at 161.

Third, the royalists concentrated on the gate, cf. 442ff., attempting to fire it, cf. 177.

Fourth, by organizing a mobile force the defenders were able to repulse into the fosse a diversionary attack, cf. Αἴαντε ... πάντοσε φοιτήτην 265ff. Whether intentionally or no (the text does not say) the attack launched by Sarpedon had the effect of diverting the strongest part of the Achaean defence from the gate that was forced by Hektor.

Fifth, inspired by the example of a priest, the attackers tackled the palisade with axes, cf. the Trojan tactics at 256ff.

Finally, when the royalists had made a breach, many of the defenders were killed and the survivors withdrew to the elevated motte and continued the fight from there, an option not available to the Achaeans (Suger, *Vita Ludovici Grossi Regis*, ed. H. Waquet (Paris 1929) 130–41).

The similarities, which arise from each army following the tactics that would occur to the mind of any commander in such circumstances, bring out the basic restraint of the Homeric narrative. Its fictions are ἐτύμοισιν ὁμοῖα (Hes. *Theog.* 27).

1–33 The narrative returns from the ships where Nestor and Patroklos were conversing to the battlefield, but before the poet develops the usual piece of general description of the fighting the mention of the Achaean ditch and wall leads the poet into a digression: the works had been begun without divine blessing and were to be obliterated by the rivers of the Troad on the morrow of the Achaeans' departure

The building of the wall was proposed by Nestor at 7.337–43 and executed at 7.436–41; its destruction was adumbrated in Zeus's reply to Poseidon's complaint (7.446–63). There are allusions in the *Iliad* to monuments in the region of Troy (the tomb of Ilos, 10.415, etc., that of an unknown warrior, 23.331) but it is unclear whether the poet wishes to imply that these were visible in his own day. See 10.415n. for the monuments in existence c. 700 B.C. The present passage reads like a naive device to explain why no Achaean wall, or its ruins, stood in the poet's day. This is the view taken by bT here and at 7.445, cf. Aristotle fr. 162 Rose [τὸ τεῖχος] οὐδ' ἐγένετο, ὁ δὲ πλάσας ποιητὴς ἠφάνισεν (= Strabo 13.1.36). It may also be noticed that since the wall is to be the centre-piece of this Book it is appropriate to comment on its history outside the time-span of the epic, cf. the story of Odysseus' bow, *Od.* 21.11–41, here (since it has no history to speak of) on the fate of the wall. For the view that the emphasis on destruction and death in these lines reflects the idea known from the *Cypria* that Zeus designed the annihilation of the race of heroes see R. Scodel, *HSCP* 86 (1982) 33–53.

The building of the wall is plausible as something that a real army might do, but it is not introduced into the *Iliad* because in the saga of Troy the Achaeans did in fact build it as related in book 7. Thucydides (1.11.1), who argued that the wall, or a wall, was built in the first year of the war, would have saved himself and Homer's commentators much speculation (see 7.327–43n.) if he had been able to recognize the existence of fiction in Homer. The point of the wall is not to record a fact but to give structure generally to the central battle for the ships and specifically to permit the introduction in this Book of an *Assault*.

Strabo (13.1.31–2) locates the ναύσταθμον near Sigeion 20 stades from classical Ilium, but also reports a place called Ἀχαιῶν λιμήν only 12 stades distant at least half of which, he says, was post-Homeric accretion to the delta of the Skamandros.

1–8 Fragments of these verses are contained in the third-century papyrus Pap. 5 (see 11.788n.). There are no plus-verses. For the papyrus' failure to mark the book division see 11.848n.

1–2 The Book begins in the same way as book 9 (see 9.1n.) with a reference to the last scene of the preceding book using the formula ὡς ὁ (οἱ) μέν ... *X* δέ (αὐτάρ *X*).

3 ὁμιλαδόν: the ὅμιλος is the mass of warriors around or behind the πρόμαχοι, so that the battle has now become general just as it was at the beginning of book 11 (11.67ff.). A simile to illustrate the ferocity of the fight could be expected to follow, but the description of battle is overtaken by the digression about the Achaean wall.

5–6 ≅ 7.448–9. This description, and especially the words τεῖχος ὕπερθεν in 4, seems to envisage the ditch and wall as a single composite fortification. That would be a sensible arrangement that increased the effective height of the wall, but it is at variance with the narrative of books 9 (see 9.67 and n.) and 10 (see 126, 194) and of this and the following Books, which envisages a space between the ditch and wall. For the purpose of this arrangement, if it has any foundation in military practice, see 65–6n.

7 *Pace* Leaf ληΐδα πολλήν at the end of this verse implies that the wall was built when the *Iliad* says it was, to defend the loot taken in Akhilleus' raids around the Troad.

9–33 Thus far what the poet has said about the Achaean wall he has said in his normal role as the observer of the Trojan war, so to speak, as the Muse unfolded it before his eyes; now he reveals his historical perspective, reporting as fact what Zeus had prophesied at 7.459–63.

11 ἔπλεν is the reading (or the implied reading) of the vulgate. It is guaranteed by the attempts, noted in T, on the part of Zenodotus (by 'apocope' of ἔπλετο) and Aristarchus (by syncope of ἔπελεν) to explain it. The form is indeed, as Leaf says, a *vox nihili*, but that is from the viewpoint of vernacular Greek. The *Kunstsprache* was exempt from the regular rules of word-formation, and the creation of an active ἔπλε(ν) beside the middle ἔπλετο would seem to be well within the limits of its inventiveness. ἦεν, the reading of Allen's '**h**' family of MSS, is clearly intrusive from verse 12.

12 τόφρα ... ἔμπεδον ἦεν: the poet speaks generally. In fact Apollo levelled a whole section of wall to speed on the Trojans' final assault, 15.355–66, 'as easily as a child knocks down a sand-castle'.

14 οἱ μὲν δάμεν, οἱ δὲ λίποντο is barely logical as an expansion of the verb of the δέ-clause. In the oral manner the poet adds to the sentence the thought that some of the Achaeans survived the war. A formula lurks behind the expression, cf. πολλοὶ μὲν ... δάμεν, πολλοὶ δὲ λίποντο (*Od.* 4.495).

17 Poseidon and Apollo are the gods concerned and act together in spite of being currently on opposite sides because, as Poseidon complained at 7.451–3, not only had the Achaeans omitted the proper hecatombs but also the κλέος of Agamemnon's wall was like to surpass that of the wall he and Apollo had built for Laomedon, an unacceptable infringement of the gods' τίμη – a good point if it is taken in isolation; however Poseidon and Apollo had swallowed a direct insult from Laomedon, see 21.442–57, and *his* wall stood notwithstanding. The two gods act, as gods usually do in the *Iliad*, as persons not as personifications of their provinces in the natural world. Poseidon was god of earthquakes, ἐνοσίχθων and ἐννοσίγαιος, in which capacity he would have been well placed to demolish a wall.

18 τεῖχος ἀμαλδῦναι must envisage a wall built in part at least of sun-dried brick. Brick walls erected on a stone footing are common at all times, e.g. at Old Smurne before 800: discussion and examples in Lawrence, *Fortification* 203–20. — μένος is 'energy'. In the Homeric view of the world there is little difference in the potential of animate and inanimate forces, hence μένος can denote the power of water (as also at 21.305, 21.383), wind

(5.524, *Od.* 5.478, 19.440) or fire (23.177, 23.238 = 24.792) as readily as the vitality of a human being or animal (horse 23.468, 23.524, mule *Od.* 7.2, lion 5.136, 20.172).

20–2 The rivers of the Troad. The Rhesos, Heptaporos, Karesos, Rhodios, and Grenikos are mentioned only here in the *Iliad*. That is not surprising, since together with the Aisepos (which flowed past Zeleia into the Propontis, 2.824–7) they do not flow across the Trojan plain. The names, however, form some sort of traditional list for they recur (except for Karesos) in the list of rivers in Hesiod *Theog.* 338–45, see West's n. *ad loc.* Hesiod's list is incoherent and suggested already to Aristarchus that Hesiod had taken the names from this passage, οὐ γὰρ ἐξενήνοχε τοὺς ποταμοὺς μὴ ὄντας ἀξιολόγους εἰ μὴ δι᾽ Ὅμηρον (Arn/A); a good point, but by no means conclusive. It is usually safer in cases such as this to think of the two poets drawing on similar traditional sources, see for example the commentators on *Od.* 8.167ff. There are, however, some indications that the tradition behind this digression is not that which provides most of the background to the *Iliad*, see nn. to 11, 23, 27, and 33. For further discussion see J. Butterworth in *Studies Webster* I 37–9.

20 The jingle 'Ῥῆσος ... Κάρησος, however handy as a mnemonic device, is uncharacteristic of Homeric/Hesiodic cataloguing style; Hesiod, *loc. cit.*, avoided it. Heptaporos, 'seven channels' (or 'fords'), is presumably a Hellenization of an aboriginal name. The Rhesos was unidentified in classical times, 'unless it be the Rhoeites' (Demetrius of Scepsis, a would-be expert on the Troad, *apud* Strabo 13.1.44). Pliny, *NH* 5.124, could find no trace of the Heptaporos, Karesos, and Rhodios either; the former was identified with the Pidys, the latter with the Dardanos by the exegetic scholia. For the courses of the Grenikos (Granicus) and Aisepos, which run well to the east of the Troad, see map 3, vol. I 251.

21 δῖός τε Σκάμανδρος: the peculiar metrics whereby Σκ- do not make position, cf. the treatment of σκέπαρνον, σκίη (Hesiod, *Erga* 589) and Ζάκυνθος, Ζέλεια, have caused much discussion. Some, e.g. Heubeck, *Würzburger Jahrbücher* 4 (1950) 201, and Wyatt, *ML* 183 n. 1, have thought that the spelling σκ represented, in a non-Greek river-name, a non-Greek unitary phoneme, but the tradition of the grammarians, e.g. Monro, *GH* 343, Debrunner, *IF* 45 (1927) 183, and Chantraine, *GH* I 110, is strongly in favour of the view that we have a licence motivated by the clash between the needs of the narrator and the structural requirements of the hexameter. The whole matter is judiciously examined – and the grammarians supported – by O. Szemerényi in *Tractata Mycenaea, Proc. of the VIIIth International Colloquium on Mycenaean Studies* (1985) 343–7. Suggestions that Σκάμανδρος is translated by its alternant Ξάνθος, or (better) that the two names are versions of the same word, though attractive, remain unproven. δῖος is unusual as an epithet of a river (otherwise only at 2.522) and it is not clear what sense should be attributed to it. Its use may reflect a misunderstanding of διιπετής, in the formula διιπετέος ποταμοῖο, as 'fallen from Zeus', on which see *LfgrE*.

23 ἡμιθέων: many heroes were half-divine in the sense that they had a god or goddess for a parent, although (save for Akhilleus) they did not enjoy exceptional physical or mental attributes in consequence, see 10.47–50n. Within his narrative Homer does not recognize them as a separate class of being and therefore has no use for the present term, which occurs only here in the *Iliad*. But the peculiarity of the present passage is that the poet is not narrating events before Troy as it were as a contemporary observer but commenting upon them from the standpoint of a later age, from which the heroes may well have seemed half-divine, cf. *h.Hom.* 31.19, 32.19. As a description of the heroes ἡμίθεος expresses a Hesiodic idea, cf. ἀνδρῶν ἡρώων θεῖον γένος, οἳ καλέονται | ἡμίθεοι (*Erga* 160–1). For that reason, for Hesiod, they did not die like other men but were translated by Zeus to the Isles of the Blessed. For Homer all heroes of whatever parentage are human and mortal, and this is an important part of the poet's conception of their predicament as they struggle for κῦδος, see Griffin, *HLD* 81ff.

25 ἐννῆμαρ: T notes that the poet εὐεπίφορος ἐστὶν εἰς τὰ ἐννέα, cf. 6.174n. and [Plutarch], *Vita Hom.* 145, and the number indeed enjoyed a certain popularity (21× in *Il.*), on which see F. B. Anderson, *CJ* 50 (1954–5) 131–8. The nine-day flood is emblematic of divine power, yet at 15.355–66 (simile of the sand-castle) Apollo displayed even greater power by his swift destruction of the κάματος καὶ ὀϊζύς (cf. μογέοντες 29) of the Achaeans. Callistratus is reported (T) to have read ἐν δ' ἦμαρ, a silly conjecture lest Zeus and Apollo should seem to spend nine days in demolishing what men had taken one to build.

26 συνεχές: *Od.* 9.74 has the same metrics. The long ῡ is unexpected but analogous to other lengthened prefixes of -εχ-: ὑπείρεχον (2.426, etc.), πᾶρέχῃ (*Od.* 19.113), as if < (ϝ)έχω not (σ)έχω. The formula συνεχὲς αἰεί is a member of an adverbial set: ἀσφαλὲς αἰεί, νωλεμὲς αἰεί, etc.

27 Poseidon's trident is so familiar a part of his iconography that it is remarkable it should be mentioned only here in the *Iliad*. It occurs twice in the *Odyssey* (4.506, 5.292). Poseidon may be thought to have used his trident on this occasion but it is really a permanent adjunct of the god, the pictorial equivalent of his Homeric epithets.

28–29 The θεμείλια are 'footings'. They make level the base of the super-structure of the wall where the ground is rocky and are normally wider than the superstructure so as to spread the load, see 258n. (κρόσσαι). φιτρῶν καὶ λάων is a nondescript expression, but it stuck in the poet's mind, see 21.314.

30 ἀγάρροον Ἑλλήσποντον is almost certainly formular, though unique in this case and position, cf. Ἑλλήσποντος ἀγάρροος (2.845). The -ρρ- of ἀγάρροον reflects the antecedent -σρ-, as ἀγάννιφος an earlier -σν-. The epithet is, of course, well justified as a general description. Modern charts show a westward current of 5.5 km per hour.

33 καλλίρροον ὕδωρ is an under-represented formula, absent from the *Odyssey* and the main body of the *Iliad*. It occurs also at 2.752 in the Catalogue (and in a spurious plus-verse 21.382a) but enjoyed favour in *HyAp.* (241, 380) and in the Hesiodic school (*Erga* 737, frr. 70.18, 185.12 M–W).

34–59 After his note on the Achaean Wall the poet devotes the rest of the book to the account of its defence. He begins in the usual way with a General Description of the battle, ornamented by a simile (41–8), as the Achaeans scramble to safety behind their trench and wall. Hektor probes the Achaeans' outer defences, but his horses refuse the ditch

35 ἀμφὶ ... δεδήει (< δαίω): literally 'blaze', but an established metaphor, cf. 6.328–9, and a possible use of πῦρ at 177 below.

36–7 It is odd that Aristarchus (Arn/A) did not recognize that the δούρατα are the same as the φιτροί of 29, but took them as spears hurled (βαλλόμενα 37) against the towers.

37 The scourge of Zeus appears again at 13.812, where see n. Zeus's terrible weapon, the thunderbolt, suggested the crack of a whip and its effect (so bT here and the D scholia to 13.812). But Zeus reserves his ultimate weapon for use against gods, cf. 8.405, 15.117, 21.198 (although he used one against Diomedes at 8.133), and no literal thunderbolt can be intended here. Zeus is exerting his power from Ida and driving on the armies like herds of horses. For this reminder of the influence of Zeus on the battle see 11.74–83n.

41–8 The simile describes the actions of a boar or lion at bay but not intimidated by hunters; it stalks up and down, makes rushes at the men, and is killed as a result of its very resolution. One is surprised then to find that all this illustrates, not the actions of one of the defending commanders, but Hektor (49). Fränkel, *Gleichnisse* 67, compares the boar-simile used of the beset Odysseus at 11.414–18, and, taking στρέφεται (2 and 47) as the point of comparison, tentatively suggests that verses 41–6 are traditional and partially adapted to their present use by the addition of 47–8 which present the boar, and so Hektor, as looking for a weak spot. T make a similar point, calling everything that does not immediately apply to Hektor ποιητικὸς κόσμος. (On similes, or some similes, as traditional 'runs' see C. M. Bowra, *Tradition and Design* 116–19.) W. C. Scott, *The Oral Nature of the Homeric Simile* (Leiden 1974) 61, sees the parallel in the present example not between the actions of the parties but in their feelings, viz. their impetuosity and frustration. This is accepted by Moulton, *Similes* 47–8. Even if not the primary point, feelings are implicit in most comparisons with animate subjects. The disjunction 'boar or lion' occurs also at 11.293 'to strengthen the essential idea of the comparison', here latent aggression (Edwards, vol. v 37).

41–2 ὅτ' ἂν ... στρέφεται: when a simile has been introduced by ὡς ὅτε with the subjunctive it may be continued paratactically by verbs in the present indicative (Goodwin, *Syntax* 210), but the indicative (as it must be) in direct construction with ἂν astonishes, however, cf. 1.67n. and *Od.* 10.410–12 ὅτ' ἂν ... σκαίρουσι (on which see Chantraine, *GH* II 356) and *Od.* 24.88–9 ὅτε κεν ... ζώννυνταί τε νέοι καὶ ἐπεντύνονται ἄεθλα (where emendation is metrically possible). The construction does not recur before Hellenistic times.

41 The expression κύνεσσι καὶ ἀνδράσι θηρευτῇσι recurs in the nominative at 11.549 (= 15.272) as κύνες τε καὶ ἀνέρες ἀγροιῶται: the hunters of Homeric similes are peasants not sportsmen.

43 πυργηδόν: seen from the front the line of men resembles a wall (πύργος). The same word occurs also at 13.152 and 15.618, and the same formation of troops at 4.334, 4.347. It is glossed as κατὰ τάξιν τείχους by Hsch., and as διάταξις στρατιωτικὴ τετραγωνοειδὴς κατὰ πλινθίον συντεταγμένη by Eust. 829.10, i.e. 'close-packed', cf. 16.212–14 ὡς δ' ὅτε τοῖχον ἀνὴρ ἀράρῃ πυκινοῖσι λίθοισι | ... ὡς ἄραρον κόρυθές τε καὶ ἀσπίδες ὀμφαλόεσσαι. At 15.615ff. Hektor fails to break the ranks because they are πυργηδὸν ἀρηρότες – 'rock solid', as a simile there explains. The πύργος could also be an offensive formation, cf. 105n. 'Turris' was a term of the Roman army (Gell. 10.9.1; cf. Dion. Hal. *Ant. Rom.* 6.33).

44–5 ἀκοντίζουσι θαμειὰς | αἰχμάς: an instance of Kirk's 'violent enjambment' where the end of line does not coincide with any point of natural articulation of the sentence, see *YCS* 20 (1966) 107. This particular phrase, however, is formular, cf. 14.422–3. There is another example of violent enjambment at 51–2, ἐπ' ἄκρῳ | χείλει. At 50–1 οὐδέ οἱ ἵπποι | τόλμων ὠκύποδες is weaker, an instance of 'integral enjambment', cf. 54–5, 55–6. The whole passage 43–59 is well-enjambed, though most instances are of the weak, 'progressive' sort exemplified by ἀπὸ γὰρ δειδίσσετο τάφρος | εὐρεῖ', 52–3, cf. also 49–50, 53–4, 56–7. This kind of composition reflects the tension of this dramatic moment as the Trojans close up to the Achaean lines.

46 ἀγηνορίη δέ μιν ἔκτα: cf. φθίσει σε τὸ σὸν μένος (6.407), which also refers to Hektor. That Hektor's courage was his undoing is part of Homer's conception of that hero. For the thought cf. ἑή τέ μιν ὤλεσεν ἀλκή (16.753), of Patroklos.

49–50 Delebecque, *Cheval* 77, finds fault with this passage because it seems to envisage that chariotry might contemplate leaping such an obstacle as the Achaean ditch as if they were mounted cavalry. The crucial point, however, is what the poet thought it a plausible fiction to affirm: at 8.179 he makes Hektor assert that his horses easily τάφρον ὑπερθορέονται and in a fine hyperbole at 16.380 he imagines the immortal horses of Akhilleus doing just that, while the mortal teams were wrecked. The speech of Pouludamas (61–79) shows that the poet was well aware of the effectiveness of earthworks as a defence against chariotry. Even so Hektor's team, for epic horses, put up an unimpressive performance: the heroic horses of central Asian epic traditions take rivers in their stride, see A. Hatto in Hainsworth (ed.), *Traditions of Heroic and Epic Poetry* ii (London 1989) 108ff. — ἐλίσσεθ' ἑταίρους: the etymology of λίσσομαι is unclear, but the initial λ- always makes position in the *Iliad* (except at 16.46 ὡς φάτο λισσόμενος), probably by analogy with words having a genuinely original σλ-. The lengthening is applied to the prefix in all four augmented forms that occur in the *Iliad*, cf. 6.45, 9.585, 21.71, and this is often marked by MSS and edd. by the spelling -λλ- (as OCT marks at 9.585). Odyssean usage is altogether less regular. ἐλίσσεθ', 'pleaded', expresses a humble posture (cf. 11.610) for a commanding officer and combines awkwardly with ἐποτρύνω in 50 (ἀρχοὺς λισσομένῳ at 5.491 is a different situation). Hence Nicanor discussed the possibility of reading εἰλίσσεθ' here (which would neatly pick up στρέφεται from 47) but rejected it on the grounds that to separate ἑταίρους from the principal verb and construe it with ἐποτρύνων in the next verse would be an un-Homeric division of phrases, in fact a very violent enjambment. There is strong enjambment in this passage, cf. 44n., but in no case does it lead to a break in sense in the fifth foot of the verse. LSJ (s.v. ἐλίσσω) construe with ἑταίρους and translate 'rallied his comrades' – but Hektor is here very much on the offensive.

50–4 Four enjambed verses express the excitement of this moment. The progressive enjambments of 50–1, 52–3, and 53–4 are straightforward and ἵπποι | – – ὠκύποδες is formular (3× *Il.* 1× *Od.*). The violent enjambment of ἐπ' ἄκρῳ | χείλει (cf. 44–5n.) is an almost onomatopoeic description of the chariots teetering on the brink of the Achaean ditch.

53 σχεδόν: 'at close quarters', the usual sense of σχεδόν, is unintelligible here: hence 'at a bound', cf. αὐτοσχέδιος, 'offhand' (Monro), 'in serried ranks' (Leaf). Perhaps = σχεδόθεν; Hektor's horses have shied at the ditch, they cannot leap it *from the edge* (but might in the poet's imagination if they took a run at it, like Patroklos' horses at 16.380).

54–7 H. Drerup, *Arch. Hom.* o 100, visualizes a stockaded earthwork as the fortification described by these verses. That is the sort of structure the circumstances would demand and permit, yet the poet seems to describe a more substantial edifice, being constrained perhaps by the traditional diction for an assault on a city: see 258n. The σκόλοπες, for example, were part of the reinforcement of the town-wall of Skherie in *Od.* 7.44–5. Here they are ὀξέες – the slight emphasis that the runover position confers marks this as a significant quality, i.e. it is the upper end that is sharpened – as if intended to impale an enemy attacking the ditch. The extensive use of mud-brick and unconsolidated material even in permanent fortifications makes it impossible to verify the details of the Homeric description from extant remains of town-walls in Ionia or elsewhere in Greece. κρημνοὶ ἐπηρεφέες, literally 'overhanging', must be an impressionistic or hyperbolical description of the heaped-up earth, unless the σκόλοπες are thought to project horizontally. ἀμφοτέρωθεν is possibly poetical elaboration. In practice an earthwork is more formidable if the soil is thrown up on one side. ὕπερθεν: i.e. on the crest of the κρημνοί, so as to form a breastwork. Lattimore's rendering (*The Iliad of Homer* (Chicago 1951)), 'the surface of the floor was thickset with pointed palisades', is more consistent with Pouludamas' description at 63–4 (q.v.) than with the Greek in this verse. The ditch plays an important role in the assault until 199, after which it disappears from view until 15.344. It does not impede the attacks of Sarpedon or Hektor.

56 ἠρήρει: the subject is τάφρος. ἔστασαν (not ἵστασαν as in OCT) is the transmitted form and was accepted by Aristarchus. It is philologically improbable as a genuine alternative to ἔστησαν as a 3rd person plural of the causative aorist, though that would not have deterred ἀοιδοί from creating it. It may be retained, as also at 2.525 and probably at 18.346, for the erection of the stakes is not a process such as would call for an imperfect tense. (The quasi-homophone ἔστασαν at 55 is the pluperfect, an awkward jingle to the modern ear.)

60–107 The pause at the ditch enables the poet to set the scene by means of a speech from Pouludamas for an assault en règle. Pouludamas explains to Hektor the hazard presented by the ditch and proposes they make the assault as infantry. Hektor accepts this sensible advice and dismounts. The Trojans divide themselves into five companies, each under three commanders

58 ἐύτροχον ἅρμα is probably formular, cf. 8.438, but has a duplicate ἐύξοον ἅρμα at 2.390. The formula system around ἅρμα is weakly developed (θοὸν ἅρμα 3×, καμπύλον ἅ. and ἀγκύλον ἅ. 1× each). καμπύλον and ἀγκύλον are borrowed from the formula system of the bow.

59 πεζοί is predicative with εἰ τελέουσι, 'if they do it on foot'. μενοίνεον, like ὁμόκλεον (15.658), ἤντεον (7.423), and ἐσύλεον (v.l. at 5.48), represents a transfer from the -άω to the -έω conjugation attested only in these metrically convenient forms; it would have been facilitated by the ambivalent -ησαν in the aorist, see Meister, *Kunstsprache* 77–8.

60 = 210. Πουλυδάμας is son to the Trojan elder Panthoos (3.146). There is a passing reference to him at 11.57 but he appears here for the first time in his characteristic role as giver of sound advice to Hektor. Uncharacteristic, however, is Hektor's reaction at 80; he was pleased. A more gripping idea widely exploited in heroic poetry is that the hero, from an excess of heroic virtue, rejects pleas and counsel to act in a prudent but less than heroic manner, see Introduction 49. So Asios (110ff.) disdained Pouludamas' manifestly sound advice to attack on foot and charged the gate in his chariot. This aspect of the hero asserts itself in subsequent exchanges between Hektor and Pouludamas (210ff., 13.726ff., 18.254ff.), where Pouludamas' caution sets off Hektor's recklessness. Pouludamas survived the *Iliad* and apparently the war. Virg. *Aen.* 2.318ff. records the death of the father (or any rate of a Panthous) at the sack of Troy but not that of the son. Pouludamas was a fighting hero as well as councillor, see 14.449–64, 15.339, 15.453–7, 15.518, 17.597–600. His arguments, however, are always concerned with safety and not with honour (contrast Odysseus at 11.404–10). Pouludamas fulfils most of the criteria for a character of the poet's invention: he has no role outside the *Iliad*, his role within the poem is well defined but not indispensable, his name is a straightforward formation (likewise his father Panthoos and brother Euphorbos), and nothing he does or says is not explicable by its immediate context. For his role *vis-à-vis* Hektor see M. Schofield, *CQ* 36 (1986) 18–22.

61–79 The first of Pouludamas' four speeches. The others are 12.211–29, 13.726–47, 18.254–83. There is a certain sameness between them, not perhaps deliberate (as was argued by Lohmann, *Reden* 178–82) but because the poet has a pattern for speeches of prudent admonition, cf. Nestor's speeches of tactical advice, 2.337–68, 7.327–43, 10.204–17.

63–4 The σκόλοπες are now 'in the ditch'. If Pouludamas' description is consistent with 54–7 he must, not unreasonably, make no distinction between the wall of the ditch and the face of the κρημνοί above where the σκόλοπες (55) were set ὕπερθεν, hence ''Tis crowned with pointed stakes' (Earl Derby). ποτὶ δ' αὐτούς: 'close behind' (Leaf) is the required sense but is not easily understood from the phrase, still less from the widely attested reading περὶ δ' αὐτούς.

65–6 These verses, with 49–54, offer some account of the purpose of the ditch. It keeps the enemy chariotry at a distance and restricts the manoeuvres of the forces that cross it, forcing them to deploy within range of the walls and preventing their retreat, cf. 16.368–9. The use of an outwork to supplement the main defensive wall is common from the mid-seventh century on Greek sites, see Lawrence, *Fortification* 279–88. The ditch at Vrulia in Rhodes *c.* 650 B.C. was sited so as to leave a space of 4–5 m before the wall; at Athens the fifth-century works near the Dipylon Gate allowed for a similar gap. One may suppose that the *Iliad* envisaged some such interval in the passages that speak of the ditch. στεῖνος: στεῖνος ὁδοῦ κοίλης 23.419 suggests that the 'narrow space' here is the confines of the ditch itself where it would indeed be difficult to fight effectively, mounted or on foot. Pouludamas would have a better point than this trite observation if we could take him to mean '⟨and even if we could cross⟩ we could not dismount from our chariots and fight effectively because the space on the other side is too narrow and dangerous'. καταβήμεναι: a sense 'to dismount (from the chariots *scilicet* after descending into the ditch)' is urged by Willcock, *Commentary ad loc.*

68 Pap. 69 has βούλετο νίκην, a familiar formula (4×) and combined with Τρώεσσι δέ at 7.21 and 16.121. ἵετ' ἀρήγειν and the vulgate βούλετ' ἀρήγειν are both unique phrases.

70 = 13.227 = 14.70. "αἰσχρὸν γὰρ τόδε γ' ἐστὶ καὶ ἐσσομένοισι πυθέσθαι", said Agamemnon of a failure to take Troy at 2.119. But to die νώνυμνος, unremembered and without hope of meaningful survival, is a fate even worse than the shameful (δυσκλέης) return feared by Agamemnon (2.115 = 9.22).

71–2 ὑποστρέψωσι: intransitive, = 'if they should rally', cf. ἐλιχθέντων at 74. παλίωξις (< παλι-ϝίωξις) is 'counter-attack' after a rally. ἐνιπλήξωμεν is also intransitive = 'be forced into'.

75 This is a standard formular verse (8× *Il.* 2× *Od.*).

76–7 πρυλέες: see 11.49n. Verses 77 + 84–5 = 11.47–9, but are now applied to the Trojans.

79 ὀλέθρου πείρατ' ἐφῆπται: see 6.143n. The metaphorical sense 'fasten the shackles of destruction upon' is thoroughly investigated by A. Bergren, ΠΕΙΡΑΡ *in Early Greek Poetry* (American Philol. Ass. 1975) 21–62.

80–1 = 13.748–9, the only other place where Hektor accepts Pouludamas' advice, cf. 231n. Verse 81 is a formular one (8× with minor variations).

83 Pouludamas spoke to Hektor and the Trojan captains (61), and it must not be thought that he could be heard by the rest of the army. The troops follow the example rather than the orders of their commander.

84–5 = 11.47–8, where the subject was the Achaeans, an instance of the dexterity with which the poet manipulates these runs of verses.

87–107 No division of the Trojan army into five or any other number of regiments is implied elsewhere; it was probably invented to add graphic detail to a momentous occasion, cf. the five leaders of the Pylians, 4.295–6 and the catalogue of the Myrmidons at 16.168ff., also in five divisions. Observe the artificial note of symmetry introduced by the recurrent pattern of one principal with two seconds. The principal Trojan captains are listed (after the demise of Asios) at 14.425–6 as Πουλυδάμας τε καὶ Αἰνείας καὶ δῖος Ἀγήνωρ | Σαρπηδών τ᾽, ἀρχὸς Λυκίων, καὶ Γλαῦκος ἀμύμων. (Very different lists of Trojan champions are given at 13.790–4 and 17.215–18.) There can be little doubt in the present context that such a catalogue should anticipate the form of the subsequent narrative, which would then tell of each assault in turn, rather as does Aeschylus in *Th.* and as the *Thebais* would have done. That would imply that the Achaean wall was pierced by five gates (an idea mooted by bT), but the number is nowhere specified, see introduction to this Book. In the event the theme disintegrates after the attack of Asios and in spite of some tentative attempts fails to re-establish itself. Yet the poet seems to recall his failure to tell of Aineias' attack when he brings him back into the fray at 13.458ff.: Aineias had been hanging back allegedly 'because Priam did not honour him', the occasion and manner of Priam's neglect being unstated. For the other personnel see nn. *ad locc.* T tries to relate the names to the entries in the Trojan Catalogue but without much success. The divisions do not attack in the order named here, but that of Asios first, then Hektor, Sarpedon, and finally Hektor again.

87 A quasi-formular verse, see 3.1n., here used to introduce a list of commanders, not to resume the narrative with the advance of the troops after a catalogue.

91 Κεβριόνης, a bastard son of Priam, was promoted Hektor's charioteer at 8.318 after the death of Arkheptolemos, see 11.521n. He fights alongside Pouludamas at 13.790 and is slain in his chariot by Patroklos at 16.733ff.

92 ἄλλον: the failure to assign a name to this worthless substitute is uncharacteristic. S. E. Bassett, *The Poetry of Homer* (Berkeley 1938) 256, notes similar anonymity only at 13.211 and 394.

93 Alkathoos, like Asios below, is killed in book 13 (424ff.). He appears only here and in 13 where, however, he is elevated into a son-in-law of Ankhises (428), and styled the best man in Troy.

94 Helenos was οἰωνοπόλων ὄχ᾽ ἄριστος at 6.76 but there is no other allusion to his mantic role in the *Iliad*. In the *Cypria* he prophesied the dire outcome of Paris' journey to Sparta. He has a considerable role in book 13 with five mentions, three of them in association with Deiphobos. Deiphobos, mentioned here for the first time, was a full brother to Hektor. Athene took his appearance to lure Hektor to his death (22.226ff.). There are two mentions of him in the *Odyssey*: 8.517, as the opponent of Odysseus and Menelaos at the taking of Troy, and 4.276 (athetized by Aristarchus, but defended by West, *Odyssey ad loc.*), as accompanying Helen on her inspection of the Wooden Horse. In the *Little Iliad* he married Helen after the death of Paris; that is nowhere stated in Homer, but seems to be hinted at in the Odyssean passages.

95–6 This Asios meets his death at 13.384–93 at the hands of Idomeneus. His home Arisbe is on the south shore of the Hellespont above Abudos. Note that 96–7 = 2.838–9 q.v. Another, undistinguished, Asios was full brother of Hekabe (16.717ff.). Asios is a senior figure; the Adamas at 140, etc. is certainly his son. There is also Phainops Ἀσιάδης, Ἀβυδόθι οἰκία ναίων, mentioned at 17.583, whose father may be the same as the present Asios or an echo of him. The name is not as 'Asiatic' as it may appear; an Asios was a genealogical poet of Samos, and an *a-si-wi-jo* is recorded at Cnossos (Df 1469, etc.). His father's name Hurtakos recalls the Lycian toponym *urtaqijahñ* and, perhaps more significantly, coincides with a place in Crete, cf. Phaistos at 5.43. Aristarchus (Arn/A) noted that the epanalepsis, Ἄσιος . . . | Ἄσιος, is typical of the *Iliad*, but occurred only once in the *Odyssey* (1.22–3).

96–7 = 2.838–9. ποταμοῦ ἀπὸ Σελλήεντος is independently formular, but the river at 2.659 and 15.531 flowed near Ephure, not into the Hellespont. See 15.531n.

98–9 Aineias has not been seen in action since his ignominious encounter with Diomedes at 5.297–317, nor indeed does he take part in the sequel in spite of this foreshadowing (as it must naturally be taken) of his assault.

100 These sons of Antenor are associated with Aineias in the Catalogue (2.819–23). Verses 99–100 = 2.822–3 with οὐκ οἶος for Αἰνείας.

101–2 Sarpedon and Glaukos, commanders of the Lycians (see 292n.), are the only leaders of the ἐπίκουροι of any consequence in the *Iliad* and play a role in the fighting second only to that of Hektor. Sarpedon slew Tlepolemos, the principal Achaean casualty in the first half of the *Iliad*, and meets his own death at the hands of Patroklos at 16.419ff. He and Glaukos were cousins, see the genealogy at 6.196–9 and 16.419–683n. Asteropaios here enters the epic for the first time. He has no role in the attack on the Achaean wall, but reappears in books 17 and 21. He was a leader of the Paeonians, not mentioned in the Catalogue (2.848–50), and perhaps for that reason as well as to increase the pathos of his death, is described as a recent reinforcement for the Trojans when he confesses his identity to Akhilleus at 21.153–60. It is the lack of first-rank fighting men among them that confines the ἐπίκουροι to one brigade; elsewhere it is implied they were numerous (2.130, 4.438, 17.154–5).

103–4 The pronouns οἱ (nom. plur.) and οἱ (dat. sing.) refer to Glaukos with Asteropaios and to Sarpedon respectively. The couplet explains the inclusion of Asteropaios, for Glaukos would be an automatic choice. None of the leaders of the more distant allies listed at 2.840–75 were worthy to stand beside the two Lycians.

105 ἀλλήλους ἄραρον may describe the formation called the πύργος when the army stands on the defensive, see 43n. and cf. 13.129–35 and

16.211–17 where the troops mass for a charge. In the present case the Trojans are assaulting fortifications and concentrating their attacks at particular points. Leaf was probably wrong to imagine a 'rudimentary sort of *testudo*', unless 'rudimentary' is stressed, for a more than rudimentary *testudo* would call for the rectangular shield of the Roman legionary, but he was right to recognize that the tactics of siege warfare are in question. The Trojan squads are to rush the gates. When they attack they do so βόας αὔας | ὑψόσ' ἀνασχόμενοι (137–8). For βόεσσι = 'shields' see 137n. τυκτῆσι: *vox propria* as epithet of a leather shield, cf. ὅ οἱ Τυχίος κάμε τεύχων, | σκυτοτόμων ὄχ' ἄριστος (7.220–21), of Aias' shield ἑπταβόειον.

106 The participle λελιημένοι, 'eager', is the only part in use of a defective verb. Some connexion, or confusion, with λιλαίομαι seems probable, see Chantraine, *Dict.* s.v., but cannot be directly established.

107 It would be natural to take the subjects of the infinitives σχήσεσθαι and ἐν ... πεσέεσθαι to be the Trojans, as in 9.235 (see n.) and (probably) 17.639; but when the verse recurs at 126, again with Trojans as subject of the leading verb, the subject of the infinitives is expressed, and is Ἀχαιούς. On that analogy some commentators (e.g. Leaf, tentatively) understand Δαναούς here and translate σχήσεσθαι as 'hold out' and πεσέεσθαι as 'die'.

108–194 Asios, leading the third division of the Trojan forces, refuses to dismount. The gate before him is open, but the Lapithai, Leonteus and Polupoites, advance to defend it and frustrate Asios' attack. After reflecting on the difficulty of his task the poet gives the two Lapithai a short aristeia

108–72 Asios tries to force the gate. This, the attacks of Hektor (195–289 and 442–71), Sarpedon (378–435), and Patroklos' onslaught (16.698–711), make up our corpus, such as it is, of archaic siege poetry in the narrow sense. Since a frontal assault on the enemy's walls is as much a climax of battle poetry as it is of battle, and since the siege scene has its place in the repertory of Mycenaean art (see Webster, *Mycenae to Homer* 58–63), these scenes are likely to be a remnant of a significant part of Late Helladic and Dark Age ἀοιδή. The well-designed bastions, casemates, and sally ports of Mycenaean fortifications are testimony to the art of defending (and by implication to the art of attacking) such works. Asios' mounted attack, however – two horses, two men, and a vehicle are a wasteful means of bringing two spears into action in a situation where every hand counted – is not war but magnificent poetic imagination. When Asios meets his death at the hands of Idomeneus at 13.384ff. he fights in the normal way, on foot, but with his chariot close at hand. The presence of his chariot within the fortifications in that passage and the oddity of his mounted assault here has been used as an argument for the dependence of the Asios episode on the narrative of book 13, cf. Von der Mühll, *Hypomnema* 206. The assaults of Asios, Hektor, and Sarpedon would naturally be launched simultaneously, and perhaps are to be so understood, but in the usual epic manner are narrated as if sequential.

111 For the suggestion that either ἡνίοχος or θεράπων is a personal name here see 13.386n. It is unusual for the charioteer not to be named in these contexts.

113–17 This foreshadowing of Asios' death reads like the setting up of an immediate narrative goal, like the prediction of Agamemnon's injury at 11.191ff., but Asios does not in fact die in the assault on the wall, in whose defence Idomeneus plays no recorded part, in spite of the fact that his station was νηῶν ἐπ' ἀριστερά. The *aristeia* of Idomeneus marks the first stage of the Achaean counter-attack (13.361ff.), and Asios was his second victim (13.383–93).

113 νήπιος (-ον, etc.) is highly formular (18× *Il.*, 9× *Od.* as runover word in the first foot) and therefore probably a traditional way in which the narrator, in spite of his apparent objectivity, intruded a personal comment on his story, see Edwards, vol. v 5.

115 = 8.499. Ἴλιος is normally feminine in the epic. A neuter form Ἴλιον αἰπύ is attested only at 15.71 (see n.), where Aristarchus emended it away. ἠνεμόεσσα is the regular epithet in this position (7× and *HyAphr* 280), cf. 3.305n.

118–19 εἴσατο, 'charged', is aorist of (ϝ)ίεμαι, see 11.358 and n. Arn/A refer the form to εἶμι, as did the poet at least sometimes: the digamma is ignored at 13.90, 17.285. ἐπ' ἀριστερά: the 'normal orientation when there is movement from one part of the battlefield to another' (Fenik, *TBS* 41): see also 11.498 and 5.355n. The poet can say ἐπὶ δεξιόφιν παντὸς στρατοῦ (13.308), but that expression is not formular. Oddly, formulas for movement to the right are lacking. 'Left' usually means left from the Achaean viewpoint (so Cuillandre, *La Droite et la gauche* 99), and it was νηῶν ἐπ' ἀριστερά where Asios was slain, cf. 13.674–6. But it remains odd that his opponents here are leaders of a Thessalian contingent, some of the Thessalians at least being brigaded on the Achaean right, see 11.5–9n. and introduction to this Book. Aristarchus (Arn/A) on the strength of this passage stationed the Lapithai next to Idomeneus, i.e. on the left. The matter is surprisingly difficult to resolve, cf. 13.681n., and the attempt may be futile; the narrative as usual is focused on the foreground and works through a cast of characters rather than a strategic plan. — The poet seems to envisage some means of passing the ditch in front of the gate. Over it the Achaeans are streaming σὺν ἵπποισιν καὶ ὄχεσφι, and Asios, mounted, follows. Any ancient or medieval audience would recognize the situation and its danger: the Trojans are about to pass the Achaean defences by mingling with the fugitives.

120–1 To shut the gates on fugitives must have been a desperate decision, cf. the dilemma of Priam at 21.531–6. The Lapithai, however, are not *enfants perdus*, fighting a delaying action with the gates closed at their backs. They are following a recognized tactical plan: προπάροιθε πυλάων ὑψηλάων | ἔστασαν (131–2), cf. 22.35–6 προπάροιθε πυλάων | ἑστήκει of Hektor's first design to resist Akhilleus. This is not as rash as it may seem since they are supported by the troops manning the wall, cf. 153. The alternative was stated by Hekabe, ἄμυνε δὲ δήϊον ἄνδρα | τείχεος ἐντὸς ἐών (22.84–5), as do the Aiantes (265ff.). — The ὀχεύς is to be understood as a massive wooden drawbar sliding in some sort of fitments on the back of the doors, see also 456n. where the gate has two ὀχῆες. The gates of the Achaean camp appear to be thought of as mere apertures in the curtain wall, vulnerable to frontal assault. This is very simple fortification but convenient for heroic attack and defence. The gates of the LH citadels at Tiryns, Midea, Mycenae, and Gla vary according to the terrain but are always designed to force an enemy attacking a gate into a confined area dominated by the defence; see the plans of Mycenae, etc., Sp. Iakovides, *Arch. Hom.* E 170ff. In Ionia the gateways of Old Smurne, Melia, and Miletos were formed by making one sector of wall overlap the next, with similar effect. Projecting towers, which enable defensive 'fire' to harass a force attacking the curtain wall at an enfilading angle, come into regular use in Greece only in the sixth century. See generally Lawrence, *Fortification* 246–62.

125 κεκλήγοντες: the Aeolic declension of the perfect participle is well attested and clearly right (see 16.430n.), although bastard forms in -ῶτες had invaded the paradosis deeply enough for Aristarchus to have hesitated: κεκληγῶτες καὶ κεκλήγοντες διχῶς αἱ Ἀριστάρχου (Did/A) at 13.30). -οντες, unlike the singular -ων, could not be directly Ionicized.

126 For the construction of this verse and the sense of πεσέεσθαι see 107n.

127–53 The account of the fight put up by the Lapithai is unclear. The two Lapithai are first outside the gates (131 προπάροιθε), then inside (142 ἔνδον ἐόντες), then outside again (145 πρόσθε). Suggested remedies have been to place 141–53 after 128 (or rather 130), or to condemn either 131–40 or 141–53. Leaf argues that 124–40 relate the situation that Asios found confronting him while 141–4 explain how it had arisen and 145–53 take the narrative back to the point reached at 140. That obliges him to render the imperfect ὄρνυον at 142 as 'had been inciting'. In the narrative of a fast-moving situation in which the poet's eye, as it were, leaps from point to point problems of this kind arise as easily as they can be exaggerated. The sequence of thought would be smoother if the vulgate ἔνδον ἐόντας *sc.* the Achaeans were read in 142 for Aristarchus' ἐόντες *sc.* the Lapithai. They can encourage the troops from their station outside the gates.

127ff. Verses 127–31 are contained in Pap. 432, for which see 11.265n. Verses 128–40, 176–91, 249–63, 355–71, 399–414, and 446–59 are contained in Pap. 121 + Pap. 342. (The two papyri are from the same roll, according to G. M. Bolling, *Journal of Egyptian Archaeology* 14 (1928) 78.) The stichometry used by the scribe indicates that he wrote up to five plus-verses between 192 and 249, two certainly after 347 and 350 corresponding to 360a and 363a in the parallel passage, and at least four more between 263 and 355, or 371 and 398, or 414 and 446. No more precise indications survive.

127–38 Zenodotus and Aristophanes read the dual throughout this passage according to Did/AT (so ἐπερχομένω 136 in Pap. 59). The dual is obviously impossible at some points, e.g. εὗρον 127, and introduces improbable hiatus in 127–8. Nevertheless it was adopted by Leaf.

128 Despite the fame of their battle with the Centaurs the Lapithai were an embarrassment to genealogists, see West, *Catalogue* 85–6. As a tribe they have no role in the Trojan saga and accordingly have only the briefest mention in the *Iliad*, here and at 181. They are mentioned once in the *Odyssey* at 21.297. Their leaders, Polupoites and Leonteus, are listed in the Catalogue as coming from northern Thessaly (2.738–47), without a note of their tribe, and *their* father Peirithoos is mentioned at 1.263 in Nestor's recollection of the fight with the Centaurs. They took part in the Games of Patroklos (23.836–7). The oddity is the neglect of the tribal name in the earlier allusions.

130 T reports a plus-verse (τινὲς ἐπάγουσιν), υἱὸν ὑπερθύμοιο Κορώνου Καινεΐδαο (130a = 2.746). The commentator takes the addition seriously and praises the style of the passage in the light of it: παρατήρει τὸ ποικίλον τῆς ἐπαγγελίας; he means the alternation between father's name + own name and own name + father's name. One of T's τινές is Pap. 432, which also inserts the verse as 190a. Pap. 121 omits the verse here but has it as 190a. For further discussion see West, *Ptolemaic Papyri* 99–101, who thinks its omission was accidental (*contra* van der Valk, *Researches* II 408–1). — βροτολοίγῳ ἶσον Ἄρηϊ: an extravagant compliment, though not so extravagant as Agamemnon's comparison to Zeus, Ares, and Poseidon at 2.478–9. The formula is otherwise reserved for Akhilleus and Hektor, see 11.604. Leonteus is ὄζος Ἄρηος at 188 and twice elsewhere, but that formula is clearly generic (applied to seven heroes in the *Iliad* and four others in the Hesiodic corpus).

132–6, 146–51 G. Murray objected that 'People who stand firm in front of a gate, like oaks, are not very like wild boars that rush out and tear up the undergrowth' (*Rise* 247). bT affirm reasonably enough that the oak represents firmness (as 135–6 indicate) and the boar firmness + aggression. But between the two similes the narrative moves on; at 131 the Lapithai are awaiting the onslaught, at 145 they move to repel it. At 151, however, it is made clear that the *tertium comparationis* of the second simile is the noise of gnashing teeth and clashing armour. For the gnashing teeth cf. 11.416, 13.474–5.

132 ὑψικάρηνοι is a *hapax legomenon*, apparently a variation of ὑψίκομος, the regular epithet of the oak (2× *Il.*, 4× *Od.*, and 2× in Hesiod).

134 An impressive four-word verse. ῥίζῃσι ... διηνεκέεσ' ἀραρυῖαι is a formula under-represented in the *Iliad*; it recurs, with ἀρηρώς, at Hesiod, *Theog.* 812, where the roots are metaphorical.

137–8 τεῖχος is used loosely, for Asios is attacking the gate, cf. 443 (τεῖχος) with 445ff. (πύλαι). The action of holding up the shield is natural in the circumstances, cf. the posture of the figures on the Silver Siege Vase from Shaft Grave IV at Mycenae (Lorimer, *HM* 142, fig. 4). No particular formation, like the Roman *testudo*, seems to be intended, for which ἀραρίσκειν would be the appropriate verb. The Siege Vase draws attention to an omission from the Homeric account, the absence of covering 'fire' from archers. For sophisticated Near Eastern siege methods see the silver bowl from Amathous (*Arch. Hom* N 10) and the discussion in Lawrence, *Fortification* 13–30. — For βοῦς in the sense of '(leather) shield' see 105 and 7.238. On the evidence of the *Iliad* βόας αὔας is not formular as a word-group, but the idea that the shield requires cured and toughened hide recurs in βῶν | ἀζαλέην, 7.238–9.

139–40 Note the Greek names, other than Iamenos, of these Trojans. Of Asios' satellites Iamenos and Orestes die at 193 and the rest along with their leader in book 13. Ἰάμενός can only be linked with ἰάομαι by popular etymology; von Kamptz, *Personennamen* 166, 349, suspects the presence of the Anatolian suffix -*mn*-. It is odd that the names of important figures in the wider Trojan saga – Orestes here, Helenos at 5.707 – should be used for these insignificant characters. Yet the *Iliad* needs an extensive onomasticon and avoids confusion of mind in its audience by making that Helenos an Achaean and this Orestes a Trojan. There is, however, an Achaean Orestes at 5.705, and another Oinomaos at 5.706, as if the names somehow formed a group.

141–2 The reference of οἱ is evidently to Polupoites and Leonteus (τώ would be better, cf. 131, 135, 145), verses 137–40 being parenthetic. The pronoun was sufficiently obscure for some MSS to change ἐϋκνήμιδας Ἀχαιούς to the nominative, but that would require ὄρνυον to be intransitive, which is impossible. For the vulgate reading ἔνδον ἐόντας see 127–53n. ἧος (εἵως codd.) is 'for a little time', as at 13.143, 15.277, 17.730.

143–4 = 15.395–6. ἰαχή τε φόβος τε is formular (4× and once in the dative). ἰαχή is certainly from Ϝιαχή and probably from σϝιαχή, see Chantraine, *Dict.* s.v. ἠχή, hence the length of the final syllable of γένετο.

145–51 The simile has caused difficulty by beginning as an illustration of the tactics of Leonteus and Polupoites, making sudden charges like wild boars, and ending with the noise of missiles against their armour, like boars whetting their tusks. The poet's picture of the action does not stand still during the simile, but *via* the image of the boars passes from movement to sound.

147–8 δέχαται is the 3rd person plural (< δέκ*η*ται – the -χ- is Attic) corresponding to the 3rd person singular δέκτο (2.420, 15.88), participle δέγμενος, etc. (2.794, 9.191, 18.524 (also ποτι-, ὑπο-)), and infinitive δέχθαι (1.23 = 1.377), to which the *Odyssey* adds an imperfect ἐδέγμην (*Od.* 9.513, 12.230). These forms are best regarded as the present and imperfect forms of an athematic conjugation of the root δεκ-, partly reinterpreted in the historic forms as aorists, see Chantraine, *GH* I 296, and 9.191n., and Shipp, *Studies* 63. κολοσυρτός: also at 13.472, in a similar context, a rather derogatory word, 'rabble'. The hunting party, it must be supposed, are not like the noble pursuers of the Calydonian boar (9.543), but peasants whose crops have been damaged. δοχμώ τ᾿ ἀΐξαντε: an authentic detail, the tusks of the boar do not point forwards, cf. λικριφὶς ἀΐξας (*Od.* 19.451), of the boar that wounded the young Odysseus.

149 ὑπαὶ δέ τε κόμπος ὀδόντων (= 11.417): in the midst of all this action (ὑπαί) there is heard the gnashing of the boar's teeth.

151 For the resumed narrative picking up a secondary point in the simile, here the sound of gnashed teeth by the sound of weapons on armour. Ameis–Hentze compare 13.492–5, where the troops follow their leader like sheep the ram, at which the shepherd is delighted, his pleasure being then echoed by that of Aineias, and 15.623–9, where Hektor's charge is compared to a wave crashing on a ship and terrifying the sailors, whose terror is then picked up by the terror of the Achaeans.

153 καθύπερθε is clearly used adjectivally with λαοῖσιν. It would in classical Greek require a verbal form (e.g. ἱσταμένοις) to give it construction. Zenodotus read λάεσσι (Did/A) for λαοῖσι, which would be awkwardly followed by οἱ in 154. No details are given in the *Iliad* of special works to improve the defensibility of the gate; the λαός have manned the battlements and hurl their missiles over the heads of Polupoites and Leonteus.

155 σφῶν τ᾿ αὐτῶν: the same orthography and the same phrase recurs at 19.302, but σφέων (monosyllabic) at 18.311 without αὐτῶν in a more archaic usage. The most archaic form is σφείων (metrically lengthened from dissyllabic σφέων), only in the formula ὦσαν ἀπὸ σφείων (3×).

156–8 This neat simile of the snowstorm anticipates the longer and more famous comparison at 278–89 (see nn. *ad loc.*). The parallelism between the assault of Asios and Hektor's first attack is emphasized by the relative rarity and brevity of other snow similes (only 3.222 (a short comparison) and 19.357–8) except where snow is an adjunct to hail or the like (10.7, 15.170, and 22.152). The image is usually that of falling snow (νιφάδες), not snow on the ground (χιών).

160 αὖον, literally 'dry', must mean a harsh, grating noise, cf. 13.441 and nn. to 13.404–10. But the juxtaposition with αὖτευν or αὖσεν is suspicious, as if some etymological connexion was felt to exist, as was suggested by M. Leumann, *Mus. Helv.* 14 (1957) 50.

161 The army had to bake its bread, so μυλάκεσσι, 'millstones', may be taken literally, in spite of their minimal effect on the Trojan helmets. Aias felled Hektor μυλοειδέϊ πέτρῳ at 7.270, a rock 'as big as a millstone', but that was on the battlefield, not a few yards from the huts and ships. At 380 we learn that the Achaeans had their ammunition ready beforehand on the battlements.

162 = 15.397, *Od.* 13.198. πεπλήγετο μηρώ is a formular gesture (4×, and recast with the verb in the sigmatic aorist in place of the archaic reduplicated form at 16.125, *HyDem* 245; for other references see 15.113–14n.); the concomitant dual is therefore probably an archaism too. What the gesture means (impotent rage) is unhelpfully glossed by ἀλαστήσας at 163. Chantraine, *Dict.* s.v. ἀλάστωρ, is unusually hesitant about this word and pronounces a derivation from ἄλαστος (as if = 'to find a situation "insufferable"') artificial. But the man who calls Zeus a liar at 164 can easily be imagined to exclaim (to use a mild rendering) 'Confound it!'

164–5 Asios' excessive language – and to call Zeus φιλοψευδής is excessive – exemplifies his exasperation: it is not hubristic in the sense that it calls for punishment, and Zeus reacts at 173 with indifference. Zeus does not fulfil all men's hopes, cf. 18.328, and it is natural for Homeric heroes to blame him, or the gods in general, when things go wrong. At 9.21 Agamemnon complained of the ἀπάτη of Zeus.

166 χεῖρας ἀάπτους is a common formula (10× *Il.*, 3× *Od.*). The general sense 'irresistible hands' makes it inappropriate in combination with σχήσειν, 'withstand'. The primary force of the adjective is evidently 'inexpressibly (strong)' and its primary form ἄ-(ϝ)επ-τος. The attested form is by diectasis of a hypothetical ἄπτος resulting from the contraction of vowels after the lapse of digamma. Aristophanes actually read ἀέπτους (Hrd/A at 1.567). See further 13.318n. Ancient interpretations (see *LfgrE*) link the word with ἅπτομαι, and so perhaps did the poet.

167–70 Wasps are the subject of a simile at 16.259–65 (see n.), and bees at 2.87–90. The rarity of these aggressive and/or useful insects in similes is unexpected, but insects are rare altogether; cicadas appear at 3.151–2, flies at 16.641–3 and 17.570–2, and grasshoppers at 21.12–13. bT, who hold (on 10.5) that there is a correlation between a character and the subject chosen for comparison, suggest that Asios' choice of insects is intended to be derogatory. That may be so, but this is one of those theses where favourable instances are counted and counter-examples ignored: the Achaeans at 2.87 and the Myrmidons at 16.259 are not subjects of adverse comment. αἰόλος is used in the epic as an attribute of a most heterogeneous group of nouns: of a horse's feet, wasps, gadflies, maggots, and of metallic objects. It appears to mean 'flickering' ('lebending-schimmernd', Mette, *LfgrE*). Ancient interpretations oscillate between ποικίλος and εὐκίνητος. Similes of parent defending young are found at 16.259–65 (wasps again), 17.133–7 (lioness), *Od.* 20.14–15 (bitch): vivid comparisons to an audience whose fighting men too often had to do just that, cf. 8.56–7, 11.242, 15.497–9, 17.223–4, 21.587–8, and especially such expressions as μαρνάμενος ὀάρων ἕνεκα σφετεράων (9.327), and *Od.* 8.525 ἄστεϊ καὶ τεκέεσσιν ἀμύνων νηλεὲς ἦμαρ. It is unusual for similes to occur in speeches (cf. 9.323–4n.); for half the speech to be so taken up is unparalleled, see Scott, *Simile* 50.

168 ὁδῷ ἔπι παιπαλοέσσῃ: cf. κατὰ παιπαλόεσσαν ἀταρπόν in another simile at 17.743. In the narrative the epithet is applied to an island at 13.33 ≅ 24.78 and *Od.* 15.29, and to a mountain at 13.17. The sense 'rough' would suit all of these, but the way in which it is to be understood in the similes is complicated by the expression Φοίνικες πολυπαίπαλοι, 'very devious', at *Od.* 15.419, as if the road favoured by the wasps was 'winding'. This and other ramifications of the word are examined by Shipp, *Essays in Mycenaean and Homeric Greek* (Melbourne 1961) 48–51.

170 θηρητῆρας is odd, unless the poet is now thinking exclusively of the bees and, though it is not mentioned, their honey. At 16.259, more realistically, it is pestering children against whom the wasps defend themselves.

171 Wasps or bees are a natural comparison for a crowd, but that association is here misleading; they are not cited here as a swarm of insects but as a type of tenacity, so that (*pace* Leaf *et al.*) the point of the simile is not nullified by the phrase καὶ δύ' ἐόντε. Aristarchus (Arn/A) took ἥρωας at 165 to mean πάντας κοινῶς, but Asios, true to the ideology of Homeric battle, can see only the two Lapithai.

172 κατακτάμεν ἠὲ ἁλῶναι: a variant (only here) of the fatalistic comments ἠέ τῳ εὖχος ὀρέξομεν ἠέ τις ἡμῖν (2×, cf. 22.130), ἤ τ' ἔβλητ' ἤ τ' ἔβαλ' ἄλλον (11.410), etc.

175–8 A glance at the general situation is by no means out of place after the narrative of Asios' attack, but these verses were not found in Zenodotus and were athetized by Aristophanes and Aristarchus (Did/AT). The latter found 175 derivative from 15.414 ἄλλοι δ' ἀμφ' ἄλλῃσι μάχην ἐμάχοντο νέεσσιν, and objected to the intrusion of the poet's personality in 176, to the premature mention of fire at 177 anticipating Hektor's words at 15.718, to the separation of τεῖχος from λάϊνον at 177–8, and to the feeble remark about the pro-Achaean gods at 179: all of which seems hypercritical. For modern discussions, generally in favour of excision, see G. Jachmann, 'Vom frühalexandrinischen Homertext', *Nachrichten der Akad. Göttingen* (1949) 169–87. Aristarchus had another reason for rejecting any reference to a plurality of gates: his monograph Περὶ τοῦ ναυστάθμου mentioned in the scholia (Arn/A) to 10.53, 11.166, 11.807, 12.258, 15.449 argued (implausibly, but see 3.145n.) that the camp had only one gate, that eventually stormed by Hektor. Aristarchus also objected to the ethnicon Λαπίθαι in 181, a verse that should therefore be added to the athetesis. The passage is indeed badly put together, piling up the extent of the battle, the poet's incapacity, fire, the desperation of the Achaeans, the vexation of the gods, and the resolution of the Lapithai. Homer's mind is not usually so butterfly. However, some verses of transition between Hektor's prospective κῦδος at 174 and the successes of the Lapithai at 182ff. are desirable. The exegetical scholia detect a certain Ὁμηρικὴ ἐνάργεια in the lines.

176 The poet confesses his ἀπορία, cf. 2.484ff., and the rhetorical question τίς κεν ... εἴποι 17.260–1 (see n. *ad loc.*). The fact that the description of battle is said, unsurprisingly, to be difficult is an indication that the poet recognized the problem and at least strove to attain a degree of clarity and cohesion, an aim in which in great measure he succeeded. — ἀργαλέον (< ἀλγ-αλέον by dissimilation of λ ... λ): a dead metaphor, like English 'taking *pains*'. θεὸν ὥς: the self-reference and the point of comparison ('as if I had the abilities of a god') are alike unique. The proper use of this old formula (θεὸς (ϝ)ώς etc., 11× *Il.*, 6× *Od.*) is to express admiration for appearance or status.

177–8 περὶ τεῖχος ὀρώρει θεσπιδαὲς πῦρ | λάϊνον: the poet needs a run-over word but λάϊνον is ill-chosen. Applying fire to defences is a standard tactic of besieging forces but to *wooden* gates or *wooden* superstructures. Metaphorical fire can be ruled out; θεσπιδαὲς πῦρ (7× *Il.*, 1× *Od.*) is always literal fire. The use of fire against the gates or fabric of the wall, which seems to be envisaged here, does not arise in the account of the Trojan assault; fire is reserved for the ships, e.g. 198, 441 below.

178 καὶ ἀχνύμενοί περ: the two participles ἀχνύμενος and ἐσσύμενος, both regular at the verse-end with περ (15× and 3× respectively), are neatly shifted to a medial position by prefixing καί (8× and 3×). They are something of a special case, for of the other participles used with περ at the verse-end only ἐχθόμενος is so treated (*Od.* 4.502).

180 Pap. 121 had a different verse, ὡς Τρώεσσιν ἄρηγε πατὴρ Ζεύς,] κῆδε δ' Ἀχαιούς (*suppl.* Allen, *alii alia*), but Aristarchus (Arn/A on 175) ignored the reading and criticized the vulgate.

181 συμβάλλειν πόλεμον, 'join battle', as we should say, is not exactly paralleled in the epic but is clearly related to such expressions as σὺν δ᾽ ἐβάλοντο μάχεσθαι at 377, etc. συμβάλλειν μάχην and analogous expressions are common in tragedy.

182–94 With these succinct statements of the exploits of the Lapithai cf. 16.306–50, although that is an altogether more vigorous passage. Victim and wound are named, but without pathetic anecdotes. *Aristeiai* may degenerate into mere lists, cf. the laconic notice of Hektor's exploits at 11.289–309. This is the big moment for the Lapithai in the *Iliad*; they have not been heard of since the Catalogue (except for one verse at 6.29) and will not be met again until the Funeral Games of Patroklos. The casualties of book 11 bring these lesser figures (and Menestheus among the leaders, 331ff.) to the fore.

182 Ἔνθ᾽ αὖ marks the resumption of the narrative after a digression, cf. 4.1n. Unfortunately for the authenticity of 175–81 the digression might as easily have been Asios' protest to Zeus as the poet's comments on the battle.

183–94 The victims of the two Lapithai have the usual Greek names of minor Trojans. For Antimakhos see 11.123n., and for Iamenos and Orestes 139n. above.

183–6 The 'bronze-cheeked' helmet, the 'bronze' helm, and the 'bronze' spear-point is tired, or rather routine style. The parallel verses, 20.397–400, have αἰχμὴ ἱεμένη, but that was Akhilleus' spear in a more impassioned episode. Some MSS have ἱεμένη here by contamination with 20.399. Verses 185–6 ≅ 11.97–8 (see n. *ad loc.*). It is to be remarked that Pap. 121 replaces the head wound (184–7) with a single verse 183a, ending]περησεν, but of uncertain suppletion (= 13.652?).

186 δάμασσε δέ gives a pleasing but probably unintentional jingle after Δάμασον at 183.

187 For the aural echo of this line at 11.422 see n. *ad loc.*

189 The hit κατὰ ζωστῆρα is presumably fatal. Aias (5.615) and Menelaos (17.578) inflicted lethal wounds through this inadequate protection of the abdomen, the former passage describing the result: νειαίρη δ᾽ ἐν γαστρὶ πάγη δολιχόσκιον ἔγχος. On the other hand his ζωστήρ saved Agamemnon at 11.236, in spite of Iphidamas' putting weight behind the spear.

190–198 Parts of these verses, preceded by two plus-verses 189a and b, are preserved in Pap. 121 and 432 (see 11.265n.).

192 ὁ δ᾽ ὕπτιος οὔδει ἐρείσθη (or οὖδας ἔρεισε, as Aristarchus preferred): for the reading see 11.144n. Antiphates is thrown on his back by the force of the blow, a result that would follow more naturally from a spear-thrust, as is the case in book 11. The Homeric sword seems to be normally used as a hacking weapon, e.g. 11.146; see Lorimer, *HM* 271.

194 'Brought them to the ground' is a grim formular periphrasis

(= 16.418 = 8.277 if genuine), made all the grimmer by the epithet
πουλυβοτείρῃ. It is to be noted that the pathetic combination of creation
and destruction is enshrined in the traditional diction of the epic, cf. 3.243–
4 and n.

*195–289 Hektor is about to launch an attack when an omen appears. It is cautiously
interpreted by Pouludamas. Hektor angrily rejects the omen and leads his men in an
attempt to make a breach in the wall. The Aiantes stiffen the defence as both sides
shower each other with missiles*

The poet returns to the pattern of the previous episode: a cautionary
speech from Pouludamas, Hektor's reaction, Trojan attack, and successful
Achaean defence. Though arguing that the structure of this Book is a
repetition of a basic thematic pattern, Fenik, *Homer and the Nibelungenlied*
28–33, has a somewhat different analysis, making the first episode consist
of A: Trojan charge (34–59), B: Pouludamas and reaction (60–107),
C: Asios attacks (108–94), balanced by A': Trojan charge (195–9), B':
Pouludamas and reaction (200–89), C': Sarpedon attacks (290–436). The
length of the constituent parts, the distribution of similes, and the device of
the catalogue (which must represent a starting-point) argue for the analysis
here adopted.

In the event the attack is the Trojans' collectively rather than Hektor's
personally and the narrative of fighting is cast in general terms. The simile
of the snowflakes (278–86) links this episode to that of Asios (108–74), cf.
the simile at 156–58, so that the two passages should be viewed as a whole
and the ill-tempered exchange of Pouludamas and Hektor (210–50) and
the defence of the Aiantes (265–76) subsumed within it. The appearance of
the Aiantes anticipates their more elaborate defence at 329–377.

195–9 A rather rambling sentence, a product of the cumulative 'speaker's style'; the οἳ ῥ' of 199 is the antecedent of the relative clause οἳ ...
ἕποντο at 196, to which a further relative clause, 197–8, is appended.
Verses 197–8 = 89–90 with verbal variation at the end of the second line.

199 ἔτι marks the linear form of the narrative. It is of course implausible
that the crack force under Hektor and Pouludamas should spend the whole
time of Asios' assault and repulse in contemplation of the ditch. The epic
narrative moves forward in time, sometimes sideways, but never backwards. So here the account of Hektor's attack reverts to the point at which
it was left at 109, but is made to follow that of Asios.

200–50 The point of the omen of the snake and the eagle, Pouludamas'
interpretation, and Hektor's response lies in its clarification of Hektor's
attitude at this critical moment. He has put his trust in Zeus and this not
only spurs him on but blinds him to the significance of every warning.

Omens do not occur ἄνευ θεοῦ but, though it is clear that this omen was sent by Zeus, there is absent any unambiguous statement to that effect. That conceals the incongruity of Zeus at once warning the Trojans to desist and urging them to attack, cf. 252–3. — Eagle and snake, the bird of Zeus and the symbol of chthonic power, make up a powerful omen, probably a favourite combination in the mantic art, to judge from the parody in Aristophanes, *Eq.* 197–8.

200 ὄρνις is ambiguously a bird, in apposition to αἰετός in 201, or a bird-omen, as is more likely. Omens are usually bird-omens in the epic, e.g. 8.247 and 24.315 where the bird is also an eagle and where it is specifically sent by Zeus (cf. Διὸς τέρας here at 209 and [Διὸς] τεράεσσι at 256). For a detailed study of Homeric divination see H. Stockinger, *Die Vorzeichen im homerischen Epos* (Munich 1959).

201 ὑψιπέτης is to be linked with πέτομαι, 'fly', not πίπτω, as LSJ suggest, see Shipp *Studies* I 67: ὑψιπέτης is from ὑψιπετέτης by haplology. — ἐπ' ἀριστερά: to the left of the Trojans (Arn/A); we are looking at the ominous eagle from their standpoint. λαὸν ἐέργων, only here and in the repeated line 219, reflects the fundamental sense of ἐέργω, 'bar the way'. The eagle flew *across the front of the army* from right to left, i.e. from East to West, as appears from 240, since the Trojans are facing North.

202 φοινήεντα: like the snake at 2.308, δράκων ἐπὶ νῶτα δαφοινός. *noun* + φέρων ὀνύχεσσι πέλωρον is formular, cf. *Od.* 15.161. πέλωρος is 'portentous' rather than specifically 'huge', and connotes indeterminate menace, like τέρας at 209.

205 ἰδνωθείς: 'twisting itself backwards'; the word is used, e.g. 2.266, of one 'doubled up' in pain.

208 ὄφιν (root ŋgʷhis) is an Aeolism, although that has no relevance for the remarkable metrics: ∪∪ for −∪. Wyatt, *ML* 231 rightly rejects Schulze's insinuation that the aspirate could make position, but the metrics remain unexplained. The στίχοι μείουροι of the ancient metricians are a statement of the problem, not its answer. Hipponax also makes the first syllable long, represented by the spelling ὄπφις, fr. 28.2 and 6 West, cf. for the spelling ὀκχέω, Pind. *Ol.* 2.67 (also ὀκχή and ὄκχος) for ὀχ-, and νυκχάζω = νύσσω Hsch. Compounds, ὀφιόεις and ὀφιόδειρος, also lengthen the first syllable, but for acceptable metrical reasons.

210 ≅ 13.725 (with εἰ μή for δὴ τότε). θρασὺν Ἕκτορα: the epithet is used 6× of Hektor, usually in the normal way, i.e. as a general characterization without allusion to the immediate context, cf. 60 where there is no question of Pouludamas' restraining an impetuous commander. Here Hektor is certainly pressing his luck although Pouludamas is not made to say so. At 13.726, however, Pouludamas begins "Ἕκτορ, ἀμήχανός ἐσσι", as if picking up the epithet.

211–29 For Pouludamas' speeches of admonition see 61–79n. Hektor's attitude, 'quite inexplicable after Polydamas' speech in 8off.' (Leaf), reflects the traditional roles of the two heroes. Heroism is enhanced if the hero is given the opportunity to act unheroically, and rejects it, even if as here the rejection has hubristic overtones.

211 ἀεὶ … ἐπιπλήσσεις: an allusion to the role of prudent adviser, presumably traditional, of Pouludamas in the Trojan saga. Pouludamas has no part in the *Iliad* before this Book and his previous intervention (61–79) had been welcome. — ἀεί, with ᾱ, is attested also at 23.648 and *Od.* 15.379. East Ionic retained the diphthong, αἰεί.

212 οὐδὲ μὲν οὐδέ is emphatic (not connective as at 10.299); the full phrase ἐπεὶ οὐδὲ μὲν οὐδὲ ἔοικε is formular (= *Od.* 21.319).

213 δῆμον was probably rendered by Horace when he wrote *plebs eris*, *Ep.* 1.1.59, but is not really intelligible ἀντὶ τοῦ δημότην. The form is generally understood as being a spelling for δήμγον, i.e. δήμιον, 'of the people', with the same orthography as πότνα for πότνια (*Od.* 5.215, etc.), see Chantraine, *GH* I 170. The *apparatus criticus* to OCT refers to T. W. Allen's paper in *CR* 20 (1906) 5 proposing δῆμον(α) from a form δήμων meaning 'prudent', a bold remedy for a real problem: why should Pouludamas, son of one of Priam's councillors and ἑταῖρος of Hektor (18.251), associate himself with the δῆμος? Hektor is as good as a king and has a king's temper; accordingly Pouludamas speaks ingratiatingly, 'It is the business of your humble servant σὸν κράτος ἀέξειν, but …'; cf. Diomedes to Agamemnon at 9.32. Hektor's response is to threaten his councillor with immediate execution for cowardice in the face of the enemy (247–50).

213–14 For the phrase pattern οὔτ' ἐνὶ βουλῇ | οὔτε ποτ' ἐν πολέμῳ cf. ἢ ἐν ἀέθλῳ | ἠὲ καὶ ἐν πολέμῳ, 16.590. The two phrases are brought into the same verse at 2.202, οὔτε ποτ' ἐν πολέμῳ ἐναρίθμιος οὔτ' ἐνὶ βουλῇ.

217–27 Pouludamas is no θεοπρόπος, cf. 228–9, but Homeric omens do not usually seem to demand much in the way of arcane knowledge for their interpretation. The eagle, of course, is the bird of Zeus, as the hawk is of Apollo (*Od.* 15.526), and indicates the provenance of the omen, cf. 24.315–20. Note that Pouludamas' description of the omen embodies an interpretation absent from the narrator's text: the eagle, he says, was taking prey *home* to its *young*.

218 ὄρνῑς ἦλθε is Aristarchus' correction of the paradosis ὄρνῑς ἐπῆλθε. Homer has ὄρνῑς ἐνὶ μεγάροισι in the paradosis at 24.219, where emendation to ὄρνῑς ἐν μ. would be easy, but ὄρνῑς at 9.323. The -ῑ- is long in the oblique cases and should be so in the nominative, but both quantities are found in later poets.

219 (= 201) is clearly intrusive, an instance of 'concordance interpolation'. It is omitted by the most important MSS.

221-2 With Pouludamas' οἰκία and τεκέεσσι compare Akhilleus' μάστακα and νεοσσοί 9.323-4. The sentimentality, of course, helps to make the interpretation convincing.

225 ναῦφιν is a notable archaism, preserving the plural function of -φι and retaining the -αυ- diphthong because the form was unknown to the Ionic vernacular, see Shipp, *Studies* I 3-4, 7. The case fluctuates, as usual with -φι, between dative and genitive. ναῦφι always means the ships of the Achaean encampment, and bears that meaning also at its single appearance in the *Odyssey* (14.498).

228ff. Parts of 228-38 and 246-65 are contained in Pap. Sorb. 4 (Cadell, *Papyrus de la Sorbonne* I (Paris 1966)). The text, unlike that of Pap. 121, diverges only in trivial respects from the vulgate.

230 Zenodotus read τὸν δ' ἠμείβετ' ἔπειτα μέγας κορυθαίολος Ἕκτωρ (Arn/A), a clear case of the substitution of one formula for another. Zenodotus' reading is less apposite than the ὑπόδρα ἰδών formula. It is surprising that more such variants are not recorded, cf. 444.

231-50 An important characterizing speech. Hektor is made to ignore an omen again at 13.821-32. For Hektor's happy-go-lucky (or fatalistic) approach to war and contempt for divination cf. his words to the dying Patroklos: "Πατρόκλεις, τί νύ μοι μαντεύεαι αἰπὺν ὄλεθρον; | τίς δ' οἶδ' εἴ κ' Ἀχιλεύς, Θέτιδος πάϊς ἠϋκόμοιο, | φθήη ἐμῷ ὑπὸ δουρὶ τυπεὶς ἀπὸ θυμὸν ὀλέσσαι;" (16.859-61). Verse 231 = 18.285, where Hektor rejected Pouludamas' advice on a more serious matter. Verses 231-4 = 7.357-60 (with Ἀντῆνορ for Πουλυδάμα) where Paris is given this short 'run' of verses as part of his refusal to surrender Helen. bT interpret Hektor's character from a hostile standpoint; he is said to be boastful, vacillating, and (bT to 22.91) θρασὺς καὶ ἕτοιμος, ἀλόγιστος δὲ καὶ οὐ μεταβλητός. That judgement mirrors their attribution of a φιλέλλην bias to the poet.

231 Πουλυδάμα: Zenodotus (Did/A) preferred the philologically correct vocative in -αν (< -αντ), Aristarchus the analogical -α, after the vocative of masculine a-stems.

232 The joining of μῦθον with νοῆσαι brings out clearly the way in which μῦθος (but not ἔπος) implies the intention of the speaker, cf. μῦθος ἀπήμων 12.80 where the implication is that Hektor recognized that Pouludamas was trying to be helpful.

234 For Hektor's blaming the gods for Pouludamas' supposed folly see 9.377n.

235-6 Hektor refers to the message relayed to him by Iris at 11.200-9 that he would reach the ships and be victorious until nightfall. Ζηνὸς μὲν ἐριγδούποιο: cf. 15.293 and Hesiod *Theog.* 41 for the same formula (without μέν). Expressions made with the analogical case-forms of Ζεύς usually show no obvious marks of antiquity or settled usage: Ζ. Ὀλυμπίου (and Ζ. ...

'Ολυμπίου), Ζ. ἐριβρεμέτεω (*hapax legomenon*), Ζ. κελαινεφέϊ, Ζ. Κρονίωνα (and Ζ. ... Κρονίωνος), πανομφαίῳ Ζ. (*hapax legomenon*). Ζηνὸς ἐριγδούποιο is therefore most likely to be derived from ἐρίγδουπος πόσις Ἥρης (4× *Il.*, 3× *Od.*).

237–43 Hektor's fine words make a memorable heroic speech, appropriate both to his dramatic role as leader and to the tragic movement of the *Iliad*. Hektor relies, as he thinks, on the promise of Zeus given at 11.207–10, but to any pious mind his words would represent a fatal delusion. In tragedy contempt for oracles is always a sure precursor of doom. In general, however, the epic takes a rational view, accepting omens as a confirmation or discouragement of decisions already taken but not allowing them to determine action, cf. the sceptical attitude of Eurumakhos at *Od.* 2.181–2 ὄρνιθες δέ τε πολλοὶ ὑπ' αὐγὰς ἠελίοιο | φοιτῶσ', οὐδέ τε πάντες ἐναίσιμοι.

237 τύνη is an emphatic 2nd person pronoun found 5× elsewhere in the *Iliad*, (5.485, 6.262, 16.64, 19.10, 24.465). According to Wathelet, *Traits éoliens* 286–7, the form is probably an Aeolism – or a very remote archaism; see also 16.64–5n. It is entirely absent from the *Odyssey* but is found three times in Hesiod. Apollonius liked the word (8× in the *Argonautica*).

239–40 The Greek οἰωνοσκόπος faced north, hence the sunrise lay on his right and the sunset on his left. The same language is used to indicate west and east at *Od.* 9.26 ['Ιθάκη] πρὸς ζόφον, αἱ δέ τ' ἄνευθε πρὸς ἠῶ τ' ἠέλιόν τε.

243 This famous verse is ejected by Lohmann, *Reden* 219, as upsetting the parallelism of Pouludamas' speech and Hektor's response. ἀμύνεσθαι περὶ πάτρης is formular, cf. 15.496, 24.500. At 15.497–8 defending the πάτρη is justified as defending ἄλοχος, παῖδες, οἶκος, and κλῆρος, but that is Hektor exhorting lesser Trojans, and generals must appeal to the self-interest of their men not only to an altruistic sense of social obligation. Effectively Hektor's οἶκος is Troy. The well-rounded heroic character, *pace* Finley, *World* 116, acknowledges the claims of the community (cf. 310–28), but even in Hektor's own case those claims rank lower than his sense of honour and shame (cf. 22.99–130).

247–50 Hektor's words to a man of Pouludamas' standing are exceedingly harsh, cf. Idomeneus' gentle reproach of Meriones at 13.249–53. The charge of cowardice, which at this moment we have no evidence to refute, is quite unjustified by the sequel; he is ranked beside Aineias, Agenor, Sarpedon, and Glaukos at 14.425–6, rescued Satnios and scored a success at 14.449–57, and fought well in book 15. It is likely that the plus-verse in Pap. 121, ἀλλ' ἐπ[εο πτολεμόνδε καὶ ἄλλους ὄρνυθι λαούς (= 19.139) *vel sim.*, was inserted to end Hektor's speech on a courteous note, cf. the plus-verses at 1.543a, 6.433–9, and 22.126a. The generalization ἠέ τιν' ἄλλον at 248 is actually Hektor's justification, the λαός being the regular target of such threats (2.391, 13.232, 15.348). (The shirkers of rank at 4.336 and 4.368 were not so menaced.) Like other intemperate threats in the *Iliad* it is nowhere carried out.

250 ≅ 11.433 ≅ 16.861 ≅ 18.92 with variations in the first foot.

251–64 A remarkable passage of siege-poetry without parallel in the *Iliad*: one could wish for more in exchange for tired passages of spear-fighting. Siege-poetry naturally had its typical motifs and vocabulary of which such passages as this furnish a brief glimpse. The siege is at the heart of the stories of Oikhalia, Thebes, and Kaludon, and must have formed a large part of ἀοιδή from the earliest times. We must expect it to have developed a diction as rich as that deployed for open warfare in the *Iliad*. For siege scenes in the graphic art of the Mycenaean age see 108–72n.; unfortunately none shed light on the problems posed by the Trojan attack on the Achaean wall.

252 The Trojans charge *en masse* with a great war whoop, cf. the μεγάλη ἰαχή in the similar scene at 15.379–84, where the Trojan advance is likened to a μέγα κῦμα θαλάσσης.

256 This verse echoes the pattern of 135, χείρεσσι πεποιθότες ἠδὲ βίηφι, cf. also 153. βίη is of course the Trojans' strength of arm not that of Zeus. Like prudent soldiers at any time they back up their trust in god with practical measures. At this point Hektor's force has somehow passed the ditch that gave them so much pause without our being told a word about their surmounting that formidable obstacle. This is one indication of many in this Book that the poet's faultless fluency in handling the battle on the open plain does not extend to the special context of fighting from or against fortifications.

257 A force attacking a wall hopes either to scale it or breach it. Scaling, unless the wall has a batter (cf. 16.702) or is very roughly made, requires ladders, κλίμακες, or something similar, as envisaged at Aesch. *Th.* 466, Eur. *Phoen.* 180–1, 488–9. Unless these lurk under the mysterious κρόσσας of 258 (see n. *ad loc.*) they are absent from the narrative of the Trojan assault, for the goal of the attacking force is consistently expressed by τεῖχος ῥηγνύναι (12.90, 198, 223–4, 257, 261–2, 418, 440), 'make a breach'. They do this by levering out key parts of the structure, στήλας ἐμόχλεον (259), a detail that is not taken up subsequently, probably because the great heroes could not be represented as labouring like sappers; or they could demolish the battlements protecting the fighting platform (397–9), after which in the present narrative they can swarm over. But sometimes at least τεῖχος includes the gates pierced in the wall in that sector; thus at 443 Hektor's division rushes the τεῖχος and Hektor himself smashes the gate. The professional way to do this would presumably be to ram it (cf. Thuc. 2.76), fire it, or hack it with axes, but that would be teamwork not the heroic action of a single leader of men; so Hektor is made to achieve the same end single-handed by a superhuman feat of boulder-hurling.

258–60 The passages in addition to the present one that shed some light on the nature of the Achaean wall as the poet conceived it are 7.436–41 (its construction), 7.461–3 (its destruction), 12.3–32 (its destruction in detail), 12.177–8, 12.397–9 (its damage), 15.361–4 (its partial destruction). Since the aim of an attacking force is τεῖχος ῥηγνύναι and the destruction of the wall by flood is described as τεῖχος ἀμαλδύνειν (7.463, 12.18, 12.32), the poet cannot have in mind the Cyclopean masonry of the Mycenaean citadels of the mainland, or be using diction devised for their description. The stated materials for the construction of the wall were φιτροί, 'logs' (12.29), and λᾶες, 'stones', (12.29, 12.178), and in the context of the *Iliad* it is a hastily improvised defence completed in one day. One may compare the works achieved by the Athenian army in two and half days at Delion in 424 B.C., cf. Thuc. 4.90 τάφρον μὲν κύκλῳ περὶ τὸ ἱερὸν καὶ τὸν νεὼν ἔσκαπτον, ἐκ δὲ τοῦ ὀρύγματος ἀνέβαλλον ἀντὶ τείχους τὸν χοῦν, καὶ σταύρους παρακαταπηγνύντες, ἄμπελον κόπτοντες τὴν περὶ τὸ ἱερὸν ἐσέβαλλον καὶ λίθους ἅμα καὶ πλίνθον ἐκ τῶν οἰκοπέδων τῶν ἐγγὺς καθαιροῦντες, καὶ παντὶ τρόπῳ ἐμετεώριζον τὸ ἔρυμα. πύργους τε ξυλίνους κατέστησαν ᾗ καιρὸς ἦν. Where an army was less apprehensive of immediate attack it would, like the Peloponnesians before Plataea in 429, make use of mud-brick, digging the material out of a trench alongside the wall, see Thuc. 2.78. τεῖχος ἀμαλδύνειν would be an appropriate description of the effects of water on such material. Homer, however, conceives the ditch as separated from the wall (see 65–6n.) and having its own ramparts. However, the substantial foundations and superstructure described in these verses are more appropriate to permanent town-walls than to an improvised fieldwork, cf. the description of the walls of Skherie at *Od.* 7.44–5, and are reminiscent of the walls of Old Smurne and their reconstructed timber fittings, as described by J. V. Nicholls, *BSA* 53–4 (1958–9) 112–13, figs. 34, 35, and more briefly by H. Drerup, *Arch. Hom.* o 44–7. Descriptions of walls are a necessary part of siege-poetry, but fieldworks (except here) do not figure in Iliadic battle scenes and specific diction for them seems to be lacking. — κρόσσαι is an Ionic word with some currency in late Greek. It was intelligible to Herodotus or his informants, see *History* 2.125 ἀναβαθμῶν τὰς μετεξέτεροι κρόσσας, οἱ δὲ βωμίδας ὀνομάζουσι, describing the stepped construction of the Great Pyramid (see A. L. Lloyd, *Herodotus Book ii* III (Leiden 1988) 67–8), cf. Porphyry 1.180.8 τοὺς προβεβλημένους τοῦ τείχους λίθους. Aristarchus was uncertain, cf. Arn/A κρόσσας ἐν μὲν τοῖς ὑπομνήμασι κεφαλίδας, ἐν δὲ τῷ περὶ τοῦ ναυστάθμου κλίμακας. If ladders are meant then πύργων must be understood to be genitive of the point of aim (λείπει τὸ κατά, bT). Scaling ladders were a tactic of Near Eastern armies from an early period, see the illustrations in *Arch. Hom* N 10–11, and from the standpoint of Hellenistic siegecraft may have seemed obvious, yet they are clearly out of place here: one need look no further for their absence than the account of Sarpedon's near-successful attack at 375 and 397–9. The κρόσσαι have been thought to describe, in a way that can hardly now be conjectured, the construction of the parapet (the κεφαλίδες of Aristarchus): the compound πρόκροσσοι (14.35 (see n.), Hdt. 7.188) may mean 'in echelon' but is itself less than clear. Lorimer's suggestion, *HM* 433, that at its base 'the Greek wall had a strong "batter"' is possible, though her reference to the (no longer visible in the first millennium) batter 'such as forms the almost sole surviving part of the great wall of Hissarlik vi' does not help. The θεμείλια (28) of many archaic and classical town-walls extend beyond the superstructure and may be stepped, see Lawrence, *Fortification* 201–7. The sole other mention of this feature in the *Iliad*, κροσσάων ἐπέβαινον at 444, does not help to determine the sense. The ἐπάλξεις are battlements which give the wall height as well as protecting its defenders; they are clearly thought of as relatively flimsy, for Sarpedon can break them away with one wrench of his heroic arm (397–9), so as to make a 'practicable' breach. (The escaping Plataeans did the same, Thuc. 3.23.) The στῆλαι προβλῆτες must be vertical members, of stone or timber (φιτροί, 29), necessary to hold the improvised materials in position, or to support the superstructure of a permanent wall. It is not clear why they should project (in the manner of a buttress?), unless the poet has in mind some architectural practice which has left no trace in archaeology.

262 χάζοντο κελεύθου (= 11.504) must be understood as 'get out of their way' (so Leaf). No literal κέλευθος can be in question.

263 ῥινοῖσι βοῶν φράξαντες ἐπάλξεις is explained by bT as τὰ διάκενα τῶν ἐπάλξεων φράξαντες τοῖς ὅπλοις. The Achaeans formed a front on top of their wall like the solid formation in the field described by φράσσω/φράσσομαι (see 13.126–35n.).

265–75 The Aiantes exhort their men. *Kampfparänesen* are part of the typology of the Homeric battle. Latacz, *Kampfdarstellung* 246–50, lists 65 examples, 38 on the Achaean side against 27 on the Trojan. Only occasionally, as at 310ff. below, do the speakers rise to eloquence. — The poet must mean by Αἴαντε Aias son of Telamon and Aias son of Oïleus, as is clearly the case at 335–6. For the probable idea that the dual primitively signified 'Aias and one other, *sc.* Teukros' see 13.46n. and J. Wackernagel, *Kleine Schriften* I (Göttingen 1953) 538–46. The ambiguity could lead to confusion, see 13.177–8n.

265 κελευτιόων (also 13.125) exemplifies a productive epic formation (Risch, *Wortbildung* 321), common in the participle. It may be understood as an intensive or iterative alternative to κελεύω, though no such force is evident in e.g. ἀκροκελαινιόων, θαλπιόων, or φαληριόων.

267–8 μειλιχίοις ... νείκεον is an easy zeugma and avoids an awkwardly complex sentence. The Aiantes adopted the same tactics as Odysseus at 2.188–206: gentle words for the βασιλῆες and ἔξοχοι ἄνδρες, threats for the other ranks.

269 μεσήεις: cf. φοινήεις at 202–20. These forms, listed by Risch, *Wortbildung* 154, are the precursors of an extensive component of the classical and post-classical poetic vocabulary. μεσήεις is a *hapax legomenon*.

270 πω: i.e. 'in any way', see 15.426–8n.

271 For ἔπλετο in the sense 'has turned out to be' cf. 15.227, and see Monro, *HG* 66. The usage requires ἔπλετο to be aorist in tense.

273–4 On whose side is the ὁμοκλητήρ? The Aiantes would be understandably afraid that their men might run when they heard the shout of the attacking Trojans (the vulgate ἀκούων, present tense, would require this interpretation); ὁμοκλέω and ὁμοκλή refer to the cries of a commander to his own men (or horses), so that the ὁμοκλητήρ here should be the Achaean officer. ὁμοκλητῆρος ἀκούσας goes with both clauses, μή τις ... and ἀλλὰ πρόσω ..., but is awkwardly put inside the negative part of the sentence. Aias, or the poet, slips into the language of a commander urging his men to *advance*, πρόσω ἴεσθε, as if they were out on the plain, not manning the battlements.

277 προβοῶντε, 'cheering *on*' (Leaf), is doubtless the sense of the compounded verb. In 'some of the ὑπομνήματα' (Did/A) Aristarchus interpreted the form as προβάοντε, i.e. 'moving forward', a participle unknown to the epic.

278–86 Simile of the snowflakes, cf. 156–8n. and Moulton, *Similes* 64–6. 'One of the finest descriptions of nature in ancient poetry' (Leaf), with more imaginative touches than usual: the snowflakes as the κῆλα of Zeus, κοιμάω of winds dropping, the lotus-fields, and the 'plashing' (προσπλάζον) wave. The simile, unlike that at 156–8, envisages a steady snowfall (which echoes the relentless nature of the bombardment), not a blizzard, and lays stress on the silence of the scene (κοιμήσας ... ἀνέμους, κῦμα ... ἐρύκεται); the narrative, after recalling the *tertium comparationis* (λίθοι ... θαμειαί, 287, cf. νιφάδες ... θαμειαί, 278), emphasizes the din of battle. Similes must always be inexact, so that some irrelevance is almost inevitable, but rarely does the ποιητικὸς κόσμος (see 41–8n.) diverge so remarkably from the narrative.

278 For the construction of τῶν see the resumptive verse 287; the stones fell 'to either side of them'.

280 κῆλα is used of divine missiles, the arrows of Apollo at 1.53 and Zeus's thunder and lightning, no less, at Hesiod, *Theog.* 707, and is a strong word for snowflakes; but this is no ordinary snowfall, it χέει ἔμπεδον and blankets everything.

283 λωτοῦντα, by contraction of λωτό(ϝ)εντα, is the reading of Aristarchus (Arn/A) and OCT, but would be the only adjective in -όεις so contracted in the *Iliad*. (The *Odyssey* offers the enigmatic καιροσέων at 7.107). The vulgate reading λωτεῦντα is preferable phonologically, but would be the participle of an otherwise unattested λωτέω. The sense 'covered in lotus' is unaffected. λωτεῦντα was known to Hesychius who glosses it as ἀνθοῦντα.

284 ἀκταῖς offers another orthographical problem. Instances of -αις as opposed to normal Ionic -ης are rare (also 1.238, *Od.* 5.119, 22.471), but strongly attested where they occur. It is hasty to class such forms as Attic, which dialect had -ασι, -ησι until the fifth century. For detailed discussion see G. M. Bolling, *Language* 22 (1945) 261–4.

285 ἐρύκεται must be passive (*pace* Leaf). The snow blankets even the waves and prevents their breaking.

287 λίθος is normally masculine in the epic, whether the meaning is 'a stone' (for throwing) or 'stone' (the material). The feminine is found only here and at *Od.* 19.494.

289 βαλλομένων: masculine. The reciprocal sense of the middle voice, 'as they bombarded each other', is clear, though surprisingly without parallel in this common verb, but cf. νυσσομένων (14.26 = 16.637) for an identical usage.

290–412 Sarpedon, commander of the Lycians, intervenes. He summons Glaukos to join him and in a famous speech utters a lapidary statement of the heroes' code. His attack on the wall comes near to success

Taken as a whole the assault of Sarpedon and Glaukos is a repetition of the assault of Asios (108–94). As usual when a motif is repeated after a short interval the second occurrence is in a more elaborate form:

    I. Asios attacks 110–26
        Opposed by Polupoites and Leonteus 127–53
        Missiles and snowflake simile 154–61
        Asios admits failure 162–72
    II. Sarpedon (with Glaukos) attacks 290–330
        Opposed by Menestheus and the Aiantes 331–99
        (Missiles and snowflake simile 278–89)
        Sarpedon admits failure 400–12

Already from 265 the narrative has lost its special character as siege-poetry and now continues to revert in its themes to an ordinary open battle. A

warrior (Sarpedon) encourages his comrade (Glaukos); they go off to battle; an inferior opponent (Menestheus) calls for assistance; a major warrior
(Aias with Teukros) joins him and averts the danger (with 331–91 cf.
11.463–501).

Sarpedon's ranking as a hero has already been established by his slaying
of Tlepolemos (5.627–59); it is confirmed now by his near-success at carrying the Achaean wall. He is thus established, as e.g. Aineias is not, in the
mind of the poet's audience as the one hero on the Trojan side, other than
Hektor himself, who is capable of confronting Patroklos (16.419–507).

290–4 It is hard to understand why Leaf should condemn these lines
as 'practically meaningless,' except as a consequence of his view that in
one version of the assault Sarpedon was successful, a trace of which he finds
at 16.558 [Σαρπήδων] ὃς πρῶτος ἐσήλατο τεῖχος Ἀχαιῶν. The assaults
of Asios, Sarpedon, and Hektor form a crescendo, moving from repulse
through near-success to triumph. By keeping up the pressure and dis-
tracting the Aiantes the Lycian assault paves the way for Hektor's, as 290
indicates.

292–307 Although the poet is ready enough when it suits him to exercise
a composer's privilege to know what his characters cannot know, his normal
narrative stance is that of an observer who must infer the unseen from the
seen. As an observer he has a choice between two kinds of rhetorical
language, both alien to later and modern thought. He can say, as at 292,
that a god impelled the man to act or, as at 307 and of the same event, that
the man's θυμός impelled him to act. It is natural for an observer of
Sarpedon's assault to say that he was inspired by a god (292); that describes
and at the same time explains its impetuosity: it is also natural to say that
he was inspired by his θυμός (307). There is no contradiction, nor even what
some have called 'common-sense carelessness' in these descriptions. The
common ground is that both figures of speech describe action in terms of an
impulse emanating from outside, or at least distinct from, the man himself.
It is even possible, if a man has 'second thoughts' to speak of a ἕτερος θυμός
(*Od.* 9.302). Homer has no word for the 'self' (neither has ordinary non-
technical language), but it does not follow that he lacked the concept: see
R. Gaskin, *CQ* 40 (1990) 1–10. That human and divine motivation were,
at least originally, parallel explanations of action was affirmed by Nilsson,
GgrR 363–5, and reaffirmed in an important paper by A. Lesky, *Sitz.
Heidelberger Akad. Wiss., Phil.-Hist. Klasse* (1961) 4. The more rigorous
view, that Homeric man had no will of his own, was developed by B. Snell
in various works, e.g. *The Discovery of the Mind*, trans. T. G. Rosenmeyer
(Oxford and Cambridge, Mass., 1953), and especially by Erbse, *Funktion
der Götter*. The view taken here is that in the language of the heroes gods
are an externalization of inner impulses, in the language of the poet an

externalization of his conviction that behind the events he describes was a guiding force. Neither mode of description implies that the action is in any way morally different from action that is merely stated: see Adkins, *Merit and Responsibility* 10–17, Dodds, *Greeks and the Irrational* 8–18. Figurative language should imply that the action is vigorous or resolute enough to call for an elaborated description, but is easily devalued; θυμὸς ἀνῆκε is a formula (8× with variants), stronger than θυμὸς ἀνώγει (15× in *Il.* with variants).

292 Sarpedon (unlike Glaukos) has a possible Lycian name, cf. J. Sundvall, *Die einheimischen Namen der Lykier*, 2nd edn (Aalen 1963) 29, 251, and 5.663n., and is clearly conceived as ruling in the area known classically as Lycia, cf. the exploits of his ancestor Bellerophon (6.171–90), improbable as that might seem for an ally of the Trojans. The classical Lycians preferred to call themselves Τερμίλαι; it is possible that the Greek name unwittingly preserves the second-millennium designation of the Lukka lands, uncertainly located somewhere in western Anatolia.

293 λέονθ' ὡς βουσὶν ἕλιξιν is an unusually extended 'short simile' with ambivalent syntax; understand Σαρπήδονα (ἐπ)όρμενον with λέονθ' rather than Ζεὺς ὤρσεν. The brief simile anticipates the longer lion simile that follows at 299: for this narrative pattern see 13.298–303n. and Moulton, *Simile* 19–22. Another instance is the repetition of the whirlwind motif at 11.297 and 11.305–8. The short comparison may serve to prompt its subsequent elaboration, but at the same time the recurrent image has a cumulative effect on the imagination of the audience. — ἕλιξι, 'twisted', *sc.* with respect to the horns, puzzled the scholiasts who took it for a colour term ('black'), see 9.466–9n.

294–6 For the action of the charging warrior – and the construction of his shield cf. 13.803–4. The short description of Sarpedon's equipment is an instance of what the scholia call αὔξησις; it enhances the standing of the warrior in the eyes of the poet's audience. — ἐλαύνειν, cf. ἐξήλατον at 295, is the *vox propria* for the process of working bronze into a convex sheet to form the outer cover of the shield. The same process is described, with more emphasis on the leather inside, at 7.219–23. Aristarchus, thinking of the seven hides of Aias' shield, read ἐξήλατον followed by ἤλασεν (Hrd/A) – and betrayed his penchant for exotic interpretation. Zenodotus fell into the same trap at 9.130.

297 The ῥάβδοι, which run round the shield, are different from the κάνονες of 13.407 (see n.). It is hard to say what is meant: ῥαβδοειδέσι ῥαφαῖς (ex A) merely restates the problem. H. Borchhardt translates 'Drähten' (*Arch. Hom.* ε 3), LSJ suggest 'studs', Willcock 'stitches' (cf. ῥάπτειν, 'stitch').

298 δύο δοῦρε τινάσσων (only here) is a neat description of a Late Dark

Age warrior going into action with his two spears – a clear indication that he intends to throw them. It says much for the conservatism of Homeric diction that this useful and apposite phrase has failed to enter the formular repertoire.

299–306 The finest lion simile in the *Iliad*. The lion in the epic is a generic idea, a type of fearless aggressive behaviour (ἀγηνορίη), and the fiercest animal known to the Homeric imagination. This lion is a hero in its own right; it is inspired by its θυμὸς ἀγήνωρ to attempt a well-nigh impossible task (ἐς πυκινὸν δόμον ἐλθεῖν, like the assault on the wall); it will not retreat in the face of resistance, but will be victorious or die. As often the simile clarifies the emotional colour of the narrative rather than the action to which it ostensibly relates; Sarpedon too, we understand, is resolved to carry the wall or die in the attempt, as he himself says at 328 below. — The whole simile of this mountain-bred lion must be compared with *Od.* 6.130–4 (similar phrases underlined):

> βῆ δ' ἴμεν ὥς τε λέων ὀρεσίτροφος, ἀλκὶ πεποιθώς,
> ὅς τ' εἶσ' ὑόμενος καὶ ἀήμενος, ἐν δέ οἱ ὄσσε
> δαίεται· αὐτὰρ ὁ βουσὶ μετέρχεται, ἢ ὀΐεσσιν
> ἠὲ μετ' ἀγροτέρας ἐλάφους· <u>κέλεται δέ ἑ γαστήρ</u>
> <u>μήλων πειρήσοντα καὶ ἐς πυκινὸν δόμον ἐλθεῖν.</u>

The lion's hunger, which in the *Iliad* gives it high courage, is capped in the *Odyssey* by its physical distress in order to make the point that it acted out of sheer necessity, χρειὼ γὰρ ἵκανε.

301 πυκινὸν δόμον, here a farmstead (ἔπαυλις Arn/A), is an expression suitable for the dwelling of Amuntor (10.267) or, in the form πυκινὸν δῶ, for that of Zeus. The epic lacks diction for the description of a humble or rural dwelling, cf. grand arrangements at Eumaios' pig-farm, *Od.* 14.5–15.

302 παρ' αὐτόφι provides a useful dactyl for the fourth foot in place of αὐτοῖσι, cf. 11.44–5n. and Chantraine, *GH* I 239–40.

304 δίεσθαι is normally transitive in Homer (= 'put to flight'). A passive use occurs also at 23.475.

305–6 The lion is heroic even in its fatalism (cf. 11.410, 12.172 and nn.), and is credited with the same motives as Sarpedon expresses at 328, an unusual correlation of a detail in a simile with *oratio recta*. With 306 compare 11.675 ἔβλητ' ἐν πρώτοισιν ἐμῆς ὑπὸ χειρὸς ἄκοντι (Nestor recounting his Elean exploit). There ἐν πρώτοισι had its natural sense, 'among the front ranks, *sc.* of his own side'. Here the expression is absurd unless it has lost its proper meaning and become an empty formula, meaning little more, as Leaf says, than 'like a hero'.

309ff. In spite of his accession of spirit Sarpedon is made to call for aid and the narrative (to 378 and beyond) enters the pattern described by

Fenik (*TBS* 24ff.): a Trojan associates a friend in the fight; his adversary calls for aid; the attack is repulsed: cf. 5.166–310 and 13.455–539.

310–21 These famous verses constitute the clearest statement in the *Iliad* of the imperatives that govern the heroic life and their justification. It is, as Sarpedon puts it, a kind of social contract: valour in exchange for honour, see Adkins, *Merit and Responsibility* 34–6. Honour comes first, for only the founders of dynasties gained their thrones by first showing valour (like Bellerophon, 6.171–95); their successors inherited their status, and might, as here, have to remind themselves of the obligations that it entailed. At least Sarpedon admits obligations (which is more than Akhilleus does) in addition to the reward of κλέος, but we are still some way from the ξυνὸν ἐσθλόν for which Tyrtaeus fought, fr. 12.15 West.

311 = 8.162 (where Hektor jeers at the honours Diomedes *used* to receive) and is evidently a formular verse that spells out the traditional idea of what it was to be honoured. ἕδρη means participation in the feasts of the ἄριστοι, cf. the dishonour anticipated for the orphaned Astuanax at 22.498: "ἔρρ' οὕτως. οὐ σός γε πατὴρ μεταδαίνυται ἡμῖν." The feast was also the means by which the leader 'honoured' his subordinates and thereby implicitly imposed obligations on them, cf. 4.340–4 (Agamemnon in reproach of Menestheus and Odysseus) τίπτε καταπτώσσοντες ἀφέστατε . . . | πρώτω γὰρ καὶ δαιτὸς ἀκουάζεσθον ἐμεῖο, and Hektor to his allies at 17.225–8 ('I have bribed and fed you well, now fight!'). For κρέασι cf. 7.321, where Aias is honoured νώτοισι διηνεκέεσσι. Note, however, that there is no trace of the *comitatus*-relationship of the Germanic heroic age, in which the chieftain maintained and enriched his henchmen. There are no Homeric formulas corresponding to the OE *sinces* (*goldes, beaga*) *brytta*(*n*), 'giver of treasure (gold, rings)', *goldwine gumena*, 'gold-friend of heroes', and *sinc-*(*gold-*)*gifa*, 'treasure-(gold-)giver'. πλείοις δεπάεσσιν probably means that their cups were kept full at the feast, cf. 4.261–3 and n. where Idomeneus enjoys the privilege of his cup 'always standing full' in contrast to the meaner allowance of the Ἀχαιοί.

313 ≅ 6.195 (to ἀρούρης). The τέμενος is that granted by the Lycians to Bellerophon (6.194). There is allusion to τεμένη of gods in the formula τέμενος βωμός τε θυήεις (2× *Il.*, 1× *Od.*), but those described in the text are secular, the private property of kings: see Edwards on 18.550–1 and Hainsworth on *Od.* 6.293. Vineyard and cornland are specified for the τέμενος offered to Meleagros (9.578–80). — Xanthos, the modern Eşen Çayı (marked Koca Çayı on some maps), is the greatest of the Lycian rivers and its valley forms the heart of the country, the πίων δῆμος of 16.437. Sirbis, mentioned by T and Strabo (14.3.6), was an alternative, or native, name. The river is naturally mentioned in connexion with Sarpedon, cf. 2.876 and 6.172. The classical city of Xanthos, situated in the lower valley, is not mentioned by Homer, whose knowledge of the region is limited. εὐρεῖα is a generic epithet of places (Helike, Krete, Sparta, Troy, as well as Lycia); by the standards of those places it would be a reasonable description of the Xanthos valley.

316 (= 4.342). μάχης καυστείρης: note the metaphorical epithet. Fires (conflagrations, not domestic hearths), being destructive and well-nigh irresistible, make effective similes for advancing heroes or armies (19×). See also 17.736–41 and n., where bT observe that the extended simile at that point is here compressed into a single metaphorical word.

317 ὄφρα τις ὧδ' εἴπῃ (εἴπῃσι) is formular, cf. 7.300; note the neglected digamma (ϝείπῃ), a rare feature within formulas.

318 ἀκλεέες is a hypercorrection based on the strange statement in Did/A and T that Aristarchus read an unmetrical ἀκλεές "ὡς τὸ δυσκλέα" (9.22). Aristarchus may have intended ἀκλεῖες, cf. εὐκλεῖας (10.281) etc., against the vulgate ἀκληεῖς with -η- after the declension of Ἡρακλέης etc. Eust. and a few MSS read ἀκλειεῖς. The contraction, whether -ει- or -η-, is normal in the paradosis for parts and compounds of κλέος, δέος, and σπέος (Chantraine, *GH* I 7, 10–11). Ludwich corrected to ἀκλέες, ⟨οἵ⟩; van der Valk, *Researches* II 184, suggested varying interpretations of an ambiguous ΑΚΛΕΕΣ.

322–8 Compare Sarpedon's philosophy of battle with that of Odysseus, 19.233–7 and nn., and Hektor's fatalism at 6.488–9, μοῖραν δ' οὔ τινά φημι πεφυγμένον ἔμμεναι ἀνδρῶν, | οὐ κακόν, οὐδὲ μὲν ἐσθλόν, ἐπὴν τὰ πρῶτα γένηται. The verses do not follow logically on 310–21 but give a second, personal, and more heroic reason for fighting: if life were certain we could forgo renown (cf. Akhilleus' argument at 9.410–16), but life is uncertain, so let us fight well and make sure of good repute. Pindar expressed the same sentiment, *Ol.* 1.132, and it is not uncommon in various traditions of heroic poetry, e.g. *Beowulf* 1384, 'Each must expect an end to living in this world; let him who may win glory before death'; *Gilgamesh*, 'If I fall I leave behind me a name that endures' (p. 23 in the Penguin translation). It does not suit Sarpedon's argument to admit that the pursuit of κῦδος through battle is as likely to stimulate aggression as it is to galvanize defence, cf. Nestor's youthful exploits 11.670–761.

323 ἀγήρω τ' ἀθανάτω τε (also 17.444): the basic shape of the formula is –∪∪ ἀθάνατος καὶ ἀγήραος –∪∪–∪, but the contraction of ἀγήραος to ἀγήρως permitted many variants to arise: see R. Janko, *Mnem.* 34 (1981) 382–5.

326–7 The γάρ-clause, which may be translated 'since . . .', gives the reason for ἴομεν at 328. This 'inversion,' as Monro calls it (*HG* 317) is common in the *Iliad* but absent from the *Odyssey*. OCT normally punctuates with a colon after the γάρ-clause. — A κήρ is a death-demon, more personified (or objectified, as in the *kerostasia*-scenes, 8.69, 22.209) than μοῖρα, less so than δαίμων, see 9.411n. Sarpedon's comments are comparatively mild. At 13.283 the coward 'thinks of the κῆρες and his teeth chatter'; what he thinks of is described at 18.535–8 ὀλοὴ Κὴρ | ἄλλον ζωὸν ἔχουσα νεούτατον, ἄλλον ἄουτον, | ἄλλον τεθνηῶτα κατὰ μόθον ἕλκε ποδοῖιν, and with Lucanesque horrors at [Hesiod], *Aspis* 248–57:

> αἱ δὲ μετ' αὐτοὺς
> Κῆρες κυάνεαι, λευκοὺς ἀραβεῦσαι ὀδόντας,
> δεινωποὶ βλοσυροί τε δαφοινοί τ' ἄπλητοί τε
> δῆριν ἔχον περὶ πιπτόντων. πᾶσαι δ' ἄρ' ἵεντο
> αἷμα μέλαν πιέειν. ὃν δὲ πρῶτον μεμάποιεν
> κείμενον ἢ πίπτοντα νεούτατον, ἀμφὶ μὲν αὐτῷ
> βάλλ⟨ον ὁμῶς⟩ ὄνυχας μεγάλους, ψυχὴ δὲ [Ἀϊδόσδε] κατῆεν
> Τάρταρον εἰς κρυόενθ'. αἱ δὲ φρένας εὖτ' ἀρέσαντο
> αἵματος ἀνδρομέου, τὸν μὲν ῥίπτασκον ὀπίσσω,
> ἂψ δ' ὅμαδον καὶ μῶλον ἐθύνεον αὖτις ἰοῦσαι.

328 Sarpedon can face the uncertainty of battle (ξυνὸς Ἐνυάλιος καί τε κτανέοντα κατέκτα, 18.309), because a brave end too is glorious, cf. 22.304–5 μὴ μὰν ἀσπουδί γε καὶ ἀκλειῶς ἀπολοίμην, | ἀλλὰ μέγα ῥέξας τι καὶ ἐσσομένοισι πυθέσθαι. The glorious death in battle is a notion easily abused, especially by arm-chair poets: *dulce et decorum est pro patria mori* (Horace, *Carm.* 3.2.13); 'Yet do their beating breasts demand the strife, / And thirst of glory quells the love of life' (Addison, *The Campaign*). Homer does not pretend that any form of death is 'sweet' and his heroes do not 'demand the strife'; they enter it from a sense that it is their duty, their μοῖρα. Sarpedon's present bid for fame is ennobled by his fatalism. — The ellipse of ὀρέξει from ἤέ τις ἡμῖν led to the intrusion of a plus-verse reported by Arn/A, δώσει ἀποκτάμενος κλυτὰ τεύχεα καὶ δόρυ μακρόν, cf. 9.415–16n.

331 This is Menestheus' first appearance since he was reproved by Agamemnon during the Ἐπιπώλησις (4.327–48). His unheroic performance is typical; at 13.190–7 he extricates Amphimakhos while Aias holds off the Trojans, and at 13.685 he, with many others, cannot hold off Hektor. His lieutenant is killed at 15.329, after which the poet forgets him. His particular talent, not exemplified in the *Iliad*, was to marshal the fighting men and their horses, 2.553–5 (athetized by Zen., but read in the fifth century according to Hdt. 7.161). For the implications of this 'dismal record' (as Page called it) of the Athenian leader see 2.552n. The genealogy of the Athenian royal house recorded by late sources is a heroic effort of systemization. Menestheus son of Peteos son of Orneus was put in the fourth generation from Erekhtheus; the 'legitimate' line of Aigeus – Theseus was linked through two Pandions to the first Kekrops. See West, *Catalogue* 103–9, and Page, *HHI* 173–5, for a tabulation of the sources. In truth the parochial mythology of Athens was remarkably, and surely significantly, isolated from that of the wider heroic world. Μενε-σθεύς is a *Kurzform* for Μενε-σθένης, which would not scan in the nominative. An alternative form of the name, for different persons, is Μενέσθιος (7.9, 16.173).

332–3 παπταίνειν is always a symptom of fear, as explicitly at 11.546. πύργον: the best *sense* would be given to these two verses if in 332 πύργος is taken to be a 'bastion' protecting Menestheus' gate and in 333 to be the phalanx of defending spearmen, cf. πυργηδόν 43 and n., but the collocation of different uses of the word would be strangely harsh. Leaf, with some reason, contends that in Homer πύργος refers generally to a fortification rather than specifically to a 'tower', so that Menestheus may be said to be defending a sector of the wall, his πύργος, and looks along it, ἀνὰ πύργον, to the adjacent sectors for support.

334 For ἀρήν, 'disaster', see 14.484–5n. and West on Hesiod, *Theog.* 657. This ἀρή is an old word of uncertain origin and formation (conjectures in Chantraine, *Dict.* s.v.), which survived in the formulas ἀρὴν ∪∪ – ∪ ἀμύνειν (3× *Il.*, 2× *Od.* with a variant at *Od.* 22.208) and ἀρῆς ἀλκτῆρα (2× *Il.*).

335–6 For the sense of Αἴαντε see 265–76n. If 336 is original (there is no athetesis), the poet understood Αἴαντε as the two Aiantes. Teukros had been wounded by Hektor and taken to his hut at 8.324–9, which may account for this tardy realization that a battle was taking place, but no direct allusion is made in this Book to his previous injury.

337 βώσαντι: βω- is the Ionic contraction of βοη-. γεγωνεῖν implies 'reach by shouting', 'make to hear', as in the Odyssean formula ὅσσον (ὅσον) τε γέγωνε βοήσας (4×).

340 πᾶσαι . . . ἐπῴχατο (so Aristarchus, Arn/Did/A): πάσας . . . ἐπῴχετο was read by Zenodotus and appears in the majority of MSS. ἐπῴχατο, 3rd person plural of the pluperfect of ἐπέχειν, is cited in Ap. Soph. *Lex.*, and may have been what Aristarchus intended to write (= ἐπωχλισμέναι ἦσαν, Ap. Soph., ἐπικεκλιμέναι ἦσαν, ἐπέκειντο, bT), although the scholiasts are insistent that ἐπῴχατο (διὰ τοῦ α καὶ σὺν τῷ ι) was his reading: that would be from ἐποίγω (ἐπιϝοίγω would probably be the Homeric form), for the sense of which ('close') the late compound προσοίγνυμι may be compared. The plural verb carries with it the change of πάσας to πᾶσαι (= 'the whole'). Aristarchus wished to have only one gate in his text and appears therefore to have emended the vulgate, which may stand, see van der Valk, *Researches* I 575–80. With ἐπῴχετο understand ἀϋτή, 'noise of battle', from 338 as subject. — πυλέων: Ionic εω (by metathesis of an immediately antecedent ηο) is normally scanned as a single syllable in the epic as in the Ionic iambographers, cf. Chantraine, *GH* I 64, as if it were phonetically diphthongal. But metathesized εω is often dissyllabic in Attic and may occasionally be so in the epic, cf. Ἀκρόνεως, Ἀναβησίνεως (*Od.* 8.111, 8.113), which, however, are from νᾶϝος. Anapaestic πυλέων occurs also at 7.1.

342 As a line introducing direct speech but not containing a verb of speaking 342 is paralleled by 9.224 and 10.476 (see nn). The immediate passage into direct speech adds an impression of urgency to Menestheus' words. — Αἴαντα: Zenodotus (ArnDid/A), followed by Pap. 9 and part of the medieval paradosis, emended to Αἴαντε here and in 343, because of the following plural and dual at 353 and 354. The singular is clearly right, as the following ἀμφοτέρω μὲν μᾶλλον shows. Zenodotus made the same emendation at 15.301. Θοώτης, 'swift', is a significant herald name, see 9.170n. ὀνοματοθετικὸς ὁ ποιητής, as Didymus commented.

343–4 Aias is the best fighter on the Achaean side still capable of wielding a spear and, as the sequel shows, defence is his *forte*. That is sufficient reason for Menestheus' appeal. There is no suggestion in the *Iliad* that their being neighbours at home gave Athenian Menestheus a special claim to Salaminian Aias' aid. The additive syntax of Menestheus' remarks ('Fetch Aias – or rather both of them') conveys his alarm.

346 Zenodotus (Arn/A) took ὧδε in a local sense, 'against this point', a function that Aristarchus wished to deny to the word. Zenodotus then changed ὧδε at 359 in the herald's speech to κεῖσε, 'against that point', just as τῇδε at 345 becomes κεῖθι at 358. For ὧδε = 'hither' cf. 10.537n.

347 ζαχρηεῖς, 'powerful' (5.525, 13.684), probably represents a primitive ζαχραϝέες (χραύω) with the Aeolic intensive prefix ζα-, as in ζαής, ζάθεος. τελέθουσι is present because the Lycian leaders, who were mighty before (πάρος 346) are mighty still.

349 = 362: ἀλλά περ qualifies the whole sentence 'but at least let Telamonian Aias come by himself'. ἄλκιμος Αἴας is not a free alternant of the formula φαίδιμος Αἴας (6×), but occurs only here (and in the repeated verse 362) as part of the expanded expression Τελαμώνιος ἄλκιμος Αἴας. ἄλκιμος properly belongs to the formula ἄλκιμος υἱός (9× *Il.* only), where it does indeed alternate with φαίδιμος. Note that ὄβριμος, which might seem especially suitable for the massive Aias, is a special epithet of Hektor (4×) and Ares (5×) and in other respects is of very restricted use.

350 This verse was athetized by Aristophanes and Aristarchus (Arn/A). They objected to Teukros' being specially summoned since he always fought alongside his half-brother. Consequently 363 in the delivery of the message and 371 in the narrative were also rejected.

353–4 Verse 353 ≅ 17.707 (with θέων for κιών); 354 = 4.285. χαλκοχιτώνων, used once with Ἐπειῶν at 4.437, is properly the epithet of Ἀχαιῶν (22× *Il.*, 2× *Od.*). Ἀργείων ἡγήτορε χαλκοχιτώνων is formed similarly to the epithet phrase in the whole-verse address to Aineias, Τρώων βουληφόρε χαλκοχιτώνων, and also to the description of Stikhios, Βοιωτῶν ἡγήτορα χαλκοχιτώνων (15.330). The open vowel at the end of these case-forms of ἡγήτωρ precludes the usual complement ἠδὲ μέδοντες. In 354 Αἴαντ᾽, Ἀργείων ἡγήτορε is independently formular (2×).

356 μίνυνθά περ: 'if only (περ) for a short time', as at 23.97. The herald adds a persuasive point on his own account. ἀντιάσητον: a short-vowel subjunctive would be expected in the sigmatic aorist, but would be unmetrical (ἀντιάσετον −∪∪∪−) in this verb. Leaf read the optative ἀντιάσαιτον, which has negligible MS support.

363 This verse was athetized by Aristarchus, cf. 350n. τόξων ἐῢ εἰδώς: Teukros is the Achaean archer *par excellence*, having *aristeiai* at 8.273ff. and 15.442ff. He demonstrates his skill at 386–8 below, but scores only one success on this occasion, and that not fatal. Despite his special expertise Teukros fights on occasion as a spearman (13.170–82).

365 αὐτίκ' Ὀϊλιάδην: Zenodotus read αὐτίκ' ἄρ' Ἰλιάδην, perhaps by correction of αὐτίκα Ὀϊλιάδην with *scriptio plena*. Chantraine, *GH* I 116–17, admits the possibility that initial 'Ο- was not originally syllabic but an abnormal indication of *w*-. Οἴτυλος (2.585) and of course Ὀϊλεύς would be other instances. See also 11.93n. and 13.66–7n. In the text itself the formula Ὀϊλῆος ταχὺς Αἴας (9×) and four other instances of Ὀϊλ- fall after the caesura and 'Ο- must be syllabic.

366 Aias has been resisting Hektor's crack troops; he cannot leave that sector unsupported. Lukomedes, to whom with the other Aias it is entrusted, is more than a name; he appeared in good company among the captains of the watch at 9.84 and will appear in better at 19.240. He was known to the *Little Iliad* also (fr. 12 Davies). Nevertheless his elevation to a post of responsibility draws attention to the weakness of the Achaean front rank. Idomeneus and Meriones are away on the left still preparing for action; Menelaos, last mentioned at 11.487, has dropped out of sight.

368–9 = 13.752–3 but with ἐπαμύνω for ἐπιτείλω.

370 This movement by Aias results in the repulse of the Lycians and a temporary stalemate. We may imagine that his departure enabled Hektor (whom he had been facing) to press home his attack, but the poet does not say so. The two Aiantes are together again at 13.46ff.

371 ὅπατρος hints at Teukros' bastardy; he was not ὁμογάστριος. Bastards in the epic take their rank from their father. Homer does not mention Teukros' mother – Laomedon's daughter Hesione according to Eust. 713.25 and D on 8.284.

372 This Pandion is otherwise unknown. In the context of the Athenian contingent the name must be an echo of Pandion, the mythical king of Athens (or kings in some genealogies). Thinking that Teukros was capable of carrying his own bow Aristarchus rejected the line (Arn/T).

373–4 The repeated ἵκοντο strikes the modern ear as clumsy, but the epic style makes no special effort to avoid such repetition, cf. Hainsworth on *Od.* 7.116.

375 ἐρεμνῇ λαίλαπι ἴσος is a formular comparison, used at 20.51 of Ares himself. Nestor was κελαινῇ λ. ῖ. in his younger days (11.747). A storm is a favourite image for Trojan attacks in this part of the *Iliad*, cf. 11.297, 12.40, 13.334, 13.795 (ἀέλλη), 11.306 (λαῖλαψ). The cumulative effect of such repetition conveys a more vivid impression of the Trojan attack than any narrative statement.

377 For σὺν δ' ἐβάλοντο μάχεσθαι see 181n. The middle συμβάλλομαι usually means 'meet with', but need not be corrected.

379 Ἐπικλῆα μεγάθυμον: -κλῆα μεγάθυμον (Βαθυ-, Διο-, Ἐπι-, Ὀϊ-, Πατρο-) is formular. The initial μ- of μέγας and its compounds regularly makes position, as if < σμ-, but without etymological justification.

381 This large stone that lay so handy by the battlements, as if by chance, is an echo of actual siege tactics, the preparation of dumps of heavy boulders for dropping on assailants, cf. Thuc. 4.115, Eur. *Phoen.* 1143, 1157–8, 1177. — ῥέα: the monosyllabic pronunciation, beside disyllabic ῥεῖα, has caused some surprise: an Ionic colloquialism according to Meister, *Kunstsprache* 193.

382 χείρεσσ' ἀμφοτέρῃς is a correction of Aristarchus (so van der Valk, *Researches* II 617–18) for χειρί γε τῇ ἑτέρῃ of the vulgate, but has considerable MS support. Aristarchus thought the reading of the vulgate reflected adversely on Aias' strength, cf. 450n., it being no surprise if Aias could hurl a stone which a modern man could not grasp with *one* hand. Note ἔχοι, not βάλοι; the modern man could not even get his hands round it. The vulgate reading is so odd that χειρί γε τῇ ἑτέρῃ could conceivably be the remains of a verse following 383; Aias threw the stone with one hand, cf. Hektor's exploit, 452. For the motif 'only he could ...' cf. 449, 11.637, 16.142, 24.456.

383 οἷοι νῦν βροτοί εἰσ' is formular (4× *Il.*, ὅσσοι ... *Od.* 8.222 in a different context). bT at 5.304 comment that it shows the poet 'was much later than heroic times', apparently a controversion of Aristarchus' view that Homer was an Athenian living shortly after the Trojan war.

384 Aias catches Epikles as he clambers up the wall. The φάλαρα of a helmet (see 16.106), implied by the epithet τετραφάληρον, are obscure, see 5.743–4n., but probably distinct from the φάλοι, at least originally. Lorimer, *HM* 242, identifies the φάλαρα as metal plates.

384–6 ≅ *Od.* 12.412–14 (a fall from a ship's deck) with variation of the third verse. Verses 385–6 ≅ 16.742–3 (from ὁ δ' ἄρ' ἀρνευτῆρι) with a well-made chariot in place of the high tower. The ἀρνευτήρ, 'acrobat', performs cartwheels and somersaults, cf. Patroklos' jeer at 16.745 "ἦ μάλ' ἐλαφρὸς ἀνήρ, ὡς ῥεῖα κυβιστᾷ." The word must be connected with ἀρνειός, 'ram', but is hardly known outside Homer (here, 16.742, and *Od.* 12.413), a vivid vernacular term alongside the formally correct but still largely Homeric κυβιστητήρ (16.750, 18.605, *Od.* 4.18).

386 Cf. *Od.* 12.414 κάππεσ' ἀπ' ἰκριόφιν, λίπε δ' ὀστέα θυμὸς ἀγήνωρ, and 16.743 κάππεσ' ἀπ' εὐεργέος δίφρου, λίπε δ' ὀστέα θυμός, where the victim is Kebriones. Smashing a head with a large rock is one of the motifs of battle, cf. 11.349ff. (Diomedes knocks out Hektor).

387–8 Glaukos' wound is remembered at 16.508ff. (but not at 14.426), when because of it he is unable to come to Sarpedon's aid. He there prayed to Apollo for a cure. For the absence of such prayers in books 11–12 see 11.273n. Glaukos' quality as a warrior must largely be taken on trust; he is given minor successes at 7.13ff. and 16.593ff., but did not assist Sarpedon when he was injured at the slaying of Tlepolemos (5.627–67). Glaukos died at Troy at the hands either of Aias (Quint. Smyrn. 3.214ff.) or Agamemnon (Hyginus 113). The kings of Lycia traced their ancestry to him (Hdt. 1.147). Verse 388 is rearranged and divided between verses at 16.511–12 ἐπεσσύμενον βάλεν ἰῷ | τείχεος ὑψηλοῖο. τείχεος goes with ἐπεσσύμενον, 'as he was dashing at the wall'.

393 ὅμως is a neologism for epic ἔμπης, otherwise only at *Od.* 11.565 (ὁμῶς OCT).

394 In spite of the peril of the Achaeans this Alkmaon is the only named casualty on their side, cf. 11.310–64n. In the absence of any anecdote to amplify this brief notice of Alkmaon's death it is idle to speculate on the identity of his father Thestor, cf. Κάλκας Θεστορίδης, 1.69 and n. Arn/A denies that this Thestor is the same as Kalkhas' father, but cites no authority.

397–8 πᾶσα διαμπερές should imply something about the construction of the wall and its superstructure. In the poet's imagination Sarpedon brings down the breastwork as it were in one piece all along a stretch of wall. A wooden structure with long horizontal members might come down in that way, but not masonry.

398 ἕλχ' is effective placed in enjambment at the beginning of the verse to emphasize Sarpedon's action. The device is formular, however, cf. 17.126 and the habitual placing (9×) of elided νύξ' in that position.

400–3 Sarpedon has a fortunate escape, saved by his baldric. A spear-cast can be anticipated and parried, but not an arrow. So too Aias had cause to bless his τελαμῶνε (those of shield and sword) at 14.402–6. Alternatively, a warrior who lets a shot past his shield, if not killed on the spot, is saved by his ζωστήρ (4.186 (Menelaos), 11.236 (Agamemnon)). The ζωστήρ (and doubtless the τελαμών too) was unreliable protection; Aias (5.615), Leonteus (12.189), and even Menelaos (17.578) drove their spears clean through it. — ὁμαρτήσανθ': understand the dual ὁμαρτήσαντε in agreement with Αἴας καὶ Τεῦκρος; the two heroes acted 'simultaneously'.

402–3 The poet is more explicit than he was at 5.662, where the interference of Zeus was almost casual (πατὴρ δ' ἔτι λοιγὸν ἄμυνεν). Sarpedon is preserved now because the poet needs him later, or as he puts it in book 16 (433–8), it was Sarpedon's fate to die at the hands of Patroklos and not by the ships. The omission of 403 by Pap. 342 seems accidental; the verse is dispensable but is read by two other early texts.

404–5 = 7.260–1, but with οὐδέ for ἣ δέ, a bold adaptation of a formular verse by substitution, see Introduction 15. ἣ δέ is read here by some MSS, an obvious example of 'concordance corruption'. The tactic, pushing the opponent back by brute force, is typical of Aias, see also 13.192–3.

407 ἐέλδετο, 'desired', is more exclusively epic than ἐέλπετο and has considerable MS support, including Pap. 9; it is marginally preferable. Leaf's objection to the construction of ἔλπομαι with the aorist ἀρέσθαι (< ἄρνυμαι), however, is not well founded, cf. Goodwin, *Syntax* 45–6.

408 = 16.421 (with καθαπτόμενος) and ≅ 12.467 with the substitution of Τρώεσσιν in the first hemistich.

409–12 The leader's complaint that he cannot do everything recurs, from the Achaean side, at 20.354–63. Perhaps a typical motif; 410 = 20.356, but there is no other language in common between the two passages.

412 ἐφομαρτεῖτε: the dual ἐφομαρτεῖτον would not have troubled Zenodotus, who could accept the concord with genuinely plural subject, but in spite of its MS support, cf. 8.191 = 23.414, is clearly impossible after Λύκιοι. The Lycian pair of course are Sarpedon himself and Glaukos, now *hors de combat*. — πλεόνων κτλ.: 'many hands make light work'. Sententiousness, apart from the concatenation of aphorisms in Aineias' speech to Akhilleus (20.200–58), is more characteristic of the Odyssean style, cf. *Od.* 6.29–30 and Hainsworth's note *ad loc.*

413–71 The Achaeans rally and the battle hangs momentarily in the balance. The Book then concludes with a truly epic moment. Hektor inspires the Trojans for a second assault and bursts through the gates, spears in hand. The Trojans swarm over the wall

The passage has been justly praised from antiquity for its vigour, cf. bT πανταχόθεν ἐκίνησε τὴν ἐνέργειαν, ἐκ τοῦ βαλόντος, ἐκ τῶν διαρριπτομένων σανίδων, ἐκ τοῦ εἰσπηδῶντος καὶ φοβερὸν βλέποντος, ἐκ τῶν ὑπερβαινόντων τὸ τεῖχος, καθ' ὃ μέρος ἔρρηξε Σαρπήδων, ἐκ τῶν εἰστρεχόντων εἰς τὰς πύλας, καθ' ὃ μέρος αὐτὸς ἔρρηξεν αὐτὰς ὁ Ἕκτωρ.

414 βουληφόρος is epithet of Sarpedon at 5.633 but does not, as epithet, appear to have specific significance, least of all in the midst of battle. (Verse 414 in book 10 is different; βουληφόροι is there predicative.) Its use in formulas is principally as a metrical alternative to ἡγήτωρ.

415–16 The first verse is formular (= 11.215 ≅ 16.563 ≅ Hesiod, *Theog.* 676). To resist the Lycians' final effort the Achaeans mass behind their battlements. This must be the sense of τείχεος ἔντοσθεν, cf. 380–1 where τείχεος ἔντος implies παρ' ἔπαλξιν. The breach opened by Sarpedon (397–9) was not so great after all. — σφισι refers to both Lycians and Achaeans, as if οἱ δέ (413) and Ἀργεῖοι δέ (415) were subjects of parallel clauses in the same sentence.

417–8 The battle reaches an impasse. The image and some of the language recurs at 15.405–9 αὐτὰρ Ἀχαιοὶ | Τρῶας ἐπερχομένους μένον ἔμπεδον, οὐδὲ δύναντο | παυροτέρους περ ἐόντας ἀπώσασθαι παρὰ νηῶν· | οὐδέ ποτε Τρῶες Δαναῶν ἐδύναντο φάλαγγας | ῥηξάμενοι κλισίῃσι μιγήμεναι. — Δαναῶν ... | τεῖχος: B. Giseke, *Homerische Forschungen* (Leipzig 1864) 47–8, an early study of word position in Homer, noted the rarity of this kind of enjambment in which a genitive noun is placed in the verse preceding the noun on which it depends. τεῖχος Ἀχαιῶν (223, 5×) is precluded here by the parallelism of 418 with 411.

421–4 The point of comparison in the simile is unusually recondite – the farmers are quarrelling over a foot or two of ground, so the two sides are no more than the battlements' breadth apart. οὔροισι is from οὖρος (Attic ὅρος), 'boundary stone', rather than οὖρον, an obscure measure of distance mentioned at 10.351, 23.431, and *Od.* 8.124. There is even a verb for the fraudulent adjustment of ὅροι, ἀπούρισσειν (22.489). ἐπιξύνῳ: a common field, distinct from the τεμένη of the aristocracy, cf. the *ki-ti-me-na* and *ke-ke-me-na ko-to-na* of the Pylos Tablets. For ἴσης, 'fair share', cf. 11.705.

423 Zenodotus read ὀλίγῃ ἐνὶ χώρῃ (Did/A), as at 17.394. χῶρος, 'piece of ground', is better here than χώρη, 'space' (which is appropriate in book 17).

424 αὐτέων: the Ionic genitive in -έων (< -άων), unless its use gives a rhythm ∪ – –, occurs for the most part in the first half of the verse, where diction is looser and old formulas are infrequent: so in books 9–12 πασέων (9.330), ἀγορέων (9.441), πολλέων (9.544), ὁπλέων (11.536 = 20.501), βουλέων (12.236), πυλέων (∪∪–, 12.340), cf. κριθῶν (*sic*) 11.69. A plus-verse βάλλον ἀμυνόμενοι χαλκήρεσιν ἐγχείῃσι looks like an alternative to 425–6 (= 5.452–3), so van der Valk, *Researches* II 561.

425–6 = 5.452–3 (see nn. *ad loc.*). The enjambment is formally 'violent' in that the adjective βοείας precedes the noun ἀσπίδας, but βοείη can be substantivized and the second verse understood as standing in apposition to it. The λαισήϊα are very obscure, see H. Borchhardt, *Arch. Hom.* E 52–3. Arn/A records among other conjectures that they are long shields, as if the word stood in contrast with εὐκύκλους. Herodotus (7.91) uses the word for Cilician equipment made of rawhide (ὠμοβοέη) and distinguished from ἀσπίδες. λαισήϊον, like κρόσσαι, appears to be an Ionic word unfamiliar to other dialects.

428 Turning to retreat is fatal to many Homeric soldiers, either because they wear no *thorex* or because the *thorex* provides inadequate protection when uncovered by the shield, cf. 11.447. ὅτεῳ: Zenodotus was undoubtedly right against the vulgate (and Aristarchus') ὅτῳ, cf. *Od.* 2.114.

430–2 When the battle closes to hand-to-hand fighting, there is no nimble leaping onto chariots for a quick retreat. Men fall in their ranks and a bloodbath naturally follows, cf. 4.451 = 8.65, cf. 15.715, 16.639, 17.360. — ἐρράδατ(ο): for this peculiar perfect in -δ-, a testimony to the linguistic vitality of the *Kunstsprache*, see Chantraine, *GH* i 435. It recurs at *Od.* 20.354, cf. ἀκηχέδαται (< ἀχέειν) in some MSS at 17.637 and ἐληλάδατο (< ἐλαύνειν) in the vulgate at *Od.* 7.86. The -δ- must be derived from dental stems such as ἐρείδειν (which has a perfect ἐρηρέδαται, 23.284, 23.329, *Od.* 7.95). Similar forms from verbs in -άζειν, -ίζειν occur in the Ionic of Herodotus. T imagine a ῥάζω, a ghost word in this sense. The repetition of Ἀχαιῶν at the end of 431 and 432 does not trouble the poet, cf. 373–4 and n.

433–5 Simile of the spinning woman, presumably a free widow. For comparisons drawn from women's work cf. 4.141 (ivory-staining), and 23.760 (weaving). Spinning, however, is usually represented as the work of the women of the heroic household, no matter what their status, e.g. *Od.* 6.305–7 (Arete and her slave-women). As an image, scales express balance, as here, or the moment of decision, when the balance inclines in one direction, as at 8.69, 22.209. The scales of Zeus, however (8.69, 22.209), symbolize another idea, that of being 'weighed in the balances, and ... found wanting'. ἀληθής is 'honest', 'conscientious' ('ehrlich' Ameis–Hentze), a sense not repeated in the epic, but that is not objectionable in a simile, cf. ἀληθὴς νόος at Pind. *Ol.* 2.167. Leaf conjectures, unnecessarily, a primitive sense 'not forgetful'. ἔχον is intransitive, 'hold on', but a transitive ἔχει must be understood from it as the verb of the simile. ἀεικέα expresses humiliation inflicted on another ('mit der Nebenbedeutung "hässlich", "schmählich", "verabscheuungswürdig"'), *LfgrE* s.v., cf. the ἀεικέσσι πληγῇσι with which Thersites was threatened (2.264 and 22.395n.), not, *pace* Plutarch, *Mor.* 19c (on 23.24), the shame that falls, or ought to fall, on the doer of wicked deeds, hence an ἀεικὴς μισθός is a 'pittance', presumably a portion of the thread spun or similar payment in kind. Aristarchus was momentarily puzzled, suggesting ἀνεικέα or ἀμεμφέα, before settling for ἀεικέα = εὐτελῆ (Did/A). The pathetic touch caught the imagination of later poets, cf. Ap. Rhod. 4.1062–7, Virg. *Aen.* 8.408–13.

436 = 15.413, where the simile concerns the use of the line (στάθμη), not scales (σταθμός), as if the idea ἐπὶ ἶσα τέτατο were somehow associated in the singer's mind with the sound σταθμ-. For the metaphor of tension see 11.336n. — After the pause during the simile the narrative surges forward to the climax. With Zeus's blessing (as the poet knows) Hektor urges on his men for a final effort. They charge the wall in a body and clamber over the battlements, but the climax, the great heroic deed, is reserved for the hero, for Hektor.

438 ≅ 16.558, where the reference is to Sarpedon, not Hektor, cf. 3.356 = 7.250, where Πριαμίδαο refers in the first verse to Paris, in the second to Hektor. The economical use of the same diction with a different reference is oral style. — ἐσήλατο: the sigmatic aorist of ἄλλομαι must represent the vernacular form contemporary with the epic. It is a remarkable conservatism that it occurs only in this repeated phrase and probably in the subjunctive at 21.536, whereas the archaic athematic aorist ἆλτο occurs more than 50×.

439 ≅ 8.227, etc. (7×, with Δαναοῖσι). It is of course Hektor who shouts, but Aristarchus (Arn/A) suggested that Zeus is the subject of ἤϋσεν on the grounds that this was a more than mortal shout. For the same reason Zenodotus substituted ἐπεὶ θεοῦ ἔκλυον αὐδήν in the second half of 444.

443 The sector that Hektor attacked and carried is most easily understood to be that abandoned by Aias and Teukros when they came to the rescue of Menestheus. But the thread of the narrative is not easily followed. The statement at 290–2 associated Hektor with Sarpedon and there is no indication of a change of scene in the short passage 424–32 between the two similes, the first of which certainly refers to the Lycian attack, the second most probably to Hektor's forces. Then at 13.679–82 Hektor is fighting 'where he first surmounted the wall, where were the ships of Aias and Protesilaos'. But we are left to wonder which Aias and where was the ship of Protesilaos. The centre of the Achaean camp, defended at 13.313 by both Aiantes and Teukros and visible from Akhilleus' quarters on the right, seems to be a satisfactory location. In that case Hektor attacked opposite the ships of the Lesser Aias and his namesake moved back to his former station (or his movement to rescue Menestheus is overlooked) in the fighting of book 13.

444 ἀκαχμένα δούρατ' ἔχοντες is formular (cf. 17.412), but a relatively recent addition to the poet's diction: the τ-stem in the oblique cases of δόρυ occurs only 14× in the *Iliad* against 167 occurrences of the archaic stem without suffix; ἀκαχμένα is of doubtful etymology (*LfgrE* offer no firm suggestion), but its alternation with κεκορυθμένος in the formulas of arming make the sense, 'tipped', clear. In that case the formula (ἔγχος) ἀκαχμένον ὀξεῖ χαλκῷ (10.135 etc.) is the better usage. Zenodotus' reading ἐπεὶ θεοῦ ἔκλυον αὐδήν, cf. 15.270, looks like an instance of formula substitution, see 230n., but not in this case by inadvertence; the god is Zeus, understood as the speaker of the two verses of direct speech.

448 The ἄμαξα is a four-wheeled cart, cf. ἄμαξαι | ... τετράκυκλοι (*Od.* 9.241–2). The chariot (ἅρμα, δίφρος) is for personal transport and a strictly military vehicle. ἀπ' οὔδεος ὀχλίσσειαν: the phrase recurs at *Od.* 9.242 in the description of the Kuklops' doorstop. The motif 'such as not *x* could lift' is formular, see 382n.

449 = 5.304 (Diomedes) = 20.287 (Aineias). The hurling of large rocks is one of the rare breaches of realism in the *Iliad* and one of the few indications that the heroes were thought to possess preternatural strength. There is no indication at all that they were thought to be of preternatural size, although in classical times when their supposed mortal remains came to light they were regularly reported to be of appropriately heroic dimensions, seven to twelve cubits, e.g. Hdt. 1.68 (Orestes), Plutarch, *Thes.* 36 and *Cim.* 8 (Theseus), Paus. 1.35.3 (Aias), 1.35.5 ('Asterios'), 8.29.3 ('Orontes'), Philostr. *Her.* 8.3 (Peleus?), Phlegon *FGH* III no. 257 F 36 ix Jacoby (Idas). — Stones are handy and general missiles (12.154, 16.774), but not despised either by the front ranks (4.517, etc.: 11 instances).

450 The verse was omitted by Zenodotus and athetized by his successors (Did/A); they took it as an adverse comment on Hektor's heroic strength if Zeus had to lighten the stone. The verse was read, however, by Pap. 342 (saec. ii).

452–3 χειρὶ λαβὼν ἑτέρῃ: a tribute to Hektor's strength of arm, but not, or not merely, poetic exaggeration. Hektor is fighting in the normal way, spears in one hand, cf. 465, and picks up the boulder in the other. For a similar scene see 16.733–6, where Patroklos holds his spear in his left hand while hurling a stone at Kebriones. In this case Hektor does not hurl the stone (cf. φέρε, 453) until he is at close quarters and uses it as a sort of battering ram.

454 εἴρυντο here is from ῥύομαι, at 18.69 from ἐρύω; in both cases εἰρύατο would be expected as the normal Ionic form. — στιβαρῶς is substituted for the formular πυκινῶς with ἀραρυίας (cf. 9.475, 21.535) because of the preceding πύκα. στιβαρός is otherwise an archaism preserved by formular conservatism.

455–6 For city gates see S. Iakovides, *Arch. Hom.* E 219. The ὀχῆες are substantial drawbars (μοχλοί Arn/A). It would be natural to think of these as horizontal beams working from opposite directions (ἐπημοιβοί) and secured, when in position, by a vertical bolt (κληΐς). This would duplicate the single ὀχεύς envisaged at 121, 291, and 13.124. The scholia, however, take ἐπημοιβοί to mean that the ὀχῆες crossed over each other ἐξ ἑκατέρας φλιᾶς ἕνα, ἐπαλλασσομένους κατὰ μέσον, a possible but unlikely arrangement.

457–66 The fine description of Hektor in his moment of triumph, rising through a series of lightly enjambed varied verses to a fine threefolder, does justice to the zenith of his fortunes. This great epic moment makes an impressive half-way point of the *Iliad* and the perfect note on which to conclude a ῥαψῳδία. Note the rarity of ornamental epithets in this tense

Book Twelve

passage and down to 470 – only in the brief formulas φαίδιμος Ἕκτωρ and νυκτὶ θοῇ, cf. bT to 22.61 (Priam's vision of the sack of Troy) δαιμονίως δὲ ταῦτα ὑπ᾽ ὄψιν ἤγαγεν ἐν βραχεῖ, χρησάμενος ἅμα καὶ ἀπεριέργως ταῖς λέξεσι· οὐ γὰρ ὑψορόφους ἢ δαιδαλέους θαλάμους λέγει οὐδὲ θύγατρας καλλικόμους ἢ καλλισφύρους, ἀλλ᾽ ἀπήλλακται τῶν ἐπιθέτων αὐτῷ τὰ δυστυχοῦντα τῶν σωμάτων: see 22.61–5n. Metrically the passage races forward with many medial sentence-breaks, skewed sentences, light enjambments, and two fine threefolder verses (464, 466).

The present are almost the circumstances that Akhilleus had envisaged at 9.650–5, the eleventh hour at which he would intervene; almost, but not quite, for the Trojans have only carried the wall and in the few moments before they can reach the ships Zeus turns his eyes to other things (13.1–9). The course of the Great Battle then repeats itself with a temporary Achaean success followed by their decisive rout.

459 The θαιροί are pivots, working in hollows cut in the threshold and lintel, that served the same purpose as hinges, to secure the gate in position and permit it to turn. Hektor does not burst the gate open; he smashes it out of its seating in the masonry.

462–3 The comparison of an advancing warrior, bent on wreaking great deeds, to night is all the more effective for being imprecise, cf. the descent of Apollo at 1.47 νυκτὶ ἐοικώς. Hektor's complexion, we are to imagine in spite of his standard epithet φαίδιμος in 462, is livid ('black as night') with the fury and effort of his attack. This contrasts, as Eust. noted, with the terrifying flashing of his battle gear, λάμπε δὲ χαλκῷ | σμερδαλέῳ.

464 The adverbial σμερδαλέον (καθ᾽ ἑτέραν γραφήν Eust.) would be a more straightforward syntax, but σμερδαλέῳ is secure as an epithet of χαλκῷ at 13.192 in verses conceptually similar to 463–4.

465 For the alternatives οὐκ ἄν (most MSS) and οὔ κεν (Aristarchus) see 13.288–9n. The vulgate reading (and *lectio difficilior*) ἐρυκάκοι for ἐρύκακεν (Aristarchus and some late MSS) is equally acceptable in the epic in the sense 'would have held back', cf. 5.311 καί νύ κεν ἔνθ᾽ ἀπόλοιτο ... Αἰνείας, 'A would have perished', and the other examples cited in Goodwin, *Syntax* 161–2. The past indicative is the classical construction.

466 νόσφι θεῶν anticipates the intervention of Poseidon that immediately follows (13.10ff.). πυρὶ δ᾽ ὄσσε δεδήει: Hektor is berserk, cf. 13.474 (a raging boar), 15.607 (Hektor), 15.623 (Hektor again), and the formula φλογὶ εἴκελος etc. (7×). He is λυσσώδης at 13.53. The image is apposite here but already well-established, see 8.299, 9.238. 9.305. Blazing eyes (always ὄσσε, not ὄμματα or ὀφθαλμοί except at 13.474) are symptomatic of fury, whether of battle-fury or plain anger, cf. 1.104, 19.16–17, 19.365–6, and 2× in *Od.* See also the remarkable description of Hektor at 15.605–10. The neuter dual ὄσσε, like the neuter plural, construes with singular verb,

365

cf. 23.477, *Od.* 6.131–2, and see Schwyzer, *Gr. Gr.* II 50 (ὄσσε is the only word cited). For the similes of night (463) and fire cf. a fine passage from *Manas*, 'In his eyes a furnace blazed. A living dragon it was ... His look was like the midnight's look, angry as a cloudy day' (cited by Bowra, *HP* 99).

469–71 Verse 471 = 16.296. The scene, the Trojans pouring over the wall and the intense din of battle, is repeated at 15.395–6, where Patroklos is roused by the noise to emerge at last from Eurupulos' hut. The narrative line as always is sequential on the surface, which results in implausibilities such as the prolonged inaction of Nestor and Patroklos while the slaughter continues around them. For the view that the sequential series of events in books 12–15, or some of them, should be understood as simultaneous see 15.262–404n.

The book ends on a cliff-hanging note with the conclusion of the first Achaean attack – retreat episode. It would be a good place for the singer to pause. How long he paused, however, is a moot point, for books 12 and 13 are securely linked by anticipation and recall. The leaders of the catalogue (12.88–102) supply the slain in book 13; Pouludamas repeats his advice to Hektor; Menestheus continues, and concludes, his undistinguished career; atrocious slayings (11.146, 11.261) recur at 13.202 and 14.497; minor details of expression are kept in mind: πᾶς δ' ἄρα χαλκῷ | σμερδαλέῳ (13.191–2) blends πᾶς δ' ἄρα χαλκῷ (11.65) and χαλκῷ | σμερδαλέῳ (12.463–4), and σθένεϊ μεγάλῳ (12.224) recurs at 13.193.

INDEX

An index of Greek words appears at the end of vol. VI.

Index

atrocity, 50, 73, 139, 197–8, 241, 273
Attic forms, Atticism, 184, 191, 207, 209, 261, 275
audience: of ἀοιδή, 37–8, 289; of heroic poetry, 50, 197, 248; of *Iliad*, 60, 62, 76, 86, 92, 108, 120, 138, 140, 150, 219, 227, 245, 269, 270, 275, 282, 287, 290
Augeias, 301
augment, 126, 159
Aulis, 62, 66, 77
aural echo, 105, 177, 188, 195
Austin, N., 162, 295
Automedon, 88, 90, 91, 291

Bacchylides, 109, 130, 131, 132, 133
Bakker, E. J., 72
baldric, 219, 220, 221–2, 281; saves warrior, 359
Bannert, H., 132
barbarity: *see* atrocity
Bassett, S. E., 10, 233, 327
bastards: Achaean, 237, 357; of Priam, 237, 277, 280
bathing scene, 209
bathtub, 74, 209
battle: hand to hand, 228, 362; mode of narrating, 227-8, 257, ideology of, 227–8, 336; rally, 227, 231, 247, 257, 260, 276; retreat, 260, 271, 275, 277, 282, 284, 362; rout, 230; tactics of, 247, 260, 263, 266, 287; typology of, 235, 257, *see also aristeia*
Bechtel, F., 179, 215
Beck, W., 25
Beekes, J. R. S., 8
Bekker, I., 97
Bentley, R., 69, 95, 98, 104
Beowulf, see Old English heroic poetry
Bergren, A., 326
berserker, 48, 96, 99, 365
Bethe, E., 75
Beye, C. R., 232
Bienor, 233, 234
blazon, 221, 281
boar, 201, 258, 262, 271, *see also* simile; Calydonian, 131, 133, 137, 159, 334
boast, victor's, 268, 269, 273, 358
Boedeker, D., 25
Bolling, G. M., 74, 113, 123, 206, 245, 281, 308, 322, 348
book division, 56–7, 312
Bölte, F., 296, 298
Bömer, F., 130
book 9, function of, 56–7
book 10: differs from *Iliad*, 156, 169, 170, 186, 191; differs from *Odyssey*, 157, 168, 186; links with books 8 and 9, 152, 163,

177; general character of, 153; linguistic character of, 154, 161; 'Odyssean' elements/language, 154, 160, 165, 166, 169, 170, 173–4, 178, 185, 192, 200, 205, 207; philhellenism of, 153, 158; plan of, 155; pretentious thought or language, 157, 159, 160, 166, 169, 171, 172, 178, 185, 201; problem of, 151–5, style of, 155; van Thiel's theory, 153
book 12: construction of, 313; links with book 13, 271, 366
booty/loot/plunder, 75, 105–6, 108, 145, 155, 189, 197, 292
Borchhardt, J., 178, 179, 222; H., 220
bowdlerization, 122
Bowra, C. M., 21, 32–3, 38, 44–5, 48, 98, 100, 321, 366
Brandenburg, H., 250, 285
Braun, M., 33
Bremmer, J. N., 126–7
Brenk, F. E., 120
brideprice, 77, 251
Briseis, 73, 75, 76, 86, 106–7, 108, 110, 111, 112, 134, 143, 144, 145, 146
brothers fight as pairs, 231, 236–7, 247
Brugmann, K., 117, 240
Bruns, G., 292
Burkert, W., 87, 113, 122, 132, 273, 308
Burr, V., 77
Butterworth, J., 319

Calhoun, G. M., 213
Callistratus, 320
camp, Achaean, 39, 42, 189, 313–14, 363; *see also* gates
catalogue, list, 78, 118, 134, 159, 174, 196, 212, 225, 257, 259, 271, 277, 313, 319, 326–7, 338
Catalogue of Ships, 70, 77, 78, 108, 118, 122, 196, 214, 243, 289, 298, 302, 321, 327; Trojan, 196, 225, 262–3, 327, 328, 338
Catalogue of Women, 130
Catling, H. W., 217, 218, 219
Carpenter, R., 124
Carruba, O., 177
cattle raid, 136, 296
Chadwick, H. M., 41; and N. K., 32–3; J., 77, 161, 162, 223, 246, 252, 259, 292, 293
chant, 35–6
Chantraine, P., 104, 123, 134, 142, 147, 206, 224, 266, 319, 322, 335, and *passim*
characterization, 61, 63, 73, 76, 94, 102, 141, 164, 167, 176, 187, 189, 213, 284, 303, 304, 342, 351
chariot, 41, 120, 180, 187, 189, 202, 204, 207, 224, 234, 239, 246, 279, 323, 325,

Index

372

Index